DISCARDED

Benchmark Papers in Geology

Series Editor: Rhodes W. Fairbridge
Columbia University

A selection from the published volumes in this series

Volume

1. ENVIRONMENTAL GEOMORPHOLOGY AND LANDSCAPE CONSERVATION, Volume I: Prior to 1900 / *Donald R. Coates*
2. RIVER MORPHOLOGY / *Stanley A. Schumm*
6. SLOPE MORPHOLOGY / *Stanley A. Schumm and M. Paul Mosley*
8. ENVIRONMENTAL GEOMORPHOLOGY AND LANDSCAPE CONSERVATION, Volume III: Non-Urban / *Donald R. Coates*
12. ENVIRONMENTAL GEOMORPHOLOGY AND LANDSCAPE CONSERVATION, Volume II: Urban Areas / *Donald R. Coates*
21. GLACIAL DEPOSITS / *Richard P. Goldthwait*
22. PLANATION SURFACES: Peneplains, Pediplains, and Etchplains / *George F. Adams*
25. ENVIRONMENTAL GEOLOGY / *Frederick Betz, Jr.*
26. LOESS: Lithology and Genesis / *Ian J. Smalley*
27. PERIGLACIAL PROCESSES / *Cuchlaine A. M. King*
28. LANDFORMS AND GEOMORPHOLOGY: Concepts and History / *Cuchlaine A. M. King*
39. BEACH PROCESSES AND COASTAL HYDRODYNAMICS / *John S. Fisher and Robert Dolan*
41. DRAINAGE BASIN MORPHOLOGY / *Stanley A. Schumm*
42. COASTAL SEDIMENTATION / *Donald J. P. Swift and Harold D. Palmer*
59. KARST GEOMORPHOLOGY / *M. M. Sweeting*
63. EROSION AND SEDIMENT YIELD / *J. B. Laronne and M. P. Mosley*
80. RIVER NETWORKS / *Richard S. Jarvis and Michael J. Woldenberg*

Related Titles

　　THE ENCYCLOPEDIA OF GEOMORPHOLOGY / *Rhodes W. Fairbridge*

Benchmark Papers in Geology / 80

A BENCHMARK® Books Series

RIVER NETWORKS

Edited by
RICHARD S. JARVIS
and
MICHAEL J. WOLDENBERG

State University of New York
at Buffalo

Hutchinson Ross Publishing Company

Stroudsburg, Pennsylvania

Copyright ©1984 by **Hutchinson Ross Publishing Company**
Benchmark Papers in Geology, Volume 80
Library of Congress Catalog Card Number: 83-5898
ISBN: 0-87933-106-2

All rights reserved. No part of this book covered by the copyrights hereon may be reproduced or transmitted in any form or by any means—graphic, electronic, or mechanical, including photocopying, recording, taping, or information storage and retrieval systems—without written permission of the publisher.

86 85 84   1 2 3 4 5
Manufactured in the United States of America.

LIBRARY OF CONGRESS CATALOGING IN PUBLICATION DATA
Main entry under title:
River networks.
  (Benchmark paper in geology; 80)
  Includes bibliographies and indexes.
  1. Rivers—Addresses, essays, lectures. 2. Watersheds—Addresses, essays, lectures. 3. Geomorphology—Addresses, essays, lectures, I. Jarvis, Richard S.
II. Woldenberg, Michael J. III. Series.
GB1204.R58 1984   551.48'3   83-5898
  ISBN 0-87933-106-2

Distributed worldwide by Van Nostrand Reinhold Company Inc., 135 W. 50th Street, New York, NY 10020.

CONTENTS

Series Editor's Foreword — ix
Preface — xi
Contents by Author — xiii

Introduction — 1

PART I: HORTON'S LAWS OF DRAINAGE COMPOSITION

Editors' Comments on Papers 1 Through 5 — 8

1 HORTON, R. E.: Erosional Development of Streams and Their Drainage Basins; Hydrophysical Approach to Quantitative Morphology — 15
Geol. Soc. America Bull. **56**:281-300 (1945)

2 MELTON, M. A.: A Derivation of Strahler's Channel-Ordering System — 37
Jour. Geology **67**:345-346 (1959)

3 SCHUMM, S. A.: Evolution of Drainage Systems and Slopes in Badlands at Perth Amboy, New Jersey — 39
Geol. Soc. America Bull. **67**:602-611 (1956)

4 MAXWELL, J. C.: Quantitative Geomorphology of the San Dimas Experimental Forest, California — 51
Office of Naval Research Project 389-042, Technical Report No. 19, Dept. Geology, Columbia University, New York, pp. 22-24, 65, 67, and 68 (1960)

5 STRAHLER, A. N.: Quantitative Geomorphology of Drainage Basins and Channel Networks — 56
Handbook of Applied Hydrology, section 4-II, V. T. Chow, ed., McGraw-Hill, New York, pp. 4-39–4-76 (1964)

PART II: THE RANDOM MODEL OF DRAINAGE COMPOSITION

Editors' Comments on Papers 6 Through 13 — 96

6 SHREVE, R. L.: Statistical Law of Stream Numbers — 108
Jour. Geology **74**:17-37 (1966)

7 SHREVE, R. L.: Infinite Topologically Random Channel Networks — 129
Jour. Geology **75**:178-186 (1967)

8 SHREVE, R. L.: Stream Lengths and Basin Areas in Topologically Random Channel Networks — 138
Jour. Geology **77**:397-414 (1969)

Contents

9	**LIAO, K. H., and A. E. SCHEIDEGGER:** A Computer Model for Some Branching-Type Phenomena in Hydrology *Internat. Assoc. Sci. Hydrology Bull.* **13**:5-13 (1968)	156
10	**WERNER, C., and J. S. SMART:** Some New Methods of Topologic Classification of Channel Networks *Geog. Analysis* **5**:271-295 (1973)	165
11	**JARVIS, R. S., and A. WERRITTY:** Some Comments on Testing Random Topology Stream Network Models *Water Resources Research* **11**:309-318 (1975)	190
12	**JAMES, W. R., and W. C. KRUMBEIN:** Frequency Distributions of Stream Link Lengths *Jour. Geology* **77**:544-554, 563-565 (1969)	200
13	**MOCK, S. J.:** A Classification of Channel Links in Stream Networks *Water Resources Research* **7**:1558-1566 (1971)	214

PART III: NETWORK GROWTH AND SPACE FILLING

Editors' Comments on Papers 14 Through 18		224
14	**GLOCK, W. S.:** The Development of Drainage Systems: A Synoptic View *Geog. Review* **21**:475-482 (1931)	230
15	**HORTON, R. E.:** Erosional Development of Streams and Their Drainage Basins; Hydrophysical Approach to Quantitative Morphology *Geol. Soc. America Bull.* **56**:331-355 (1945)	238
16	**SCHUMM, S. A.:** Evolution of Drainage Systems and Slopes in Badlands at Perth Amboy, New Jersey *Geol. Soc. America Bull.* **67**:617-622 (1956)	263
17	**MORISAWA, M.:** Development of Drainage Systems on an Upraised Lake Floor *Am. Jour. Sci.* **262**:340-354 (1964)	269
18	**DACEY, M. F., and W. C. KRUMBEIN:** Three Growth Models for Stream Channel Networks *Jour. Geology* **84**:153-163 (1976)	284

PART IV: RIVER NETWORKS AND DRAINAGE BASIN GEOMORPHOLOGY

Editors' Comments on Papers 19 Through 24		296
19	**LEOPOLD, L. B., and J. P. MILLER:** Ephemeral Streams—Hydraulic Factors and Their Relation to the Drainage Net *U.S. Geol. Survey Prof. Paper 282-A*, 1956, pp. 16-24	302
20	**WARNTZ, W.:** Stream Ordering and Contour Mapping *Jour. Hydrology* **25**:209-227 (1975)	312
21	**CHORLEY, R. J., and P. F. DALE:** Cartographic Problems in Stream Channel Delineation *Cartography* **7**:150-162 (1972)	331

22	**GREGORY, K. J., and D. E. WALLING:** The Variation of Drainage Density Within a Catchment *Internat. Assoc. Sci. Hydrology Bulletin* **13**:61-68 (1968)	**345**
23	**KIRKBY, M. J.:** Tests of the Random Network Model, and Its Application to Basin Hydrology *Earth Surf. Processes* **1**:197-212 (1976)	**353**
24	**SMART, J. S.:** Quantitative Characterization of Channel Network Structure *Water Resources Research* **8**:1487-1496 (1972)	**369**

Author Citation Index — 379
Subject Index — 383
About the Editors — 386

SERIES EDITOR'S FOREWORD

The philosophy behind the Benchmark Papers in Geology is one of collection, sifting, and rediffusion. Scientific literature today is so vast, so dispersed, and, in the case of old papers, so inaccessible for readers not in the immediate neighborhood of major libraries that much valuable information has been ignored by default. It has become just so difficult, or so time consuming, to search out the key papers in any basic area of research that one can hardly blame a busy person for skimping on some of his or her "homework."

This series of volumes has been devised, therefore, as a practical solution to this critical problem. The geologist, perhaps even more than any other scientist, often suffers from twin difficulties—isolation from central library resources and immensely diffused sources of material. New colleges and industrial libraries simply cannot afford to purchase complete runs of all the world's earth science literature. Specialists simply cannot locate reprints or copies of all their principal reference materials. So it is that we are now making a concerted effort to gather into single volumes the critical materials needed to reconstruct the background of any and every major topic of our discipline.

We are interpreting "geology" in its broadest sense: the fundamental science of the planet Earth, its materials, its history, and its dynamics. Because of training in "earthy" materials, we also take in astrogeology, the corresponding aspect of the planetary sciences. Besides the classical core disciplines such as mineralogy, petrology, structure, geomorphology, paleontology, and stratigraphy, we embrace the newer fields of geophysics and geochemistry, applied also to oceanography, geochronology, and paleoecology. We recognize the work of the mining geologists, the petroleum geologists, the hydrologists, and the engineering and environmental geologists. Each specialist needs a working library. We are endeavoring to make the task of compiling such a library a little easier.

Each volume in the series contains an introduction prepared by a specialist (the volume editor)—a "state of the art" opening or a summary of the object and content of the volume. The articles, usually some twenty to fifty reproduced either in their entirety or in significant extracts, are selected in an attempt to cover the field, from the key papers of the last century to fairly recent work. Where the original works are in foreign languages, we have

Series Editor's Foreword

endeavored to locate or commission translations. Geologists, because of their global subject, are often acutely aware of the oneness of our world. The selections cannot therefore be restricted to any one country, and whenever possible an attempt is made to scan the world literature.

To each article, or group of kindred articles, some sort of "highlight commentary" is usually supplied by the volume editor. This commentary should serve to bring that article into historical perspective and to emphasize its particular role in the growth of the field. References, or citations, wherever possible, will be reproduced in their entirety—for by this means the observant reader can assess the background material available to that particular author, or, if desired, he or she too can double check the earlier sources.

A "benchmark," in surveyor's terminology, is an established point on the ground that is recorded on our maps. It is usually anything that is a vantage point, from a modest hill to a mountain peak. From the historical viewpoint, these benchmarks are the bricks of our scientific edifice.

RHODES W. FAIRBRIDGE

PREFACE

This volume presents key papers in fluvial network analysis. All but one were published after 1945, the date of Robert E. Horton's classic article. During the two subsequent decades, work on fluvial networks followed the Horton-Strahler tradition and developed the morphometric approach. Horton's geometric series laws described river networks with simple equations, which had a profound effect when presented as graphs. However, the graphs gave a false impression of precision; much information was lost in averaging network properties over stream orders. Horton had also attempted to relate his laws to hydrophysical processes and space filling. These goals have been only partially achieved.

Because of the shortcomings of the Hortonian approach, the link-based probabilistic approach introduced by Ronald L. Shreve has achieved considerable acceptance. The precise characterization of the network is better preserved using link-based measures, and several investigators have shown that Horton's laws could be generated by probabilistic means, bypassing physical and spatial considerations. Subsequent developments of the link-based approach have led to an increased understanding of the impact of environmental and spatial constraints on network topology and metrics.

Biologists have been reluctant to give up the Hortonian approach (they use Strahler orders), partly because the inherent generalization is seen to be a virtue, allowing compact models of form and/or flow for systems that can be very large. Additionally, some impressive evidence on the impact of physical constraints has come from the analysis of arteries, veins, airways, and Purkinje (brain) cells. Our current understanding of the pattern of topological variation in botanical trees seems to indicate a stronger role for genetics and space filling.

Each of the two editors of this book advocate some of the points of view briefly summarized above. Richard Jarvis has worked with the link-based approach, using the random model as a null hypothesis in order to detect deviations from randomness in rivers. Michael Woldenberg has searched for physical or spatial impacts in streams and in biological networks. We hope that these different approaches, and the debates they have provoked, are reflected in the selection of papers and our commentaries.

Several other volumes in the Benchmark series complement the work

Preface

on river networks presented here. In particular, *Drainage Basin Morphology* (Schumm, 1977) would be an excellent companion to this book. It contains the entire text of Horton's 1945 paper and almost all of Schumm's 1956 article. We have excerpted these two pivotal works here, focusing on their contributions to the study of the river network *per se*. The river network is clearly an integral part of the spatial assemblage of landforms that make up a drainage basin. All scientists concerned with the analysis of treelike networks, including those in fields other than fluvial geomorphology, should consider the characteristics of drainage basins as the context in which river networks develop. Further work on fluvial processes and river channel forms is contained in the volume on river morphology (Schumm, 1972).

We have organized our selection of Benchmark papers around four themes. The first two sections review chronologically the two major models of drainage composition: Horton's laws in Part I, and the random model in Part II. The review of the history of branch ordering in Part I and the historical comments in Part II were written by Michael Woldenberg. The evolution of channel networks and space filling within drainage basins are covered in Part III. Finally, Part IV deals with some applications of river network analysis to a variety of problems in drainage basin geomorphology and hydrology.

Michael Woldenberg wishes to thank the following organizations for financial support during the preparation of this volume: the State University of New York at Buffalo, the Johnson Fund of the American Philosophical Society, and the Minna James Heineman Fund administered by the Senior Scientists Program of N.A.T.O. Finally, we acknowledge the intellectual stimulus of the Philomorphs of Cambridge, Massachusetts.

RICHARD S. JARVIS
MICHAEL J. WOLDENBERG

REFERENCES

Horton, R. E., 1945, Erosional Development of Streams and Their Drainage Basins; Hydrophysical Approach to Quantitative Morphology, *Geol. Soc. America Bull.* **56:**275-370.

Schumm, S. A., 1956, Evolution of Drainage Systems and Slopes in Badlands at Perth Amboy, New Jersey, *Geol. Soc. America Bull.* **67:**597-646.

Schumm, S. A., 1972, *River Morphology,* Benchmark Papers in Geology, volume 2, Dowden, Hutchinson & Ross, Stroudsburg, Pa., 429p.

Schumm, S. A., 1977, *Drainage Basin Morphology,* Benchmark Papers in Geology, volume 41, Dowden, Hutchinson & Ross, Stroudsburg, Pa., 353p.

CONTENTS BY AUTHOR

Chorley, R. J., 331
Dacey, M. F., 284
Dale, P. F., 331
Glock, W. S., 230
Gregory, K. J., 345
Horton, R. E., 15, 238
James, W. R., 200
Jarvis, R. S., 190
Kirkby, J. J., 353
Krumbein, W. C., 200, 284
Leopold, L. B., 302
Liao, K. H., 156
Maxwell, J. C., 51

Melton, M. A., 37
Miller, J. P., 302
Mock, S. J., 214
Morisawa, M., 269
Scheidegger, A. E., 156
Schumm, S. A., 39, 263
Shreve, R. L., 108, 129, 138
Smart, J. S., 165, 369
Strahler, A. N., 56
Walling, D. E., 345
Warntz, W., 312
Werner, C., 165
Werritty, A., 190

INTRODUCTION

This book traces the important contributions of river network analysis to the study of fluvially eroded landscapes. Quantitative analyses by European hydraulic engineers of the physical relationships between channel form, resistance, and velocity were known in England by the beginning of the nineteenth century (Young, 1807). It is entirely possible that Hutton and Playfair knew of this work, but perhaps only after Playfair published his exposition of Hutton's ideas (Playfair, 1802). Gilbert (1877) is a classic early example of process-oriented work in fluvial geomorphology. However, the Davisian paradigm, and the debate over certain of its interpretations by its detractors, dominated geomorphic thought for the first half of the twentieth century. While Davis (1909) was concerned with the evolution of landforms over long spans of geologic time, the focus of more recent research has been on the response of landforms to current processes. River network analysis has been part of the revolution, or shift in paradigm in the sense of Kuhn (1962), that replaced the Davisian explanatory description of landforms with studies of process and morphometry.

The river network has long been recognized as an essential element in models of fluvial landscape evolution and organization. Network morphology has been used to express the stage of landscape development, and network parameters have been employed as indicators of the influence of geologic structure. In recent years network characteristics themselves have become a primary object of research.

Prior to Horton (1945), river networks were treated largely in a qualitative manner by geomorphologists. The pattern of drainage was seen as a useful indicator of geological control over landscape:

> It is evident that drainage patterns may reflect original slope and original structure or the successive episodes by which the surface has been modified, including uplift, depression, tilting, warping, folding, faulting, and jointing, as well as deposition by the sea, glaciers, volcanoes, wind, and rivers.... Moreover, as streams are long lived ... they may embody a long record of the geologic history of a region. (Zernitz, 1932, p. 498)

Introduction

Drainage patterns were generalized and classified into types indicative of particular geologic settings: dendritic, trellis, rectangular, radial, annular, parallel, pinnate, anastomotic, angulate, centripetal, and collinear. Many of these terms persist in general usage today. Although Zernitz (1932) viewed drainage patterns as "the key to landscape," the main question being posed was that of the relative importance of geologic structure and contemporary process in molding landscape to its present stage of evolution. Davis noted in his exposition of the geographical cycle of erosion that:

> The simple consequent drainage of youth is modified by the development of subsequent drainage lines, so as to bring about an *increasing adjustment of streams to structure,* than which nothing is more characteristic of the mature stage of the geographical cycle. (Davis, 1899, p. 492; Davis's emphasis)

The few attempts to treat drainage as channel networks whose branching structure might yield useful geomorphic information (e.g., Gravelius, 1914) made little impact.

Quantitative techniques, especially mathematical and graphical presentation, were first applied in Horton's seminal paper of 1945 in the attempt to create a unified model of a fluvially eroded surface. Horton understood that the very core of this model should be an analysis of the morphometry of the drainage network. All other elements of the model, although full of valuable insights, serve to explain the evolution of the drainage network. As the network develops, it tends to be in adjustment with the spatial elements of the land surface. Thus, Horton's paper begins with a statement of Playfair's law:

> Every river appears to consist of a main trunk, fed from a variety of branches, each running in a valley proportioned to its size, and all of them together forming a system of valleys connecting with one another, and having such a nice adjustment of their declivities that none of them join the principal valley either on too high or too low a level; a circumstance which would be infinitely improbable if each of these valleys were not the work of the stream which flows in it. (Playfair, 1802, p. 102)

Horton saw the complementarity between his and the Davisian model;

> The author has considered stream development and drainage-basin topography wholly from the view point of the operation of hydrophysical processes. In the Davis theory the same subject is treated largely with reference to the effects of antecedent geologic conditions and subsequent geologic changes. The two views bear much the same relation as two pictures of the same object taken in different lights—the results are not necessarily in conflict; each supplements the other. The hydrophysical concept appears to be more fundamental because it carries back to the original, newly exposed surface. (Horton, 1945, p. 367)

Introduction

The profession agreed; Horton's strategy for research became dominant, and with this strategy came a strong emphasis on quantitative geomorphology. Indeed, for nearly two decades after 1945 the words "quantitative geomorphology" in the title of an article were virtually synonymous with "a Hortonian drainage network analysis." To the extent that he opened the door for the quantitative analysis of fluvial landscapes, Horton's innovation and use of river network analysis, based on the topological concept of stream order, provided the key. Horton agreed with Playfair's realization that although river channels occupy but a tiny proportion of land surface area, they appear to play a major role in coordinating valleys and organizing space. While Playfair's use of the term *system* may be fortuitous, present-day geomorphologists can readily identify the river channel network as the linkage in the drainage basin system between a morphological subsystem of valley slope and channel forms and the cascading subsystem of the drainage basin hydrologic cycle (Chorley and Kennedy, 1971).

Having chosen the network as the focus of study, Horton made a crucial innovation that has had far-reaching consequences for the study of branching networks in geomorphology, as well as for several biological disciplines. He ordered branches centripetally—that is, from the twigs to the trunk. The reversal of the centrifugal, historical, or generational ordering direction commonly used in biology allowed for a closer correlation between order and measures of flow and size. This ordering reflected Horton's emphasis of the morphometric-process orientation over the historical development approach. Thus, Horton abandoned Davis's "life cycle" of a landscape, a biological frame of reference, in the interest of a better understanding of hydrophysical processes.

The topologic notion of centripetal stream order, introduced by Horton (1932, 1945) and modified by Strahler (1952), provided the framework of Horton's laws of drainage composition. Networks and basins were shown to exhibit a systematic hierarchical organization. The mathematical implications of Playfair's law were elegantly revealed, and the high degree of mutual adujustment between some of the morphologic components of fluvial landscapes was quantitatively established. By the end of the Hortonian era in the late 1960s, the influence of Strahler and his students had helped to release fluvial geomorphology from the straitjacket of the Davisian cycle. Drainage basins were seen as open systems in dynamic equilibrium, and nowhere was that dynamic equilibrium better displayed than in the hierarchical organization of river networks and the mutual adjustments of stream networks, basin areas, and channel and valley-side slopes.

Many studies in fluvial geomorphology that have little or no

Introduction

interest in river network properties *per se* still use them to define a sample of basins. With Horton's ordering system the outlet of a stream of a given order drains a basin of the same order, which is physically defined by a system of ridges (Woldenberg, 1969). In an individual basin, the outlet may be determined by some external feature that fixes a local base level—such as outflow into a lake or ocean or junction with a major river whose entire basin is beyond the scope of interest. But when a sample of drainage basin replicates is required for statistical analysis, a river network property most commonly provides the basis for defining basins. Indices of network size, such as order or magnitude, have proved very popular, not least because the only measurement process required is enumeration.

By the same principles, the river network can also be used to reference valley locations within drainage-basin space. River channel networks consist of nodes and links. Nodes are either sources (stream heads) or junctions. Links are unbroken reaches of channel that connect either a source to a junction (exterior links) or a junction to another junction or outlet (interior links). Drainage-basin space can be allocated to valleys, bounded laterally by divides and enclosing the area that drains directly to a link, or to a downstream sequence of links. Valleys can then be referenced to the links that drain them, and the link can be identified by the properties of the subnetwork that drains into it. As noted by Curtis et al. (1965): "The position of a site in a drainage basin may be referred to the orders of steams comprising the drainage net."

Horton also addressed the hydrological processes that generate stream flow. From considerations of infiltration and slope geometry he built a model of overland flow. Rill channels compete for flow and space and finally develop into stream channels. Stream channels subdivide the available space so that eventually channel, basin area, channel slope, and valley-side slope are linked in both the hydrologic and geomorphologic systems. The entire process is governed by physical laws. Subsequent research has revealed a more complex process of subsurface and return flow, so the Hortonian overland flow model is restricted in application to areas of impermeable surface (Kirkby and Chorley, 1967). While this and other details of his model may be modified, Horton's general methods remain unchallenged; they echo the principles of Gilbert on the importance of studying process in order to explain form, and form in order to understand process.

In spite of Horton's stated goal of relating his ratios and laws of drainage composition to the infiltration capacity and environmental factors of slope and climate (Horton, 1945, pp. 290, 339), very little was actually accomplished toward these ends. Furthermore, attempts to relate the topology to stream flow hydrographs were not successful in any quantitative way. The paradigm of Horton-Strahler stream network analysis had lost its vigor by 1965.

The Hortonian era ended as it had begun, with a basic reformulation of the way networks are classified. The revision appeared in two papers by Shreve in 1966 and 1967, which replaced the concept of stream order by that of link magnitude. Magnitude is another topologic index, given by the number of sources ultimately tributary to a link. Bifurcating networks of equal magnitude have equal numbers of sources and links and are thus of equal complexity. Shreve made the initial assumption that all topologically distinct channel networks (TDCN) of a given magnitude are equally probable. Hence the probability of occurrence of a network, or group of topologically classed networks, could be calculated using combinatorial analysis. Such probabilities are the mathematical expression of Shreve's fundamental geomorphic hypothesis that "in the absence of geologic controls a natural population of channel networks will be topologically random" (Shreve, 1966, p. 27).

The success of the combinatorial random models in predicting Horton's laws of drainage composition, along with certain other statistical regularities that were not anticipated by these laws, posed a challenge to those who attempted to link hydrophysical process to network topology. If very small networks, of magnitude six or less, could be shown to be topologically random, then there would in theory be no scope for physical or space-filling constraints to cause systematic patterns in network topology at this scale, provided the surface was free of geological controls. While topological randomness could not be definitively established for large-magnitude streams in a direct test, certain properties of large networks were found to be consistent with topological randomness (Smart, 1969, 1972).

Further probing of the properties of topologically random networks by James and Krumbein (1969) and by Mock (1971) has led to the discovery that large networks seem to deviate from topological randomness in certain systematic ways. This behavior may stem from space-filling constraints imposed by the network itself, rather than constrictions in available space due to geological structure (Flint, 1980; Abrahams, 1980; Jarvis and Sham, 1981). Other studies suggest that basin slope has an impact on river network topology (Abrahams, 1977; Woldenberg, 1977a, 1977b).

REFERENCES

Abrahams, A. D., 1977, The Factor of Relief in the Evolution of Channel Networks in Mature Drainage Basins, *Am. Jour. Sci.* **277**:626–646.

Abrahams, A. D., 1980, Divide Angles and Their Relation to Interior Link Lengths in Natural Channel Networks, *Geog. Analysis* **12**:157-171.

Chorley, R. J. and B. A. Kennedy, 1971, *Physical Geography, A Systems Approach,* Prentice-Hall, London, 370 p.

Introduction

Curtis, L. F., J. C. Doornkamp, and K. J. Gregory, 1965, The Description of Relief in Field Studies of Soils, *Jour. Soil Sci.* **16:**16-30.

Davis, W. M., 1899, The Geographical Cycle, *Geog. Jour.* **14:**481-504.

Davis, W. M., 1909, *Geographical Essays,* D.W. Johnson, ed., Ginn, Boston, 777p., (republished 1954, Dover, New York).

Flint, J. J., 1980, Tributary Arrangements in Fluvial Systems, *Am. Jour. Sci.* **280:**26-45.

Gilbert, G. K., 1877, *Report on the Geology of the Henry Mountains,* U.S. Geological Survey Rocky Mountain Region, Government Printing Office, Washington, D.C., 170p.

Gravelius, H., 1914, *Flüsskunde, Band I,* Goschenesche Verlagshandlung, Berlin and Leipzig, 176p.

Horton, R. E., 1932, Drainage-Basin Characteristics, *Am. Geophys. Union Trans.* **13:**350-361.

Horton, R. E., 1945, Erosional Development of Streams and Their Drainage Basins; Hydrophysical Approach to Quantitative Morphology, *Geol. Soc. America Bull.* **56:**275-370.

James, W. R., and W. C. Krumbein, 1969, Frequency Distributions of Stream Link Lengths, *Jour. Geology* **77:**544-565.

Jarvis, R. S., and C. H. Sham, 1981, Drainage Network Structure and the Diameter-Magnitude Relation, *Water Resources Research* **17:**1019-1027.

Kirkby, M. J., and R. J. Chorley, 1967, Throughflow, Overland Flow, and Erosion, *Internat. Assoc. Sci. Hydrology Bull.* **12**(3):5-21.

Kuhn, T. S., 1962, *The Structure of Scientific Revolutions,* University of Chicago Press, Chicago, 172p.

Mock, S. J., 1971, A Classification of Channel Links in Stream Networks, *Water Resources Research* **7:**1558-1566.

Playfair, J., 1802, *Illustrations of the Huttonian Theory of the Earth,* Cadell and Davies, London, 528p., (republished 1956, Dover, New York).

Shreve, R. L., 1966, Statistical Law of Stream Numbers, *Jour. Geology* **74:**17-37.

Shreve, R. L., 1967, Infinite Topologically Random Channel Networks, *Jour. Geology* **75:**178-186.

Smart, J. S., 1969, Topological Properties of Channel Networks, *Geol. Soc. America Bull.* **80:**1757-1774.

Smart, J. S., 1972, Channel Networks, *Advances in Hydroscience* **8:**305-346.

Strahler, A. N., 1952, Hypsometric (Area-Altitude) Analysis of Erosional Topography, *Geol. Soc. America Bull.* **63:**1117-1142.

Woldenberg, M. J., 1969, Spatial Order in Fluvial Systems: Horton's Laws Derived from Mixed Hexagonal Hierarchies of Drainage Basin Areas, *Geol. Soc. America Bull.* **80:**97-112.

Woldenberg, M. J., 1977a, Relation of Bifurcation Ratio to Relief Ratio in Tidal Streams (Abstract), *EOS, Am. Geophys. Union Trans.* **58:**393.

Woldenberg, M. J., 1977b, Negative and Positive Relationships of Bifurcation Ratio with Increasing Relief Ratio (Abstract), *EOS, Am. Geophys. Union Trans.* **58:**1136.

Young, T., 1807, *A Course of Lectures on Natural Philosophy and the Mechanical Arts,* 2 vols., Taylor and Walton, London (new edn. 1845).

Zernitz, E. R., 1932, Drainage Patterns and Their Significance, *Jour. Geology* **40:**498-521.

Part I
HORTON'S LAWS OF DRAINAGE COMPOSITION

Editors' Comments
on Papers 1 Through 5

1 HORTON
Excerpt from *Erosional Development of Streams and Their Drainage Basins; Hydrophysical Approach to Quantitative Morphology*

2 MELTON
A Derivation of Strahler's Channel-Ordering System

3 SCHUMM
Excerpt from *Evolution of Drainage Systems and Slopes in Badlands at Perth Amboy, New Jersey*

4 MAXWELL
Excerpt from *Quantitative Geomorphology of the San Dimas Experimental Forest, California*

5 STRAHLER
Quantitative Geomorphology of Drainage Basins and Channel Networks

In a major work, posthumously published, Horton (1945) laid the foundations for quantitative for fluvial geomorphology. It was not his first treatment of quantitative indices of drainage basin morphology (Horton, 1932), but is the most complete statement of his ideas on morphometry and its relations to hydrology, landscape evolution, and the principles of space filling. Horton's proposition of the laws of drainage composition generated a major stimulus to further research. The derivation of these laws of stream numbers, lengths, and slopes forms the first part of his 1945 article (Paper 1). Yet the laws themselves were not Horton's primary objective. He sought to develop a set of tools for quantitative landform analysis, and the first two measures he presented were stream order and drainage density.

In some ways Horton's most striking contribution was the centripetal ordering system. Instead of ordering branches of riverine trees centrifugally, in terms of a developmental sequence of generations from the trunk to the branches, Horton ordered from the fingertip tributaries down to the trunk. The generational method had been used by biologists from at least the seventeenth century to modern times. This approach was modified and applied to rivers by Gravelius (1914). However, Horton's method causes branches of the same order to be similar in size, while centrifugal orders show a poor correlation with size. For perfectly symmetrical dichotomous systems, both centrifugal and centripetal orders should correlate well with some measure of size—but perfect dichotomy is extremely rare in nature. Natural treelike systems are said to branch with asymmetry; hence a centripetal method of ordering is required for morphometric, as opposed to developmental, studies.

Horton's stream orders led to the discovery of the geometric-series laws of steam numbers and lengths, whose branching ratios form two of the five properties needed to "determine completely the composition of the stream system" (Paper 1, p. 295). The others are basin area, order, and average length of the first-order streams. These five properties determine the drainage density, in a relationship that Horton saw as a quantitative generalization of Playfair's law, wherein the "nice adjustment goes far beyond the matter of declivities" (Paper 1, p. 291). The laws of drainage composition and their relation to Playfair's law provide the conceptual basis for quantitative fluvial morphometry.

It is appropriate to digress a bit here so that we may give credit to some of the early authors who used the concept of branching order. A very early reference to the ordering of a branching system is by Winthrop (1670). Winthrop, who was governor of the colony of Connecticut, reported the discovery of an echinoderm, later referred to as *Astrophyton* (Lyman, 1878). Winthrop studied the bifurcations on each arm of the starfish and assumed, for the purpose of counting all the branches, perfect dichotomous branching. He noted that the diameters of the two distal branches at a junction are not symmetrical, but nonetheless assumed that the number of branches doubles at each generation. Later Lyman (1878) confirmed that some branches die out and gave a table from which one can reconstruct part of the topology of the network.

While Winthrop deduced a geometeric-series number law for generations of dichotomous branches, Keill (1708, 1717, 1738) extended the geometric-progression laws to predict the decrease of diameter and blood velocity in the human arterial network. From measurements of diameters of the capillaries and aorta and the average ratio of cross-sectional areas between generations at a junction, Keill was able to estimate the number of generations and the diameters at each generation. Using this information, and an estimate of the peak and average velocities of blood as it enters the aorta, Keill showed how to calculate the velocity of blood at each generation. He found the velocity must be lower in the smaller branches, a fact deduced in a somewhat related way for rivers over 200 years later (Leopold and Maddock, 1953). Keill (1738) also used the sum of an infinite geometric series to calculate the transit time for passage of the blood in the mesenteric artery. Horton used the same mathematical tools to calculate drainage density.

Young (1809) essentially repeated the methods and extended the findings of Keill in an elegant article on the circulation of the blood. It is interesting that Young studied medicine at Edinburgh University in 1797, and among the professors at the university at that time were Playfair, who was known to Young, and Hutton, who died that year. In their methods and kinds of results, Keill's book of 1708 and Young's article of 1809 are remarkably similar to the network morphometry described in the widely acclaimed book by Weibel (1963). However, all these results are flawed by the use of a generational ordering system and by the modeling assumptions of perfect dichotomy and perfect symmetry.

While Horton had copious data that fit the geometric series, Young and Keill simply imagined that such laws should exist in the arterial tree. Building on the ideas introduced by Keill, Young developed geometric-series laws for number, diameter, length, cross-sectional area, velocity, surface area, volume, and resistance. He used the formula for an infinite geometric series to calculate total volume and total resistance. The actual data available were minimal, but sufficient to allow development of the equations. Although the generational model of geometric progression equations was based on the (mistaken) idea that the number of branches at each generation increased by a power of two, we should still acknowledge Keill for the first comprehensive use of such relations, and Young for the most thorough development of these equations to model a treelike system. Horton independently rediscovered them, but this time they were stated in terms of a centripetal ordering system and provided a better morphometric model of the tree.

The first modification of Horton's work concerned the method of stream ordering, replacing Horton's ordered streams with Strahler's ordered segments. Strahler orders were formally introduced to the literature in a footnote (Strahler, 1952, p. 1120), but they rapidly preempted Horton's method as the most common basis for river network analysis. Strahler's revision was initially seen as just a simplification, avoiding the geomorphologic subjectivity of Horton's headward extension of order assignments. The revision also improved the correlation of order and size. But this view misses the point that

Strahler orders are a basic mathematical concept, not restricted to one particular kind of treelike network. The general derivation of Strahler ordering was shown by Melton (Paper 2), who also reminded geomorphologists of some other fundamental topologic properties of treelike graphs. In the light of later developments, Melton's note is an important precursor of the applications of graph theory and combinatorial probability theory in Shreve's random model (see Part II). Both Melton and Shreve cite the same book on combinatorial analysis (Riordan, 1958). Ironically, work along these lines ultimately revealed the shortcomings of Hortonian network analysis.

Two more laws of drainage composition were discovered by Schumm (Paper 3). He formalized the fourth law of drainage basin areas, which had been hinted by Horton, and then coined a fifth law for the relationship between mean basin area and channel length over successive orders. From the latter Schumm defined the constant of channel maintenance, complementing Horton's textural measures of drainage density, stream frequency, and length of overland flow. A major theme of both Horton's and Schumm's papers concerns network growth and associated landform development within a drainage basin (see further excerpts in Papers 14 and 15). Schumm also realized that growth has implications for stream orders, and he investigated how network extension increases the order of existing streams. In Paper 3 he searched for limiting values of stream length and basin area beyond which new orders appear and identified the role of interbasin areas. The topologic consequences of network extension were later examined for bifurcation ratios by Coffman et al. (1972).

One complication arising from Strahler's revision of the ordering method was that the bifurcation ratio of the two highest orders was usually less than the common ratio for the rest of the orders (Schumm, 1956; Broscoe, 1959; Paper 4). The relationships between Horton- and Strahler-ordered lengths are discussed by Broscoe (1959) and Bowden and Wallis (1964), along with various issues of network definition that will be addressed in Part IV. They showed that mean segment lengths for each Strahler order should be cumulated before calculating the relationship between order and cumulative length. This procedure allows an approximation to the length of the basin to be regressed against order. Schumm and Maxwell both proposed some modifications in the definition of bifurcation ratios, so it is often difficult to compare published values of either bifurcation ratios or stream-length ratios when different authors have used slightly different computational methods (see Smart, 1972).

In addition to the properties incorporated in the laws of drainage composition, several other network or basin properties have been found to have meaningful relationships with stream order. Broscoe

(1959) found the vertical drop in successive orders often remains constant, and, assuming the geometric progression of length with order, this relationship between stream order and relief implies a semi-log plot for stream profiles. Later, Fok (1971) and Yang (1971) also claimed that average stream relief is an arithmetic function of stream order and that riverbed profiles can be described by semi-log equations of stream relief as a function of stream length. Maxwell (Paper 4) found that both basin diameter length and relief follow increasing geometric series with order; drainage density and channel frequency decrease with order, while basin-shape elongation seems to be independent of order. The last result would tend to support Strahler's (1958) notion of the geometrical similarity of basins of different sizes. However, Hack (1957) found that mainstream length increases as the 0.6 power of basin area, and this relationship implies increasing elongation of basin shape with size. Leopold and Miller (see Paper 19) related stream discharge to order, linking the relations of discharge to drainage area and area to stream order and thus forming a bridge to the analysis of the hydraulic geometry of streams (Leopold and Maddock, 1953).

In the years after 1945, the promotion and development of Hortonian analysis was dominated by the work of Strahler and his associates. There is no better summary of the achievements of this period than the review by Strahler (Paper 5). Strahler related river network analysis to drainage basin geomorphology in the context of an open system in a steady state (see also Chorley, 1962). He developed the ideas of dimensional analysis and the geometrical similarity of drainage basins. True to Hortonian principles, he saw the study of drainage basins and channel networks as "a rigorous quantitative science capable of providing hydrologists with numerical data of practical value" (Paper 5, p. 4-40). Much more than Horton, who was content to fit his laws graphically by inspection, Strahler promoted the application of statistical methods.

By the time Paper 5 appeared in 1964, various shortcomings of Hortonian analysis were becoming apparent. Early presentations and abstracts by Shreve in 1963 and 1964 began to emphasize the law of stream numbers as a statistical relation, which Bowden and Wallis (1964, p. 769) argued was "a result of the definition of stream order rather than being due to either orderly evolution or random development." The geomorphic relevance of Horton's laws was dismissed by Milton (1966), who, like Shreve, saw the laws as outcomes of a probabilistic process. The sensitivity of Hortonian branching ratios to differences in regional geomorphic environment remained unresolved. Horton originally envisaged typical values of the bifurcation ratio ranging from "about 2 for flat or rolling drainage basins up to 3 or 4 for mountainous or highly dissected drainage basins" (1945, p. 290). The empirical validity of this suggestion was questioned very early by Strahler (1952, p. 1136). But there were still several successful developments. Chorley and Morgan (1962) used Hortonian analysis to clarify distinctions between two regions of similar relief and lithology. Eyles (1968) offered geomorphic interpretations of some deviations from Horton's laws, particularly the effects of stream rejuvenation on the law of stream numbers and the effects of the approach to cyclic old age on the laws of stream length, area, slope, and relative relief. Woldenberg (1971, 1979) argued for the existence of a limited number (eleven) of preferred hierarchies of "stream" numbers of various treelike networks of rivers, blood vessels, airways, brain cells, and botanical trees. Each hierarchy has a different bifurcation ratio, and the bifurcation ratio appears to be inversely related to the quotient of power available divided by power required (Woldenberg, 1979).

REFERENCES

Bowden, K. L., and J. R. Wallis, 1964, Effect of Stream-Ordering Technique on Horton's Laws of Drainage Composition, *Geol. Soc. America Bull.* **75:**767-774.

Broscoe, A. J., 1959, Quantitative Analysis of Longitudinal Stream Profiles of Small Watersheds, *Office of Naval Research, Project NR 389-042, Technical Report No. 18,* Dept. Geology, Columbia University, New York, 73p.

Chorley, R. J., 1962, Geomorphology and General Systems Theory, *U.S. Geol. Survey Prof. Paper 500-B,* 10p.

Chorley, R. J., and M. A. Morgan, 1962, Comparison of Morphometric Features, Unaka Mountains, Tennessee and North Carolina, and Dartmoor, England, *Geol. Soc. America Bull.* **73:**17-34.

Coffman, D. M., E. A. Keller, and W. N. Melhorn, 1972, New Topologic Relationship as an Indicator of Drainage Network Evolution, *Water Resources Research* **8:**1497-1505.

Eyles, R. J., 1968, Stream Net Ratios in West Malaysia, *Geol. Soc. America Bull.* **79:**701-712.

Fok, Y-S, 1971, Law of Stream Relief in Horton's Stream Morphological System, *Water Resources Research* **7:**201-203.

Gravelius, H., 1914, *Flüsskunde, Band I,* Goschenesche Verlagshandlung, Berlin and Leipzig, 176p.

Hack, J. T., 1957, Studies of Longitudinal Stream Profiles in Virginia and Maryland, *U.S Geol. Survey Prof. Paper 294-B,* pp. 45-97.

Horton, R. E., 1932, Drainage-Basin Characteristics, *Am. Geophys. Union Trans.* **13:**350-361.

Horton, R. E., 1945, Erosional Development of Streams and Their Drainage Basins; Hydrophysical Approach to Quantitative Morphology, *Geol. Soc. America Bull.* **56:**275-370.

Keill, J., 1708, *An Account of Animal Secretion, the Quantity of Blood in the Humane Body, and Muscular Motion,* George Strahan, London, 187p.

Keill, J., 1717, *Essays on Several Parts of the Animal Oeconomy,* George Strahan, London, 2nd ed., 233p.

Keill, J., 1738, *Essays on Several Parts of the Animal Oeconomy. The Fourth Edition to Which is Added a Dissertation Concerning the Force of the Heart, by James Jurin, M. D., F. R. S., with Dr. Keill's Answer and Dr. Jurin's Reply. Also Medicina Statica Britannica, or Statical Observations Made in England, by James Keill, M. D., Explained and Compared with the Aphorisms of Sanctorius, by John Quincy, M. D.,* George Strahan, London, 295p.

Leopold, L. B., and T. Maddock, Jr., 1953, The Hydraulic Geometry of Stream Channels and Some Physiographic Implications, *U.S. Geol. Survey Prof. Paper 252,* 56p.

Lyman, T., 1878, Mode of Forking among Astrophytons, *Boston Soc. Nat. History Proc.* **19:**102–108, and Plates 4–7.

Milton, L. E., 1966, The Geomorphic Irrelevance of Some Drainage Net Laws, *Australian Geog. Stud.* **4:**89–95.

Riordan, J., 1958, *An Introduction to Combinatorial Analysis,* Wiley, New York, 244p.

Schumm, S. A., 1956, Evolution of Drainage Systems and Slopes in Badlands at Perth Amboy, New Jersey, *Geol. Soc. America Bull.* **67:**597–646.

Smart, J. S., 1972, Channel Networks, *Advances in Hydroscience* **8:**305–346.

Strahler, A. N., 1952, Hypsometric (Area-Altitude) Analysis of Erosional Topography, *Geol. Soc. America Bull.* **63:**1117–1142.

Strahler, A. N., 1958, Dimensional Analysis Applied to Fluvially Eroded Landforms, *Geol. Soc. America Bull.* **69:**279–300.

Weibel, E., 1963, *Morphometry of the Human Lung,* Springer Verlag, Berlin, 151p.

Winthrop, J., 1670, An Extract of a Letter Written by John Winthrop, Esq., Governour of Connecticut in New England, . . . Concerning Some Natural Curiosities . . . Especially a Very Strange and Very Curiously Contrived Fish . . . *Royal Society London Philos. Trans.* **4:**1151–1153, and Figure 1, facing p. 1142.

Woldenberg, M. J., 1971, A Structural Taxonomy of Spatial Hierarchies, in *Regional Forecasting,* M. Chisholm, A. Frey, and P. Haggett, ed., Butterworth, London, pp. 147–175.

Woldenberg, M. J., 1979, A Periodic Table of Spatial Hierarchies, in *Philosophy in Geography,* S. Gale and G. Olson, eds., D. Reidel, Dordrecht, pp. 429–456.

Yang, C. T., 1971, Potential Energy and Stream Morphology, *Water Resources Research* **7:**311–322.

Young, T., 1809, The Croonian Lecture. On the Functions of the Heart and Arteries, *Royal Soc. London Philos. Trans.* **99:**1–31.

EROSIONAL DEVELOPMENT OF STREAMS AND THEIR DRAINAGE BASINS; HYDROPHYSICAL APPROACH TO QUANTITATIVE MORPHOLOGY

Robert E. Horton

[*Editors' Note:* In the original, material precedes this excerpt.]

QUANTITATIVE PHYSIOGRAPHIC FACTORS

GENERAL CONSIDERATIONS

In spite of the general renaissance of science in the present century, physiography as related in particular to the development of land forms by erosional and gradational processes still remains largely qualitative. Stream basins and their drainage basins are described as "youthful," "mature," "old," "poorly drained," or "well drained," without specific information as to how, how much, or why. This is probably the result largely of lack of adequate tools with which to work, and these tools must be of two kinds: measuring tools and operating tools.

One purpose of this paper is to describe two sets of tools which permit an attack on the problems of the development of land forms, particularly drainage basins and their stream nets, along quantitative lines.

An effort will be made to show how the problem of erosional morphology may be approached quantitatively, and even in this respect only the effects of surface runoff will be considered in detail. Drainage-basin development by ground-water erosion, highly important as it is, will not be considered, and the discussion of drainage development by surface runoff will mainly be confined to processes occurring outside of stream channels. The equally important phase of the subject, channel development—including such problems as those of the growth of channel dimensions with increase of size of drainage basin, stream profiles, and stream bends—will not be considered in detail.

STREAM ORDERS

In continental Europe attempts have been made to classify stream systems on the basis of branching or bifurcation. In this system of stream orders, the largest, most branched, main or stem stream is usually designated as of order 1 and smaller tributary streams of increasingly higher orders (Gravelius, 1914). The smallest unbranched fingertip tributaries are given the highest order, and, although these streams are similar in characteristics in different drainage basins, they are designated as of different orders.

Feeling that the main or stem stream should be of the highest order, and that unbranched fingertip tributaries should always be designated by the same ordinal, the author has used a system of stream orders which is the inverse of the European system. In this system, unbranched fingertip tributaries are always designated as of order 1, tributaries or streams of the 2d order receive branches or tributaries of the 1st order, but these only; a 3d order stream must receive one or more tributaries of the 2d order but may also receive 1st order tributaries. A 4th order stream receives branches of the 3d and usually also of lower orders, and so on. Using this system the order of the main stream is the highest.

To determine which is the parent and which the tributary stream upstream from the last bifurcation, the following rules may be used:

(1) Starting below the junction, extend the parent stream upstream from the bifurcation in the same direction. The stream joining the parent stream at

the greatest angle is of the lower order. Exceptions may occur where geologic controls have affected the stream courses.

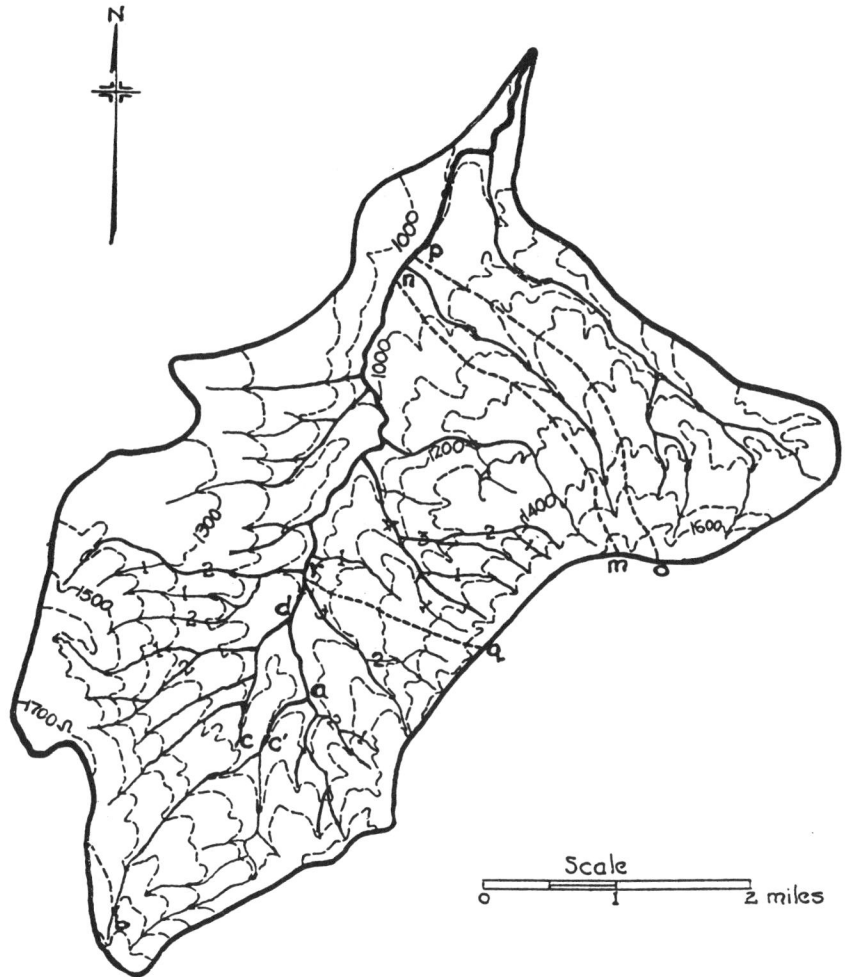

FIGURE 1.—*Well-drained basin*
(Cherry Creek, N. Y., quad., U. S. G. S.)

(2) If both streams are at about the same angle to the parent stream at the junction, the shorter is usually taken as of the lower order.

On Figure 1 several streams are numbered 1, and these are 1st order tributaries. Streams numbered 2 are of the 2nd order throughout their length, both below and above the junctions of their 1st order tributaries. The main stream is apparently $ac'b$ although it joins ad at nearly a right angle. It is probable that the original course of the stream was dcb, but the portion above dc was diverted by headwater erosion into stream ac'. The well-drained basin (Fig. 1) is of the 5th order, while the poorly drained basin (Fig. 2) is of the 2d order. Stream order therefore affords a simple quantitative basis for comparison of the degree of development in the drainage nets of basins of comparable size. Its usefulness as a basis for such comparisons is limited by the fact that, other things equal, the order of a drainage basin or its stream system generally increases with size of the drainage area.

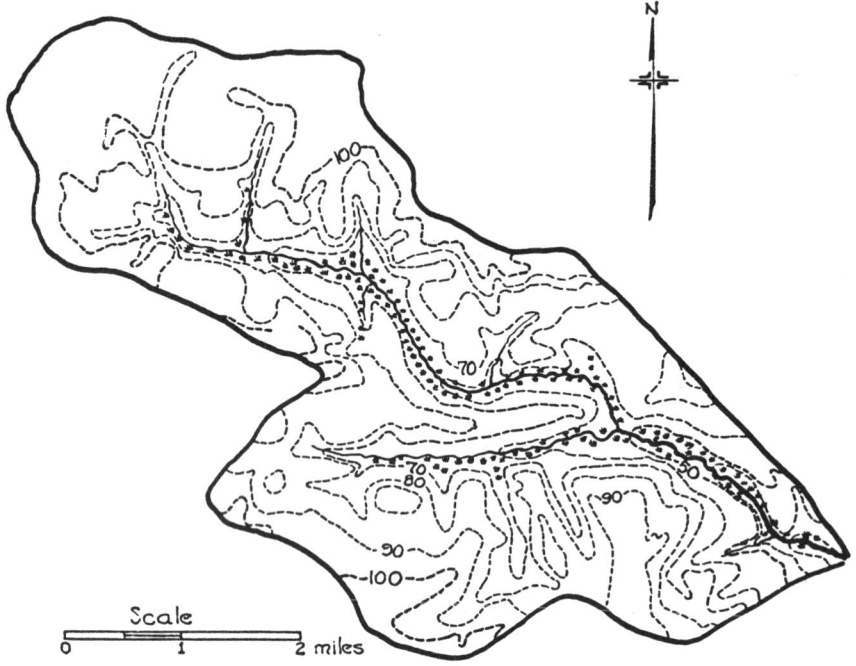

FIGURE 2.—*Flat sandy area, poorly drained*
(Bridgeton, N. J., quad. U. S. G. S.)

DRAINAGE DENSITY

Figures 1 and 2 show two small drainage basins, both on the same scale; one well drained, the other poorly drained. These terms, well drained and poorly drained, while in common use in textbooks on physiography, are purely qualitative, and something better is needed to characterize the degree of drainage development within a basin. The simplest and most convenient tool for this purpose is drainage density or average length of streams within the basin per unit of area (Horton, 1932). Expressed as an equation

$$\text{Drainage density, } D_d = \frac{\Sigma L}{A} \qquad (1)$$

where ΣL is the total length of streams and A is the area, both in units of the same system. The poorly drained basin has a drainage density 2.74, the well-drained one, 0.73, or one fourth as great.

For accuracy, drainage density must, if measured directly from maps, be determined from maps on a sufficiently large scale to show all permanent natural stream channels, as do the U. S. Geological Survey topographic maps. On these maps perennial streams are usually shown by solid blue lines, intermittent streams by dotted blue lines. Both should be included. If only perennial streams were included, a drainage basin containing only intermittent streams would, in accordance with equation (1), have zero drainage density, although it may have a considerable degree of basin development. Most of the work of valley and stream development by running water is performed during floods. Intermittent and ephemeral streams carry flood waters, hence should be included in determining drainage density. Most streams which are perennial in their lower reaches or throughout most of their courses have an intermittent or ephemeral reach or both, near their headwaters, where the stream channel has not cut down to the water table. These reaches should also be included in drainage-density determinations.

In textbooks on physiography, differences of drainage density are commonly attributed to differences of rainfall or relief, and these differences in drainage density are largely used to characterize physiographic age in the sense used by Davis (Davis, 1909; Wooldridge and Morgan, 1937). In the poorly drained area (Fig. 2) the mean annual rainfall is about 30 per cent greater than in the well-drained area (Fig. 1). Therefore some other factor or factors are far more important than either rainfall or relief in determining drainage density. These other factors are infiltration-capacity of the soil or terrain and initial resistivity of the terrain to erosion.

LENGTH OF OVERLAND FLOW

The term "length of overland flow," designated l_o, is used to describe the length of flow of water over the ground before it becomes concentrated in definite stream channels. To a large degree length of overland flow is synonymous with length of sheet flow as quite commonly used. The distinction between overland flow and channel flow is not so vague or uncertain as might at first appear. Overland flow is sustained by a relatively thin layer of surface detention. This disappears quickly—often in a few minutes—through absorption by the soil or infiltration after rain ends. Surface detention and surface runoff may, in fact, end before rain ends if, as is often the case, there is at the end of the storm an interval of residual rainfall having an intensity less than the infiltration-capacity. Channel flow is sustained by accumulated channel storage. This drains out slowly and lasts for hours or even days after channel inflow from surface runoff ends.

In addition to its obvious value in various ways in characterizing the degree of development of a drainage net within a basin, drainage density is particularly useful because of the fact that the average length of overland flow l_o is in most cases approximately half the average distance between the stream channels and hence is approximately equal to half the reciprocal of the drainage density, or

$$l_o = \frac{1}{2D_d} \qquad (2)$$

Later it will be shown that length of overland flow is one of the most important independent variables affecting both the hydrologic and physiographic development of drainage basins.

In this paper it is frequently assumed for purposes of convenience that the average length of overland flow is sensibly equal to the reciprocal of twice the drainage density. From considerations of the geometry of streams and their drainage areas the author has shown (Horton, 1932) that the average length of overland flow is given by the equation

$$l_o = \frac{1}{2D_d \sqrt{1 - \left(\frac{s_c}{s_g}\right)^2}} \tag{3}$$

where s_c is the channel or stream slope and s_g the average ground slope in the area.

Values of the correction factor or of the ratio $l_o/2D_d$ for different values of the slope ratio s_c/s_g are as follows:

s_c/s_g =	0.9	0.8	0.7	0.6	0.5	0.4	0.3	0.2	0.1
$l_o/2D_d$ =	1.86	1.67	1.40	1.25	1.15	1.09	1.05	1.02	1.005

The ground slope or resultant slope of the area tributary to a stream on either side is necessarily always greater than the channel slope since the ground surface has a component of slope parallel with and of the same order of magnitude as that of the stream, and in addition it has a component of slope at right angles to the stream.

Table 4 shows the average channel and ground slopes of streams in the Delaware River and some other drainage basins, derived from topographic maps. The channel slope in these instances is commonly from half to one fourth the ground slope. Often on an area which as a whole is nearly horizontal, but the surface of which is interspersed with hills, the ground slope may be and frequently is two or three times the channel slope. If the channel slope is less than one third the ground slope, the error resulting from the assumption that average length of overland flow is equal to the reciprocal of twice the drainage density may in general be neglected.

STREAM FREQUENCY

This is the number of streams, F_s, per unit of area, or

$$F_s = \frac{N}{A} \tag{4}$$

where N = total number of streams in a drainage basin of A areal units.

Values of drainage density and stream frequency for small and large drainage basins are not directly comparable because they usually vary with the size of the drainage area. A large basin may contain as many small or fingertip tributaries per unit of area as a small drainage basin, and in addition it usually contains a larger stream or streams. This effect may be masked by the increase of drainage density and stream frequency on the steeper slopes generally appurtenant to smaller drainage basins.

COMPOSITION OF DRAINAGE NET

The term "drainage pattern" is used in rather a restricted sense in many books on physiography, implying little more than the manner of distribution of a given set of tributary streams within the drainage basin. Thus, for example, with identically the same lengths and numbers of streams, the drainage pattern may be dendritic, rectangular, or radial. Neither the drainage pattern nor the drainage density, nor both, provide an adequate characterization of the stream system or drainage net in a given basin. There may be various combinations of stream numbers, lengths, and orders which will give the same drainage density, or there may be similar forms of drainage pattern with widely different drainage and stream densities. Something more is needed as a basis for quantitative morphology of drainage basins. The author has therefore coined the expression "composition of a drainage net," as distinguished from "drainage pattern." Composition implies the numbers and lengths of streams and tributaries of different sizes or orders, regardless of their pattern. Composition has a high degree of hydrologic significance, whereas pattern alone has but little hydrologic significance, although it is highly significant in relation to geologic control of drainage systems.

Cotton (1935) and others have used the term "texture" to express composition of a drainage net as related both to drainage density and stream frequency. For quantitative purposes two terms are needed, since two drainage nets with the same drainage densities may have quite different numbers and lengths of streams. Numerical values of drainage density independent of other units are needed for various purposes.

LAWS OF DRAINAGE COMPOSITION

The numbers and lengths of tributaries of different orders were determined for the streams listed in Table 1. The numbers and the lengths of streams varied with the stream order in a manner which suggested a geometrical progression. Plotting the data on semilogarithmic paper it was found (Fig. 3) that the stream numbers fall close to straight lines, and (Fig. 4) the same is true of the stream lengths. From the manner of plotting, these lines are necessarily graphs of geometrical series, inverse for stream numbers of different orders and direct for stream lengths.[1]

From the properties of geometric series, the equation of the lines giving the number N_o of streams of a given order in a drainage basin can be written

$$N_o = r_b^{(s-o)}. \qquad (5)$$

From the laws governing geometric series it is easily shown that the number N of streams of all orders is

$$N = \frac{r_b^s - 1}{r_b - 1}. \qquad (6)$$

By definition, o is the order of a given class of tributaries, s is the order of the main stream, and r_b is the bifurcation ratio.

The equation correlating the lengths of streams of different orders is, similarly,

$$l_a = l_1 r_l^{o-1}. \qquad (7)$$

---

[1] In the figure the lines of best fit were drawn by inspection. Somewhat more accurate lines could of course be obtained by the method of least squares or the correlation method. However, the agreement of the observed points with the lines located by inspection is so close in most cases that little would be gained in accuracy by the use of these methods.

TABLE 1.—Characteristics of the drainage nets of certain stream basins

Stream	Location	Type	Order of Main Stream o	Area Sq.Mi. A	No. of Streams ΣN_o	No. of 1st order streams N_1	Stream Frequency F_s	Drainage Density D_d	Aver. lgth 1st order streams L_1	Bifur-cation ratio r_b	Length ratio r_l	ΣL
(1)	(2)	(3)	(4)	(5)	(6)	(7)	(8)	(9)	(10)	(11)	(12)	(13)
Esopus Creek	Olive Bridge, N.Y.	Mountains	5	234	126	90	0.527	0.849	0.99	3.12	2.31	203.2
" "	Lower Area *	Rolling and Plains	7	426.3	361	256	.847	.818	.81	2.27	1.84	348.6
Randout "	Honk Falls, N.Y.	Mountains	4	105.	58	44	.552	1.07	1.08	3.30	2.64	112.6
Putnam Brook	Weedsport, N.Y.	Glacial, Drumlin	4	27	26	18	.963	1.95	.77	2.46	2.74	52.7
Cold Spring Brook	"	"	4	15.8	25	15	1.58	2.025	.58	2.62	2.66	32.
Crane Creek	"	"	5	45.7	48	31	1.05	2.03	.81	2.22	2.30	92.6
Ganarqua Creek	Lyons, N.Y.	"	6	299.	269	166	.899	1.628	.87	2.89	2.30	487.1
Kauka Lake	Foot of Lake, , N.Y.	Hilly, Dissected	5	161.†	170	124	1.055	1.665	1.16	3.25	1.96	268.
Seneca "	" " "	"	6	479.†	472	334	.984	1.59	.95	3.15	2.20	762.5
Owasco "	Weedsport, " **	"	5	200.	265	191	1.325	1.79	.83	3.91	2.22	358.
Thunder Bay River	Alpena, Mich. **	Glacial ~ Flat	4	—	44	33	—	—	—	3.00	—	—

*Ashokan Dam to Saugerties, N.Y. ** Data furnished by Prof. C.O. Wisler. † Land area, excluding lake.

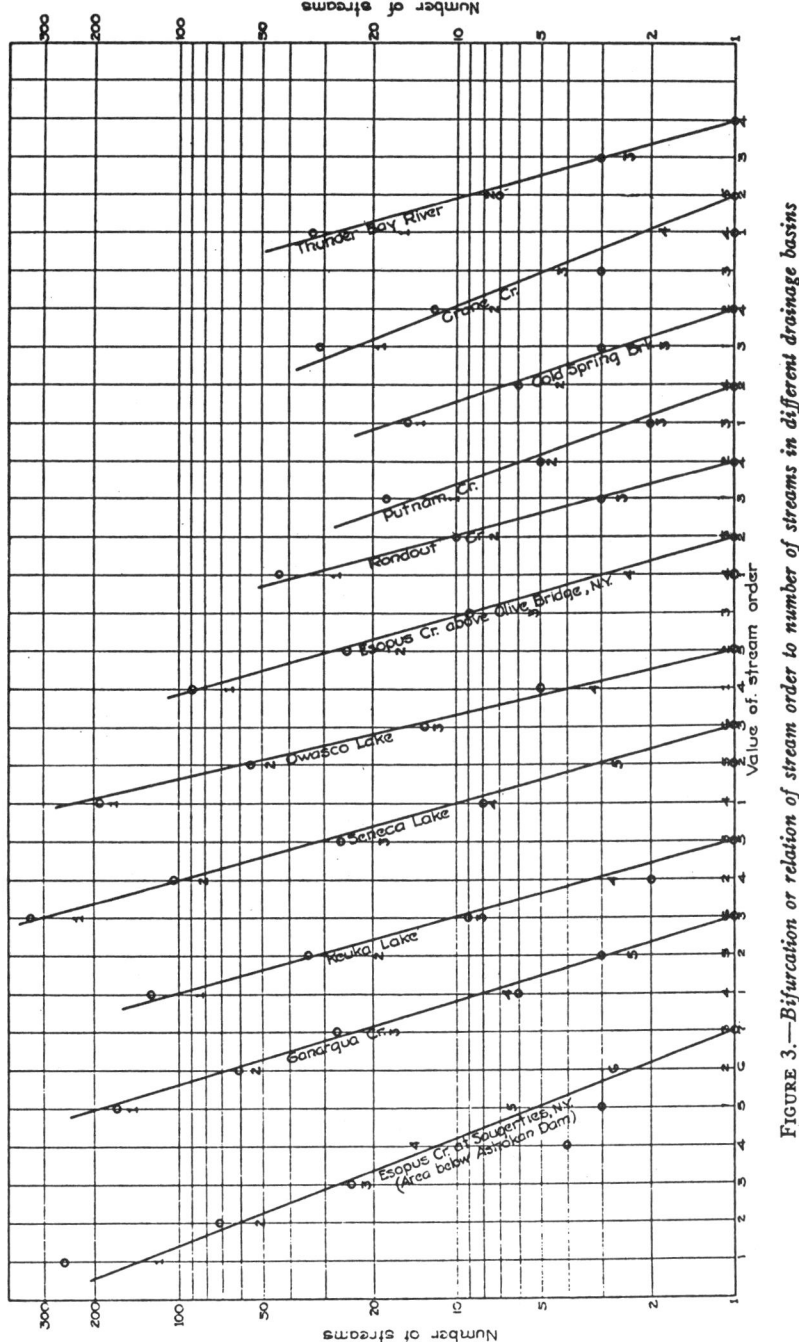

FIGURE 3.—Bifurcation or relation of stream order to number of streams in different drainage basins

These equations may appear formidable, but they are merely the statement in symbolic form of the simple algebraic laws of geometric series. Equations (5) and (7) are the most important and are readily solved by means of logarithms.

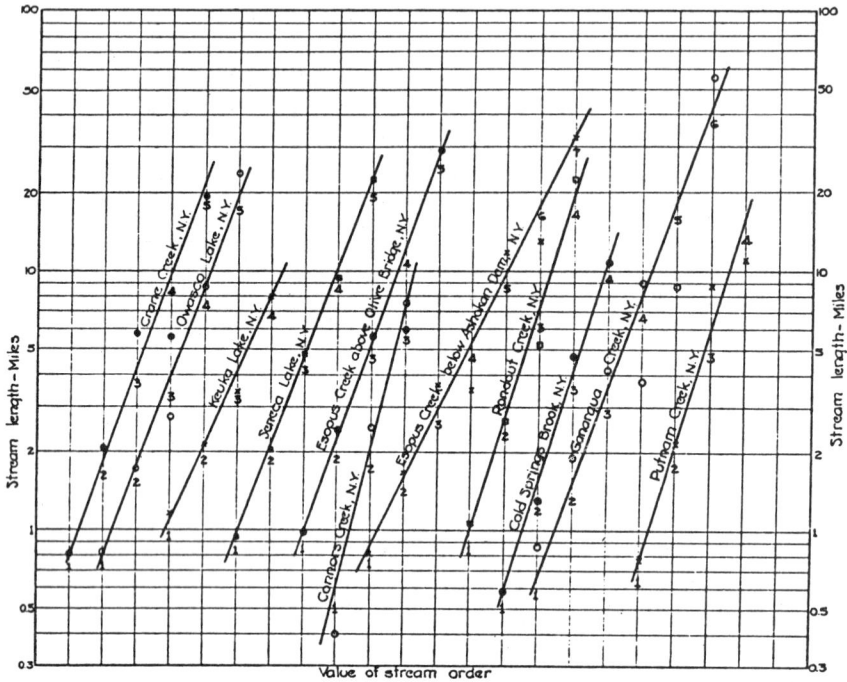

FIGURE 4.—*Relation of stream lengths to stream order in different drainage basins*

As an example, Table 2 shows the observed and computed numbers and lengths of streams of different orders, based on the following values of the variables:

$$r_b = 3.12$$
$$s = 5$$
$$r_l = 2.31$$
$$l_1 = 0.994$$

Actual stream numbers must of course be integers, while the computed numbers may be fractions. Some variation between the computed and observed stream numbers and lengths must be expected, for various reasons. Several drainage basins listed in Table 1 contain large lakes, and the drainage density is less than it would be if the lake did not exist, since there would then necessarily be a stream of the highest order traversing the lake bed. Lower Rondout Creek represents an incomplete drainage basin to which the geometric-series laws do not necessarily apply because it contains a stream or portions of streams of higher order than those originating within this particular area. For some other areas the data were derived from early editions of topographic maps which do not show all the low-order tributaries. In order that the equations shall give correct results the drainage basin must be reasonably homogeneous. This is true of the drainage basin of Esopus Creek above Olive Bridge, which is wholly mountainous. The drainage basin of lower Esopus Creek is, however, rolling and permeable, with great differences in soil, vegetal cover, rainfall, and climate, as compared with the upper basin. Upper Esopus Creek drainage basin

TABLE 2.—*Observed and computed stream lengths and stream numbers*
Drainage basin of Esopus Creek above Olive Bridge, New York.

Stream Order	Number of streams		Average stream length (miles)	
	From topographic maps	By eq. (5)	From topographic maps	By eq. (7)
1	90	94.75	0.994	0.994
2	25	30.37	2.45	2.30
3	9	9.73	5.64	5.31
4	1	3.12	6.00	12.2
5	1	1.00	29.00	28.3

has a much higher bifurcation ratio and stream-length ratio than the lower basin (Table 1), and the composition of the drainage nets is quite different, as shown graphically on Figures 3 and 4.

The importance of these equations lies both in their practical application and in the fact that they represent laws which evolve from physical processes which Nature follows rather closely in the development of stream systems under such diverse conditions as those of upper and lower Esopus Creek. The size of the drainage basin does not enter the equations directly. It is indirectly involved, since the order of the main stream would in general be higher in the larger drainage basin, for two homogeneous drainage basins of different sizes. The order of the main stream is a factor in the equations, and the drainage basin in which the main stream is of the higher order will have, in general, more tributaries of a given order.

The data given in Table 1 cover a wide range of conditions, from precipitous mountain areas, like upper Esopus Creek, and highly dissected areas, like those of Seneca and Owasco lakes, to moderately rolling and flat areas. They cover also drainage basins ranging in size from a few square miles up to several hundred square miles.

The bifurcation ratio (Table 1, column 11) ranges from about 2 for flat or rolling drainage basins up to 3 or 4 for mountainous or highly dissected drainage basins. As would be expected, the bifurcation ratio is generally higher for hilly, well-dissected drainage basins than for rolling basins.

The values of the length ratios (column 12) range from about 2 to about 3; the average is 2.32.

In the examples given in Table 1, the stream lengths were measured to stream tips as shown on U. S. Geological Survey topographic maps. If stream lengths had been measured as extended to watershed lines, the resulting stream-length ratios would have been materially reduced. If c is the average length from the stream tip to the watershed line, and l_1 and l_2 are actual average stream lengths of two successive orders, l_2 being the higher, then, as computed in Table 1,

$$r_l = \frac{l_2}{l_1}. \tag{8}$$

If measured as extended to the watershed lines,

$$r'_l = \frac{l_2 + c}{l_1 + c}. \tag{9}$$

The quantity r'_l will always be less than r_l. The average value of r_l for the streams listed in Table 1 is 2.32. If the stream lengths were extended to the watershed lines, this value would lie between 2.00 and 2.32. The theoretical value of r'_l for streams flowing into larger streams at right angles is 2.00, but r'_l will be greater for streams entering at acute angles, as do most streams on steeper slopes. The distance along the course of a stream from its mouth extended to the water shed line is called "mesh length." The use of this quantity instead of actual stream length is preferable in physiographic studies, and its use leads to closer agreement with the theoretical values.

In Figures 3 and 4, the agreement between the mean lines for the different streams and the observed data is so close that the two following general laws may be stated regarding the composition of stream-drainage nets:

(1) *Law of Stream Numbers:* The numbers of streams of different orders in a given drainage basin tend closely to approximate an inverse geometric series in which the first term is unity and the ratio is the bifurcation ratio.

(2) *Law of Stream Lengths:* The average lengths of streams of each of the different orders in a drainage basin tend closely to approximate a direct geometric series in which the first term is the average length of streams of the 1st order.

Playfair called attention to the "nice adjustment" between the different streams and valleys of a drainage basin but chiefly with reference to their declivities. These two laws supplement Playfair's law and make it more definite and more quantitative. They also show that the nice adjustment goes far beyond the matter of declivities.

TOTAL LENGTH OF STREAMS OF A GIVEN ORDER

Since the total length of streams of a given order is the product of the average length and number of streams, equations (5) and (7) can be combined into an equation for total stream length of a given order.

The total length L_o of tributaries of order o is:

$$L_o = l_1 r_b{}^{s-o} r_l{}^{o-1} \tag{10}$$

The total lengths of all streams of a given order is the product of the number of streams and length per stream. The number of streams is dependent on the bifurcation ratio r_b and increases with stream order, while the length per stream is dependent on the stream length r_l and decreases with increasing stream order. Thus the total lengths of streams of a given order should have either a maximum or a minimum value for some particular stream order. A maximum or minimum may not occur because the stream order required to give the maximum or minimum stream length may exceed the order of the main stream, in which case the total lengths of streams of a given order will either increase or decrease progressively with increasing stream order. An exception occurs where r_b and r_l are equal. Then the total lengths of streams of all orders are the same and equal to $l_1 r_b^s$. The ratio of r_l to r_b is designated ρ and is an important factor in relation both to drainage composition and physiographic development of drainage basins. As will be shown later, the value of the ratio $\rho = \dfrac{r_l}{r_b}$ is determined by precisely those factors—hydrologic, physiographic, cultural, and geologic—which determine the ultimate degree of drainage development in a given drainage basin.

By summation of the total stream lengths for different orders, as given by equation (10), the total stream length within a drainage basin can be expressed in terms of four fundamental quantities: l_1, o_s, r_b, and r_l.

CHANNEL-STORAGE CAPACITY

Natural channel storage is a principal factor in modulating flood-crest intensities as a flood proceeds down a system of stream channels. A knowledge of relative amounts of channel storage at different locations is required for various problems of flood routing and flood control. It can readily be shown that the normal channel storage at a given discharge rate in a given stream channel varies as a simple-power function of the stream length, usually less than the square of the stream length, and this relation can readily be determined from the stage-discharge relation at a gaging station. Equation (10) provides a means of determining total and average stream lengths for each stream order. From this the channel storage provided by each order of streams in the drainage basin can be determined, and by summation the total channel storage in the stream system becomes known. This illustrates the practical application of quantitative physiography to a variety of engineering problems.

Different stream systems may have substantially the same drainage density and yet differ markedly in channel-storage capacity. The higher-order stream channels have larger cross sections and contain more channel storage per unit length than lower-order streams. If r_l/r_b is high, the greater length of larger stream channels may afford greatly increased channel storage per unit of drainage area as compared with a drainage basin with the same drainage density and a lower value of r_l/r_b.

GENERAL EQUATION OF COMPOSITION OF STREAM SYSTEMS

From equation (10) the total length of streams of a given order is:

$$L_0 = l_1 r_b^{s-o} r_l^{o-1}$$

The total length of all streams in a drainage basin with the main stream of a given order s is the sum of the total lengths of streams of different orders, or:

$$\Sigma L = l_1 [r_b^{s-1} + r_b^{s-2} r_l + r_b^{s-3} r_l^2 + \cdots r_b^0 r_l^{s-1}] \tag{11}$$

This equation is cumbersome and can easily be simplified.

Let:

$$\rho = \frac{r_l}{r_b}; \quad r_l = \rho r_b \qquad (12)$$

$$L_o = l_1 \rho^{o-1} r_b^{s-1}. \qquad (13)$$

Applying subscripts 1, 2, etc., to designate the total lengths of streams of different orders:

$$\Sigma L = L_1 + L_2 + L_3 + \cdots L_s \qquad (14)$$

and from (13):

$$\Sigma L = l_1 r_b^{s-1}(\rho^{1-1} + \rho^{2-1} + \rho^{3-1} + \cdots \rho^{s-1})$$
$$= l_1 r_b^{s-1}(1 + \rho + \rho^2 + \rho^3 + \cdots \rho^{s-1}) \qquad (15)$$

The term in parentheses is the sum of a geometric series with its first term unity and a ratio ρ and is equal to:

$$\frac{\rho^s - 1}{\rho - 1}.$$

Substituting this value in equation (15):

$$\Sigma L = l_1 r_b^{s-1} \cdot \frac{\rho^s - 1}{\rho - 1}. \qquad (16)$$

The drainage density is, from (1):

$$D_d = \frac{\Sigma L}{A}.$$

Substituting the value of ΣL from (16):

$$D_d = \frac{l_1 r_b^{s-1}}{A} \cdot \frac{\rho^s - 1}{\rho - 1}. \qquad (17)$$

This equation combines all the physiographic factors which determine the composition of the drainage net of a stream system in one expression. Aside from its scientific interest in this respect, it can also be used to determine drainage density. Values of the factor $(\rho^s - 1)/(\rho - 1)$ can be obtained from Figure 5.

RELATION OF SIZE OF DRAINAGE AREA TO STREAM ORDER

Since equation (17) incorporates all the principal characteristics of the stream system of a drainage basin, it may be considered a quantitative generalization of Playfair's law. It can be written in such a form as to give any one of the quantities l_1, D_d, A, r_b, r_l, and s when the other five quantities are known. If the ratio $\rho < 1$, then, for larger values of s, ρ^s is small, and $\rho^s - 1$ may be taken as -1.0. The equation (17) may then be written:

$$s = 1 + \frac{\log[(1-\rho)D_d A/l_1]}{\log r_b}. \qquad (18)$$

If $\rho > 1$, then, for large values of s, ρ^s is sensibly the same as $\rho^s - 1$, and $\rho^s - 1$ is positive. This leads similarly to the equation:

$$(s-1) \log r_b + s \log \rho = \log \frac{(\rho-1) D_d A}{l_1}$$

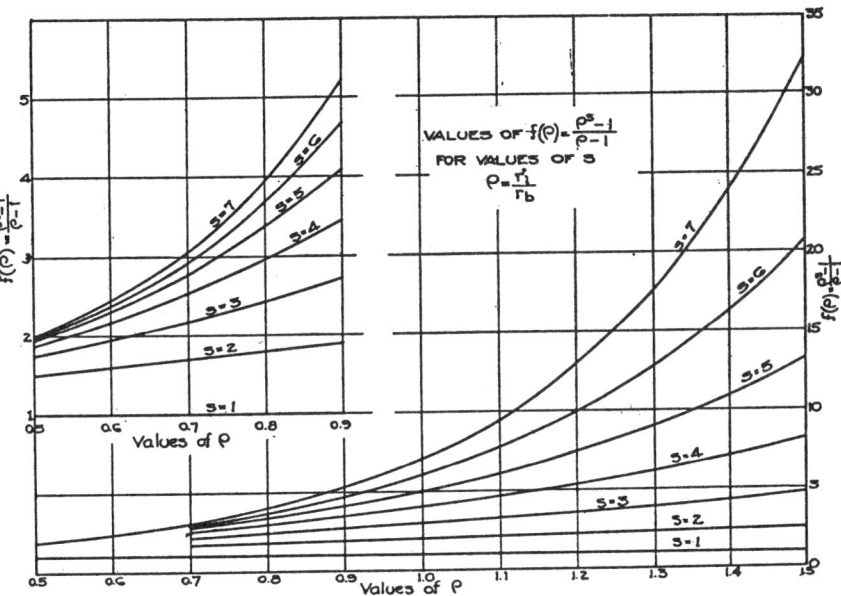

FIGURE 5.—*Diagram of factor $\rho^s - 1/\rho - 1$*

and

$$s = \frac{\log [(\rho-1) D_d A/l_1] + \log r_b}{\log r_b + \log \rho}. \tag{19}$$

The quantity $\log r_b$ is small relative to $\log (\rho - 1) D_d A$ and may be neglected, so that in either case the order of the main stream developed in a drainage basin of a given area A increases for larger values of s in proportion to the logarithm of the area A. If, for example, with given values of ρ, D_d, r_b, r_1, and l_1, an area of 10,000 square miles is required to develop a stream order s, then, under the same conditions, in a drainage basin of 100,000 square miles, the main stream would be of order one unit higher, and in a drainage basin of 1,000,000 square miles the main stream would be two units higher in order than in an area of 10,000 square miles. This shows at once why stream systems with extremely high orders do not occur—there is not room to accommodate the requisite drainage basins on the solid surface of the earth The orders of the Mississippi, Amazon, and other large rivers have not been determined accurately, but the Mississippi River quite certainly does not exceed the 20th order.

From equation (17) drainage density should vary inversely as the drainage area A, other things equal. Actually other things are not equal in drainage areas of different sizes, and, although the bifurcation ratio, stream-length ratio, and average length of

1st order streams may be the same in two drainage basins physiographically similar and of different sizes, the order s of the main stream will in general be larger for the larger drainage basin. As a result the drainage density may increase, decrease, or remain substantially unchanged in two similar drainage basins of different sizes.

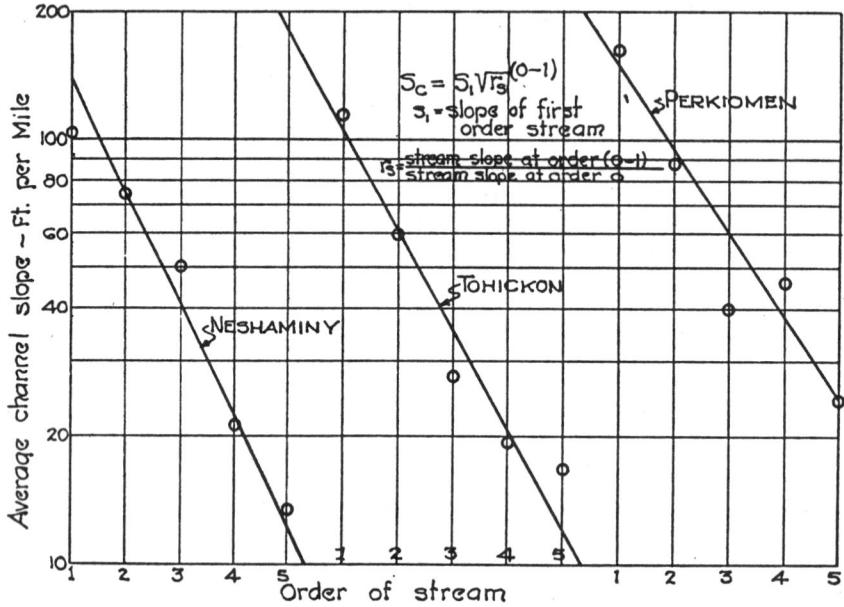

FIGURE 6.—*Law of stream slopes*
Neshaminy, Tohickon, and Perkiomen drainage basins.

LAW OF STREAM SLOPES

In addition to the various quantitative relationships between the different factors involved in drainage composition, expressed by equation (17), there are certain other quantitative relationships. The relation of stream slope to stream order in a given drainage basin is hinted in Playfair's law. As an illustration, the slopes of streams of different orders in the Neshaminy, Tohickon, and Perkiomen drainage basins have been plotted in terms of stream order (Fig. 6), and there is a fairly definite relationship between slope of the streams and stream order, which can be expressed by an inverse geometric-series law.

DETERMINATION OF PHYSIOGRAPHIC FACTORS FOR DRAINAGE BASINS

To determine completely the composition of a stream system it is necessary to know: (1) the drainage area, A, (2) the order s of the main stream, (3) the bifurcation ratio r_b, (4) the stream length ratio r_l, and (5) the length l_s of the main stream or preferably the average length l_1 of 1st order streams. If these data are given, then the drainage density, stream frequency, and other characteristics of the stream system can be determined by calculation, using the equations which have been given.

From equation (5):
$$N_0 = r_b^{(s-o)}.$$

If $o = s - 1$:
$$N_{s-1} = r_b.$$

This shows that the bifurcation ratio r_b is equal to the number of streams of the next to the highest order for the given drainage basin.

If the stream numbers for different stream orders are plotted on semilog paper (Fig. 3), the bifurcation ratio r_b can be determined by simply reading from the average line the number of streams of the second highest order.

From equation (7):
$$l_o = l_1 r_l^{o-1}.$$

If $o = 2$,
$$\frac{l_2}{l_1} = r_l.$$

The stream length ratio r_l can therefore be obtained by dividing the average stream length of any order by the average stream length of the next lower order, the values of stream lengths being read from the diagram of stream lengths plotted in terms of stream order. It is preferable to use these data rather than actual measured values, as the number of streams of a given order—particularly the higher order streams—may not be exactly the normal number for the given drainage composition. Stream numbers can, of course, be only integers, and there may be either two, three, or four streams of the second highest order in a given drainage basin where there should be three.

In Table 1 and Figures 3 and 4, the stream lengths and numbers of all orders were determined directly from topographic maps. Where this is done the order s becomes known directly.

In analyzing the drainage net of a stream system it is desirable to trace, with different colors for each order, the stream system from the base map. When the higher-order streams are determined some of the lower-order streams may prove to be the head-water portions of higher-order streams. Figure 7 shows the drainage basin of Hiwassee River above Hiwassee, Georgia, with 1st order streams shown by dotted lines and stream orders indicated by figures.

The determination of stream lengths and orders by direct measurement from maps which are on a sufficiently large scale to show all 1st order streams is so laborious as to be practically prohibitive except for smaller drainage basins.

Fortunately, all the required quantities—l_s, l_1, r_b, r_l, and D_d—can be determined from smaller-scale maps from which the lower-order tributaries are omitted. The maps must show correctly the streams for several of the higher orders. The order of the main stream is of course unknown since it is not in general known which of the lower orders of streams are omitted from the map. The streams shown are assigned orders assuming that the main stream has an unknown order s, the next lower order of stream shown is designated 2, and so on. The number of streams of each assumed

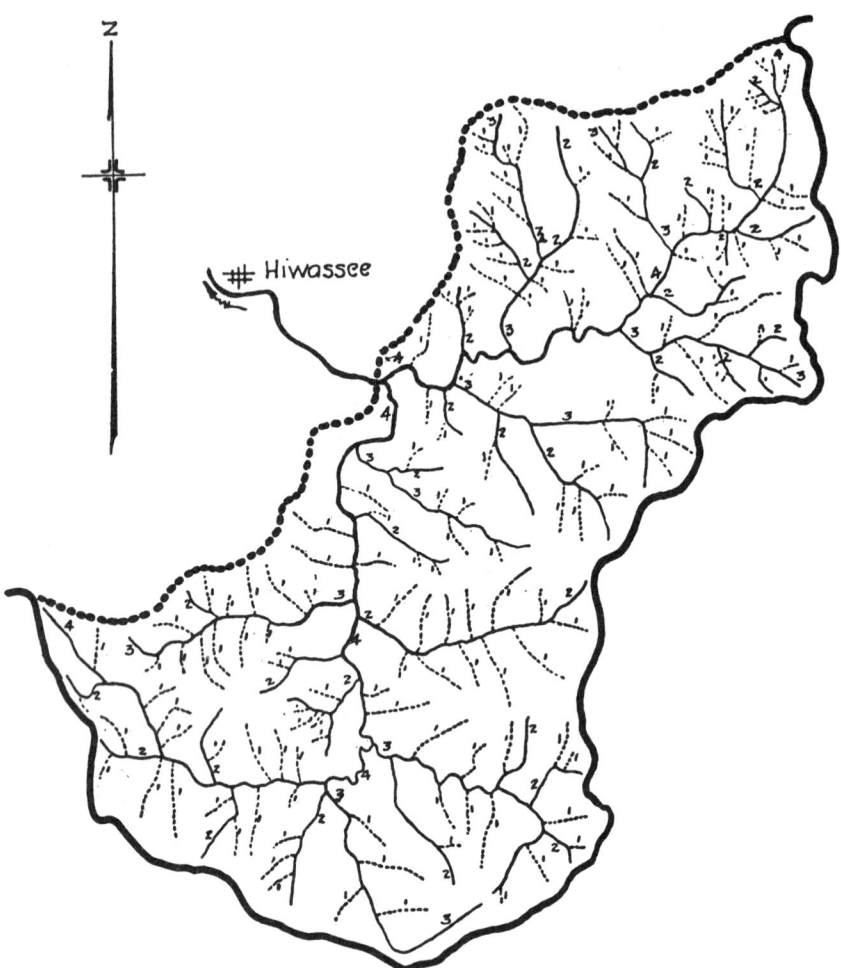

Order	No. of streams	Length miles	Aver. length miles
1	146	72	0.49
2	32	41	1.28
3	9	32.8	3.65
4	2	24.6	12.30
		170.4	

Drainage area = 82.8 sq. mi

D_d = 2.06

FIGURE 7.—*Drainage net, upper Hiwassee River*

order is counted, their stream lengths measured from the map, the results tabulated as follows and plotted as shown by Figure 8A.

Data for Perkiomen Creek

Order	Assumed inverse order	Number of streams	Average stream length (miles)
s	1	1	20.5
s − 1	2	2	13.75
s − 2	3	10	3.61
s − 3	4	32	1.39

If it is assumed that the main stream is of the
4th order, then $l_1 = 1.38$ miles;
5th order, then $l_1 = 0.50$ mile;
6th order, then $l_1 = 0.20$ mile.

Since l_1 is not far from half a mile, the main stream is of the 5th order. From line B (Fig. 8) the number of 2d order streams is 3.15. This is the bifurcation ratio. From line A the lengths of 2d and 1st order streams are, respectively, 1.38 and 0.52 miles. This gives the stream length ratio:

$$r_l = \frac{1.38}{0.52} = 2.70.$$

Data for at least four stream orders are required to determine the order of the main stream from incomplete data by this method. Care must also be used in determining the lines A and B accurately to secure correct results.

The values of the stream lengths as far as known are then plotted on semilog paper (Fig. 8A), in terms of inverse stream orders, a line of best fit drawn to represent the plotted points and this line extended downward to stream length unity or less.

To determine the order of the main stream it is necessary to know the order of magnitude but not the exact value of the average length of streams of the 1st order. The length l_1 of streams of the 1st order is rarely less than a third of a mile, a value which is approached as a minimum limit in mountain regions with heavy rainfall, as in the southern Appalachians. Also it is rarely greater than 2 or 3 miles, values which are approached as maximum limits under some conditions in arid and semiarid regions. Data from which the order of magnitude of l_1 can be determined are always available from some source. In general all that is required is to know whether l_1 is of the order of half a mile, 1 mile, or 2 miles or more. The point at which the stream length shown by the line ab (Fig. 8A) extended downward has a value about the same as the known value of l_1 for the given order indicates the order of the main stream.

This method for determining the order of the main stream is of limited value in some drainage basins, particularly large drainage basins, such as that of the Mississippi River, which are not homogeneous, and where there may be large variations in the length of 1st order streams in different portions of the drainage basins, so that the order of magnitude of l_1 may be difficult to determine. A small portion of a drainage basin, with suitable conditions of high rainfall, steep slopes, etc., may add several units to the value of s for the main stream, although it has little effect on the weighted average value of l_1 for the drainage basin as a whole. For basins which are reasonably homogeneous the method is accurate. Proof of its validity is readily obtained by applying this method to a drainage basin where the values of l_1 and the drainage density D_d have been determined from measurements on a map showing streams of all orders, but using in the determination only the data for streams of higher orders. This was done in preparing Figure 8, which is of the 5th order, although only data for the first four stream orders were used in the computation, it being assumed that l_1 was of an order of magnitude between 1 and 1.5.

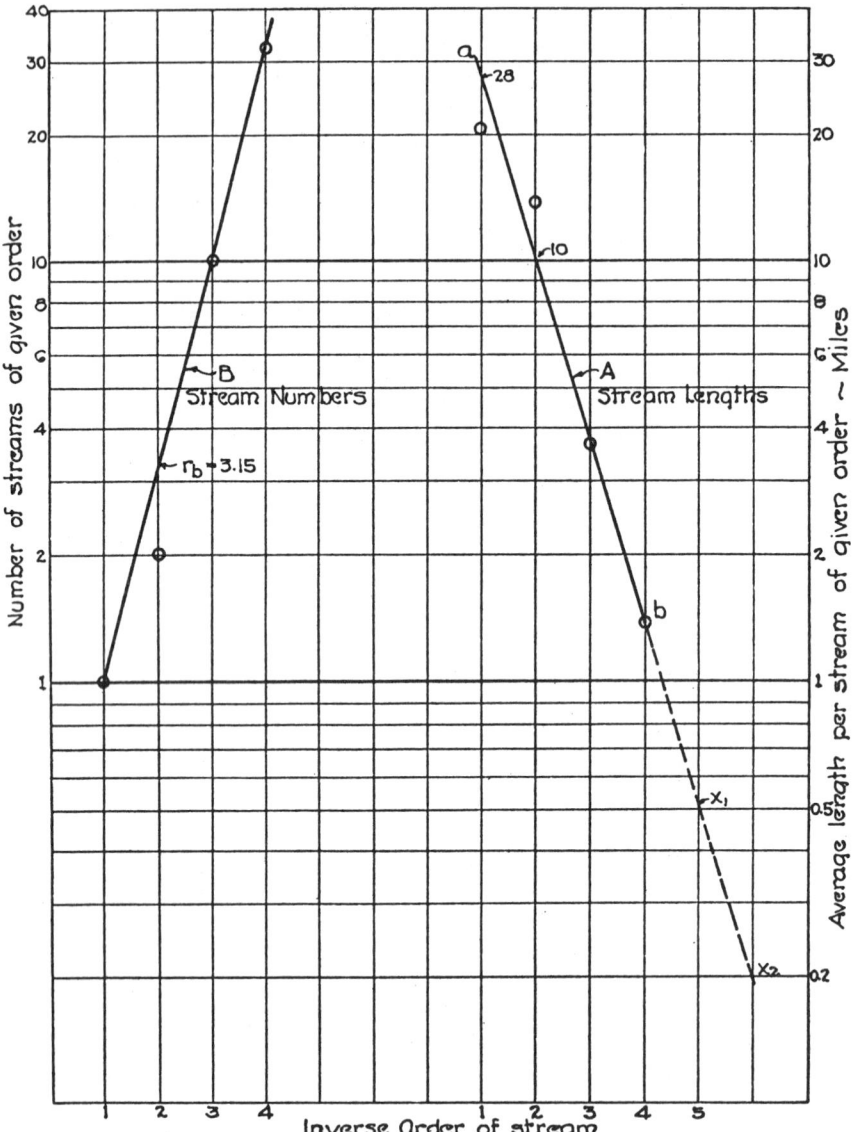

FIGURE 8.—*Graphical determination of stream characteristics*

This determination of s gives also the average length l_1 of 1st order streams. The bifurcation ratio r_b and the stream-length ratio r_l are determined by the slopes of the lines A and B on Figure 8. It is not necessary to know the order of the main stream to determine these quantities. When r_b, r_l, A, s, and l_1 are known, the drainage density can be determined by means of equation (17).

This method of determining s has the advantage that it is at least as accurate when applied to large as when applied to smaller drainage basins. In general, data for more stream orders will be available from a map for a large drainage basin than for a small basin.

Table 3 shows the drainage composition of Neshaminy, Tohickon, and Perkiomen Creek stream systems, derived in the manner described, together with the drainage

TABLE 3.—*Observed and computed drainage densities, Neshaminy, Tohickon, and Perkiomen creeks*

Item		Neshaminy Below Forks	Tohickon Point Pleasant	Perkiomen Near Frederick
1	Stream	Neshaminy	Tohickon	Perkiomen
2	Location	Below Forks	Point Pleasant	Near Frederick
3	Drainage area, square miles	139.3	102.2	152.0
	Computed values:			
4	Stream order from map	5	5	5
5	l_s	35.0	33.0	27.0
6	r_b	3.45	3.00	3.15
7	r_l	2.92	2.85	2.70
8	$\rho = r_l/r_b$	0.85	0.95	0.86
9	$f(\rho)$	3.75	4.50	3.80
10	r_b^{s-1}	41.6	81.0	98.4
11	r_b^{s-1}/A	1.02	0.79	0.65
12	(11) × (9)	3.82	3.56	2.47
13	l_1	0.50	0.53	0.52
14	(12) × (13) = D_d	1.91	1.89	1.28
15	Drainage density from map	1.60	1.91	1.24

densities as computed by equation (17) and as derived from direct measurement from topographic maps.

Drainage densities computed by equation (17) will usually be somewhat higher than those derived directly from maps if stream lengths are measured directly and only to the fingertips of the stream channels, because the stream lengths and mesh lengths are sensibly identical for higher-order streams, whereas there may be 10 to 25 per cent or even 50 per cent difference between stream length and mesh length for low-order streams. In computing drainage density from values of l_1, r_b, and r_l obtained graphically, the computed value corresponds more nearly to drainage density expressed in terms of mesh length than in terms of actual stream length for lower-order streams.

[*Editors' Note:* Material has been omitted at this point.]

ERRATUM

Page 283, third line from the bottom should read: "... The poorly drained basin has a drainage density of 0.73; the well-drained one, 2.74 or four times as great."

REFERENCES

[*Editors' Note:* Only the references cited in the preceding excerpt are reproduced here.]

Cotton, C. A., 1935, *Geomorphology of New Zealand, Part I,* p. 57.
Davis, W. M., 1909, *Geographical Essays,* Ginn & Co., Boston, 777p.
Gravelius, H., 1914, *Flusskunde,* Goschen'sche Verlagshandlung, Berlin, 176p.
Horton, R. E., 1932, Drainage Basin Characteristics, *Am. Geophys. Union Tr.,* pp. 350–361.
Wooldridge, S. W., and Morgan, R. S., 1937, *The Physical Basis of Geography,* Longmans, Green & Co., London, 435p.

A DERIVATION OF STRAHLER'S CHANNEL-ORDERING SYSTEM[1]

MARK A. MELTON

University of Chicago

ABSTRACT

Channel order, according to the Strahler system, is a simple mathematical concept that can be derived from the notion of a rooted tree without first postulating the existence of a single downstream direction on each channel segment. The Strahler system is probably unique in this respect.

The channel-ordering system, as modified by A. N. Strahler (1952, p. 1120, n.) from that originally proposed by R. E. Horton (1945, p. 281–282), can be drived from concepts of elementary combinatorial analysis without the introduction of arbitrary or non-mathematical geomorphic concepts.

We state that an ideal channel net is a finite rooted tree with two kinds of points other than the root: (1) a set of inner points (junctions) with three lines arrayed from each and (2) a set of outer points (heads) with one line arrayed from each; the lines represent channels (fig. 1) (Riordan, 1958, p. 110 ff.). Implicit in this definition is the knowledge that the channel net, considered as a linear graph,[2] is connected (i.e., all points are joined by some path), and no slings or lines in parallel exist (i.e., the path between any two points is unique, or no islands exist). The procedure to be presented can be generalized with some complication to include the existence of islands, but we shall not do so. The root of the tree is a unique fixed point that corresponds to the mouth of the channel net.

The direction along any path from an outer point to the root is defined as the downstream direction. It follows that for any inner point, or junction, two lines are always upstream and one line is downstream. To every point except the root there corresponds exactly one line, which can be taken as the line immediately downstream. Thus, the total number of points is always one more than the number of lines. It may

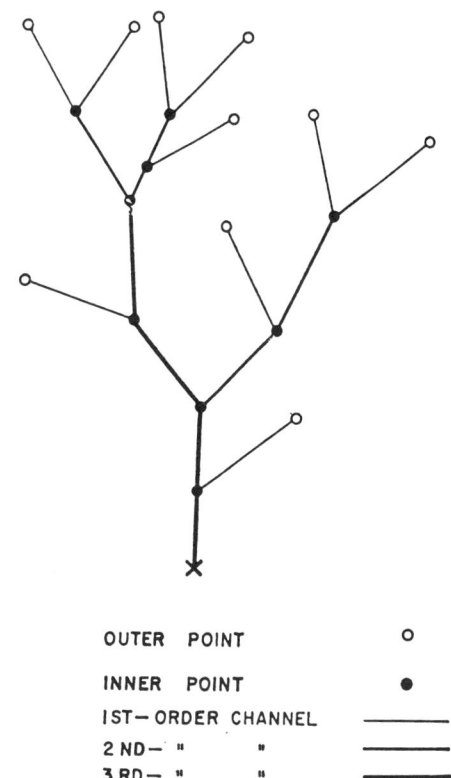

FIG. 1.—Ideal channel net (rooted tree) showing inner and outer points and channel orders.

also be shown that the number of lines is always $2n_0 - 1$, where n_0 is the number of outer points (heads) and where the number

[1] Manuscript received February 13, 1959.

[2] The channel net, as a linear graph, bears the same relation to the actual channel system as a stickman bears to a human being.

of inner points plus the root equals the number of outer points.

We shall use the following rule which is entirely implicit in our stated conditions: When any line is cut off at its downstream end, the point at the lower end must vanish, as two-lined points are not permitted. If two upstream lines are cut off simultaneously from the same point, that point need not vanish, as it then becomes a one-lined point.

We shall now proceed with the derivation of channel order.

1. Each line which terminates upstream at an outer point is cut off from the tree at its downstream end. This set of lines is the set of first-order channels.

It should be noted that points where two first-order channels joined remain in the net, but all points where a first-order channel joined some other line must "evaporate." We now have a *new* and smaller, rooted tree, consisting as before of one-lined and three-lined points.

2. Each line which terminates upstream at an outer point is cut off from the tree at its downstream end. This set of lines is the set of second-order channels.

As before, we now have a new, smaller, rooted tree with one-lined and three-lined points (provided, of course, that we did not start with a second-order channel net, in which case we would now have only the root left). The operation can be repeated u times, and each successive operation defines the set of channels of order equal to the number of times the operation has been performed. When the last operation is completed, the root of the uth-order channel net may or may not vanish, depending on whether it is the head of a channel of order $u + 1$, not represented in the original net.

The significance of such a derivation lies not in making the concept of order any clearer, although it may do so, but in showing that channel order according to the Strahler system is a simply defined mathematical concept. The Strahler ordering system is probably unique in this respect, as all others involve from the beginning the notions of a downstream direction, entrance angles, size of channels, etc. In this case, the only notion needed was that of a rooted tree, which we get from combinatorial analysis; and the only arbitrary restriction was that there be one-lined and two-lined points only, so that the tree will correspond to ideal channel nets. Even the notion of a downstream direction follows from these.

ACKNOWLEDGMENTS.—The writer is indebted to Professor A. N. Strahler, Columbia University, and to Mr. Leigh N. Ortenburger, Palo Alto, California, for critically reading the manuscript and suggesting modifications, all of which were incorporated.

REFERENCES CITED

HORTON, R. E., 1945, Erosional development of streams and their drainage basins: Geol. Soc. America Bull., v. 56, p. 275–370.

RIORDAN, JOHN, 1958, An introduction to combinatorial analysis: New York, John Wiley & Sons.

STRAHLER, A. N., 1952, Hyposometric (area-altitude) analysis of erosional topography: Geol. Soc. America Bull., v. 63, p. 1117–1142.

3

Reprinted from pages 602–611 of *Geol. Soc. America Bull.* **67**:597–646 (1956), courtesy of the Geological Society of America

EVOLUTION OF DRAINAGE SYSTEMS AND SLOPES IN BADLANDS AT PERTH AMBOY, NEW JERSEY

S. A. Schumm

[*Editors' Note:* In the original, material precedes this excerpt.]

In all the drainage basins studied the streams are assigned order numbers following the method outlined by Strahler (1952b, p. 1120) whereby the higher stream-order numbers are not extended headward to include smaller tributaries, but refer to segments of the main channel (Fig. 9). With the Horton classification, the higher stream-order numbers include the smallest headward extension of the main stream. Using Strahler's method, the two major channels joining at point H (Pl. 1) are third-order; using Horton's method, the south tributary would be the extension of the fifth-order channel and would be eliminated from studies involving third-order channels. This method will be referred to again in a discussion of channel lengths.

The fifth-order basin mapped includes 3531 feet of drainage channels within an area of 31,027 square feet. The drainage density (Horton, 1945, p. 283), equal to the sum of the channel lengths in miles divided by the area of the drainage basin in square miles, is 602, indicating that within an area of this type 602 miles of drainage channels occur for every square mile of drainage basin. This value is indicative of the fine texture of the area. Although the density is high compared to a typical value of 5 to 20 for humid regions, it is not high for badland topography.

Within the mapped area the first-, second-, and third-order stream basins show a transition from maturely developed topography near the mouth of the main stream, where the main channel has widened the valley until small segments of flood plain have developed, to progressively more youthful basins toward its head, where the tributaries are eroding into portions of the undissected surface of the fill.

The mean length of the first-order channels is 10.1 feet, and the mean drainage area is 85.0 square feet, indicating the small scale of the topography. The hypsometric integral (Strahler, 1952b) for the entire fifth-order network is 70 per cent, indicating that erosion has removed a minimum of 30 per cent of the total mass of the basin. This figure is reasonably accurate because the upper surface of the terrace into which the system developed is still preserved in the headwater areas. Although the terrace is not a natural deposit and the drainage is developing on a small scale, investigation of principles of drainage-network development is aided by knowledge of several factors not available in the study of the geomorphic evolution of other areas.

The homogeneity of the fill aided development of an insequent drainage pattern on the terrace. The rapid erosion developed youthful V-valleys with steep straight slopes descending from convex or sharp-crested divides. The longitudinal profile of the main channel, typical of streams growing headward into an upland surface, had a concave lower segment and an upper convexity where degradation was most rapid. Tributary profiles varied with stage from convex-up, where the streams were unable to maintain themselves against the rapid degradation of the main channel in the headwater areas, to concave-up where the main channel appeared to be at grade.

Stream-channel erosion with sheet and rill erosion on the slopes were the dominant geomorphic processes observed. Wind erosion was negligible, but frost action became important during the winter months.

CHARACTERISTICS OF THE DRAINAGE NETWORK

Components of the Drainage Network

Morphometric studies of drainage-network components at Perth Amboy included measurements of all stream-channel lengths and drainage-basin areas for all stream orders, so that each component could be studied independently. Stream-order analysis permits comparison of the drainage network developed on the Perth Amboy terrace with patterns originating under natural conditions. Horton (1945) proposed certain laws of drainage composition which assume an orderly development of the geometrical qualities of an insequent drainage system. These laws were applied to data obtained from morphometric measurements on the Perth Amboy map (Pl. 1) to determine whether they conformed; if they did, conclusions from the Perth Amboy study might apply to other larger areas. Geometry of two other fifth-order basins was measured for comparison with Perth Amboy basin (Table 2): Chileno Canyon basin (Chileno Canyon, California,

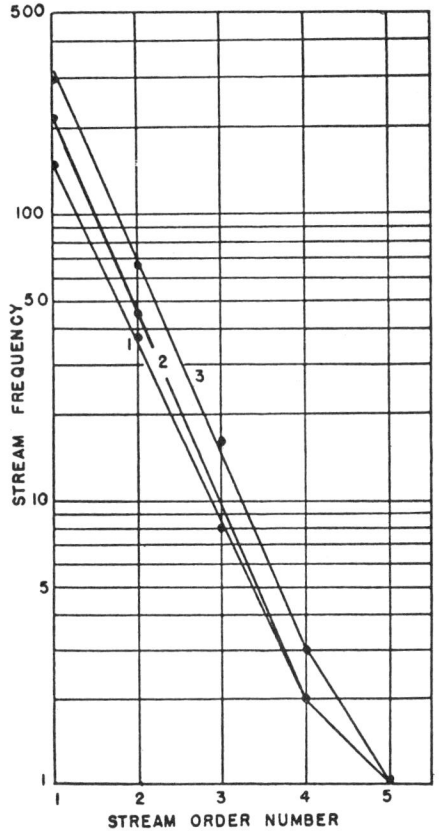

FIGURE 2.—RELATION OF NUMBER OF STREAMS OF EACH ORDER TO ORDER NUMBER
(1) Perth Amboy, (2) Chileno Canyon, (3) Hughesville area

quadrangle) and Mill Dam Run basin (Hughesville, Maryland, quadrangle).

The law of stream numbers, first of Horton's laws of drainage composition, is stated as follows (Horton, 1945, p. 291): "The numbers of streams of different orders in a given drainage basin tend closely to approximate an inverse geometric series in which the first term is unity and the ratio is the bifurcation ratio." If a geometric series exists, a straight-line series of points results where the numbers of streams of each order are plotted on a logarithmic scale on the ordinate against order numbers on an arithmetic scale on the abscissa. This has been done in Figure 2, in the manner of Horton's graphs. All three sets of points show a marked up-concavity at the lower end, suggesting that the geometric progression is not closely observed in the higher orders, but the Perth Amboy data show general similarity with the rest

TABLE 1.—METHOD OF DERIVING WEIGHTED MEAN BIFURCATION RATIO

1 Stream order	2 Number of streams	3 Bifurcation ratio	4 No. of streams involved in ratio	5 Products of columns 3 and 4
1	214			
		4.78	259	1238.0
2	45			
		5.63	53	298.4
3	8			
		4.00	10	40.0
4	2			
		2.00	3	6.0
5	1			

Total number of streams used in Col. 4 = 325.
Sum of products of Col. 5 = 1582.4.
Weighted mean bifurcation ratio = $\frac{1582.4}{325}$ = 4.87.

and there is no reason to believe that any fundamental dissimilarity exists.

The weighted mean of the Perth Amboy bifurcation ratio is 4.87. Bifurcation ratio is the ratio of the total number of streams of one order to that of the next higher order (Horton, 1945, p. 280), e.g., a basin with 20 second-order channels and 60 first-order channels would have a bifurcation ratio between these two orders of 3. Because of chance irregularities, bifurcation ratio between successive pairs of orders differs within the same basin even if a general observance of a geometric series exists. To arrive at a more representative bifurcation number Strahler (1953) used a weighted-mean bifurcation ratio obtained by multiplying the bifurcation ratio for each successive pair of orders by the total number of streams involved in the ratio and taking the mean of the sum of these values (Table 1).

The second law stated by Horton (1945, p. 291) concerns stream lengths: "The average lengths of streams of each of the different orders in a drainage basin tend closely to approximate a direct geometric series in which the first term is the average length of streams of the first order."

lengths although the value of the length of the fifth-order stream is low in two cases Because integer values only are used for order numbers continued channel development might be ex-

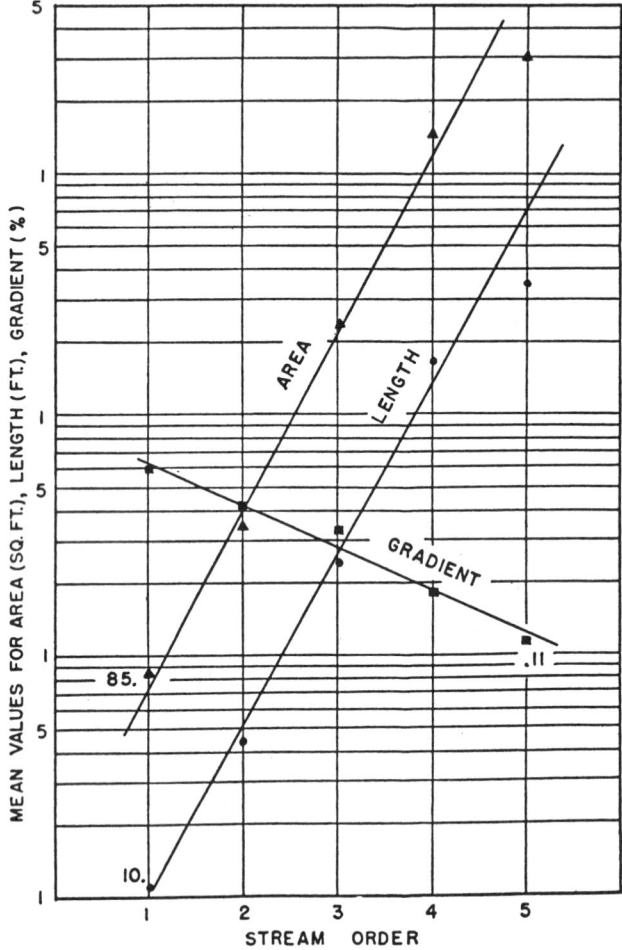

FIGURE 3.—RELATION OF MEAN BASIN AREA, MEAN STREAM LENGTH, AND MEAN STREAM GRADIENT TO STREAM ORDER

The length of streams of each order was obtained by measuring all the drainage channels within a basin of a given order; the length of the fifth-order stream at Perth Amboy is the total length of all the channels within the basin. This method differs from Horton's, but the total channel lengths may be more meaningful when considered within the area of each drainage basin. Using this method, however, the mean stream-length plots (Figs. 3, 5) for the Perth Amboy, Chileno Canyon, and Mill Dam Run systems adhere to Horton's law of stream

pected to raise the value of the fifth-order length, bringing it closer to the fitted regression line. The shortness of the fifth-order segment at Perth Amboy may be due to the truncation of the drainage pattern at the front of the terrace. In Figure 4 both the Hughesville and Perth Amboy drainage patterns have short fifth-order segments in comparison to that of the Chileno Canyon area. This may explain the low fifth-order channel lengths and areas for those two basins (Figs. 3, 5).

Horton's third law (1945, p. 295) states:

"There is a fairly definite relationship between slope of the streams and stream order, which can be expressed by an inverse geometric series law." The Perth Amboy stream slopes appear to conform (Fig. 3). In this case the gradient is obtained by dividing stream length measured from mouth to headwaters by the elevation difference.

Horton's laws may require revision because he obtained his data from old maps of small scale on which he measured as stream channels only the blue drainage symbols, thus omitting a large part of the first- and second-order channel network. His statements are sound, however, in the light of investigations made on modern topographic maps, either mapped for the purpose (Perth Amboy basin) or selected because of their large scale and detailed representation of topography (Hughesville and Chileno Canyons quadrangles). These undoubtedly afford data more precisely representative of the natural development of drainage systems than the old maps.

The writer compared the Hughesville and

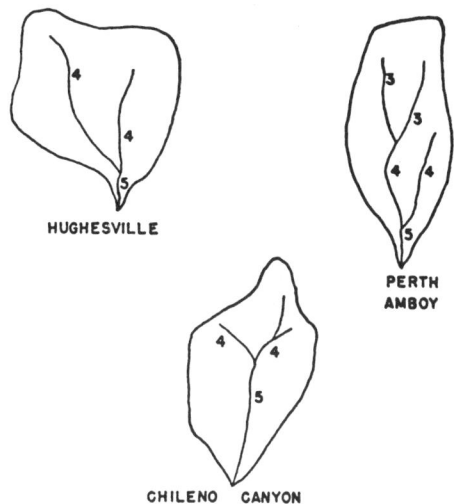

FIGURE 4.—COMPARISON OF SHAPE OF BASIN AND MAIN DRAINAGE ELEMENTS OF THREE AREAS

Numbers indicate order of main drainage channels

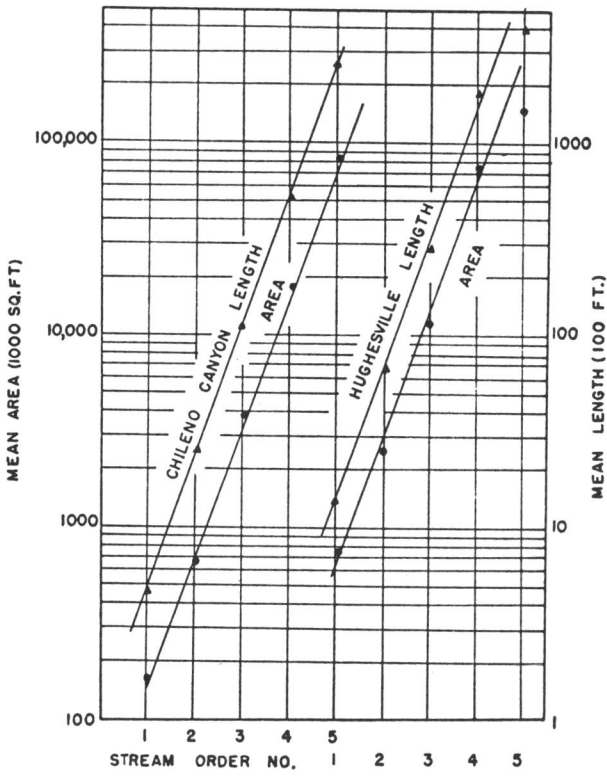

FIGURE 5.—RELATION OF MEAN BASIN AREA AND MEAN STREAM LENGTH TO STREAM ORDER

TABLE 2.—DRAINAGE-NETWORK CHARACTERISTICS

Basin	Order number	Number of streams	Mean length (ft.)	Mean area (sq. ft.)	Mean gradient (%)
Perth Amboy	1	214	10.1	85.0	59.9
	2	45	40.4	343	40.6
	3	8	242	2360	33.7
	4	2	1660	14600	18.2
	5	1	3530	31000	11.1
Chileno Canyon	1	296	482	167000	....
	2	66	2560	872000	....
	3	16	11400	3890000	....
	4	3	51100	18100000	....
	5	1	254000	86100000	....
Hughesville	1	150	1420	781000	....
	2	37	6860	2540000	....
	3	8	28400	12000000	....
	4	2	180000	78800000	....
	5	1	397000	154000000	....

length of channels close to the maximum value, perhaps obtainable only by detailed remapping in the field.

Further investigations included map measurement by polar planimeter of all drainage-basin areas. Horton (1945, p. 294) inferred that mean drainage-basin areas of each order should form a geometric series. A plot of the mean areas of stream basins of each order for the three basins compared above (Figs. 3, 5) reveals this relationship. A fourth law of drainage composition may therefore be formulated in the style set by Horton: the mean drainage-basin areas of streams of each order tend to approximate closely a direct geometric series in which the first term is the mean area of the first-order basins. It could be assumed that such a relationship would exist if there were any connection between the length of a stream and the size of its drainage basin.

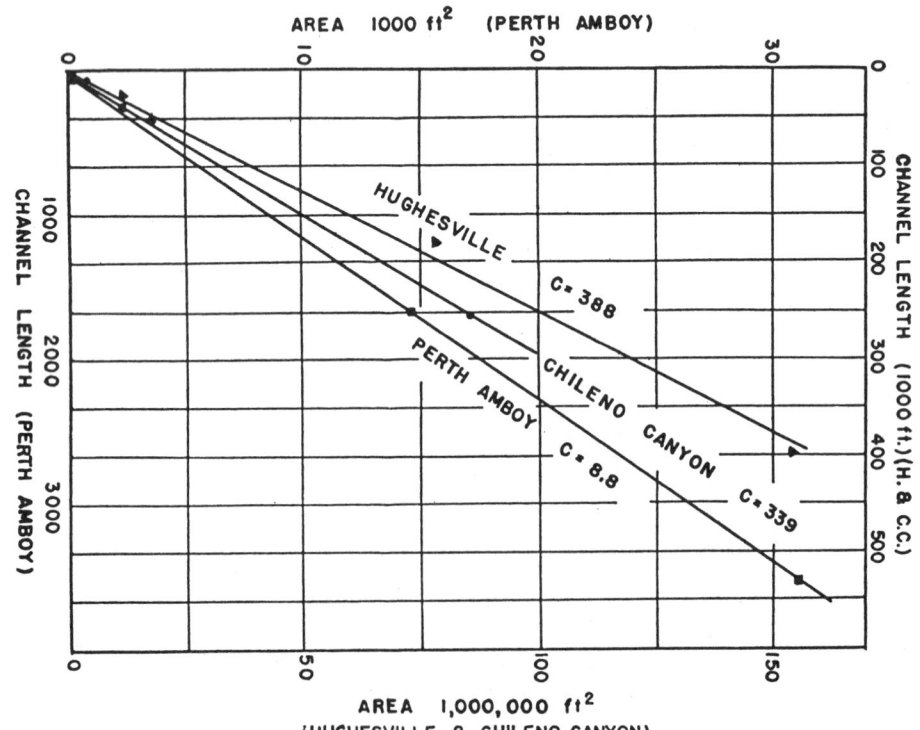

FIGURE 6.—RELATION OF MEAN STREAM LENGTH OF EACH ORDER TO MEAN BASIN AREA OF EACH ORDER

Chileno Canyon maps with aerial photographs so that the blue drainage lines could be extended to what appeared to be the correct length and small tributaries were also added to the drainage pattern. This method brought the

In Figures 3 and 5 the parallelism of the plots of mean stream length and mean drainage-basin area is striking and suggests a directly proportional relationship between the two. Figure 6 shows a plot of the mean drainage-basin areas and mean stream-channel lengths for the three areas. The scatter of the Perth Amboy data is slight around a regression line fitted by the method of least squares and is described by the regression equation $Yc = 56.8 + 8.77X$. The ratio between mean area and length values is thus approximately 9. The calculated ratio for the Chileno Canyon basin is 339 and for the Mill Dam Run basin 388.

The significance of the ratio is that it represents in square feet the area required to maintain 1 foot of drainage channel. It is the quantitative expression of one of the most important numerical values characteristic of a drainage system: the minimum limiting area required for the development of a drainage channel. This value, *the constant of channel maintenance*, is a measure of texture similar to drainage density; it is in fact, equal to the reciprocal of drainage density multiplied by 5280 (because the channel-maintenance ratio is expressed in square feet while drainage density is expressed in miles). Along with drainage density this constant is of value as a means of comparing the surface erodibility or other factors affecting surface erosion and drainage-network development. A related texture measure is Horton's (1945) length of overland flow, the distance over which runoff will flow before concentrating into permanent drainage channels. The length of overland flow equals the reciprocal of twice the drainage density.

The discovery of the above relationship permits statement of a fifth law of drainage composition: the relationship between mean drainage-basin areas of each order and mean channel lengths of each order of any drainage network is a linear function whose slope (regression coefficient) is equivalent to the area in square feet necessary on the average for the maintenance of 1 foot of drainage channel. This law requires an orderly development of any drainage network, for the extension of any drainage system can occur only if an area equal to the constant of channel maintenance is available for each foot of lengthening drainage channel.

Limiting Values of Drainage Components

In addition to a lower limiting area necessary for channel maintenance there may be expected upper limits to basin areas and stream lengths of each order beyond which new tributaries or bifurcation occurs, forming new basins. These

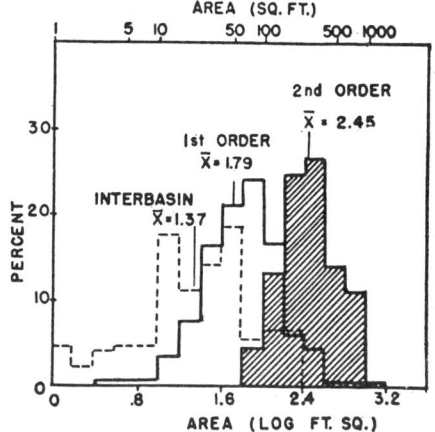

FIGURE 7.—FREQUENCY-DISTRIBUTION HISTOGRAMS OF THE LOGS OF DRAINAGE-BASIN AREA

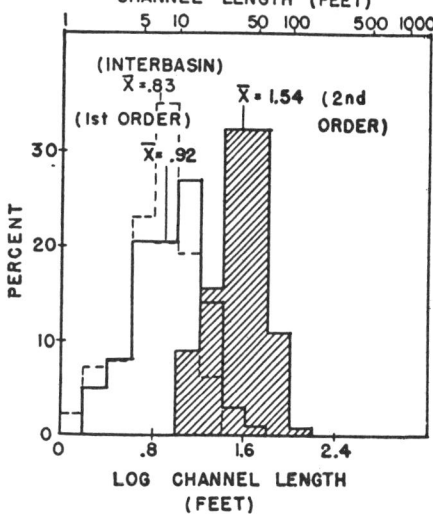

FIGURE 8.—FREQUENCY-DISTRIBUTION HISTOGRAMS OF THE LOGS OF STREAM-CHANNEL LENGTHS

relationships would appear in frequency-distribution histograms of the basin areas and stream lengths of each order and further confirm the principle of a channel-maintenance constant.

Frequency-distribution histograms of the stream lengths and basin areas show a marked right skewness, which appears to be corrected by plotting log values on the abscissa (Figs. 7, 8; Tables 3, 4). All measurements are made on a topographic map and are therefore taken from the horizontal projection of the drainage-basin elements rather than from true lengths and surface areas. Frequency-distribution study is limited to the first two orders by the small number of streams in the third and higher orders. A study of the first- and second-order basin areas and interbasin areas may be adequate, however, to determine if a transition phase exists between orders.

TABLE 3.—FREQUENCY DISTRIBUTIONS OF LOGS OF CHANNEL LENGTHS*

Sample	Class mid-values in logs of lengths in feet										$\bar{X}$	s	N
	0.3	0.5	0.7	0.9	1.1	1.3	1.5	1.7	1.9	2.1			
First order channels	11	17	45	45	58	30	6	2	...	...	.92	.302	214
Second-order channels	...	...	...	...	4	7	14	14	5	1	1.54	.21	45

* In this and all following tables and figures, $\bar{X}$ is the arithmetic mean, s is the standard deviation, and N is the number of items in each sample.

TABLE 4.—FREQUENCY DISTRIBUTIONS OF LOGS OF DRAINAGE-BASIN AREAS

Sample	Class mid-values in logs of area in square feet															$\bar{X}$	s	N
	0.3	0.5	0.7	0.9	1.1	1.3	1.5	1.7	1.9	2.1	2.3	2.5	2.7	2.9	3.1			
First-order areas	...	2	2	6	17	34	45	50	34	12	8	1	1	1	...	1.79	.19	214
Second-order areas	...	...	...	...	..	..	..	..	2	7	11	12	7	5	1	2.45	.284	45

quate, however, to determine if a transition phase exists between orders.

Between adjacent drainage basins are *interbasin areas*, those roughly triangular areas which have not developed a drainage channel (Fig. 9), but which drain directly into a higher-order channel. The histograms of first- and second-order basin areas and interbasin triangular areas are superimposed in Figure 10 (Table 5); the histograms of first- and second-order stream lengths are compared with maximum interbasin-slope lengths in Figure 11 (Table 6). Figures 7 and 8 compare the histograms of the logarithms of basin area, channel length, interbasin areas, and interbasin maximum lengths. The discussion of limiting values of drainage components may be followed on either set of figures.

An overlap between the areas of each histogram suggests that transformation from first to second order takes place within a wide range of values. In Figure 10 interbasin areas show a sharp decrease in frequency for areas above 50 square feet, which is well below the mean of the first-order areas. Of the 27 interbasin areas over 50 square feet, 12 seemed capable of developing a channel at any time; the remaining 15 were irregular, wider than long, or were on rounded spurs where the divergence of orthogonals downslope prevents the concentration of runoff. From this investigation alone it is difficult to set limiting area above which channel development may be expected on the interbasin areas, especially since the comparison of triangular interbasin areas with elliptical first-order basins is questionable.

Areas of first-order basins rise sharply at the 10-square-foot class limit. Two first-order basins of less than 10 square feet were mapped by Strahler and Coates, but a field check revealed that these did not contain permanent drainage channels. The fact that areas of less than 10 square feet are remarkably free of drainage channels coincides with the concept of a con-

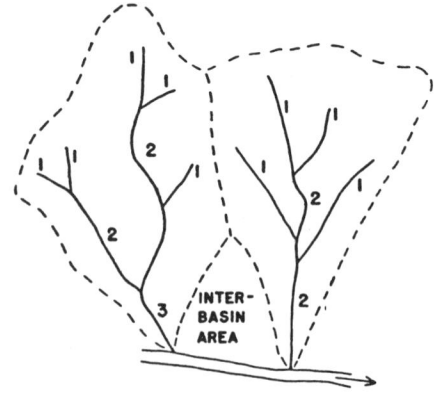

FIGURE 9.—POSITION OF INTERBASIN AREA AND METHOD OF CLASSIFYING STREAMS BY ORDER NUMBER

stant of channel maintenance of about 9 (8.77). Thus, no permanent channel will develop without a drainage area of about 10 square feet, while the channel can lengthen only with the average increment of 9 square feet of area for each additional foot of length.

Most of the overlap between the first- and second-order areas falls between 50 and 150 square feet, although some first-order areas range up to 650 square feet. Again an inspection

CHARACTERISTICS OF THE DRAINAGE NETWORK

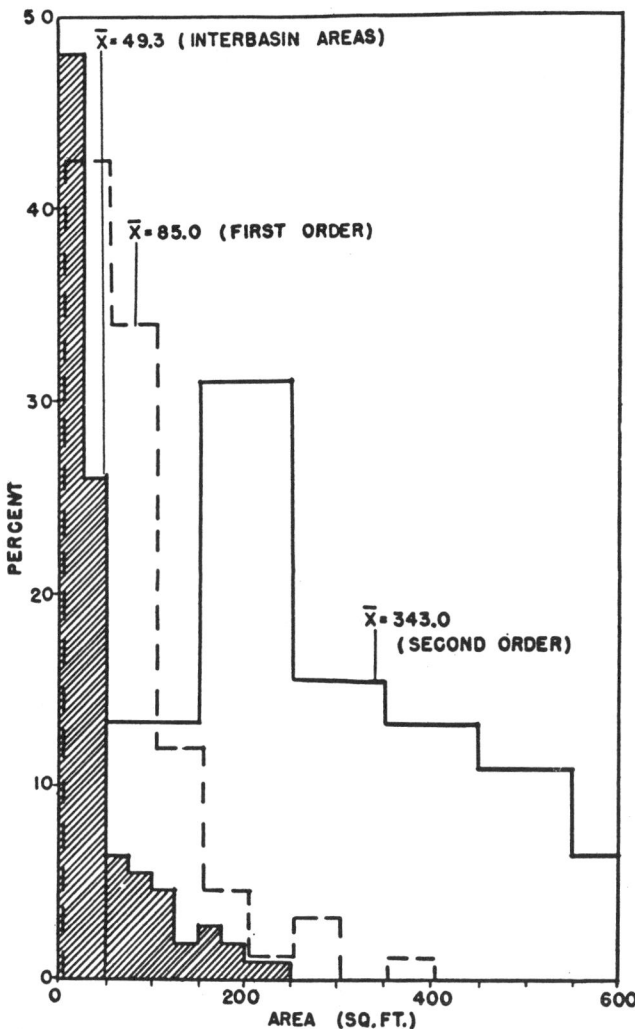

FIGURE 10.—FREQUENCY-DISTRIBUTION HISTOGRAMS OF FIRST- AND SECOND-ORDER BASIN AREAS AND INTERBASIN AREAS

TABLE 5.—FREQUENCY DISTRIBUTIONS OF FIRST- AND SECOND-ORDER DRAINAGE-BASIN AREAS AND INTERBASIN AREAS

Sample	Class mid-values in square feet													$\bar{X}$	s	N
Mid-values	30	80	130	180	230	280	330	380	430	480	530	580	630			
First-order areas	91	73	26	10	3	7	0	2	0	0	0	1	1	85	80	214
Mid-values	100	200	300	400	500	600	700	800	900	1000	1100	...	...	...	...	...
Second-order areas	6	14	7	6	5	3	2	0	1	0	1	...	...	343	218	45
Mid-values	12.5	37.5	62.5	87.5	112.5	137.5	162.5	187.5	212.5	237.5	..	...	...	...	...	...
Interbasin areas	51	28	7	5	5	3	4	3	1	1	..	...	...	49.3	49	108

of individual basin characterstics within the zone of histogram overlap is profitable. Of the 46 first-order areas greater than 110 square feet, 29 are of very youthful basins including basins it seems a fair generalization that first-order channels with areas greater than 100 square feet are unstable and ready for subdivision.

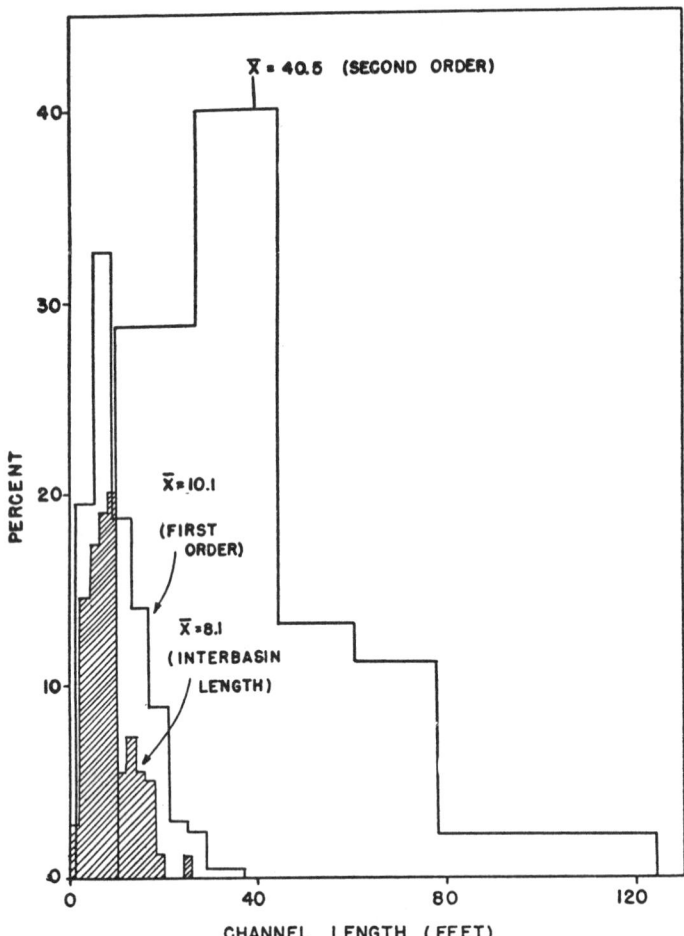

FIGURE 11.—FREQUENCY-DISTRIBUTION HISTOGRAMS OF FIRST- AND SECOND-ORDER CHANNEL LENGTHS AND MAXIMUM INTERBASIN LENGTHS

broad, gently sloping surfaces with only traces of channels on the flat undissected divide areas. With further development these would evolve to a higher order, for their longitudinal profiles are still essentially convex-up, retarding rapid tributary extension into their headwater areas. Thirteen of the 46 are narrow almost rill-like basins unable to broaden because of adjacent more aggressive basins. The remaining 4 of the 46 first-order basins larger than 110 square feet have no obvious reason for not developing into second-order channels. Although it is difficult to explain peculiarities of individual drainage

The smallest second-order channel area is 65 square feet. The class limits of the second-order areas within the overlap are 50 and 150 square feet (Fig. 10). Within this size range are six second-order basins which have developed tributaries recently and are capable of enlarging by headward extension so that the lowest-frequency class of the second-order area histogram would disappear unless replaced by new units created by bifurcation of first-order channels. Youthfulness of the entire system at Perth Amboy prevents the recognition of narrow transition zones between orders. A similar study in a fully extended mature drainage system might show sharper distinctions.

In accordance with the fifth law of drainage composition, stream-length frequency distributions are similar to the area distributions. Maximum interbasin-slope lengths cannot be directly compared to actual stream lengths because a channel developing on the interbasin surface will not extend the entire length of the slope. Nevertheless, a sharp drop in frequency at 10 feet suggests that at lengths above this runoff surfaces are unstable in form and will tend to develop channels (Fig. 11). Twenty-six interbasin areas with lengths greater than 10 feet had no channels. Seven were very narrow with little drainage area. The remaining 19, as previously noted under the discussion of interbasin areas, are irregular or on rounded spurs, while 4 seem capable of developing channels.

The lower values for first-order stream lengths are not significant because all channels must originate from a point and then lengthen. The region of transition between first- and second-order stream lengths lies between 9 and 17 feet, but 17 feet is not the upper limit of first-order lengths. Of 27 streams longer than 17 feet, 20, within basins considered previously under the discussion of areas, were in very youthful or narrow basins; the remaining 7 seemed capable of change. All but 1 of the 12 second-order channels between 10 and 17 feet will continue to develop, eliminating these streams from the frequency class. Youthfulness of the area probably masks a more distinct transition zone.

Within the Perth Amboy drainage network there are recognizable limits to the areas and lengths of streams of each order. First-order streams have an upper limiting length between 9 and 17 feet and an upper limiting area between 65 and 110 square feet. The limited number of stream orders considered and the subjective evaluation of parts of the data make it more appropriate to set a lower limit below which higher orders cannot exist. The first-order streams require more than 10 square feet for development; second-order streams will not normally evolve from first orders until the drainage area is equal to 65 square feet and the first-order channel is longer than 10 feet.

The writer remapped the drainage pattern in 1952 and compared it with the pattern mapped in 1948, aiding the study of channel alterations within the zones of transition. In all cases the addition of channels occurred only in basins above the size limits set from the frequency-distribution analysis. No channels developed on areas less than 10 square feet. Four new channels developed on interbasin areas, all but one (46.5 sq. ft.) greater than 50 square feet. Twelve new tributaries developed on first-order channels, forming several new second-order basins. Each new basin was youthful (developing headward into the as yet undissected fills), and almost all exceeded 110 square feet. Four were within the transition zone between first- and second-order areas. The newer field study, therefore, seems to confirm the existence of the zones of transition and upper limiting values of development related to the constant of channel maintenance. The constant of channel maintenance, therefore, may be applied to the as yet undissected portions of a drainage system to aid in the prediction of areas of future sediment loss.

TABLE 6.—FREQUENCY DISTRIBUTIONS OF FIRST- AND SECOND-ORDER CHANNEL LENGTHS AND INTERBASIN LENGTHS

Sample	Class mid-values in feet													$\bar{X}$	s	N
Mid-values	3	7	11	15	19	23	27	31	35							
First-order lengths	42	70	40	30	19	6	5	1	1					10.1	6.08	214
Mid-values	18.5	35.5	52.5	68.5	86.5	103.5	120.5									
Second-order lengths	13	18	6	5	1	1	1							40.4	23.4	45
Mid-values	1	3	5	7	9	11	13	15	17	19	21	23	25			
Interbasin lengths	3	16	18	21	23	5	8	5	5	2	0	0	2	8.06	4.17	108

[*Editors' Note*: Material has been omitted at this point.]

REFERENCES

[*Editors' Note:* Only the references cited in the preceding excerpt are reproduced here.]

Horton, R. E., 1945, Erosional Development of Streams and Their Drainage Basins; Hydrophysical Approach to Quantitative Morphology, *Geol. Soc. America Bull.,* v. 56, p. 275-370.

Strahler, A. N., 1952, Hypsometric (Area-Altitude) Analysis of Erosional Topography, *Geol. Soc. America Bull.,* v. 63, p. 1117-1142.

Strahler, A. N., 1953, Revisions of Horton's Quantitative Factors in Erosional Terrain, Paper read before Hydrology Section of Am. Geophys. Union, Washington, D.C., May 1953.

4

Reprinted from pages 22-24, 65, 67, and 68 of *Office of Naval Research Project NR389-042, Technical Report No. 19,* Dept. Geology, Columbia University, New York, 1960, 95p.

QUANTITATIVE GEOMORPHOLOGY OF THE SAN DIMAS EXPERIMENTAL FOREST, CALIFORNIA

James C. Maxwell

[*Editors' Note:* In the original, material precedes this excerpt.]

Relief, Relief Ratio, and Relative Relief

Only the small sets of fourth-order properties and the incomplete sets of perimeter logarithms and relative relief logarithms had been found to meet the prerequisites for analysis of variance. The fourth-order sets probably met conditions only because the small number of values in each set provided scant basis for discrimination of non-homogeneities of variances. The two incomplete first-order sets provided only three watershed means and variances, instead of five. Analysis of variance showed that differences between means of fourth-order relief ratio logarithms were significant at the five-percent level but not at two percent. Differences between log relief fourth-order means were significant at ten percent but not at five percent. No significance was found to differences between the three first-order log relative relief means. Other orders of the several relief properties had between-means to pooled variance ratios ranging from approximately 6 to 36.

Perimeter, Elongation and Circularity

Differences between the three watershed means of first-order perimeter logarithms were found to be significant at three percent but not at two percent. Only the fourth-order sets of elongation logarithms met the requisites of normality and homogeneity of variances; means of these sets had no significant differences. The ratios of between-means to pooled variances for the second- and third-order logarithms of elongation were quite small. This indicates that differences between the watershed means may be non-significant. Large differences between the variances make accurate evaluation of the analysis of variance results impossible. The sets of first-order circularity and of logarithms of circularity had variances which were non-homogeneous, consequently their means could not validly be compared by analysis of variance. The variances ratios for these sets were moderately large. The inconclusive results of tests of these three measures of drainage basin size and shape suggest that there may be no important differences between watersheds for second-order and higher order values of these properties but that there probably are differences between first-order watershed averages.

Drainage Density and Channel Frequency

The sets of logarithms of second-order drainage density, and of second-order channel frequency were normally distributed with homogeneous variances. The differences between the means of these sets were highly significant. Variance ratios of means of the third-order drainage density logarithms and channel frequency logarithms indicate significant differences between means of these properties, if the moderate (significant at one-half percent) departures from homogeneity of variances do not invalidate the analyses of variance for these properties. Fourth-order drainage density logarithms had valid significant differences between watershed means. The between-means to pooled variance ratio of fourth-order channel frequency logarithm means indicated significant differences between watershed means, although the measurement sets did not have homogeneous variance. Logarithms of first-order drainage and channel frequency sets, which had non-homogeneous variances, had between to pooled variance ratios of, respectively, 70 and 64. The results of analysis of variance of log drainage density and log channel frequency means indicate that these properties provide a significant basis for distinguishing differences and similarities between watersheds.

DRAINAGE COMPOSITION

R. E. Horton (1945) formulated from observed relationships a group of laws of drainage composition relating numbers of streams, stream lengths, stream slopes, and basin areas respectively to order number, by geometric series. The geometric ratios of these series were called respectively the bifurcation ratio, length ratio, slope ratio, and area ratio. The law of basin areas had been implied by Horton but was first explicitly stated by Schumm (1956, p. 606). Schumm also established a new law of drainage composition which related basin areas and channel lengths as a linear function whose slope was designated the constant of channel maintenance. Because these laws were postulated to be geometric series, graphs of the relationships on semi-logarithmic coordinates appear as sets of points lying on straight lines, with slopes which are the geometric ratios. For convenience these ratios are referred to below as watershed ratios to distinguish them from other ratios. Each of the watershed ratios has a single value for each watershed. The relationship of eight geomorphic properties to basin order was investigated in the present study. Figures 10 through 17 are graphs of the laws of drainage composition based on these eight properties. Logarithms, base 10, of the watershed ratios are given in each case, because these are the regression coefficients of the regressions of the logarithms of each property on order.

The law of stream numbers, as stated by Horton, seems to apply well to the San Dimas watersheds (Figure 10). The logarithms of bifurcation ratios were all similar, the greatest being 0.70, for Fern Canyon, and the least 0.62 for Upper East Fork. The San Dimas channel length-order data do not seem to fit a geometric series closely (Figure 11). In the five watersheds studied, the fifth-order channel segment is shorter than would be expected if a semilog linear relation based on the first four orders were extended to the fifth order. In other words, the functions appear to be concave up when plotted on semilogarithmic coordinates. Strahler (1953) found similar relations for several other watersheds. Much of this apparent departure from linearity may be due to Strahler's revision of Horton's method of stream ordering. Horton considered the length of a fifth-order stream to extend from the mouth of a fifth-order watershed to the head-water extremity of its furthest fingertip tributary. Strahler's revision, which eliminated subjective choices about the trunk stream, considers the fifth-order segment to extend only from a junction with a fifth-order (or higher order) segment up to the highest confluence of two fourth-order segments. Such fifth-order segments would, on the average, be shorter than fifth-order streams as defined by Horton. Broscoe (1959, p. 5) gave a similar explanation for this apparent non-linearity. When more data are available, for sixth-order or higher order watersheds, it will be possible to ascertain which method of ordering yields results most closely fitting Horton's law and, conversely, what function best fits channel lengths as defined by Strahler.

Mean basin area measurements seem to follow closely the law of basin areas as stated by Schumm (1956, p. 606). The logarithms of watershed area ratios were all between 0.71 and 0.72 except that for Fern Canyon which was 0.78 (Figure 12). A plot of mean basin diameters on a logarithmic scale versus channel order is very closely fitted by a straight line (Figure 13). From this observation another law of drainage basin composition can be formulated: the mean diameter of basins of each order within a higher order watershed tend closely to approximate a direct geometric series in which the first term is the mean diameter of the first-order basins and the ratio is the diameter ratio.

Logarithmic plots of mean drainage basin relief (or, more exactly, diameter relief) against order also fall close to straight lines (Figure 14). Hence, a law of basin relief, which describes this relation, is postulated: the mean relief of basins of each order in a watershed tend closely to follow a direct geometric series in which the first term is the mean relief of the first-order basins and the ratio is the watershed relief ratio. Obviously this law will be valid only for watersheds of low to intermediate order; the maximum regional relief quickly becomes a limiting factor as order increases. It is unfortunate that the phrase "relief ratio" thus has two meanings. The use of "relative relief" for the relief of the diameter would improve terminology if that term had not already been used by Melton for the ratio of relief to perimeter. The logarithm of watershed relief ratio found in this study ranged from 0.21 for Volfe Canyon to 0.26 for Fern Canyon. It is notable that Fern Canyon had the largest watershed ratios for stream numbers, channel lengths, basin areas and relief. The significance of this fact has not yet been determined.

The derived geomorphic properties of elongation, drainage density, and channel frequency showed much less variation with basin order (Figures 15, 16, and 17). The largest value of the slope of mean elongation plotted logarithmically against order was 0.015. In general, the mean elongation of first-order basins was less than that of higher order basins. This may indicate that first-order basins start as insequent gullies unaffected by processes which control the shape of better integrated higher order basins, or it may indicate that a recent rejuvenation affected the shape of many first-order basins but has not yet affected the higher order basins. It is probable that in regions characterized by dendritic drainage patterns, elongation is independent of order.

The semi-logarithmic graph of drainage density against order showed that this property decreases with increase in order (Figure 16). The points scatter widely about a straight line, but all watersheds show the same inverse relationship. No consistency in the departures from linearity was apparent. The largest value of decrease in log drainage density per unit increase in order was 0.025, for Fern Canyon; the least was 0.019, for Volfe Canyon. Semilogarithmic plots of channel frequency against order showed a relationship similar to that of drainage density (Figure 17). Departures of the plotted points from straight lines were less than those of the drainage density—order plots. The logarithm of channel frequency ratio was largest for Fern Canyon (-0.079); least for Wolfskill Canyon, (-0.063). The larger channel frequencies in the Big Dalton drainage, Watersheds VIII and IX, compared with corresponding orders in the San Dimas drainage, Watersheds I, II, and III, are apparent on the graphs. A similar but less conspicuous segregation can be seen on the drainage density-order graphs. This tendency of channel frequency-order plots to segregate into groups suggests that channel frequency may be a useful property for distinction between watersheds which are in the same physiographic province but which have subtle geomorphic and hydrologic differences.

[*Editors' Note:* Material has been omitted at this point.]

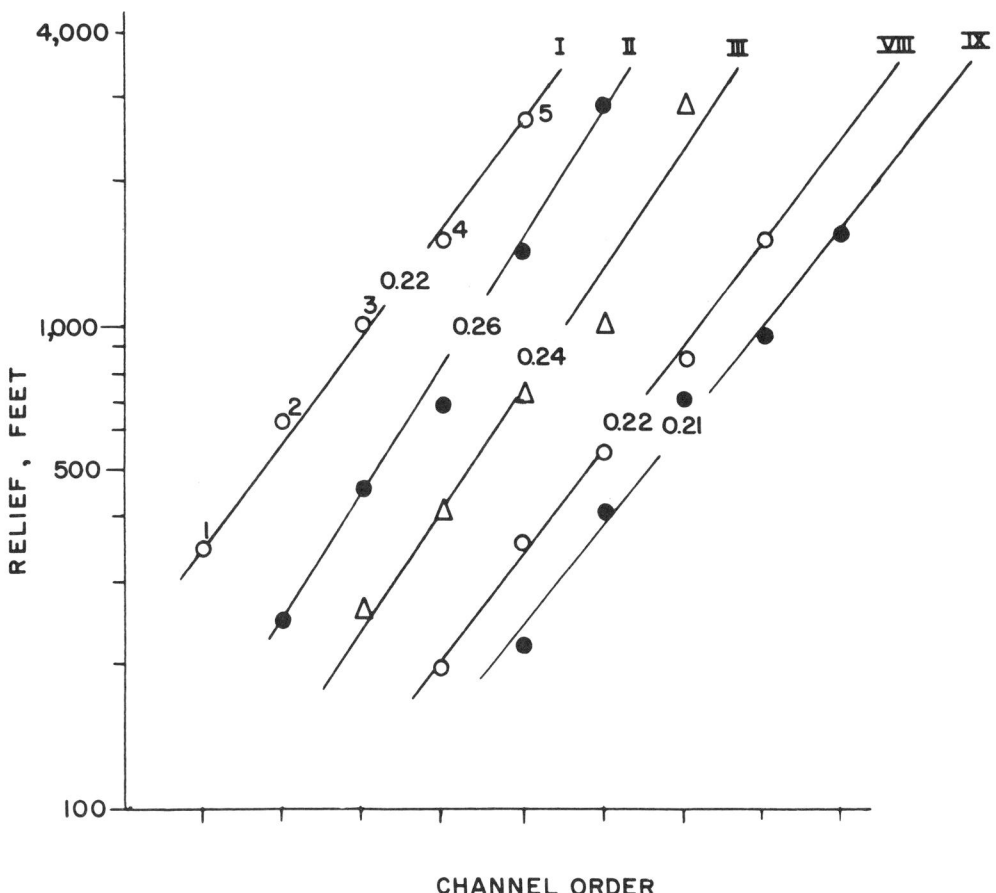

Figure 14. Relation of relief to order.

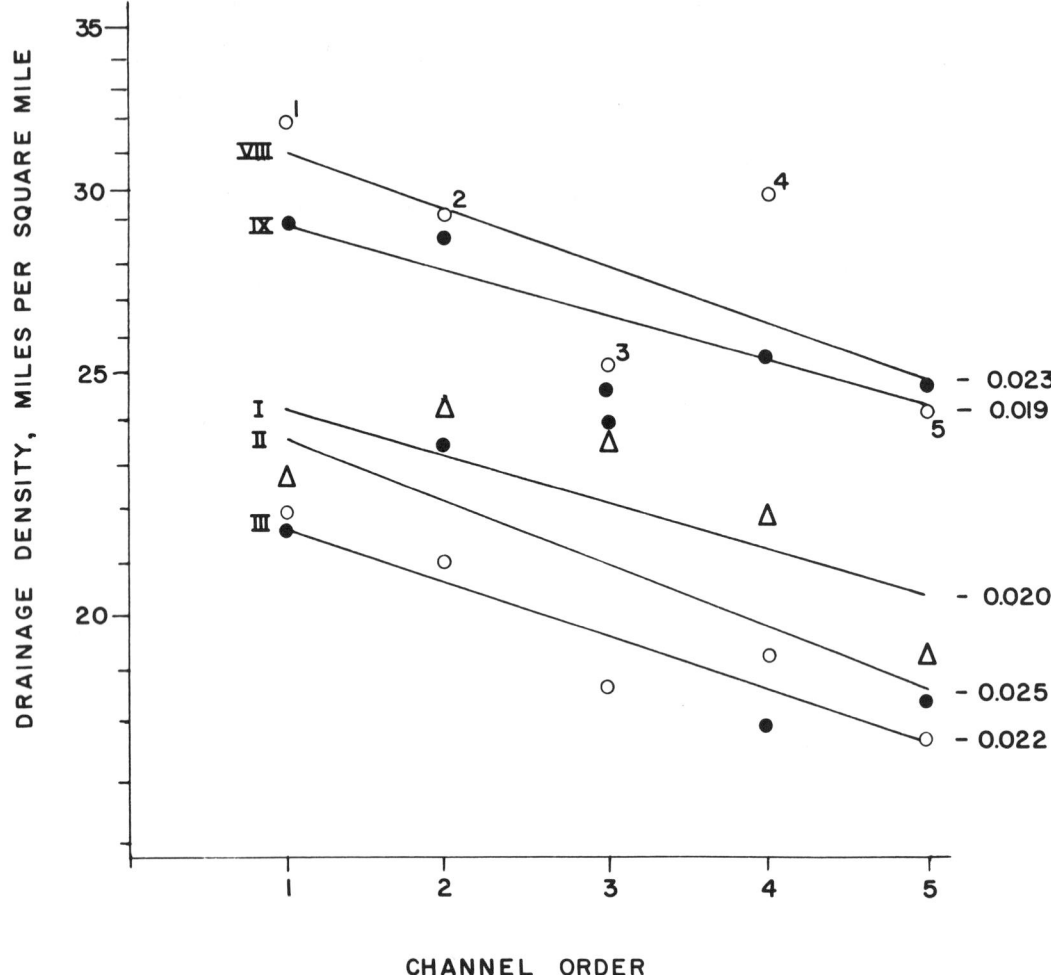

Figure 16. Relation of drainage density to order.

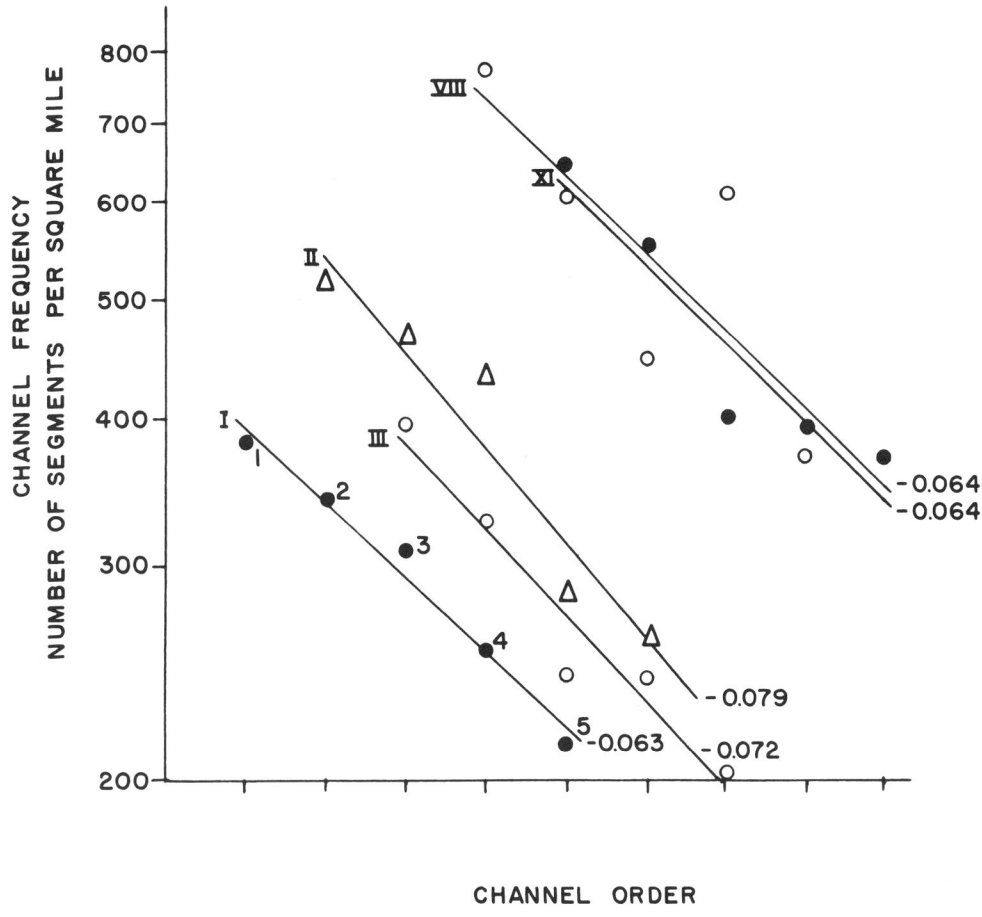

Figure 17. Relation of channel frequency to order.

REFERENCES

[*Editors' Note:* Only the references cited in the preceding excerpt are reproduced here.]

Broscoe, A. J., 1959, Quantitative Analysis of Longitudinal Stream Profiles of Small Watersheds, *Office of Naval Research, Geography Branch, Project NR 389-042, Tech. Rept. No. 18* (Columbia University, New York), 73pp.

Horton, R. E., 1945, Erosional Development of Streams and Their Drainage Basins; Hydrophysical Approach to Quantitative Morphology, *Geol. Soc. Amer. Bull.*, v. 56, p. 275-370.

Schumm, S. A., 1956, Evolution of Drainage Systems and Slopes in Badlands at Perth Amboy, New Jersey, *Geol. Soc. Amer. Bull.*, v. 67, p. 597-646.

Strahler, A. N., 1953, Revisions of Horton's Quantitative Factors in Erosional Terrain. Hydrology Section, Am. Geophys. Union, Washington, D.C., 1953 (Abstract).

5

Copyright ©1964 by McGraw-Hill Book Company
Reprinted by permission from pages 4-39–4-76 of *Handbook of Applied Hydrology*,
Section 4-II, V. T. Chow, ed., McGraw-Hill, New York, 1964, 1465p.

QUANTITATIVE GEOMORPHOLOGY OF DRAINAGE BASINS AND CHANNEL NETWORKS

ARTHUR N. STRAHLER, *Professor of Geomorphology, Columbia University.*

I. Introduction.. 4-40
II. Basic Concepts... 4-40
    A. Open Systems and Steady States......................... 4-40
    B. Dimensional Analysis...................................... 4-41
    C. Statistical Analysis... 4-42
    D. Plan of Morphometric Analysis.......................... 4-43
III. Linear Aspects of the Channel System........................ 4-43
    A. Stream Orders.. 4-43
    B. Stream Lengths... 4-45
    C. Length of Overland Flow................................. 4-47
IV. Areal Aspects of Drainage Basins............................... 4-48
    A. Arrangement of Areal Elements......................... 4-48
    B. Frequency Distribution of Basin Areas................. 4-48
    C. Law of Stream Areas...................................... 4-48
    D. Relation of Area to Length............................... 4-49
    E. Relation of Area to Discharge............................ 4-50
    F. Basin Shape (Outline Form).............................. 4-51
    G. Drainage Density.. 4-52
    H. Constant of Channel Maintenance...................... 4-54
    I. Stream Frequency... 4-55
V. Relief (Gradient) Aspect of Drainage Basins and Channel Networks.. 4-56
    A. Channel Gradients... 4-56
        1. Single-channel Profiles................................ 4-56
        2. Cause of Profile Upconcavity........................ 4-57
        3. Fitted Regression Functions......................... 4-57
        4. Derivative Functions.................................. 4-59
        5. Profile Segmentation.................................. 4-60
        6. Composite Profiles.................................... 4-60
        7. Channel Slope as a Function of Order............. 4-60
        8. Main-stream-slope Factor............................ 4-61
    B. Channel-cross-section Geometry......................... 4-61

          C. Ground-surface Gradients................................. 4-61
             1. Relationship of Ground and Channel Slopes............ 4-61
             2. Maximum Valleyside Slopes.......................... 4-62
             3. Total Surface-slope Distribution...................... 4-63
          D. Relief Measures... 4-65
             1. Relief... 4-65
             2. Relief Ratios....................................... 4-66
          E. Ruggedness and Geometry Numbers...................... 4-67
          F. Hypsometric (Area-Altitude) Analysis.................... 4-68
      VI. Theory of Drainage-basin Dynamics......................... 4-69
          A. Statement of Variables.................................. 4-69
          B. Solution by Pi Theorem................................. 4-70
          C. Steady-state Relationships............................. 4-71
          D. Upsets of Steady State................................. 4-71
     VII. Observed Complex Relations among Hydrologic and Geometric
          Properties... 4-72
          A. Control of Basin Geometry by Climatic Factors.......... 4-72
          B. Relation of Basin Geometry to Stream Flow.............. 4-72
    VIII. Notations.. 4-73
      IX. References.. 4-74

I. INTRODUCTION

Under the impetus supplied by Horton [1, 2], the description of drainage basins and channel networks was transformed from a purely qualitative and deductive study [3] to a rigorous quantitative science capable of providing hydrologists with numerical data of practical value. Horton's work was supplemented by Langbein [4], then developed in detail by Strahler [5-11] and his Columbia University associates [14-18, 21, 22, 25, 26, 39, 66, 68].

This section treats quantitative land-form analysis as it applies to normally developed watersheds in which running water and associated mass gravity movements, acting over long periods of time, are the chief agents in developing surface geometry. Emphasis is upon the geometry itself, rather than upon the dynamic processes of erosion and transportation which shape the forms (see Sec. 17-I for erosion and transportation).

II. BASIC CONCEPTS

A. Open Systems and Steady States

Of fundamental importance is the concept of a drainage basin as an open system tending to achieve a steady state of operation. Strahler [5, p. 676] applied open-system biologic concepts [12] to a graded drainage system. An open system imports and exports matter and energy through system boundaries and must transform energy uniformly to maintain operation. In a drainage basin the land surface within the limits of the basin perimeter constitutes a system boundary through which precipitation is imported. Mineral matter supplied from within the system and excess precipitation leave the system through the basin mouth. In a graded drainage basin the steady state manifests itself in the development of certain topographic characteristics which achieve a time-independent state. Erosional and transportational processes meanwhile produce a steady flow (averaged over periods of years or tens of years) of water and waste from the basin. Potential energy of position is transformed into kinetic energy of water and debris motion or into heat. Considered over a very long span of time, however, continual readjustment of components in the steady state is required as relief lowers and available energy diminishes. The topographic forms will correspondingly show a slow evolution.

Where geologic events have brought into being a new land mass not previously acted upon by running water, the steady state is preceded by a transient state in which a new channel system grows and deepens rapidly as the ground slopes are transformed to contribute most efficiently to the drainage network. In the terminology of the earlier, classical descriptive geomorphology, the transient state was referred to as the stage of youth in the cycle of erosion; the steady state, as the stage of maturity [3].

Validity of the Horton system of fluvial morphometry depends upon the theory that, for a given intensity of erosion process, acting upon a mass of given physical properties, the conditions of surface relief, slope, and channel configuration reach a time-independent steady state in which morphology is adjusted to transmit through the system just the quantity of debris and excess water characteristically produced under the controlling regimen of climate. Should controlling factors of climate or geologic material be changed, the steady state will be upset. Through a relatively rapid series of adjustments, serving to reestablish a steady state, appropriate new values of basin geometry are developed [11, pp. 295-296]. In brief, steady state manifests itself by invariant geometry; transient state, by rapid changes in geometry in which new sets of forms replace the old.

B. Dimensional Analysis

Dimensional analysis forms a sound basis for study of the geometrical and mechanical aspects of drainage basins [11]. The fundamental dimensions of length, mass, and time, whether used singly or combined as products, suffice to define all geometrical and mechanical properties of a drainage basin. Many of the form elements have the simple dimension of length, for example, stream length, basin perimeter, or basin

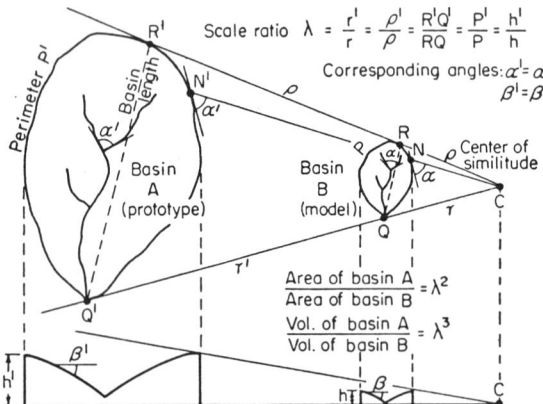

Fig. 4-II-1. Geometrical similarity of two drainage basins. (*After Strahler* [11, p. 291; 10, p. 914].)

relief. Measures of area have the dimension of length squared; volumes, the dimension of length cubed. Another class of geometrical properties consists of the dimensionless ratios of one length property to another. Dimensionless ratios describe pure shape, or form, irrespective of absolute size. For tables of land-form parameters and their dimensional properties, see Ref. 11, pp. 282-283.

Geometrical similarity is an important concept of dimensional analysis applied to drainage basins. Systems of land forms evolving from the same geologic processes and materials possess a high degree of geometrical similarity, an attribute that makes possible the recognition and classification of land forms. Figure 4-II-1 shows the meaning of geometrical similarity as applied to two drainage basins which differ in size but not in shape. Basins A and B are said to be *homothetic* [13, pp. 14–20], because any two corresponding points in the basins lie on the same radius vector from a center of similitude, i.e., are *collinear*.

The points Q' and Q mark the mouths of the basins, at corresponding distances r' and r from the center of similitude. Two other corresponding points are R' and R, collinear and located at distances ρ' and ρ, respectively, from the center of similitude. For reasons that are self-evident from considerations of Euclidian geometry of similiar triangles,

$$r' = \lambda r \quad \text{and} \quad \rho' = \lambda \rho \qquad (4\text{-II-}1a)$$

where λ is the linear scale ratio. Consequently,

$$\lambda = \frac{r'}{r} = \frac{\rho'}{\rho} \qquad (4\text{-II-}1b)$$

which is to say that the radius vectors of any two collinear points are always in the ratio λ. Hence, in geometrically similar drainage basins, the distances between corresponding points in the system have the same scale ratio. In geometrical similarity, the tangents to corresponding points on curved lines in the two systems are always equal. In Fig. 4-II-1 the tangents of α' and α at the points N' and N are equal, whereas the degrees of curvature at corresponding points on the two figures are inversely related to the linear scale ratio.

In summary, two drainage basins are geometrically similar when all corresponding land-form elements having the dimension of length are in the same ratio λ, when all corresponding measures having the dimension of inverse of length are in the scale ratio $1/\lambda$, and when those of dimension length squared are in the same ratio, λ^2. Furthermore, all dimensionless properties must have identical values in the corresponding parts of both systems. Although perfect similarity is not to be expected in drainage basins, a high degree of similarity has been found over a great size range when planimetric (horizontal) aspects are considered [11, pp. 292–294]. Lack of similarity among drainage basins may result from strong geologic inhomogeneities which distort the basin shapes.

As applied to scale-model studies, the ratio λ is taken as the ratio of length in prototype to length in model. Mechanical (kinematic and dynamical) similarity between basins is not treated here, but would be essential aspects of model studies.

C. Statistical Analysis

Application of principles of mathematical statistics to quantitative geomorphology is essential if meaningful conclusions are to be achieved (see Sec. 8 for statistical methods). Groups of measurements of drainage-basin characteristics constitute samples drawn from vastly greater populations [8]. At the outset of any investigation, a sampling procedure must be designed to assure the highest possible degree of objectivity in selection of observations. Use of grids or randomly selected orthogonal coordinates may provide a means of sampling the surface characteristics of a watershed where operator bias must be avoided. Tables of random numbers can provide unbiased selection of sample elements from among many individual items, or can provide random azimuths and distances for unbiased field traverses.

Mathematical statistics is concerned with the making of inferences from a small sample about the characteristics of a vast population whose absolute parameters can never be known. Tests are concerned with ascertaining the probability of being right or wrong in stating some hypothesis concerning the relation of one or more samples to the population or populations from which they have been drawn.

In practice, a particular geometric property of a drainage basin, for example, the length of stream segments, is sampled by measuring from maps or air photographs or by direct field surveys. When a sample of, say, 50 or 100 measurements is thus obtained, the standard methods of frequency-distribution analysis are used [8, pp. 2–6]. The individual measurements, termed variates, are grouped into classes, and the nature of the distribution examined. If strongly skewed, a logarithmic transformation of variates may be required. The mean $\bar{x}$, variance s^2, and standard deviation s of the population, as estimated from the sample, are next computed, and serve to describe the geomorphic property in objective and useful terms. Next, the sample frequency distribution is compared with the normal, or Gaussian, distribution, and a test performed to assure that the normal distribution can be assumed [8, pp. 8–10]. Many geometric properties of drainage basins, particularly those having the dimensions of length, area, or volume, are characteristically log-normal in distribution, whereas other properties, particularly dimensionless ratios and angular values, tend to be arithmetically normal in distribution [18]. Melton [14] collected an extensive body of morphometric data on drainage basins and discussed the sample-size requirements for use in statistical tests.

Two or more samples can be compared by statistical tests to reach a decision as to whether the samples are likely to have been drawn from the same or from different populations [8, pp. 10–17]. Such tests are essential to avoid unwarranted assumptions as to the significance of the observed differences in means and variances of the samples themselves.

Relationship of a dependent variable to an independent variable, as, for example, the influence of infiltration capacity upon drainage density, is treated by regression analysis [8, pp. 18–24]. Linear and nonlinear equations may be used to obtain the best fit of data. Significance of the observed relationship can be evaluated by rigorous tests. Multiple regression, in which the combined effect of several independent variables upon one dependent variable can be considered, has been extensively used in drainage-basin analysis [15–17]. Machine methods of multiple-correlation-and-regression analysis have been introduced [18].

D. Plan of Morphometric Analysis

Systematic description of the geometry of a drainage basin and its stream-channel system requires measurement of linear aspects of the drainage network, areal aspects of the drainage basin, and relief (gradient) aspects of channel network and contributing ground slopes. Whereas the first two categories of measurement are planimetric (i.e., treat properties projected upon a horizontal datum plane), the third category treats the vertical inequalities of the drainage-basin forms. Although not free from inconsistencies, the above plan of morphometric analysis is useful operationally and is followed throughout the remainder of this section.

III. LINEAR ASPECTS OF THE CHANNEL SYSTEM

A. Stream Orders

The first step in drainage-basin analysis is designation of stream orders, following a system introduced into the United States by Horton [2, pp. 281–282] and slightly modified by Strahler [7, p. 1120]. Melton [19, pp. 345–346] has explained the mathematical concepts involved. Assuming that one has available a channel-network map including all intermittent and permanent flow lines located in clearly defined valleys, the smallest fingertip tributaries are designated order 1 (Fig. 4-II-2). Where two first-order channels join, a channel segment of order 2 is formed; where two of order 2 join, a segment of order 3 is formed; and so forth. The trunk stream through which all discharge of water and sediment passes is therefore the stream segment of highest order.

Usefulness of the stream-order system depends on the premise that, on the average, if a sufficiently large sample is treated, order number is directly proportional to size of the contributing watershed, to channel dimensions, and to stream discharge at that place in the system. Because order number is dimensionless, two drainage networks differing greatly in linear scale can be compared with respect to corresponding points in their geometry through use of order number. After the drainage-network

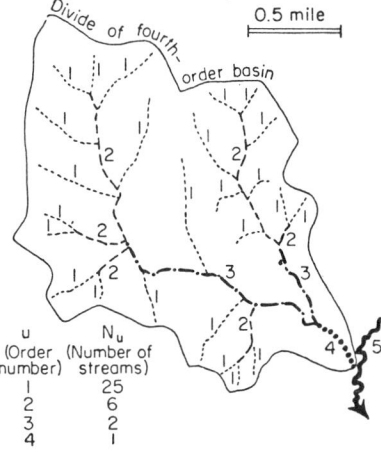

FIG. 4-II-2. Designation of stream orders. (*After Strahler* [10, p. 914].)

elements have been assigned their order numbers, the segments of each order are counted to yield the number N_u of segments of the given order u (Fig. 4-II-2).

It is obvious that the number of stream segments of any given order will be fewer than for the next lower order but more numerous than for the next higher order. The ratio of number of segments of a given order N_u to the number of segments of the higher order N_{u+1} is termed the *bifurcation ratio* R_b:

$$R_b = \frac{N_u}{N_{u+1}} \qquad (4\text{-II-}2)$$

The bifurcation ratio will not be precisely the same from one order to the next, because of chance variations in watershed geometry, but will tend to be a constant throughout the series. This observation is the basis of Horton's [2, p. 291] *law of stream numbers*, which states that the numbers of stream segments of each order form an inverse geometric sequence with order number, or

$$N_u = R_b^{k-u} \qquad (4\text{-II-}3)$$

where k is the order of the trunk segment, and the other terms are as previously defined. The law has received verification by accumulated data from many localities [7, p. 1137; 20, p. 18; 21, p. 603; 22, p. 1002; 16, p. 48]. When logarithm of number

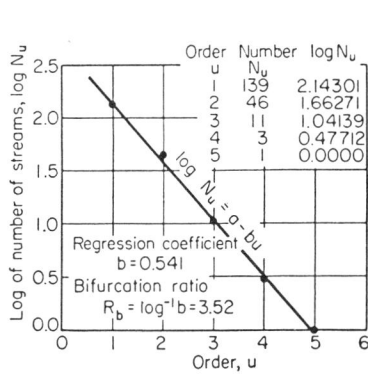

FIG. 4-II-3. Regression of number of stream segments on order. (*After Strahler* [10, p. 915], *based on data by Smith* [22, p. 1003].)

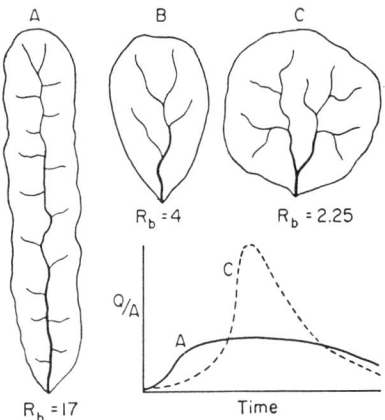

FIG. 4-II-4. Hypothetical basins of extreme and moderate bifurcation ratios, with schematic hydrographs.

of streams is plotted against order, most drainage networks show a linear relationship, with small deviation from a straight line (Fig. 4-II-3).

Calculation on an average value of R_b for a given channel network can be made by determining the slope of the fitted regression of logarithm of numbers (ordinate) on order (abscissa) [23]. The regression coefficient b is identical with the logarithm of R_b. In Fig. 4-II-3 the bifurcation ratio is estimated to be 3.52, which means that, on the average, there are $3\frac{1}{2}$ times as many channel segments of any given order as of the next higher order.

Bifurcation ratios characteristically range between 3.0 and 5.0 for watersheds in which the geologic structures do not distort the drainage pattern. The theoretical minimum possible value of 2.0 is rarely approached under natural conditions. Because the bifurcation ratio is a dimensionless property, and because drainage systems in homogeneous materials tend to display geometrical similarity, it is not surprising that the ratio shows only a small variation from region to region.

Abnormally high bifurcation ratios might be expected in regions of steeply dipping rock strata where narrow strike valleys are confined between hogback ridges. Basin A in Fig. 4-II-4 shows such an elongate basin compared with a normal basin (basin B) and one approaching the theoretical minimum value of 2.0 (basin C). The effects of such distortions upon maximum flood discharges, assuming precipitation and other controls to be the same throughout, are suggested by hydrographs (Fig. 4-II-4). Whereas the elongate basin with high R_b would yield a low but extended peak flow, the rotund basin with low R_b would produce a sharp peak. Basin B would lie somewhere between these two extremes.

Horton [2, p. 286] shows that the total number of streams of all orders in a network can be computed if the bifurcation ratio R_b, and trunk order k are known:

$$\sum_{i=1}^{k} N_u = \frac{R_b^k - 1}{R_b - 1} \tag{4-II-4}$$

B. Stream Lengths

Mean length $\bar{L}_u$ of a stream-channel segment of order u is a dimensional property revealing the characteristic size of components of a drainage network and its contributing basin surfaces. Channel length is measured with the chartometer (map measurer) directly from the map and therefore represents the true length somewhat shortened by projection upon a horizontal plane [24]. Because in practice all segments of a given order within the specified drainage network are measured successively without pause for recording, the cumulative length appears on the dial of the chartometer. To obtain the mean length of channel $\bar{L}_u$ of order u, the total length is divided by the number of segments N_u of that order, thus:

$$\bar{L}_u = \frac{\sum_{i=1}^{N} L_u}{N_u} \tag{4-II-5}$$

Treating each channel segment as a statistical variate, the frequency distribution of segment lengths of a given order was studied by Miller [25], who observed that the distribution of first- and second-order segments was strongly skewed to the right. Schumm [21, p. 607] corrected this skewness by use of logarithm of length. It is recommended that logarithmic transformation of the raw data be made before grouping into classes. Computation of mean, variance, and standard deviation can then be made on a logarithmic basis as in Fig. 4-II-5 [8, pp. 7-8].

The first-order stream channel with its contributing first-order drainage-basin surface area should be regarded as the unit cell, or building block, of any watershed. Because first-order drainage basins tend to be geometrically similar over a wide range of sizes, it matters little what length property is chosen to provide the characteristic measurement of size by which systems are compared from region to region. Thus, while length of first-order channel is a convenient and easily obtained length measure, it might be equally valid to select basin perimeter, basin length, drainage density, or square root of basin area as alternative indices of scale of the unit basin.

As expected, mean length of channel segments of a given order is greater than that of the next lower order but less than that of the next higher order. Horton [2, p. 291] postulated that the length ratio R_L (which is the ratio of mean length $\bar{L}_u$ of segments of order u to mean length of segments of the next lower order $\bar{L}_{u-1}$) tends to be constant throughout the successive orders of a watershed. He was therefore able to state the *law of stream lengths*, that the mean lengths of stream segments of each of the successive orders of a basin tend to approximate a direct geometric sequence in which the first term is the average length of segments of the first order:

$$\bar{L}_u = \bar{L}_1 R_L^{u-1} \qquad (4\text{-II-}6)$$

If the law of stream lengths is valid, a plot of logarithm of stream length (ordinate)

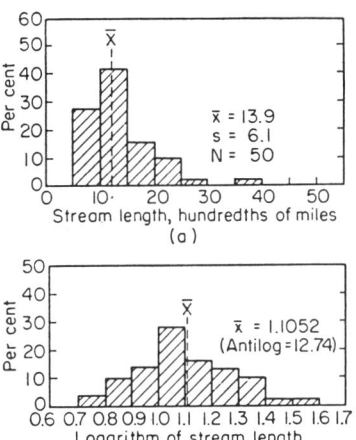

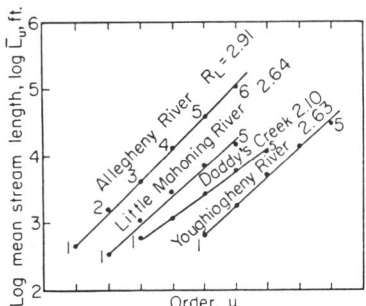

FIG. 4-II-5. Histogram showing (a) arithmetic distribution of lengths of first-order streams developed on Copper Ridge dolomite, Virginia; (b) distribution of logarithms of same stream lengths. Frequencies computed and grouped from logs of variates. (*After Strahler* [8, pp. 7–8], based on data from *Miller* [25, table 2].)

FIG. 4-II-6. Regression of logarithm of stream-segment length on order for four drainage basins in the Appalachian Plateau Province. (*After Morisawa* [17, p. 48].)

as a function of order (abscissa) should yield a set of points lying essentially along a straight line (Fig. 4-II-6). Confirmation of the law seems amply demonstrated by data from many watersheds [21, pp. 604–605; 20, p. 13; 17, pp. 49–50; 26, p. 5].

As with the law of stream numbers, the law of stream lengths is essentially an exponential function defined only for integer values of the independent variable. The length ratio R_L is therefore obtained as the antilogarithm of the regression coefficient b of a line fitted by inspection or by least-squares method to the plot of logarithm of stream length on order (Fig. 4-II-6).

Verification of Horton's laws of stream numbers and lengths supports the theory that geometrical similarity is preserved generally in basins of increasing order. In other words, a basin of the third order would tend to be geometrically similar to the second-order basins which lie within it, and these in turn would be similar to the first-order basins within them. Hack [27, pp. 63–64] casts doubt on this theory by finding that stream length (measured cumulatively from the stream head) varies as the 0.6 power of area in basins spanning nearly four orders (0.01 to 100 sq mi). An exponent of 0.5 is required if geometrical similarity is to be perfectly preserved, whereas the observed value of 0.6 requires that basins become somewhat longer and narrower as their size increases.

Of interest in the estimation of channel storage capacity for an entire watershed is Horton's [2, p. 291] observation that the laws of stream numbers and lengths can be combined as a product to yield an equation for the total length of channels of a given order u, knowing only the bifurcation and length ratios, the mean length $\bar{L}_1$ of the first-order segments, and the order of the trunk segment, thus:

$$\sum_{i=1}^{N} L_u = \bar{L}_1 R_b^{k-u} R_L^{u-1} \qquad (4\text{-II-}7)$$

Furthermore, Horton [2, p. 293] shows that the total length of channels for all orders of a watershed of order k can be estimated as

$$\sum_{i=1}^{k} \sum_{i=1}^{N} L_u = \bar{L}_1 R_b^{k-1} \frac{R_{Lb}^{k} - 1}{R_{Lb} - 1} \qquad (4\text{-II-}8)$$

where
$$R_{Lb} = \frac{R_L}{R_b}$$

A somewhat different approach to a measure of stream length representative of a given drainage basin does not use the Horton stream-order concept, but instead measures length L_{ca} from basin mouth (or other reference point on a stream such as a gage) to a point on the main stream channel opposite the computed center of gravity (centroid) of the total drainage area [28; 29; 30, p. 456; 31].

Snyder [28, p. 450] found from study of a large number of basins that the lag in time between center of mass of surface-producing runoff and resulting peak discharge at a given station varied as the 0.6 power of distance in miles from station to center of area. Taylor and Schwartz [29, p. 235] found distance L_{ca} from gage to computed center of gravity (centroid) of drainage area to be a significant factor in unit-hydrograph lag (Sec. 14).

C. Length of Overland Flow

Surface runoff follows a system of downslope flow paths from the drainage divide (basin perimeter) to the nearest channel. This flow net, comprising a family of orthogonal curves with respect to the topographic contours, locally converges or diverges from parallelism, depending upon position in the basin. Horton [2, p. 284] defined *length of overland flow* L_g as the length of flow path, projected to the horizontal, of nonchannel flow from a point on the drainage divide to a point on the adjacent stream channel. He noted [2, p. 284] that "length of overland flow is one of the most important independent variables affecting both the hydrologic and physiographic development of drainage basins." (See also Sec. 14.)

During evolution of the drainage system, L_g is adjusted to a magnitude appropriate to the scale of the first-order drainage basins and is approximately equal to one-half the reciprocal of the drainage density [2, p. 284].

Because the number of starting points on a basin perimeter is infinite, the choice of flow path to represent length of overland flow must be specified. An average length can be computed from measurements of a number of paths emanating from points uniformly spaced around the entire basin perimeter or extended upward from uniformly spaced points along the channel. A maximum length can be obtained for any given first-order basin by taking the longest possible flow path contributing to the tip of the first-order channel [26, pp. 6, 39].

A particular case of the length of overland flow is that used to describe the length of a triangular element of ground surface lying between two adjacent tributary basins and the larger stream they join. The relationships of these surfaces, which drain directly into channels of order higher than first, without themselves being included in any lower-order basin, are described below in the discussion of basin areas. The maximum horizontal length of one such element of surface, from its apex to the adjacent channel, is here designated as *interbasin length* L_0.

IV. AREAL ASPECTS OF DRAINAGE BASINS

A. Arrangement of Areal Elements

The perimeters of all first, second, and higher orders of basins may be drawn on the topographic map of a watershed. The area A_u of a basin of a given order u is defined as the total area projected upon a horizontal plane, contributing overland flow to the channel segment of the given order and including all tributaries of lower order (Fig. 4-II-2). For example, the area of a basin of the fourth order, A_4, would cumulate the areas of all first-, second-, and third-order basins, plus all additional surface elements, known as *interbasin areas*, contributing directly to a channel of order higher than first [21, p. 608].

In Fig. 4-II-7, A_2, the area of the second-order basin, consists of the sum of the two first-order basins plus the areas of two interbasin areas contributing directly to the second-order channel segment, and may be written as

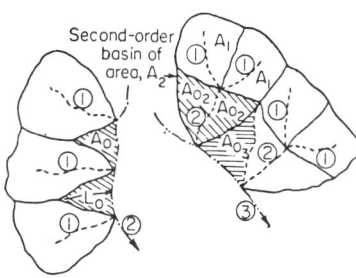

FIG. 4-II-7. Interbasin areas contributing runoff directly to second- and third-order channel segments.

$$A_2 = \sum_{i=1}^{N} A_1 + \sum_{i=1}^{N} A_{O_2} \qquad (4\text{-II-}9)$$

where A_{O_2} is the area of an interbasin area contributing to a second-order segment.

In the general case, the total area A_u of a basin of the order u may be written as

$$A_u = \left(\sum_{i=1}^{N} A_1 + \sum_{i=1}^{N} A_2 + \cdots + \sum_{i=1}^{N} A_{u-1} \right)$$
$$+ \left(\sum_{i=1}^{N} A_{O_1} + \sum_{i=1}^{N} A_{O_2} + \cdots + \sum_{i=1}^{N} A_{O_u} \right) \qquad (4\text{-II-}10)$$

B. Frequency Distribution of Basin Areas

The areas of drainage basins of a given order can be measured by planimeter from a map on which the perimeters have been outlined for each order. Frequency distribution of areas has been studied by Miller [25, p. 14] and Schumm [21, p. 607], who found that a strong right skewness in the distributions could be largely corrected by using the logarithm of area (Fig. 4-II-8). For a given order, area characteristics can be described in terms of mean, variance, and standard deviation computed from the sample. Although individual basin areas deviate widely from the mean, the means themselves show a progressive increase with order.

C. Law of Stream Areas

Horton [2, p. 294] inferred that mean drainage-basin areas of progressively higher orders should increase in a geometric sequence, as do stream lengths. Schumm [21, p. 606] expressed this relationship in a *law of stream areas:* the mean basin areas of stream of each order tend closely to approximate a direct geometric sequence in which the first term is the mean area of the first-order basin. This law may be written as

$$\bar{A}_u = \bar{A}_1 R_a{}^{u-1} \qquad (4\text{-II-}11)$$

where $\bar{A}_u$ is mean area of basins of order u, $\bar{A}_1$ is mean area of the first-order basins, and R_a is an area ratio analogous to the length ratio R_L.

As with stream length, the regression of logarithm of basin area on order is linear (Fig. 4-II-9). Morisawa [17, p. 51] confirmed this relationship in representative watersheds of the Appalachian Plateau Province. Leopold and Miller [20, pp. 19–20] found the law to apply to basins of ephemeral streams in central New Mexico.

D. Relation of Area to Length

Assuming the validity of the laws of stream lengths and basin areas, in which both properties are related in an exponential function with order, length should be related to area by a power function. Morisawa [17, pp. 12, 58–61] plotted both logarithm of mean stream length and logarithm of cumulative length against logarithm of basin area for each order of representative basins of the Appalachian Plateau Province, obtaining highly linear relationships (Fig. 4-II-10).

Absolute stream length, measured headward to the divide from a given point on a stream, plotted against area of watershed contributing to the stream above the given point, also shows a strongly linear relationship when the logarithms of both variables

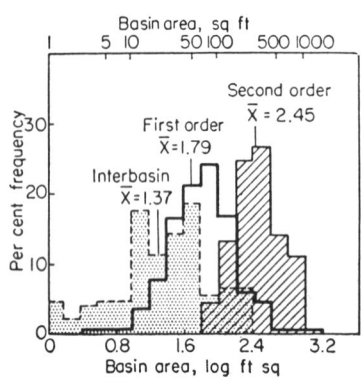

FIG. 4-II-8. Frequency distributions of logarithm of basin area for interbasin, first-order, and second-order areas at Perth Amboy badlands. (*After Schumm* [21, p. 607].)

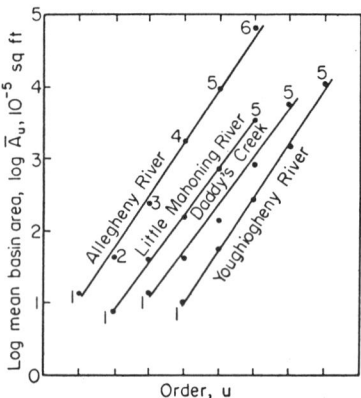

FIG. 4-II-9. Regression of logarithm of basin area on order for four drainage basins of the Appalachian Plateau Province. (*After Morisawa* [17, p. 51].)

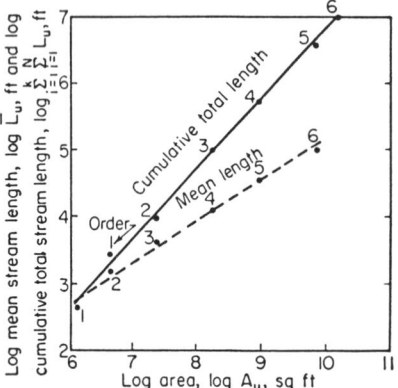

FIG. 4-II-10. Relation of stream length to basin area, order for order, for Allegheny River. (*After Morisawa* [17, p. 58].)

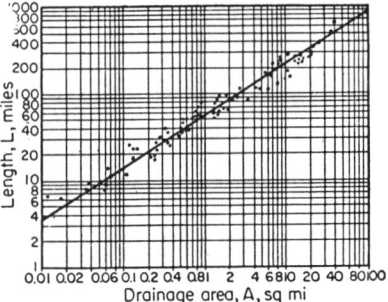

FIG. 4-II-11. Relation of stream length to drainage area for seven areas in Virginia and Maryland. (*After Hack* [27, p. 64].)

are used. Hack [27, p. 64] demonstrated the applicability of the power function relating length and area as thus defined for streams in seven areas of Virginia and Maryland (Fig. 4-II-11). He used the equation

$$L = 1.4 A^{0.6} \qquad (4\text{-II-}12)$$

where L is stream length in miles measured to a point on the drainage divide, and A is area in square miles. He plotted 400 similar measurements made by Langbein [4, p. 145] at gaging stations in the northeastern United States and found the same equation to apply. Hack noted [27, p. 64] that if geometrical similarity is to be preserved as a drainage basin increases in area downstream, the exponent in the above equation should be 0.5. An observed exponent larger than 0.5 requires that drainage basins change their overall shape in a downstream direction, becoming longer and narrower as they enlarge. Hack [27, pp. 65–67] further examined the relationships between area and length in terms of Horton's laws of drainage-network composition, showing that the area A_u of a basin of order u can be derived as

$$A_u = \bar{A}_1 R_b^{u-1} \frac{R_{Lb}^{u} - 1}{R_{Lb} - 1} \qquad (4\text{-II-}13)$$

where $\bar{A}_1$ is the mean area of first-order basins, R_b is the bifurcation ratio, and R_{Lb} is Horton's term for the ratio of length ratio to bifurcation ratio. This equation gives close agreement with the actual plot of logarithm of length as a function of logarithm of area for the watershed of Christian's Creek, Virginia [27, p. 67].

E. Relation of Area to Discharge

Empirical equations relating stream discharge to basin area have long been in general use in the form

$$Q = jA^m \qquad (4\text{-II-}14)$$

where Q is some measure of discharge in cfs, such as the mean annual flood; A is the watershed area in suitable areal units; and the constants j and m are derived by fitting a regression line to the available data. The exponent m generally falls in the range 0.5 to 1.0 [32, p. 329].

For example, Hack [27, p. 54] plotted average discharge (cubic feet per second) against drainage area (square miles) on logarithmic paper for all gaging stations in the Potomac River basin and fitted a regression line with an exponent of 1.0 (Fig. 4-II-12). From this he concluded that studies of relationship of basin area with respect to other variables, such as order, channel, slope, channel width, and stream length, would apply, by direct proportionality to average annual discharge as well.

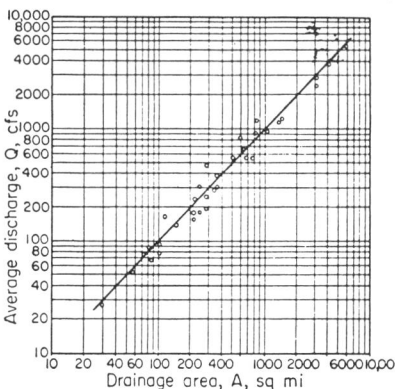

Fig. 4-II-12. Relation of discharge to drainage area for all gaging stations in the Potomac River basin, fitted by a regression line with coefficient of 1. (*After Hack* [27, p. 54].)

Leopold and Miller [20, pp. 23–24] found that for 12 streams of central New Mexico the discharge-area relationship can best be described by the equation

$$Q_{2.3} = 12 A^{0.79} \qquad (4\text{-II-}15)$$

where $Q_{2.3}$ is flood discharge in cfs equaled or exceeded in 2.3 years, and A is drainage area in sq mi. They were then able to combine the discharge-area graph with an order-area graph to show the relationship of discharge to stream order.

F. Basin Shape (Outline Form)

The shape, or outline form, of a drainage basin, as it is projected upon the horizontal datum plane of a map, may conceivably affect stream-discharge characteristics. As explained above, long narrow basins with high bifurcation ratios would be expected to have attenuated flood-discharge periods, whereas rotund basins of low bifurcation ratio would be expected to have sharply peaked flood discharges.

Horton [33, pp. 303–304] described the outline of a normal drainage basin as a pear-shaped ovoid. He depicted the average outline of six great rivers of the world by a composite of their perimeters reduced to equal basin area and superimposed on one another. He regarded the pear shape as one proof that drainage basins are formed largely by sheet-erosion processes acting upon an initially inclined surface.

Quantitative expression of drainage-basin outline form was made by Horton [1, p. 351] through a form factor R_f, which is the dimensionless ratio of basin area A_u to the square of basin length L_b, thus:

$$R_f = \frac{A_u}{L_b^2} \qquad (4\text{-II-}16)$$

In its inverted form, L_b^2/A_u, this ratio was used in unit hydrograph applications by the U.S. Army Corps of Engineers [34].

Miller [25, p. 8] used a dimensionless *circularity ratio* R_c, defined as the ratio of basin area A_u to the area of a circle A_c having the same perimeter as the basin. He found that circularity ratio remained remarkably uniform in the range 0.6 to 0.7 for first- and second-order basins in homogeneous shales and dolomites, indicating the tendency of small drainage basins in homogeneous geologic materials to preserve geometrical similarity. By contrast, first- and second-order basins situated on the flanks of moderately dipping quartzite strata of Clinch Mountain, Virginia, were strongly elongated and had circularity ratios of between 0.4 and 0.5 generally.

Schumm [21, p. 612] used an *elongation ratio* R_e, defined as the ratio of diameter of a circle of the same area as the basin to the maximum basin length. This ratio runs between 0.6 and 1.0 over a wide variety of climatic and geologic types. Values near to 1.0 are typical of regions of very low relief, whereas values in the range 0.6 to 0.8 are generally associated with strong relief and steep ground slopes.

The inappropriateness of a circle as the standard figure of reference in comparison with a pear-shaped drainage basin, which has a sharply defined point at the mouth, led Chorley, Malm, and Pogorzelski [35, pp. 138–141] to use as a model the lemniscate function

$$\rho = L_b \cos p\theta \qquad (4\text{-II-}17)$$

where ρ and θ are radius and angle, respectively, in polar coordinates. L_b is basin length measured from mouth to most distant point on the perimeter, and p is a coefficient which determines the rotundity of the basin. When $p = 1$, the basin outline is a circle. Basin area A_u is obtained by integration of Eq. (4-II-17) between the limits $-\pi/2p$ and $+\pi/2p$, giving

$$A_u = \frac{\pi L_b^2}{4p} \qquad (4\text{-II-}18)$$

and

$$p = \frac{\pi L_b^2}{4 A_u} \qquad (4\text{-II-}19)$$

Thus the coefficient p, which expresses rotundity, is readily obtained by substitution of measurements of basin length and basin area. The degree of approach of actual basin form to the pure lemniscate form is measured by a *lemniscate ratio*, the ratio of perimeter of the lemniscate to actual perimeter of the basin.

Morisawa [36, pp. 587–591] tested the effectiveness of the above measures of basin outline form as factors in the hydrology of a watershed. For 25 watersheds of the Appalachian Plateau, regressions of the runoff-rainfall ratio on five measures of form showed a significant regression coefficient at the 5 per cent level only with elongation ratio R_e and circularity ratio R_c, but the standard error of estimate is relatively high in both cases. From this it is concluded that controls other than drainage-basin outline form dominate the hydrologic characteristics of a basin.

G. Drainage Density

An important indicator of the linear scale of land-form elements in stream-eroded topography is *drainage density* D, introduced into the American hydrologic literature by Horton [1, p. 357; 2, p. 283]:

$$D = \frac{\sum_{i=1}^{k} \sum_{i=1}^{N} L_u}{A_u} \qquad (4\text{-II-}20)$$

Thus D is simply the ratio of total channel-segment lengths cumulated for all orders within a basin to the basin area (projected to the horizontal). Dimensionally, this ratio reduces to the inverse of length, L^{-1}. Horton used units of miles per square mile, and most later workers followed suit. Drainage density may be thought of as an expression of the closeness of spacing of channels. If geometrical similarity exists between two drainage systems, their drainage densities will be related in the same ratio as the inverse of the linear scale ratio (Fig. 4-II-1). Thus, broadly considered, drainage density is simply one of several linear measures by which the scale of features of the topography can be compared.

Measurement of drainage density is made from a map with the planimeter and chartometer. If a complete morphometric analysis is being made, the necessary stream lengths and basin areas will have been measured in the course of the analysis. An average drainage-density value for each order can be computed and designated $D_1, D_2, \ldots, D_k$ through the highest order k. Extreme care must be taken to include all permanent stream channels to their upper ends. Checking in the field and on air photographs is an essential step in verification of topographic maps. A rapid approximation method of drainage-density determination is described by Carlston and Langbein [37].

Drainage-density measurements have been made over a wide range of geologic and climatic types of the United States. The lowest values, between 3.0 and 4.0 miles/sq mi, are observed in resistant sandstone strata of the Appalachian Plateau Province [38, pp. 658–659; 17, pp. 84–86] (Fig. 4-II-13A). Values in the range 8 to 16 are typical of large areas of the humid central and eastern United States on rocks of moderate resistance under a deciduous forest cover [7, p. 1135; 39, pp. 19, 59] (Fig. 4-II-13B). Comparable values are found in parts of the Rocky Mountain region [15, table 2], but in the drier areas of that region values range from 50 to 100.

Coast ranges of southern California, where strongly fractured and deeply weathered igneous and metamorphic rocks have evolved under a dry-summer subtropical climate, show drainage-density values in the range 20 to 30 (Fig. 4-II-13C) [38, p. 659; 7, p. 1135; 18, appendix I], but where weak Pleistocene sediments are exposed, values of D rise to 30 to 40. A still higher order of magnitude of drainage density is observed in badlands, developed on weak clays barren of vegetation. Smith [22, p. 999] measured values of 200 to 400 in Badlands National Monument, S.D. (Fig. 4-II-13D). Schumm [21, p. 616] measured values as high as 1,100 to 1,300 in badlands developed on weak clay at Perth Amboy, N.J.

Factors controlling drainage density are the same as those that control the characteristic length dimension of any group of first-order basins. A complete discussion is not appropriate here. In general, low drainage density is favored in regions of highly resistant or highly permeable subsoil materials, under dense vegetative cover, and where relief is low. High drainage density is favored in regions of weak or impermeable subsurface materials, sparse vegetation, and mountainous relief. A

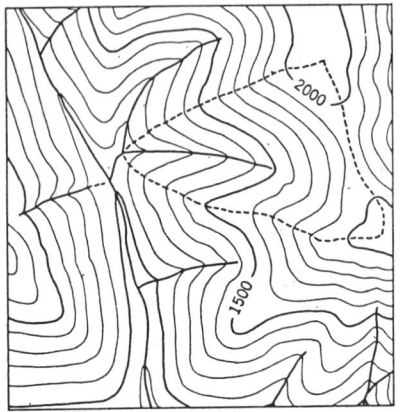

A. Low drainage density or coarse texture, Driftwood, Pennsylvania, Quadrangle.

B. Medium drainage density or medium texture, Nashville, Indiana, Quadrangle.

C. High drainage density or fine texture, Little Tujunga, California, Quadrangle.

D. Extremely high drainage density or ultrafine texture, Cuny Table West, South Dakota, Quadrangle.

FIG. 4-II-13. Topographic maps of 1 sq mi each, illustrating natural range in drainage density. (*From maps of the U.S. Geological Survey. Reproduced by permission from Strahler, Physical Geography, copyright by John Wiley & Sons, Inc., New York, 1960.*)

comprehensive study of drainage-density controls by Melton [15, pp. 33–35] used multiple-regression-and-correlation analysis in which drainage density is the dependent variable with respect to Thornthwaite's precipitation-effectiveness index[1] and infiltration capacity, vegetative cover, surface roughness, and a runoff-intensity index as independent variables. Of these, only surface roughness has no significant correlation with drainage density. The strongest related factor appears to be

[1] PE index $= 10 \sum_{1}^{12} (P/E)$, where P is the average precipitation for each month, and E the average evaporation for each month. It is a measure of the availability of moisture to vegetation. (See also Subsec. 11-V-B.)

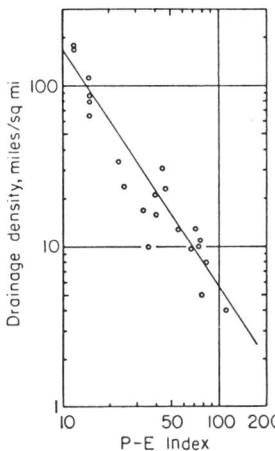

FIG. 4-II-14. Regression of drainage density on Thornthwaite's precipitation-effectiveness index for 22 small drainage basins of Colorado, Arizona, New Mexico, and Utah. (*After Melton* [15, p. 73].)

Thornthwaite's *PE* index, with a simple correlation coefficient of -0.943; a two-variable regression of this relationship is shown in Fig. 4-II-14.

Horton [2, p. 293] combined the laws of stream numbers and lengths with his definition of drainage density to yield

$$D_u = \frac{\bar{L}_1 R_b{}^{u-1}}{A_u} \frac{R_{Lb}{}^u - 1}{R_{Lb} - 1} \qquad (4\text{-II-}21)$$

where D_u is the drainage density of an entire basin of order u. Horton noted that this equation combined all the geometric factors which determine the composition of the drainage net of a stream system into one expression. This can be regarded as the quantitative statement of a major part of *Playfair's classic law of streams*[1] stated in 1802.

The average length of overland flow $\bar{L}_g$ is approximately half the average distance between stream channels and is therefore approximately equal to half the reciprocal of drainage density [2, p. 284]:

$$\bar{L}_g = \frac{1}{2D} \qquad (4\text{-II-}22)$$

In order to take into account the effect of slope of the stream channels and valleysides, Horton [2, p. 285] refined this generalization to read

$$\bar{L}_g = \frac{1}{2D \sqrt{1 - (\theta_c/\theta_g)}} \qquad (4\text{-II-}23)$$

where θ_c is channel slope, and θ_g is average ground slope in the area.

H. Constant of Channel Maintenance

Schumm [21, p. 607] used the inverse of drainage density as a property termed *constant of channel maintenace C*. Thus

$$C = \frac{1}{D} = \frac{A_u}{\sum_{i=1}^{k} \sum_{i=1}^{N} L_u} \qquad (4\text{-II-}24)$$

This constant, in units of square feet per foot, has the dimension of length and therefore increases in magnitude as the scale of the land-form units increases. Specifically, the constant C tells the number of square feet of watershed surface required to sustain one linear foot of channel. The relation of C to stream order is shown in Fig. 4-II-15 [10, p. 917], in which logarithm of basin area (ordinate) is plotted against logarithm of cumulative stream length (abscissa). Both lengths and areas are those measured when projected to a horizontal plane. For three basins shown, the series of points

---

[1] The law of streams originally stated by John Playfair reads as follows: "Every river appears to consist of a main trunk, fed from a variety of branches, each running in a valley proportioned to its size, and all of them together forming a system of valleys connecting with one another, and having such a nice adjustment of their declivities that none of them join the principal valley either on too high or too low a level; a circumstance which would be infinitely improbable if each of these valleys were not the work of the stream which flows in it."

numbered 1 to 5, represent the data for successive orders within each basin. In each basin the points fall close to a straight line of 45° slope, indicating that a linear relationship may be used. If the logarithm of the intercept is read at log stream

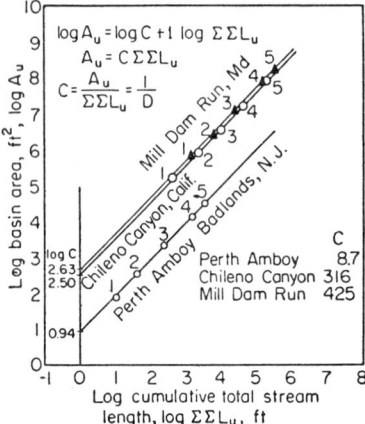

Fig. 4-II-15. Constant of channel maintenance through successive orders of three drainage basins. (*Data by Schumm* [21, p. 606], *modified by Strahler* [10, p. 917].)

length = 0 and the antilog of this intercept is taken, the constant of channel maintenance C for the whole basin is obtained. The value of $C = 8.7$ in the Perth Amboy badlands means that, on the average, 8.7 ft^2 of surface is needed to support each linear foot of channel. By contrast, 316 ft^2 of surface is required to support one foot of channel in the Chileno Canyon watershed of the San Gabriel Mountains.

I. Stream Frequency

Horton [1, p. 357; 2, p. 285] introduced *stream frequency* (or *channel frequency*) F as the number of stream segments per unit area, or

$$F = \frac{\sum_{i=1}^{k} N_u}{A_k} \qquad (4\text{-II-25})$$

where $\sum_{i=1}^{k} N_u$ is the total number of segments of all orders within the given basin of

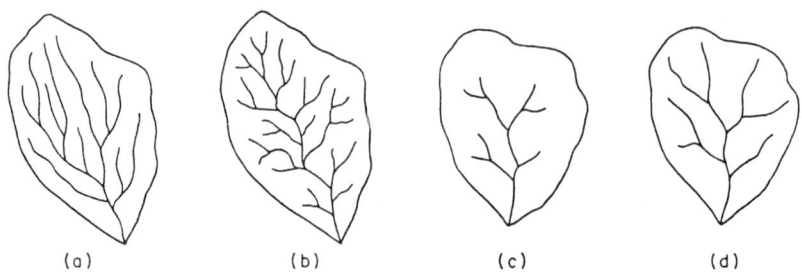

Fig. 4-II-16. Hypothetical basins *a* and *b* have the same drainage densities but different stream frequencies; basins *c* and *d* have the same stream frequencies but different drainage densities.

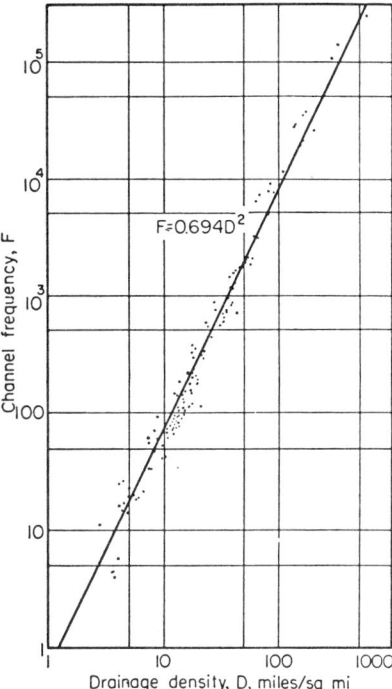

FIG. 4-II-17. Regression of channel frequency on drainage density for 156 drainage basins. (*After Melton* [16, p. 37].)

order k, and A_k is the area of that basin in square miles. Stream frequency has the dimensions L^{-2}.

Melton [16, pp. 35–54] analyzed in detail the relationships between drainage density and stream frequency, both of which measure the texture of the drainage net, but each of which treats a distinct aspect. As shown in Fig. 4-II-16, it is possible to construct two hypothetical drainage basins having the same drainage density but different stream frequency, and on the other hand, it is possible to have two basins of the same frequency but different density. Melton tested this possible range of variation in nature by plotting F versus D for 156 drainage basins covering a vast range in scale, climate, relief, surface cover, and geologic type (Fig. 4-II-17). Remarkably small scatter exists, showing that the relationship of density to frequency tends to be conserved as a constant in nature. The slope of a least-squares line was not significantly different from 2.0, from which Melton [16, p. 36] derived the dimensionally correct equation

$$F = 0.694 D^2 \qquad (4\text{-II-}26)$$

and from this the dimensionless number F/D^2, which tends to approach the constant value 0.694, despite vast variations in linear scale.

V. RELIEF (GRADIENT) ASPECT OF DRAINAGE BASINS AND CHANNEL NETWORKS

A. Channel Gradients

1. **Single-channel Profiles.** The longitudinal profile of a stream channel may be shown graphically by a plot of altitude (ordinate) as a function of horizontal distance (abscissa) (Fig. 4-II-18A). Altitude is commonly stated in feet or meters above the sea-level datum; distance, in miles or kilometers from stream head, stream mouth, or some other convenient reference point. For streams of large discharge and high order, a considerable factor of vertical exaggeration is used, whereas for streams of low order in regions of strong relief, none may be required.

A single-channel profile follows one channel continuously despite the junction of tributaries of equal or lower stream order [26, p. 5]. Within a given basin that part of the profile following the trunk stream of highest order is unambiguous, whereas to continue the profile headward into channels of lower order requires choice of one of two alternatives at the head of each segment of a given order. Choice may be governed by which branch falls most directly in line with the higher-order segment or which branch leads eventually to the longest total stream length in the entire basin.

Where profiles are plotted from topographic maps, stream elevation is estimated from the contour crossings, the distinction between stream bed and stream surface in streams of low order being undetermined or neglected as trivial. Where, however, the profile of a perennial stream of large discharge is plotted, the elevation of the stream surface may be defined as the elevation of mean low water, or actual lowest low water [40, pp. 624–626; 41, p. 650], or as the elevation at some rigorously defined stage, such as the mean or median annual discharge. Actual elevation of the stream bed along the thalweg, or line of maximum depth in channel cross section, is used instead of stream-surface elevation where attention is focused upon processes of scour and aggradation [40, p. 622] and where profiles are made from direct instrumental field surveys in streams of small discharge [42, p. 11].

2. Cause of Profile Upconcavity. Single-channel profiles of almost all streams, under a wide range of climatic and geologic conditions, show *upconcavity*, i.e., a persistent downstream decrease in gradient. Causes of upconcavity cannot be treated in detail here. Gilbert [43, pp. 103–104, 107–108] explained upconcavity as an effect of increasing stream discharge. His *law of declivities* states that declivity (gradient) bears an inverse relation to discharge because, as discharge increases, channel cross-section increases, reducing proportionately the frictional losses of the stream and enabling it to carry its bedload on a lesser slope.

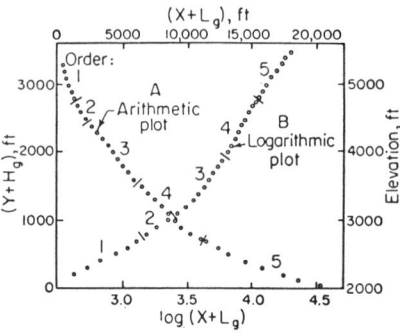

FIG. 4-II-18. Single-channel longitudinal profile of Chileno Canyon, California. (*A*) Arithmetic plot; vertical exaggeration ×5. (*B*) Logarithmic plot. Terms defined in Fig. 4-II-19. (*After Broscoe* [26, p. 72].)

Others have attributed upconcavity to decreasing caliber (diameter) of bed-load particles downstream [40; 44, pp. 660–662], using the reasoning that a lesser gradient suffices for the transport of finer bed materials.

3. Fitted Regression Functions. The longitudinal stream profile may be fitted by an equation expressing the statistical regression of elevation Y as the dependent variable on distance X as the independent variable. Four simple regression equations may be considered [26, pp. 5–6]:

1. Simple linear form, in which both altitude and distance are plotted on arithmetic scales. A straight line on such a plot is represented by the regression equation of basic form

$$Y = a - bX \qquad (4\text{-}II\text{-}27)$$

Although useful in providing a visual impression of the longitudinal profile (Fig. 4-II-18), the arithmetic plot typically yields a strong upconcave-profile line to which the linear equation is poorly fitted.

2. Exponential form, in which altitude is on a logarithmic scale while horizontal distance is on an arithmetic scale. A straight line on such a plot is represented by the basic regression equation

$$\log Y = a - bX \qquad (4\text{-}II\text{-}28)$$

3. Logarithmic form, in which altitude is plotted on an arithmetic scale on the ordinate against distance scaled logarithmically on the abscissa (Fig. 4-II-18). A straight line on such a plot is represented by the regression equation of the basic form

$$Y = a - b \log X \qquad (4\text{-}II\text{-}29)$$

4. Power form (log-log form), represented by the basic regression equation

$$\log Y = \log a - b \log X \qquad (4\text{-}II\text{-}30)$$

With appropriate definitions of Y and X, the exponential, logarithmic, and power functions are capable of making upconcave profiles more nearly approximate straight lines and therefore minimizing the deviations from the ideal mathematical expression selected for description and prediction.

A serious problem in plotting the stream profiles in exponential, logarithmic, and power forms is the selection of meaningful reference points from which the arbitrary constants of these equations are derived [26, p. 6]. Assignment of arbitrary constants does not affect the linear equation. In Eq. (4-II-29), where X is defined as distance downstream from the profile head, the equation cannot be solved for $X = 0$, because logarithm of zero is not defined. If an arbitrary constant C is added to X, the stream head may be plotted, for when $X = 0$, $Y = a - b \log C$. An element of horizontal distance has thus been added to the stream head to define the origin, or reference point,

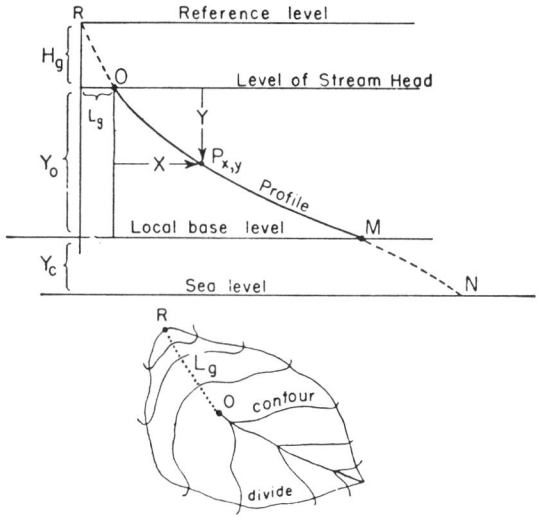

Fig. 4-II-19. Reference points in profile plotting.

Points:
    R reference point
    O stream head
    M end of segment, gaging station, or local base level
    N mouth at sea level

Constants:
    L_g horizontal distance of overland flow on orthogonal from reference point R to head O
    H_g vertical drop from R to O
    Y_o vertical distance from stream head O to local base level M
    Y_c vertical distance between local base level and sea level

Variables:
    Y drop in elevation from stream head O to any point P on stream profile
    X horizontal distance from stream head O to any point P on stream profile

(*After Broscoe* [26, p. 39].)

for the measurement of downstream distance. Degree of curvature of the plotted profile now depends upon the arbitrary constant selected, enabling the equation to be so adjusted as to fit closely a given stream profile. In so doing, however, the application of the logarithmic function as a general case is greatly impaired.

Broscoe [26, p. 6] proposed that the arbitrary constant in the logarithmic function be unambiguously defined by selecting a reference point R on the drainage divide of the watershed, where it is intersected by a profile line projected in the upstream direction along the longest path of overland flow leading to the channel head. The length of this line is equivalent to the term L_g, defined previously as length of overland flow. Justification for use of maximum L_g is that, during the evolution of the drainage basin, L_g has been adjusted in magnitude to the scale of the first-order drainage basins and is approximately equal to one-half of the reciprocal of drainage density.

Figure 4-II-19 shows a complete definition of reference point and constants in stream-profile plotting. In the logarithmic equation, the horizontal distance X is now replaced by the term $X + L_g$. Correspondingly, a constant of vertical distance H_g is defined as the elevation difference between the point R and the head of the stream channel O. The variable Y is then defined as vertical drop from O to any point P on the stream. The variable X is defined as the horizontal distance in the downstream direction from O to any point P. In the regression equations, then, the origin of numerical values shifts from point O to point R; the dependent variable becomes $Y + H_g$; the independent variable becomes $X + L_g$.

Using the new definitions, Eqs. (4-II-27) to (4-II-30) can be rewritten, respectively, as:

Linear: $\quad\quad\quad\quad Y + H_g = a + b(X + L_g)$ $\quad\quad\quad\quad$ (4-II-31)
Logarithmic: $\quad\quad\,\, Y + H_g = a + b \log (X + L_g)$ $\quad\quad\quad\,$ (4-II-32)
Exponential: $\quad\quad\,\,\, \log (Y_c + Y_0 - Y) = -b(X + L_g)$ $\quad\quad\quad\,$ (4-II-33)
Power: $\quad\quad\quad\quad\,\, \log (Y_c + Y_0 - Y) = \log a - b \log (X + L_g)$ $\quad\,$ (4-II-34)

4. Derivative Functions. A vexing problem of arbitrary constants arises in Eq. (4-II-33). In most exponential plots of stream profiles [40, 44–46], sea level is

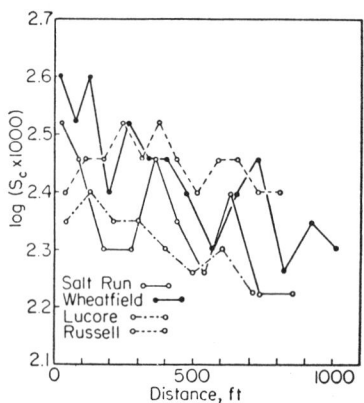

FIG. 4-II-20. Exponential relation of channel slope to downstream distance from stream head for four first-order stream-channel segments of the Appalachian Plateau in north-central Pennsylvania. (*After Broscoe* [26, p. 45].)

taken as the arbitrary reference level. Although sea level is a natural, readily defined geologic feature, related to stream development, there are good reasons to think that sea level does not relate dynamically to the control of stream slope in the upper reaches of the stream. Rubey [46, p. 134] has stated succinctly the reasons for concluding that the level of water body into which a stream flows controls the vertical position of the profile, but not its shape.

A solution to the problem of an arbitrary base of reference is to examine the relation of stream slope S_c to distance downstream, where S_c is defined as dY/dX. Differentiation removes reference to sea level, which is in effect a constant of integration in Eqs. (4-II-31) to (4-II-34). Differentiation yields:

Linear: $\quad\quad\quad S_c = b$ $\quad\quad\quad\quad\quad\quad\quad\quad\quad\quad\quad\quad\quad$ (4-II-35)

Logarithmic: $\quad\,\, S_c = \dfrac{b}{X + L_g}$ $\quad\quad\quad\quad\quad\quad\quad\quad\quad\quad\,$ (4-II-36)

Exponential: $\quad\, \log S_c = \log b - b(X + L_g)$ $\quad\quad\quad\quad\quad\,\,\,$ (4-II-37)
Power: $\quad\quad\quad \log S_c = \log ab - (b + 1) \log (X + L_g)$ $\quad\,\,\,$ (4-II-38a)

or, letting $a' = \log ab$, and $b' = b + 1$,

$$\log S_c = a' - b' \log (X + L_g) \quad\quad\quad (4\text{-II-}38b)$$

An example of the exponential slope plot [Eq. (4-II-37)] of four stream segments of the first order is shown in Fig. 4-II-20. To the extent that the observed points fall on a straight, sloping line, the exponential profile can be used. If a fitted regression line has a slope not different from zero, the linear equation is suggested (Russell Hollow, in Fig. 4-II-20). Shulits [40, pp. 624–626] and Yatsu [44, pp. 656–659] use exponential plots of slope as a function of distance and seem to have accepted the exponential form as the best description of stream profiles. Hack [27, pp. 69–70] fitted the power-slope function [Eq. (4-II-38b)], to several streams of Virginia and Maryland. Broscoe [26, pp. 45, 72] observed that the logarithmic plot [Eq. (4-II-36)] gave a good approach to a straight line for several single-channel profiles (Fig. 4-II-18). No generalization as to the best description of the single-channel longitudinal profile seems yet warranted in view of such divergent observations.

5. Profile Segmentation. That the longitudinal profile of a stream channel consists of series of connected segments, "each differing from those that adjoin it, but all closely related parts of one system," has been pointed out by Mackin [47, p. 491], who states further that "each segment has the slope that will provide the velocity required for transportation of all of the load supplied to it from above, and this slope is maintained without change as long as controlling conditions remain the same." To describe a single-channel profile by one continuous mathematical function is therefore unrealistic in failing to take segmentation into account, but may nevertheless be useful in certain applications.

Abrupt changes in gradient marking the discontinuities between adjoining channel segments may result from changes in discharge-load ratios, in caliber of load, or in channel characteristics [44, p. 657; 47, p. 491; 48, p. 819].

Considering the convergence of a drainage network into channel segments of increasing order, it is obvious that the formation of a segment of a given order by the junction of two segments of the next lower order will normally mark an abrupt reduction in gradient, for reasons explained by Gilbert's law of declivities, discussed above. Between tributary junctions the profile may be expected to approach a straight line of uniform slope, discounting the slight upconcavity to be expected from gradual increases in discharge and load from directly contributing valleyside slopes. Actual plots of single-channel profiles do not show obvious segmentation associated with changes from one order to the next [26, pp. 44, 72], but the principle is strongly displayed in the composite profiles described below.

6. Composite Profiles. A composite stream profile combines the segments of a given order within the watershed into a single average segment whose vertical drop is the mean drop of all the segments and whose horizontal distance is the mean horizontal length of all the segments (Fig. 4-II-21). The average slope of the channel segments of a given order is thus the slope of the hypotenuse of a right triangle defined by the average vertical drop and the average horizontal distance. Triangles for each order are connected in sequence to produce the composite profile shown in Fig. 4-II-21.

The succession of order segments of the composite profile may be fitted, if desired, by a continuous mathematical function, using one of the four forms [Eqs. (4-II-31) to (4-II-34)]. Similarly, the derivative equations of slope [Eqs. (4-II-35) to (4-II-38b)] may be fitted to the composite profile by plotting slope of the segment against horizontal distance $X + L_g$, measured to the mid-point of the segment. Details and examples are given by Broscoe [26, pp. 8, 16, 29–30, 46, 73], who found that the composite profiles are best fitted by a logarithmic equation.

7. Channel Slope as a Function of Order. The average slope of segments of a given order in a drainage net, measured as described above, will obviously be less than the average slope for the next lower order but greater than that for the next higher order. Horton [2, p. 295] expressed this relationship in a *law of stream slopes*, an inverse-geometric-series law, which is analogous to the law of stream numbers.

$$\bar{S}_u = \bar{S}_1 R_s^{k-u} \qquad (4\text{-II-}39)$$

where $\bar{S}_u$ is average slope of segments of order u; $\bar{S}_1$ is average slope of first-order segments; R_s is a constant slope ratio, analogous to bifurcation ratio; and k is the order of the highest-order segment.

The law of stream slopes has been applied to many watersheds [17, pp. 9–10, 52–53;

20, p. 21; 21, p. 605; 26, p. 15] and appears to be generally valid, provided that the geologic materials in which the channels are carved are free of strong inhomogeneities.

8. Main-stream-slope Factor. Use of a single numerical value representing slope of the main stream of a drainage basin has been made by Taylor and Schwartz [29, pp. 235–238, 244]. Their slope factor, S_{st}, termed equivalent main-stream slope, is the slope, in feet per foot, of a uniform channel having the same length as the

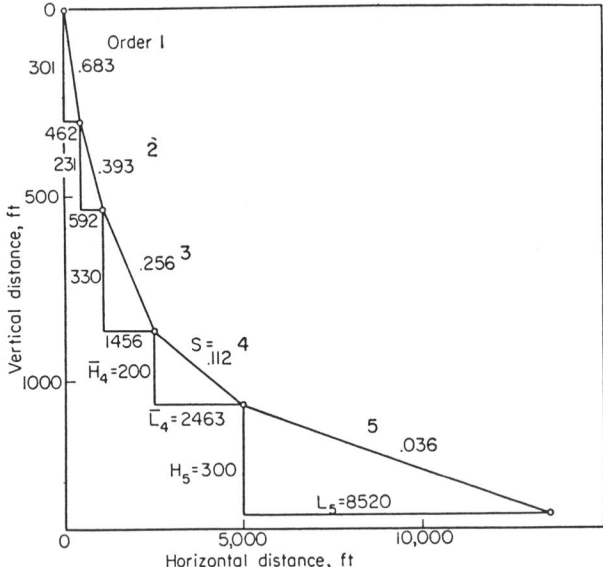

FIG. 4-II-21. Composite profile of stream segments of five orders in the Chileno Canyon watershed, California. (*After Broscoe* [26, p. 72].)

longest watercourse and an equal time of travel. This slope factor proved to be a significant drainage-basin characteristic influencing unit-hydrograph lag and peak flow of 20 basins ranging from 20 to 1,600 sq mi in the North and Middle Atlantic States. For further discussions of a main-stream-slope factor, see Refs. 31, 34, and 49

B. Channel-cross-section Geometry

In this section the channel network has been treated only as a system of branching lines, without consideration of the fact that channels have finite depths and widths and that these parameters change systematically as the channels are followed downstream or with fluctuations of discharge. The field of hydraulic geometry of streams, which relates width, depth, cross-sectional area, and form to such factors as distance, gradient, discharge, and load, is treated in Sec. 17-II of this handbook. Detailed treatment given in Refs. 20, 27, 42, and 50 to 53 constitutes an integral part of the field of quantitative geomorphology of drainage basins and channel systems.

C. Ground-surface Gradients

1. Relationship of Ground and Channel Slopes. The inclinations, or gradients, of the ground-surface elements of a watershed are closely tied in with its channel gradients and relief (elevation differences). In mountainous regions, where relief is great, erosion intensity is correspondingly high. Steep slopes contribute large quantities of relatively coarse textured detritus to channels, which must have steep gradients to enable stream flow to transport the debris as bed load through the channel system. In regions of low relief, slopes are gentle and shed relatively small quantities of fine-textured detritus, which in turn requires correspondingly low channel gradients for its transport. Strahler [5, p. 689] has observed a close quantitative relationship of

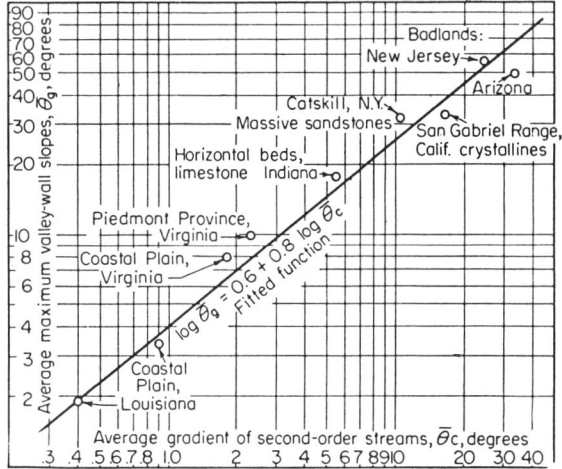

Fig. 4-II-22. Relation of valleyside slope to slope of immediately adjacent stream channel in nine maturely dissected regions of widely different relief, climate, and rock type, fitted by least squares with a power-regression equation. (*After Strahler* [5, p. 689].)

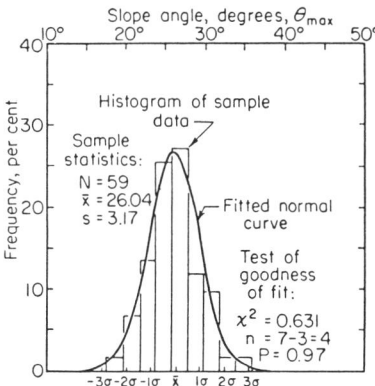

Fig. 4-II-23. Histogram of frequency distribution of maximum valleyside-slope angles fitted by a normal curve and tested for goodness of fit. Field measurements from dissected Santa Fe formation near Bernalillo, N.M. (*After Strahler* [5, p. 683].)

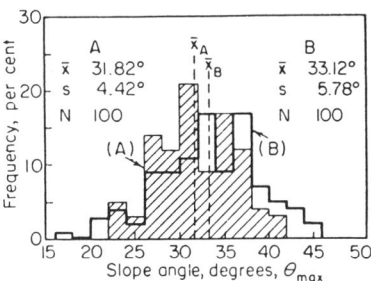

Fig. 4-II-24. Comparison of valleyside-slope samples in homogeneous clastic rocks in western Virginia. (*A*) Athens formation, shale; (*B*) Pennington formation, interbedded sandstone and shale. (*After Strahler* [8, p. 15]; *data from Miller* [25, p. 18].)

power form between channel slope θ_c and valleyside slope θ_g over a wide range of geographical regions (Fig. 4-II-22).

2. Maximum Valleyside Slopes. A significant indicator of overall steepness of ground slopes in a watershed is the maximum valleyside slope θ_{max}, measured at intervals along the valley walls on the steepest parts of the contour orthogonals running from divides to adjacent stream channels.

Maximum valleyside slope has been sampled over a wide variety of geologic and climatic environments [5, 15, 16, 21, 22, 25, 39, 54, 55]. A sample of 50 to 100 or more slope readings, taken according to a plan of uniformly spaced sample points, may be measured directly in the field with the Abney level or with dividers and scale from topographic maps of suitably large scale and high degree of accuracy. The variates of the sample may then be grouped into classes and treated by standard procedures of frequency-distribution analysis, including calculation of arithmetic mean, variance, standard deviation, skewness, and goodness of fit to the normal curve (Fig. 4-II-23) (see Sec. 8-I). These statistics not only serve to describe the slope characteristics of a region, but they may be used in rigorous statistical tests of differences in means and variances between two regions or among several regions. For example, valleyside-slope samples collected by Miller [25] from adjacent localities of somewhat different lithologic composition prove to have significantly different variances when tested by the F ratio of sample variances [8, p. 15] (Fig. 4-II-24).

Based on field and map data from a large number of small watersheds in Arizona, Colorado, and New Mexico, Melton [16, p. 46] found by regression analysis that valleyside slope θ_{max} may be estimated by the equation

$$\theta_{max} = 27.53 \frac{\Sigma L_u^{0.25} H^{0.5}}{(\sqrt{A_u})^{0.75}} \qquad (4\text{-II-40})$$

where ΣL_u is total channel length in the basin in miles, H is total basin relief in ft, and A_u is basin area in sq mi. These exponents show that area and relief have the greatest effect on valleyside slope, whereas channel length is less important.

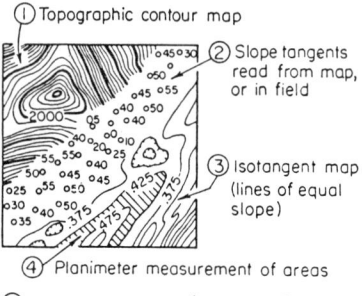
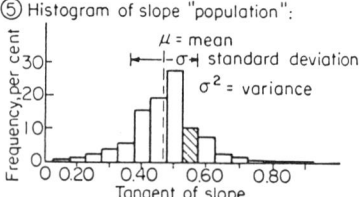

FIG. 4-II-25. Construction of isotangent slope map and slope-frequency histogram. (*After Strahler* [9, p. 575].)

3. Total Surface-slope Distribution. Slope conditions over an entire watershed may be shown by means of a slope map [9], which shows distribution of the degree of surface inclination. Procedure is as follows (Fig. 4-II-25): (1) A good contour topographic map is obtained. (2) Slopes of short segments of line normal to the contours are determined at many points over the map. Tangent or sine of slope angle may be recorded, depending upon the function desired. (3) The readings are contoured with lines of equal slope (isotangents or isosines). (4) The areas between successive slope contours are measured with planimeter and summed for each slope class. (5) This summation yields a slope frequency-percentage distribution from which mean, variance, and standard deviation can be computed.

Figure 4-II-26 shows topographic and isotangent maps compared for two small drainage basins in the Appalachian Plateau of north-central Pennsylvania. Figure 4-II-27 shows the resulting slope histogram for the area within the square. Remarkable similarity in both means and variances is typical of basins throughout a geologically uniform region.

Construction of slope maps and their areal measurement is extremely time-consuming. Essentially, the same information can be obtained by random-coordinate and grid sampling [9, pp. 589-594]. In the *random-coordinate method* a sample square is scaled in 100 units of length on a side. From a table of random numbers the coordinates of sample points are drawn for whatever size sample is desired (Fig. 4-II-28). The *grid-square method* achieves similar results, but is not flexible as to sample size. Point samples, easily and quickly taken, compare favorably in frequency-distribution properties with samples obtained by planimetry of a slope map.

4-64 QUANTITATIVE GEOMORPHOLOGY

A method of estimating the average slope of the ground surface within a drainage basin was used by Horton [56] and is described in detail by Wisler and Brater [32, pp. 46–47]. Average slope of each contour belt is computed, after which the average slope of the entire basin is computed, weighting each contour belt according to proportionate area. Strahler [7, pp. 1125–1128] describes a similar procedure and depicts a mean-slope profile for the complete basin.

Chapman [57] developed a method of analyzing both azimuth and angle of slope from contour topographic maps. Although based on petrofabric methods and designed largely for use in geologic analysis of terrain, his method might be applied to a watershed as a means of assessing both slope steepness and orientation simultaneously. For discussions of more general methods of slope analysis, see Refs. 31, 34, and 58 to 63.

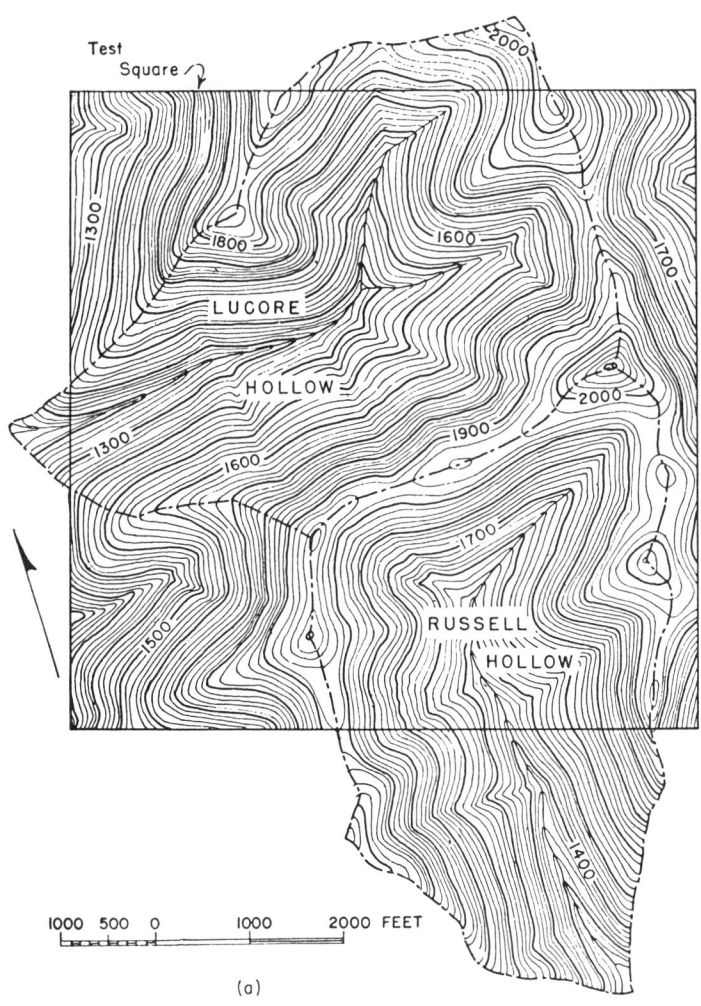

FIG. 4-II-26. Topographic contour map (a) and isotangent slope map (b) compared for two
(*Topography by U.S. Geological*

D. Relief Measures

1. Relief. *Relief H* is the elevation difference between reference points defined in any one of several ways. *Maximum relief* within a region of given boundary is simply

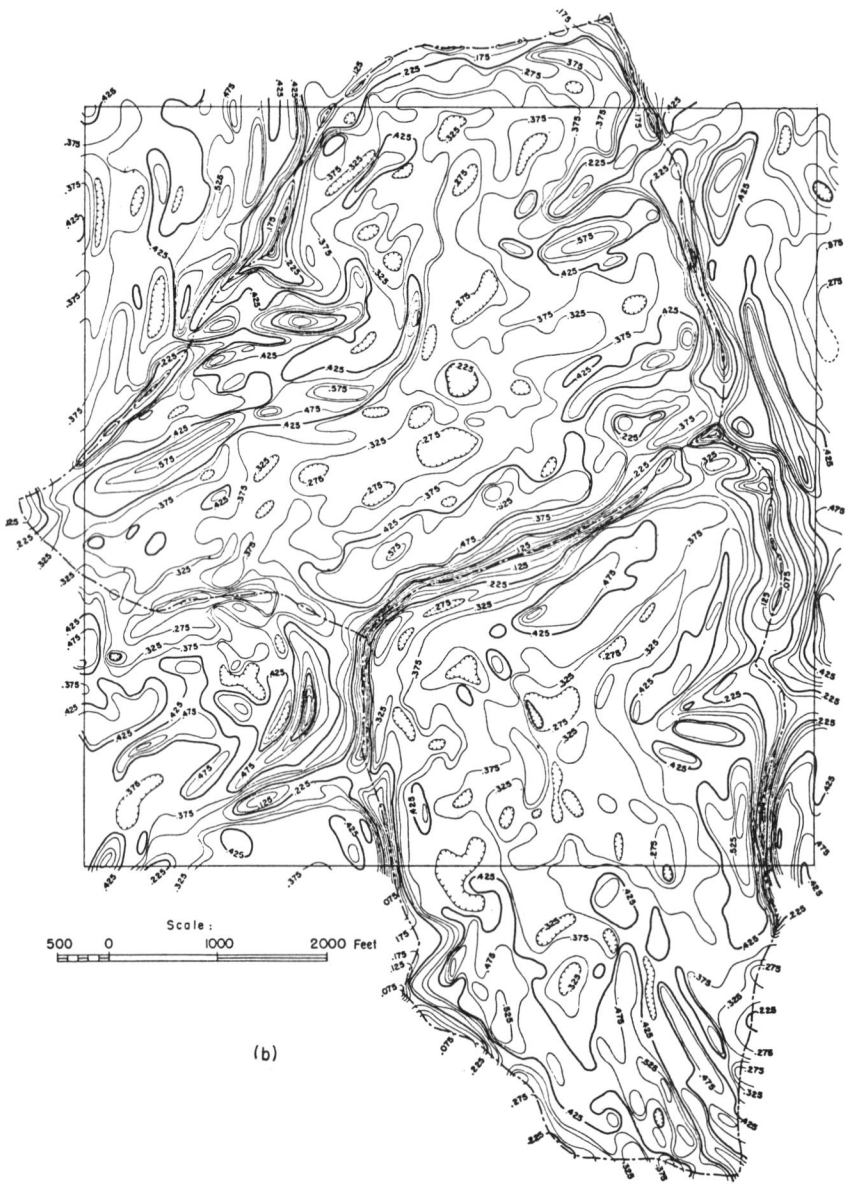

(b)

small drainage basins and an overlapping sampling square. Emporium, Pa., Quadrangle. Survey. *After Strahler* [9, pp. 586, 590].)

the elevation difference between highest and lowest points. *Maximum basin relief* is the elevation difference between basin mouth and the highest point on the basin perimeter, usually stated in units of feet or meters. Schumm [21, p. 612] measured basin relief along "the longest dimension of the basin parallel to the principal drainage line." Maxwell [18] measured relief along the basin diameter, an axial line found by use of rigorously defined criteria. Still another basin-relief measure may be obtained by determining the mean height of the entire basin perimeter above the mouth, thus minimizing the spurious effects of sharply pointed summits. Whatever criteria are

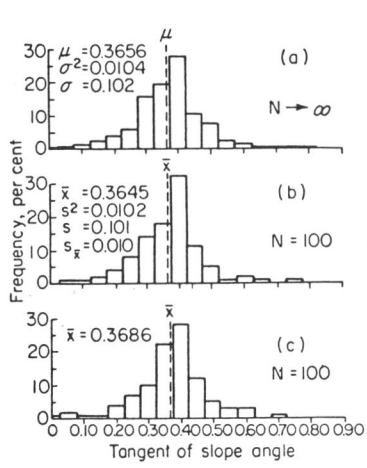

Fig. 4-II-27. Frequency-distribution histograms compared for sample square outlined in Fig. 4-II-26. (*a*) Total, or population, distribution measured by planimeter from isotangent map; (*b*) random-coordinate sample; (*c*) grid sample. (*After Strahler* [9, p. 592].)

Fig. 4-II-28. Sampling of slope by random-coordinate and grid-square methods. (*After Strahler* [9, p. 591].)

selected for measuring basin relief, they may be applied to basins of a given order to yield a mean basin relief $\bar{H}_u$ of basins of order u.

Still another means of measuring relief is to take the elevation difference between a point on drainage divide and another on the nearest adjacent stream channel, where both points lie at the ends of a line orthogonal to the contours (e.g., the surface-flow path) [11, p. 295].

Relief measures are indicative of the potential energy of a drainage system present by virtue of elevation above a given datum. In the absence of information as to the horizontal distances over which the relief measurement applies, however, one cannot directly relate relief to ground and channel slopes.

2. Relief Ratios. When basin relief H is divided by the horizontal distance on which it is measured, there results a dimensionless *relief ratio* R_h [21, p. 112]. Taking vertical and horizontal distances as legs of a right triangle, relief ratio is equal to the tangent of the lower acute angle and is identical with the tangent of the angle of slope of the hypotenuse with respect to the horizontal. The relief ratio thus measures the overall steepness of a drainage basin and is an indicator of the intensity of erosion processes operating on slopes of the basin.

Schumm [21, p. 112] measured relief ratio R_h as the ratio of maximum basin relief to horizontal distance along the longest dimension of the basin parallel to the principal drainage line. Melton [15, p. 5] used relative relief R_{hp}, expressed in per cent, as

$$R_{hp} = \frac{100H}{5{,}280P} \qquad (4\text{-II-}41)$$

where H is maximum basin relief in ft, and P is basin perimeter in miles.

Use of the perimeter as a horizontal-length dimension does away with difficulties of locating a suitable axial line in the basin but has the shortcoming that minor crenulations of the perimeter may greatly increase its length without representing any actual change in characteristic areal dimensions of the basin. Maxwell [18] used basin diameter as the horizontal distance for calculation of a relief ratio.

Possibility of a close correlation between relief ratio and hydrologic characteristics of a basin is suggested by Schumm [64], who found that sediment loss per unit area is closely correlated with relief ratio (Fig. 4-II-29). The significant regression with small scatter suggests that relief ratio may prove useful in estimating sediment yield if the appropriate parameters for a given climatic province are once established.

Maner [65] used a relief-length ratio in correlation with sediment-delivery rates of watersheds in the Red Hills area of southern Kansas, western Oklahoma, and western Texas. This ratio yielded a higher correlation with sediment delivery rate than did relief and length treated together as variables. Moreover, it gave a much closer correlation than did other individually treated geometrical factors of length-width ratio of basin, sediment-contributing area, basin relief alone, or average land slope.

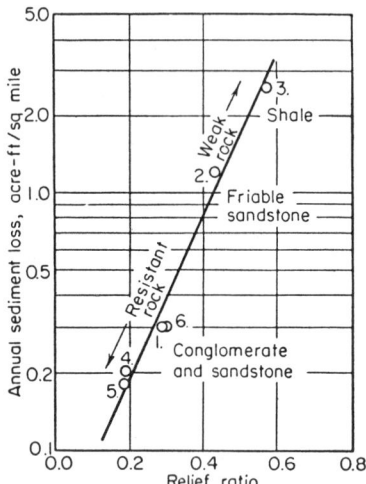

FIG. 4-II-29. Relation of sediment loss to relief ratio for small drainage basins in six localities of the Colorado Plateau Province. (*After Schumm* [64, p. 218].)

E. Ruggedness and Geometry Numbers

To combine the qualities of slope steepness and length, a dimensionless *ruggedness number* HD is formed of the product of relief H and drainage density D, where both terms are in the same units. If D should be increased while H remains constant, the average horizontal distance from divides to adjacent channels is reduced, with an accompanying increase in slope steepness. If H is increased while D remains constant, the elevation difference between divides and adjacent channels will also increase, so that slope steepness increases. Extremely high values of the ruggedness number occur when both variables are large, that is, when slopes are not only steep but long as well [11, p. 289]. Observed values of the ruggedness number range from as low as 0.06 in the subdued relief of the Louisiana coastal plain to over 1.0 in coast ranges of California or in badlands on weak clays.

The dimensionless property of slope can be introduced into the ruggedness number in the following way. Consider that the horizontal distance between a drainage divide and the adjacent stream channel is equal to about one-half the reciprocal of the drainage density D [2, p. 284] and that local relief H is measured as the vertical drop from divide to adjacent channel. Thus the slope S_g of the ground surface from divide to stream will be related to H and D by the equation

$$S_g = H \times 2D \qquad (4\text{-II-}42a)$$

where S_g is the tangent of the ground slope θ_g in degrees. Then

$$\frac{HD}{S_g} = \frac{1}{2} \qquad (4\text{-}II\text{-}42b)$$

Because the geometrical relations of H, D, and S_g will not be those of a perfect right triangle, the constant ½ should be replaced by some dimensionless constant, determined empirically, that will differ little from unity, despite a wide range in the ruggedness number (numerator). Strahler [11, p. 296] computed values of HD/S_g,

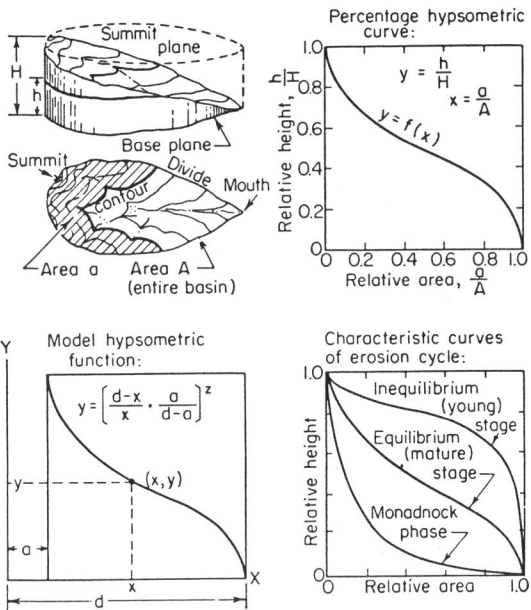

Fig. 4-II-30. Definitions and functions in hypsometric analysis of small drainage basins. (*After Strahler* [10, p. 919].)

named the *geometry number*, and found them to fall in the range 0.4 to 1.0 for six regions differing greatly in the individual components of D, H, and S_g. From this it was concluded that the geometry number tends to be conserved about a common value and that a change in any one of the three components is compensated for by changes in one or both of the other two, thus tending to keep the product constant.

F. Hypsometric (Area-Altitude) Analysis

Hypsometric analysis, or the relation of horizontal cross-sectional drainage-basin area to elevation, was developed in its modern dimensionless form by Langbein [4], who applied it to large watersheds. Application to small drainage basins of low order has been made by Strahler [7], Miller [25], Schumm [21], and Coates [39]. Similar methods have been described by Golding and Low [31].

Figure 4-II-30 illustrates the definition of the two dimensionless variables involved in hypsometric analysis. Taking the drainage basin to be bounded by vertical sides and a horizontal base plane passing through the mouth, the relative height y is the ratio of height of a given contour h to total basin height (relief) H. Relative area x is the ratio of horizontal cross-sectional area a to entire basin area A. The percentage hypsometric curve is a plot of the continuous function relating relative height y to relative area x. As shown in Fig. 4-II-30 (lower right), the shape of the hypsometric curve varies in early geologic stages of development of the drainage basin, but once a steady state is attained (mature stage), tends to vary little thereafter, despite lowering relief [7, pp. 1128–1132]. Isolated bodies of resistant rock may form prominent hills (monadnocks) rising above a generally subdued surface; the result is a distorted hypsometric curve, termed the *monadnock phase*.

Certain dimensionless attributes of the hypsometric curve, useful for comparative purposes, include the integral or relative area lying below the curve, the slope of the curve at its inflection point, and the degree of sinuosity of the curve. Many hypsometric curves seem to be closely fitted by the model function shown in Fig. 4-II-30 (lower left), although no rational basis is known for using this function. Hypsometric curves plotted for hundreds of small basins in a wide variety of regions and conditions show generally stable curve properties where the rock masses are homogeneous and the erosion stage is conventionally described as mature. Small but distinct differences in curve form from region to region appear to exist.

In hydrologic applications the hypsometric curve can be of use where some hydrologic factor, such as precipitation or evaporation, varies with altitude, or where the vegetative cover shows an altitude stratification. Langbein [4, p. 141] states: "For example, snow surveys generally show an increase in depth of cover and water equivalent with increase in altitude; the area-altitude relation provides a means for estimating the mean depth of snow or its water equivalent over a drainage basin."

VI. THEORY OF DRAINAGE-BASIN DYNAMICS

A. Statement of Variables

In quantitative studies of geomorphic processes and forms, the relationships between form elements, described above, and causative factors need to be expressed by dimensionally correct rational equations. It has already been noted that drainage basins developed in homogeneous bedrock materials under a given set of climatic conditions tend to develop a characteristic linear-scale dimension. Because of the tendency to geometrical similarity of the horizontal, or planimetric, aspects of such systems, one is free to select any property having the dimension of length or a product of length (inverse of length, length squared) to serve as the indicator of characteristic size of the elements in the system. Thus one might select mean length of first-order stream channels, or the mean perimeter of second-order basins, or the mean area of first-order basins. One of the most extensively known scale measures is drainage density D, the length of channels per unit area of watershed. Drainage density has the dimension of inverse of length, L^{-1}, and varies from values as high as 500 to 1,000, where first-order basins are only a few feet across, to values as low as 2 to 3, where the first-order basins are about a half mile wide. Drainage density is therefore used as the dependent variable in developing an equation relating the horizontal scale of the land-form units to a series of independent or controlling variables:

$$D = f(Q_r, K, H, \rho, \mu, g) \qquad (4\text{-II-}43)$$

All terms of this equation, together with their definitions and dimensional properties, are explained in Table 4-II-1.

The first independent variable, runoff intensity Q_r, combines rainfall intensity and infiltration capacity in a single term. Rainfall intensity represents a major climatic control; infiltration capacity, a major physical factor, expresses state of the ground surface and subsoil. Both components have the dimensions of velocity LT^{-1}; runoff intensity is simply the excess of rainfall intensity over infiltration capacity.

The second independent variable is an *erosion proportionality factor* K, defined by Horton [2, p. 324] as the ratio of erosion intensity to eroding force. Erosion intensity has the dimensions of mass rate of removal per unit area; eroding force, the dimensions of force per unit area. Thus K has the dimensions $L^{-1}T$, the inverse of velocity, and may be thought of as a measure of the erodibility of the ground surface.

Relief H, the third independent variable, represents the vertical dimension of the basin geometry and may vary independently of the horizontal scale. Relief represents potential energy of the system and is directly related to its total erosion intensity. Relief may be measured in various ways, described above, but is most meaningful in the analysis when defined as local, or basin, relief.

Table 4-II-1. Factors Controlling Drainage Density

Symbol	Term	Dimensional quality	Dimensional symbol
D	Drainage density	Length divided by area	$\frac{L}{L^2} = L^{-1}$
Q_r	Runoff intensity	Volume rate of flow per unit area of surface	$\frac{L^3T^{-1}}{L^2} = LT^{-1}$
K	Erosion-proportionality factor	Mass rate of removal per unit area divided by force per unit area	$\frac{ML^{-2}T^{-1}}{ML^{-1}T^{-2}} = L^{-1}T$
H	Relief	Length	L
ρ	Density of fluid	Mass per unit volume	ML^{-3}
μ	Dynamic viscosity of fluid	Mass per unit length per unit time	$ML^{-1}T^{-1}$
g	Acceleration of gravity	Distance per unit time per unit time	LT^{-2}

The remaining variables—density ρ, viscosity μ, and acceleration of gravity g—are significant properties of a fluid system, introduced here because the drainage system is developed by water erosion on slopes and in channels, acting in a force field of gravity. Note that the first four variables involve no mass dimension; hence an analysis limited to these four would include only geometric and kinematic factors of time and length. Introduction of mass through density and viscosity brings force into the analysis and makes possible scale-model comparisons.

B. Solution by Pi Theorem

The variables of Eq. (4-II-43) may be grouped into the functional relationship

$$f'(D, Q_r, K, H, \rho, \mu, g) = 0 \qquad (4\text{-II-}44)$$

The seven variables in this function may be reduced to four through application of the pi theorem (Sec. 7, Subsec. II-B). Solution of the four pi terms, described in detail by Strahler [11, p. 290], yields a function of four dimensionless groups:

$$\phi\left(HD, QK, \frac{Q_r\rho H}{\mu}, \frac{Q_r^2}{Hg}\right) = 0 \qquad (4\text{-II-}45)$$

Solving for drainage density gives

$$D = \frac{1}{H}f\left(Q_rK, \frac{Q_r\rho H}{\mu}, \frac{Q_r^2}{Hg}\right) \qquad (4\text{-II-}46)$$

The term HD is the ruggedness number, previously described as expressing essential geometrical characteristics of the drainage system. It may be replaced by the dimensionless geometry number HD/S_g explained above, without affecting the dimensionless nature of the group. The second term, Q_rK, is the *Horton number*, expressing the relative intensity of the erosion process in the drainage basin. The third term, $Q_r\rho H/\mu$, is a form of the Reynolds number, in which Q takes the place of the velocity term and H the characteristic length. The fourth term, Q_r^2/Hg, is a form of Froude number. Reduction of the seven variables into four dimensionless groups focuses attention upon dynamic relationships, simplifies the design of controlled empirical observations, and establishes conditions essential to the validity of comparisons of models with prototypes.

C. Steady-state Relationships

Conditions for a steady state within a drainage basin are such that, for a given Horton number (i.e., for a given intensity of erosion process), values of local relief, slope, and drainage density reach a time-independent steady state in which basin geometry is so adjusted as to transmit through the system just that quantity of runoff and debris characteristically produced under the controlling climatic regime.

D. Upsets of Steady State

Consider possible upsets and readjustments of the steady state. If a forested land surface is denuded of its vegetative cover and intensively cultivated, the Horton

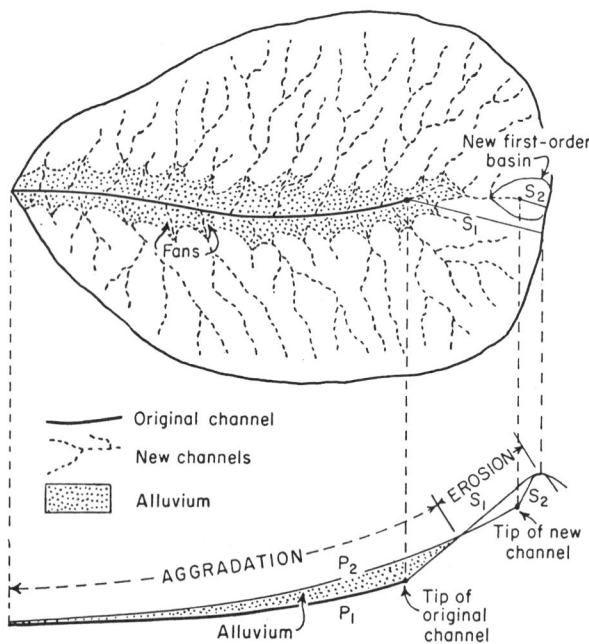

Fig. 4-II-31. Drainage-density transformation accompanying severe, accelerated slope erosion and development of badlands. (*After Strahler* [11, p. 297].)

number will undergo a sharp increase, either through increase in runoff intensity or surface susceptibility to erosion or through simultaneous increase in both. In compensation, basin geometry is altered by gully development to increase greatly the drainage density, to increase channel and ground-surface gradients, but to decrease the local relief [11, p. 296].

When transformation has been completed, a new set of drainage-basin forms, very much smaller in characteristic-length dimension, has replaced the original basins. A new steady state of erosion is achieved on a much higher level of intensity. Thus, badlands, from which sediment is produced at a rapid rate, replace the former long, gentle, smooth slopes of the land. Many new channel segments of first, second, and third orders have come into existence where formerly a single first-order basin had been (Fig. 4-II-31). Steepening of main-stream channel gradients through aggradation is also a characteristic result of the transformation. The various manifestations of accelerated soil erosion are thus seen to be related to a general theory of drainage-basin dynamics.

VII. OBSERVED COMPLEX RELATIONS AMONG HYDROLOGIC AND GEOMETRIC PROPERTIES

A. Control of Basin Geometry by Climatic Factors

Students of quantitative geomorphology of drainage basins have attempted to relate empirically one or more of the geometric elements of drainage basins to several independent variables, including climatic, vegetative, and hydrologic factors. Statistical methods of correlation and regression have been applied to observational data on basin geometry, precipitation and runoff, vegetative cover, geologic type, and soils.

Melton [15] used multiple-regression-and-correlation analysis upon 23 small drainage basins of Arizona, Colorado, New Mexico, and Utah. Multiple-correlation analyses showed that valleyside slopes and drainage density are related to climate and to properties of mantle and vegetal cover. Slopes were found to be higher with greater values of infiltration capacity and Thornthwaite's precipitation-effectiveness index (see Subsec. IV-G) but to vary inversely with soil strength and runoff intensity-frequency. Melton found that drainage density varies directly with per cent of bare area and runoff intensity-frequency, but inversely with precipitation-effectiveness index and infiltration capacity, confirming Horton's infiltration theory of erosion. Melton [54] carried his analysis further by examining the correlation structure of morphometric properties of drainage systems and their controlling agents. He classified variable systems by the presence and direction of feedback among the variables

Chorley [66] attempted to establish the relationship of basin geometry to climate by a comparative study of three areas of similar gross geology but greatly different climate. A climate-vegetation index, combining mean annual rainfall, mean monthly precipitation in 24 hr, and Thornthwaite's precipitation-effectiveness index, was computed for each region. The climate-vegetation index was found to be closely correlated with ogarithms of stream length, basin area, and drainage density.

B. Relation of Basin Geometry to Stream Flow

Effect of drainage-basin characteristics upon unit-hydrograph lag and peak flow has been reported by Taylor and Schwartz [29], using the data of 20 basins ranging in area from 20 to 1,600 sq mi, and located in the North and Middle Atlantic States. Drainage area, length of longest watercourse, main-stream length to centroid of area, and equivalent main-stream slope were judged the most significant geometrical variables.

A regression of peak stream discharge upon factors of topography, basin area, and rainfall was determined empirically by Potter [67, p. 69] for 51 basins in the Appalachian Plateau. Potter's T factor, representing basin geometry, is the ratio of longest length of principal stream to square root of average channel slope from head to mouth. The T factor was judged to be significant in multiple regression with basin area and measures of rainfall intensity and frequency.

Morisawa [17, pp. 16–17] substituted other geomorphic properties for Potter's T factor in an effort to explain still more of the observed variance. When relief ratio, circularity ratio, and frequency of first-order streams were combined as a product to yield a new T factor, multiple regression for 10 of Potter's basins on rainfall intensity and frequency yielded an equation in which the standard error of estimate was considerably reduced and a high correlation was established with peak intensity of runoff. In another study, Morisawa [68] established significant regressions for average runoff and peak runoff on stream length, relief ratio, and shape ratio within subdivisions of a single small watershed.

Maxwell [18] used digital computers to relate stream-discharge characteristics to several elements of drainage-basin geometry in the San Dimas Experimental Forest of southern California. He computed multiple correlations between peak discharge and storm rainfall, cover density, antecedent rainfall, and nine geomorphic properties taken five at a time. The geomorphic variables considered were fifth-order area and diameter; means of second-order area, diameter, relief, drainage density, channel frequency, and relief ratio; and watershed bifurcation, length, diameter, and area ratios. It was concluded that fifth- and second-order areas or diameters, together with second-order drainage density and relief ratio, provide a good estimate of the variability in peak discharge which can be explained by geomorphic variation between watersheds.

VIII. NOTATIONS

A watershed area above gage or other reference point, sq mi
A_c area of a circle of same perimeter as basin, sq mi
A_u area of basin of order u, sq mi
$\bar{A}_u$ mean area of basins of order u, sq mi
A_0 area of interbasin area, ft^2, sq mi
A_1 area of a first-order basin, sq mi
a cross-sectional area of basin at a given contour level, sq mi; a numerical constant
b regression coefficient, dimensionless
C constant of channel maintenance, ft^2/ft; a constant of integration
D drainage density, mi/sq mi
D_u drainage density of entire basin of order u, mi/sq mi
D_1 drainage density of first-order basins, mi/sq mi
F stream frequency; channel frequency, no./ sq mi
g acceleration of gravity, ft/sec^2
H basin relief, ft
H_g elevation difference; stream head to divide reference point, ft
$\bar{H}_u$ mean relief of basins of order u, ft
h height of given contour above basin mouth, ft
i item number in summation
j a constant, dimensionless
K erosion proportionality factor, sec/ft
k highest stream order in a given basin, no.
L stream length from gage to point on divide, mi
L_b basin length, mi
L_{ca} main-stream length from gage to centroid, mi
L_g length of overland flow, ft, mi
$\bar{L}_g$ mean length of overland flow, ft, mi
$\bar{L}_u$ mean length of stream segments of order u, mi
$\sum_{i=1}^{N} L_u$ total length of stream segments of order u, mi
L_0 interbasin length, ft, mi
$\bar{L}_1$ mean length of first-order stream segments, mi
m an exponent, dimensionless
N_u number of stream segments of order u, no.
P basin perimeter, ft, mi
p constant in lemniscate model of basin shape, dimensionless
Q discharge, cfs
Q_r runoff intensity, fps
$Q_{2.3}$ discharge equaled or exceeded in 2.3 years, cfs
R_a basin-area ratio, dimensionless
R_b bifurcation ratio of stream segments, dimensionless
R_c circularity ratio, dimensionless
R_e elongation ratio, dimensionless
R_f form ratio of basin, dimensionless
R_h relief ratio, dimensionless

R_{hp} relative relief, dimensionless
R_L length ratio of stream segments, dimensionless
R_{Lb} ratio of R_L to R_b, dimensionless
R_s slope ratio of stream segments, dimensionless
S_c channel slope, ft/ft, %
S_g ground-surface slope, ft/ft, %
S_{st} equivalent main-stream slope, ft/ft, %
$\bar{S}_u$ mean slope of stream segments of order u, ft/ft, %
$\bar{S}_1$ mean slope of first-order stream segments, ft/ft, %
s standard deviation, estimated from sample
s^2 variance, estimated from sample
u a given order of stream segments, no.
X horizontal distance downstream from stream head, ft, mi
x relative area of horizontal cross section to basin area, dimensionless
$\bar{x}$ arithmetic mean of a sample
Y vertical distance downward from stream head, ft
Y_c elevation difference between local base level and sea-level datum, ft
Y_0 elevation difference between stream head and local base level, ft
y relative height of given contour above basin mouth, dimensionless
λ linear scale ratio in model analysis, dimensionless
μ viscosity (absolute or dynamic) of a fluid; population mean (statistical)
ρ density of a fluid; radius vector in polar coordinates
$\sum_{i=1}^{N}$ summation of terms from 1st to nth
σ population standard deviation
σ^2 population variance
θ angle in polar coordinates
θ_c gradient of stream channel, deg
θ_g gradient of ground surface, deg
$\theta_{\max}$ maximum angle of valleyside slopes, deg

IX. REFERENCES

1. Horton, R. E.: Drainage basin characteristics, *Trans. Am. Geophys. Union*, vol. 13, pp. 350–361, 1932.
2. Horton, R. E.: Erosional development of streams and their drainage basins: hydrophysical approach to quantitative morphology, *Bull. Geol. Soc. Am.*, vol. 56, pp. 275–370, 1945.
3. Davis, W. M.: "Geographical Essays," Ginn and Company, Boston, 1909. (Reprinted 1954 by Dover Publications, Inc., New York.)
4. Langbein, W. B., and others: Topographic characteristics of drainage basins, *U.S. Geol. Surv. Water-Supply Paper* 968-C, 1947.
5. Strahler, A. N.: Equilibrium theory of erosional slopes approached by frequency distribution analysis, *Am. J. Sci.*, vol. 248, pp. 673–696, 800–814, 1950.
6. Strahler, A. N.: Dynamic basis of geomorphology, *Bull. Geol. Soc. Am.*, vol. 63, pp. 923–938, 1952.
7. Strahler, A. N.: Hypsometric (area-altitude) analysis of erosional topography, *Bull. Geol. Soc. Am.*, vol. 63, pp. 1117–1142, 1952.
8. Strahler, A. N.: Statistical analysis in geomorphic research, *J. Geol.*, vol. 62, pp. 1–25, 1954.
9. Strahler, A. N.: Quantitative slope analysis, *Bull. Geol. Soc. Am.*, vol. 67, pp. 571–596, 1956.
10. Strahler, A. N.: Quantitative analysis of watershed geomorphology, *Trans. Am. Geophys. Union*, vol. 38, pp. 913–920, 1957.
11. Strahler, A. N.: Dimensional analysis applied to fluvially eroded landforms, *Bull. Geol. Soc. Am.*, vol. 69, pp. 279–300, 1958.
12. Von Bertalanffy, Ludwig: The theory of open systems in physics and biology, *Science*, vol. 111, pp. 23–28, 1950.
13. Duncan, W. J.: "Physical Similarity and Dimensional Analysis," Edward Arnold (Publishers) Ltd., London, 1953.
14. Melton, M. A.: List of sample parameters of quantitative properties of landforms: their use in determining the size of geomorphic experiments, *Project* NR 389-042, *Tech. Rept.* 16, Columbia University, Department of Geology, ONR, Geography Branch, New York, 1958.

REFERENCES

15. Melton, M. A.: An analysis of the relations among elements of climate, surface properties, and geomorphology, *Project* NR 389-042, *Tech. Rept.* 11, Columbia University, Department of Geology, ONR, Geography Branch, New York, 1957.
16. Melton, M. A.: Geometric properties of mature drainage systems and their representation in an E_4 phase space, *J. Geol.*, vol. 66, pp. 35–54, 1958.
17. Morisawa, M. E.: Relation of quantitative geomorphology to stream flow in representative watersheds of the Appalachian Plateau Province, *Project* NR 389-042, *Tech. Rept.* 20, Columbia University, Department of Geology, ONR, Geography Branch, New York, 1959.
18. Maxwell, J. C.: Quantitative geomorphology of the San Dimas Experimental Forest, California, *Project* NR 389-042, *Tech. Rept.* 19, Columbia University, Department of Geology, ONR, Geography Branch, New York, 1960.
19. Melton, M. A.: A derivation of Strahler's channel-ordering system, *J. Geol.*, vol. 67, pp. 345–346, 1959.
20. Leopold, L. B., and J. P. Miller: Ephemeral streams: hydraulic factors and their relation to the drainage net, *U.S. Geol. Surv. Profess. Paper* 282-A, 1956.
21. Schumm, S. A.: Evolution of drainage systems and slopes in badlands at Perth Amboy, New Jersey, *Bull. Geol. Soc. Am.*, vol. 67, pp. 597–646, 1956.
22. Smith, K. G.: Erosional processes and landforms in Badlands National Monument, South Dakota, *Bull. Geol. Soc. Am.*, vol. 69, pp. 975–1008, 1958.
23. Maxwell, J. C.: The bifurcation ratio in Horton's law of stream numbers (abstract), *Trans. Am. Geophys. Union*, vol. 36, p. 520, 1955.
24. Morisawa, M. E.: Accuracy of determination of stream lengths from topographic maps, *Trans. Am. Geophys. Union*, vol. 38, pp. 86–88, 1957.
25. Miller, V. C.: A quantitative geomorphic study of drainage basin characteristics in the Clinch Mountain area, Virginia and Tennessee, *Project* NR 389-042, *Tech. Rept.* 3, Columbia University, Department of Geology, ONR, Geography Branch, New York, 1953.
26. Broscoe, A. J.: Quantitative analysis of longitudinal stream profiles of small watersheds, *Project* NR 389-042, *Tech. Rept.* 18, Columbia University, Department of Geology, ONR, Geography Branch, New York, 1959.
27. Hack, J. T.: Studies of longitudinal stream profiles in Virginia and Maryland, *U.S. Geol. Surv. Profess. Paper* 294-B, 1957.
28. Snyder, F. F.: Synthetic unit-graphs, *Trans. Am. Geophys. Union*, vol. 19, pp. 447–454, 1938.
29. Taylor, A. B., and H. E. Schwartz: Unit-hydrograph lag and peak flow related to basin characteristics, *Trans. Am. Geophys. Union*, vol. 33, pp. 235–246, 1952.
30. Linsley, R. K., M. A. Kohler, and J. L. H. Paulhus: "Applied Hydrology," McGraw-Hill Book Company, Inc., New York, 1949.
31. Golding, B. L., and D. E. Low: Physical characteristics of drainage basins, *Proc. Am. Soc. Civil Engrs., J. Hydraulics Div.*, vol. 86, no. HY3, pp. 1–11, 1950.
32. Wisler, C. O., and E. F. Brater: "Hydrology," John Wiley & Sons, Inc., New York, 1959.
33. Horton, R. E.: Sheet erosion: present and past, *Trans. Am. Geophys. Union*, vol. 22, pp. 299–305, 1941.
34. "Unit Hydrograph Compilations," U.S. Corps of Engineers, Department of the Army, Washington District, Civil Works Invest., Project CW 153 (three volumes 1949; one volume 1954).
35. Chorley, R. J., Donald E. G. Malm, and H. A. Pogorzelski: A new standard for estimating drainage basin shape, *Am. J. Sci.*, vol. 255, pp. 138–141, 1957.
36. Morisawa, M. E.: Measurement of drainage-basin outline form, *J. Geol.*, vol. 66, pp. 587–591, 1958.
37. Carlston, C. W., and W. B. Langbein: Rapid approximation of drainage density: line intersection method, *U.S. Geol. Surv. Water Resources Div., Bull.*, p. 11, Feb. 10, 1960.
38. Smith, K. G.: Standards for grading texture of erosional topography, *Am. J. Sci.*, vol. 248, pp. 655–668, 1950.
39. Coates, D. R.: Quantitative geomorphology of small drainage basins of southern Indiana, *Project* NR 389-042, *Tech. Rept.* 10, Columbia University, Department of Geology, ONR, Geography Branch, New York, 1958.
40. Shulits, Samuel: Rational equation of river-bed profile, *Trans. Am. Geophys. Union*, vol. 22, pp. 622–631, 1941.
41. Shulits, Samuel: Graphical analysis of trend profile of a shortened section of river, *Trans. Am. Geophys. Union*, vol. 36, pp. 649–654, 1955.
42. Miller, J. P.: High mountain streams: effects of geology on channel characteristics and bed material, *New Mexico Bur. Mines & Mineral Resources*, Mem. 4, 1958.

43. Gilbert, G. K.: Report on the geology of the Henry Mountains, U.S. Geographical and Geological Survey of the Rocky Mountain Region, Washington, D.C., 1877.
44. Yatsu, Eiju: On the longitudinal profile of the graded river, *Trans. Am. Geophys. Union*, vol. 36, pp. 655–663, 1955.
45. Krumbein, W. O.: Sediments and the exponential function, *J. Geol.*, vol. 45, pp. 577–601, 1937.
46. Rubey, W. W.: Geology and mineral resources of the Hardin and Brussels quadrangles (Illinois), *U.S. Geol. Surv. Profess. Paper* 218, 1952.
47. Mackin, J. H.: Concept of the graded river, *Bull. Geol. Soc. Am.*, vol. 59, pp. 463–512, 1948.
48. Woodford, A. O.: Stream gradients and Monterey Sea Valley, *Bull. Geol. Soc. Am.*, vol. 62, pp. 799–852, 1951.
49. Benson, M. S.: Channel-slope factor in flood frequency analyses, *Proc. Am. Soc. Civil Engrs., J. Hydraulics Div.*, vol. 85, no. HY4, pp. 1–9, 1959.
50. Lane, E. W.: Stable channels in erodible material, *Trans. Am. Soc. Civil Engrs.*, vol. 102, pp. 123–194, 1937.
51. Leopold, L. B., and Thomas Maddock, Jr.: The hydraulic geometry of stream channels and some physiographic implications, *U.S. Geol. Surv. Profess. Paper* 252, 1953.
52. Leopold, L. B.: Downstream change of velocity in rivers, *Am. J. Sci.*, vol. 251, pp. 606–624, 1953.
53. Wolman, M. G.: The natural channel of Brandywine Creek, Pennsylvania, *U.S. Geol. Surv. Profess. Paper* 271, 1955.
54. Melton, M. A.: Correlation structure of morphometric properties of drainage systems and their controlling agents, *J. Geol.*, vol. 66, pp. 442–460, 1958.
55. Melton, M. A.: Intravalley variation in slope angles related to microclimate and erosional environment, *Bull. Geol. Soc. Am.*, vol. 71, pp. 133–144, 1960.
56. Horton, R. E.: Derivation of runoff from rainfall data, Discussion, *Trans. Am. Soc. Civil Engrs.*, vol. 77, pp. 369–375, 1914.
57. Chapman, C. A.: A new quantitative method of topographic analysis, *Am. J. Sci.*, vol. 250, pp. 428–452, 1952.
58. Wentworth, C. K.: A simplified method of determining the average slope of land surfaces, *Am. J. Sci.*, 5th ser., vol. 20, pp. 184–194, 1930.
59. Smith, Guy-Harold: The relative relief of Ohio, *Geograph. Rev.*, vol. 25, pp. 272–284, 1935.
60. Raisz, Irwin, and Joyce Henry: An average slope map of New England, *Geograph. Rev.*, vol. 27, pp. 467–472, 1937.
61. Calef, Wesley: Slope studies of northern Illinois, *Trans. Illinois Acad. Sci.*, vol. 43, pp. 110–115, 1950.
62. Calef, Wesley, and Robert Newcomb: An average slope map of Illinois, *Ann. Assoc. Am. Geographers*, vol. 43, pp. 305–316, 1953.
63. Ruhe, R. V.: Graphic analysis of drift topographies, *Am. J. Sci.*, vol. 248, pp. 435–443, 1950.
64. Schumm, Stanley: The relation of drainage basin relief to sediment loss, *Intern. Union Geodesy Geophys., Tenth Gen. Assembly* (Rome), *Intern. Assoc. Sci. Hydrol. Publ.* 36, vol. 1, pp. 216–219, 1954.
65. Maner, S. B.: Factors affecting sediment delivery rates in the Red Hills physiographic area, *Trans. Am. Geophys. Union*, vol. 39, pp. 669–675, 1958.
66. Chorley, R. J.: Climate and morphometry, *J. Geol.*, vol. 65, pp. 628–638, 1957.
67. Potter, W. D.: Rainfall and topographic factors that affect runoff, *Trans. Am. Geophys. Union*, vol. 34, pp. 67–73, 1953.
68. Morisawa, M. E.: Relation of morphometric properties to runoff in the Little Mill Creek, Ohio, drainage basin, *Project* NR 389-042, *Tech. Rept.* 17, Columbia University, Department of Geology, ONR, Geography Branch, New York, 1959.

ERRATUM

Page 4-60, the exponent in Equation (4-II-39) should read: "$u-1$."

Part II

THE RANDOM MODEL OF DRAINAGE COMPOSITION

Editors' Comments
on Papers 6 Through 13

6 SHREVE
Statistical Law of Stream Numbers

7 SHREVE
Infinite Topologically Random Channel Networks

8 SHREVE
Stream Lengths and Basin Areas in Topologically Random Channel Networks

9 LIAO and SCHEIDEGGER
A Computer Model for Some Branching-Type Phenomena in Hydrology

10 WERNER and SMART
Some New Methods of Topologic Classification of Channel Networks

11 JARVIS and WERRITTY
Some Comments on Testing Random Topology Stream Network Models

12 JAMES and KRUMBEIN
Excerpts from *Frequency Distributions of Stream Link Lengths*

13 MOCK
A Classification of Channel Links in Stream Networks

Within a period of three years, from 1966 to 1969, the era of Hortonian analysis in fluvial geomorphology was effectively terminated. Horton's laws of drainage composition, which had been viewed as reflecting the orderly evolution of channel networks and their drainage basins, were shown to be derivable from a link-based random model. Because this model has fewer assumptions than the Hortonian one and explains some results that Horton's laws could not, it won many adherents. Tests of the randomness of network topology led to new methods of network classification and the development of probability distributions for different classes. Also, the testing of link-length distributions led to the development of link-type classifications, along with the probabilities of their occurrence under the random model. These link types in turn made possible further refinements of link-length distribution models and enabled geomorphologists to test for space-filling constraints in the horizontal plane and for the effects of relief and slope on river network topology. Thus, the random model can serve as a standard of comparison, allowing better visualization of the roles of space filling and basin relief.

The random model was established in two papers by Shreve and one by Smart. In his first paper Shreve tackled Horton's law of stream numbers as a statistical relation arising from the application of stream ordering to a large number of randomly merging stream channels (Paper 6). He coined the "fundamental geomorphological hypothesis . . . that in the absence of geologic controls a natural population of channel networks will be topologically random" (Paper 6, p. 27). When stream ordering is applied to such a population, the most probable networks obey Horton's law of stream numbers. Shreve successfully tests his model and also elucidates various statistical properties of Horton- and Strahler-order numbers. In his second paper Shreve generalizes the theory to infinite topologically random channel networks (Paper 7). Since the individual basins we study are not isolated in space, they can be viewed as samples from an infinite channel network. The first postulate of the random topology model thus becomes: In the infinite topologically random channel network, all topologically distinct channel networks of a given magnitude occur with equal frequency. A similar hypothesis of topological randomness was also developed around this time by Scheidegger (1966, 1967, 1968; Paper 9).

The second postulate of the random model of drainage composition concerns channel lengths and was derived by Smart: For drainage networks developed under similar environmental conditions, the exterior and interior link lengths are independent random variables with a single common distribution for each type (Smart, 1972, 1976). Existence of this postulate was hinted by Shreve (Paper 7) and initially developed by Smart (1968). From Smart's work on stream lengths and basin areas in ordered networks, and from further extensions by Shreve (Paper 8), it became apparent that, like the law of stream numbers, Horton's other laws of lengths and areas were no more than the outcome of applying ordering to a system that conforms with the random model of drainage composition. These papers also explain other results of Hortonian analysis, including Schumm's constant of channel maintenance (see Paper 3), the fit to the stream-length law (Bowden and Wallis, 1964), and Melton's (1958) relation between channel frequency and drainage density (see Paper 5). Perhaps most important, these founding papers of the random model firmly established the mathematics of treelike networks in the study of river basins, with links to combinatorial analysis (see historical comments that follow) and to theories of branching processes and random walks. Though very successful, powerful, and elegant, the hypothesis of randomness was not accepted without qualification by all geomorphologists (Shreve, 1975; Werritty, 1972; Howard, 1971, 1972):

While the number of TDCN was the basic means of classification used in the initial development of the random model, several other new methods of topological classification of channel networks soon followed. Smart (1969) defined ambilateral classes of TDCN by grouping those that could be made identical by reversing the right/left arrangement of tributary junctions. This generalization permits comparison with networks of dispersion in porous media, where the three-dimensional net precludes distinction of the right- or lefthandedness of tributaries. Liao and Scheidegger (1969) gave algorithms for ambilateral class numbers in a three-dimensional random graph model. Topologic path lengths were identified by Liao and Scheidegger (Paper 9), who investigated the mean and maximum height of arborescences. These measures, termed link distances, were applied to natural river channel networks by Jarvis (1972), and a comprehensive theoretical treatment was provided by Werner and Smart (Paper 10). Werner and Smart defined the total path length of a network, the mean exterior path length, and the network diameter. Path length indices offer topologic analogs of some important metric properties used in drainage basin hydrology. They reveal the topologic foundation of Hack's (1957) relation between mainstream length and drainage area (Shreve, 1974; Jarvis and Sham, 1981). They also provide ways of quantifying network size much more precisely than basin order and have been used to reveal scale dependencies in network morphometry, such as the correlation between interior and exterior link lengths, which increases with network diameter (Jarvis, 1976).

With all these different methods available for classifying channel networks, there were many ways of testing the random topology model. Jarvis and Werritty (Paper 11) investigated the information losses inherent in classifications that group TDCN. Due to the rapid proliferation of TDCN with increasing network magnitude, it soon becomes practically impossible to obtain sufficient natural replicates to test the random model directly with TDCN. But when TDCN are grouped into classes, the information losses become so great the results may have little meaning as a test of the random model.

Another type of sampling problem may occur when testing a group of small-magnitude networks for topological randomness. Spatial distribution and orientation may not be taken into account, although they can be very important factors in topologic configuration. Abrahams (1975) has shown that for two basins in Australia, while sets of magnitude 4 networks did not differ from a topologically random expectation, when disaggregated according to direction of flow the random hypothesis had to be rejected. The geographical segregation of types of TDCN was attributed to microclimatic effects, and the orientation of slopes to the direction of prevailing winds when the networks were formed.

Besides geological and climatic controls, the constraints of space filling and a notion of the available potential energy or power are still missing from the random model of drainage composition. The development of streams is ultimately a physical process, and therefore it must take place in the arena of three-dimensional space. Recent research has begun to investigate these effects with work on space filling and potential energy, which developed as an outgrowth of examinations of link-length distributions and topologic structural compaction.

The appropriate distribution for stream-link lengths was sought by several workers and led to new classifications of link topology and geometry. Smart (1968) suggested a negative exponential distribution for interior link lengths, while Shreve (Paper 8) indicated a gamma density with shape parameter of 2. The major study of this problem was carried out by James and Krumbein (Paper 12). Their introduction of the concepts of cis and trans links and chains opened network analysis to the evaluation of the constraints of space filling. The terms *cis* and *trans* were borrowed from the analysis of treelike molecules in organic chemistry and refer to a link, or chain of links, bounded by same-sided (cis) or opposite-sided (trans) tributaries. James and Krumbein found that the proportions of cis and trans links along some streams free from geological controls differ from the random model expectation of 50 percent. There is an excess of trans links, which may be explained in terms of stream capture of neighboring external links on the same side of the channel during growth, thus eliminating very short cis links. They also presented a composite gamma-distribution model for link lengths and established the existence of different types of interior links.

The distinction of link types was extended by Mock (Paper 13) into a full classification of interior and exterior links, based on the tributary magnitudes upstream and downstream of a junction. Mock gave the probability of occurrence of each type in a population of topologically random networks. Abrahams found that differences in link-length distributions depend on link type and the type of link joined downstream (1976, 1980a; Abrahams and Campbell, 1976; Smart, 1981). He further showed that divide angle and link length are related to link type (Abrahams, 1980b).

Flint (1980) explored the suggestion of James and Krumbein that there may be other differences in topology due to differences in the propensity of tributary streams to branch on either side of a channel. He distinguished eight types of chains that might occur on a tributary of a larger stream—four on the inside of the space between tributary and main stream, and four on the outside. Empirical tests show a higher frequency of branches on the outside of natural channels than in a topologically random tree, suggesting a tendency to deviate from a purely random configuration.

Although the distribution of available relief and slope determines the potential energy of a fluvially eroded surface, there has not been much work relating network morphometry and topology to these properties of the drainage basin. Distribution of link slopes and downstream change in relation to order, magnitude, and discharge have been examined by Flint (1974, 1976). Power functions of link slope against magnitude give empirical results consistent with the well-known hydraulic geometry equations. Horton's (Paper 1, p. 290) suggestion that the bifurcation ratio would decrease with slope or relief has not been substantiated by subsequent work. Bifurcation ratios seem to vary little, with a mean of approximately 4.0, exactly as expected under the random model (see Paper 7). However, Abrahams (1977) showed that the bifurcation ratio between orders 1 and 2 increases with the relief ratio of third-order basins, while Woldenberg (1977a) found an inverse relationship for fourth- and fifth-order basins of low relief developed on tidal flats. There is a possibility that bifurcation ratio declines with relief ratio for relief ratio less than 0.01 and then increases with relief ratio for terrestrial rivers (Woldenberg, 1977b).

Presently, development of the random model approach continues. It can be seen as a kind of null hypothesis. In carefully designed situations, deviations from random model expectations can be assigned to specific causes. Detailed reviews and major recent applications are covered in Smart (1972, 1973, 1978), Werritty (1972), Smart and Werner (1976), and Jarvis (1977).

The first papers in this section chronicle the replacement of the Hortonian model by the random model in fluvial studies. The latter papers test the random model and discover the constraints caused by space filling, relief, and slope. We see that link types coupled with random expectations have become a powerful tool for drainage basin analysis.

Many other fields of scientific enquiry deal with treelike networks whose mathematical properties are similar to those of river channel networks. Geomorphologists should be aware of many opportunities for a profitable exchange of ideas and methods. A brief introduction to some of these applications is included in this section.

While the future potential of the Horton and other centripetal ordering systems for fluvial studies is bleak, this is not the case in the analysis of organic branching networks. Studies of lungs (Woldenberg et al., 1970; Horsfield, 1981a, 1981b; Cumming, 1981), livers (Woldenberg, 1968), brain cells (Berry et al., 1975; Hollingworth and Berry, 1975; Berry and Bradley, 1976a, 1976c), and woody trees (Holland, 1969; Woldenberg, 1968, Oohata and Shidei, 1971; Tomlinson, 1978; Steingraeber et al., 1979; Borchert and Slade, 1981) reflect a continuing use and evaluation of the Hortonian approach to network analysis. Many of the lung studies develop models that describe the morphometry and function of the lung with great economy in the way Keill (1708), Young (1809), and Horton (Paper 1) suggested. Some investigators believe bifurcation ratios are related to function in organic systems. There is good reason to suspect that the hydraulic geometries of "channel" links in airways and arteries optimize some cost function (Murray, 1926; Roy and Woldenberg, 1982). If the links reflect some aspect of optimality, then perhaps optimality also affects or is affected by network topology (Leopold, 1971). Branching ratios are meaningful in the human lung (Woldenberg et al., 1970); Horsfield (1980) indicated that lung airways branch so that resistance and entropy production are minimized. Woldenberg (1979) suggested that for rivers and lungs, when the ratio of power available to power required is high, then the bifurcation ratio is low, and vice versa.

Network topology has been simulated in several ways not used by geomorphologists. Horsfield (1972) demonstrated the usefulness of a Strahler-ordered connectivity matrix for modeling the lung. A related approach in computer simulation of botanical trees is based on the repeating nature of a few branching patterns, each of which has some probability of occurrence. This work grew out of a fusion of automata and formal language theory from computer science with developmental biology (Frijters and Lindenmayer, 1976; Lindenmayer, 1977; Frijters, 1978; Lück et al., 1977).

There is a large literature on link-based network analysis of brain cells (Smit et al., 1971-72; Hollingworth and Berry, 1975; Berry and Bradley, 1976a, 1976b; Bradley and Berry, 1978; McConnell and Berry, 1978a, 1978b; Sadler and Berry, 1982; Sadler et al., 1982; van Pelt and Verwer, 1983). The branching in these networks of Purkinje cells, although two-dimensional, has been mapped and simulated only at the level of the ambilateral class. The topology and metric geometry of Purkinje cell networks are strongly affected by environmental influences.

The work in the biological sciences suggests that fluvial geomorphologists might well reexamine the Horton model from the standpoint of modeling large systems to assess various optimality criteria and environmental effects. If the form of organic treelike networks is as closely related to function as studies of the lung illustrate, and to environment as some work by neuro-anatomists suggests, then we need more sensitive tests of river networks to determine how they are affected by environmental controls (see Paper 24). At the same time, network analysts in biology could usefully apply the recent advances in the study of river networks that stem from the development of the random model of drainage composition.

SOME HISTORICAL COMMENTS

Calculations of the number of topologically distinct channel networks (Paper 6) and of the number of ambilateral classes (Paper 10) are both combinatorial problems that have a long history. Following Etherington (1937), the solution of the TDCN problem is equivalent to the number of interpretations of x^n in a general noncommutative, nonassociative algebra. The ambilateral class problem addresses the number of interpretations of x^n in a general commutative nonassociative algebra.

In order to evaluate the probability of a network topology, we need to know how many TDCN and ambilateral classes there are. An iterative solution for the number of TDCN was suggested by Euler (de Segner, 1758-59), who posed the problem in terms of the number of ways a convex polygon may be divided into triangles by means of its diagonals. Euler derived the solution for polygons with a few sides and told de Segner, who devised an algorithm for generating the solution for many-sided polygons. Unfortunately de Segner made an arithmetic error, which was noticed by several subsequent authors. Lamé (1838) derived a more elegant iterative formula that had evidently been published by Euler without proof in 1758. Catalan (1838, 1839) provided the first closed expression for the problem. Cayley (1859) represented this combinatorial problem with tree diagrams and redevised an exact solution. The form of the equation commonly cited today is that of Catalan (1838), not Cayley, though Cayley's formula can be easily transformed to Catalan's. This whole problem has a more detailed history, and interested readers can find a good review in Brown (1965), with additional work by Feller (1957), Tomari (1974), and Silberger (1969). The TDCN problem has applications in organic chemistry concerned with the enumeration of isomers (Cayley, 1874, 1875). Polya (1937) wrote a major treatise on the subject, dealing with all sorts of tree topologies, not just those with two daughter branches emanating from each junction.

There is no known closed expression for the number of ambilateral trees. An iterative solution was made by Wedderburn (1927) and later by Etherington (1937, 1939). Recursive relations were given by Werner and Smart (Paper 10), and Liao and Scheidegger (1969). The problem of the number of TDCN grouped within each ambilateral class also remains unsolved (Harding, 1971), although improved algorithms for iterative solution have been developed (van Pelt and Verwer, 1983).

Further classifications of network topology have been applied to river channel networks in recent years. Many useful algorithms for path-length properties are presented by Werner and Smart (Paper 10). Applications of random walk theory and development of the network topologic width and asymmetry properties are given by Kirkby (Paper 23) and Ferguson (1980).

REFERENCES

Abrahams, A. D., 1975, Topologically Random Channel Networks in the Presence of Environmental Controls, *Geol. Soc. America Bull.* **86:**1459-1462.

Abrahams, A. D., 1976, Evolutionary Changes in Link Lengths: Further Evidence for Stream Abstraction, *Inst. British Geographers Trans.*, new series **1:**225-230.

Abrahams, A. D., 1977, The Factor of Relief in the Evolution of Channel Networks in Mature Drainage Basins, *Am. Jour. Sci.* **277:**626-646.

Abrahams, A. D., 1980a, Channel Link Density and Ground Slope, *Assoc. Am. Geographers Annals* **70:**80-93.

Abrahams, A. D., 1980b, A Multivariate Analysis of Chain Lengths in Natural Channel Networks, *Jour. Geology* **88:**681-696.

Abrahams, A. D., and R. N. Campbell, 1976, Source and Tributary-Source Link Lengths in Natural Channel Networks, *Geol. Soc. America Bull.* **87:**1016-1020.

Berry, M., and P. M. Bradley, 1976a, The Application of Network Analysis to the Study of Branching Patterns of Large Dendritic Fields, *Brain Research* **109:**111-132.

Berry, M., and P. M. Bradley, 1976b, The Growth of the Dendritic Trees of Purkinje Cells in Irradiated Agranular Cerebellar Cortex, *Brain Research* **111:**361-387.

Berry, M., and P. M. Bradley, 1976c, The Growth of Dendritic Trees of Purkinje Cells in the Cerebellum of the Rat, *Brain Research* **112:**1-35.

Berry, M., T. Hollingworth, E. M. Anderson, and R. M. Flinn, 1975, Application of Network Analysis to the Study of the Branching Patterns of Dendritic Fields, *Adv. Neurol.* **12:**217-245.

Borchert, R., and N. A. Slade, 1981, Bifurcation Ratios and the Adaptive Geometry of Trees, *Bot. Gaz.* **142:**394-401.

Bowden, K. L., and J. R. Wallis, 1964, Effect of Stream-Ordering Technique on Horton's Laws of Drainage Composition, *Geol. Soc. America Bull.* **75:**767-774.

Bradley, P., and M. Berry, 1978, Quantitative Effects of Methyloxy-methanol Acetate on Purkinje Cell Dendritic Growth, *Brain Research* **143:**499-511.

Brown, W. G., 1965, Historical Note on a Recurrent Combinatorial Problem, *Am. Math. Mon.* **72:**973-977.

Catalan, E., 1838, Note sur une equation aux différences finies, *Jour. Math. Pures Appl.* **3:**508-516.

Catalan, E., 1839, Solution d'une probleme de combinaisons, *Jour. Math. Pures Appl.* **4:**74.

Cayley, A., 1859, On the Analytical Forms Called Trees. Second Part, *London, Edinburgh, Dublin Philos. Mag. Jour. Sci.* **18:**374-378.

Cayley, A., 1874, On the Mathematical Theory of Isomers, *London, Edinburgh, Dublin Philos. Mag. Jour. Sci.* **47:**444-446.

Cayley, A., 1875, On the Analytical Forms Called Trees, with Application to the Theory of Chemical Combinations, *Report British Assoc. Advancement Sci.* **45:**257-305.

Cumming, G., 1981, The Structure of the Pulmonary Circulation, in *Scientific Foundations of Respiratory Medicine,* J. G. Scadding, G. Cumming, and W. M. Thurlbeck, eds., Heinemann, London, pp. 71-77.

de Segner, J. A., 1758-59, Modorum quibus figurae planae rectilineae per diagonales dividuntur in triangula, *Akad. Nauk SSSR, Leningrad, Acad. Sci. Imp. Petropolitanae,* 1758-1759, pp. 203-210.

Etherington, I. M. H., 1937, Non-Associative Powers and a Functional Equation, *Math. Gaz.* **21:**36-39.

Etherington, I. M. H., 1939, On Non-Associative Combinations, *Royal Soc. Edinburgh Proc.* **59:**153-162.

Feller, W., 1957, *An Introduction to Probability Theory and Its Applications, Volume 1,* Wiley, New York.

Ferguson, R. I., 1980, Topologic Asymmetry of Drainage Networks: the L Index and Its Applications, *Jour. Geology* **88:**457-465.

Flint, J. J., 1974, Stream Gradient as a Function of Order, Magnitude, and Discharge, *Water Resources Research* **10:**969-973.

Flint, J. J., 1976, Link Slope Distribution in Channel Networks, *Water Resources Research* **12:**645-654.

Flint, J. J., 1980, Tributary Arrangements in Fluvial Systems, *Am. Jour. Sci.* **280:**26-45.

Frijters, D., 1978, Principles of Simulation of Inflorescence Development, *Annals Bot.* **42:**549-560.

Frijters, D., and A. Lindenmayer, 1976, Developmental Descriptions of Branching Patterns with Paracladial Relationships, in *Automata, Languages, Development,* A Lindenmayer and G. Rozenberg eds., North Holland Publishing Company, Amsterdam, pp. 57-73.

Hack, J. T., 1957, Studies of Longitudinal Stream Profiles in Virginia and Maryland, *U. S. Geological Survey Prof. Paper 294B,* pp. 45-97.

Harding, E. F., 1971, The Probabilities of Rooted Tree-Shapes Generated by Random Bifurcation, *Adv. Appl. Probab.* **3:**44-77.

Holland, P. G., 1969, The Maintenance of Structure and Shape in Three Mallee Eucalypts, *New Phytologist* **68:**411-421.

Hollingworth, T., and M. Berry, 1975, Network Analysis of Dendritic Fields of Pyramidal Cells in the Neocortex and Purkinje Cells in the Cerebellum of the Rat, *Royal Soc. London Philos. Trans.,* ser. B, **270:**227-264.

Horsfield, K., 1972, *Analysis and Modeling of Branching Systems,* Ph.D. thesis, University of Birmingham, England.

Horsfield, K., 1980, Are Diameter, Length and Branching Ratios Meaningful in the Lung? *Jour. Theor. Biol.* **87**:773-784.

Horsfield, K., 1981a, The Science of Branching Systems, in *Scientific Foundations of Respiratory Medicine,* J. G. Scadding, G. Cumming, and W. M. Thurlbeck, eds., Heinemann, London, pp. 45-54.

Horsfield, K., 1981b, The Structure of the Tracheobronchial Tree, in *Scientific Foundations of Respiratory Medicine,* J. G. Scadding, G. Cumming, and W. M. Thurlbeck, eds., Heinemann, London, pp. 54-77.

Howard, A. D., 1971, Simulation of Stream Networks by Headward Growth and Branching, *Geog. Analysis* **3**:29-50.

Howard, A. D., 1972, Problems of Interpretation of Simulation Models of Geologic Processes, in *Quantitative Geomorphology: Some Aspects and Applications,* M. Morisawa, ed., State University of New York, Publications in Geomorphology, Binghamton, New York, pp. 61-82.

Jarvis, R. S., 1972, New Measure of the Topologic Structure of Dendritic Drainage Networks, *Water Resources Research* **8**:1265-1271.

Jarvis, R. S., 1976, Link Length Organization and Network Scale Dependencies in the Network Diameter Model, *Water Resources Research* **12**:1215-1225.

Jarvis, R. S., 1977, Drainage Network Analysis, *Prog. Phys. Geog.* **1**:271-295.

Jarvis, R. S., and C. H. Sham, 1981, Drainage Network Structure and the Diameter-Magnitude Relation, *Water Resources Research* **17**:1019-1027.

Keill, J., 1708, *An Account of Animal Secretion, the Quantity of Blood in the Humane Body, and Muscular Motion,* George Strahan, London, 187p.

Lamé, M., 1938, Extrait d'une lettre de M. Lamé à M. Liouville sur cette question: Un polygone convexe étant donné, de combien de manières peut-on le partager en triangles au moyen de diagonales? *Jour. Math. Pures Appl.* **3**:505-507.

Leopold, L. B., 1971, Trees and Streams: The Efficiency of Branching Patterns, *Jour. Theor. Biol.* **31**:339-354.

Liao, K. H., and A. E. Scheidegger, 1969, Branching-Type Models of Flow Through Porous Media, *Internat. Assoc. Sci. Hydrology Bull.* **14**(4):137-145.

Lindenmayer, A., 1977, Paracladial Relationships in Leaves, *Dtsch. Bot. Ges. Ber.* **90**:287-301.

Lück, H. B., J. Lück, and P. Rouane, 1977, Non-linear Patterns of Complex Ramification Schemes in Higher Plants (Proposition for an Insight), *Dtsch. Bot. Ges. Ber.* **90**:277-285.

McConnell, P., and M. Berry, 1978a, Effects of Undernutrition on Purkinje Cell Dendritic Growth in the Rat, *Jour. Comp. Neurol.* **177**:159-172.

McConnell, P. and M. Berry, 1978b, The Effects of Refeeding After Neotonal Starvation on Purkinje Cell Dendritic Growth in the Rat, *Jour. Comp. Neurol.* **178**:759-772.

Melton, M. A., 1958, Geometric Properties of Mature Drainage Systems and Their Representation in an E_4 Phase Space, *Jour. Geology* **66**:35-56.

Murray, C. D., 1926, The Physiological Principle of Minimum Work. I. The Vascular System and the Cost of Blood Volume, *Nat. Acad. Sci. Proc.* **12**:207-214.

Oohata, S., and T. Shidei, 1971, Studies on the Branching Structure of Trees. I. Bifurcation of Trees in Horton's Law, *Japanese Jour. Ecol.* **21**:7-14.

Polya, G., 1937, Kombinatorische Anzahlbestimmungen für Gruppen, Graphen und Chemische Verbindungen, *Acta Math.* **68:**145-253.

Roy, A. G., and M. J. Woldenberg, 1982, A Generalization of the Optimal Models of Arterial Branching, *Bull. Math. Biol.* **44:**349-360.

Sadler, M., and M. Berry, 1983, Vertex Analysis of the Growth of Purkinje Cell Dendritic Fields of the Mouse, *Stereology,* in press.

Sadler, M., M. Berry, and D. Widdett, 1983, Morphometric Study of the Development of Purkinje Cell Dendritic Trees in the Mouse Using Vertex Analysis, *Jour. Microsc.,* in press.

Scheidegger, A. E., 1966, Stochastic Branching Processes and the Law of Stream Orders, *Water Resources Research* **2:**199-203.

Scheidegger, A. E., 1967, Random Graph Patterns of Drainage Basins, in *Hydrological Aspects of the Utilization of Water,* International Association of Scientific Hydrology, Pub. No. 76, pp. 415-425.

Scheidegger, A. E., 1968, Horton's Law of Stream Numbers, *Water Resources Research* **4:**655-658.

Shreve, R. L., 1974, Variation of Mainstream Length with Basin Area in River Networks, *Water Resources Research* **10:**1167-1177.

Shreve, R. L., 1975, The Probabilistic-Topologic Approach to Drainage-Basin Geomorphology, *Geology* **3:**527-529.

Silberger, D., 1969, Occurrence of the Integer $(2n-1)!/n!(n-1)!$ *Ann. Soc. Math. Pol., Ser. I: Commentat. Math.* **13:**93-96.

Smart, J. S., 1968, Statistical Properties of Stream Lengths, *Water Resources Research* **4:**1001-1014.

Smart, J. S., 1969, Topological Properties of Channel Networks, *Geol. Soc. America Bull.* **80:**1757-1774.

Smart, J. S., 1972, Channel Networks, *Adv. Hydroscience* **8:**305-346.

Smart, J. S., 1973, The Random Model in Fluvial Geomorphology, in *Fluvial Geomorphology,* M. Morisawa, ed., Proceedings of the Fourth Annual Geomorphology Symposium, State University of New York, Binghamton, New York, pp. 27-49.

Smart, J. S., 1976, Joint Distribution Functions for Link Lengths and Drainage Areas, in *Random Processes in Geology,* D. F. Merriam, ed., Springer-Verlag, New York, pp. 112-123.

Smart, J. S., 1978, The Analysis of Drainage Network Composition, *Earth Surf. Processes* **3:**129-170.

Smart, J. S., 1981, Link Lengths and Channel Network Topology, *Earth Surf. Processes and Landforms* **6:**77-80.

Smart, J. S., and C. Werner, 1976, Applications of the Random Model of Drainage Basin Composition, *Earth Surf. Processes* **1:**219-233.

Smit, G. J., H. B. M. Uylings, and L. Veldmaat-Wansink, 1971/72, The Branching Pattern in Dendrites of Cortical Neurons, *Acta Morphol. Neerl.-Scand.* **9:**253-274.

Steingraeber, D. A., L. J. Kascht, and D. H. Franck, 1979, Variation of Shoot Morphology and Bifurcation Ratio in Sugar Maple (*Acer Saccharum*) Saplings, *Am. Jour. Botany* **66:**441-445.

Tomari, D., 1974, Formulae for Well-Formed Formulae and Their Enumeration, *Australian Math. Soc. Jour.* **17**(2):154-162.

Tomlinson, P. B., 1978, Some Qualitative and Quantitative Aspects of New Zealand Divaricating Shrubs, *New Zealand Jour. Botany* **16:**299-309.

Van Pelt, J., and R. W. H. Verwer, 1983, The Exact Probabilities of Branching Patterns Under Terminal and Segmental Growth Hypotheses, *Bull. Math. Biol.* **45:**264-285.

Wedderburn, J. H. M., 1922, The Functional Equation, $g(x^2)=2ax+(g(x))^2$, *Ann. Math.* **24:**121-140.

Werritty, A., 1972, The Topology of Stream Networks, in *Spatial Analysis in Geomorphology,* R. J. Chorley, ed., Methuen, London, pp. 167-196.

Woldenberg, M. J., 1968, *Hierarchical Systems: Cities, Rivers, Alpine Glaciers, Bovine Livers and Trees,* Ph.D. dissertation, Columbia University, New York.

Woldenberg, M. J., 1977a, Relation of Bifurcation Ratio to Relief Ratio in Tidal Streams (Abstract), *Am. Geophys. Union Trans.* **58:**393.

Woldenberg, M. J., 1977b, Negative and Positive Relationships of Bifurcation Ratio with Increasing Relief Ratio (Abstract), *Am. Geophys. Union Trans.* **58:**1136.

Woldenberg, M. J., 1979, A Periodic Table of Spatial Hierarchies, in *Philosophy in Geography,* S. Gale and G. Olson, eds., D. Reidel, Dordrecht, Holland, pp. 429-456.

Woldenberg, M. J., G. Cumming, K. Horsfield, K. Prowse, and S. Singhal, 1970, Law and Order in the Human Lung, *Harvard Papers in Theoretical Geography Number 41,* 56p.

Young, T., 1809, The Croonian Lecture. On the Functions of the Heart and Arteries, *Royal Soc. London Philos. Trans.* **99:**1-31.

STATISTICAL LAW OF STREAM NUMBERS[1]

RONALD L. SHREVE
University of California, Los Angeles

ABSTRACT

The statistical nature and remarkable generality of Horton's law of stream numbers suggest the speculation that the law of stream numbers arises from the statistics of a large number of randomly merging stream channels in somewhat the same fashion that the law of perfect gases arises from the statistics of a large number of randomly colliding gas molecules. The fact that networks with the same number of first-order Strahler streams are comparable in topological complexity suggests equating "randomly merging stream channels" with a topologically random population of channel networks, defined as a population within which all topologically distinct networks with given number of first-order streams are equally likely. In a topologically random population the most probable networks approximately obey Horton's law but exhibit certain systematic deviations. For networks with given number of first-order streams, the most probable network order is that which makes the geometric mean bifurcation ratio closest to 4. For networks with both order and number of first-order streams specified, the most probable networks have the property that the bifurcation ratio of the second-order streams is always close to 4 and, hence, that the bifurcation ratios respectively decrease, remain unchanged, or increase with order and the corresponding curves on the Horton diagram are respectively concave upward, straight, or concave downward according as the geometric mean bifurcation ratio is less than, equal to, or greater than 4. Statistical comparison of these properties with 172 published sets of stream numbers strongly supports the conclusion that, as speculated, populations of natural channel networks developed in the absence of geologic controls are topologically random and, hence, that the law of stream numbers is indeed largely a consequence of random development of channel networks according to the laws of chance.

INTRODUCTION

In a paper now famous among students of geomorphology and hydrology Robert E. Horton in 1945 published two remarkable laws of drainage composition connecting the numbers and the lengths of the streams of different order in a river network. Horton's law of stream numbers states that "the numbers of streams of different orders in a given drainage basin tend closely to approximate an inverse geometric series in which the first term is unity and the ratio is the bifurcation ratio" (Horton, 1945, p. 291; see also 1932, p. 356). This law was chosen for investigation in the present paper because it involves only the relative arrangement of the streams in a channel network without regard to their length, shape, or orientation, and is therefore more amenable to mathematical analysis than the law of stream lengths and similar laws subsequently proposed by others (Schumm, 1956, p. 604, 606, 607; Morisawa, 1962, p. 1033–1034, 1035).

Horton's law of stream numbers is essentially a statistical relationship, inasmuch as the phrase, "tend closely to approximate an inverse geometric series," indicates both the central values and the dispersion of the stream numbers. In other words, Horton's law indicates the distribution of natural river networks among the possible sets of stream numbers, the most probable networks according to Horton being those with stream numbers close to inverse geometric series. It is thus a particular example of the general notion of a *law of stream numbers*, defined in this paper as the statistical distribution of a natural or theoretical population of channel networks among the possible sets of stream numbers determined by a specified system of stream ordering. Despite appearances, however, Horton's law is not fully quantitative, for it gives neither the exact distributions nor even the central values.

Horton (1945, p. 303) believed that his law of stream numbers is relatively insensitive to lack of isotropy and homogeneity in the bedrock, but that departures from the law "will, however, be observed, and if other

[1] Manuscript received February 8, 1965. Publication No. 274, Institute of Geophysics and Planetary Physics, University of California, Los Angeles, Calif. 90024.

conditions are normal these departures may in general be ascribed to effects of geologic controls." Since 1945 investigators working in many different areas have confirmed this insensitivity, showing that both the geometric-series form and the bifurcation ratio are characterized by considerable independence of the detailed geomorphic processes at work in any particular channel network, which in turn implies very general basic causes.

These characteristics of Horton's law suggest the speculation that in the absence of *geologic controls*, defined in this paper as systematic inhomogeneity or anisotropy in bedrock or environment, the population of natural channel networks is governed primarily by the general tendency of erosional processes to produce arborescent networks and secondarily, or perhaps not at all, by local environmental factors. This leads naturally to the further speculation that the law of stream numbers arises from the statistics of a large number of randomly merging stream channels in somewhat the same fashion that the law of perfect gases arises from the statistics of a large number of randomly colliding gas molecules.

The object in this paper is to give substance to these heuristic ideas and to explore some of their theoretical ramifications by elucidation of the mathematical properties of Horton's law and by examination of a particular definition of "randomly merging stream channels."

HORTON'S LAW OF STREAM NUMBERS

In mathematical terms Horton's law of stream numbers states that

$$H_\omega \approx h_\omega, \quad (1a)$$

where $\approx$ denotes approximate equality, H_ω is the number of Horton streams of order ω in a given drainage basin, and h_ω is the corresponding term in the geometric series defined by

$$h_\omega = R_H^{\Omega-\omega}, \quad (1b)$$

in which R_H is the Horton bifurcation ratio and Ω is the order of the basin, which is by definition equal to the order of the highest-order stream in the basin.

In the system of classifying streams according to order devised by Horton (1945, p. 281),

unbranched fingertip tributaries are always designated as of order 1, tributaries or streams of the 2d order receive branches or tributaries of the 1st order, but these only; a 3d order stream must receive one or more tributaries of the 2d order but may also receive 1st order tributaries. A 4th order stream receives branches of the 3d and usually also of lower orders, and so on.

To determine which is the parent and which the tributary stream upstream from the last bifurcation, the following rules may be used:

(1) Starting below the junction, extend the parent stream upstream from the bifurcation in the same direction. The stream joining the parent stream at the greatest angle is of the lower order. Exceptions may occur where geologic controls have affected the stream courses.

(2) If both streams are at about the same angle to the parent stream at the junction, the shorter is usually taken as of the lower order.

Some workers (Leopold and Miller, 1956, p. 16; Brush, 1961, p. 155; Leopold and Langbein, 1962, p. A15) have followed Horton's system of determining stream orders, but others (Schumm, 1956, p. 602; Melton, 1957, p. 2; Coates, 1958, p. 4; Smith, 1958, p. 999, 1003; Maxwell, 1960, p. 9; Morisawa, 1962, p. 1028), in order to avoid the necessity of subjective decisions inherent in Horton's system, have adopted a somewhat different system introduced by Strahler (1952, p. 1120 n.; see Melton, 1959, for alternative definition). In Strahler's system "the smallest, or 'finger-tip,' channels constitute the first-order segments," somewhat as in Horton's system, but a "second-order segment is formed by the junction of any two first-order streams; a third-order segment is formed by the joining of any two second-order streams, etc."

The application of these two systems to a particular stream network is illustrated in figures 1 and 2.

Stream numbers for a given network determined according to the Strahler system cannot in general be the same as those deter-

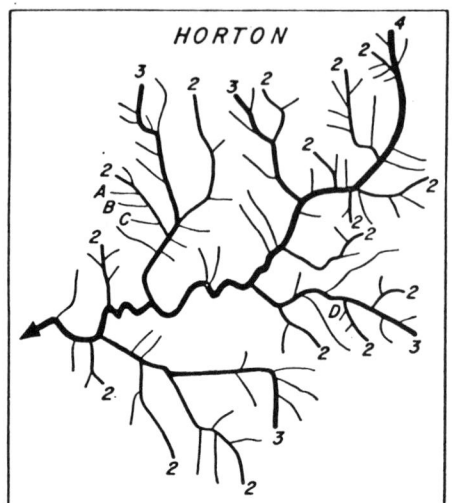 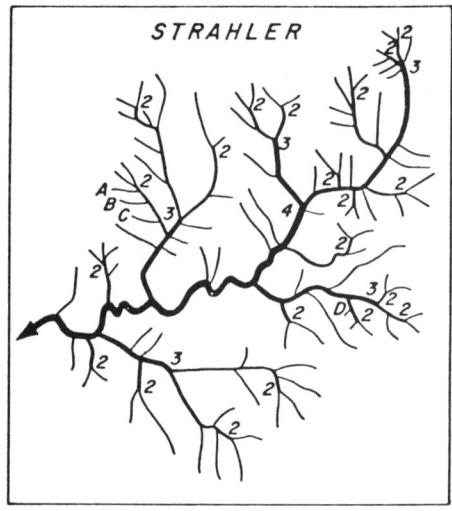

Fig. 1.—Horton and Strahler definitions of stream order applied to channel network of Hightower Creek, upper Hiwassee River, Towns County, northern Georgia (redrawn from Horton, 1945, p. 297). Order indicated by number near upstream end of respective streams. Unnumbered streams are first order. If streams A, B, C, or D were actually second order, rather than first, then network would be fifth order, rather than fourth.

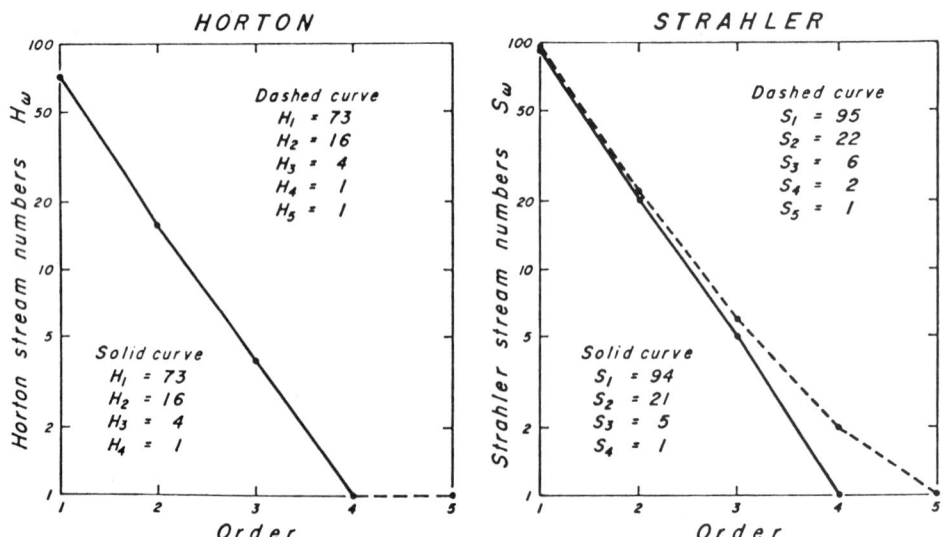

Fig. 2.—Horton diagrams for channel network of Hightower Creek as shown in fig. 1. Solid curves for network as shown. Dashed curves for fifth-order network resulting if one of streams A, B, C, or D were actually second order.

mined according to the Horton system; nevertheless, the Strahler stream numbers appear to approximate inverse geometric series (Schumm, 1956, p. 603; Smith, 1958, p. 1002; Maxwell, 1960, p. 61; Morisawa, 1962, p. 1929) differing from the Horton series only in the magnitude of the bifurcation ratios. In analogy with equation (1),

$$S_\omega \approx s_\omega, \quad (2a)$$

where S_ω is the number of Strahler streams of order ω and s_ω is the corresponding term in the geometric series defined by

$$s_\omega = R_S^{\Omega-\omega}, \quad (2b)$$

in which R_S is the Strahler bifurcation ratio. Both this relationship and Horton's original one are commonly termed *Horton's law of stream numbers*.

BASIC CONCEPTS AND METHODS

The channels and lakes, if any, upstream of an arbitrarily chosen channel cross section, termed the *outlet* of the network, collectively comprise a *channel network*, also called a *drainage network*, *stream network*, or *river network*. The points farthest upstream in a channel network are termed *sources*. The point of confluence of two channels is a *fork*. The term *link* will refer to a section of channel reaching without intervening forks from either a fork or a source at its upstream end to either a fork or the outlet at its downstream end.

Correct, or at least consistent, identification of sources and channels on maps and air photographs and in the field is of fundamental importance in the study of channel networks. The problems involved have therefore been recognized and investigated by many workers (Horton, 1945, p. 284; Leopold and Miller, 1956, p. 2–4, 16–19; Melton, 1957, p. 1, 7; Morisawa, 1957; Maxwell, 1960, p. 24–25), and will not be discussed further in this paper.

Confluences of more than two channels precisely at a single place are exceedingly rare in nature, and for the purpose of analysis are usually judiciously resolved into two or more forks. Lakes fed by multiple inlets and islands bounded by branching channels pose similar difficulties, however, that are not so easily resolved. Although Horton (1945, p. 289) evidently was not bothered by such difficulties, most workers seem to have avoided them by choosing to study networks without lakes or islands, such as those normally associated with mature topography.

The *Horton bifurcation ratio* R_H is conventionally determined from the slope $-\log R_H$ of the straight line

$$\log h_\omega = (\Omega - \omega) \log R_H \quad (3a)$$

that passes through $(\Omega, 0)$ and "best fits" the points on a *Horton diagram*, which is a plot of $\log H_\omega$ versus ω. The *Strahler bifurcation ratio* R_S, which can never be less than 2, is found in analogous fashion from a plot of $\log S_\omega$ versus ω, also called a Horton diagram. Maxwell (1960, p. 12), on the other hand, has argued that the "best" straight line should not be required to pass through $(\Omega, 0)$. As either method would lead to the same conclusions, the conventional definition will be used in this paper.

The method of least squares leads straightforwardly to the formula

$$\log R_H = \frac{6}{\Omega(\Omega-1)(2\Omega-1)} \times \sum_{\omega=1}^{\Omega-1} (\Omega - \omega) \log H_\omega \quad (3b)$$

for R_H. This equation gives the value of R_H for which the root-mean-square deviation

$$D_H = \left[\frac{1}{\Omega}\sum_{\omega=1}^{\Omega-1}(\log H_\omega - \log h_\omega)^2\right]^{1/2} \quad (3c)$$

is a minimum. Equation (3c) may be written in terms of R_H in the useful form

$$D_H = \left[\frac{1}{\Omega}\sum_{\omega=1}^{\Omega-1}(\log H_\omega)^2 - \tfrac{1}{6}(\Omega-1)(2\Omega-1)(\log R_H)^2\right]^{1/2} \quad (3d)$$

The corresponding formulas relating to the Strahler bifurcation ratio may be obtained by writing R_S, S_ω, s_ω, and D_S, respectively, for R_H, H_ω, h_ω, and D_H in (3).

The unqualified term *bifurcation ratio* or the term *bifurcation ratio of streams of order ω* will refer to B_ω as defined by the equation (see Melton, 1958, p. 44)

$$B_\omega = S_{\omega-1}/S_\omega. \quad (4a)$$

This ratio, which can never be less than 2, is the average number of Strahler streams of order $\omega - 1$ tributary to each Strahler stream of order ω, and is therefore the Strahler bifurcation ratio obtained by considering only streams of order ω and $\omega - 1$. In terms of B_ω the Strahler stream numbers are given by

$$S_\omega = B_{\omega+1} B_{\omega+2} \ldots B_\Omega,$$
$$\omega = 1, 2, \ldots, \Omega - 1, \quad S_\Omega = 1, \quad (4b)$$

where Ω is the order of the channel network. An analogous definition may be made in terms of Horton stream numbers (Horton, 1945, p. 280), but will not be used in this paper.

The *geometric mean bifurcation ratio* B, which also can never be less than 2, will be defined by the equation

$$B = (B_2 B_3 \ldots B_\Omega)^{1/(\Omega-1)} = S_1^{1/(\Omega-1)}, \quad (4c)$$

where Ω is the order of the channel network. It is equal to the Strahler bifurcation ratio which would be computed from the slope of the straight line that passes through the two end points $(1, \log S_1)$ and $(\Omega, 0)$ on a Horton diagram. The quantity B, therefore, though closely similar to the Strahler bifurcation ratio R_S, does not depend upon either Horton's law or "best fits." In a channel network obeying Horton's geometric-series law, B would be exactly equal to R_S.

Horton (1945, p. 290) believed that R_H is greater "for hilly, well-dissected drainage basins than for rolling basins," being about 3 to 4 for the former and only about 2 for the latter. Strahler has found, however, that R_S, which should be closely correlated with R_H and therefore with relief, is instead completely uncorrelated with relief (1952, p. 1136) and, further, that it "is highly stable and shows a small range of variation from region to region or environment to environment, except where powerful geologic controls dominate," its range being from 3 to 5 but its usual value being about 4 (1957, p. 914). Histograms of R_H and R_S are given for comparison in figure 3. In a different type of investigation Morisawa (1962, p. 1042, table 6) has shown, moreover, that R_S is not highly correlated with peak flow, with mean runoff, or with mean annual discharge from watersheds in the Appalachian Plateau, the correlation coefficients ranging from .10 to .26. Thus, although Horton's law of stream numbers is intimately and intricately connected with the law of stream lengths and with other geometric properties of drainage systems (Melton, 1958, p. 44–46, 53), the bifurcation ratio is largely independent of the other geomorphic and hydrologic variables and of the environment.

STREAM ORDERS AND STREAM NUMBERS

According to my interpretation the *Horton order* of a link in a stream network may be determined by means of the following four rules: (1) a set of contiguous links of order ω extending from a given fork upstream to a source is termed a *provisional Horton stream* of order ω; (2) each link originating at a source is initially considered to be a provisional Horton stream of order 1; (3), if two provisional Horton streams of the same order ω join, then the resultant link downstream has order $\omega + 1$ and that tributary stream is reclassified as order $\omega + 1$, which either (a) enters the junction in a direction more nearly parallel to the head of the resultant link, or (b), in case both enter at about the same angle, is longer, or (c) is for some other reason, such as the presence of geologic controls, considered to be the parent stream; and (4), if two provisional Horton streams of different order join, then the resultant link downstream has order equal to that of the tributary of higher order.

Recasting Strahler's definition in parallel terms, the *Strahler order* of a link in a stream network may be determined by means of the following four rules: (1) a set of contiguous links of order ω extending from a given fork upstream to a fork where two links of order $\omega - 1$ join is termed a *provisional Strahler stream* of order ω; (2) each link originating at a source is initially considered to be a provisional Strahler stream of order 1; (3), if two provisional Strahler streams of the same order ω join, then the resultant link downstream has order $\omega + 1$; and (4), if two provisional Strahler streams of different order

of higher order. The highest order stream may be either complete or incomplete, though it is often arbitrarily considered to be complete. A network whose highest order stream is complete is by extension a *complete network* (Strahler, 1952, p. 1120; Melton, 1957, p. 2; Morisawa, 1962, p. 1028–1029), and the converse.

The order of a channel network or drainage basin is defined as being the order of its highest order stream. The Strahler order of

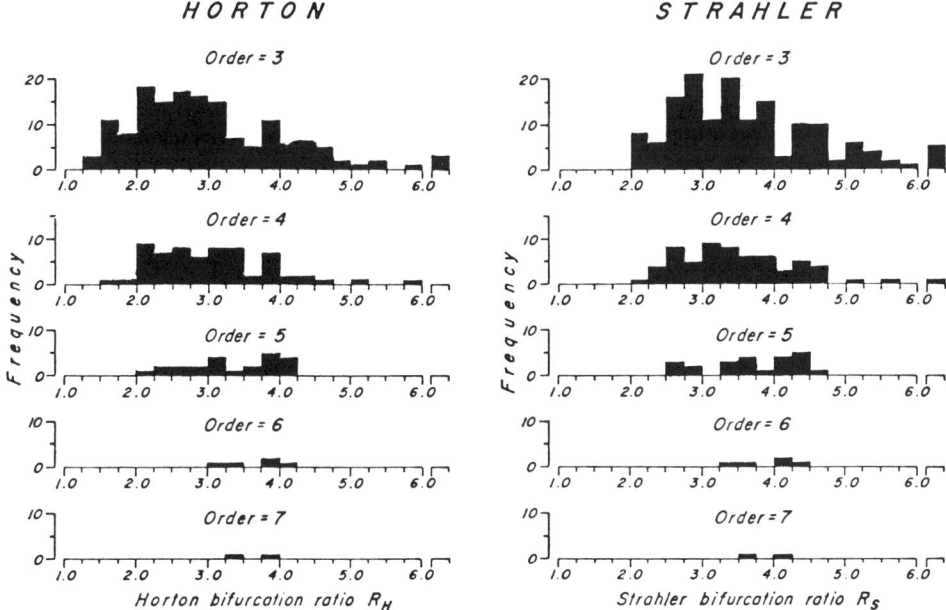

Fig. 3.—Histograms of Horton and Strahler bifurcation ratios R_H and R_S, respectively, for 246 natural networks for which usable sets of stream numbers have been published (references in table 1). Lower limit included and upper limit excluded in each interval. Ratios equal to or greater than 6.0 lumped in separate interval at right.

join, then the resultant link downstream has order equal to that of the tributary of higher order. The Strahler definition of stream order thus differs from the Horton definition only in the omission of the somewhat arbitrary reclassification in rule (3) and in the revision this necessitates in rule (1).

In both systems, after the order of all links has been determined, the qualification *provisional* is dropped, and all streams except the one of highest order are considered *complete*, because they debouch into streams

any network is fixed by the arrangement of links within the network itself. The Horton order of an incomplete network, on the other hand, depends upon the arrangement of links in the larger network of which the given network is part. If a given network is complete or arbitrarily considered to be complete, its Horton and Strahler orders will be equal.

In either system the effect of disregarding all streams of the lowest a orders is to diminish the apparent order of the remaining streams by a; thus, in such cases streams of actual order ω appear to be of order $\omega - a$. In certain cases, as illustrated in figure 1, omission or addition of a single first-order stream can change the apparent order of the entire network (Maxwell, 1960, p. 24–25).

The Strahler system of stream ordering, unlike the Horton system, is purely topological, for it refers only to the interconnections and not to the lengths, shapes, or orientations of the links comprising a network. Surprisingly, however, the "subjective decisions inherent in Horton's system" have no influence upon the resultant stream numbers. In fact, even when the criteria used are completely arbitrary, the Horton stream numbers associated with a network that is complete or arbitrarily considered to be complete are entirely unaffected by the reclassification in rule (3). This conclusion follows from the observation that every Horton stream of order ω consists of ω Strahler streams, one of each order from 1 to ω, laid end to end in sequence, and every Strahler stream is part of one and only one Horton stream, as may be seen in figure 1; hence,

$$S_\omega = \sum_{a=\omega}^{\Omega} H_a, \quad \omega = 1, 2, \ldots, \Omega, \quad (5a)$$

and, conversely,

$$H_\omega = S_\omega - S_{\omega+1},$$
$$\Omega = 1, 2, \ldots, \Omega - 1, \quad H_\Omega = 1, \quad (5b)$$

from which the assertion results directly, inasmuch as the S_ω are unambiguously defined. Equations (5) enable conversion of stream numbers from one system to the other without the lengthy classification and counting otherwise required; and they show that in any channel network which is complete or arbitrarily considered to be complete the number of first-order Strahler streams is equal to the total number of Horton streams.

COMPARISON OF THE TWO LAWS

A number of authors (Schumm, 1956, p. 603; Melton, 1957, p. 5; Smith, 1958, p. 1002; Maxwell, 1960, p. 12; Morisawa, 1962, p. 1029) have either stated or implied that the law expressed by (2) is Horton's law of stream numbers. If the two laws (1) and (2) were in fact equivalent, the series terms in (1b) and (2b) would satisfy the relations (5). Direct substitution in (5b) leads to the set of equations

$$R_H^{\Omega-\omega} = R_S^{\Omega-\omega} - R_S^{\Omega-\omega-1},$$
$$\Omega = 1, 2, \ldots, \Omega - 1, \quad (6)$$

whose only real solution is $R_H = 0$, $R_S = 1$; hence, inasmuch as R_S can never be less than 2, (1) and (2) cannot be mathematically equivalent, but are different physical laws. The system of determining stream orders must therefore be explicitly and unambiguously specified in every investigation involving Horton's law of stream numbers, a point which has not always been appreciated, as Bowden and Wallis have pointed out (1964, p. 768).

The root-mean-square deviation D_S is less than D_H in 210 of the 246 natural networks for which usable sets of stream numbers have been published (references in table 1). Although this sample is undoubtedly not strictly random, at least it consists entirely of networks selected by other authors for other purposes, and it comprises all the data given in each reference except for those few unusable cases in which, in descending order of frequency, stream numbers were given only as points on insufficiently detailed Horton diagrams, the stated total number of Horton streams disagreed with the actual sum, stream numbers from several networks were summed or averaged, or one of the ratios B_ω was less than 2.

Detailed data and references are presented in figure 4 and table 1 (logarithms to base 10 used).

If p is the probability that in a randomly chosen natural network the root-mean-square deviation D_S will be less than the root-mean-square deviation D_H, then the probability $P(n; N, p)$ that $D_S < D_H$ in exactly n of N randomly chosen networks is

$$P(n; N, p) = \binom{N}{n} p^n (1-p)^{N-n}. \quad (7)$$

Hence, on the undoubtedly shaky assumption that the present sample of 246 networks is random, the maximum-likelihood estimate of p (Mood, 1950, p. 152–161) is $p_m = 210/246 = 0.855$, and the 0.95 confidence interval for p (Mood, 1950, p. 233–237) is $0.811 < p < 0.899$. More detailed results are presented in table 1. In the cases where N was 2, 5, 23, and 64, respectively, the exact equations (Mood, 1950, p. 234) and *Tables of the Cumulative Binomial Probability Distribution* (Harvard University, Staff of the Computation Laboratory, 1955)

SYSTEMATIC DEVIATIONS

Both Schumm (1956, p. 603) and Maxwell (1960, p. 12) have called attention to the fact that many of their curves of log S_ω versus ω are distinctly concave upward. An example based on stream numbers given by Morisawa (1962, p. 1036) is shown in figure 5. This concavity suggests replacing (2) by

$$S_\omega \approx c_\omega, \quad (8a)$$

$$\log c_\omega = [(\Omega - \omega)/(\Omega - 1)] \times [1 - a(\omega-1)] \log S_1, \quad (8b)$$

TABLE 1

ANALYSIS OF PUBLISHED STREAM NUMBERS*

	Order					
	All	3	4	5	6	7
Networks.........	246	152	64	23	5	2
$D_S < D_H$	210	125	58	20	5	2
$D_C < D_S$	241	152	62	20	5	2
$D_C < D_H$	244	151	63	23	5	2
Mean D_H	0.140	0.129	0.162	0.150	0.115	0.184
Mean D_S	0.068	0.061	0.082	0.080	0.056	0.106
Mean D_C	0.013	0.000	0.026	0.044	0.040	0.099
Estimate p_m.....	0.855	0.823	0.907	0.870	1.000	1.000
Confidence interval for p..........	0.811–0.899	0.763–0.883	0.827–0.966	0.720–0.973	0.478–1.000	0.158–1.000
Confidence........	0.95	0.95	0.95	0.95	0.95	0.95
Mean a..........	0.128	0.160	0.095	0.042	0.013	0.010
Median a........	0.110	0.143	0.110	0.054	0.015	0.010
Confidence interval for a..........	0.084–0.139	0.139–0.224	0.075–0.127	0.001–0.073	0.012–0.039	0.010–0.011
Confidence........	0.95	0.95	0.97	0.96	0.97	0.50

* Data from Horton (1945, p. 287–288, 290, 297, 302, 306), Leopold and Miller (1956, p. 17), Schumm (1956, p. 606), Melton (1957, table 2, facing p. 88), Coates (1958, p. 51, 53), Smith (1958, p. 1003), Maxwell (1960, p. 71–83), and Morisawa (1962, p. 1036–1037).

were used. In the cases where N was 152 and 246, respectively, the normal approximation (Mood, 1950, p. 236) was used. Except for networks of order 6 and 7, for which insufficient data are available, these results indicate that the Strahler stream numbers for the population sampled generally approximate inverse geometric series more closely than do the corresponding Horton stream numbers.

where the parameter a, like the bifurcation ratio, is adjusted to give the "best fit" to a plot of Strahler stream numbers on a Horton diagram. Equation (8b) represents a parabolic curve that passes through $(1, \log S_1)$ and $(\Omega, 0)$ on the Horton diagram and is concave upward, straight, or concave downward when a is positive, zero, or negative, respectively. Thus, inasmuch as a will generally be greater for Horton stream numbers than for Strahler stream numbers, it is a suitable measure for investigation of the concavity noted by Schumm and Maxwell.

The method of least squares leads to the formula

$$a = \frac{5}{(\Omega^2 - 2\Omega + 2)}$$
$$\times \left[\frac{\Omega - 1}{2} - \frac{6}{\Omega(\Omega - 2) \log S_1} \right. \quad (9a)$$
$$\left. \times \sum_{\omega=2}^{\Omega-1} (\Omega - \omega)(\omega - 1) \log S_\omega \right]$$

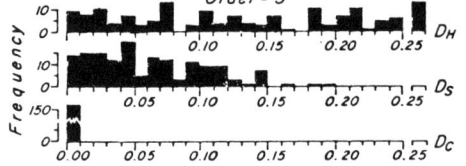

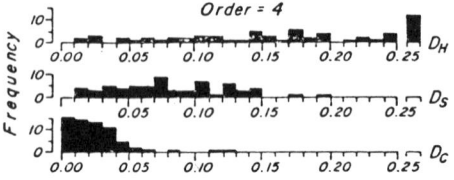

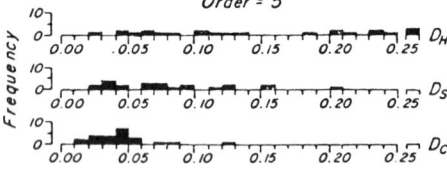

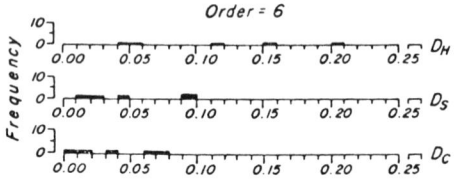

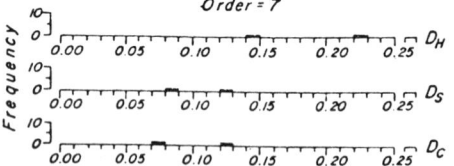

FIG. 4.—Histograms of root-mean-square deviations D_H, D_S, and D_C. Lower limit included and upper limit excluded in each interval. Deviations equal to or greater than 0.25 lumped in separate interval at right.

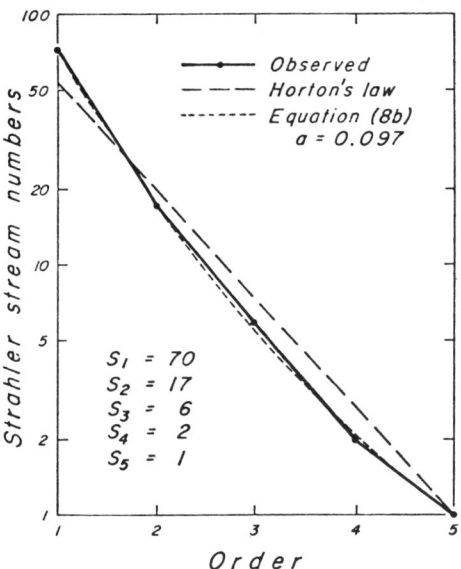

FIG. 5.—Horton diagram for Home Creek, 3 km. (2 mi.) east of New Philadelphia, Tuscarawas County, eastern Ohio (data from Morisawa, 1962, p. 1036), showing Horton's law (long dashes) and law (8b) (short dashes).

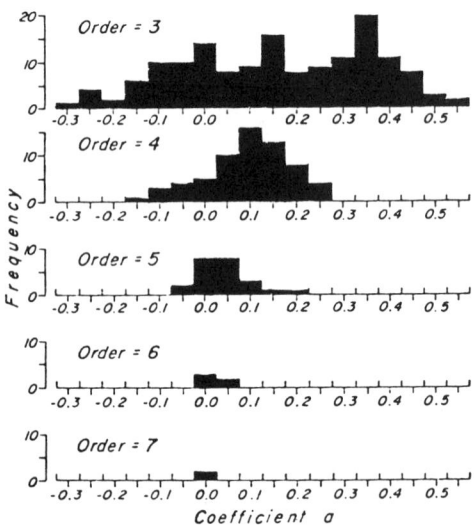

FIG. 6.—Histograms of parameter a in law (8b). Lower limit included and upper limit excluded in each interval. Positive a corresponds to Horton diagrams that are concave upward, and the converse.

for the value of a giving the "best fit" in the sense that the root-mean-square deviation D_c is a minimum. The formula for D_c analogous to (3d) is

$$D_c = \left[\frac{1}{\Omega}\sum_{\omega=2}^{\Omega-1}(\log S_\omega)^2 \right.$$
$$- \frac{2\log S_1}{\Omega(\Omega-1)}\sum_{\omega=2}^{\Omega-1}(\Omega-\omega)\log S_\omega \quad (9\mathrm{b})$$
$$+ \frac{(\Omega-2)(\log S_1)^2}{30\Omega(\Omega-1)}\{5(2\Omega-3)$$
$$\left. - a^2\Omega(\Omega^2 - 2\Omega + 2)\}\right]^{1/2},$$

which is easy to evaluate because the two sums are byproducts of the computation of R_S and D_S. Results of numerical computations for the 246 networks previously analyzed are presented in table 1 and figures 4 and 6. The multimodal character of the histogram for third-order networks in figure 6 is due to the fact that for small networks the permissible values of a are more widely spaced than the class intervals.

Except for the data of Horton (1945) the sample mean values of a summarized in table 1 are consistently positive, showing that the curves for the 246 networks analyzed do indeed tend to be slightly concave upward. Unfortunately, an estimate and confidence interval for the population mean cannot be given because the distribution of a is unknown. An estimate and confidence interval for the population median, however, can be obtained by distribution-free methods (Mood, 1950, p. 387–390). The population median a as estimated by the sample median for the 246 networks is 0.110, and the 0.95 confidence interval for a is $0.084 < a < 0.139$, again assuming a random sample. As before, the exact equations (Mood, 1950, p. 388–389) were used when N was 2, 5, 23, and 64, whereas the normal approximation (Mood, 1950, p. 389) was used when N was 152 and 246. Both the mean and median values of a decrease monotonically with increasing network order, thereby tending to substantiate the speculation to this effect originally made by Smith (1958, p. 1002) on the basis of only five networks. Evidently the law of stream numbers for natural channel networks is not quite the simple relationship proposed by Horton.

"RANDOMLY MERGING STREAM CHANNELS"

Perhaps the most natural and certainly the most direct realization of "randomly merging stream channels" for theoretical purposes is achieved by graphical construction according to rules whose action is governed by chance events such as the drawing of shuffled cards or random numbers, the particular rules and probabilities used implicitly defining the theoretical population generated. A fine example of a network produced by this method has been published by Leopold and Langbein (1962, p. A18; reproduced by Leopold, Wolman, and Miller, 1964, p. 418), although unfortunately the authors omitted the rules for avoiding or eliminating closed loops and dead-end spirals. A slight modification of their method has already been partially automated on a small-scale digital computer by Schenck (1963).

The graphical method has a number of advantages in addition to being natural and direct: it is relatively nonabstract and nonmathematical; it involves the same methods of sampling and analysis as natural networks; and, perhaps most important, by simple manipulation of pattern and probabilities, it is capable of simulating the effects of geologic controls, the evolution of channel networks, and possibly even the results of environmental variations. On the other hand, it has several major disadvantages: it requires rather highly simplified basic stream patterns in order to be practical; it inherently involves Monte Carlo methods which not only make difficult the control of parameters, such as the number of first-order streams or the order of the network, but also, as will be shown, entail almost astronomical numbers of trials because of the vast number of possible cases even for relatively small networks; and, finally, it does not directly provide the quantities of interest, such as stream order and number, which must be obtained by the same laborious methods that are applied to natural networks.

Because of these latter characteristics the graphical method is impractical for computing the probability of occurrence of a network with a given set of stream numbers or other arbitrarily specified parameters; hence, it is unsuited for detailed investigation of the law of stream numbers for the theoretical population of networks implicitly defined by its rules and probabilities. Moreover, it unavoidably encompasses network properties that are not explicitly involved in the Strahler system of stream ordering, which is purely topological, or in the law of stream numbers, which is entirely enumerative. This paper therefore adopts an alternative definition of "randomly merging stream channels," which involves only network topology and simple enumeration.

For simplicity and convenience in the remainder of this paper the Strahler system of stream ordering will be used exclusively.

TOPOLOGICALLY RANDOM POPULATION

In any network such as the usual channel network associated with mature topography in which one and only one path exists between any two points and in which every link either joins at each end to two other links or connects at one end to two other links and terminates at the opposite end in a source or, in one case, the outlet, the number of links l and the number of forks f are related to the number of sources n by the equations

$$l = 2n - 1, \quad (10a)$$

and

$$f = n - 1, \quad (10b)$$

which follow by induction from the facts that networks with only one source have only one link and no forks and that addition of a source to any network increases the number of links by two and the number of forks by one. These relationships were first explicitly stated by Melton (1959, p. 345), although they result directly from two general topological theorems respectively deduced in the famous paper on the Königsberg bridges by Euler (1741) and in a little-known work on topology by Listing (1847; also 1862; see Cayley, 1873, for English summary, reprinted in 1895, p. 540-547). The conditions stated at the beginning of this paragraph, which in practice are not particularly restrictive, define the idealized concept of channel network assumed in the remainder of this paper.

Equations (10) and (5) show that channel networks with equal numbers of links have equal numbers of forks, sources, Horton streams, and first-order Strahler streams; and are therefore comparable in topological complexity, as illustrated in figure 7. This suggests equating "randomly merging stream channels" with a *topologically random* population of channel networks, defined as a population within which all topologically distinct networks with given number of links are equally likely. *Topologically distinct* networks, illustrated in figure 7, in contradistinction to *topologically identical* networks, illustrated in figure 8, are those whose schematic map projections cannot be continuously deformed and rotated in the plane of projection so as to become congruent.

The fundamental geomorphological hypothesis that emerges from these strictly heuristic and somewhat abstract considerations is that in the absence of geologic controls a natural population of channel networks will be topologically random. Though intuitively attractive this hypothesis is by no means self-evident, for the possibility exists that certain of the possible topologically distinct networks might be statistically promoted or inhibited, not by gross geologic controls, but by the subtle interaction of the links in networks, or as Playfair put it (1802, p. 102) the "nice adjustment," mediated by the interdependence of slope and channel processes. Justification of the hypothesis therefore ultimately rests upon comparison with natural networks, which for lack of other data means statistical analysis of published sets of stream numbers, hence the emphasis in this paper.

Far more than this, however, is latent in the definition of topologically random channel networks. It can predict, without any adjustable parameters, not only the law of stream numbers as shown in this paper but also such quantities as the probability that a link chosen at random will drain a basin having a given order or a given number of links. Thus, it can supply both the basic distributions and the sampling requirements for meaningful statistical analysis of any of the enumerative properties of natural networks; it provides a mathematically simple and well-defined model for the deeper elucidation of the topological properties of natural networks; and, perhaps most important, it constitutes the necessary starting point for derivation of the non-enumerative properties of drainage basins, such as the law of stream lengths.

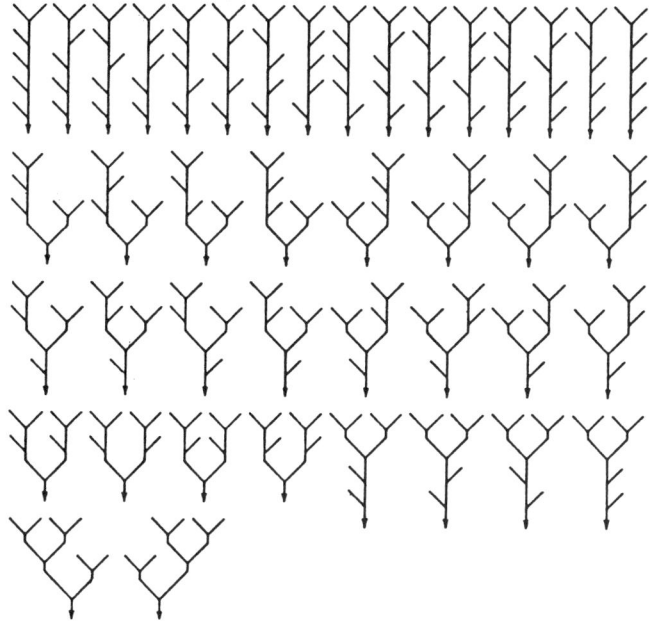

FIG. 7.—Schematic diagrams of the $N(6) = 42$ topologically distinct channel networks with $l = 11$ links and $n = 6$ first-order Strahler streams or six Horton streams. In a topologically random population these networks would all be equally likely. Top row shows the possible second-order networks, for which $\Omega = 2$, $B = 6.00$, $N(6;2) = 16$, $p(6;2) = 16/42 = 0.381$, $N[6,1] = 16$, and $p[6,1] = 16/16 = 1.000$. Bottom four rows show the possible third-order networks, for which $\Omega = 3$, $B = 2.45$, $N(6;3) = 26$, $p(6;3) = 26/42 = 0.619$, $N[6,2,1] = 24$, $p[6,2,1] = 24/26 = 0.923$ (first three of the four rows), $N[6,3,1] = 2$, and $p[6,3,1] = 2/26 = 0.077$ (last row). Arrowhead indicates outlet in each diagram.

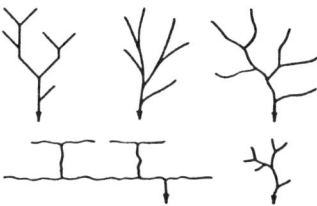

FIG. 8.—Topologically identical channel networks. Arrowhead indicates outlet. Note that network topology, stream pattern, and drainage density, though perhaps physically connected, are mathematically distinct concepts.

COMBINATORIAL PROPERTIES

The number of topologically distinct channel networks having n sources, denoted by $N(n)$, may be computed from the recursion formula

$$N(n) = \sum_{i=1}^{n-1} N(i) N(n-i),$$
$$N(1) = 1, \quad n = 2, 3, \ldots .$$
(11)

The general term in the sum is the number of topologically distinct networks with n

sources formed by combination of the $N(i)$ distinct networks having i sources with the $N(n-i)$ distinct networks having $n-i$ sources in all possible pairs. The result follows by summation over all permissible values of i.

Similarly, the number of topologically distinct channel networks of order Ω having n sources, denoted by $N(n; \Omega)$, may be computed from the recursion formula

$$N(n; \Omega) = \sum_{i=1}^{n-1} \Big[N(i; \Omega-1) \\ \times N(n-i; \Omega-1) + 2N(i; \Omega) \\ \times \sum_{\omega=1}^{\Omega-1} N(n-i; \omega) \Big], \quad (12)$$

$$N(1;1) = 1, \quad N(n;1) = 0,$$
$$N(1;\Omega) = 0, \quad n = 2, 3, \ldots,$$
$$\Omega = 2, 3, \ldots.$$

The first product in the general term of the sum on i accounts for the creation of networks of order Ω by combination of two of order $\Omega-1$; and the second accounts for the combination of networks of order Ω with those of lower order.

The problem of finding a simple closed expression for $N(n)$ was first solved by Cayley (1859; reprinted in 1891, p. 112–115), whose solution, after slight manipulation and conversion of notation, is

$$N(n) = \frac{1}{l}\Big[\frac{l(l-1)\ldots(l-n+1)}{n(n-1)\ldots 1}\Big] \\ = \frac{1}{l}\binom{l}{n}, \quad (13)$$

in which $l = 2n - 1$ as before.

The number of topologically distinct channel networks of order Ω having $n_1, n_2, \ldots, n_{\Omega-1}, 1$ streams of order $1, 2, \ldots, \Omega-1, \Omega$, respectively, denoted by $N[n_1, n_2, \ldots, n_{\Omega-1}, 1]$, is given by the formula

$$N[n_1, n_2, \ldots, n_{\Omega-1}, 1] \\ = \prod_{\omega=1}^{\Omega-1} 2^{(n_\omega - 2n_{\omega+1})} \binom{n_\omega - 2}{n_\omega - 2n_{\omega+1}}. \quad (14)$$

The general term of the product is the number of topologically distinct ways that the n_ω streams of order ω may be arranged as tributaries to the streams of higher order in the network. Of these n_ω streams $2n_{\omega+1}$ must join in pairs to form the $n_{\omega+1}$ streams of order $\omega+1$, leaving $r_\omega = n_\omega - 2n_{\omega+1}$ remaining streams of order ω tributary to the $l_{\omega+1} = 2n_{\omega+1} - 1$ links of order $\omega+1$ or higher present before the lower-order streams are added to the network. The binomial coefficient in (14) is the number of distinct ways that the r_ω streams may be divided among the $l_{\omega+1}$ links (Riordan, 1958, p. 6–7). The factor 2^{r_ω} is the number of distinct patterns in which the remaining streams may join these links, inasmuch as each must enter from either the right or the left. The general term in (14) is independent of the arrangement of the higher-order links; hence, the number $N[n_1, n_2, \ldots, n_{\Omega-1}, 1]$ is simply the product of the individual terms for all orders from $\Omega-1$ down to 1.

The set of stream numbers $[n_1, n_2, \ldots, n_{\Omega-1}, 1]$ is subject to the restriction, implied by the definition of stream order, that every network must contain at least two streams of order $\omega-1$ for each stream of order ω, for $\omega = 2, 3, \ldots$. This is equivalent to the restriction

$$r_\omega = 0, 1, \ldots. \quad (15a)$$

When $n = n_1$ is given, the r_ω must satisfy the equation

$$r_1 + 2r_2 + \ldots + 2^{\Omega-2} r_{\Omega-1} \\ = n - 2^{\Omega-1}. \quad (15b)$$

A unique set $[r_1, r_2, \ldots, r_{\Omega-1}]$ exists for each set $[n_1, n_2, \ldots, n_{\Omega-1}, 1]$, and the converse; therefore, the number of different sets of stream numbers with n and Ω given is the same as the number of solutions in integers of (15b) subject to the restriction (15a), which in turn is the number $D(n; \Omega)$ of partitions of $n - 2^{\Omega-1}$ into parts $1, 2, \ldots, 2^{\Omega-2}$, each of which may appear zero, one, or more times. Riordan (1958, p. 117–123) has discussed various methods of calculating this number, the simplest of which leads to the useful recursion formula

$$D(n;\Omega) = D(n - 2^{\Omega-2};\Omega - 1)$$
$$+ D(n - 2^{\Omega-2};\Omega),$$
$$n = 2^{\Omega-1}, 2^{\Omega-1} + 1, \ldots,$$
$$D(n;\Omega) = 0, \quad (16)$$
$$n = 1, 2, \ldots, 2^{\Omega-1} - 1,$$
$$\Omega = 2, 3, \ldots,$$
$$D(1;1) = 1, D(n;1) = 0,$$
$$n = 2, 3, \ldots.$$

Horton's law, as shown in figure 9. In other words, inherent in the definition of stream order is the corollary that no channel network, indeed no arborescent network of any kind, can depart indefinitely far from Horton's geometric-series law.

LAW OF STREAM NUMBERS

The law of stream numbers for topologically random channel networks is readily found from the combinatorial properties just derived. The procedure is to divide the num-

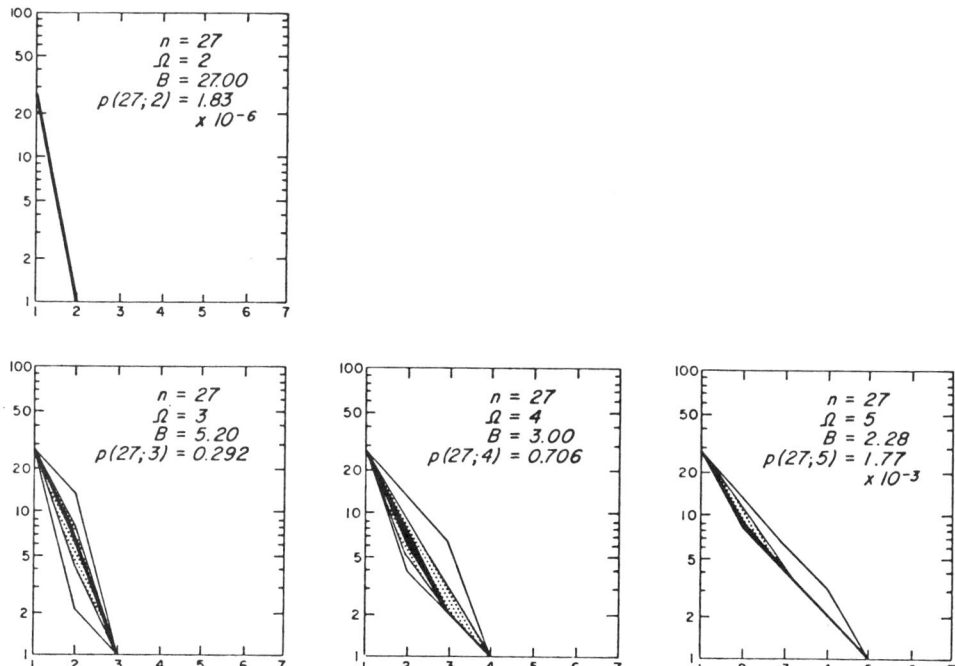

FIG. 9.—Statistics of population of topologically random channel networks with 27 first-order streams. Vertical coordinate is Strahler stream number (logarithmic scale); horizontal coordinate is stream order. Black area contains most probable 50 per cent of networks. Black and dotted areas together contain most probable 95 per cent of networks. Outer parallelogram contains all possible networks.

The fact that for every stream of given order, except the first, there must be at least two streams of the next lower order means that on a Horton diagram the points for any channel network with given order and given number of first-order streams will necessarily lie within a relatively restricted parallelogram-shaped region whose long diagonal is the locus of points which exactly satisfy

ber of topologically distinct networks $N[n_1, n_2, \ldots, n_{\Omega-1}, 1]$ given by (14) corresponding to each possible set of stream numbers by the total number $N(n;\Omega)$ given by (12) or by summation in order to obtain for specified n and Ω the normalized, or probability, distribution $p[n_1, n_2, \ldots, n_{\Omega-1}, 1]$ of the population of topologically random networks among the sets of stream numbers.

A flow diagram of this procedure, with main emphasis on the algorithm for systematically and exhaustively generating the sets of stream numbers, is given in figure 10. The distribution $p(n; \Omega)$ of the population of networks with specified n among the possible orders is found by dividing the number $N(n; \Omega)$ by the total number $N(n)$ given by (13) or by (11).

The computation was programmed in FORTRAN and executed on an IBM 7094 digital computer. Storage requirements were determined by means of (16). Do-it-yourself floating-point routines were required, because the large numbers involved (up to 10^{56}) exceeded the built-in capacity of the machine (only up to 10^{38}). The program is limited by size of memory to computations with n less than about 100.

Values of $N(n)$, $p(n; \Omega)$, and $D(n; \Omega)$ for various values of n and Ω and of $p[n_1, n_2, \ldots, n_{\Omega-1}, 1]$ for the various values of Ω when $n = 27$ are given in tables 2, 3, and 4.

The computations, whose results are displayed graphically in figures 9, 11, and 12, show that in a topologically random population of channel networks the most probable networks approximately obey Horton's geometric-series law, as speculated, but exhibit certain systematic deviations. For networks with given number n of first-order streams the most probable network order Ω is that which makes the geometric mean bifurcation ratio $B = n^{1/(\Omega-1)}$ closest to 4. For networks with both n and Ω given the most probable networks have the property that the bifurcation ratio of the second-order streams B_2 is always close to 4 and, hence, that the bifurcation ratios respectively decrease, remain unchanged, or increase with order and the corresponding curves on the Horton diagram are respectively concave upward, straight, or concave downward according as the geometric mean bifurcation ratio is less than, equal to, or greater than 4.

Comparison of these results with several typical natural networks is highly encouraging, as illustrated in figures 13 and 14.

STATISTICAL COMPARISON

The null hypothesis to be tested is that a random sample of sets of stream numbers from natural networks not subject to systematic inhomogeneity or anisotropy in bedrock or environment could have been drawn from a topologically random population. An appropriate statistical test for this hypothesis is the goodness-of-fit test described by Mood (1950, p. 270–271), inasmuch as the foregoing theoretical analysis provides the necessary expected frequencies.

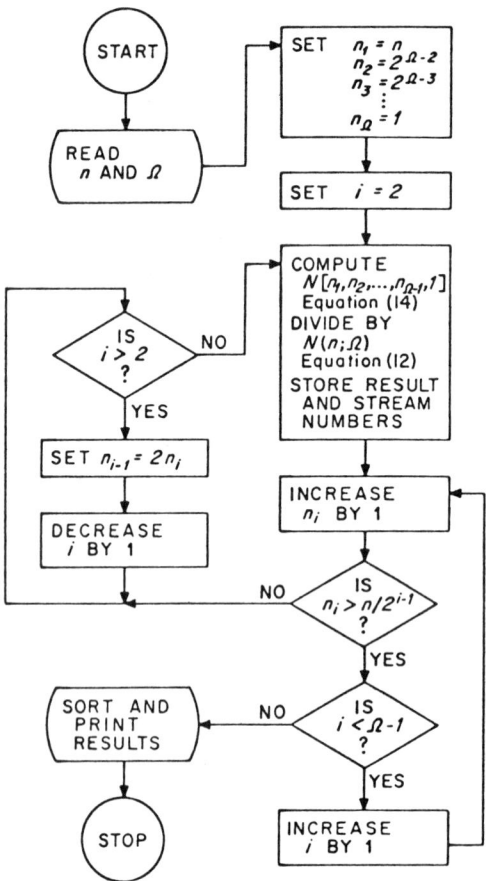

FIG. 10.—Flow diagram of procedure for computing law of stream numbers for population of topologically random channel networks with given number of first-order streams n and given order Ω. Main emphasis is on algorithm for systematically and exhaustively generating the sets of stream numbers.

The data available for analysis consist of 172 published sets of stream numbers selected from the 246 sets previously analyzed (references in table 1). All 152 third-order sets were admitted on the assumption that by virtue of their generally small size their basins would be relatively free of geologic controls. Only 18 fourth-order and 2 fifth-order sets were retained, the rest being rejected because of geologic controls, inadequate descriptions, or too large n. Because these 172 sets of stream numbers are in many cases from basins selected on the basis of size or, more frequently, order, they do not collectively constitute a random sample, but must be subdivided into separate samples corresponding to the various combinations of n and Ω. Whether these separate samples actually are random, as necessarily assumed in the following analysis, cannot be determined with certainty, because most authors vouchsafe few, if any, details about their method of selecting basins for investigation.

Unfortunately, nearly all of these samples are too small for meaningful statistical analysis, the majority consisting of just one set of stream numbers and only four, all third-order, containing 10 or more sets of stream numbers. Analysis of these four samples by means of the goodness-of-fit test indicates that, as hoped, they could have been drawn

TABLE 2

TOPOLOGICALLY DISTINCT NETWORKS

n	$N(n)$	$p(n;\Omega)$					
		$\Omega=2$	$\Omega=3$	$\Omega=4$	$\Omega=5$	$\Omega=6$	$\Omega=7$
6	42	0.381	0.619				
16	9.695×10^6	$.169 \times 10^{-2}$	.753	0.245	0.103×10^{-6}		
25	1.290×10^{12}	$.650 \times 10^{-5}$	.357	.642	$.772 \times 10^{-3}$		
27	1.837×10^{13}	$.183 \times 10^{-5}$	.292	.706	$.177 \times 10^{-2}$		
50	5.096×10^{26}	$.552 \times 10^{-12}$	$.194 \times 10^{-1}$	.874	.106	0.243×10^{-7}	
64	9.430×10^{34}	$.489 \times 10^{-16}$	$.307 \times 10^{-2}$	.743	.254	$.382 \times 10^{-5}$	0.106×10^{-3}
75	3.115×10^{41}	$.303 \times 10^{-19}$	$.683 \times 10^{-3}$	.617	.382	$.437 \times 10^{-4}$	$.347 \times 10^{-2}$
100	2.275×10^{56}	0.139×10^{-26}	0.201×10^{-4}	0.361	0.638	0.122×10^{-2}	0.115×10^{-1}
200	1.29×10^{116}						
500	1.35×10^{296}						
1000	5.12×10^{596}						

TABLE 3

SETS OF STREAM NUMBERS

n	$D(n;\Omega)$							
	$\Omega=3$	$\Omega=4$	$\Omega=5$	$\Omega=6$	$\Omega=7$	$\Omega=8$	$\Omega=9$	$\Omega=10$
6	2							
16	7	9	1					
25	11	25	10					
27	12	30	14					
50	24	132	190	46				
64	31	225	455	201	1			
75	36	306	744	436	14			
100	49	576	2024	1980	284			
200	99	2401	18424	46420	32694	2790		
500	249	15376	3.101×10^5	2.231×10^6	5.680×10^6	4.388×10^6	5.436×10^6	
1000	499	62001	2.542×10^6	3.814×10^7	2.159×10^8	4.419×10^8	2.693×10^8	2.287×10^7

TABLE 4
Topologically Distinct Networks with 27 First-Order Streams

n_1	n_2	n_3	n_4	n_5	$p[\ldots]$	Sum	n_1	n_2	n_3	n_4	n_5	$p[\ldots]$	Sum
27	1	....	....	....	1.000	1.000	27	11	3	1	....	0.106×10^{-2}	0.999
							27	11	2	1	....	$.604 \times 10^{-3}$	1.000
27	6	1	....	....	0.319	0.319	27	11	4	1	....	$.353 \times 10^{-3}$	......
27	7	1	....	....	.254	.573	27	12	3	1	....	$.382 \times 10^{-4}$	......
27	5	1	....	....	.211	.784	27	10	5	1	....	$.380 \times 10^{-4}$	......
27	8	1	....	....	.109	.892	27	12	4	1	....	$.191 \times 10^{-4}$	......
27	4	1	....	....	$.691 \times 10^{-1}$	.962	27	11	5	1	....	$.189 \times 10^{-4}$	......
27	9	1	....	....	$.249 \times 10^{-1}$	.987	27	12	2	1	....	$.164 \times 10^{-4}$	......
27	3	1	....	....	$.988 \times 10^{-2}$	.996	27	12	5	1	....	$.204 \times 10^{-5}$	......
27	10	1	....	....	$.293 \times 10^{-2}$	0.999	27	13	3	1	....	$.326 \times 10^{-6}$	......
27	2	1	....	....	$.468 \times 10^{-3}$	1.000	27	13	4	1	....	$.228 \times 10^{-6}$	......
27	11	1	....	....	$.162 \times 10^{-3}$	......	27	13	2	1	....	$.109 \times 10^{-6}$	......
27	12	1	....	....	$.351 \times 10^{-5}$	......	27	13	5	1	....	$.407 \times 10^{-7}$	......
27	13	1	....	....	0.191×10^{-7}	......	27	12	6	1	....	$.227 \times 10^{-7}$	......
							27	13	6	1	....	0.136×10^{-8}	......
27	7	2	1	....	0.263	0.263							
27	6	2	1	....	.198	.461	27	9	4	2	1	0.451	0.451
27	8	2	1	....	.169	.630	27	8	4	2	1	.281	.733
27	8	3	1	....	$.845 \times 10^{-1}$	.715	27	10	4	2	1	.212	.945
27	7	3	1	....	$.657 \times 10^{-1}$	.780	27	11	4	2	1	$.352 \times 10^{-1}$	.980
27	5	2	1	....	$.656 \times 10^{-1}$	.846	27	10	5	2	1	$.114 \times 10^{-1}$	.992
27	9	2	1	....	$.542 \times 10^{-1}$	.900	27	11	5	2	1	$.566 \times 10^{-2}$	.997
27	9	3	1	....	$.452 \times 10^{-1}$	.946	27	12	4	2	1	$.191 \times 10^{-2}$	0.999
27	6	3	1	....	$.165 \times 10^{-1}$	.962	27	12	5	2	1	$.612 \times 10^{-3}$	1.000
27	10	3	1	....	$.106 \times 10^{-1}$	.973	27	13	4	2	1	$.228 \times 10^{-4}$	......
27	10	2	1	....	$.851 \times 10^{-2}$	.981	27	12	6	2	1	$.136 \times 10^{-4}$	......
27	4	2	1	....	$.716 \times 10^{-2}$	.988	27	13	5	2	1	$.122 \times 10^{-4}$	......
27	9	4	1	....	$.452 \times 10^{-2}$	.993	27	12	6	3	1	$.113 \times 10^{-5}$	......
27	8	4	1	....	$.282 \times 10^{-2}$	.996	27	13	6	2	1	$.814 \times 10^{-6}$	......
27	10	4	1	....	0.213×10^{-2}	0.998	27	13	6	3	1	0.678×10^{-7}	......

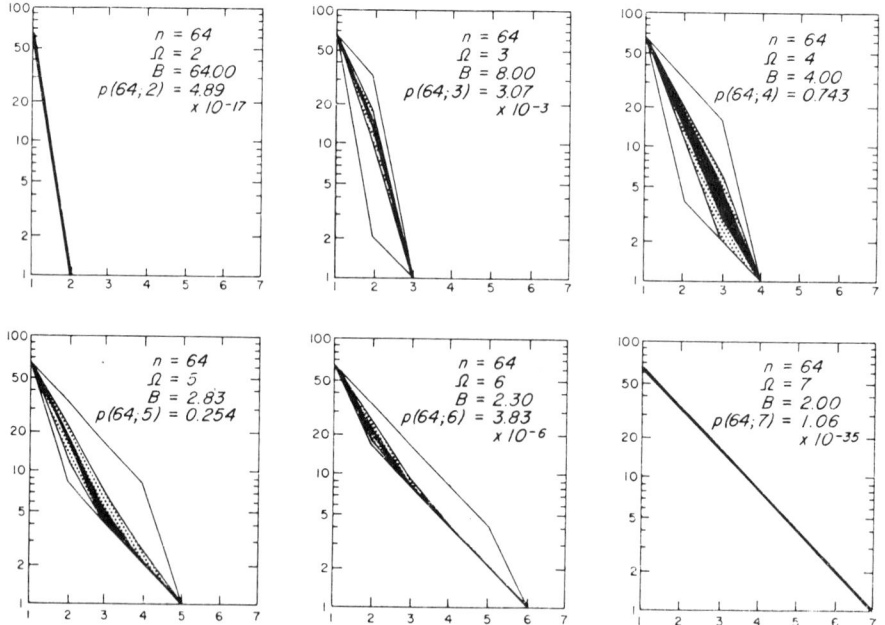

Fig. 11.—Statistics of population of topologically random channel networks with 64 first-order streams. Coordinates and symbols same as in fig. 9.

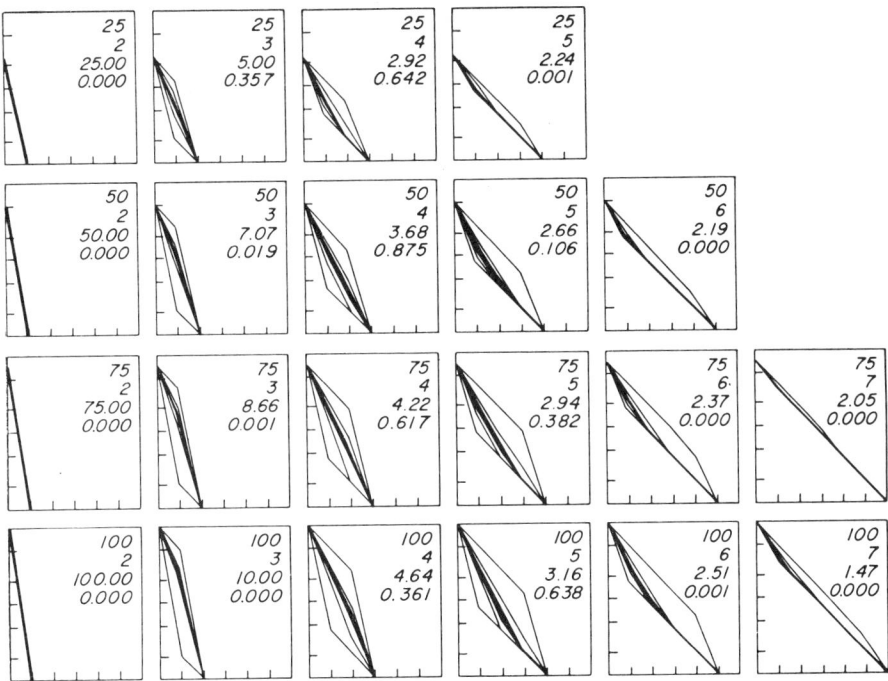

Fig. 12.—Statistics of four populations of topologically random channel networks with 25, 50, 75, and 100 first-order streams, respectively, for comparison. Coordinates and symbols same as in fig. 9, except dotted pattern omitted. The four numbers in each diagram are, from top to bottom, n, Ω, B, and $p(n;\Omega)$.

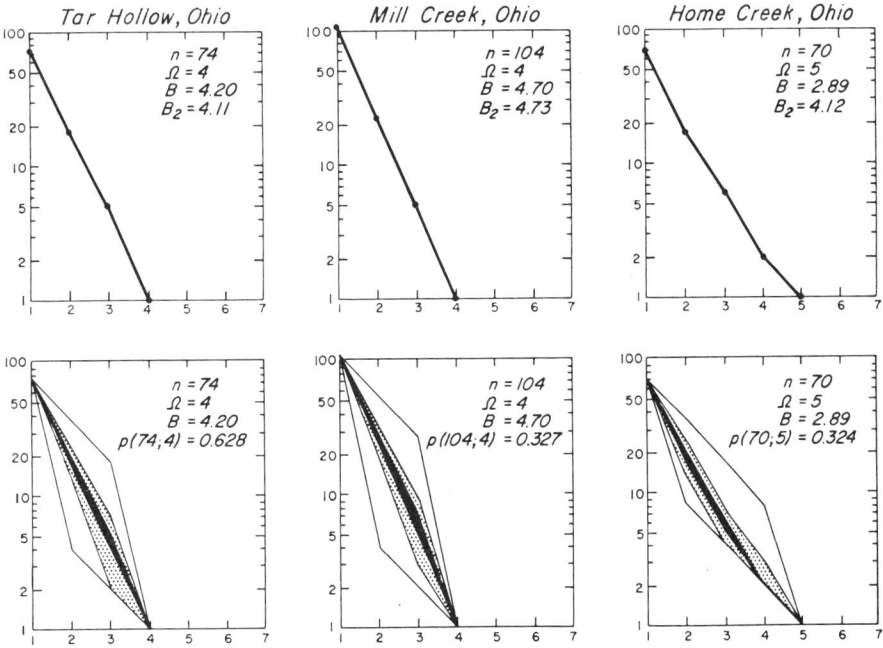

Fig. 13.—Three natural channel networks with similar and relatively homogeneous and isotropic bedrock and environment compared with corresponding topologically random populations (data from Morisawa, 1962, p. 1036).

from a topologically random population, for in none of the four cases was the null hypothesis rejected at the .05 significance level. Details and references are given in tables 5 and 1, respectively. In each case the χ^2 approximation was used (Mood, 1950, p. 259, 271, 424), and the effect of sampling without replacement was assumed negligible.

In a somewhat less straightforward approach designed to utilize all of the available data, the topologically random population was divided into four equal groups, from the most probable 25 per cent of the networks to the least probable, and the 172 observed sets of stream numbers classified accordingly. Networks with probabilities overlap-

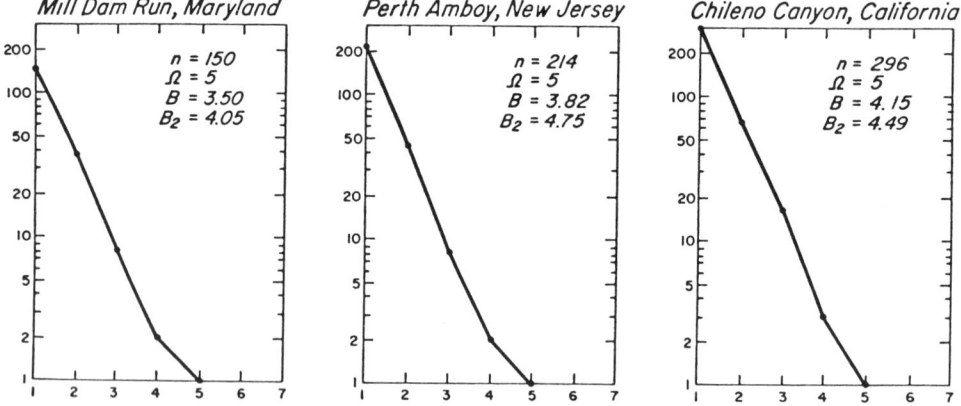

FIG. 14.—Three natural channel networks with dissimilar but relatively homogeneous and isotropic bedrock and environment (data from Schumm, 1956, p. 605). Just as in a topologically random population the concavity of the curves decreases practically to zero as B increases approximately to 4.

TABLE 5

STATISTICAL ANALYSIS

n_1	n_2	n_3	Observed	Expected	Likelihood Ratio λ	$-2 \ln \lambda$*	Decision at .05
9	2	1	10	7.31	0.233	2.91	Accept
9	3	1	4	6.09		(2, 5.99)	
9	4	1	0	0.60			
11	2	1	6	3.56	.279	2.55	Accept
11	3	1	4	6.24		(3, 7.81)	
11	4	1	2	2.08			
11	5	1	0	0.12			
13	2	1	1	1.69	.367	2.01	Accept
13	3	1	7	5.08		(4, 9.49)	
13	4	1	2	3.56			
13	5	1	1	0.64			
13	6	1	0	0.02			
14	2	1	4	1.19	0.030	7.04	Accept
14	3	1	3	4.46		(5, 11.1)	
14	4	1	4	4.16			
14	5	1	0	1.11			
14	6	1	0	0.08			
14	7	1	0	0.00			

* Figures in parentheses are number of degrees of freedom for χ^2 distribution and critical value for rejection at .05 significance level, respectively.

ping two or more groups were divided proportionally, an observed network with the stream numbers [27, 8, 2, 1], for example, being counted as 0.23 in the second most probable group and 0.77 in the third (see table 4 for the relevant probabilities). The goodness-of-fit test was then applied to the observed frequencies in the four classes, which by their construction have equal expected frequencies. The null hypothesis, that the sample could have been drawn from a topologically random population, was not rejected at the .05 significance level for networks free of geologic controls; but it was rejected for fourth-order networks selected without regard to such controls. Details and references are given in table 6. As before, in each case the χ^2 approximation was used, and the effect of sampling without replacement was assumed negligible.

These statistical comparisons strongly support the conclusion that populations of natural channel networks developed in the absence of geologic controls are topologically random (which does not, however, imply that the lengths, shapes, and orientations of the links necessarily are also random) and therefore that, as proposed, the law of stream numbers is indeed largely a consequence of random development of the topology of channel networks according to the laws of chance.

ACKNOWLEDGMENTS.—The numerical computations were carried out on the IBM 7094 and associated equipment of the Computing Facility of the University of California, Los Angeles. Especially appreciated is much valuable information and assistance freely given by F. H. Hollander, F. Schneider, and I. Beatty. Financial support in the form of fellowships from the National Science Foundation and the University of California is gratefully acknowledged.

TABLE 6

MODIFIED STATISTICAL ANALYSIS

Networks; Order	Geologic Controls	Observed	Expected	Likelihood Ratio λ	$-2 \ln \lambda$*	Decision at .05
172; 3, 4, 5	No[1,2,3]	34.92 38.09 47.33 51.66	43 43 43 43	0.118	4.26 (3, 7.81)	Accept
152; 3	No[1]	32.44 34.33 41.37 43.86	38 38 38 38	.305	2.37 (3, 7.81)	Accept
18; 4	No[3]	2.48 3.76 3.96 7.80	4.5 4.5 4.5 4.5	.196	3.26 (3, 7.81)	Accept
60; 4	Yes[4]	8.44 6.31 16.38 28.87	15 15 15 15	0.000	20.03 (3, 7.81)	Reject

* Figures in parentheses are number of degrees of freedom for χ^2 distribution and critical value for rejection at .05 significance level, respectively.

[1] Data for third-order networks same as in table 1.

[2] Data for fourth-order networks from Schumm (1956, p. 606), Melton (1957, table 2, facing p. 88), Smith (1958, p. 1003), Maxwell (1960, p. 79–82), and Morisawa (1962, p. 1026–1027, 1036–1037).

[3] Data for fifth-order networks from Maxwell (1960, p. 81) and Morisawa (1962, p. 1026, 1036).

[4] Data same as in table 1, except networks with n greater than about 100 omitted.

REFERENCES CITED

Bowden, K. L., and Wallis, J. R., 1964, Effect of stream-ordering technique on Horton's laws of drainage composition: Geol. Soc. America Bull., v. 75, p. 767-774.

Brush, L. M., 1961, Drainage basins, channels, and flow characteristics of selected streams in central Pennsylvania: U.S. Geol. Survey Prof. Paper 282-F, p. 145-181.

Cayley, A., 1859, On the analytical forms called trees: Philos. Mag., v. 18, p. 374-378.

——— 1873, On Listing's theorem: Messenger Math., v. 2, p. 81-89.

——— 1891, Collected mathematical papers, v. 4: Cambridge, University Press.

——— 1895, Collected mathematical papers, v. 8: Cambridge, University Press.

Coates, D. R., 1958, Quantitative geomorphology of small drainage basins of southern Indiana: New York, Columbia University, Dept. Geol., Office of Naval Res. Project NR 389-042, Tech. Report No. 10, 67 p.

Euler, L., 1741, Solutio problematis ad geometriam situs pertinentis: Commentarii Academiae Scientarum Petropolitanae (U.S.S.R., Akademiia Nauk, Leningrad), v. 8, p. 128-140.

Harvard University, Staff of the Computation Laboratory, 1955, Tables of the cumulative binomial probability distribution: Cambridge, Mass., Harvard University Press, 503 p.

Horton, R. E., 1932, Drainage basin characteristics: Am. Geophys. Union Trans., p. 350-361.

——— 1945, Erosional development of streams and their drainage basins: hydrophysical approach to quantitative morphology: Geol. Soc. America Bull., v. 56, p. 275-370.

Leopold, L. B., and Langbein, W. B., 1962, The concept of entropy in landscape evolution: U.S. Geol. Survey Prof. Paper 500-A, p. A1-A20.

——— and Miller, J. P., 1956, Ephemeral streams: hydraulic factors and their relation to the drainage net: U.S. Geol. Survey Prof. Paper 282-A, p. 1-37.

———, Wolman, M. G., and Miller, J. P., 1964, Fluvial processes in geomorphology: San Francisco, W. H. Freeman & Co., 522 p.

Listing, J. B., 1847, Vorstudien zur Topologie: Göttingen, Die Studien, p. 811-875.

——— 1862, Der Census räumlicher Complexe oder Verallgemeinerung des Euler'schen Satzes von den Polyedern: Göttingen, Königliche Gesellschaft der Wissenschaften, Abhandlungen, v. 10, p. 97-180.

Maxwell, J. C., 1960, Quantitative geomorphology of the San Dimas Experimental Forest, California: New York, Columbia University, Dept. Geol., Office of Naval Res. Project NR 389-042, Tech. Report No. 19, 95 p.

Melton, M. A., 1957, An analysis of the relations among elements of climate, surface properties, and geomorphology: New York, Columbia University, Dept. Geol., Office of Naval Res. Project NR 389-042, Tech. Report No. 11, 102 p.

——— 1958, Geometric properties of mature drainage systems and their representation in an E_4 phase space: Jour. Geology, v. 66, p. 35-56.

——— 1959, A derivation of Strahler's channel-ordering system: Ibid., v. 67, p. 345-346.

Mood, A. M., 1950, Introduction to the theory of statistics: New York, McGraw-Hill Book Co., 433 p.

Morisawa, M. E., 1957, Accuracy of determination of stream lengths from topographic maps: Am. Geophys. Union Trans., v. 38, p. 86-88.

——— 1962, Quantitative geomorphology of some watersheds in the Appalachian Plateau: Geol. Soc. America Bull., v. 73, p. 1025-1046.

Playfair, J., 1802, Illustrations of the Huttonian theory of the earth: Edinburgh (facsimile reprint by University of Illinois Press, Urbana, 1956), 528 p.

Riordan, J., 1958, An introduction to combinatorial analysis: New York, John Wiley & Sons, 244 p.

Schenck, H., Jr., 1963, Simulation of the evolution of drainage-basin networks with a digital computer: Jour. Geophys. Res., v. 68, p. 5739-5745.

Schumm, S. A., 1956, Evolution of drainage systems and slopes in badlands at Perth Amboy, New Jersey: Geol. Soc. America Bull., v. 67, p. 597-646.

Smith, K. G., 1958, Erosional processes and landforms in Badlands National Monument, South Dakota: Geol. Soc. America Bull., v. 69, p. 975-1008.

Strahler, A. N., 1952, Hypsometric (area-altitude) analysis of erosional topography: Geol. Soc. America Bull., v. 63, p. 1117-1142.

——— 1957, Quantitative analysis of watershed geomorphology: Am. Geophys. Union Trans., v. 38, p. 913-920.

7

Copyright ©1967 by The University of Chicago
Reprinted from *Jour. Geology* **75**:178-186 (1967), by permission of The University of Chicago Press

INFINITE TOPOLOGICALLY RANDOM CHANNEL NETWORKS[1]

RONALD L. SHREVE

University of California, Los Angeles

ABSTRACT

Individual channel networks ordinarily are portions of far larger, essentially infinite, networks. The over-all network is by definition at infinite topologically random network if the populations of subnetworks within it are topologically random. From such a network, the probability of randomly drawing a link, a subnetwork, or a basin with Strahler order ω is $1/2^\omega$; and that of randomly drawing a stream of order ω is $3/4^\omega$. The probability of drawing a link of magnitude μ, that is, one having μ sources ultimately tributary to it, is equal to the probability of a first passage through the origin at step $2\mu - 1$ in a symmetric random walk, a fact which suggests a useful mathematical analogy between random walks and infinite topologically random networks. Assuming uniform link length equal to the constant of channel maintenance, which in turn is the reciprocal of drainage density, the probability distributions for links and streams of various orders may be interpreted as crude geomorphological "laws" analogous to Horton's laws of drainage composition. These distributions predict geometric-series "laws" in which, using Strahler orders, the bifurcation ratio is 4, the link-number ratio is $\frac{1}{2}$, the length ratio is 2, the cumulative-length ratio is 4, and the basin-area ratio is 4, all in good agreement with the observed ratios. They also predict values of $\frac{4}{3}$ and $\frac{2}{3}$, respectively, for the dimensionless ratios of total number of Strahler streams to network magnitude and of Strahler stream frequency to the square of the drainage density, in agreement with the values of 1.34 and 0.694 found empirically.

INTRODUCTION

Individual channel networks in nature do not ordinarily exist independently, but are portions of far larger networks that for practical purposes are essentially infinite. The hypothesis that in the absence of geologic controls natural networks will be topologically random (Shreve, 1966, p. 27) thus implicitly contains the corollary that in the over-all infinite network, which will be termed an *infinite topologically random channel network*, all topologically distinct subnetworks with the same number of sources occur with equal frequency. The purposes of this paper are to deduce some of the geomorphologically significant probability distributions associated with these infinite topologically random networks, to demonstrate the close connection of such networks with random walks, and to derive theoretically several of the well-known empirical "laws" of geomorphology.

DEFINITIONS

Most of the specialized terms used in this paper—such as *link, fork, source, topologi-* *cally identical, topologically distinct,* and *topologically random*—have been defined in a previous publication (Shreve, 1966, p. 20, 27). Strahler stream orders (1952, p. 1120 n.; Shreve, 1966, p. 21-22) will be used exclusively. The terms *channel network* or, for convenience, simply *network* will refer to the idealized concept of channel network (Shreve, 1966, p. 27) in which one, and only one, path exists between any two points and in which at its upstream end each link either connects to two other links or terminates in a source. Stated negatively, and somewhat less precisely, no lakes with multiple inlets, no islands of major extent, and no confluences of more than two channels at a single place are permissible in the idealized channel networks considered in this paper. The terms *exterior link* and *interior link* will signify links terminating at their upstream ends in sources and forks, respectively. In these terms, Melton's relationships (1959, p. 345; Shreve, 1966, p. 27) state that every idealized network with μ sources will have $2\mu - 1$ links, of which μ are exterior links and $\mu - 1$ are interior links.

The phrase *link drawn at random* will signify a link selected in such a way that all links in the specified target population, which may be either real or hypothetical,

[1] Manuscript received April 8, 1966; revised August 9, 1966. Publication No. 494, Institute of Geophysics and Planetary Physics, University of California, Los Angeles, California 90024.

are equally likely to be drawn (see Mood and Graybill, 1963, p. 141–142). It is completely equivalent to the phrases *network drawn at random* or *basin drawn at random*, because each link of given magnitude or order or both in a population of networks is the outlet of a single subnetwork of the same magnitude or order or both. Actually drawing links or networks at random from natural populations is not easily accomplished; nevertheless, for meaningful statistical analysis it is an absolute necessity.

CONCEPT OF MAGNITUDE

The *magnitude* of a link in a channel network is herein defined by the following two rules. (1) Each exterior link has magnitude 1. (2) If links or magnitude μ_1 and μ_2 join, then the resultant link downstream has magnitude $\mu_1 + \mu_2$. The application of these rules to a typical channel network is illustrated in figure 1. By induction, the magnitude of a link is equal to the total number of sources ultimately tributary to it. Magnitude is thus a purely topological concept, for it involves only the interconnections and not the lengths, shapes, or orientations of the links comprising the network. Like the systems of stream ordering of Horton (1945, p. 281), Strahler (1952, p. 1120 n.), and, more recently, Scheidegger (1965, p. B188), the concept of magnitude assumes the existence of sources, that is, of objectively describable points that in fact or by definition are the points farthest upstream in a channel network.

In analogy with basin order, the magnitude of a channel network or drainage basin is equal to the magnitude of its highest magnitude link. Thus, if two networks are tributary to the same link, the resultant network has magnitude equal to the sum of the magnitudes of the two tributary networks. Networks with equal magnitudes have equal numbers of links, forks, sources, Horton streams, and first-order Strahler streams, and are therefore comparable in topological complexity (Shreve, 1966, p. 27). A reasonable conjecture is that they are comparable in other ways as well.

Despite its apparent complexity, the system of stream ordering proposed by Scheidegger (1965) is simply related to the concept of magnitude. If the Scheidegger order and the magnitude of a link (or network) are denoted by X and μ, respectively, then

$$X = \log_2 2\mu, \qquad (1)$$

in which $\log_2$ signifies the logarithm to base 2.

According to Scheidegger (1965, p. B188–B189), if the second-order streams as classified by his system "are treated as first-order

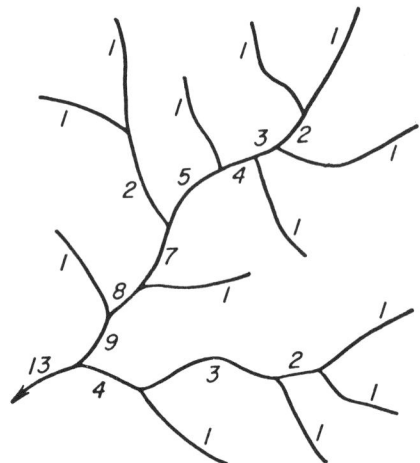

FIG. 1.—Link magnitudes for a typical channel network.

streams, then all orders are simply reduced by one." Equation (1) makes it easy to see, however, that this statement is incorrect, unless the previous first-order streams are treated as zero-order streams that contribute to the order of the higher-order streams even though, as Scheidegger himself states (1965, p. B188), they are in fact non-existent in nature. Thus, one of the main advantages of the Horton and Strahler systems (Shreve, 1966, p. 22–23) is lost in the Scheidegger system.

PROBABILITY DISTRIBUTIONS

The probability $p(\mu, \omega)$ that a link drawn at random from an infinite topologically random network will have specified magnitude μ and Strahler order ω can be computed from the recursive relationship

$$p(\mu, \omega) = \tfrac{1}{2} \sum_{a=1}^{\mu-1} [p(a, \omega-1) \times p(\mu-a, \omega-1) + 2p(a, \omega) \sum_{\beta=1}^{\omega-1} p(\mu-a, \beta)], \quad (2)$$

$$p(1,1) = \tfrac{1}{2}, \quad p(\mu, 1) = 0,$$
$$p(1, \omega) = 0, \quad \mu, \omega = 2, 3, \ldots.$$

can be derived either in the same direct fashion or by summation using (2). Proceeding directly,

$$u(\omega) = \tfrac{1}{2}\Big[u(\omega-1)^2 + 2u(\omega)\sum_{\beta=1}^{\omega-1} u(\beta)\Big], \quad (3)$$

$$u(1) = \tfrac{1}{2}, \quad \omega = 2, 3, \ldots,$$

and

$$v(\mu) = \tfrac{1}{2} \sum_{a=1}^{\mu-1} v(a) v(\mu-a), \quad (4)$$

$$v(1) = \tfrac{1}{2}, \quad \mu = 2, 3, \ldots.$$

TABLE 1

INFINITE TOPOLOGICALLY RANDOM CHANNEL NETWORKS

μ	$p(\mu,\omega)$							$v(\mu)$
	$\omega=2$	$\omega=3$	$\omega=4$	$\omega=5$	$\omega=6$	$\omega=7$	$\omega=8$	
1								0.50000
2	0.12500							.12500
3	.06250							.06250
4	.03125	0.00781						.03906
5	.01562	.01172						.02734
6	.00781	.01270						.02051
7	.00391	.01221						.01611
8	.00195	.01111	0.00003					.01309
9	.00098	.00983	.00011					.01091
10	.00049	.00856	.00022					.00927
20	.00000	.00181	.00141	0.00000				.00322
50	.00000	.00002	.00070	.00009	0.00000			.00080
100	.00000	.00000	.00010	.00018	.00000	0.00000		.00028
200	.00000	.00000	.00000	.00009	.00001	.00000	0.00000	.00010
500	.00000	.00000	.00000	.00000	.00002	.00000	.00000	.00002
1000	0.00000	0.00000	0.00000	0.00000	.00001	0.00000	0.00000	.00001
$u(\omega)$	0.25000	0.12500	0.06250	0.03125	0.01562	0.00781	0.00391	

The factor $\tfrac{1}{2}$ is the probability of drawing an interior link; and the sum on a accounts for the various ways that pairs of smaller networks can be tributary to this link to give it the specified μ and ω. Recursive relationships for the marginal probabilities

$$u(\omega) = \sum_{\mu=1}^{\infty} p(\mu, \omega)$$

and

$$v(\mu) = \sum_{\omega=1}^{\infty} p(\mu, \omega)$$

As before, the factor $\tfrac{1}{2}$ is the probability of drawing an interior link; and the remaining factor accounts for the various ways that pairs of smaller networks can be tributary to this link to give it the specified μ or ω.

Representative values of $p(\mu, \omega)$, $u(\omega)$, and $v(\mu)$ are presented in table 1. For any particular magnitude the distribution of probabilities with order has a relatively sharp peak, whereas for any particular order the distribution with magnitude has a relatively broad peak; hence, in a topologically random population magnitude more precisely characterizes a network than does order.

A closed expression for $u(\omega)$ can readily be derived from (3). Summation of the first $\omega - 1$ terms of $u(\omega)$ gives, using (3),

$$2\sum_{\beta=1}^{\omega-1} u(\beta) = \left[\sum_{\beta=1}^{\omega-1} u(\beta)\right]^2 - u(\omega-1)^2 + 1. \quad (5a)$$

Completing the square, taking the square root, and substituting into (3) leads to the relationship

$$2u(\omega) = u(\omega - 1),$$
$$u(1) = \tfrac{1}{2}, \quad \omega = 2, 3, \ldots, \quad (5b)$$

from which

$$u(\omega) = 1/2^\omega, \quad \omega = 1, 2, \ldots, \quad (5c)$$

follows by mathematical induction.

A closed expression for $v(\mu)$ can be derived from (4) by means of the generating function $R(r)$, where

$$R(r) = \sum_{\mu=1}^{\infty} v(\mu) r^\mu. \quad (6a)$$

Squaring both sides of (6a) and collecting the coefficients of like powers of r gives

$$R^2 = \sum_{\mu=2}^{\infty} r^\mu \sum_{\alpha=1}^{\mu-1} v(\alpha) v(\mu - \alpha); \quad (6b)$$

hence, using (4),

$$R^2 = 2R - r,$$
$$R = 1 - (1 - r)^{1/2}, \quad (6c)$$

from which

$$v(\mu) = \frac{2^{-(2\mu-1)}}{2\mu - 1} \binom{2\mu - 1}{\mu},$$
$$\mu = 1, 2, \ldots, \quad (6d)$$

follows by the binomial expansion. The minus sign is chosen in the quadratic formula because the power-series expansion in (6a) represents the branch of the curve of R versus r that passes through the origin.

The distribution $v(\mu)$ can also be derived from the probability $w(\mu; M)$ of drawing a link of magnitude μ at random from a topologically random population of networks of magnitude M. This probability is

$$w(\mu; M)$$
$$= \frac{(M-\mu+1)N(M-\mu+1)N(\mu)}{(2M-1)N(M)}, \quad (7a)$$

where $N(\mu)$ is the number of topologically distinct networks of magnitude μ. The denominator is equal to the total number of links of all magnitudes in the population of $N(M)$ networks of magnitude M; and the numerator is therefore the number of links of magnitude μ in this population, which in turn is the number of ways that the $N(\mu)$ networks of magnitude μ can be attached to the $M - \mu + 1$ sources of each of the $N(M - \mu + 1)$ networks of magnitude $M - \mu + 1$ to form networks of magnitude M.

Substitution of Cayley's closed expression for $N(\mu)$,

$$N(\mu) = \frac{1}{2\mu - 1} \binom{2\mu - 1}{\mu} \quad (7b)$$

(Shreve, 1966, p. 29), gives

$$w(\mu; M)$$
$$= \frac{1}{2\mu - 1} \binom{2\mu}{\mu} \binom{2(M-\mu)}{M-\mu} \Big/ \binom{2M}{M}, \quad (7c)$$

from which (6d) follows by taking the limit as M approaches infinity.

Representative values of $w(\mu; M)$ are presented in table 2.

For any network magnitude M the greatest (or modal) probability is that of drawing a link of magnitude 1, inasmuch as

$$w(1; M) = M/(2M - 1) \geq \tfrac{1}{2}. \quad (8)$$

At the other end of the distribution, however, for $M > 3$ the probability of drawing a link of magnitude M is greater than that of drawing one of magnitude $M - 1$. This is because networks of magnitude M always have one link of that magnitude, whereas they very often have no links of the next smaller magnitude and very rarely have two, which is the maximum possible. Setting the ratio of two successive terms equal to 1 and solving for μ shows that the minimum in the distribution is located approximately at $\mu = 3(M + 1)/4$.

The probability $s(\omega)$ of drawing a Strahler stream of order ω at random from the streams (not links) comprising an infinite topologically random network can be derived from (5c) and (6d) by noting that, because in any network the links whose tributaries are both of order $\omega - 1$ are in one-to-

could readily be tested against natural populations of channel networks by means of the goodness-of-fit test (see, e.g., Siegel, 1956, p. 42–52, 59–60, and Mood and Graybill, 1963, p. 308–309).

CONNECTION WITH RANDOM WALKS

A symbolic representation of any channel network can be constructed as follows. Start at the outlet and traverse the network, always turning left at forks and reversing direction at sources, until the outlet is again

TABLE 2

POPULATIONS OF FINITE TOPOLOGICALLY RANDOM CHANNEL NETWORKS

M	$w(\mu;M)$							
	$\mu=1$	$\mu=2$	$\mu=3$	$\mu=4$	$\mu=5$	$\mu=6$	$\mu=7$	$\mu=8$
1	1.00000							
2	0.66667	0.33333						
3	0.60000	.20000	0.20000					
4	0.57143	.17143	.11429	0.14286				
5	0.55556	.15873	.09524	.07936	0.11111			
6	0.54545	.15152	.08658	.06494	.06061	0.09091		
7	0.53846	.14685	.08158	.05828	.04895	.04895	0.07692	
8	0.53333	.14359	.07832	.05439	.04351	.03916	.04103	0.06667
9	0.52941	.14118	.07602	.05183	.04031	.03455	.03258	.03529
10	0.52632	.13932	.07430	.05001	.03819	.03183	.02858	.02786
20	0.51282	.13167	.06772	.04360	.03151	.02445	.01992	.01683
50	0.50505	.12756	.06445	.04072	.02882	.02185	.01737	.01428
100	0.50251	.12627	.06346	.03987	.02805	.02115	.01671	.01365
200	0.50125	.12563	.06297	.03946	.02769	.02082	.01640	.01336
500	0.50050	.12525	.06269	.03922	.02748	.02063	.01623	.01320
1000	0.50025	.12512	.06259	.03914	.02741	.02057	.01617	.01314
∞	0.50000	0.12500	0.06250	0.03906	0.02734	0.02051	0.01611	0.01309

one correspondence with the streams of order ω,

$$s(2)/s(1) = v(2)/v(1) = \tfrac{1}{4} \qquad (9a)$$

and

$$s(\omega + 1)/s(\omega) = \tfrac{1}{2}u(\omega)^2/\tfrac{1}{2}u(\omega - 1)^2$$
$$= \tfrac{1}{4}, \quad \omega = 2, 3, \ldots \qquad (9b)$$

These equations define a geometric series with ratio $\tfrac{1}{4}$, from which

$$s(\omega) = 3/4^\omega, \quad \omega = 1, 2, \ldots, \qquad (9c)$$

follows by mathematical induction.

The distributions (5c), (6d), and (9c)

reached. During the traverse, generate a sequence of I's and E's by recording an I the first time a given interior link is traversed and an E the first time a given exterior link is traversed. Each link will be traversed twice but recorded only once.

If a right turn instead of a left turn is made at each fork, a different sequence will result, which is the sequence for the mirror-image network. The new sequence will not be the reverse of the original, however; and, in general, symmetry in the network will not be evident in the sequence, and vice versa. The reverse sequence is generated by turning right and recording the I's and E's the second time given links are traversed rather than the first time. The mirror-image and reverse sequences, although necessary for certain types of investigation, will not be used in this paper.

Topologically identical networks will have identical sequences, and topologically distinct networks will have different unique sequences. Obviously, some possible sequences, such as all I's or all E's, cannot correspond to channel networks. Sequences corresponding to networks of more than one link, for instance, always begin with I and end with two successive E's. More generally, because of the fact that in any network or subnetwork the number of interior links is always exactly one less than the number of exterior links, only those sequences are possible in which, as they are recorded, the number of E's never exceeds the number of I's except at the terminal E. Put another way, if the I's count $+1$ and the E's count -1, then the partial sums can never be negative, except for the last, which will be -1. Thus, on a graph the curve of partial sums may fall to the level of the origin, but it does not drop below it until the terminal E.

The steps from network to sequence to graph are illustrated in figure 2.

Graphs like that of figure 2 occur widely in the theory of random walks; and it is worthwhile to compare their properties with those of topologically random networks. The graphs dropping below the axis for the first time at step $2\mu - 1$ correspond to the topologically distinct networks with $2\mu - 1$ links; hence, the number of such graphs is $N(\mu)$, as shown directly by Feller (1957, p. 71; see Shreve, 1966, p. 29, for derivation in terms of networks). In random-walk terminology $N(\mu)$ different one-dimensional paths make a first passage of the origin at step $2\mu - 1$. Following the analogy further, if the graphs are generated by unbiased coin tossing, counting heads as I and tails as E, then the probability that the graph will drop below the axis, that is, that a first passage will occur, at step $2\mu - 1$ is equal to $v(\mu)$ (Feller, 1957, p. 73–75). Thus, the probability that a link drawn at random from an infinite topologically random network will have magnitude μ, thereby defining a subnetwork with $2\mu - 1$ links, is exactly the same as the probability that in a symmetric random walk the first passage of the origin will occur at step $2\mu - 1$ (Feller, 1957, p. 76).

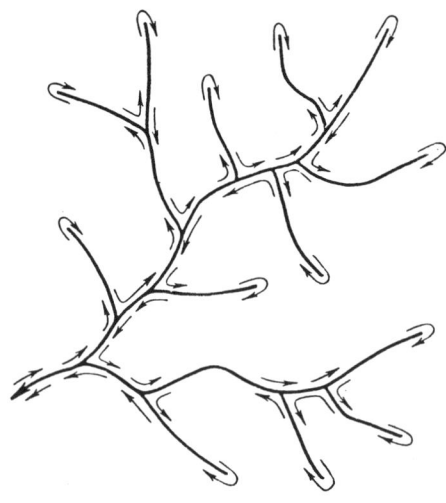

$I\ IE\ I\ I\ IE\ E\ I\ E\ I\ I\ I\ E\ E\ E\ E\ E\ I\ I\ IE\ E\ E\ E$

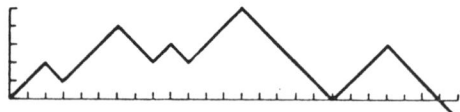

FIG. 2.—Symbolic and graphical representations of a typical channel network.

A symmetric random walk can be regarded as the outcome of a sequence of Bernoulli trials with probability of "success" equal to $\frac{1}{2}$ (Feller, 1957, p. 135, 311); hence, in the infinite sequence of I's and E's corresponding to an infinite topologically random network, E appears at any specified position with probability $\frac{1}{2}$ regardless of the pattern anywhere else in the sequence. All possible subsequences are equally likely to appear, corresponding to the definition of topologically random networks (for proof of the zero probability of occurrence of "pathological" sequences, such as all E's, see Feller, 1957, p. 189-197).

In the sequence corresponding to an infinite network that is not topologically random, on the other hand, although the two letters appear in equal numbers as required by Melton's relationships, the probability that E appears at a specified position is not necessarily $\frac{1}{2}$. Instead, it depends upon the preceding pattern of letters, corresponding to the fact that certain network topologies, hence certain letter sequences, are preferentially developed.

As random walks and Bernoulli trials occur widely in fields ranging from nuclear physics to gambling, their theory is highly developed in many different guises (see, e.g., Feller, 1957, chaps. iii, xi, xiii, xiv); hence, the analogy with infinite topologically random channel networks makes available for application a vast body of theorems and solutions.

GEOMORPHOLOGICAL "LAWS"

The law of large numbers (Feller, 1957, p. 141-142, 189-191) in conjunction with (9c) implies that, in random samples from an infinite topologically random network, the average number of Strahler streams of successive orders will, as the number of samples increases, tend toward a geometric series with ratio $\frac{1}{4}$. Similarly, in conjunction with (5c), it implies that the average number of links of successive orders will tend toward a geometric series with ratio $\frac{1}{2}$. In analogy with Horton's laws of drainage composition, these relationships might be termed the "law of stream numbers" and the "law of link numbers," respectively, although, like Horton's laws, they are not true statistical laws in the sense proposed in my paper on the law of stream numbers (Shreve, 1966, p. 17). Combining these two "laws" leads to the further relationship that the average number of links per stream increases with order as a geometric series with ratio 2.

Derivation of a "law of stream lengths" requires a hypothesis concerning the lengths of individual links. The simplest, and one that does not appear to be too far from the truth, is that all of the links have the same length. In this case, the "law of stream lengths" corresponding to the previous crude "laws" would state that the average length of streams increases with order as a geometric series with ratio 2. In like manner, the average total length of streams in basins of given order would increase with successive orders approximately as a geometric series with ratio 4, in good agreement with observation (e.g., Schumm, 1956, p. 604-605).

Suggestive as these geomorphological "laws" are, they are based upon averages over an infinite population and so, like Horton's laws (Shreve, 1966, p. 17), do not supply the complete distributions needed for statistical analysis of observations made on natural populations. Moreover, the hypothesis of constant link length amounts to using the average link length. A better hypothesis, for example, might be that the link lengths have a log-normal distribution (M. A. Melton, unpublished analysis; Schumm 1956, p. 607-608) with mean inversely proportional to drainage density, or perhaps with exterior links having one mean and interior links another. Surprisingly, the statistics of natural link lengths, or even of stream lengths, has not received much investigation beyond the work of Schumm (1956, p. 607-608) on the badlands at Perth Amboy.

The total length L of channels in a basin of magnitude μ is

$$L = l(2\mu - 1), \qquad (10a)$$

where l is the link length, which is assumed constant. Similarly, the area A of the basin may be written

$$A = \kappa l^2 (2\mu - 1), \qquad (10b)$$

in which the dimensionless coefficient κ is a constant if, as will be assumed, the drainage density

$$D = L/A = 1/(\kappa l) \qquad (10c)$$

is uniform, as would be the case in mature topography developed in a homogeneous environment. Elimination of l between (10a) and (10c) gives κ in terms of commonly measured network parameters,

$$\kappa = (2\mu - 1)/LD. \qquad (10d)$$

For the 11 networks tabulated by Melton which are definitely free of geologic controls (1957, Table 2, facing p. 88; Chinle Badlands N and S, Finley and Adams Canyon I and II, Sycamore Canyon I and II, Whipple Basin, Mesa Gulch, Dory Hill Basin, Peters Dome Basin, and Cerro Pavo Basin), the mean value of κ is 0.96. Thus, from (10b) the average basin area drained by each link is approximately that of a square of side l; and from (10c) the constant of channel maintenance (Schumm, 1956, p. 607) is approximately equal to the mean link length. Assuming $\kappa = 1$, $\mu \gg 1$, and noting from (9c) that the bifurcation ratio is approximately $\frac{1}{4}$, so that (Shreve, 1966, p. 21)

$$\mu \approx 4^{\omega-1}, \qquad (10e)$$

where μ and ω are the basin magnitude and order, respectively, and $\approx$ denotes approximate equality, leads to a "law of basin areas,"

$$A \approx (2/D^2)4^{\omega-1} \qquad (10f)$$

The basin-area ratio is thus 4, again in good agreement with observation (e.g., Schumm, 1956, p. 604–605).

Because from (9c) the bifurcation ratio is approximately $\frac{1}{4}$, a simple summation for $\mu \gg 1$ shows that the total number S_S of Strahler streams in networks of magnitude μ will on the average be close to $4\mu/3$; hence, for all networks of sufficient size, the average ratio S_S/μ will be approximately $\frac{4}{3}$, in agreement with the mean observed ratio of 1.34 for the 11 networks free of geologic controls tabulated by Melton, whose magnitudes range from 19 to 111.

Once more assuming $\kappa = 1$, $\mu \gg 1$, defining $F_S = S_S/A$, and using (10b) and (10c), leads to the approximate relationship

$$F_S/D^2 \approx \tfrac{2}{3}. \qquad (11a)$$

This may be compared with the empirical equation

$$F_S/D^2 \approx 0.694 \qquad (11b)$$

obtained by Melton (1958, p. 36–37) by analysis of data from 156 drainage basins. For the 11 networks previously considered, the mean value of F_S/D^2 is 0.71.

In terms of links rather than Strahler streams, the relationship is exactly

$$F/D^2 = \kappa, \qquad (12)$$

where F is the average number of links per unit area. This equation is tautological, inasmuch as it follows directly from the definitions of F, D, and κ; it does not depend upon constant link lengths, uniform drainage density, or topologically random networks. Similarly, the ratio F_S/D^2 investigated by Melton (1958, p. 37) is exactly equal to κ divided by the number of links per Strahler stream. Part of the scatter in his diagram of F_S versus D is therefore due to variations in network topology, as he recognized (Melton, 1958, p. 37, 38, 43–46); and the remainder is due to fluctuations in κ. Use of the channel link (a theoretical concept unrecognized at the time) rather than the Strahler stream as the basic channel unit would have eliminated the scatter due to topological variations and reduced the problem to investigation of the behavior of the conceptually simple quantity κ.

ACKNOWLEDGMENTS.—Especially appreciated are the free use of computing time and other facilities generously furnished by the Department of Geological Sciences at Harvard University, where I was Honorary Research Fellow in Geology when this paper was written. Also appreciated are the careful reading and useful suggestions made by M. A. Melton, who reviewed the manuscript for publication. The numerical computations were carried out on the IBM 7094 and associated equipment of the Harvard Computing Center. Earlier financial support from the University of California is also gratefully acknowledged.

REFERENCES CITED

Feller, W., 1957, An introduction to probability theory and its applications: New York, John Wiley & Sons, v. 1, 461 p.

Horton, R. E., 1945, Erosional development of streams and their drainage basins; hydrophysical approach to quantitative morphology: Geol. Soc. America Bull., v. 56, p. 275–370.

Melton, M. A., 1957, An analysis of the relations among elements of climate, surface properties, and geomorphology: New York, Columbia University, Dept. Geol., Office of Naval Res. Project NR 389 042, Tech. Report No. 11, 102 p.

────── 1958, Geometric properties of mature drainage systems and their representation in an E_4 phase space: Jour. Geology, v. 66, p. 35–56.

────── 1959, A derivation of Strahler's channel-ordering system: *Ibid.*, v. 67, p. 345–346.

Mood, A. M., and Graybill, F. A., 1963, Introduction to the theory of statistics (2d ed.): New York, McGraw-Hill Book Co., 443 p.

Scheidegger, A. E., 1965, The algebra of stream-order numbers: U.S. Geol. Survey Prof. Paper 525-B, p. B187–B189.

Schumm, S. A., 1956, Evolution of drainage systems and slopes in badlands at Perth Amboy, New Jersey: Geol. Soc. America Bull., v. 67, p. 597–646.

Shreve, R. L., 1966, Statistical law of stream numbers: Jour. Geology, v. 74, p. 17–37.

Siegel, S., 1956, Nonparametric statistics for the behavioral sciences: New York, McGraw-Hill Book Co., 312 p.

Strahler, A. N., 1952, Hypsometric (area-altitude) analysis of erosional topography: Geol. Soc. America Bull., v. 63, p. 1117–1142.

8

Copyright ©1969 by The University of Chicago
Reprinted from *Jour. Geology* **77**:397-414 (1969), by permission of The University of Chicago Press

STREAM LENGTHS AND BASIN AREAS IN TOPOLOGICALLY RANDOM CHANNEL NETWORKS[1,2]

RONALD L. SHREVE
University of California, Los Angeles, California 90024

ABSTRACT

In order to comprehend the geometry of drainage basins and channel networks, which is prerequisite to explaining their mechanics, it is necessary to understand the close connection between network topology and such planimetric elements as stream lengths and basin areas. Topologically random channel networks constitute an important theoretical case. In an infinite topologically random network, (1) the expected magnitude of a randomly drawn link of order ω is $(2^{2\omega-1} + 1)/3$, (2) $\frac{2}{3}$ of all links and $\frac{1}{6}$ of the interior links head streams, (3) complete subnetworks of any given order have the same distribution of magnitudes as all networks of that order, which seems to make little difference whether or not basins chosen for investigation are complete, (4) the probability that a randomly drawn stream of order ω will consist of λ links is $2^{-(\omega-1)}(1 - 2^{-(\omega-1)})^{\lambda-1}$, and (5) the average stream of order Ω will have $2^{\Omega-1} - 1$ tributaries entering from the sides, of which $2^{\Omega-\omega-1}$ will on the average be of order ω. Link lengths measured on 1:24,000-scale maps of eastern Kentucky are approximated more closely by a gamma density with parameter $\nu = 2$ than by either a log normal or an exponential. The mean length of the exterior links is almost twice that of the interior links, in agreement with the findings of others. In an infinite topologically random channel network whose interior link lengths are gamma distributed with $\nu = 2$, (1) the densities of the logarithms of the stream lengths are slightly left-skewed and increase in dispersion with increasing order, and (2) the densities of the logarithms of the Schumm total length of all streams in a subbasin of given order are highly symmetrical, decrease slightly in dispersion with increasing order, and for orders 1 and 2 agree well with Schumm's observations at Perth Amboy, New Jersey. If the link lengths are exponentially distributed, then the stream lengths will also be exponentially distributed. In finite topologically random channel networks with specified stream numbers, the expected number of links per stream and per subnetwork of given order are given by closed but complicated formulas, from which the expected stream lengths and Schumm lengths can be calculated. As observed in natural networks, in a topologically random population, (1) the expected stream lengths do not satisfy Horton's geometric-series law as well as the expected stream numbers, whereas the expected Schumm lengths do, (2) on Horton diagrams the curves are straightest for the most probable networks, and are concave upward or downward for networks of order lower or higher, respectively, than the most probable, and (3) the geometric-mean stream-length and Schumm-length ratios are about 2 and 4.5, respectively. The corresponding results for basin areas are exactly the same as for Schumm lengths. In the Perth Amboy basin studied by Schumm, the average area draining directly overland into unit length of channel is not a constant independent of the particular position of the channel in the basin as he proposed, but is less for exterior links than for interior links. Substantial differences in the relative areas draining into sources and in other geomorphic characteristics are not reflected in Horton diagrams because the Horton variables are averages that are mainly determined by network topology. Of most fundamental significance, therefore, are not the Horton variables, but the more elementary quantities, such as link lengths and source areas.

INTRODUCTION

The way in which the planimetric elements of a drainage basin are put together is intimately connected with the topology of the channel network. Indeed, certain geomorphological relationships, such as the laws of drainage composition proposed by Horton (1945, p. 286–291), apparently are in large part the result of randomness in network topology (Shreve 1966, 1967; Smart 1968). Thus, in order to comprehend the geometry of drainage basins and channel networks, which is prerequisite to explaining their mechanics, it is necessary to understand the perhaps dominant topological effects. The purpose of this paper is to investigate these effects in the important theoretical case of stream lengths and basin areas in topologically random channel networks.

DEFINITIONS

All of the specialized geomorphological terms used in this paper have been defined

[1] Manuscript received September 30, 1968; revised January 16, 1969.

[2] Publication 709, Institute of Geophysics and Planetary Physics, University of California, Los Angeles, California 90024.

in previous publications (Shreve 1966, p. 20, 22, 27; 1967, p. 178-179). Strahler stream orders will be used throughout (Strahler 1952, p. 1120; Shreve 1966, p. 21-22). The term *channel network* will refer to idealized networks with no lakes, no islands, and no junctions with more than two tributary channels. A *complete* network is one that discharges into a stream of higher order. *Sources* are the points farthest upstream in a network; their existence as objectively describable points in natural networks is a fundamental assumption of the theory. *Exterior links* are the reaches of channel from the sources to the highest *forks;* and *interior links* are the reaches between the forks. The *magnitude* of a link is equal to the number of sources upstream of it; and the magnitude of a channel network or drainage basin is equal to the magnitude of its outlet link. A *link drawn at random* is one selected in such a way that all links in the specified target population are equally likely to be drawn. An *infinite topologically random channel network* is a network of infinite extent in which all topologically distinct subnetworks of equal magnitude occur with equal probability. Finally, the *expectation*, or *expected value*, of a random variable will, as usual (Feller 1957, p. 207; 1966, p. 5), signify the mean, or first moment, of its probability density.

PROBABILITY DENSITIES

Let $p(\mu, \omega)$ be the probability that a link drawn at random from an infinite topologically random network will have magnitude μ and order ω. Then $p(\mu, \omega)$ satisfies the recursive relationship

$$p(\mu, \omega) = \tfrac{1}{2} \sum_{a=1}^{\mu-1} [p(a, \omega - 1) \\ \times p(\mu - a, \omega - 1) \\ + 2p(a, \omega) \sum_{\beta=1}^{\omega-1} p(\mu - a, \beta)] , \quad (1)$$

$$p(1, 1) = \tfrac{1}{2}, \quad p(\mu, 1) = 0 ,$$
$$p(1, \omega) = 0 , \quad \mu, \omega = 2, 3, \ldots$$

(Shreve 1967, p. 180); and therefore the generating function (Feller 1957, p. 248)

$$R_\omega(r) = \sum_{\mu=1}^{\infty} p(\mu, \omega) r^\mu \quad (2a)$$

must satisfy

$$R_\omega = \tfrac{1}{2} R_{\omega-1}^2 + R_\omega \sum_{\beta=1}^{\omega-1} R_\beta , \quad (2b)$$
$$R_1 = \tfrac{1}{2} r , \quad \omega = 2, 3, \ldots .$$

The marginal probability (Feller 1957, p. 201)

$$u(\omega) = \sum_{\mu=1}^{\infty} p(\mu, \omega) , \quad (3a)$$

which is the probability of drawing at random a link of order ω and unspecified magnitude, and the expectation (Feller 1957, p. 207)

$$E_\omega(\mathbf{\mu}) = \sum_{\mu=1}^{\infty} \mu \, p(\mu, \omega) \Big/ u(\omega) , \quad (3b)$$

which is the expected value of the magnitude μ for links of order ω drawn at random, can be found from (2b) without first finding explicit formulas for R_ω or $p(\mu, \omega)$, because from (2a)

$$u(\omega) = R_\omega(1) \quad (3c)$$

and

$$E_\omega(\mathbf{\mu}) = R'_\omega(1)/u(\omega) , \quad (3d)$$

where $R'_\omega = dR_\omega/dr$. Following convention (Mood and Graybill 1963, p. 45), $\mathbf{\mu}$ is boldface to indicate that it is a random variable and not, as in $p(\mu, \omega)$, the argument of a function.

Rewriting (2b) with the index ω decreased by 1 and eliminating the sum between the original and the rewritten equations leads to

$$\frac{R_{\omega-1}}{R_\omega} - 2 = \left(\frac{R_{\omega-2}}{R_{\omega-1}} - 2\right) \\ \times \left(\frac{R_{\omega-2}}{R_{\omega-1}} + 2\right). \quad (4a)$$

By induction, using (3c) and the fact that

$R_1(1) = u(1) = \frac{1}{2}$ and $R_2(1) = u(2) = \frac{1}{4}$ from (2b),

$$\frac{u(\omega - 1)}{u(\omega)} - 2 = 0 ; \quad (4b)$$

hence,

$$u(\omega) = 1/2^\omega, \quad \omega = 1, 2, \ldots, \quad (4c)$$

an important result that was derived by a different method in a previous publication (Shreve 1967, p. 181).

Solving (2b) for R_ω, differentiating, substituting in (3d), and using (4c) leads to

$$E_\omega = 2E_{\omega-1} + \sum_{\beta=1}^{\omega-1} 2^{\omega-\beta-1} E_\beta , \quad (5a)$$

$$E_1 = 1, \quad \omega = 2, 3, \ldots.$$

Rewriting this with the index ω decreased by 1 and eliminating the sum in the same manner as before then gives

$$4E_{\omega-1} - E_\omega = 4E_{\omega-2} - E_{\omega-1} . \quad (5b)$$

By induction, using the fact that $E_1 = 1$ and $E_2 = 3$ from (5a),

$$4E_{\omega-1} - E_\omega = 1 ; \quad (5c)$$

hence,

$$E_\omega(\mu) = (2^{2\omega-1} + 1)/3 , \quad (5d)$$
$$\omega = 1, 2, \ldots.$$

Let $s(\omega)$ be the probability of drawing at random a stream of order ω from the streams (not the links) comprising an infinite topologically random network; and let q be the probability of drawing at random a link that heads a stream. Then, because $s(\omega)$ is the same as the probability of drawing at random a link of order ω from the links that head streams, $q\,s(\omega)$ is the probability of drawing at random an interior link with two tributary links of order $\omega - 1$. Thus, using (4c),

$$q\,s(\omega) = \tfrac{1}{2}[u(\omega - 1)]^2 = 1/2^{2\omega-1} , \quad (6a)$$
$$\omega = 2, 3, \ldots,$$

(Shreve 1967, p. 180) and

$$q\,s(1) = u(1) = \tfrac{1}{2} ; \quad (6b)$$

but

$$\sum_{\omega=1}^{\infty} s(\omega) = 1 ; \quad (6c)$$

hence,

$$q = \sum_{\omega=1}^{\infty} 1/2^{2\omega-1} = \tfrac{2}{3} . \quad (6d)$$

Thus, $\tfrac{2}{3}$ of all links and $\tfrac{1}{6}$ of the interior links head streams. Finally, substituting (6d) in (6a) and (6b),

$$s(\omega) = 3/4^\omega, \quad \omega = 1, 2, \ldots, \quad (6e)$$

a formula that was obtained by a less revealing method in a previous publication (Shreve 1967, p. 182).

Let $c(\mu, \omega)$ be the probability of drawing at random from an infinite topologically random network a link that is the outlet of a complete network of magnitude μ and order ω. This is the same as the probability of drawing a link with one tributary of magnitude μ and order ω and the other of unspecified magnitude and order ω or greater. Thus,

$$c(\mu, \omega) = \tfrac{1}{2}[2p(\mu, \omega) \sum_{\beta=\omega}^{\infty} u(\beta)] ; \quad (7a)$$

and, using (4c) and summing the series,

$$c(\mu, \omega) = p(\mu, \omega)/2^{\omega-1} . \quad (7b)$$

The significance of this result is that complete networks of any given order in an infinite topologically random network have the same distribution of magnitudes as all networks of that order. This explains why it seems to make little difference whether or not basins chosen for geomorphological investigation are complete.

The probability that a link drawn at random will be the outlet of a complete network of order ω is

$$\sum_{\mu=1}^{\infty} c(\mu, \omega) = 1/2^{2\omega-1} \quad (8)$$
$$\omega = 1, 2, \ldots,$$

which, as should be expected, is identical to the probability of drawing a link that heads a stream.

Let $f(\lambda; \omega)$ be the probability that a stream of order ω drawn at random from an infinite topologically random network will consist of λ links; and let q_ω be the probability that a link of order ω drawn at random will be the terminal link of a stream, that is, the outlet link of a complete network. Then, using the rule for conditional probabilities (Feller 1957, p. 105) and substituting (4c) and (8),

$$q_\omega = \sum_{\mu=1}^{\infty} c(\mu, \omega) \bigg/ u(\omega) = 1/2^{\omega-1}. \quad (9a)$$

In topologically random networks the fact that a particular link is not a terminal link in no way influences the probability that the next link downstream will be one; therefore, $f(\lambda; \omega)$ is geometric,

$$f(\lambda; \omega) = q_\omega(1 - q_\omega)^{\lambda-1}$$
$$= 2^{-(\omega-1)}(1 - 2^{-(\omega-1)})^{\lambda-1}, \quad (9b)$$
$$\lambda, \omega = 1, 2, \ldots.$$

The expected number of links in streams of order ω is (Feller 1957, p. 210)

$$E_\omega(\lambda) = 1 + (1 - q_\omega)/q_\omega = 2^{\omega-1}. \quad (9c)$$

Thus, the expected number of links per stream increases with order as a geometric series with ratio 2, as found previously by a different argument (Shreve 1967, p. 184).

Let $T(\omega; \Omega)$ be the probability that a stream chosen at random from the streams that debouch into the sides (but not the heads) of the streams of order Ω in an infinite topologically random network will have order ω; and let $t(\omega, \Omega)$ be the probability that a link drawn at random will have tributaries of order ω and Ω, where $\omega < \Omega$. Then

$$T(\omega; \Omega) = t(\omega, \Omega) \bigg/ \sum_{\beta=1}^{\Omega-1} t(\beta, \Omega) \quad (10a)$$

but, using (4c),

$$t(\omega, \Omega) = \tfrac{1}{2}[2u(\omega)u(\Omega)] = 1/2^{\Omega+\omega}$$
$$\omega = 1, 2, \ldots, \Omega - 1 \quad (10b)$$
$$\Omega = 2, 3, \ldots;$$

hence,

$$T(\omega; \Omega) = 2^{\Omega-\omega-1}/(2^{\Omega-1} - 1),$$
$$\omega = 1, 2, \ldots, \Omega - 1, \quad (10c)$$
$$\Omega = 2, 3, \ldots.$$

According to (9c) an average stream of order Ω in an infinite topologically random network will consist of $2^{\Omega-1}$ links and will therefore have $2^{\Omega-1} - 1$ tributaries discharging into it from the sides; and according to (10c) $2^{\Omega-\omega-1}$ of these tributaries will on the average be of order ω, as suggested by Smart (personal communication).

LINK LENGTHS

Practically nothing is known about the statistical distribution of the lengths of links in natural channel networks. Schumm (1956, p. 607–608) concluded from his measurements in badlands basins at Perth Amboy that the distribution of first-order stream lengths, that is, of exterior link lengths, is log normal. He did not report interior link lengths. M. A. Melton (personal communication), on the basis of unpublished studies of various basins in the western United States, has reached the same conclusion concerning both exterior and interior links. Smart (1968, p. 1011–1012) measured link lengths on maps of basins in Missouri, Virginia, and Arizona. He found distributions qualitatively similar to those of Schumm and Melton, but concluded from a goodness-of-fit test that, except for the paucity of very short links, the distributions could be exponential, as suggested by computer simulation (Smart et al. 1967) using the model proposed by Leopold and Langbein (1962, p. A18). M. J. Kirby (personal communication) has found that links measured in the field fit an exponential distribution fairly well, but that those measured on maps fit a distribution more like the log normal.

W. C. Krumbein and I, with the help of students in a class, have studied map link lengths in thirty networks selected at random from the drainage basins of magnitude 10 tributary to Rockhouse and Wolf creeks, Martin County, eastern Kentucky. Local relief is a few hundred feet, and drainage density is about 10 miles of channel per square mile. Bedrock is flat-lying relatively homogeneous coal-bearing Pennsylvanian sandstone. Modern 1:24,000-scale topographic and geologic maps published by the U.S. Geological Survey completely cover the area. Sources and channels were drawn on the maps by eye on the basis of contour curvature, and link lengths were measured as the straight-line distances between the ends of the links. The resulting histograms (fig. 1) are right-skewed like the log normal, in agreement with the findings of the previous investigators.

Interestingly, although the two histograms have the same general form, the mean length of the exterior links is almost twice that of the interior links. A similar difference has been reported by Melton (personal communication) and Smart (1968, p. 1012) and is implied by the published data of Schumm

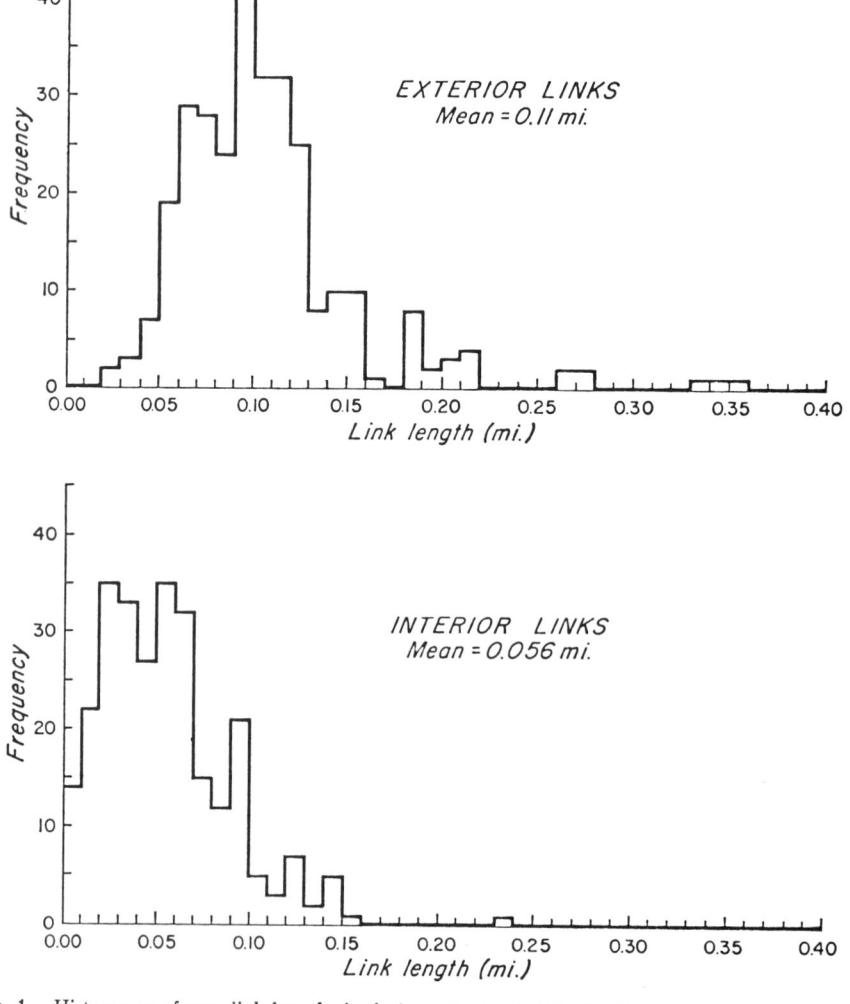

FIG. 1.—Histograms of map link lengths in drainage basins in Martin County, eastern Kentucky

(1956, p. 607–608) and Melton (1957, table 2, facing p. 88). Thus, the first-order streams, which consist of exterior links, must be considered separately from the higher-order streams, which consist of interior links, and the conclusion from (4c) that in infinite topologically random networks the average length of streams increases with order as a geometric series

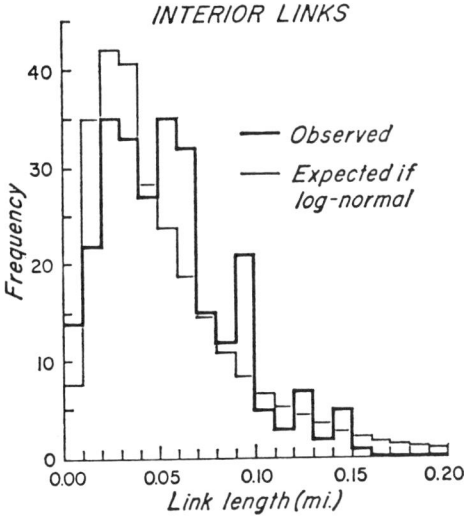

FIG. 2.—Comparison of observed distribution of link lengths from figure 1 with log normal fitted using maximum-likelihood estimators of parameters (Aitchison and Brown 1957, p. 39).

with ratio 2 (Shreve 1967, p. 184) must be restricted to streams of second and higher order.

The log normal density (fig. 2) is but one of many possible right-skewed densities that might fit the histogram for interior links in figure 1. Another possibility is one of the family of gamma densities

$$g_{\nu,a_i}(l_i) = a_i^\nu l_i^{\nu-1} \exp(-a_i l_i)/\Gamma(\nu) , \quad (11a)$$
$$\nu, a_i > 0 ,$$

in which ν, which is not necessarily an integer, is a shape parameter and

$$a_i = \nu/E(l_i) , \quad (11b)$$

where $E(l_i)$ is the expected (Feller 1966, p. 5) interior link length. Of the two densities, the gamma with $\nu = 2$ (fig. 3) fits better than the log normal, although neither fits very well. Moreover, it is mathematically convenient and it reduces to the exponential density in the special case $\nu = 1$ (fig. 4). For these reasons, therefore, and not because of any particular geomorphological significance, (11a) with $\nu = 2$ and a_i independent of order will be assumed to be a reasonable approximation to the truth in the derivations that follow.

STREAM LENGTHS

The lengths L_ω of streams of order ω greater than 1 are the sums of random numbers λ of links of random length l_i, where λ and l_i have the densities $f(\lambda; \omega)$ and

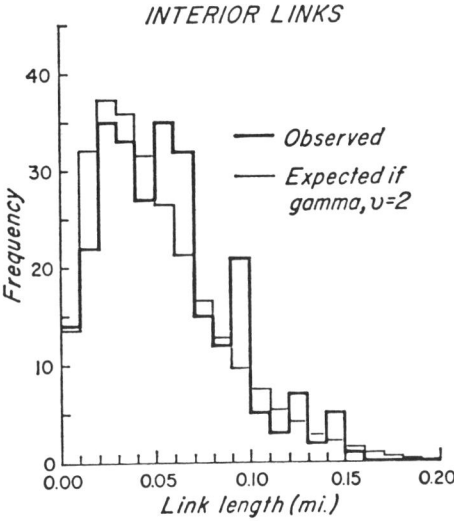

FIG. 3.—Comparison of observed distribution of link lengths from figure 1 with gamma with parameters $\nu = 2$ and $a_i = 2/\bar{l}_i$, where $\bar{l}_i$ is the observed mean length. Maximum-likelihood estimators of parameters (Mood and Graybill 1963, p. 181; Chapman 1956, p. 499) are $\nu = 2.02$ and $a_i = \nu/\bar{l}_i$.

$g_{\nu,a_i}(l_i)$ given by (9b) and (11a). They are therefore random variables with densities

$$h_\omega = \sum_{\lambda=1}^\infty f(\lambda; \omega) g_{\nu,a_i}^{\lambda *} , \quad (12a)$$

(Feller 1966, p. 53), where the superscript $\lambda *$ signifies the λ-fold convolution of g_{ν,a_i}

143

with itself (Feller 1966, p. 144). Although they occur in a similar context, the densities f and g are not the same as those defined by Smart (1968, p. 1005). Substituting (9b) and (11a) into (12a), using the fact that $g_{\nu,a} * g_{\mu,a} = g_{\nu+\mu,a}$ (Feller 1966, p. 46) and letting $p_\omega = 1 - 2^{-(\omega-1)}$ gives

$$h_\omega = p_\omega^{-1+1/\nu}(1 - p_\omega)a_i \exp(-a_i L_\omega)$$
$$\times \sum_{\lambda=1}^{\infty}(p_\omega^{1/\nu}a_i L_\omega)^{\lambda\nu-1}\Big/\Gamma(\lambda\nu), \quad (12b)$$

in which Γ is the gamma function (Dwight 1961, p. 209). For $\nu = 2$ the infinite series is that for the hyperbolic sine; hence, finally

$$h_\omega(L_\omega) = \frac{a_i \exp(-a_i L_\omega)}{2^{\omega-1}(1 - 2^{-(\omega-1)})^{1/2}}$$
$$\times \sinh\{a_i L_\omega[1 - 2^{-(\omega-1)}]^{1/2}\}, \quad (12c)$$
$$L_\omega > 0, \quad \omega = 2, 3, \ldots.$$

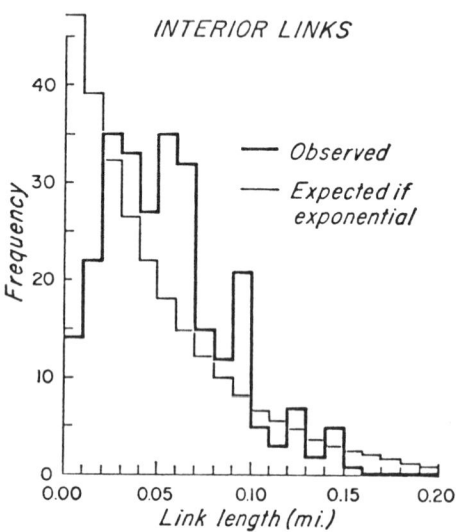

FIG. 4.—Comparison of observed distribution of link lengths from figure 1 with exponential fitted using maximum-likelihood estimator of expected link length.

Alternatively, this result could be found by Laplace transforming (12a) (Feller 1966, p. 414), making a partial-fraction decomposition, and then using a standard table of inverse transforms.

The densities h_ω are shown in figures 5 and 6. The broad, relatively flat distributions in figure 5, particularly for the higher orders, explain the common observation (Smart 1968, p. 1007) that the lengths of the single main streams in basins studied usually seem abnormal compared to the averaged lengths generally computed for the lower orders.

If the link lengths are exponentially distributed, as proposed by Smart and Kirkby, then $\nu = 1$, and from (12b) (or Feller 1966,

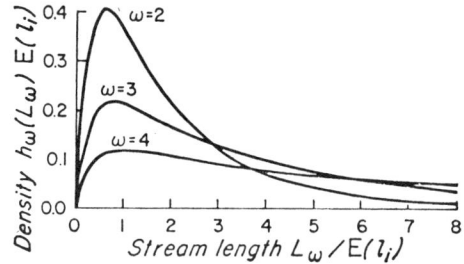

FIG. 5.—Densities of stream lengths in infinite topologically random channel network if interior link lengths are gamma-distributed with $\nu = 2$. The quantity $E(l_i)$ is the expected (or overall population mean) interior link length.

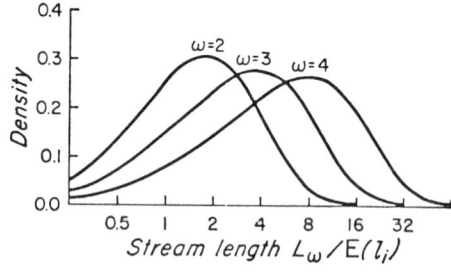

FIG. 6.—The densities of figure 5 transformed so that the horizontal coordinate is the logarithm of stream length, in accordance with common practice in plotting observed lengths.

p. 54) the stream lengths will also be exponentially distributed (figs. 7 and 8). Unlike the gamma, the exponential density for link lengths has some heuristic appeal because of its "lack of memory." This property is perhaps best exemplified by radioactive decay. The remaining lifetime of a radioactive nucleus is a random variable that is independent of the present age and has the same distribution as the lifetime itself. Only the exponential has this property (Feller 1966, p. 8). In the case of links, knowledge that a link exceeds a certain length would give no information as to how much it exceeds it. Put another way, if such a link is traversed in equal infinitesimal increments of length, the probability of termination is the same in each increment. Such a hypothesis is attractive because of its simplicity. Moreover, the computer experiments of Smart et al. (1967) show that the link lengths in

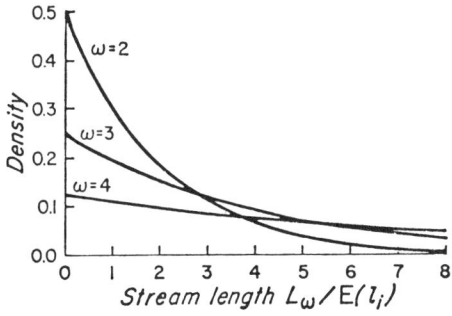

FIG. 7.—Densities of stream lengths in infinite topologically random channel network if interior link lengths are exponentially distributed.

the discrete model of channel networks proposed by Leopold and Langbein (1962, p. A18) are geometrically distributed (Smart 1968, p. 1010–1011), which suggests that in the continuous limit they might be exponentially distributed.

On the other hand, the hypothesis that link lengths are exponentially distributed is not so closely connected with symmetry requirements as the hypothesis that channel networks are topologically random, and therefore is not so immediately plausible. Also, the model of Leopold and Langbein is not geomorphologically very realistic. Real channel networks generally grow headward, and, unlike their counterparts in the model, compete for drainage area, adjust to the competition (Schumm 1956, p. 617–622), and sometimes even gain or lose whole blocks of territory by capture. Thus, it is not obvious on a priori grounds

alone that the distribution of link lengths should be exponential, or indeed what it should be. Nor, for that matter, is it obvious that the distribution of interior link lengths should be independent of order and magnitude. Clearly, careful field measurements in real channel networks are badly needed.

SCHUMM LENGTHS

Unfortunately, h_ω cannot be compared with the histograms published by Schumm (1956, p. 607, 610) because the stream lengths of given order as defined by him (p. 604) are not the mean lengths of individual streams of that order but are instead the mean total lengths of all the streams in sub-basins of that order. Thus, Schumm's stream lengths include exterior links, so that finding the densities corresponding to $h\omega$ is considerably more difficult.

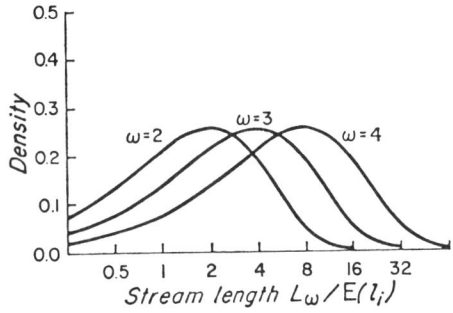

FIG. 8.—The densities of figure 7 transformed so that the horizontal coordinate is the logarithm of stream length. The curves all have the same shape; the modal lengths increase with order as a geometric series with ratio 2.

For subnetworks of magnitude μ, the Schumm length is the sum of μ exterior link lengths and $\mu - 1$ interior link lengths. In an infinite topologically random network, therefore, its density is

$$h_\omega^s = \sum_{\mu=2}^{\infty} p(\mu, \omega) g_{\nu,a_e}^{\mu *} * g_{\nu,a_i}^{(\mu-1)*} \Big/ u(\omega) , \quad (13a)$$

$$\omega = 2, 3, \ldots ,$$

assuming, for lack of better information, that both exterior and interior link lengths are gamma-distributed with the same ν and expectations ν/a_e and ν/a_i. Not only is (13a) more complicated than (12a), but also no general explicit formula for $p(\mu, \omega)$ or its bivariate generating function is known, although univariate formulas for successive values of ω can be calculated from (2b). For $\omega = 2$, the density $p(\mu, \omega)/u(\omega)$ is particularly simple, namely, from (1) and (4c),

$$p(\mu, 2)/u(2) = 1/2^{\mu-1}, \quad \mu = 2, 3, \ldots, \tag{13b}$$

which is a geometric density. Substituting (13b) into (13a), letting $\nu = 2$, and Laplace transforming the result gives

$$\mathbf{L}(h_2^S) = \sum_{\mu=2}^{\infty} \frac{1}{2^{\mu-1}} \left(\frac{a_e}{s+a_e}\right)^{2\mu}$$
$$\times \left(\frac{a_i}{s+a_i}\right)^{2(\mu-1)}, \tag{13c}$$
$$= \tfrac{1}{2} a_e^4 a_i^2 / \{(s+a_e)^2 [(s+a_e)^2 \times (s+a_i)^2 - \tfrac{1}{2} a_e^2 a_i^2]\},$$

in which, following custom, s denotes the variable in the frequency domain. The quartic in square brackets in the denominator is the difference of two squares; hence, it can be factored into the product of two quadratics, which in turn can be factored by means of the quadratic formula. The result is

$$(s + r_k) = s + \tfrac{1}{2}(a_e + a_i) \\ \pm \tfrac{1}{2}[(a_e - a_i)^2 \pm 2\sqrt{2}\, a_e a_i]^{1/2}, \tag{13d}$$

where the four factors corresponding to the subscript k are given by the four possible combinations of plus and minus signs. Note that r_k will be complex for certain values of a_e and a_i. For $a_e, a_i > 0$ these factors are distinct from each other and from $s + a_e$ except when

$$a_e/a_i = (1 + \sqrt{2}) \\ \pm \sqrt{2}(1 + \sqrt{2})^{1/2}, \tag{13e}$$

that is, when $a_e/a_i = 0.22$ or 4.6. Hence, the right-hand side of (13c) can be decomposed into partial fractions,

$$\mathbf{L}(h_2^S) = \frac{a}{(s+a_e)^2} + \frac{b}{s+a_e}$$
$$+ \frac{c_1}{s+r_1} + \frac{c_2}{s+r_2} \tag{13f}$$
$$+ \frac{c_3}{s+r_3} + \frac{c_4}{s+r_4},$$

where, unless a_e/a_i satisfies (13e),

$$a = -a_e^2, \quad b = 0, \tag{13g}$$
$$c_1 = \tfrac{1}{2} a_e^4 a_i^2 / [(a_e - r_1)^2 (r_2 - r_1) \\ \times (r_3 - r_1)(r_4 - r_1)],$$

and c_2, c_3, and c_4 are given by cyclic permutation of the numerical subscripts in the last formula. Thus, finally, using a standard table of inverse transforms,

$$h_2^S(L_2^S) = -a_e^2 L_2^S \exp(-a_e L_2^S) \\ + \sum_{k=1}^{4} c_k \exp(-r_k L_2^S), \tag{13h}$$
$$L_2^S, a_e, a_i > 0,$$
$$a_e/a_i \neq (1 + \sqrt{2}) \\ \pm \sqrt{2}(1 + \sqrt{2})^{1/2}.$$

The expectation of this density is

$$\mathbf{E}(L_2^S) = 3\mathbf{E}(l_e) + 2\mathbf{E}(l_i), \tag{13i}$$

in agreement with (5d).

By the same process, using (2b), the density of third-order Schumm lengths is

$$h_3^S(L_3^S) = -a_e^2 L_3^S \exp(-a_e L_3^S) \\ + \sum_{k=1}^{4} c_k \exp(-r_k L_3^S) \\ + \sum_{k=1}^{8} d_k \exp(-t_k L_3^S), \tag{14a}$$
$$L_3^S, a_e, a_i > 0,$$

where r_k is given by (13d) and

$$l_k = \tfrac{1}{2}(a_e + a_i) \pm \tfrac{1}{2}[(a_e - a_i)^2 \\ \pm 2\sqrt{2a_e a_i}(1 \pm \tfrac{1}{2}\sqrt{2})^{1/2}]^{1/2}, \quad (14b)$$

and, provided the thirteen roots r_k, l_k, and a_e are all different,

$$c_1 = \tfrac{1}{16} a_e^8 a_i^6 / [(a_e - r_1)^2 (r_2 - r_1) \\ \times (r_3 - r_1)(r_4 - r_1)(l_1 - r_1) \\ \times (l_2 - r_1) \ldots (l_8 - r_1)],$$

$$d_1 = \tfrac{1}{16} a_e^8 a_i^6 / [(a_e - l_1)^2 (r_1 - l_1) \\ \times (r_2 - l_1) \ldots (r_4 - l_1) \\ \times (l_2 - l_1)(l_3 - l_1) \ldots (l_8 - l_1)], \quad (14c)$$

and $c_2, c_3, c_4, d_2, d_3, \ldots, d_7$ and d_8 are given by cyclic permutation of the numerical sub-

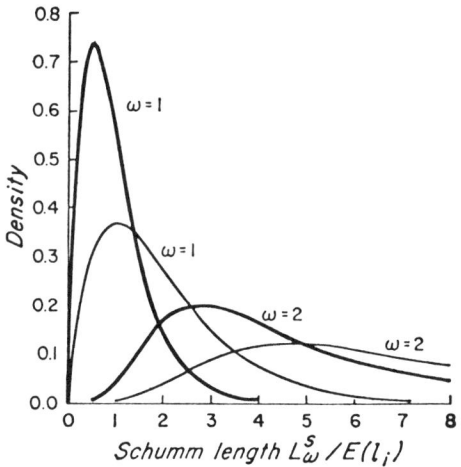

FIG. 9.—Densities of Schumm total stream lengths in infinite topologically random channel network if exterior and interior link lengths are gamma-distributed with $\nu = 2$ and expectations $E(l_e)$ and $E(l_i)$, where $E(l_e)/E(l_i) = 1$ (dark curves) and $E(l_e)/E(l_i) = 2$ (light curves).

scripts in the last two formulas. The expectation of density (14a) is

$$E(L_3^S) = 11E(l_e) + 10E(l_i). \quad (14d)$$

The densities g_{2,a_e}, h_2^S, and h_3^S are shown in figures 9 and 10, and are compared with Schumm's histograms in figure 11. The agreement between the calculated and the observed histograms is highly encouraging. Especially interesting is the lower dispersion and higher symmetry of the higher-order densities compared to the lower-order ones in figures 10 and 11; it suggests the conjec-

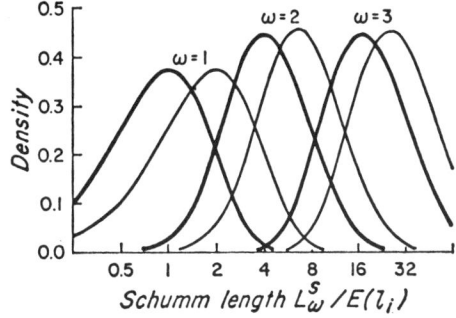

FIG. 10.—The densities of figure 9 transformed so that the horizontal coordinate is the logarithm of Schumm total stream length. Increasing the ratio $E(l_e)/E(l_i)$ merely shifts curves to right.

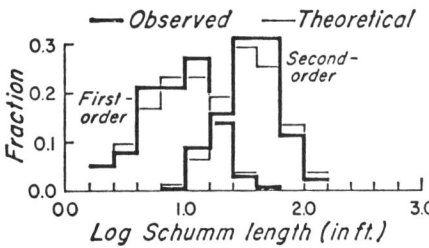

FIG. 11.—Comparison of theoretical and observed histograms of Schumm total stream length for the Perth Amboy, New Jersey, badlands basin studied by Schumm (1956, p. 607). First-order theoretical density assumed gamma with $\nu = 2$; second-order calculated for infinite topologically random channel network assuming interior link lengths also gamma-distributed with $\nu = 2$. Expected exterior and interior link lengths were taken equal to the observed means.

ture that, as a consequence of the central-limit theorem (Mood and Graybill 1963, p. 149–150), the densities of the higher-order lengths may be approximately log normal independently of the specific densities of link lengths and subbasin magnitudes.

The observed mean interior link length $\bar{l}_i$ needed as the estimator of $E(l_i)$ in computing the theoretical histograms of figure 11 was calculated from the data of Schumm (1956, p. 606, table 2) using the equation

$$L = \mu \bar{l}_e + (\mu - 1)\bar{l}_i, \quad (15)$$

where $\bar{l}_e$ and L are the mean first-order and the total stream lengths in a basin of magnitude μ (tables 1 and 2). Using these estimators in (13i) gives an expected second-order Schumm length of 43.2 feet, which compares well with the average (for forty-five subbasins) of 40.4 feet found by Schumm.

1966, p. 21–22). In order to avoid the ambiguity inherent in Horton's system, Strahler (1952, p. 1120) proposed the slightly different system used in this paper, which is now the one most commonly used. Unfortunately, stream lengths defined by Strahler's system do not fit Horton's law very well (Strahler 1952, p. 1137; 1957, p. 915; Broscoe 1959, p. 5; Maxwell 1960, p. 23; Bowden and Wallis 1964, p. 769–770); hence, modification of the content of the law

TABLE 1

MEASURED LENGTHS AND AREAS*

Basin	μ	L (Ft)	$\bar{l}_e$ (Ft)	A (Ft²)	$\bar{a}_f$ (Ft²)
Perth Amboy, N.J.	214	3.53×10^3	10.1	3.10×10^4	85.0
Chileno Canyon, Calif.	296	2.54×10^5	482.	8.61×10^7	1.67×10^5
Mill Dam Run, Md.	150	3.97×10^5	1420.	1.54×10^8	7.81×10^5

* Data from Schumm (1956, p. 606, table 2).

TABLE 2

DERIVED LENGTHS, AREAS, AND RATIOS

Basin	$\bar{l}_i$ (Ft)	$\bar{a}_i$ (Ft²)	$\bar{a}_s$* (Ft²)	$\bar{l}_e/\bar{l}_i$	$\bar{a}_f/\bar{a}_i$	$\bar{a}_s/\bar{a}_f$*
Perth Amboy, N.J.	6.43	60.3	-9.7	1.57	1.41	-0.11
Chileno Canyon, Calif.	3.77×10^2	1.24×10^5	8.42×10^3	1.28	1.35	0.05
Mill Dam Run, Md.	1.24×10^3	2.47×10^5	4.97×10^5	1.15	3.16	0.64

* Calculated assuming c in (21) is independent of position of channel in basin.

HORTON'S LAW

Horton's law of stream lengths states that "the average lengths of streams of each of the different orders in a drainage basin tend closely to approximate a direct geometric series in which the first term is the average length of streams of the 1st order" (Horton 1945, p. 291). The "streams of each of the different orders" are those defined by Horton's system of ordering, which involves subjective classification of one of the streams entering each fork as *trunk* and the other as *tributary* (Shreve

or of the definition of its terms has been proposed by a number of investigators. Strahler (1957, p. 915), for example, suggested changing the law to state that the total length of channel of each order varies inversely as some power of the order. Broscoe (1959, p. 5) and Bowden and Wallis (1964, p. 770) suggested that the geometric-series progression with order could be preserved by substituting the sum of the average stream lengths from the first through a given order, which they termed *cumulative mean length*, for the average stream length of that order. The cumulative lengths are approximations to the Horton lengths when the Strahler system of ordering is used. In a similar vein, Schumm (1956, p. 604) suggested using the average total length of channels in the subbasins of the given order.

At first sight it is surprising that such modifications should seem necessary, because (Mood and Graybill 1963, p. 147) the average stream lengths should cluster around the expected lengths (in the sense that, as the number of measurements increases, the mean observed lengths should approach arbitrarily close to the expected lengths with probability 1), and in infinite topologically random networks, according to (9c), the expected lengths will increase with order as a geometric series just as required by Horton's law. The explanation is that the population whose expectation is given by (9c) is not the one to which Horton's law refers. First, natural networks probably are not strictly topologically random. Such evidence as exists, however, suggests that in many, if not most, areas free of geologic controls they are not far from it (Shreve 1966, p. 31–36; 1967, p. 184–185; Smart, personal communication). Second, as already mentioned, the mean length of the exterior links in a basin generally is significantly greater than that of the interior links. This fact probably explains some of the concave-upward curvature in Horton diagrams of logarithm of stream length versus order reported by Broscoe (1959, p. 5) and Maxwell (1960, p. 62, fig. 11; note that text on p. 23 contradicts the figure). Third, and most important, regardless of which system of ordering is used, Horton's law applies to average stream lengths in finite networks, whereas (9c) refers to average stream lengths in infinite networks. Thus, comparison with (9c) is not necessarily proper, except as an indicator of general behavior (as in Shreve 1967, p. 184).

Expected average Strahler stream lengths in finite topologically random channel networks with given order and magnitude can be calculated in terms of the expected interior and exterior link lengths $\mathbf{E}(l_i)$ and $\mathbf{E}(l_e)$ independently of the specific distributions of the link lengths, assuming as before that the distribution of interior link lengths is independent of order, magnitude, or any other characteristic. With this assumption, the expected average length of streams of order 1 is $\mathbf{E}(l_e)$, and that of streams of order $\omega > 1$ is equal to the product of $\mathbf{E}(l_i)$ and the expected average number of links per stream of order ω. The expected average number of links per stream in turn is the average of $\mathbf{E}(\nu_\omega)$ over all of the possible sets of stream numbers, weighted according to the probability of occurrence of each set, where

$$\mathbf{E}(\nu_\omega) = \prod_{\beta=2}^{\omega} (n_{\beta-1} - 1) \big/ (2n_\beta - 1), \quad (16)$$

$$\omega = 2, 3, \ldots, \Omega,$$

(Smart 1968, p. 1007) is the expected number of links per stream of order ω in networks with stream numbers $n_1, n_2, \ldots, n_{\Omega-1}, 1$. For a topologically random population of networks of given magnitude and order, the sets of stream numbers and their probabilities can be computed by means of the algorithm and formulas given in a previous paper (Shreve 1966, p. 29, 31).

The expected average total channel lengths of Schumm can be calculated in similar fashion from the weighted average of $\mathbf{E}(\xi_\omega)$ over the possible sets of stream numbers, where

$$\mathbf{E}(\xi_\omega) = 1 + \sum_{\beta=2}^{\omega} \prod_{\alpha=2}^{\beta} 2(n_{\alpha-1} - 1) \big/ (2n_\alpha - 1), \quad (17)$$

$$\omega = 2, 3, \ldots, \Omega,$$

is the expected number of links per subnetwork of order ω in networks with stream numbers $n_1, n_2, \ldots, n_{\Omega-1}, 1$. The expected total length per subnetwork of order ω is then $\tfrac{1}{2}\mathbf{E}(l_e)[\mathbf{E}(\xi_\omega) + 1] + \tfrac{1}{2}\mathbf{E}(l_i)[\mathbf{E}(\xi_\omega) - 1]$ from Melton's relationships (Melton 1959, p. 345; Shreve 1966, p. 27).

The cumulative mean lengths of Broscoe

can be computed simply by summation of the expected average Strahler stream lengths.

To derive (16) and (17), consider the process of constructing topologically random networks with given stream numbers $n_1, n_2, \ldots, n_{\Omega-1}, 1$ by starting with the single main stream and in cycles adding the streams of successively lower order as done by Shreve [1966, p. 29] and in the original derivation of (16) by Smart [1968, p. 1005–1007]. If after the ath cycle the expected number of links in streams of some given order ω is $E_a(\nu_\omega)$, then after the next cycle it will be

$$E_{a+1}(\nu_\omega) = E_a(\nu_\omega) R_a ,$$

$$R_a = (n_{\Omega-a} - 1)/(2n_{\Omega-a+1} - 1) ,$$

$$a = \Omega - \omega + 1, \qquad (18a)$$

$$\Omega - \omega + 2, \ldots, \Omega - 1 ,$$

$$\omega = 2, 3, \ldots, \Omega ,$$

counting addition of the streams of order $\Omega - 1$ as the second cycle. These equations express the fact that in the construction of topologically random networks, in which all topologically distinct arrangements are equally likely, the expected number of links in individual streams of a given order increases in direct proportion to the total number of links of that order and higher. Streams of order ω will consist of a single link when $a = \Omega - \omega + 1$; hence, by induction,

$$E(\nu_\omega) = \prod_{a=\Omega-\omega+1}^{\Omega-1} R_a , \qquad (18b)$$

$$\omega = 2, 3, \ldots, \Omega ,$$

from which (16) follows by letting $\beta = \Omega - a + 1$ and reversing the order of multiplication.

Similarly, if after the ath cycle the expected number of links in subnetworks of order ω is $E_a(\xi_\omega)$, then after the next cycle it will be

$$E_{a+1}(\xi_\omega) = E_a(\xi_\omega) + 2E_a(\xi_\omega)$$

$$\times (n_{\Omega-a} - 2n_{\Omega-a+1})/(2n_{\Omega-a+1} - 1)$$

$$+ E_a(\xi_\omega) + 1 ,$$

$$a = \Omega - \omega + 1, \qquad (19a)$$

$$\Omega - \omega + 2, \ldots, \Omega - 1 ,$$

$$\omega = 2, 3, \ldots, \Omega .$$

The second term on the right-hand side is the increase in the expected number of links due to addition of new tributary links along the sides of the already existing streams; and the sum of the last two terms is, from Melton's relationships (Melton 1959, p. 345; Shreve 1966, p. 27), the increase due to addition of two new tributary links at the head of each stream. As before, subnetworks that will ultimately be of order ω will consist of a single link when $a = \Omega - \omega + 1$; hence, by induction, combining the terms in (19a),

$$E(\xi_\omega) = 1 + 2R_{\Omega-1}\{1 + 2R_{\Omega-2}$$

$$\times [1 + \ldots + 2R_{\Omega-\omega+2} \qquad (19b)$$

$$\times (1 + 2R_{\Omega-\omega+1}) \ldots]\} ,$$

$$\omega = 2, 3, \ldots, \Omega ,$$

from which (17) follows by successively eliminating the parenthetical expressions.

Figures 12, 13, and 14 show Horton diagrams of the expected stream lengths and numbers for topologically random populations of networks of various magnitudes and orders. Certain generalizations are immediately apparent. First, as in natural networks, the Strahler lengths do not satisfy Horton's law nearly so well as do the Strahler numbers, whereas the Broscoe and Schumm lengths do. Second, the curves are straightest for the most probable networks, as observed in natural networks by Smart (1968, p. 1007), and, except for the first-order lengths, are concave upward for networks whose order is less than the most probable, that is, whose geometric-mean bifurcation ratio is less than about 4 (Shreve 1966, p. 31), and the converse. Finally, for μ given and $E(l_e)/E(l_i)$ in the range from 1 to 2, the geometric-mean Strahler length ratio, which, incidentally, is preferable to the arithmetic-mean ratio sometimes used, is close to 2, and the Broscoe and Schumm ratios are close to 2.5 and 4.5, respectively, in approximate agreement with observed values (Schumm 1956, p. 604–605).

BASIN AREAS

Although Horton did not specifically include basin areas in his laws of drainage composition, he implied that they should satisfy a geometric-series law like stream numbers and lengths (Horton 1945, p. 294; Schumm 1956, p. 606). This *law of basin areas*, as it was subsequently formulated by Schumm (p. 606) in the style of Horton, states that "the mean drainage-basin areas of streams of each order tend to approximate closely a direct geometric series in which the first-order term is the mean area of the first-order basins." This law not only is identical to the law of stream lengths but also can be treated theoretically in exactly the same way.

Let a_f and a_i be, respectively, the first-order areas and the double-triangular areas draining directly overland into individual interior links. Like link lengths, these areas are random variables. Judging from the data of Schumm (p. 607, 609), they are distributed according to right-skewed densities very similar to those for link lengths. In the absence of better in-

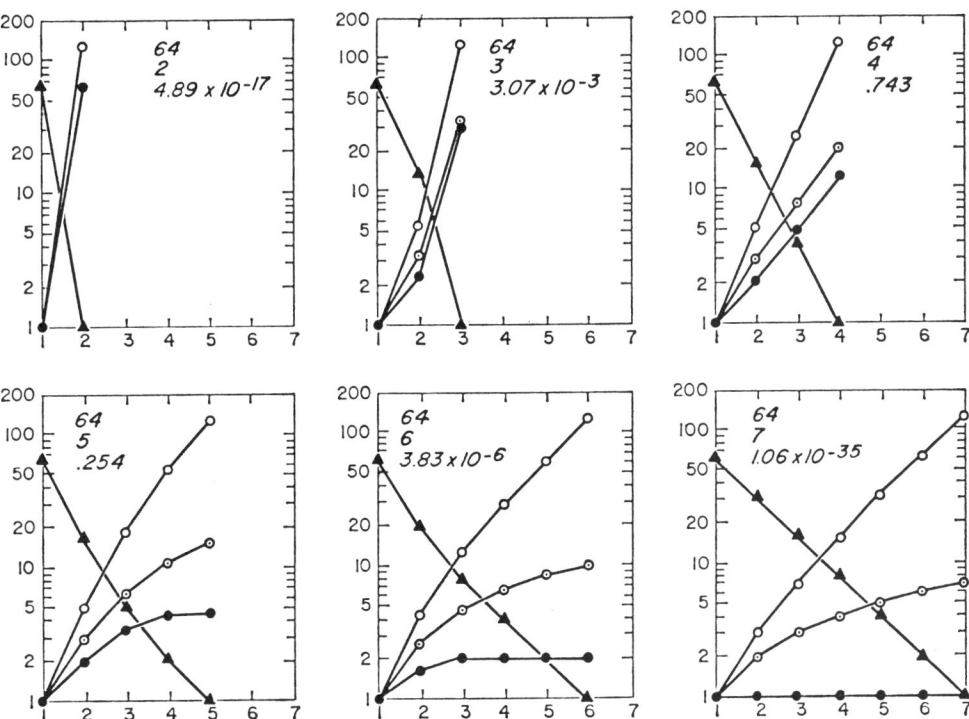

FIG. 12.—Horton diagrams of expected stream lengths and numbers for topologically random populations of networks of magnitude 64 in which expected interior and exterior link lengths are equal. Strahler stream lengths shown by solid circles, Broscoe lengths by circles with dots, Schumm lengths by open circles, and stream numbers by triangles. Unit of stream length is expected interior link length. Horizontal coordinate is stream order. The three numbers in each diagram are, from top to bottom, network magnitude, network order, and probability that a network of the given magnitude will have the specified order.

STREAM LENGTHS AND BASIN AREAS 411

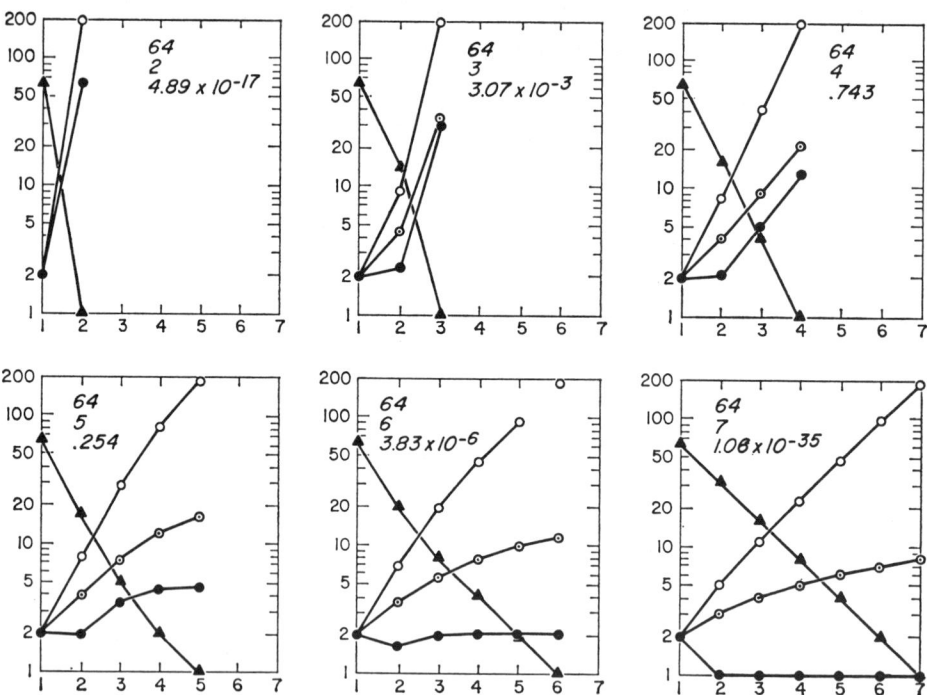

FIG. 13.—Horton diagrams of expected stream lengths and numbers for topologically random populations of networks of magnitude 64 in which expected exterior link lengths are twice expected interior link lengths. Coordinates and symbols same as in figure 12.

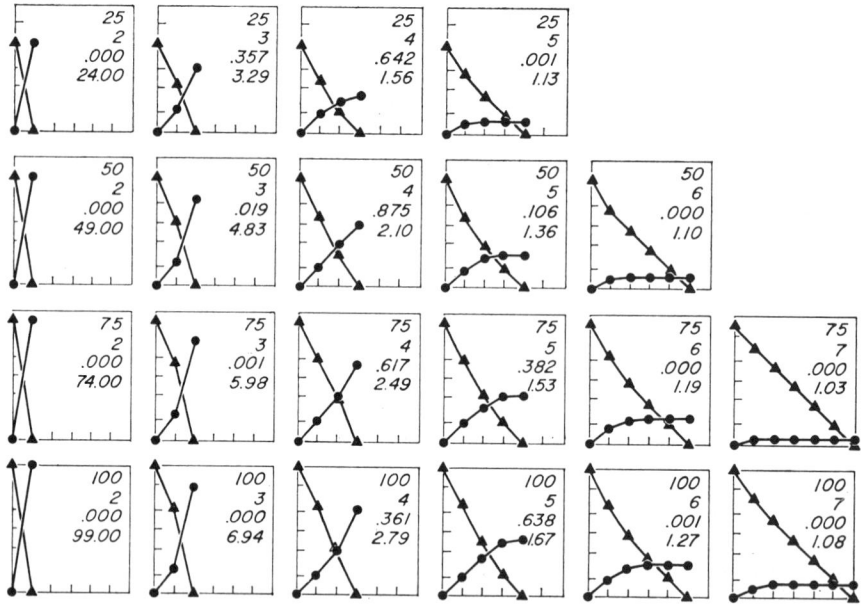

FIG. 14.—Horton diagrams of expected Strahler stream lengths and numbers for topologically random populations of networks of magnitude 25, 50, 75, and 100 in which expected interior and exterior link lengths are equal. Coordinates and symbols same as in figure 12. Fourth number in each diagram is the geometric-mean length ratio.

formation, therefore, it seems justifiable as a first approximation to assume the same type of densities, namely, gamma densities with $\nu = 2$ and expectations $E(a_f) = 2/a_f$ and $E(a_i) = 2/a_i$. With this assumption all of the previous results for Schumm total stream lengths are directly applicable to basin areas.

The theoretical densities of basin areas in infinite topologically random channel networks are shown in figures 9 and 10, and are compared with Schumm's histograms in figure 15. Again, the agreement between

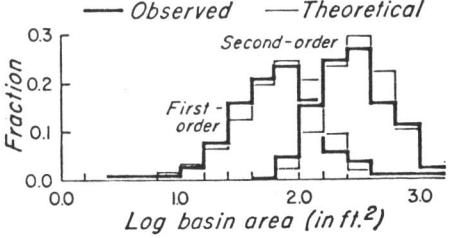

Fig. 15.—Comparison of theoretical and observed histograms of subbasin area for the Perth Amboy, New Jersey, badlands basin studied by Schumm (1956, p. 607). Assumptions same as for figure 9.

the calculated and the observed histograms is highly encouraging.

Incidentally, in the table given by Schumm (p. 608, table 4), the frequencies for the first-order areas are one column to to the left of their correct positions.

Just as in the case of link lengths, the observed mean interior area $\bar{a}_i$ needed as the estimator of $E(a_i)$ was calculated using the equation

$$A = \mu \bar{a}_f + (\mu - 1)\bar{a}_i, \qquad (20)$$

where $\bar{a}_f$ and A are the mean first-order and total areas in a basin of magnitude μ (tables 1 and 2). Using these estimators in the equation analogous to (13i) gives an expected second-order area of 376 ft^2, which may be compared with the average (for forty-five subbasins) of 343 ft^2 found by Schumm (p. 606, table 2).

Horton diagrams of the expected areas in finite topologically random channel networks are shown in figures 12, 13, and 16. Like expected lengths, expected areas do not depend upon the specific distributions of the first-order and interior areas, but only upon their expectations, provided as before that the distribution of interior areas is independent of order, magnitude, or any other characteristic. The diagrams show that the expected areas satisfy Horton's law rather well. The curves are straightest for the most probable networks, that is, for those whose geometric-mean bifurcation ratio is about 4 (Shreve 1966, p. 31), and are concave upward for networks whose order is less than the most probable, and the converse. Finally, the geometric-mean area ratio for the expected areas in the most probable networks is about 4.5, in approximate agreement with observed values (Schumm 1956, p. 604–605).

CONSTANT OF CHANNEL MAINTENANCE

Schumm (1956, p. 606–607) pointed out the nearly linear relationship between area and Schumm total stream length in drainage basins, and proposed (p. 608) that the average area c draining directly overland into unit length of channel is a constant characteristic of the bedrock and environment but independent of the particular position of the channel in the basin.

Although c seems to be the average area required to maintain unit length of channel as meant by Schumm (p. 607), it is not the *constant of channel maintenance* as defined by him, which is instead the slope in a simple linear regression model relating the average drainage area to the average total channel length in the subbasins of the various orders in a single drainage basin. Mathematically, neither c nor, contrary to the assertion by Schumm (p. 607), the constant of channel maintenance is the reciprocal of drainage density, that is, is equal to A/L, because of the contribution of the areas draining directly into the sources in the first case and the presence of the nonzero constant term in the model in the second. Practically, however, the constant of channel maintenance will be approximately equal to the reciprocal of drainage density whenever the basin area is large compared to the constant term in the model.

Incidentally, the model is valid only for the discrete points corresponding to the orders, so the meaning of the constant term is complex. In particular, it is not the average area draining into each source, as the improper procedure of setting the length equal to zero would suggest.

(tables 1 and 2). Thus, c cannot be independent of the particular position of the channel in the basin, but instead must be less for exterior links than for interior links.

The same calculation, also based on the data of Schumm, gives $\bar{a}_s/\bar{a}_f = 0.05$ for Chileno Canyon, California, and 0.64 for Mill Dam Run, Maryland. These differences are readily apparent in the basins themselves. In both the Perth Amboy basin

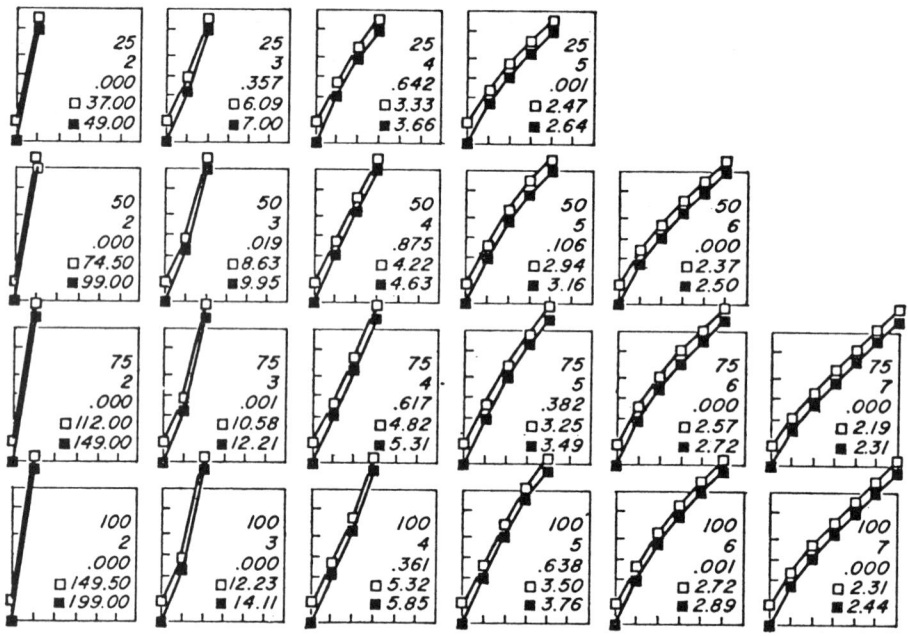

FIG. 16.—Horton diagrams of expected subbasin areas (or Schumm total stream lengths) for topologically random populations of networks of magnitude 25, 50, 75, and 100 in which the ratio of exterior to interior expected drainage areas (or link lengths) is 1 (solid squares) and 2 (open squares). Coordinates and symbols same as in figure 12. Fourth and fifth numbers in each diagram are geometric-mean area (or Schumm-length) ratios.

The proposal that c is constant is not supported by Schumm's own data from the Perth Amboy, New Jersey, badlands. This is shown by solving the identity

$$A = cL + \mu \bar{a}_s \qquad (21)$$

for the average source area $\bar{a}_s$ assuming that $c = \bar{a}_i/\bar{l}_i$ as required if it is constant. The quantities $\bar{l}_i$ and $\bar{a}_i$ can be found by means of (15) and (20). Substitution of the numerical values reported by Schumm then gives the impossible result $\bar{a}_s/\bar{a}_f = -0.11$

and Chileno Canyon, slopes are near the angle of repose, ridges are sharp, and many first-order basins are long, narrow chutes with tiny source areas at their heads. In the basin of Mill Dam Run, on the other hand, slopes are gentle, interfluves are broad, and first-order basins are more ovoid in plan with large source areas draining flat uplands.

These striking differences are not reflected in the Horton diagrams for the three basins. The stream numbers, lengths, and areas conform to Horton's laws and the bifurcation, length, and area ratios are comparable in all three basins (Schumm 1956, p. 603, 604, 605). The calculations in this and previous papers (Shreve 1966, 1967; Smart 1968) show that this lack of sensitivity to substantial differences in geomorphic character is primarily due to two factors. First, channel networks developed in the absence of geologic controls are to a considerable degree topologically random. Second, the stream lengths and areas in a Horton analysis are sums of many link lengths or their associated areas. The Horton variables, in other words, behave so well because the deviations have been averaged out. Of most fundamental significance, therefore, are not the Horton variables but the more elementary quantities, such as link lengths and source areas.

ACKNOWLEDGMENTS.—Essential unpublished information on theoretical developments was freely given by J. S. Smart, and on link lengths by Smart, M. A. Melton, W. C. Krumbein, and M. J. Kirkby. Financial support was provided by the National Science Foundation (grant GA-1137) and the University of California. The numerical computations were carried out on the IBM 360/75 and associated equipment of the UCLA Campus Computing Network.

REFERENCES CITED

AITCHISON, J., and BROWN, J. A. C., 1957, The lognormal distribution: New York, Cambridge Univ. Press, 176 p.

BOWDEN, K. L., and WALLIS, J. R., 1964, Effect of stream-ordering technique on Horton's laws of drainage composition: Geol. Soc. America Bull., v. 75, p. 767–774.

BROSCOE, A. J., 1959, Quantitative analysis of longitudinal stream profiles of small watersheds: New York, Columbia Univ. Dept. Geology, Office of Naval Research Project NR 389-042, Tech. Rept. no. 18, 73 p.

CHAPMAN, D. G., 1956, Estimating the parameters of a truncated gamma distribution: Annals of Mathematical Statistics, v. 27, p. 498–506.

DWIGHT, H. B., 1961, Tables of integrals and other mathematical data: New York, Macmillan Co., 336 p.

FELLER, W., 1957, An introduction to probability theory and its applications: New York, John Wiley & Sons, v. 1, 461 p.

——— 1966, An introduction to probability theory and its applications: New York, John Wiley & Sons, v. 2, 626 p.

HORTON, R. E., 1945, Erosional development of streams and their drainage basins; hydrophysical approach to quantitative morphology: Geol. Soc. America Bull., v. 56, p. 275–370.

LEOPOLD, L. B., and LANGBEIN, W. B., 1962, The concept of entropy in landscape evolution: U.S. Geol. Survey Prof. Paper 500–A, p. A1–A20.

MAXWELL, J. C., 1960, Quantitative geomorphology of the San Dimas Experimental Forest, California: New York, Columbia Univ. Dept. Geology, Office of Naval Research Project NR 389-042, Tech. Rept. no. 19, 95 p.

MELTON, M. A., 1957, An analysis of the relations among elements of climate, surface properties, and geomorphology: New York, Columbia Univ. Dept. Geology, Office of Naval Research Project NR 389-042, Tech. Rept. no. 11, 102 p.

——— 1959, A derivation of Strahler's channel-ordering system: Jour. Geology, v. 67, p. 345–346.

MOOD, A. M., and GRAYBILL, F. A., 1963, Introduction to the theory of statistics (2d ed.): New York, McGraw-Hill Book Co., 443 p.

SCHUMM, S. A., 1956, Evolution of drainage systems and slopes in badlands at Perth Amboy, New Jersey: Geol. Soc. America Bull., v. 67, p. 597–646.

SHREVE, R. L., 1966, Statistical law of stream numbers: Jour. Geology, v. 74, p. 17–37.

——— 1967, Infinite topologically random channel networks: Jour. Geology, v. 75, p. 178–186.

SMART, J. S., 1968, Statistical properties of stream lengths: Water Resources Research, v. 4, p. 1001–1014.

———; SURKAN, A. J.; and CONSIDINE, J. P., 1967, Digital simulation of channel networks, *in* Symposium on river morphology: Internat. Assoc. Sci. Hydrology Pub. 75, p. 87–98.

STRAHLER, A. N., 1952, Hypsometric (area-altitude) analysis of erosional topography: Geol. Soc. America Bull., v. 63, p. 1117–1142.

——— 1957, Quantitative analysis of watershed geomorphology: Am. Geophys. Union Trans., v. 38, p. 913–920.

A COMPUTER MODEL FOR SOME BRANCHING-TYPE PHENOMENA IN HYDROLOGY

K. H. LIAO and A. E. SCHEIDEGGER
University of Illinois, Urbana, Ill.

ABSTRACT

In hydrology, branching-type phenomena occur in several instances, for example in ground-water flow (splitting flow channels in a porous medium) and in the formation of a natural river network (combining, i.e., inverse branching, of small rivers to form large rivers). Such phenomena can be treated by the statistics of topological bifurcating arborescences. It is shown how ensembles of arborescences can be generated on a computer and expectation values for observables can be calculated. In this fashion, the laws of dispersion processes in flow through porous media and Horton's law of stream numbers in drainage basins are shown to be the outcome of very simple statistical assumptions.

I. INTRODUCTION AND ACKNOWLEDGEMENTS

In water resources problems, one finds instances where the branching of flow channels is of great interest: channels either split or combine, forming thereby a network. An instance of splitting flow channels is found in miscible displacement in a porous medium, an instance of combining flow channels in the formation of a natural river network in a drainage basin.

Miscible displacement in a porous medium is essentially a dispersive process (see e.g. Scheidegger, 1960). There are a number of theories, mostly based on some type of statistical mechanics, which attempt to account for the dispersion in a porous medium. It is one of the aims of the present paper actually to model such a process on a computer. In this, we confine ourselves to a linear process and follow the spread of a "spot" of (miscible) "dye" in an overall stream flowing through a porous medium.

The geometry of a drainage network is characterized by Horton's law of stream numbers: The number of river segments of different (Strahler 1957) orders present in a network form a geometric sequence. The writer has suggested earlier (Scheidegger, 1967) that this is nothing but the outcome of a complete topological randomness in channel configurations. Thus, the second aim of this paper is to test this contention.

In both instances mentioned above, the indicated aim can be accomplished by investigating the statistics of a particular type of topological "graph": viz. of "bifurcating arborescences".

The work reported in this paper was supported in part by funds provided by the United States Department of Interior, Office of Water Resources Research, as authorized under the Water Resources Act of 1964, Public Law 88-379, under grant number B-010-Illinois, agreement number 14-01-0001-1015. The computations were performed on the University of Illinois IBM 7094-1401 system operating under a grant from the National Science Foundation. Without this support, this work could not have been done. Mr. Hans Pulpan of the University of Illinois carried out some of the actual calculations; the authors wish to thank him therefor.

II. Dispersion in Porous Media

A. The Model

In setting up a suitable model for dispersion processes in porous media, we refer to the view of the passage of fluid particles through such a medium as a stochastic process. For the purposes of this paper, we consider only linear processes.

There are, of course, many ways by which a stochastic process can be modeled on a computer. We choose a particular approach in which the pore space is considered as a random medium in which the fluid moves. By virtue of the ergodic hypothesis, the consideration of ensembles of such random media is equivalent to the consideration of a time-evolutionary stochastic process, viz. of the motion of the fluid through the porous medium.

Let us now envisage that a unit mass of foreign (miscible) fluid enters a porous medium at time $t = 0$ at a particular level. This fluid, then, will spread through the medium by an essentially branching-type process. For the sake of simplicity, let us assume that each "junction" of flow paths is only a bifurcating junction. Then, the unit mass injected will spread in a geometrical form which, in graph theory, is called a "bifurcating arborescence" (see e.g. Berge, 1958). In any particular case, we might assume that one obtains a particular bifurcating arborescence with a certain number of pendant (free) vertices. We bring in the idea of randomness of the medium by considering not one particular graph, but the ensemble of all possible graphs with a given number of pendant vertices. For calculating expectation values, we assume that every possible arborescence within the given ensemble is equally probable. As noted above, by virtue of the ergodic hypothesis, the expectation value for the position of the fluid taken over an ensemble of graphs will be equal to the expectation value for the position of the fluid as a result of a stochastic branching process.

In this view of flow of fluids through a porous medium, the recombination of flow channels may be neglected. We are not concerned in this, linear, theory with the actual sideways spread of the tracer; hence, an arborescence "spreading" from its root is only a topological *model* of the process in question; in fact, some of the vertices reached may in actuality be identical in space.

Thus, we consider the ensemble of all possible bifurcating arborescences with a given number n of pendant vertices. The number N of different such graphs is (see e.g. Berge, 1958)

$$N = \frac{1}{2n-1}\binom{2n-1}{n} \tag{1}$$

Every arborescence under consideration has a certain maximum and mean "height". The maximum "height" h_{max} indicates the maximum distance at which some free vertices are situated from the root, the mean height h_{mean} indicates the mean distance of the free vertices from the root and the zeros will have a certain standard deviation σ_h^2 around their mean position. The quantities h_{max}, h_{mean}, and σ_h^2 will have a certain distribution over the ensemble, their mean values, $\bar{h}_{max}$, $\bar{h}_{mean}$, and $\overline{\sigma_h^2}$ indicate the dispersion occurring by the stochastic process. The aim, then, is to calculate the values of $\bar{h}_{max}$, $\bar{h}_{mean}$, and $\overline{\sigma_h^2}$ for ensembles of arborescences.

B. The Method of Calculation

In order to generate graphs on a computer, it is first of all necessary to have a suitable numerical representation of same. In this instance, the representation of arborescences due to Lukasiewicz (see Berge, 1958) is particularly convenient: One represents the mathematical arborescence with n pendant vertices by a left-to-right sequence (a "word") of $2n-1$ numbers, consisting of n zeros and $n-1$ ones. The word is obtained from the graph by putting 1 for each junction, zero for each pendant vertex and reading the graph from its root at the top to the bottom and from the left to the right (see fig. 1).

Conversely, a "word" of n zeros and $n-1$ ones describes one and only one bifurcating arborescence. Such a word is determined only up to cyclic permutations. Of all the possible cyclic permutations of a particular word, one and only one has the easy correspondence with the graph, starting the "reading" of the graph from its root at the top.

In principle, the task is, thus, to enumerate all possible graphs for a given number n of pendant vertices. However, the number N of different graphs in an ensemble (see eq. (1)) rapidly gets very large. An estimate (using Stirling's formula) for $n = 20$ already yields $N \approx 1.8 \times 10^9$. Since the generation of one word and the calculation of h_{max}, h_{mean}, and σ_h^2 takes a time of the order of one millisecond on a large and fast computer, it is evident that many days of computer time would be required to enumerate *all* possible graphs if n is reasonably large (say > 20).

One has no other choice, then, but to sample the possible words by a Monte Carlo technique. This is done by random-generating words of a given length, possessing the required number of zeros and ones. This is best achieved by using an available random number generator whose values X range from 0.0 to 1.0. If $X > C$, we assume that a 1 is generated, if $X < C$, a zero, where C is the probability for drawing a zero from the available zeros and ones (if $X = C$, the trial is rejected). This number C changes after every "draw" depending on what number of zeros and ones are left for the word being generated.

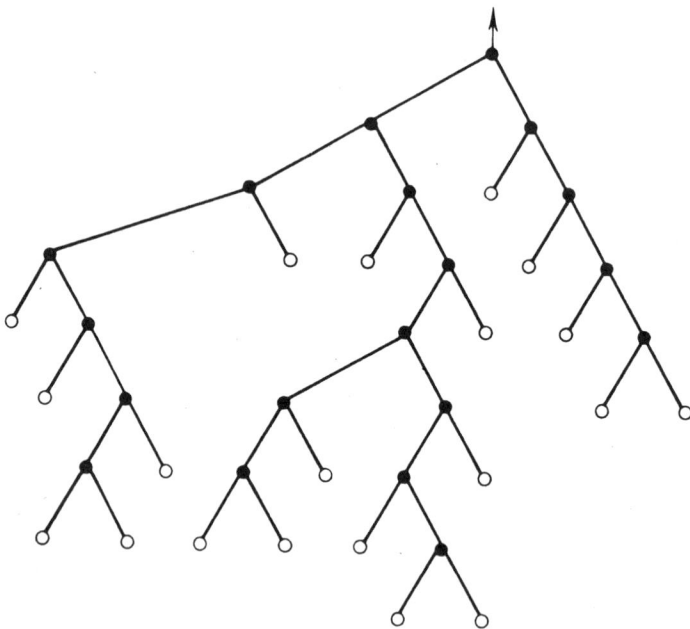

Fig. 1 — Graph represented by the word
(111101011000010111100011010000101010100)
Note $h_{max} = 8$, $h_{mean} = 5.6$.

In this fashion, a word containing the right number of zeros and ones is obtained. The next step is to find the right starting point through cyclic permutation of the random-generated word. The program tests every possible starting position, but only one gives a coherent "graph"; this is the correct one.

Next, the maximum h_{max} and mean h_{mean} heights of the random-generated graphs are calculated. For each zero, one finds its distance h_i from the vertex; the maximum of these numbers is h_{max}, the mean value is h_{mean}

$$h_{mean} = \frac{1}{n} \sum h_i \qquad (2)$$

for the particular graph under consideration. Of interest is also the standard deviation σ_h of the heights of the graph under consideration.

$$\sigma_h^2 = \frac{1}{n} \sum (h_i - h_{mean})^2 \qquad (3)$$

since this gives the spread of the pendant vertices in the graph around their mean position.

Then, the values of h_{max} and h_{mean} and σ_h^2 are stored for every graph generated. A reasonable number (up to 10,000) of graphs are random-generated and $\overline{h}_{max}$, $\overline{h}_{mean}$, and $\overline{\sigma_h^2}$ are calculated from the corresponding stored values.

The program was written in Fastran language and executed on the 7094-1401 IBM system of the University of Illinois.

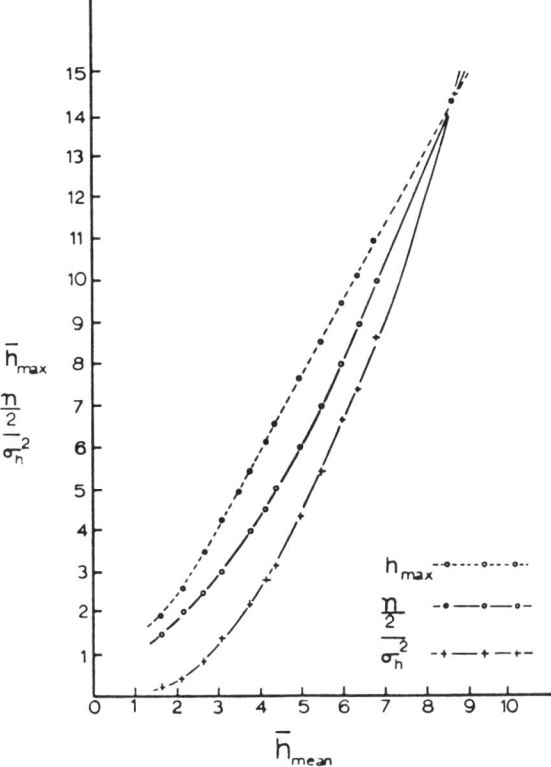

Fig. 2 — Plot of $\overline{\sigma_h^2}$ and $\overline{h}_{max}$ against $\overline{h}_{mean}$. The value of n (number of pendant vertices) is also indicated.

C. Results

In the calculations mentioned in the last section, $\bar{h}_{mean}$ represents the mean position of a "spot of dye" in a fluid stream at a certain time, then, $\overline{\sigma_h^2}$ is the spread of the dye around its mean position. The envisaged phenomenon is one-dimensional. Since, from phenomenological considerations,

$$\bar{h}_{mean} = Vt \tag{4}$$

where t is time and V the overall injection pore-velocity, we can identify $\bar{h}_{mean}$ with a measure of time in certain units, and plot $\overline{\sigma_h^2}$ against $\bar{h}_{mean}$. This has been done in figure 2 on a linear and in figure 3 on a log-log scale. At the same time, $\bar{h}_{max}$ shows the outer limit to which the dye has proceeded; this also is plotted against $\bar{h}_{mean}$ in figures 2 and 3. Since the graphic representation of the results is of necessity somewhat inaccurate, the actually obtained numbers are presented in table 1.

For a discussion of the results, one must refer to the general theory of dispersive processes. The mean square deviation is proportional to time

$$\overline{\sigma_h^2} \sim Dt \tag{5}$$

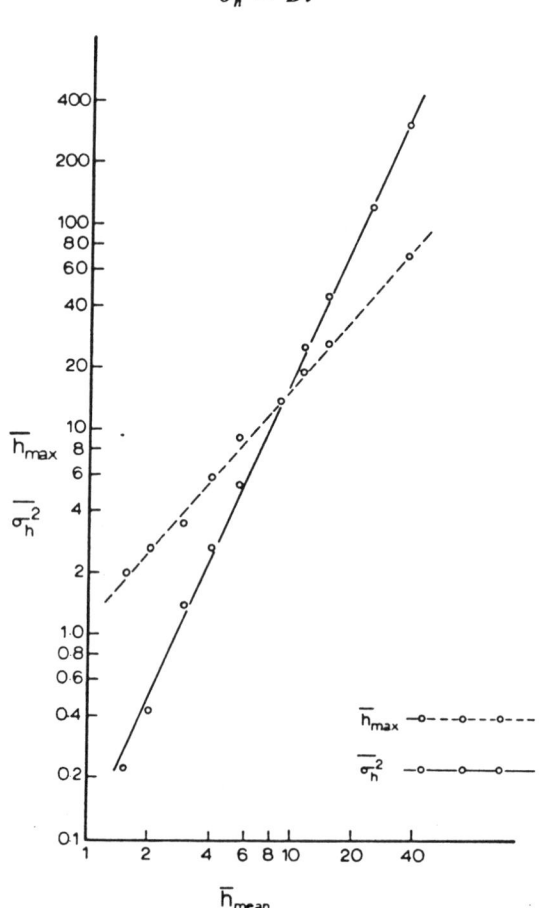

Fig. 3 — Plot of $\overline{\sigma_h^2}$ and $\bar{h}_{max}$ against $\bar{h}_{mean}$ on log-log paper.

TABLE 1

Results for model of flow through porous medium

Number of pendant vertices	Number of trials	h_{max}	h_{mean}	$\overline{\sigma_h^2}$
3	2	2.00	1.67	0.22
4	5	2.60	2.15	0.41
5	14	3.50	2.64	0.89
6	42	4.29	3.08	1.40
7	132	4.95	3.49	1.96
8	429	5.42	3.75	2.21
9	500	5.98	4.07	2.69
10	600	6.68	4.45	3.46
12	700	7.48	4.90	4.14
14	800	8.51	5.45	5.40
16	900	9.37	5.93	6.50
18	1,000	10.17	6.37	7.59
20	10,000	10.92	6.78	8.67
30	10,000	14.34	8.59	14.43
50	200	19.42	11.33	25.11
80	200	26.60	14.89	45.80
200	200	44.51	24.32	121.35
500	150	73.13	38.86	309.91

where D is the diffusivity constant (see e.g. Joos, 1934, p. 565). Thus, a plot of $\overline{\sigma_h^2}$ against h_{mean} as in figure 2 really represents a plot of Dt against Vt, or, for fixed t, a plot of D against V.

According to the general theory of miscible displacement, the relation between D and V for miscible displacement should lie between the extremes

$$D \sim V \tag{6}$$

and

$$D \sim V^2 \tag{7}$$

(see Scheidegger, 1960, p. 259).

An inspection of figure 2 shows that the curve of $\overline{\sigma_h^2}$ against h_{mean} indeed approximates a parabola. A closer check, shown in figure 3, where $\overline{\sigma_h^2}$ has been plotted against h_{mean} on log-log paper shows almost a straight line for the relationship in question, with a slope slightly above 2. Of the two possible extremal cases the present model, therefore, tends to favor the second

III. RIVER NETS

A. *The Model*

A graph-theoretical model for the representation of river networks was proposed by Scheidegger (1967), who considered a particular river network as the realization of a particular graph (bifurcating arborescence) amongst all possible graphs with a given number of pendant vertices.

In the ensemble of all possible graphs, each such graph is regarded as equally likely to be realized. It is, thus, possible to calculate "expectation values" of "observables" over the ensemble of all possible graphs with a given number of pendant vertices. Of particular interest as observables are the "height" of such graphs, and also the number of segments of the network in each Strahler order. The latter numbers lead to the bifurcation ratio; the observed constancy of the bifurcation ratio is usually referred to as Horton's (1945) law of stream numbers. A potential explanation of Horton's law lies in the conjecture that it is nothing but the expression of the complete randomness of the graph patterns. In effect, this conjecture was verified in the cited paper (Scheidegger, 1967) by hand-enumerating graphs to order 6 and by making a number of Monte Carlo trials with a pack of cards representing graphs with 20 pendant vertices. It is most desirable to carry this argument further by computerizing the approach indicated in the earlier paper.

B. *Method of Calculation*

The Monte Carlo method for generating porous media networks can easily be adapted to the problem of Horton's law of stream order numbers in a river net.

The main problem is to count in each word representing a graph how many segments of a given Strahler (1957) order the graph contains. This problem can easily be solved as follows: Start with a certain word, e.g. that represented by the graph in figure 1:

(1 1 1 1 0 1 0 1 1 0 0 0 0 1 0 1 1 1 1 0 0 0 1 1 0 1 0 0 0 0 1 0 1 0 1 0 1 0 0)

The number of zeros the word contains is equal to the number $n(1)$ of first order stream segments. Then, the computer searches for groups of the form 100. Each such sequence is replaced by the number 2, representing a second order stream segment, and each time such a replacement is made, a suitable counter, say $n(2)$, is increased by one (starting from zero). The word then has the form

(1 1 1 1 0 1 0 1 2 0 0 1 0 1 1 1 2 0 1 1 0 2 0 0 1 0 1 0 1 0 2)

The next step is to search the word for combinations $1\,XY$ where $Y, X \neq 1$. If $X \neq Y$, then the combination is replaced by max (X, Y), and nothing further is counted, if $X = Y$, the combination is replaced by the number $X + 1$ and the counter $n(X + 1)$ is increased by one. This procedure is repeated until only one number is left; the counters $n(2), n(3)$, etc. give directly the number of (Strahler) segments of order 2, 3, etc. which are present in the graph.

For the above word, the sequence is:

```
1 1 1 1 0 1 0 1 1 0 0 0 0 1 0 1 1 1 1 0 0 0 1 1 0 1 0 0 0 0 1 0 1 0 1 0 1 0 0
1 1 1 1 0 1 0 1 2 0 0 1 0 1 1 1 2 0 1 1 0 2 0 0 1 0 1 0 1 0 2
1 1 1 1 0 1 0 2 0 1 0 1 1 2 1 2 0 0 1 0 1 0 2
1 1 1 1 0 2 0 1 0 1 1 2 2 0 1 0 2
1 1 1 2 0 1 0 1 3 0 2
1 1 2 1 0 3 2
1 1 2 3 2
1 3 2
3
```

One therefore has an extremely simple means of counting out the number of Strahler-order segments present in a network given by its "word". For every graph generated, one obtains a sequence of numbers $n(1), n(2), n(3)$... etc. giving the number of segments present in each Strahler order.

Therefore, it is now easy to calculate expectation values for the numbers of Strahler segments present, by taking the averages over the graphs generated, viz. $\bar{n}(1), \bar{n}(2)$, etc. An approximation of the expected bifurcation ratios $\widetilde{B}_i$ is obtained by dividing the corresponding numbers of segments:

$$\tilde{B}_i = \frac{\bar{n}(i)}{\bar{n}(i+1)}$$

Alternatively, the bifurcation ratio can be calculated for each graph generated

$$B_i = \frac{n(i)}{n(i+1)}$$

and the bifurcation ratio averaged afterward

$$\bar{B}_i = \left[\frac{n(i)}{n(i+1)}\right]$$

Which bifurcation ratio is to be used, $\tilde{B}_i$ or $\bar{B}_i$, depends on the manner in which the latter is calculated in nature. It is often common to count the average numbers of segments in many basins, divide them, and arrive at a bifurcation ratio rather than calculating individual bifurcation ratios. The computer was programmed to calculate both possibilities.

C. *Results*

The calculations indicated above were carried out; the results are presented in table 2 (rounded to two decimals). Up to 30 free vertices, the calculations were performed with a relatively large (in relation to the number of possibilities) number of trials. It is seen that Horton's

TABLE 2

Results for model of river net

Number of pendant vertices	Number of trials	Number of segments, in Strahler order						
		1	2	3	4	5	6	7
3	2	3.00	1.00					
4	5	4.00	1.40	0.40				
5	14	5.00	1.50	0.50				
6	42	6.00	1.62	0.60				
7	132	7.00	1.86	0.70				
8	429	8.00	2.24	0.88	0.002			
9	500	9.00	2.43	0.94	0.014			
10	600	10.00	2.61	0.96	0.02			
12	700	12.00	3.18	1.07	0.08			
14	800	14.00	3.64	1.16	0.16			
16	900	16.00	4.13	1.25	0.25			
18	1,000	18.00	4.68	1.35	0.34			
20	10,000	20.00	5.11	1.46	0.43			
30	10,000	30.00	7.62	2.06	0.79	0.004		
80	200	80.00	20.20	5.10	1.50	0.46		
200	500	200.00	50.06	12.75	3.31	1.09	0.10	
500	150	500.00	129.78	31.39	8.00	2.06	0.80	0.01

TABLE 2 (continued)

Number of Pendant Vertices	Bifurcation Ratio $\tilde{B}$						Bifurcation Ratio $\bar{B}$					
	$i=1$	2	3	4	5	6	$i=1$	2	3	4	5	6
3	3.00						3.00					
4	2.86	3.50					3.20	0.80				
5	3.33	3.00					3.75	1.00				
6	3.70	2.72					4.19	1.21				
7	3.77	2.66					4.38	1.55				
8	3.57	2.53	378.00				4.02	2.11	0.005			
9	3.70	2.57	67.43				4.10	2.33	0.028			
10	3.83	2.72	48.00				4.29	2.51	0.04			
12	3.78	2.98	12.88				4.11	2.98	0.17			
14	3.85	3.13	7.09				4.16	3.26	0.33			
16	3.88	3.29	5.03				4.12	3.51	0.50			
18	3.85	3.45	3.97				4.08	3.75	0.70			
20	3.91	3.50	3.39				4.12	3.86	0.89			
30	3.94	3.70	2.61	202.36			4.08	4.16	1.84			
80	3.96	3.96	3.40	3.26			4.01	4.21	3.74	0.96		
200	3.99	3.93	3.85	3.04	10.67		4.01	4.01	4.14	3.06	0.21	
500	4.01	3.98	3.92	3.88	2.58	120.00	4.02	4.01	4.04	4.34	1.84	0.01

law of stream numbers for $\tilde{B}_i$ is fairly well satisfied, at least if a river net of a given order is fully developed. It is not surprising that discrepancies occur when a new order just starts to appear (the sampling procedure that was used makes itself felt in this case).

Although Horton's law is fairly well satisfied, there are systematic deviations inasmuch as $\tilde{B}$ decreases somewhat with stream order. This is, in fact, also found in nature.

It is remarkable that, for 20 free vertices, the computer-result for 10,000 trials is quite close to the hand-calculated result with 10 trials (Scheidegger, 1967). This gives one confidence to calculate systems with many free vertices with a relatively small number of trials. Such cases are also indicated in table 2. If the highest order in each case is again neglected, for obvious reasons, the results again bear out a remarkable constancy of the bifurcation ratio $\tilde{B}$ (Horton's law), with the usual tendency of $\tilde{B}_i$ to decrease with order i. For very large nets, the bifurcation ratios for the lowest orders (headwater region) tend to about 4. The averages of $\tilde{B}$ lie around 3.5, as corresponds to the observations in nature.

REFERENCES

BERGE, C., 1958, Théorie des graphes et ses applications. Paris : Dunod.
HORTON, R.E., 1954, Erosional development of streams and their drainage basins; hydro-physical approach to quantitative morphology. *Geol. Soc. Amer. Bull.*, **56**, 275-370.
JOOS, G., 1932, Theoretical physics. Translated by I. M. Freeman. London: Blackie and Son.
SCHEIDEGGER, A.E., 1960, The physics of flow through porous media. Revised Edition. New York: Macmillan Company.
SCHEIDEGGER, A.E., 1967, Random graph patterns of drainage basins. *Paper #157, 14th General Assembly*, U.G.G.I., Int. Assoc. Sci. Hydrol., Berne.
STRAHLER, A.N., 1957, Quantitative analysis of watershed geomorphology. *Amer. Geophys. Un. Trans.*, **38**, 913-920.

10

Copyright ©1973 by Ohio State University Press
Reprinted from *Geog. Analysis* **5**:271-295 (1973)

Some New Methods of Topologic Classification of Channel Networks

C. Werner and
J. S. Smart*

Abstract

Some new methods for the topologic classification of channel networks are proposed. These methods are all based on the concept of topologic path length, or number of links from the network outlet to a junction or source. Two parameters, the total path length (sum of all path lengths) and the diameter (largest path length) are shown to be useful in network analysis. Some advantages of these parameters are that they are easy to measure, have straightforward topologic interpretations, and are closely related to important geometric measures. Moreover, they are capable of explaining various empirical geomorphic "laws," such as the 0.6 power relation between mainstream length and area.

I. Topologically Distinct Channel Networks

In the quantitative analysis of drainage networks, it is convenient to choose for study the set of all channels above a given point in the drainage system, i.e., all channels that contribute to the discharge at that point. If the channels are idealized as single lines, the resulting figure is known in the geomorphological

---

* The research for this paper was supported in part by the Geography Programs, Office of Naval Research.

C. Werner is professor of geography at the University of California at Irvine (Wallace J. Eckert Fellow at the IBM Watson Research Center during the time of the preparation of this paper); J. S. Smart is research staff member at the Thomas J. Watson Research Center, Yorktown Heights, N.Y.

literature as a *channel network* (although in the usual mathematical terminology it would be called a *planted tree*). Figure 1 gives an example of a hypothetical channel network.

Sources are the points farthest upstream in a channel network, and the *outlet* is the point farthest downstream. A point at which two channels combine to form one is called a *junction* (we make here the usual assumption that confluences of more than two channels at a single point do not occur). *Links* are the channel segments between a source and the first junction downstream, between two successive junctions, or between the outlet and the first junction upstream. Links may be classified as *exterior* or *interior* depending on whether they have a source or a junction at the upstream end. A channel network with n sources has $n-1$ junctions and $2n-1$ links, of which n are exterior links and $n-1$ are interior links. The *magnitude* of a link is the number of sources upstream; from this definition it follows that an exterior link has magnitude unity and that the magnitude of an interior link is the sum of the magnitudes of the two links joining at its upstream end. The magnitude of a channel network is the total number of sources in the network or, what is equivalent, the magnitude of the outlet link.

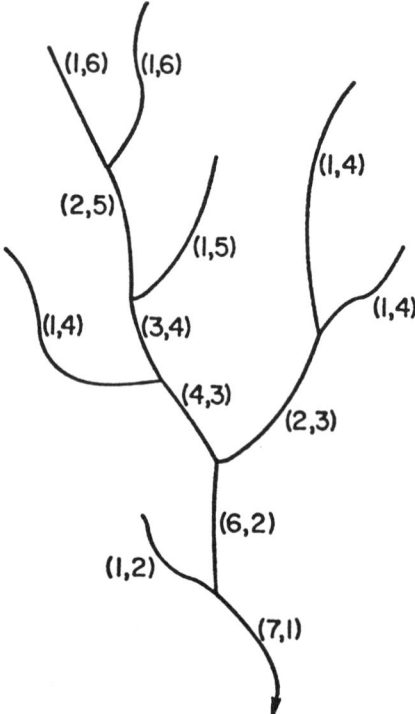

Fig. 1. A channel network of magnitude 7. The first number in each pair is the link magnitude and the second the path length to its upstream end.

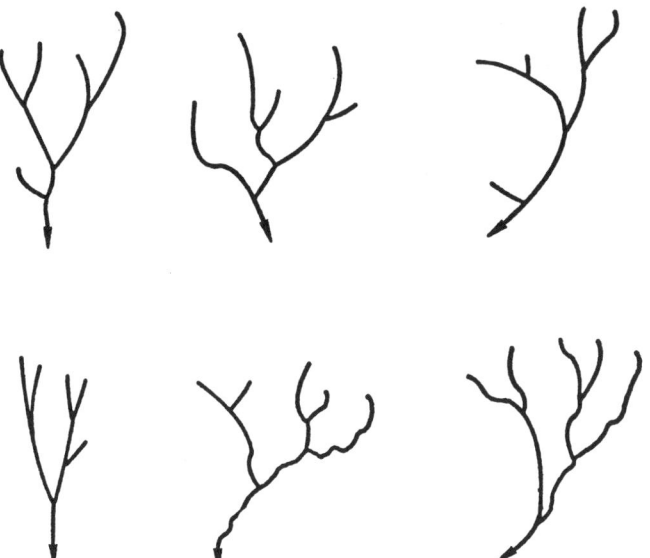

FIG. 2. Six channel networks of magnitude 5 traced from U.S.G.S. topographic maps. The first three are topologically identical and the second three topologically identical, but the two sets are topologically distinct.

The important concept of topologically identical and topologically distinct channel networks was first introduced by Shreve [17]. In a qualitative way, two networks are said to be topologically identical if one can be made congruent to the other by continuously deforming the links without removing them from the plane; some examples are shown in Figure 2. A precise definition can be given, for example, by use of the binary-string characterization of channel networks proposed by Shreve [18] and Scheidegger [16]. The topologic properties of any channel network can be specified by a string of n ones and $n - 1$ zeroes written according to the following rule: begin at the outlet and traverse the network by going left at each junction and reversing direction at each source; a zero is written whenever an interior link is traversed for the first time, and a one is written whenever an exterior link is traversed for the first time; nothing is written when the links are traversed for the second time (going toward the outlet). Thus the binary-string characterization for the channel network of Figure 1 is 0 1 0 0 1 0 0 1 1 1 0 1 1. Two channel networks are topologically identical if and only if they are represented by the same binary string; obviously, only networks with the same number of sources can be topologically identical.

The number of topologically distinct channel networks (TDCN) with n sources, $N(n)$, is known to be

$$N(n) = \frac{1}{2n-1}\binom{2n-1}{n}. \qquad (1)$$

This result was apparently first derived for tree structures by Caley [3], but the solution of an isomorphic mathematical problem, that of determining the number of ways of dissecting a convex polygonal region into triangles, goes back to deSegner, a colleague of Euler's. Values of $N(n)$ are given in Table 1, and the 14 possible TDCN for $n = 5$ are shown in Figure 3.

Shreve [17] noted that channel networks with equal numbers of sources are comparable in topological complexity since they also have equal numbers of links and junctions. He defined a topologically random population as one in which all TDCN with a given number of sources are equally likely. He then proposed the important hypothesis that a natural population of channel networks developed in the absence of geologic controls will be topologically random. This hypothesis has been tested in many different ways (see Smart [22], pp. 316–18, for a review) with the overall conclusion being that Shreve's model can be accepted as a good approximation for natural networks.

Because of the large values of $N(n)$ for even relatively small n, some method of grouping TDCN into classes is required before much quantitative investigation can be done. Ideally, the classification method should (1) provide a grouping into a manageable number of classes, (2) be reasonably easy to use, (3) have a simple topologic interpretation, and (4) emphasize any correlations that may exist between topologic and other geomorphic and hydrologic properties of drainage basins.

Strahler's [24] modification of Horton's [8] ordering scheme, which is based

TABLE 1

NUMBER OF CHANNEL-NETWORK CLASSES FOR GIVEN MAGNITUDE

n	TDCN	AMBILATERAL	PATH NUMBERS	TOTAL PATH LENGTH	DIAMETER	STREAM NUMBERS
1	1	1	1	1	1	1
2	1	1	1	1	1	1
3	2	1	1	1	1	1
4	5	2	2	2	2	2
5	14	3	3	3	2	2
6	42	6	5	5	3	3
7	132	11	9	8	4	3
8	429	23	16	12	5	5
9	1430	46	28	16	5	5
10	4862	98	50	21	6	7
11	16796	207	89	27	7	7
12	58786	451	159	34	8	10
13	2.080×10^5	983	285	42	9	10
14	7.429×10^5	2179	510	51	10	13
15	2.674×10^6	4850	914	61	11	13
16	9.695×10^6	10905	1639	72	12	18
17	3.536×10^7	24631	2938	83	12	18
18	1.296×10^8	56011	5269	95	13	23
19	4.776×10^8	1.279×10^5	9451	108	14	23
20	1.767×10^9	2.935×10^5	16952	122	15	30
40	6.804×10^{20}	8.100×10^{12}	2.015×10^9	604	34	195
60	4.059×10^{32}	3.486×10^{20}	2.396×10^{14}	1474	54	730
80	2.895×10^{44}	1.795×10^{28}	2.848×10^{19}	2728	73	2062
100	2.275×10^{56}	1.020×10^{36}	3.385×10^{24}	4378	93	4914

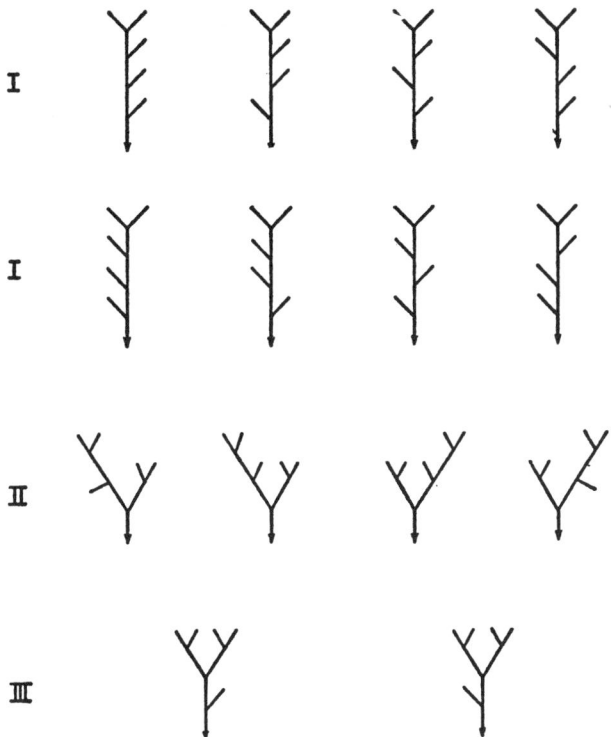

FIG. 3. The 14 TDCN for magnitude 5. The roman numerals identify the 3 ambilateral classes.

on the concept of stream numbers, has been since its inception the most commonly used method of channel-network classification, although the enumeration in terms of TDCN was not carried out until recently (Shreve [17]). The Horton-Strahler procedure satisfies our first two criteria fairly well (which observation no doubt accounts for its general use) but is not particularly successful with the last two. The information derived from a Horton-Strahler analysis typically consists of the basin order Ω and the stream numbers, mean stream lengths, and mean basin areas for orders 1 through Ω. From these quantities, the Strahler bifurcation ratio R_B, the stream-length ratio R_L, and the basin-area ratio R_A can be computed. Several attempts to find correlations between the topologic parameters in such data (order, stream numbers, and bifurcation ratio) and hydrologic variables have been unsuccessful. For example, Anderson [1] found no statistically significant relation between the Horton physiographic parameter $R_B R_S/R_L$ (R_S is the slope ratio) and either peak discharge or rate of sediment deposition for 41 watersheds in southern California. (In a subsequent discussion of this paper, Anderson reported new results which indicated that the Horton physiographic parameter did have some influence on peak discharge and that this influence varied with storm effectiveness. It may be noted that because of the high correlation between R_B and R_L [unrecognized at the time of Anderson's paper], the physiographic parameter depends only weakly on R_B.) In another study, Morisawa [14] examined data on several Appalachian Plateau drainage networks and found that R_B alone had no influence on the important hydrologic properties. A number of writers have reported finding significant correlations between basin order and such hydrologic variables as discharge and sediment load. Examination of their data, however, suggests that the correlations merely reflect the fact that all quantities involved, including basin order, are strongly dependent on basin area.

There are two possible reasons why the Horton-Strahler parameters apparently fail to give any substantial information about other geomorphic and hydrologic variables. One reason is of course that there may not be any relations between topology and the other quantities, and the other is that the Horton-Strahler method may not be effective in displaying relationships that do exist. Several authors, among them Scheidegger [15], Smart [21], Mock [13], and Jarvis [10], have proposed other topologic classification systems that were considered to be better than the Horton-Strahler method in one or more respects.

One topologic property that has been used extensively in applications of tree theory outside geomorphology is the path length. For the purposes of this paper, a *path* is the shortest route between the outlet of a channel network and a source or junction; thus, a network of magnitude n has $2n-1$ paths. The *topologic path length* is the number of links traversed in a path. It seems intuitively obvious that the topologic path lengths are rather closely related to various geomorphic and hydrologic properties, such as basin shape and peak discharge, and therefore might provide a useful basis for network classification. This paper provides a systematic survey of a sequence of topologic classification schemes based on the concept of path lengths in channel networks.

II. The Ambilateral Classification

Smart [21] suggested that TDCN of the same magnitude be grouped according to ambilateral classes. Although this method has not seen much practical application, the concept is useful as an introduction to the study of path lengths. Two channel networks belong to the same *ambilateral class* if and only if they can be made topologically identical by reversals of the right-left order at one or more junctions. Magnitude-5 networks, for example, have three ambilateral classes corresponding to the first eight, the next four, and the last two networks in Figure 3. Also, the channel network depicted in Figure 1 is one of the 16 TDCN in the fourth ambilateral class shown in Table 2. Smart argued that although hydrologic variables such as discharge and sediment load might depend on network topology, they should be essentially independent of the right-left order of subnetworks at the junctions. Since reversing the right-left arrangement leaves the link magnitudes unchanged, all networks of the same ambilateral class have the same set of magnitudes. The converse relation is, however, not always true.

TABLE 2
CLASSIFICATION METHODS FOR MAGNITUDE 7

Ambilateral Class	Number of Paths of Length 3,4,5,6,7, respectively	P_a	d
(32)	2,2,2,2,2 (32)	34 (32)	7 (32)
(8)	2,2,2,4,0 (8)	33 (8)	
(16)	2,2,4,2,0 (16)	32 (16)	6 (56)
(16)	2,4,2,2,0 (16)	31 (16)	
(16)	4,2,2,2,0 (16)		
(8)	2,4,4,0,0 (28)	30	
(4)	(12)		
(4)	4,2,4,0,0 (4)	29 (4)	5 (40)
(16)	4,4,2,0,0 (24)	28 (24)	
(8)			
(4)	4,6,0,0,0 (4)	27 (4)	4 (4)

NOTE: Values in parentheses are number of TDCN for each class.

There is no simple expression for $N'(n)$, the number of ambilateral classes for given n (Etherington [4]). Values of $N'(n)$ can, however, be calculated from the recursive relations

$$N'(1) = N'(2) = N'(3) = 1$$

$$N'(2m+1) = \sum_{i=1}^{m} N'(2m+1-i)N'(i) \qquad (2)$$

$$N'(2m) = \tfrac{1}{2} N'(m)[N'(m)+1] + \sum_{i=1}^{m-1} N'(2m-i)N'(i),$$

where m is an integer greater than 1. For large n, the ratio $N'(n+1)/N'(n)$ is approximately 2.48 (Becker [2]).

A number of problems arise in attempting to make practical use of the ambilateral scheme. First, although the ratio $N'(n)/N(n)$ becomes steadily smaller as n increases (see Table 1), the value of $N'(n)$ itself becomes very large. Second, it is difficult to find a satisfactory nonpictorial way of characterizing the classes. Finally, the problem of enumerating the TDCN for each class is still unsolved (Harding [7], pp. 52-57). Because of these and other difficulties, we shall not devote any more space to discussion of the ambilateral classification.

III. Path Lengths and Path Numbers

Each junction and source of a channel network has a topologic distance from the outlet that can be defined as the number of links in the path connecting it to the outlet. As stated in the first section, this distance will be called the topologic path length or, when there is no danger of confusion, simply the path length. Paths are classified as interior or exterior, according to whether they have a junction or a source at the upstream end. There are n exterior paths and $n-1$ interior paths in a network of magnitude n.

Every channel network has one and only one path of length 1, and the maximum possible path length for a network of magnitude n is n, which occurs when the network is second order. Thus, a channel network can be characterized topologically by a sequence of n numbers $f_1, f_2, \ldots, f_n$, where f_j is the number of paths of length j. For example, the network in Figure 1 has path numbers 1, 2, 2, 4, 2, 2, 0. In general, in writing path numbers we shall drop the zeroes, since the magnitude is specified unambiguously by

$$\sum_{j=1}^{n} f_j = 2n - 1. \qquad (3)$$

Consider the set of f_j links at the upstream ends of the paths of length j. Each of the exterior links in this set terminates in a source, and each of the interior links branches to form two paths of length $j+1$. Thus,

$$f_{j+1} \leqslant 2f_j. \qquad (4)$$

From this we see that $f_2 = 2$ and that all f_j are even for $j > 1$.

Let $f_j^{(e)}$ and $f_j^{(i)}$ denote the number of exterior and interior paths, respectively, of length j:

$$f_j^{(e)} + f_j^{(i)} = f_j = 2^{j-1} - \sum_{k=2}^{j-1} 2^{j-k} f_k^{(e)}, \qquad (5)$$

where the term 2^{j-1} on the right-hand side of the equation represents the maximum possible value of f_j. This value occurs only if all paths of length less than j are interior paths. The second term on the right-hand side provides the necessary correction when there are some exterior paths with length less than j.

$$f_j^{(i)} = \tfrac{1}{2} f_{j+1} = 2^{j-1} - \sum_{k=2}^{j} 2^{j-k} f_k^{(e)} \tag{6}$$

$$f_j^{(e)} = f_j - \tfrac{1}{2} f_{j+1} = 2 f_{j-1}^{(i)} - f_j^{(i)} \tag{7}$$

Also,

$$\sum_{j=1}^{n} \frac{f_j^{(e)}}{2^{j-1}} = 1. \tag{8}$$

From the above relations between the three sets of path numbers $f_j^{(e)}$, $f_j^{(i)}$, and f_j $(j = 1, 2, \ldots, n)$, we see that if one set is specified, the other two are also determined. The discussion in this paper will be mostly in terms of the set f_j.

We have not been able to find a simple expression for the number of different path-number classes of given magnitude, but values can be obtained with the aid of the algorithm shown schematically in Figure 4. It may be noted that all members of the same ambilateral class have the same path numbers but that the

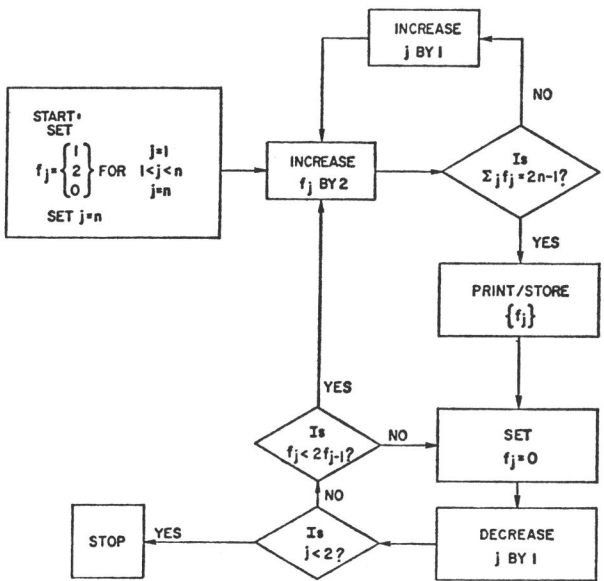

FIG. 4. Flow Chart for Determining All Path-Number Sequences.

converse is not necessarily true. From Table 1, we see that the number of classes occurring in the path-length method is significantly less than the number occurring in the ambilateral method. Table 2 illustrates the specific case of $n = 7$, in which 11 ambilateral classes give rise to 9 path-number classes.

The number of ways in which f_{j+1} paths can merge in pairs to produce $f_j^{(i)}$ interior paths of length j is

$$\binom{f_j}{\frac{1}{2}f_{j+1}} = \binom{f_j}{f_j^{(e)}} = \binom{f_j}{f_j^{(i)}}. \qquad (9)$$

Hence, the total number $\nu(f_1, f_2, \ldots, f_d; n)$ of TDCN of magnitude n having the same path numbers $f_1, f_2, \ldots, f_d$ is

$$\nu(f_1, f_2, \ldots, f_d; n) = \prod_{j=1}^{d-1} \binom{f_j}{\frac{1}{2}f_{j+1}}. \qquad (10)$$

Here d is the largest path length, or *diameter*. That is, all path numbers for $d < j \leqslant n$ are zero.

For any given magnitude n, there are two extremal sequences of path numbers corresponding to the maximum and minimum diameters. As stated previously, the maximum possible diameter is n; the corresponding path number sequence is the vector $1, 2, 2, \ldots, 2$ with n elements. All and only the 2^{n-2} TDCN of second order have this sequence in common. Networks with the minimum possible diameter do not necessarily have the maximum possible order.

Let w be the minimum possible diameter; then the corresponding path-number sequence has w nonzero elements. One possible sequence (but not the only one) is $1, 2, 4, 8, \ldots, 2^{w-2}, r$, where r is a remainder satisfying the inequality

$$a \leqslant r \leqslant 2^{w-1}.$$

$$\sum_{i=0}^{w-2} 2^i \leqslant 2n - 3 < \sum_{i=0}^{w-1} 2^i,$$

or

$$2^{w-2} \leqslant n - 1 < 2^{w-1}$$

and

$$w = \lfloor \log_2(n-1) \rfloor + 2, \qquad (11)$$

where $\lfloor x \rfloor$ means the integer part of x.

Also,

$$r = 2n - 2^{w-1}. \qquad (12)$$

The results obtained so far in this section apply without restriction to channel networks in general. If we now assume, in addition, the validity of Shreve's topologically random model, some expected parameter values of interest can be computed. In particular, the expected values of $f_j{}^{(e)}$, $f_j{}^{(i)}$, and f_j for specified n are given by the following (Smart and Werner, to be published elsewhere):

$$E[f_j{}^{(e)}; n] = \frac{2^{j-1}}{N(n)} Z(j-1, n-1), \tag{13a}$$

$$E[f_j{}^{(i)}; n] = \frac{2^{j-1}}{N(n)} Z(j+1, n), \tag{13b}$$

and

$$E[f_j; n] = \frac{2^{j-1}}{N(n)} Z(j, n), \tag{13c}$$

where

$$Z(j, n) = \frac{j}{2n-j} \binom{2n-j}{n} \tag{14}$$

(Werner, [25]). Figure 5 shows $E[f_j; n]$ for selected values of n.

IV. Total Path Lengths

Although the path-number classification has a simple topologic interpretation and has some obvious advantages over the ambilateral method, it is still not very convenient for practical use. In particular, for $n > 10$ the number of classes

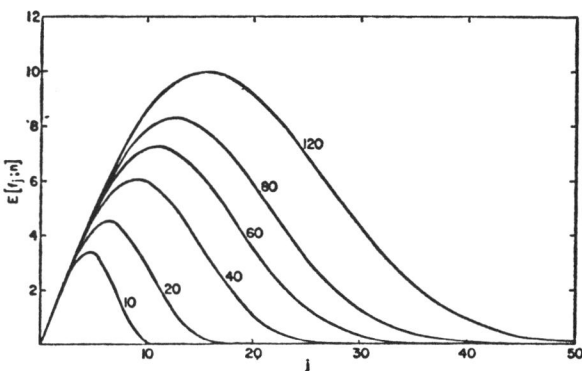

Fig. 5. $E[f_j; n]$ Versus j for $n = 10, 20, 40, 60, 80$, and 120.

becomes unmanageably large, and each class must be specified by a rather long string of numbers. Accordingly, we shall try to find a method that avoids these difficulties, while still making use of the path-length concept.

One possibility is to consider the sum of all path lengths, or *total path length* p, defined by

$$p = \sum_{j=1}^{n} jf_j. \tag{15a}$$

The total path length can of course be separated into the total exterior path length p_e and the total interior path length p_i, where

$$p = p_e + p_i, \tag{15b}$$

and

$$p_e = \sum_{j=1}^{n} jf_j^{(e)}, \tag{16a}$$

$$p_i = \sum_{j=1}^{n-1} jf_j^{(i)}. \tag{16b}$$

With the aid of equations (3) and (7), we find that

$$p_e = p_i + 2n - 1. \tag{17}$$

Thus for networks of a given magnitude, all three values, p, p_e, and p_i, are determined when one of them is known. In the network of Figure 1, $p = 49$, $p_e = 31$, and $p_i = 18$.

Since all f_j except f_1 are even, it follows from equation (15a) that p is always an odd integer; similarly, p_e and p_i are always integers. Starting with known results for small n, one can show by induction that for all TDCN of a given magnitude, the possible values of p are all odd numbers between the upper and lower limits, and the possible values of p_e and p_i are all integers between their respective upper and lower limits. As a matter of convenience, we have chosen to discuss the total path-length classification in terms of p_e, the total exterior path length. Results in terms of p_e can easily be converted to analogous statements in terms of p and p_i by the use of equations (15b) and (17).

The maximum possible total exterior path length for given n occurs when the network is of second order. In this case, the exterior path-number sequence has n elements and is of the form 0, 1, 1, ..., 1, 2. Combining this result with equation (16a) gives

$$p_e^{\max} = \tfrac{1}{2}(n^2 + 3n - 2). \tag{18}$$

The minimum possible value of p_e occurs for the same path-number sequence $(1, 2, 4, 8, \ldots, 2^{w-2}, r)$ that identified the minimum possible diameter w. (It should be noted that for $n \geqslant 9$, there exist other path-number sequences that give the minimum diameter but not the minimum path length.) The corresponding exterior path-number sequence is then a vector of length w having the form $0, 0, \ldots, 0, n\text{-}r, r$. Thus,

$$p_e^{\min} = (w-1)(n-r) + wr;$$

and with the aid of equation (12), we find

$$p_e^{\min} = n(w+1) - 2^{w-1}, \tag{19}$$

where $w(n)$ is defined by equation (11).

The number of different path-length classes for a given magnitude $N_p(n)$ is given by

$$N_p(n) = p_e^{\max}(n) - p_e^{\min}(n) + 1$$

or

$$N_p(n) = \tfrac{1}{2}(n^2 + 3n) - n(w+1) + 2^{w-1}. \tag{20}$$

These values are listed in Table 1.

The hierarchical relationship noted between ambilateral and path-number classes is continued one step further here. Whereas all members of the same path-number class have the same total path length, the converse is not true. Table 2 shows how, for $n = 7$, nine path-number classes coalesce into eight total path-length classes.

Any channel network of magnitude greater than unity may be considered as being formed from the two subnetworks that join at the upstream end of its outlet link. If one of the subnetworks has magnitude i and total exterior path length h and the other has magnitude k and total exterior path length l, the resultant network has magnitude $i + k$ and total exterior path length $h + l + i + k$. The number $\nu(p_e, n)$ of TDCN of magnitude n and total exterior path length p_e can be calculated from the recursive relation

$$\nu(p_e, n) = \Sigma \, \nu(h, i) \, \nu(l, k), \tag{21}$$

where the summation is carried out subject to the conditions $i + k = n$ and $h + l + n = p_e$, and where $\nu(1, 1) = 1$. Alternatively, this quantity is obtained as one of the results of the algorithm of Figure 4. The values of $\nu(p_e, 7)$ are listed in Table 2, and in Figure 6, $\nu(p_e, 10)$ is plotted as a function of p_e. Both sets of results indicate that for small n, $\nu(p_e, n)$ is a rather erratic function of p_e.

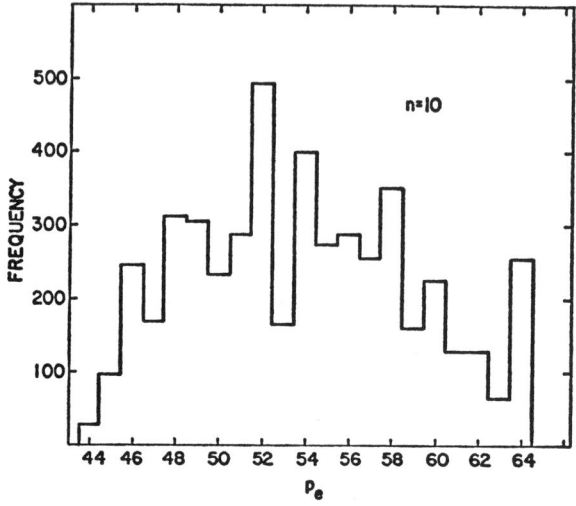

FIG. 6. The Frequency Function $\nu(p_e, 10)$.

For a topologically random population of channel networks, the expected value of p_e for given n is

$$E[p_e; n] = \frac{2^{2(n-1)}}{N(n)} \tag{22}$$

(Knuth, [11], p. 404).

An interesting relation can be established between path lengths and link magnitudes. Let n be the magnitude of a channel network and m_i be the magnitude of the ith link. Then

$$p_e = \sum_{i=1}^{2n-1} m_i \tag{23}$$

as can be seen from the fact that m_i is just the number of exterior paths traversing the ith link. Similarly,

$$p = \sum_{i=1}^{2n-1} (2m_i - 1). \tag{24}$$

An attractive feature of the total path-length method is that each network class for given magnitude is identified by a single integer, which can be readily interpreted both in terms of path lengths and in terms of link magnitudes. Other parameters that might be useful in geomorphic and hydrologic research are p_e/n, the mean exterior path length, and $p_e/(2n-1)$, the mean magnitude. Also, $p/(2n-1)$ is obviously closely related to the mean distance of travel, a parameter of considerable interest in hydrograph research. Note that all of these quantities are mean values for a specific network and should not be confused with the expected values for a topologically random population. Such an expected value for p_e/n, for example, can be obtained by dividing the right-hand side of equation (22) by n.

V. Network Diameters

The network diameter d, discussed in Section III, can evidently be used as a method of topologic classification. The maximum and minimum possible values of d were established in Section III; and by induction methods it can be shown that for given n, the diameter can take on all integer values between the upper and lower limits. The number of network diameter classes $N_d(n)$ is therefore

$$N_d(n) = n - w + 1. \tag{25}$$

As indicated in Table 1, the diameter-classification method produces significantly fewer classes than does any of the other methods; for large n, $N_d(n) \approx n$. An example of the reduction is shown in Table 2 for $n = 7$. Note that the diameter classification is not a member of the hierarchical sequence discussed previously, since TDCN with the same total path length do not necessarily have the same diameter. As a general remark about Table 2, the corresponding diagrams for large n are much more complex because the classes that combine in going from one method to the next one on the right are in general not contiguous.

There are no compact formulae for $v(d, n)$, the number of TDCN of diameter d and magnitude n, and the values must be determined by a counting procedure analogous to equation (21). A convenient approach is to consider $v'(k, n)$, the number of TDCN of magnitude n whose diameter is $\leqslant k$. Thus,

$$v'(k, n) = \sum_{j=1}^{n-1} v'(k-1, j) v'(k-1, n-j), \tag{26}$$

with

$$v'(0, j) = 0, \quad j > 0$$

$$v'(1, j) = \begin{cases} 1, & j = 1 \\ 0, & j > 1 \end{cases}$$

and

$$v'(k, j) = N(j), \quad k \geqslant j$$

$$v(d, n) = v'(d, n) - v'(d-1, n) \tag{27}$$

Values of $\nu(d, 7)$ are given in Table 2, and values of $\nu(d, 10)$ are plotted in Figure 7. Notice that the d distributions have a rather regular behavior even for small n, in contrast to the multimodal distributions for p_e.

Equations such as (21) and (27) for the number of TDCN of a given class are particularly useful in cases where Shreve's random topology model applies, because the ν values then give the relative frequencies with which the various classes may be expected to occur in natural networks. Previous tests of Shreve's model have been mainly based on stream-number and ambilateral classifications. Since diameters and total path lengths provide still other kinds of topologic measures, it is desirable also to test their distributions against the random model. As an example, we determined the network diameter for 73 magnitude-10 networks from various areas of the eastern United States. Although the selection process did not follow a strictly random sampling procedure, the sample should—at least from a "practical" standpoint—be sufficiently representative. Table 3 shows the observed distribution of diameters as well as the expected values when topologic randomness is assumed. The χ^2 test gives no reason to reject (at the 0.05 level) the hypothesis that the diameters were drawn from a topologically random population of magnitude-10 networks.

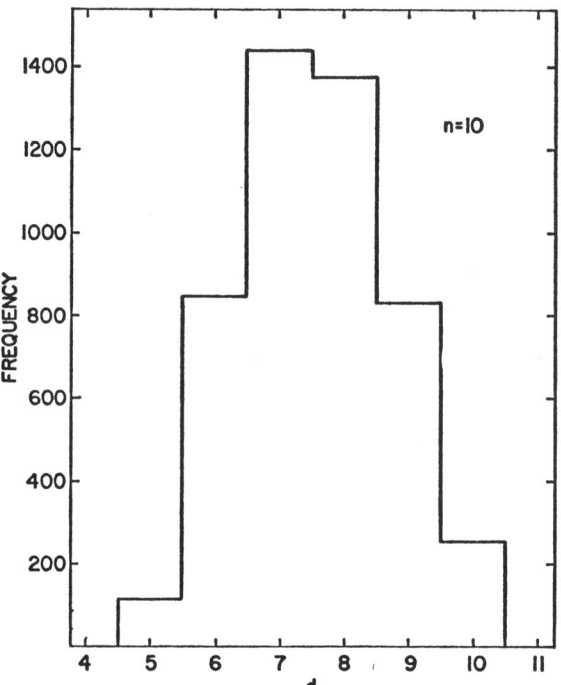

FIG. 7. The Frequency Function $\nu(d, 10)$.

TABLE 3

DIAMETER DISTRIBUTION FOR NETWORKS OF MAGNITUDE 10

Diameter	Observed Frequency	Expected Frequency	
5	1	1.7	
6	7	12.7	
7	23	21.6	$\chi^2 = 5.87$
8	20	20.7	$\chi^2_{0.05}(5) = 11.1$
9	17	12.5	
10	5	3.8	

VI. COMPUTER SIMULATION RESULTS

In order to use a topologic classification method effectively in geomorphic and hydrologic research, it is necessary, or at least highly desirable, to have the following information:

1. A parameter (or parameters) for specifying and distinguishing each class
2. The number of classes for a given network magnitude
3. The possible ranges of these parameters
4. The number of TDCN for each class
5. The statistical properties of the classification parameters for a topologically random population

In the previous three sections, we have attempted to provide such information for the path-number, total path length, and network-diameter classification methods. In most cases, the results could be given by simple algebraic expressions; where this was not possible, straightforward procedures for obtaining the desired information were described—e.g., the algorithm of Figure 4 and the summation formulas of equations (21) and (26). We must recognize, however, that practical difficulties do arise in carrying out these procedures for other than very small n. For example, the algorithm of Figure 4, which in principle can be used to obtain almost any desired information about any of the three methods, requires explicit generation of each of the different sets of path numbers for a given magnitude. For $n = 20$, this number is already almost 17,000; and for $n = 100$, it is greater than 10^{24}—and thus beyond the reach of even an electronic computer. The summation formulae also become very tedious to handle for n much larger than 100.

Some information about the behavior of the classification parameters for large magnitudes can be obtained by Monte Carlo techniques. We have devised a simple and efficient algorithm for randomly generating networks of magnitude n with each of the $N(n)$ possible TDCN having equal probability of occurrence. The results obtained by our simulation procedures thus assume the validity of Shreve's topologically random model. The individual TDCN are specified by the binary-string method described in Section I. Since the binary string contains complete topologic information about the network, all parameters of interest, such as path numbers, path lengths, and diameter, can be extracted from it. Simulation runs were made for magnitudes 10, 20, 40, 60, 80, 120, 160, and 200. In each case, a sample of 300 TDCN was generated, and the topologic parameters were analyzed statistically.

Table 4 gives some descriptive statistics for total exterior path length and network diameter. In addition, the expected values for a topologically random population, as calculated from equation (22) for p_e and from equations (26) and (27) for d, are shown for comparison. Note that p_e and d are highly correlated, with the correlation coefficient being very close to 0.9 for all n. Figure 8 presents double-logarithmic plots of $\bar{p}_e$ and $\bar{d}$ versus n. Least-squares fits of the data lead to the power law functions $1.63n^{1.52}$ and $1.98n^{0.59}$ for $\bar{p}_e$ and $\bar{d}$, respectively. The $\bar{p}_e - n$ relationship is not significantly different from the result $\pi^{1/2}n^{3/2}$ predicted for $E[p_e; n]$ by using Stirling's approximation in equation (22).

The standard deviation figures in Table 4 give some idea of the magnitude of the deviation from mean values that can be expected for single observations. It should be emphasized, however, that the distributions have appreciable asymmetry even for n as large as 200. This point is illustrated in Figures 9 and 10, which give histograms of the sample distributions of p_e and d, respectively.

Other parameters that might be useful in geomorphic research can be derived from p_e and d. As mentioned previously, p_e/n is the mean exterior path length for a network, and $p_e/(2n - 1)$ is the mean magnitude. Another possibility is the *reduced exterior path length*, $p_e/\frac{1}{2}(n^2 + 3n - 2)$, a parameter that compares p_e with its maximum possible value. Similarly, the *reduced diameter* is d/n.

All of the quantities mentioned in the previous paragraph depend rather sensitively on n. Consequently, their main use would be for comparing networks of the same magnitude. The results shown in Figure 8 suggest that the empirical parameters $p_e/n^{3/2}$ and $d/n^{1/2}$ should have distributions that are relatively independent of n and thus be useful for comparing networks of different magnitude. Figure 11 shows the approximate quartile boundaries for the two parameters. Using this figure, one can easily determine the approximate ranking of

TABLE 4

Simulation Results for p_e and d

Magnitude n	Total Exterior Path Length				Network Diameter				Corr. Coef. ρ_{pd}
	$E[p_e;n]$	$\bar{p}_e$	S.D.	C.V.	$E[d;n]$	$\bar{d}$	S.D.	C.V.	
10	53.92	53.88	5.07	0.094	7.56	7.59	1.16	0.153	0.913
20	155.5	153.5	19.1	0.125	11.92	11.80	1.97	0.167	0.904
40	444.2	431.8	72.4	0.168	18.19	18.63	3.58	0.192	0.893
60	818.6	817.8	145.1	0.177	23.04	23.00	4.80	0.209	0.911
80	1262.3	1247.9	220.3	0.177	27.16	26.82	5.21	0.194	0.905
120	2322.7	2341.8	466.6	0.199	34.10	34.84	6.95	0.200	0.896
160	3587.2*	3565.4	706.3	0.198	39.94*	40.01	8.33	0.208	0.895
200	5013.3*	5050.3	1080.2	0.214	45.13*	45.33	9.67	0.213	0.897

*Values obtained by using Stirling's approximation.

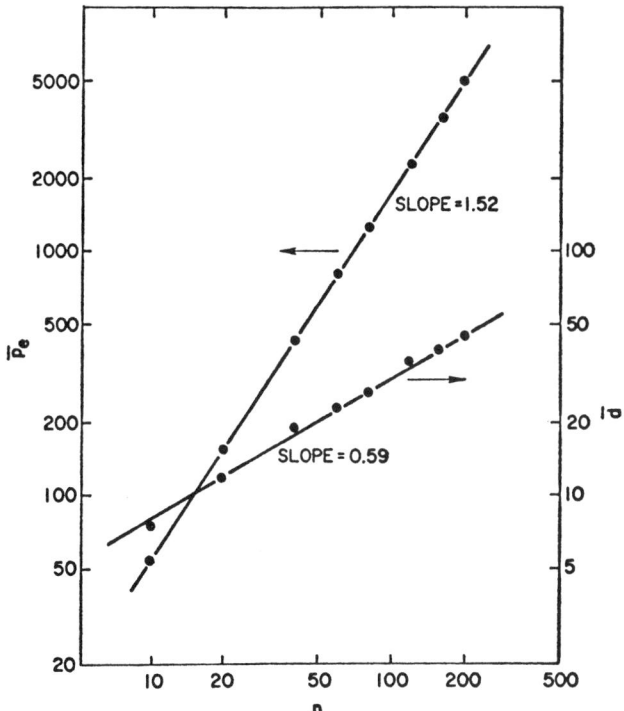

FIG. 8. Mean Values of p_e and d from Simulation Studies.

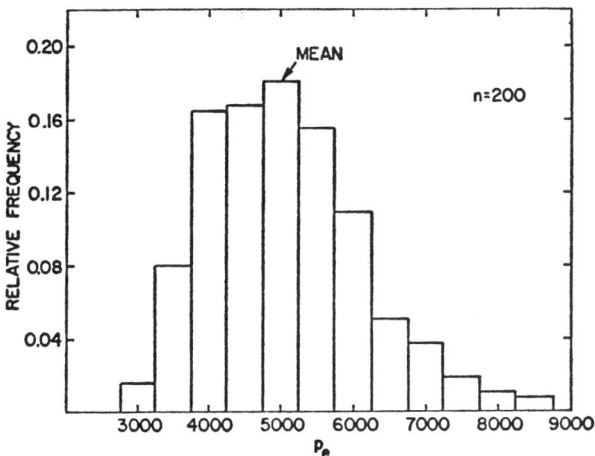

FIG. 9. Histogram of Observed Frequencies of p_e from Simulation Studies for Magnitude 200.

290 / *Geographical Analysis*

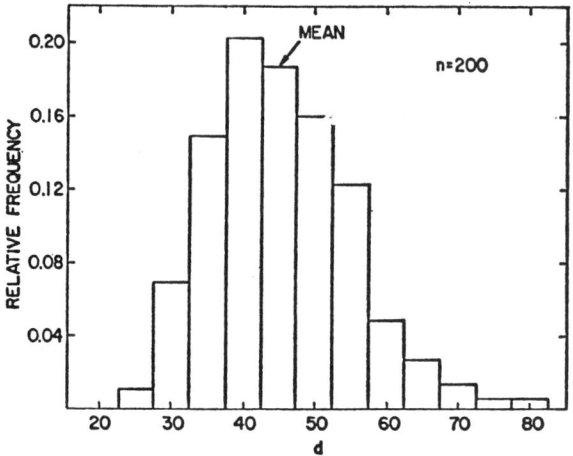

FIG. 10. Histogram of Observed Frequencies of d from Simulation Studies for Magnitude 200.

p_e and d values for an individual network in terms of a topologically random population.

VII. Some Applications

In studies on natural geomorphic systems, the relation between two variables is generally investigated by collecting paired observations and performing regression and other types of statistical analyses. In order to provide some simulated data that could be compared with actual observations, we randomly generated 200 networks with magnitudes randomly chosen in the range 20–200 and determined the diameter, total path length, and Strahler bifurcation ratio

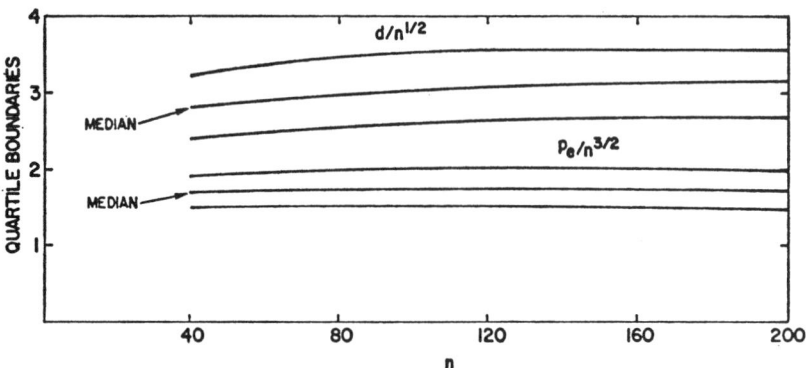

FIG. 11. Approximate Quartile Boundaries for $d/n^{1/2}$ and $p_e/n^{3/2}$ as Determined from Simulation Studies.

for each network. The diameter d is closely correlated with the mainstream length for natural drainage basins, and the magnitude n is closely correlated with the area. Theoretically, $2n - 1$ is a slightly better measure of area than n, and upon carrying out the indicated least-squares analysis, the resulting regression relation is

$$d = 1.4(2n - 1)^{0.58}. \tag{28}$$

Hack [6] and Gray [5] have both reported finding similar relationships between mainstream length and drainage area for natural networks. Both sets of data are well represented by the single relation

$$L' = 1.4 \, A^{0.584}, \tag{29}$$

where the exponent is the average of the Hack and Gray values. Here L' is the mainstream length in miles, and A is the drainage area in square miles. The near equality of the two coefficients and the two exponents of equations (28) and (29) is strikingly and presumably not completely coincidental. Approximate quantitative relations between them can be established by assuming that $L' = d\bar{l}$ and $A = (2n - 1)\bar{a}$, where $\bar{l}$ and $\bar{a}$ are, respectively, the mean-link length and mean-link drainage area for the region. With these assumptions, we find that the two exponents should be equal and that the two coefficients should be related by

$$C' = C \, K^{1/2}/\bar{a}^{(b-1/2)}, \tag{30}$$

where C' and C are the coefficients for the L'–A and $d - (2n - 1)$ regressions, respectively; $K = \bar{l}^2/\bar{a}$ is a dimensionless parameter previously studied by Smart [23]; and b is the common exponent. An evaluation of the factor $K^{1/2}/\bar{a}^{(b-1/2)}$ for 20 drainage basins in the eastern United States gave values ranging between 1.1 and 1.6 with a mean of about 1.3. Thus, the predicted relation between the two exponents is in good agreement with observation, and the predicted relation between the two coefficients is in fair agreement. In any event, it seems apparent that the empirical "law," equation (29), which has been much discussed in the literature, is in great part a consequence of the topological and geometrical randomness of natural drainage networks.

The regression of p on $2n - 1$ gives

$$p = 1.0(2n - 1)^{1.53}. \tag{31}$$

Langbein and others [12], in a study of 340 drainage basins in the northeastern United States, found the regression relation

$$P = \Sigma_k l_k a_k = 0.90 A^{1.56}, \tag{32}$$

where a_k is a partial area, l_k is the channel distance from the partial area to the outlet, and lengths and areas are measured in miles and square miles. It is evident that the variables p and P are closely related; in particular, if the a_k are chosen to be the individual link areas and if the a_k and l_k are uncorrelated, then P is an approximate geometric measure of p. If, as was done in the actual observations, the a_k are small subnetworks containing several link areas, it would appear that P and p should still have an approximate linear relationship. In this case, it follows from equation (31) that P should vary approximately as $A^{3/2}$, in excellent agreement with equation (32).

Gray [5] has also reported the regression relation

$$L_{ca} = P/A = 0.5L', \qquad (33)$$

where L_{ca} is the channel distance from the outlet to the "center of gravity" of the network. The topologic analogue of L_{ca} is $p/(2n-1)$, and from least-squares analysis of our simulation data, we find the regression relation

$$p/(2n-1) = 0.50d + 1.3 \qquad (34)$$

in essential agreement with equation (33).

The applications discussed here point up one important practical use of the topologic parameters p (or p_e) and d. Coupled with the random models of network structure, they provide explanations of observed geomorphic relations that had previously been accepted as purely empirical rules.

VIII. Discussion

Jarvis [10] and Mock [13] have each recently proposed topologic classification methods, which may be compared with ours. The Jarvis method is based on a topologic parameter E, which in our notation is given by

$$E = \sum_{k=1}^{n-1} j_k^{(i)} m_k^{(i)} k/p_e, \qquad (35)$$

where $j_k^{(i)}$ and $m_k^{(i)}$ are, respectively, the path length and magnitude for the kth interior link. This classification scheme is identical with the path-number method up to $n = 10$, but diverges from it for some higher magnitude and becomes intermediate between the path-number and total path-length methods. Although Jarvis's studies indicate that the parameter E has some discriminatory power, it is our opinion that it does not provide as good a classification method as either p_e or d, both because it requires considerably more labor and because its exact topologic interpretation is somewhat obscure.

Mock's method [13] is based on link magnitudes and hence is not very closely related to the methods discussed in this paper. His procedures—an extension of the tributary-mainstream division proposed by James and Krumbein [9]—result in two classes of exterior links and four classes of interior links. Measurements of link lengths on natural networks indicated that the four classes of interior links have different length distributions and thus suggested that the classification method has geometric as well as topologic significance. The general applicability of Mock's conclusions are in some doubt, however, because he studied trellis and rectangular networks only. Some unpublished observations by Smart on dendritic networks suggested that three of the four interior link classes have essentially the same length distribution, with only the tributary class being different. The problem needs further investigation, however. It may be noted that Mock's method is also rather tedious to apply, and geomorphologists are not apt to adopt it unless strong evidence for its usefulness is presented.

Our own results suggest that the topologic properties of channel networks can be efficiently and effectively characterized by use of the magnitude, the diameter, and possibly the total exterior path length. These parameters, particularly the magnitude and diameter, are easy to determine; and as pointed out previously, they are closely related to some important geometric quantities and can frequently be used as surrogates for these quantities in description and analysis. The high degree of correlation between p_e and d suggests that once d is obtained, the additional labor in determining p_e may not be worthwhile. On the other hand, the specification of both quantities does elucidate certain details (see, for example, in Table 2 the sequence of networks with $p_e = 30, 31, 32, 33$, and $d = 6$) that may be helpful in some investigations. Also, as shown in the last section, p_e (or p) appears to be potentially very useful in interpreting and explaining empirical geomorphic relationships.

The use of n, d, and p_e in network analysis appears to be superior to the conventional Horton-Strahler analysis with respect to both the labor involved and the information acquired. The simulation studies described in the previous section show that the correlation coefficient between the Strahler bifurcation R_B and d is about 0.2. Thus, the two types of analysis provide quite different kinds of information; and, as discussed in the introductory section, attempts to correlate the Horton-Strahler parameters with other geomorphic and hydrologic quantities have generally been unsuccessful. In an apparent exception, Smart [20] and Shreve [19] have shown that the stream numbers can be used to make reasonably accurate predictions of stream-length and basin-area ratios. Even here, however, these quantities are artifacts of the order scheme, and their relation to the actual network structure is obscure. For geometric parameters, quantities such as mean-link lengths, mean link drainage areas, and K values provide better and more easily interpreted information.

IX. SUMMARY

Several new topologic network parameters have been defined and analyzed, and examples of their application have been provided. Some advantages of using these new parameters, especially in comparison with the conventional ones, are as follows. (1) They provide alternative classifications of networks; they are easy to measure; and they have straightforward topologic interpretations. (2) They show only a weak correlation with the traditional parameters and thus provide additional information about the topology of dendritic networks. (3) They are highly correlated with morphometric network and basin parameters. Thus they can serve as approximations or substitutes for the latter, especially since they are much easier to measure. (4) They are capable of explaining various empirical geomorphic "laws," which had previously not been accounted for on theoretical grounds.

LITERATURE CITED

1. ANDERSON, H. W. "Flood Frequencies and Sedimentation from Forest Watersheds," *Trans. Amer. Geophys. Union*, 30 (1949), 567–84.
2. BECKER, H. W. "Discussion of a Problem Proposed by C. D. Olds." *Amer. Math. Monthly*, 56 (1949), 697–99.
3. CAYLEY, A. "On the Analytical Forms Called Trees," *Phil. Mag.*, 18 (1859), 374–78.
4. ETHERINGTON, I. M. H. "Non-associate Powers and a Functional Equation," *Math. Gazette*, 21 (1937), 36–39.
5. GRAY, D. M. "Interrelationships of Watershed Characteristics," *J. Geophys. Res.*, 66 (1961), 1215–23.
6. HACK, J. T. *Studies of Longitudinal Stream Profiles in Virginia and Maryland.* U.S.G.S. Prof. Paper 294-B. 1957.
7. HARDING, E. F. "The Probabilities of Rooted Tree-Shapes Generated by Random Bifurcation," *Adv. Appl. Prob.*, 3 (1971), 44–77.
8. HORTON, R. E. "Erosional Development of Streams and Their Drainage Basins: Hydrophysical Approach to Quantitative Morphology," *Bull. Geol. Soc. Amer.*, 56 (1945), 275–370.
9. JAMES, W. R. and W. C. KRUMBEIN. "Frequency Distribution of Stream Link Lengths," *J. Geol.*, 77 (1969), 544–65.
10. JARVIS, R. S. "New Measure of the Topologic Structure of Dendritic Drainage Networks," *Water Resources Res.*, 8 (1972), 1265–71.
11. KNUTH, D. E. *The Art of Computer Programming, Vol. 1: Fundamental Algorithms.* Reading, Mass.: Addison-Wesley, 1968.
12. LANGBEIN, W. B. et al. *Topographic Characteristics of Drainage Basins.* U.S.G.S. Water-Supply Paper 968-C. 1947.
13. MOCK, S. J. "A Classification of Channel Links in Stream Networks," *Water Resources Res.*, 7 (1971), 1558–66.
14. MORISAWA, M. E. "Quantitative Geomorphology of Some Watersheds in the Appalachian Plateau," *Bull. Geol. Soc. Amer.*, 73 (1962), 1025–46.
15. SCHEIDEGGER, A. E. *The Algebra of Stream-Order Numbers.* U.S.G.S. Prof. Paper 525-B (1965), B187–9.
19. ———. "Stream Lengths and Basin Areas in Topologically Random Channel Networks," *Publ. No. 76* (1967), 415–25.
17. SHREVE, R. L. "Statistical Law of Stream Numbers," *J. Geol.*, 74 (1966), 17–37.
18. ———. "Infinite Topologically Random Channel Networks," *J. Geol.*, 75 (1967), 179–86.
19. ———. "Stream Lengths and Basin Areas in Topologically Random Channel Networks," *J. Geol.*, 77 (1969), 397–414.
20. SMART, J. S. "Statistical Properties of Stream Lengths," *Water Resources Res.*, 4 (1968), 1001–14.

21. ——. "Topological Properties of Channel Networks," *Bull. Geol. Soc. Amer.*, 80 (1969), 1757–74.
22. ——. "Channel Networks." *Advances in Hydroscience*. V. T. Chow, ed. Vol. 8. New York: Academic Press, 1972.
23. ——. "Quantitative Characterization of Channel Network Structure," *Water Resources Res.*, 8 (1972), 1487–96.
24. STRAHLER, A. N. "Hypsometric (Area-Altitude) Analysis of Erosional Topography," *Bull. Geol. Soc. Amer.*, 63 (1952).
25. WERNER, C. "Expected Number and Magnitude of Stream Networks in Random Drainage Patterns," *Proc. Assoc. Amer. Geog.*, 3 (1971), 181–85.

Some Comments on Testing Random Topology Stream Network Models

R. S. JARVIS

Department of Geography, State University of New York at Buffalo, Buffalo, New York 14226

A. WERRITTY

Department of Geography, University of St. Andrews, St. Andrews, Fife, Scotland

The properties of a random topology stream network model were first introduced into fluvial geomorphology by *Shreve* [1966]. In many respects this paper and subsequent papers by *Shreve* [1967, 1969], *Smart* [1968, 1969], and *Werner* [1970, 1972] may be regarded as a stochastic reformulation of Horton's earlier work, which was devoid of explicit probabilistic elements. In this paper we wish to develop a metric to compare the relative performance of various classificatory procedures that have been introduced to test the random topology hypothesis. Then in the light of these results we shall comment upon some of the problems that arise in testing random topology models.

PROPERTIES OF THE SHREVE MODEL

Shreve's [1966, pp. 27–31] model may be derived in the following manner. If a stream network possesses n sources (i.e., first-order streams), there must exist $N(n)$ topologically distinct channel networks (TDCN's) by virtue of Cayley's expression

$$N(n) = \frac{1}{2n-1}\binom{2n-1}{n} \qquad (1)$$

A TDCN is defined as a network that when it is projected on a plane surface, cannot be continuously deformed or rotated within that surface such that it becomes congruent with any other TDCN of the same number of sources [*Shreve*, 1966, p. 27]. Shreve's basic premise for the model is that in an area uniform in lithology and free from structural controls each TDCN will occur with equal frequency.

For $n > 5$ the value of $N(n)$ increases so rapidly that a regrouping of the TDCN becomes necessary in order to test the model. For example, there are 42 TDCN's of magnitude 6, which would necessitate generating a sample of several hundred if the minimum cell requirements of goodness-of-fit tests were to be met. One of the most favored schemes for aggregating TDCN's is that based upon the *Strahler* [1964] stream-ordering method. Each stream in the network is ordered on the scale 1, 2, $\cdots$, Ω, the exterior links being of order 1 and the master stream of order Ω. The network may then be characterized by its set of stream numbers, which lists sequentially the number of streams of each order from 1 to Ω. Thus the stream set (9:4:1) would yield 9 first-order streams, 4 second-order, and 1 third-order. On the basis of the premise of equiprobable TDCN's, *Shreve* [1966, p. 29] has derived a general expression for the number of TDCN's for each set of stream numbers:

$$N(n_1, n_2, \cdots, n_{\Omega-1}, 1)$$
$$= \prod_{\omega=1}^{\Omega-1} 2^{(n_\omega - 2n_{\omega+1})}\binom{n_\omega - 2}{n_\omega - 2n_{\omega+1}} \qquad (2)$$

where $N(n_1, n_2, \cdots, n_{\Omega-1}, 1)$ denotes the number of TDCN's of order Ω having the set of stream numbers $(n_1, n_2, \cdots, n_{\Omega-1}, 1)$.

The Shreve model suffers from the problem that in order to test for nontrivial cases of n, one must aggregate the $N(n)$ TDCN's derived from (1) into some more generalized classification, e.g., their stream set numbers $N(n_1, \cdots, n_{\Omega-1}, 1)$. This is necessary in order to meet the requirements of goodness-of-fit tests. *Smart* [1969] has identified the following three properties as completely specifying the topologic characteristics of individual TDCN's: (1) the Strahler stream numbers or bifurcation ratios, (2) the location of the $n_\omega - 2n_{\omega+1}$ 'excess' tributaries of order ω, and (3) the right-left order at each junction in the network.

Only when one is testing the model by individual TDCN are all three properties specified. Aggregation of TDCN's into ambilateral classes involves discarding property 3 above [*Smart*, 1969]. Further grouping of TDCN's into their respective stream set numbers (equation (2)) involves discarding properties 2 and 3. The amount of information loss at each stage in the grouping procedure may readily be measured by Shannon's classic formula

$$H(x) = -\sum_{i=1}^{n} p_i \log_2 p_i \qquad (3)$$

where $H(x)$ equals the information content of x; x being a classification with n categories, each having an associated probability p_i [*Quastler*, 1958, p. 21].

The information content implicit in the various ways of testing Shreve's model is listed in Table 1 and is graphed in Figure 1. The maximum possible values for networks of a given magnitude, $H(\text{max})$, are given in column 7 of Table 1. These values represent the total amount of topologic information present when each TDCN is treated individually; i.e., all

TABLE 1. Information Content for Various Groupings of TDCN's of Magnitudes 4–10 (Measured in Bits)

Magnitude	$H(ss)$	$H(d)$	$H(p_e/n)$	$H(f)$	$H(\text{amb})$	$H(\text{max})$
4	0.72193	0.72193	0.72193	0.72193	0.72193	2.32193
5	0.98523	0.98523	1.37878	1.37878	1.37878	3.80735
6	1.20091	1.44117	2.16589	2.16589	2.29708	5.39232
7	1.34596	1.69524	2.70617	2.91516	3.16561	7.04439
8	1.47565	1.91010	3.37053	3.69506	4.15742	8.74483
9	1.60169	2.10300	3.76773	4.46786	5.13774	10.48180
10	1.73890	2.26026	4.21377	5.23935	6.18028	12.24733

$H(\text{max})$, each TDCN equiprobable; $H(\text{amb})$, each TDCN grouped according to its ambilateral class; $H(f)$, each TDCN grouped according to its path number classes; $H(p_e/n)$, each TDCN grouped according to its mean source height; $H(d)$, each TDCN grouped according to its maximum source height; and $H(ss)$, each TDCN grouped according to its Strahler stream set numbers.

three topologic properties are specified. In this instance since each TDCN is equiprobable, (3) reduces to

$$H(\text{max}) = \log_2 N(n) \quad (4)$$

Grouping TDCN's into their appropriate ambilateral classes results in a loss of information, as indicated by the values for $H(\text{amb})$. Classification of TDCN's according to stream set numbers further reduces the amount of topologic information present to a mere fraction of the total, $H(ss)$.

In view of these results the following guidelines are suggested in testing the Shreve model. Strictly speaking, the only complete test of the Shreve model is that for which all TDCN's are uniquely specified. But for $n > 6$ this specification is operationally not feasible, and one is forced into some degree of aggregation. If some degree of aggregation is found to be necessary, the level of aggregation and the attendant information loss should be equivalent if the results from different workers are to be strictly comparable. It would be misleading to compare two areas by a test upon ambilateral classes in the first area and a test upon stream sets in the second area. By the same token, it is not valid to compare the results within a single area if one test is upon stream sets of a given magnitude and the other test groups TDCN's of a higher magnitude according to the number of first- and second-order streams.

In more general terms, the information losses incurred up to $H(\text{amb})$ are perhaps acceptable in terms of testing the random topology model. But beyond this level the losses become excessive: stream sets for magnitude 10 networks discard 85.80% of the total information present, and those for magnitude 40 networks discard 93.54%. That such a small residue of topologic information can be described by a random combinatorial process is surely not very illuminating to the geomorphologist.

In addition to involving large information losses the use of stream set data necessitates a return to testing topologic properties within a Hortonian framework. This is not an unexpected result, for the *Shreve* [1966, p. 31] model includes Horton's law of stream numbers as a special case. One may take this a stage further and note that for a given ensemble of equiprobable TDCN's (which by definition constitute a state of maximum entropy) the law of stream numbers follows as the inevitable consequence of grouping together TDCN's into their respective stream sets [*Shreve*, 1966].

But the great problem with the classic Hortonian model was its insensitivity to different geomorphic environments; bifurcation ratios were found to lie invariably within the range 3.0–5.0 and to be very poorly correlated with other geomorphic or hydrologic variables. This insensitivity resulted from Strahler's conservative ordering system, which masked a great deal of topologic detail. One of Shreve's major contributions was the introduction of the concept of magnitude as a more precise level of network classification. This concept liberated morphometry from the Hortonian straitjacket. Given the notion of magnitude plus the concept of the TDCN, one could now examine a great many new topologic attributes, for example, right-left junctions and the distribution of excess tributaries. Once a set of models that are far more sensitive to topologic variation have been derived, it is surely a retrograde step to have to return to the Strahler stream sets in order to test the new models. When we do that, the wheel has come full circle, and we have thrown away most of the topologic detail that these new models profess to explain. However, some recent developments in the field of morphometry suggest that this bleak conclusion is possibly premature, and it is to these models that we now turn.

SOME PARTIALLY DISAGGREGATED APPROACHES

Two recent papers have suggested a series of new topologic indices that in terms of information loss lie somewhere between Smart's ambilateral classification and Shreve's stream sets. In order of increasing generality these are (1) path number classes [*Werner and Smart*, 1973]; (2) mean source height [*Jarvis*, 1972; *Liao and Scheidegger*, 1968], cf. mean exterior path length [*Werner and Smart*, 1973]; and (3) maximum source height [*Jarvis*, 1972], cf. diameter [*Werner and Smart*, 1973].

Path number classes. Each junction or source in a network can be described by a path that identifies the number of links separating it from the outlet. For a network with n sources there are n exterior paths (paths from the n sources to the outlet) and $n - 1$ interior paths (paths from each of the junctions to the outlet). Clearly, the minimum path length for a magnitude n network is 1, and the corresponding maximum value is n. Thus by grouping together paths of the same length (i.e., aggregating sources and/or junctions that in link distance terms are equidistant from the outlet) one obtains a topologic characterization of the network as a series of n numbers $f_1, f_2, \cdots, f_n$, where f_j is the number of paths of length j. The total number $\nu(f_1, f_2, \cdots, f_d; n)$ of TDCN's of magnitude n with the path numbers $f_1, f_2, \cdots, f_d$ is

$$\nu(f_1, f_2, \cdots, f_d; n) = \prod_{i=1}^{d-1} \binom{f_i}{\tfrac{1}{2} f_{i+1}} \quad (5)$$

where d is the largest path length, or maximum source height or diameter [*Werner and Smart*, 1973].

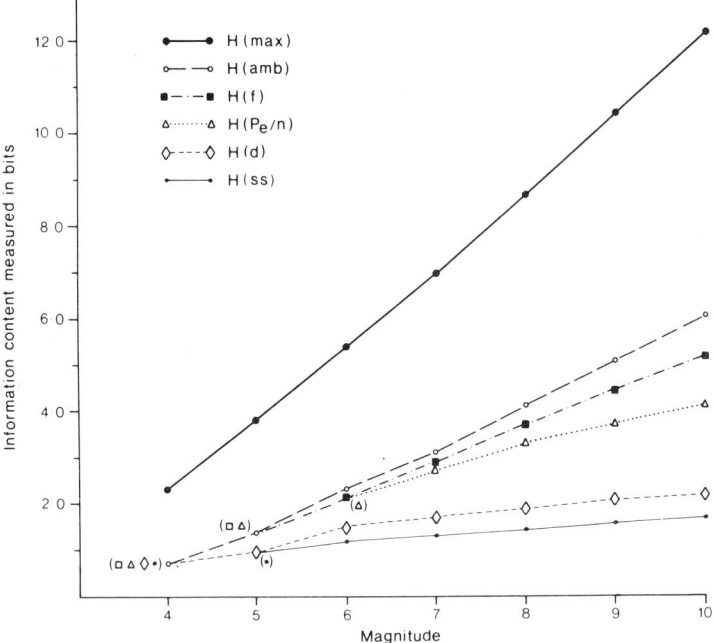

Fig. 1. Information content for various groupings of TDCN's.

Using the Shannon information metric with the probability distribution associated with (5),

$$p(f_1, f_2, \cdots, f_d; n) = \prod_{i=1}^{d-1} \binom{f_i}{\frac{1}{2}f_{i+1}} \bigg/ N(n) \quad (6)$$

we obtain values of $H(f)$ that indicate that classification of TDCN's into path number classes retains only slightly less topologic detail than that preserved at the ambilateral class level (cf. H(amb) with $H(f)$ in Table 1 and Figure 1). In comparing $H(f)$ with H(max) the information losses in percentage terms for small-magnitude networks vary between 68.91% (magnitude 4) and 57.23% (magnitude 10).

Mean source height. A measure based upon path number classes but easier to use in morphometric work is mean source height p_e/n. It may be derived in the following manner [*Werner and Smart*, 1973]. The sum of all path lengths for a given network is defined as p, a value that can be decomposed into two separate summations p_e (total exterior path length) and p_i (total interior path length). The first of these summations is given by

$$p_e = \sum_{j=1}^{n-1} j f_j^{(e)} \quad (7)$$

where $f_j^{(e)}$ is the number of exterior paths of length j. The number $\nu(p_e, n)$ of TDCN's of magnitude n and total exterior path length p_e is obtained from the recursive relation

$$\nu(p_e, n) = \sum \nu(h, i) \nu(l, k) \quad (8)$$

where $\nu(1, 1) = 1$ and the summation proceeds subject to the conditions $i + k = n$ and $h + l + n = p_e$.

Therefore the mean source height (mean exterior path length) is given by the value p_e/n, and the number of TDCN's of constant magnitude and a given value of p_e/n is identical to its associated value in the relation $\nu(p_e, n)$. Thus it follows that the required probability distribution for use with the Shannon expression is given by

$$p(p_e/n, n) = \frac{\nu(p_e/n, n)}{N(n)} = \frac{\nu(p_e, n)}{N(n)} \quad (9)$$

Values of $H(p_e/n)$ are given in Table 1 and are graphed in Figure 1. In terms of information loss the mean source height method lies midway between ambilateral classes and stream sets and on this basis would seem to offer considerable promise as a topologic index. Furthermore, it is not difficult to compute from data tabulated in binary string form [*Jarvis*, 1972, p. 1268]. As is anticipated, grouping path number classes according to their mean source height value results in a value of $H(p_e/n)$ that is considerably less than that of $H(f)$.

Maximum source height. We finally consider maximum source height as a criterion for grouping TDCN's in tests upon the Shreve random topology hypothesis. Maximum source height has already been defined as the largest path length in the set of path numbers $f_1, f_2, \cdots, f_d$ (equation (5)). The value of $\nu(d, n)$ of TDCN's of maximum source height d and magnitude n is derived from the recursive relation for $\nu'(k, n)$, the number of TDCN's of magnitude n and maximum source height $\leq k$ [*Werner and Smart*, 1973]:

$$\nu'(k, n) = \sum_{j=1}^{n-1} \nu'(k - 1, j) \nu'(k - 1, n - j) \quad (10)$$

where

$$\nu'(0, j) = 0 \quad j > 0$$
$$\nu'(1, j) = 1 \quad j = 1$$
$$\nu'(1, j) = 0 \quad j > 1$$

and

$$v'(k, j) = N(j) \quad k \geq j$$
$$v(d, n) = v'(d, n) - v'(d - 1, n) \quad (11)$$

The probability for each of the maximum source height classes is readily obtained by dividing each by the total number of TDCN's:

$$p(d, n) = v(d, n)/N(n) \quad (12)$$

Evaluating these probabilities in terms of (3) gives values of $H(d)$ that are always slightly in excess of the associated value of $H(ss)$ (Table 1 and Figure 1). It is perhaps of interest to note that although the number of classes in the maximum source height method is usually less than the number of stream sets [*Werner and Smart*, 1973, Table 1], these fewer classes retain rather more topologic detail than the stream set classes. Whereas the maximum source height takes into account the compactness of the network as well as the bifurcation structure, stream sets concentrate solely on the bifurcation structure.

IMPLICATIONS OF INFORMATION LOSSES

By means of these information losses it is now possible to measure the amount of topologic differentiation retained by classifying drainage networks at various levels—represented by Strahler stream sets, maximum source height (network diameter), mean source height, path number classes, and ambilateral classes. We also have a direct measure of the information content of each of these classificatory models, as compared with the total topologic information represented by the complete ensemble of individual TDCN's for networks of any given magnitude. It is also pertinent to examine some of the implications of the classificatory schemes with regard to the type of topologic information that is retained: for it is only by a thorough appreciation of both of these properties (type and quantity of information specified) that analyses of drainage network topology can provide any geomorphologically suggestive results.

The TDCN and ambilateral class approaches are in a sense purely specificatory models with regard to network topology, in that they simply provide a classification of pattern or arrangement of links, based upon an exact identification of the location of all branching incidences. The ambilateral class property of networks of a given magnitude n is determined by successively recording the magnitudes of the pairs of tributary links that define each of the $(n - 1)$ junctions, or branching points, in the network. If in addition, we also record the right-left arrangement of the pairs of tributary links, then the complete specification defines the TDCN property. However, classification by means of Strahler stream sets or by path number classes constitutes a further grouping within the ambilateral class framework. This is achieved by combining ambilateral classes according to certain constraints upon the type of junction combinations, or branching subdivisions, within the particular network. The Strahler model may be viewed as an order-stage branching process, as outlined by *Melton* [1959], where successive orders may be identified by a sequence of pruning operations on the exterior links defined by the removal of the previous order links. Thus whereas the property of magnitude simply indicates the amount of drainage headward of a given link, the property of Strahler order is a particular measure of the location of the link. The property of Strahler order is denoted by the degree of headward branching into like-order tributaries between the given link and the undivided first-order links at the periphery of the network. Similarly, the path number classification may be seen in terms of a headward growth model, wherein each of the links at a given link distance height from the basin mouth has an equiprobable chance of bifurcation. It may be noted that although these last two models suffer from losses of topologic specification, as derived above, they do lead to the production of parameters of network topologic structure that are amenable to analyses of other nontopologic network and basin properties. In particular, the Strahler model yields measures of bifurcation ratios, and the path number model provides various link distance or path length parameters, including the mean source height and the maximum network diameter [*Jarvis*, 1972] and many other properties developed by *Werner and Smart* [1973].

It may be helpful to attempt to assimilate some of the different properties of these various models in the context of tests of random topology model hypotheses. Given the practical problems of data collection and analysis, it would appear most reasonable to concentrate upon the particular implications of the use of Strahler stream set data by following the procedures adopted by *Shreve* [1966] and *Smart* [1969]. Nevertheless, despite the wide application of stream set classification the precise structural properties associated with this method of network characterization have remained largely unexplored. For any given stream set composition we may consider the limiting cases of the networks with the greatest and the least degree of structural compaction within the constraints of the specified stream set. It is possible to develop algorithms to generate networks representing these boundary condition cases, defined by the largest and smallest mean source height values, which are denoted by $p_{max}{}^e/n$ and $p_{min}{}^e/n$, respectively, for n sources, or first-order streams. Thus, for example, the fifth-order nets defined by the Strahler stream set (25 : 10 : 5 : 2 : 1) range from the topologically most compacted case of mean source height $p_{min}{}^e/n = 5.720$ to the most lineated case of mean source height $p_{max}{}^e/n = 9.280$. These limiting mean source height values, which have been derived for the ensemble of Strahler stream sets for networks of magnitude 25, are shown in Table 2 and Figure 2, where they are plotted against the stream set probability rank under the Shreve random topology model (an explanation of symbols used in Figures 2 and 3 is given in Table 3).

The stream sets associated with networks of any given magnitude may be distinguished first on the basis of the overall network order obtained, which in this case gives instances of second-, third-, fourth-, and fifth-order nets. Within each of these order sets, further stream set groups may be differentiated on the basis of the degree of higher-order tributary specification. Thus for a constant number of 25 first-order streams we may derive the various combinations of numbers of second- and higher-order streams. This is shown in Figure 2 by the series of order set type lines, where progression along each type line indicates an increasing number of second-order streams for the given number of higher-order streams specified for that order set type. Given the simple relationship inherent in the Strahler ordering scheme that each stream of order ω requires the presence of at least two tributary streams of order $\omega - 1$ headward of it, the sequences within and between successive order set types indicate the number of excess-order tributaries, and it is these numbers that define how precisely the Strahler stream set characterizes the network topology. The number of ways in which the excess-order tributaries may

TABLE 2. Range in Network Diameter d and Mean Source Height p_e/n Associated With Stream Set Probabilities Under the Shreve Random Topology Model for Magnitude $n = 25$ Networks

Type	Stream Set					d		p_e/n		Stream Set Probability	Rank
	N_1	N_2	N_3	N_4	N_5	max	min	max	min		
2.	25	1				25	25	13.96	13.96	0.6503×10^{-5}	33
3.	25	2	1			24	24	13.93	8.68	0.4113×10^{-3}	22
3.	25	3	1			23	10	13.80	7.20	0.7198×10^{-2}	16
3.	25	4	1			22	9	13.60	6.68	0.4103×10^{-1}	9
3.	25	5	1			21	8	13.32	6.48	0.9965×10^{-1}	4
3.	25	6	1			20	8	12.96	6.44	0.1163	3
3.	25	7	1			19	8	12.52	6.44	0.6869×10^{-1}	7
3.	25	8	1			18	9	12.00	6.56	0.2076×10^{-1}	11
3.	25	9	1			17	10	11.40	6.80	0.3114×10^{-2}	17
3.	25	10	1			16	11	10.72	7.16	0.2137×10^{-3}	26
3.	25	11	1			15	12	9.96	7.64	0.5624×10^{-5}	34
3.	25	12	1			14	13	9.12	8.28	0.3652×10^{-7}	44
4.1	25	4	2	1		21	9	13.52	6.48	0.1026×10^{-1}	15
4.1	25	5	2	1		20	8	13.24	6.20	0.7473×10^{-1}	6
4.1	25	6	2	1		19	7	12.88	6.00	0.1744	1
4.1	25	7	2	1		18	7	12.44	5.96	0.1717	2
4.1	25	8	2	1		17	7	11.92	5.92	0.7785×10^{-1}	5
4.1	25	9	2	1		16	7	11.32	5.92	0.1635×10^{-1}	12
4.1	25	10	2	1		15	7	10.64	5.96	0.1496×10^{-2}	19
4.1	25	11	2	1		14	8	9.88	6.12	0.5061×10^{-4}	29
4.1	25	12	2	1		13	8	9.04	6.32	0.4108×10^{-6}	40
4.2	25	6	3	1		18	7	12.64	6.00	0.1453×10^{-1}	13
4.2	25	7	3	1		17	7	12.20	5.88	0.4293×10^{-1}	8
4.2	25	8	3	1		16	7	11.68	5.84	0.3892×10^{-1}	10
4.2	25	9	3	1		15	7	11.08	5.80	0.1326×10^{-1}	14
4.2	25	10	3	1		14	6	10.40	5.76	0.1870×10^{-2}	18
4.2	25	11	3	1		13	7	9.64	5.84	0.8857×10^{-4}	28
4.2	25	12	3	1		12	7	8.80	5.92	0.9586×10^{-6}	38
4.3	25	8	4	1		15	7	11.28	5.92	0.1297×10^{-2}	21
4.3	25	9	4	1		14	7	10.68	5.80	0.1362×10^{-2}	20
4.3	25	10	4	1		13	6	10.00	5.76	0.3740×10^{-3}	23
4.3	25	11	4	1		12	6	9.24	5.76	0.2952×10^{-4}	30
4.3	25	12	4	1		11	7	8.40	5.84	0.4793×10^{-6}	39
4.4	25	10	5	1		12	7	9.44	5.96	0.6678×10^{-5}	32
4.4	25	11	5	1		11	7	8.68	5.92	0.1582×10^{-5}	36
4.4	25	12	5	1		10	7	7.84	5.92	0.5135×10^{-7}	42
4.5	25	12	6	1		9	8	7.12	6.32	0.5706×10^{-9}	46
5.1	25	8	4	2	1	14	7	11.12	5.76	0.3244×10^{-3}	25
5.1	25	9	4	2	1	13	6	10.52	5.72	0.3406×10^{-3}	24
5.1	25	10	4	2	1	12	6	9.84	5.72	0.9349×10^{-4}	27
5.1	25	11	4	2	1	11	6	9.08	5.72	0.7381×10^{-5}	31
5.1	25	12	4	2	1	10	6	8.24	5.72	0.1198×10^{-6}	41
5.2	25	10	5	2	1	11	6	9.28	5.72	0.5009×10^{-5}	35
5.2	25	11	5	2	1	10	6	8.52	5.72	0.1186×10^{-5}	37
5.2	25	12	5	2	1	9	6	7.68	5.72	0.3851×10^{-7}	43
5.3	25	12	6	2	1	8	6	6.96	5.72	0.8559×10^{-9}	45
5.4	25	12	6	3	1	7	6	6.48	5.72	0.7132×10^{-10}	47

be attached defines the number of TDCN's within a given stream set class, such that, for example, with the fourth-order set given by (8:4:2:1) there are no such excess-order streams, and merely specifying the stream set composition uniquely defines the TDCN for that class. The variation in the extreme values of the mean source height with increasing higher-order tributary specification is plotted directly in terms of the number of second-order streams for each order set type in Figure 3. Thus progression through each order set type, through successive order set types, and through successive order sets corresponds to increasing the higher-order tributary specification and conversely to decreasing the numbers of excess-order tributaries.

When it is borne in mind that testing random topology model hypotheses upon stream set data requires the adoption of a crude quartile ranking test devised by *Shreve* [1966], examination of some of the features apparent in Figures 2 and 3 reveals that stream set composition incorporates a wide and variable degree of topologic information, making any geomorphic interpretation of such tests extremely difficult. From inspection of Figure 3 it is evident that increasing the level of higher-order tributary specification involves a marked and consistent decline in the values for the maximum mean source height (p_{max}^e/n), indicating a strong trend toward increasing topologic structural compaction of the network. The variation in the pattern of minimum values (p_{min}^e/n) is rather more complex, owing to the constraint upon variations in the composition of higher-order tributary numbers imposed by

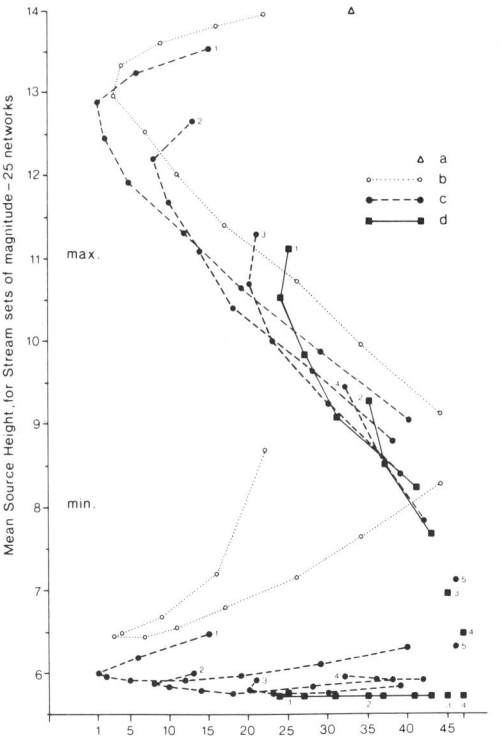

Fig. 2. Mean source height and stream set probability rank (see Table 3 for explanation of symbols).

directly into numbers of TDCN's and associated stream set probabilities under the Shreve random topology model. Therefore it would appear to be of some importance to bear in mind the effect of the absolute level of magnitude upon stream set composition variability in working with stream set data. Magnitude constraints directly affect the associated stream set probabilities under the random topology model and at the same time also affect the structural variability of networks in any chosen order set. When the trends of the order set type lines shown in Figures 2 and 3 are related, it can be seen that deviations from the most probable stream set may have a variety of implications. If the network magnitude is sufficient for the development of a wide enough range of stream set compositions, then deviation from the most probable stream set in terms of decreasing the number of higher-order tributaries will lead to a trend of increasing structural lineation, due to increasing the numbers of excess lower-order tributaries. This trend is evident in both extreme values of the mean source height measure. On the other hand, deviation from the most probable stream set in terms of increasing the number of higher-order tributaries necessarily leads to a decline in the maximum mean source height values and also to a pattern of decreasing minimum mean source height values that may remain constant and finally increase again as the magnitude constraint allows for sufficient ramification within the stream set composition.

The significance of these trends is that whereas tests of topologic randomness are capable of some interpretation in terms of topologic structure if the networks are sampled at a constant magnitude, results from stream set properties developed in networks over a wide range of magnitudes may

the absolute level of network magnitude. Thus at magnitude 25 there is sufficient scope for the development of order set types 3 and 4.1 to reveal a 'U'-shaped 'cycle' in the $p_{min}{}^e/n$ values. The declining limb may be interpreted in terms of increasing compaction of topologic structure down to the minimum of the cycle as more complex branching systems fill out the possible bifurcations at link distances near the basin mouth. Beyond the minimum point, overall compaction decreases again with increasing numbers of second-order streams, which require bifurcations further from the basin mouth in order to avoid increasing the numbers of third- and higher-order tributaries. For the other order set types the level of magnitude 25 is insufficient for development of this full cyclic pattern. If these trends are now traced back to Figure 2, the variability in structural compaction is seen to be translated

TABLE 3. Key to Symbols in Figures 2 and 3

Symbol	Order Set Type	N_1	N_2	N_3	N_4	N_5
a	2	25	1			
b	3	25	...	1		
c	4.1	25	...	2	1	
	4.2	25	...	3	1	
	4.3	25	...	4	1	
	4.4	25	...	5	1	
	4.5	25	...	6	1	
d	5.1	25	...	4	2	1
	5.2	25	...	5	2	1
	5.3	25	...	6	2	1
	5.4	25	...	6	3	1

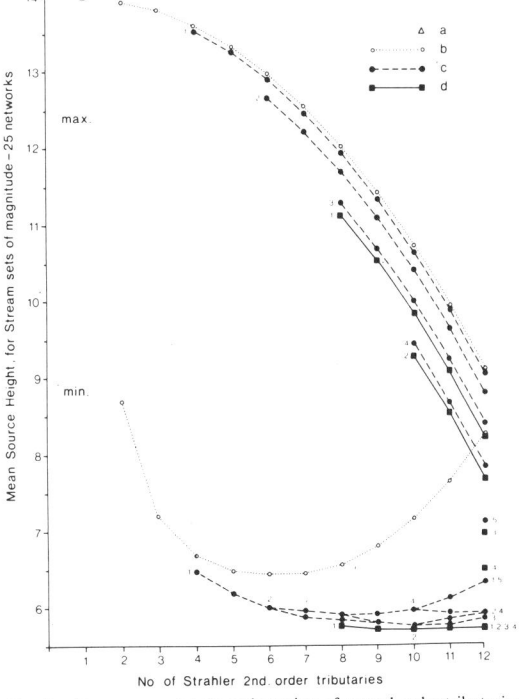

Fig. 3. Mean source height and number of second-order tributaries (see Table 3 for explanation of symbols).

well incorporate a wide variety of structural implications, making any interpretation of the model extremely difficult. Consider, for example, a sample of fourth-order networks of magnitude 25. The individual TDCN probabilities range from 0.1744 for stream set (25:6:2:1), which is in fact the most probable stream set for networks of magnitude 25, down to 0.5706×10^{-9} for stream set (25:12:6:1), which is the forty-sixth most probable stream set out of 47 for magnitude 25 networks. However, if we happened to obtain the most compacted TDCN associated with the sampled stream sets (and merely specifying the Strahler stream set composition can give no indication of whether this has occurred), then the average source height values range only from 5.760 to 6.480. On the other hand, by simply specifying the stream sets we could just as probably have obtained the least compacted network cases, in which instance the mean source height values could range from 7.120 to 13.520. When it is realized that working with empirical data often requires sampling over a wide range of network magnitudes, it is hardly surprising that interpretations of random topology model tests have had to resort to very general explanations. The model itself provides no substantive measure of the type of topologic variation in the data that is amenable to any meaningful geomorphic interpretation.

STRUCTURAL PROPERTIES OF THE RANDOM TOPOLOGY MODEL

Perhaps some indication of the general interpretation of the structural properties of the random topology model may be derived from the relationship between the number of links and the number of Strahler segments in a network, noted by *Coffman et al.* [1972]. The number of links in a network is directly related to the magnitude of the network by the simple identity

$$l = 2n - 1 \qquad (13)$$

where l is the number of links and n the number of sources, or

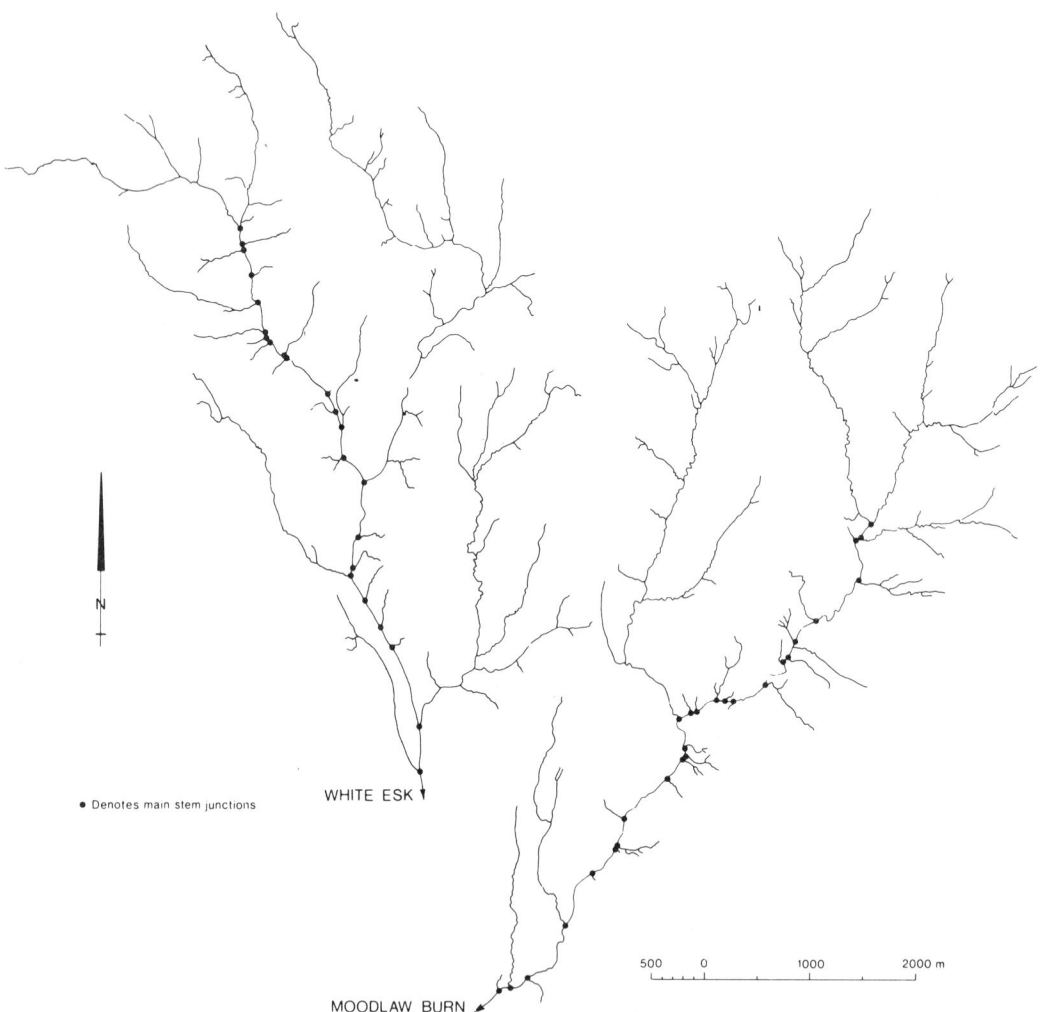

Fig. 4. Stream networks: White Esk and Moodlaw Burn.

Strahler first-order streams. Coffman et al. show that the effect of increasing orders is constrained by the family of curves

$$l = 2s - (2^\Omega - 1) \quad (14)$$

where s is the number of Strahler segments and Ω is the order of the network. Substituting in the above expression and rearranging lead to

$$s = n + (2^{\Omega-1} - 1) \quad (15)$$

Therefore we may consider the number of segments as being made up of two components, given by the first term n, which defines the number of first-order streams, and the second term $(2^{\Omega-1} - 1)$. Now $2^{\Omega-1}$ is the minimum number of sources required to generate a network of order Ω (yielding a perfect binary network in which only segments of equal order combine), and thus $(2^{\Omega-1} - 1)$ is the number of interior links in such a network. Clearly, this family of curves defines minimum threshold values for networks of specified magnitude n and order Ω, whose stream sets contain the minimum number of streams of order $\Omega - 1, \Omega - 2, \cdots, 2$. The other boundary condition noted by Coffman et al. is given by the relation

$$l = s \quad (16)$$

and on substituting for magnitude this leads to

$$s = n + (n - 1) \quad (17)$$

In other words, the maximum number of segments for a given number of sources is given by the maximum number of interior links defining separate Strahler segments, so that the second term in the general expression is equal to $(n - 1)$. In effect, this maximizes the number of streams of order $\Omega - 1, \Omega - 2, \cdots, 2$. It may be noted from Figure 2 that this does not necessarily produce the most compacted network for the specified order set. Thus, for example, the most topologically compact fourth-order network of magnitude 25 is given by stream sets (25:10:4:1), (25:11:4:1), or (25:10:3:1) and not by the maximum order-bifurcating system, which would yield stream set (25:12:6:1).

From a sample of 106 drainage network systems in northern Indiana, *Coffman et al.* [1972, p. 1502, Figure 7] demonstrate a marked stabilization in the trend of bifurcation ratios observed with increasing network size. In terms of the relationship between numbers of links and Strahler segments a large-magnitude network of order Ω behaves very much like networks of order $\Omega + 1$ at that magnitude level. From the interrelationships between magnitude and structural compaction properties discussed above it would not appear unreasonable to speculate that the consistency observed by Coffman et al. reflects a general tendency for the topologic structure of the network to evolve toward a pattern of increasing compactness. Indeed, it may well be that the overall regularity found in many tests of random topology model hypotheses merely serves to identify in large-magnitude networks a tendency toward increasing compactness of topologic structure, manifested by a simple bifurcating system filling space in competition with neighboring systems.

APPLICATION OF TOPOLOGIC MODELS TO SMALL SAMPLE STUDIES

Finally, we consider the type of information yielded by the application of topologic models to the case of local-scale or subregional studies, which because of sampling difficulties are necessarily focused upon a small number of individual basin units. This type of problem is not very amenable to treatment within either TDCN, ambilateral class, or stream set terms, in that the first two methods provide no useful measures for small sample analysis and the last method suffers from all the problems of overgeneralization developed above.

Thus we may consider the topologic information contained in two adjacent Strahler fourth-order networks located in the southern uplands of Scotland and mapped from the *Ordnance Survey* [1968] 1:25,000 topographic sheet NT20/30 (Figure 4) for Moodlaw Burn (magnitude 84) and the headwaters of the White Esk (magnitude 80). In any comparative analysis of these basins an important attribute of the topologic form of the networks would appear to be the effects of successive subnesting of subtributary systems along the main stem of the networks. It is not unreasonable to suppose that this topologic property is of some importance in controlling the hydrologic responses of the drainage basin system to precipitation input events, reflecting the phasing of throughputs within the system over both time and space. When the simple test proposed by *Werritty* [1972] is applied, it is found that Moodlaw Burn maintains very broadly a much more probable stream set composition under the random topology model throughout virtually all of its course. This relationship is plotted in Figure 5, where p is the probability of a given set of stream numbers occurring under the random model hypothesis and p_{max} is the probability of the most probable stream set for the given magnitude. However, computing the various structural measures proposed by *Jarvis* [1972] (mean and maximum source height values) provides a much more specific indication of the effects of successive junctions. These values are shown in Figure 6, and the locations of differences between the two network structures are more clearly revealed. Further refinements become possible in the case of mean source height, because *Werner and Smart* [1973] have provided algorithms for deriving the absolute limits plus the expectation of p_e/n. Thus inspection of Figure 6b reveals a marked contrast between the very lineated or elongate headwaters of the White Esk and the much more compact headwaters of the Moodlaw Burn. Above magnitude 40 both streams have a tendency to increasing elongation, this tendency becoming very marked in the high-magnitude reaches of the Moodlaw Burn, which

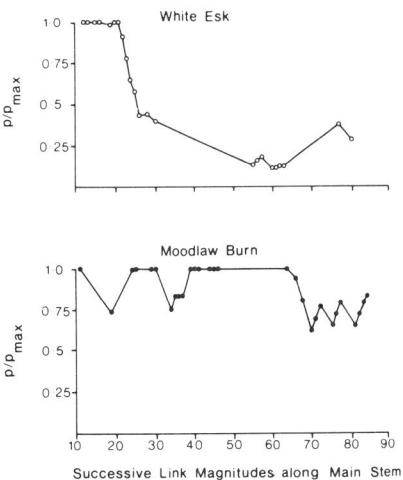

Fig. 5. Relative probability of stream set numbers along main stem.

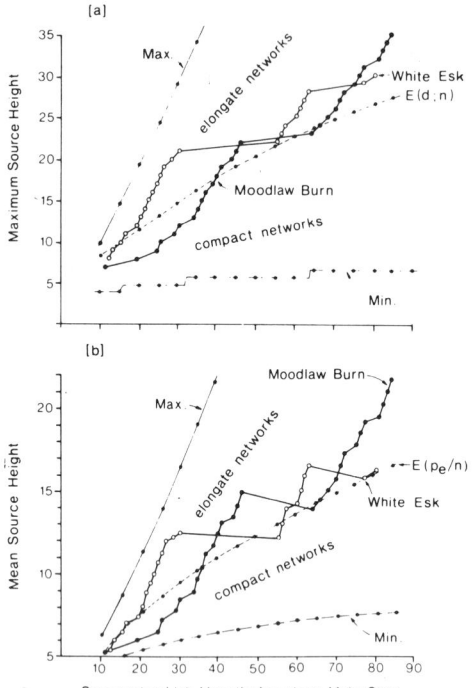

Fig. 6. Changes in simple structure measures along main stem. (*a*) Maximum source height. (*b*) Mean source height.

departs markedly from the expected values predicted by the Shreve model. The White Esk, on the other hand, conforms much more closely to the model in its higher reaches. The two simple structural measures (mean source height and maximum source height) provide useful parameters of network properties, which can be incorporated with other investigations using nontopologic attributes.

The most basic problem in applying random topology hypotheses is precisely what useful information such models provide the geomorphologist: a question that has received remarkably little attention. Analyses of bifurcation ratios, derived from Strahler stream set number distributions, have frequently proved these measures to be of extremely low discriminatory power, and given the massive losses of information involved and the variable type of structural information retained, this is perhaps hardly surprising. With analyses based upon TDCN or ambilateral class data the problem arises that neither of these methods, by its very nature, leads to the generation of topologic parameters that are capable of geomorphic interpretation at anything but the crudest level of generality. The derivation of link distance or path length measures would appear to offer a rather more fruitful line of approach, the model being geared toward a more precise quantification of drainage network topologic structure and permitting immediate comparisons at both within- and between-magnitude levels by means of parameters like those developed by *Werner and Smart* [1973]. At least it is to be hoped that future work in topologic analysis of network systems will recognize the need for the development of more meaningful parameters for hypothesis testing and interpretation.

Conclusion

The problem of testing random topology models directly on any but the smallest networks involves such severe information losses in terms of topologic detail that the interpretation of randomness or deviations from randomness becomes extremely difficult. Indeed, regrouping of TDCN's into stream sets results in such massive losses of topologic detail that one must doubt whether such tests are of any significance to the geomorphologist. The introduction of some intermediate classificatory methods provides a possible solution to this problem in that much more topologic information is retained. These new models are also of interest because for the first time they incorporate topologic parameters that correlate well with other geomorphic variables. However, most of the commonly applied measures (e.g., bifurcation ratios) contain very little information that is capable of any geomorphic interpretation beyond the crudest level of generality.

It is surely appropriate now, some 25 years after the first applications of topologic classificatory schemes to drainage networks, to call for a reappraisal of the types of parameters that these models incorporate. The introduction of link distance-based parameters may at least provide some notions of structural compactness that may be developed more directly in association with the metric and spatial properties of the drainage basin. Thus new questions will be raised to be tested in the field and thereby to lead to a more sophisticated method of dividing space in terms of the process response function of the drainage basin system.

Acknowledgments. We wish to thank C. Werner and J. S. Smart for providing us with a prepublication version of their joint paper and for allowing us to incorporate some of their findings into this paper. We also wish to acknowledge the helpful comments provided by R. J. Chorley during the preparation of this paper and the support of Natural Environment Research Council postgraduate training awards held at the Department of Geography, Cambridge University.

References

Coffman, D. M., E. A. Keller, and W. N. Melhorn, New topologic relationship as an indicator of drainage network evolution, *Water Resour. Res.*, *8*(6), 1497–1505, 1972.
Jarvis, R. S., New measure of the topologic structure of dendritic drainage networks, *Water Resour. Res.*, *8*(5), 1265–1271, 1972.
Liao, K. H., and A. E. Scheidegger, A computer model of some branching-type phenomena in hydrology, *Bull. Int. Ass. Sci. Hydrol.*, *13*(1), 5–13, 1968.
Melton, M. A., A derivation of Strahler's channel-ordering system, *J. Geol.*, *67*, 345–346, 1959.
Ordnance Survey, 1:25,000 map, 2nd ser., Chessington, Surrey, England, 1968.
Quastler, H., A primer on information theory, in *Symposium on Information Theory in Biology*, edited by H. P. Yockey, R. L. Platzman, and H. Quastler, pp. 3–49, Pergamon, London, 1958.
Shreve, R. L., Statistical law of stream numbers, *J. Geol.*, *74*(1), 17–37, 1966.
Shreve, R. L., Infinite topologically random channel networks, *J. Geol.*, *75*(2), 178–186, 1967.
Shreve, R. L., Stream lengths and basin areas in topologically random channel networks, *J. Geol.*, *77*(4), 397–414, 1969.
Smart, J. S., Statistical properties of stream lengths, *Water Resour. Res.*, *4*(5), 1001–1014, 1968.
Smart, J. S., Topological properties of channel networks, *Geol. Soc. Amer. Bull.*, *80*, 1757–1774, 1969.
Strahler, A. N., Quantitative geomorphology of drainage basins and channel networks, in *Handbook of Applied Hydrology*, edited by V. T. Chow, pp. 4/40–4/74, McGraw-Hill, New York, 1964.
Werner, C., Horton's law of stream numbers for topologically random channel networks, *Can. Geogr.*, *14*(1), 57–66, 1970.

Werner, C., Two models for Horton's law of stream numbers, *Can. Geogr.*, *16*(1), 50–68, 1972.

Werner, C., and J. S. Smart, Some new methods of topologic classification of channel networks, *Geogr. Anal.*, *5*, 271–295, 1973.

Werritty, A., The topology of stream networks, in *Spatial Analysis in Geomorphology*, edited by R. J. Chorley, pp. 167–196, Methuen, London, 1972.

(Received October 3, 1973;
revised October 9, 1974.)

12

Copyright ©1969 by The University of Chicago
Reprinted from pages 544-554 and 563-565 of *Jour. Geology* **77**:544-565 (1969), by permission of The University of Chicago Press

FREQUENCY DISTRIBUTIONS OF STREAM LINK LENGTHS[1]

W. R. JAMES[2] AND W. C. KRUMBEIN

Department of Statistics, Princeton University, Princeton, New Jersey 08540; and
Department of Geological Sciences, Northwestern University, Evanston, Illinois 60201

ABSTRACT

Shreve's concept of infinite topologically random channel networks focuses attention on exterior and interior channel links, which are the basic elements of the network. The population distribution of link lengths has importance in its relation to the statistical properties of entire networks, and it plays a basic role in computer simulation models for generating stream patterns. Published data on link lengths are sparse, and earlier workers have inclined toward a lognormal model for the length distribution of exterior links (Strahler first-order streams). More recently, Smart has proposed an exponential model for interior links, on the basis of a postulated link-generating mechanism. The model agrees with observed interior link lengths except for a deficiency of short links as required by his theory. Analysis of interior links in a magnitude 1311 basin shows that the probability of successive tributaries entering main channels from the same side is only about two-thirds the probability of opposite-side entry. These higher-order structures in the data (i.e., the spatial arrangement of successive tributaries) display a first-order Markovian property in sequences of link type. These structures are examined in their substantive context, and a composite gammalike population density for interior link lengths is developed theoretically. This density contains the higher-order structures and agrees, at least approximately, with observed relations in main channels of magnitude 10 or greater.

INTRODUCTION

Renewed interest in frequency distributions of link lengths (Smart 1968) has been stimulated by Shreve's (1966, 1967) introduction of the concept of topologically random channel networks. The basic element in Shreve's approach is the channel link, which may be exterior or interior, terminating at its upstream end in a source or fork, respectively. The exterior link is identical with Strahler's (1952) first-order stream, and interior links are channels that constitute the inner portion of the network.

In view of the basic importance of links and their interrelationships, it is apparent that the population distributions of link lengths, both exterior and interior, deserve detailed consideration. Not only are these distributions important in their relation to the statistical properties of entire networks, but they play a primary role in the development of channel network simulation models, such as that developed by Leopold and Langbein (1962). Obviously, if simulated networks are to have properties similar to those of real-world networks, the underlying population distributions must be the same.

Published data on link lengths are sparse. The earliest example known to us is that of Strahler (1954), who presented histograms of fifty first-order stream lengths (exterior links) based on unpublished thesis material from Victor C. Miller. Strahler showed that a lognormal distribution fits the data reasonably well. Schumm (1956) pointed out the likelihood that first-order streams are distributed lognormally with respect to length, but virtually no further studies of this kind were made until Shreve's papers made it clear that the subject requires further consideration.

A preliminary study of the observed distributions of exterior and interior link lengths in eastern Kentucky was made on thirty networks with graduate student aid in a course offered at the University of California at Los Angeles by Shreve and Krumbein in early 1968. The observational data are to be given in a subsequent

---

[1] Manuscript received January 20, 1969; revised April 17, 1969.

[2] Present address: Coastal Engineering Research Center, Washington, D. C. 20016.

report. The distributions are right-skewed and resemble lognormal distributions, with the mean length of exterior links about twice that of interior links. Initial statistical analysis of the data was undertaken at Northwestern University in the summer of 1968. Our approach is based on theoretical insights provided by Smart (1968), and we express our appreciation to him for making his material available to us in manuscript form. Shreve (1969) sent us his conclusions regarding the population distributions of the link length data collected at UCLA, which are mentioned later.

The purpose of this paper is to examine the adequacy of some models for link length distributions by study of the higher-order structures in observed link length data. By "higher-order structures" we refer to the spatial elements in the sequence of interior links along main channels composed of links having moderate to high magnitude. These spatial sequences are lost when link length data are assembled into histograms. By systematically recording the spatial elements it becomes possible to test the sequences for Markovian or other kinds of dependencies. Our data, collected from a magnitude 1311 drainage basin in eastern Kentucky, and supplemented by geomorphological arguments, are used to develop a probabilistic model of link length distribution that approximately fits the observed data and does contain the dependencies to be described.

LOGNORMAL, GAMMA, AND EXPONENTIAL MODELS

In addition to the lognormal distribution proposed by Strahler (1954) and Smart's (1968) exponential model, Shreve (1969) proposes a gamma distribution for interior link lengths as a convenient starting point for further analysis of stream networks. These three models are introduced briefly here as a foundation for later consideration in terms of link-generating mechanisms.

The *lognormal distribution*, treated in detail by Aitchison and Brown (1957), is discussed here in terms of logarithms of the measured variate X (= link length). If the log of X to any base is normally distributed, then X is lognormally distributed. Let $L = \log X$; then

$$n(L;\mu_L,\sigma_L) = \frac{1}{\sigma_L\sqrt{(2\pi)}} e^{-(L-\mu_L)^2/2\sigma_L^2}, \quad (1)$$

where μ_L and σ_L^2 are, respectively, the population mean and variance in L terms.

The *gamma distribution*, described in Krumbein and Graybill (1965, p. 99), has the following form:

$$G(X;r,\beta) = \frac{X^{r-1}e^{-X/\beta}}{\Gamma(r)\beta^r}, \quad (2)$$

where r and β are the population parameters, and $\Gamma(r) = (r-1)!$. Shreve (1969) found by maximum-likelihood estimation that the UCLA data has $r = 2.02$, and our data give similar results. Hence, we set $r = 2$, and for the convenience of having all terms in the numerator, we define a new β that is the reciprocal of the β in equation (2), to obtain:

$$g(X;2,\beta) = \beta^2 X e^{-\beta X} \quad (3)$$

For the gamma distribution the parameters r and β are related to the population mean and variance as follows:

$$E[X] = \frac{r}{\beta}; \quad \text{for} \quad r = 2, \quad E[X] = \frac{2}{\beta};$$

$$\text{Var}[X] = \frac{r}{\beta^2}; \quad \text{for} \quad r = 2, \quad (4)$$

$$\text{Var}[X] = \frac{2}{\beta^2}$$

The *exponential density* has the form (Smart 1968):

$$e(X;\lambda) = \lambda e^{-\lambda X}, \quad (5)$$

where the single parameter is λ. The relation of λ to the expectation and variance of X is:

$$E[X] = \frac{1}{\lambda}$$
$$\text{Var}[X] = \frac{1}{\lambda^2}. \quad (6)$$

Our version of the gamma distribution in equation (2) was selected so that when $r = 1$, it reduces to the exponential distribution with parameter β. The expression is algebraically equivalent to the form of gamma distribution used by Shreve (1969).

A RATIONAL APPROACH TO LINK LENGTH DISTRIBUTIONS

The search for empirical models is sometimes necessary in preliminary studies of newly quantified variates, but it is inadequate for "explaining" or understanding the underlying mechanism that generates the variate under study. If an understanding of the probabilistic framework of the link-generating process is to be attained, it seems to us that the only realistic approach is to start with basic assumptions that are reasonable from a substantive point of view, and from these to derive a variety of statistical properties. Observational data may then be gathered to test the derived properties and hence the initial substantive assumptions.

Smart's (1968) approach to link length distributions follows such a rational plan. On the basis of computer-simulated channel networks by Smart et al. (1967), based on a model by Leopold and Langbein (1962), which were found to display a geometric probability distribution for first-order streams (i.e., exterior links), Smart starts with the assumption that the downstream point at which the channel will make a junction (and thus terminate) is equally likely to occur in any single length increment ΔX. We may rephrase this more naturalistically and in its continuous equivalent by stating that, as a channel network develops by exterior links cutting their way upstream into the upland, the point at which a channel bifurcates (thus forming the upstream end of an interior link) is equally likely to occur in any single link length segment, dX, beyond the last bifurcation. Without implying any specific generating process, we may extend this to more fully developed channels by stating that the point along such a channel at which a tributary enters is equally likely to occur in any length increment, dX, along the channel, regardless of the positions of entry of other tributaries. We shall refer to this last statement as the exponential model of interior link length distribution.

The exponential model is intuitively very attractive because it is simple and because many implied statistical properties can be directly derived from it. Smart compared the exponential density with observed frequency distributions of natural link lengths and concluded that the model was satisfactory as a starting point, although he noted that, contrary to what the exponential density requires, natural networks show a dearth of very short links.

Our own studies have almost invariably produced the same results; that is, we find significantly fewer very short links than the model predicts. The χ^2 tests on our and other available data on sample distributions do not allow us to accept the hypothesis that any of them were drawn from an exponentially distributed population.

Despite this discrepancy, the exponential model provides a logical starting point because it is an independent-events model which assumes essentially no structure in link length sequences. The discrepancies suggest that some form of dependence is present, however, and it is here that the analysis of higher-order structures in the data are of value. As stated earlier, histograms of observed values of a variate that is areally distributed do not reveal possible dependencies in the position of individual links in the spatial sequence. These can be brought out, however, by examining the links sequentially; this may suggest additional ideas about the link-generating process.

We have developed a method of measuring links so that the sequence structure can be observed. We then present a framework of substantive assumptions regarding the generation of link lengths, which at least begins to account for the structures we observe in link sequences.

OPPOSITE-SIDE AND SAME-SIDE LINKS

The exponential model makes no distinction between lengths of links of different magnitude (except for magnitude 1 and >1), nor does it provide for distinctions between junctions involving links of similar magnitude and junctions of links having widely different magnitudes. Trunk streams with main channel links of high magnitude invariably have a large number of first- and second-order tributaries. It is difficult for us to imagine the junction of a first-magnitude link and a hundred-magnitude link as a bifurcation, in the sense that the original stream split at this point during its growth into the upland and continued to grow in two different directions. We believe that a low-magnitude link entering a link of noticeably greater magnitude can be thought of as a tributary link that enters a main channel from the "right" or "left" side, rather than considering every fork to be a bifurcation with no "handedness." Thus, as we follow along a main channel, defined as the succession of the higher-order links at each junction, we operationally define a junction as being "right-handed" if as we move upstream the channel "turns" to the right (or receives a tributary with maximum link of lower magnitude from the left), and vice versa for "left-handed" junctions.

With this definition of handedness we can represent a sequence of links along a main channel by following the higher-magnitude link upstream to each junction and recording a series of R's and L's to represent the direction of turn. Interior links can thus be classified into two groups—those bounded by junctions of opposite handedness and those bounded by junctions of the same handedness. We call these "opposite-side links," and "same-side links," respectively. A third class of links we cannot classify, as "turns" occur when both branches of a stream at a given junction have the same magnitude. Perhaps these represent true bifurcations, though we reserve the term for subsequent more critical examination.

We are indebted to R. L. Shreve for suggesting the terms *cis* and *trans* for same-side and opposite-side links, respectively. These terms permit clear differentiation between two categories of same-side links that become important later in our analysis, when we shall need to distinguish between individual same-side links, terminated at both ends by same-side entry of tributaries, and chains of links, in which the successive same-side tributaries have one or more intervening opposite-side tributaries.

The diagram of figure 1 makes this distinction clear. The horizontal line is the main channel, and the vertical lines are tributaries of lower-magnitude links entering as shown. Examples of individual same-side (cis) links and strings of links (cis chains) terminated by same-side tributary entry are labeled. Opposite-side (trans) links, which are shown as single links, can also be combined into trans chains, as described later.

If the exponential model is valid, cis links and trans links should occur with equal frequency and possess the same underlying population density of link length distribution. On an intuitive basis we postulate that, if low magnitude tributaries enter a main channel very close to each other and on the same side, one may capture the other during a period of heavy runoff or during the normal course of downcutting. Hence, a junction and a very short link would be removed from the main channel, but the same number of interior links would remain in the network. Thus, although a short link is removed from the main channel, a new one is created to connect the newly formed junction of the two tributaries with the main stream.

Inasmuch as our analysis applies to main channels, a link from this sequence of links is removed if our postulate is correct. On the other hand, we see no reason for assuming a similar interaction between tributaries entering the main channel from opposite sides. As a first approximation we assume at this point that no such influence is present.

If our assumptions are correct, they may

explain the dearth of very short links along well-developed main channels. However, we would also expect to find a greater proportion of trans links than of cis links; and we would expect the observed lengths of trans and cis links to be samples from different statistical populations. In order to test whether these implications hold, and also to have sequential link data for other forms of analysis, we applied our operational measurement procedure as described in the next section.

MEASUREMENT OF LINK SEQUENCES

After the drainage pattern is drawn on the topographic sheet, and the magnitude of each interior link indicated, observation begins with the link of highest magnitude and proceeds upstream. Figure 2 is an example of a complete fourth-order (Strahler) basin with its highest-magnitude link having magnitude 64. We start upstream along this link and note that at the first junction the main channel link (of magnitude 59) "turns" to the right. Hence an R is entered in the first column of table 1. At the next junction the main channel, now of magnitude 58, turns to the left, and an L is entered in the second double-spaced line of table 1. On the intervening line in the second column of the table we record the link magnitude, 59, between these two turns. The

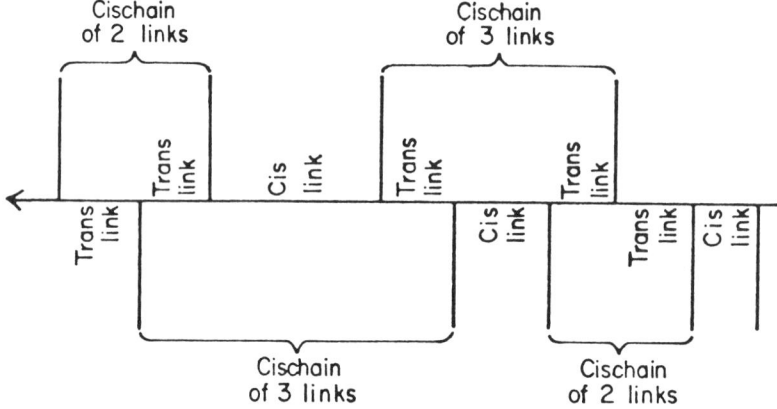

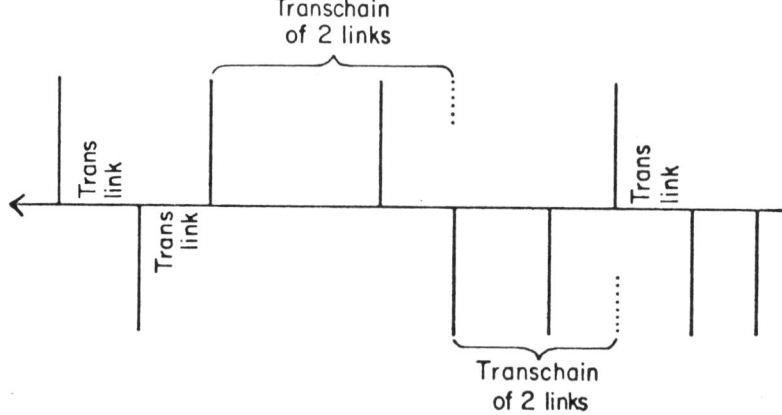

Fig. 1.—Diagram of main stream channel with tributary links of lower magnitude indicated as vertical lines. Upper diagram shows terminology for cis and trans links and identifies cis chains. Bottom diagram shows same stretch of channel with trans chains (discussed in later part of paper) designated.

length of link 59 is recorded in column 3 on the same line with the link magnitude. For convenience of statistical computation we enter the length to the nearest 1/50 inch. These figures can readily be converted to ground lengths by multiplying them by 40 feet = 1/50 inch.

The R and L marking the bounds of link 59 indicate that this is a trans link. We now proceed to the next junction, where the main channel (magnitude 57) again turns to the left. Thus link 58 has the symbol L at both ends and is thus a cis link. We follow this procedure upstream until the main channel link of magnitude 10 is reached. We terminate each sequence at the tenth magnitude to avoid the increased subjectivity of defining exterior links near basin margins. Our limiting magnitude is probably safely between eight and twelve. In addition, if an entering tributary differs in magnitude by less than five from the main channel magnitude, we terminate the sequence. New sequences are then started upstream from these junctions, providing that the streams are still of magnitude greater than ten. For simplicity we have omitted the tributary that enters with magnitude 13 from the left. We are aware these special rules are not desirable in the context of complete channel network analysis. This initial approach, however, is restricted to main channels which presumably have undergone some link adjustments of the kind already mentioned, plus other changes to be discussed below.

We follow our rules in figure 2, which yields a run of 22 R's and L's as shown on the bottom of table 1. In this example there are 12 trans links (i.e., RL or LR) and 9 cis links (RR or LL).

FREQUENCIES OF CIS AND TRANS LINKS

Our measurements were made along Middle Fork of Rockcastle Creek, Martin County, Kentucky, from its inception at the southwestern county line northward through Thomas and Inez quadrangles (1:24,000) to a point about a mile south of the town of Inez, which represents a subarea boundary in the original UCLA class data. The area is underlain by flat-lying Pennsylvanian sandstone and shale, essentially free of geologic controls that might distort the almost classical dendritic pattern of the stream network.

Middle Fork of Rockcastle Creek attains a magnitude of 1311 at our stopping point,

TABLE 1

MAIN CHANNEL SEQUENCE OF TURNS, LINK MAGNITUDE, AND LENGTH

Main Channel Turn*	Main Channel Link Magnitude	Link Length in Units of 1/50 Inch
R	59	13
L	58	4
L	57	11
L	52	5
R	51	14
R	50	10
L	47	13
R	34	14
R	33	6
L	32	13
L	31	10
L	30	4
L	28	11
R	27	13
R	26	16
L	22	11
R	20	9
L	16	19
R	15	10
L	13	20
R	11	10
R	10	19

* Upstream sequence of main channel turns: R L L L R R L R R L L L L R R L R L R L R R.

and a census was taken of all streams of magnitude 10 or higher in the manner described. The total data matrix includes 485 interior links in thirty-eight separate sequences, of which only fifteen contained fewer than four links. A count of link frequencies gave 293 trans links and 192 cis links, or 60.4 percent trans links. These are mutually exclusive categories, so that, assuming independence, the frequency of link type is binomially distributed, with probability p for trans links and $(1 - p)$ for cis links. Further, the total number of links is sufficient for use of the gaussian approximation to the binomial probabilities. If the target population contains an equal proportion of links of each type, the expected number of links of each type from a sample of 485 links is 242.5. The probability of drawing a sample of this size ($N = 485$) with a deviation of fifty or more links from a population with $p = .5$ is less than .00001, which leaves little doubt that these two kinds of links occur in different proportions in the target population.

These results, somewhat startling to us, relate to Shreve's model of infinite topological randomness for stream networks (Shreve 1966, 1967). The basic assumption in Shreve's hypothesis is that all topologically

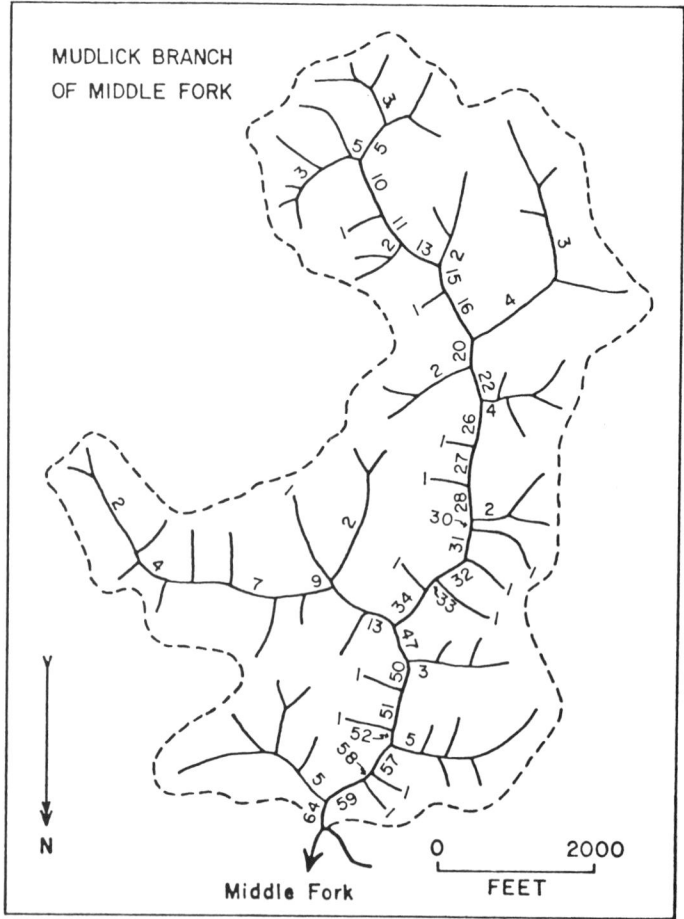

FIG. 2.—A magnitude 64 drainage basin with link magnitudes indicated. This diagram is to be used in connection with table 1. Basin is located in south-central part of Inez quadrangle, Kentucky.

distinct networks of given magnitude have equal probabilities of occurring. Now, the magnitude of a given network remains unchanged if the order of the sequence of turns (R's and L's) or the proportion of R's versus L's is changed. However, any such change in this sequence necessarily requires that the network represented by the new sequence be topologically distinct from the old. As this adjustment does not change magnitude, the new sequences must occur with the same probability as the old. This holds for any sub-sequence within a network as well as for entire networks. Hence for any segment of a main stream represented by a sequence of R's and L's, Shreve's hypothesis implies that any other sequence of R's and L's (keeping the total number of R's plus L's constant) could have occurred with equal probability. A specific example is that the sequence LLLLLL should occur with the same probability as LRLRLR. We have seen in this section that this does not appear to be the case for natural stream networks.

It is, however, important to point out that this particular contradiction to Shreve's hypothesis in no way affects the various theoretical properties thus far derived from it. Derivations, to this point in time, have involved relations between magnitude and Strahler or Horton stream order. As a consequence, topological subgroups have been defined on the basis of the number of bifurcations (junctions between links of equal magnitude or order) where no handedness is involved. Subgroup probabilities are determined by *summing across all topological classes that our finding predicts would not occur with equal probability*. Our results carry no implications regarding the probable number of bifurcations in networks of given magnitude.

FREQUENCIES OF VERY SHORT CIS AND TRANS LINKS

In addition to recording the sequence of main channel turns, we measured each interior link in the data set. Histograms were then prepared of the lengths of trans and cis links, as well as of both types pooled.

Figure 3 shows these histograms with frequencies expressed as proportions for direct comparison. The distributions clearly suggest a major difference in the frequency of short links in the two lower histograms.

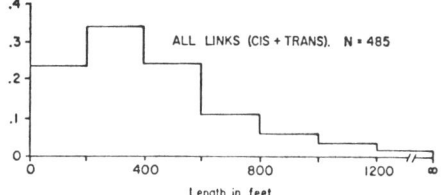

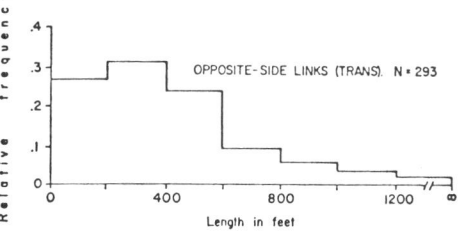

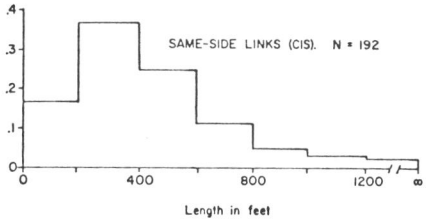

FIG. 3.—Observed distributions of interior link lengths of magnitude 10 and greater from Middle Fork of Rockcastle Creek, Inez and Thomas quadrangles, Kentucky. The top histogram shows all links, which are divided into trans and cis links in the lower two histograms.

This lends support to the earlier assumption of assimilation of short cis links. A statistical test of this difference can readily be made. The proportion of links in the shortest link length class for the whole sample of 485 links is .231. Under the null hypothesis that all links are drawn from the same length population, this value is an estimate of the probability that a link drawn at random will fall into the shortest class. For a sample of 192 links, the expected number of shortest links is 44.35. The observed frequency for cis links is thirty-two. Again, using the gaussian approximation, the probability of drawing thirty-two or fewer links in this class is less than .006. We may thus safely conclude that there are fewer very short cis links than very short trans links.

The implications of these findings is that the simple exponential model is not supported by observational data with respect to the occurrence of the two types of links disclosed by the study of link sequences. This does not say that this model may not provide an acceptable initial link-generating process, but it strongly suggests that channel adjustments of one sort or another may have to be superimposed to account for networks that are already reasonably well developed by the time observations are made.

quential arrangement of our data permits other spatial implications to be examined. Even without a specific link-generating model in mind, such further examination is worthwhile because it may permit us to reject some possible models before we attempt to develop a specific one.

One structure that deserves examination is that of sequential dependence in link types. To study this we prepared a fourth-order Markov transition probability matrix, from which the corresponding third-, second-, and first-order matrices can be derived. The fourth-order matrix was chosen because our data record is too short for any higher orders. The tally matrix and its corresponding probability matrix are given in table 2.

The manner of compiling this matrix can be shown with the summary run at the bottom of table 1. We note that the first four symbols, RLLL, are followed by R. This would be entered as a tally mark on the corresponding line of table 2. Next we shift one symbol at a time to the right in table 1, to obtain the sequence LLLR followed by

TABLE 2

FOURTH-ORDER MARKOV TALLY MATRIX AND TRANSITION PROBABILITY MATRIX OF SEQUENCE OF MAIN CHANNEL TURNS

Previous States				Followed by			Transition Probabilities	
$i-4$	$i-3$	$i-2$	$i-1$	L	R	Total	L	R
L	L	L	L	6	11	17	.353	.647
L	L	L	R	7	14	21	.333	.667
L	L	R	L	8	22	30	.267	.733
L	L	R	R	14	6	20	.700	.300
L	R	L	L	10	15	25	.400	.600
L	R	L	R	32	16	48	.667	.333
L	R	R	L	17	12	29	.586	.414
L	R	R	R	7	6	13	.538	.462
R	L	L	L	10	10	20	.500	.500
R	L	L	R	20	9	29	.690	.310
R	L	R	L	15	25	40	.375	.625
R	L	R	R	18	7	25	.720	.280
R	R	L	L	10	14	24	.417	.583
R	R	L	R	12	9	21	.571	.429
R	R	R	L	7	8	15	.467	.533
R	R	R	R	6	3	9	.667	.333
Totals				199	187	386	...	...

FURTHER ANALYSIS OF STRUCTURE IN LINK SEQUENCES

In addition to disclosing differences between two kinds of interior links, the se-

R, then LLRR followed by L, and so on.

It is evident from inspection of the values in table 2 that some sort of sequential dependence of link types is present in the data, in that sequences LRLR and RLRL are noticeably more frequent than others. This was anticipated from the finding that trans links are more common than cis links.

The simplest form of dependence is a lag-one first-order Markov property, and the tally and transition probability matrices for this are shown in table 3. The entries are obtained by considering state $(i-1)$ in the legend on the left of table 2 and summing over the appropriate lines in the tally matrix. Thus, the entry LL in table 3 is found by summing the L-column in the matrix of table 2 for all legends with state $(i-1) = L$.

A χ^2 test on table 3, using the procedure of Anderson and Goodman (1957) rejects the hypothesis that successive channel turns are independent events. The question that now remains is whether the nonequality of transition probabilities in the fourth-order matrix is due to this simple first-order dependence. This can be tested by computing the expected fourth-order tally matrix from a probability tree with the stationary probabilities of table 3, thus including only first-order dependence. This was done, and a χ^2 test fails to reject the hypothesis of no significant differences between observed and expected values. It thus seems safe to assume that no linear dependence, other than a first-order Markov property, is present in sequences of link junction types, at least for strings of four adjacent junctions.

These results do not preclude the possibility of some structure in the sequence of link lengths, or of interactions between link type and link length. We looked into these possibilities by computing serial correlation coefficients as well as serial cross-correlation coefficients between link type and link length. None of the correlation coefficients through lag 10 is highly significant. Thus, although sequences of junction types possess a first-order Markovian property, other first-order Markovian properties appear to be lacking in sequences of ten adjacent junctions. This does not rule out higher-order properties in longer link sequences, but our analysis suggests that such dependencies are probably small.

The net results of our sequential analysis of link types and link lengths are that sequences of junction types possess a first-order Markovian property, and this property suggests that there are actually two different kinds of interior stream links. We shall accordingly use these properties of the data in our approach toward a probabilistic link length model.

TABLE 3

FIRST-ORDER MARKOV TALLY MATRIX AND TRANSITION PROBABILITY MATRIX OF LINK SEQUENCES FROM TABLE 2

Previous State, $i-1$	Followed by			Transition Probabilities	
	L	R	Total	L	R
L	83	117	200	.415	.585
R	116	70	186	.624	.376
Totals...	199	187	386	...	...

DEVELOPMENT OF A LINK LENGTH MODEL

Our modified and extended version of Smart's exponential model for link length distribution can be thought of as resulting from a stochastic process model in the following way. As a stream cuts into the uplands, it bifurcates from time to time and continues migrating in separate directions. If the rate of migration and the probability of bifurcation are considered to be constant with time, this bifurcating process would lead to the exponential density for link length distribution, as long as no later events occur to change the pattern as it is initially created.

We see no reason to assume that later events will not affect the initial pattern. Although field observations on temporal changes in stream networks are sparse, Schumm (1956) found some striking changes in the Perth Amboy, New Jersey, badlands within a period of 4 years (1948-1952). These included the development of new tributaries in the triangular interdivide area between two earlier branches of an established channel, as well as the elimination of some tributaries by lateral expansion of a more competent neighbor, or by reduction of the junction angle to some minimum, followed by collapse of the divide and union of the streams. During the same interval bifurcation occurred at the growing tips of first-order streams.

Schumm's findings support the inference that channel adjustments may occur rather early in the history of growing stream networks; we believe that even along well-developed main channels relatively remote from the bifurcating edge of the system, new tributaries can develop in the triangular interdivide areas lying between adjacent same-side tributaries.

Another suggestion, regarding events on opposite sides of the main channel, was made to us by Dr. John W. Tukey of Princeton University. He pointed out that adjacent tributaries entering from the same side require a watershed or divide between them, whereas no such requirement holds for tributaries entering from opposite sides. Certainly cis links and trans links seem to arise from different statistical populations, and these differences appear intuitively to us to have been produced by the kinds of changes that Schumm observed, as well as by possible differences in the influence of closely spaced tributaries entering on the same side of the channel as opposed to closely spaced tributaries entering from opposite sides.

In the light of the possibility that the number of links (and hence the lengths of the links) along a main channel may have undergone modification with time, we decided to approach the problem of "explaining" link length distribution in the next most simple fashion. We assumed that the generating process operates independently on each side of the main channel, so that the distribution of channel lengths between successive tributaries entering the main channel from one side (i.e., all cis links and cis chains in the diagram of figure 1) would be the same as on the other side, without regard to the presence or absence of intervening trans junctions.

Inasmuch as a cis link can be considered as a cis chain of one link, we shall use the term *cis chain* as inclusive of all main channel stretches lying between successive same-side tributaries. Where we use the term *cis link* specifically, it will refer to a one-link cis chain.

If a satisfactory model can be developed for the distribution of cis chain lengths in the above inclusive sense, it is then possible by purely combinatorial methods to derive the distributions of all interior link lengths, trans link lengths, cis link lengths, etc. Thus the first problem is to set up a reasonable model for the total cis chain length distribution.

We are influenced here by the gammalike flavor carried by observed distributions of link lengths, as well as by Shreve's (1968) finding that the r in equation (2) is close to 2.0. Although Shreve considered all links, without regard to their grouping into cis and trans categories, we shall show that adoption of a gamma density with $r = 2$ for cis chain lengths gives rise to a surprisingly good basic model.

[*Editors' Note:* Material has been omitted at this point.]

primarily related to opposite-side stream phenomena.

Our development in this paper involves fairly well-developed stream channels as they are observed in nature. We offered the tentative hypothesis that such networks involve an initial stochastic link-generating process followed by link adjustments along the more fully developed main channel downstream. The initial link-generating

TABLE 6

COMBINATORIAL FEATURES THAT CAN BE DERIVED DIRECTLY FROM A PROBABILISTIC LINK LENGTH MODEL

A. Derivation of length distributions of:
   Cis chains
   Trans chains
   Cis links
   Trans links
   All links (cis + trans)
   k links of various sorts
   k chains of various sorts
   Virtually any combination of the above
B. Derivation of discrete probability distributions of:
   Number of links in cis chains
   Number of links in trans chains
   Number of links and chains of the following sorts in channels of given length:
      Cis chains
      Trans chains
      Cis links
      Trans links
      All links (cis + trans)

CONCLUDING REMARKS

The preceding section suggests that, once a basic link length model has been developed, it provides the basis for deriving a number of statistical properties associated with the larger aspects of stream networks. Yet the model and its extensions are valid only to the extent that underlying substantive aspects of the networks are also satisfied. In our case it is apparent that though the initial model $f_{cc}(X)$ in equation (7) behaves well, the distribution of all stream link lengths (cis + trans) in $f_{cl}(X)$ of equation (9) derived from the initial model involves substantive features not fully recognized. It seems apparent, however, that these substantive elements are primarily related to opposite-side stream phenomena.

process presumably operates by bifurcations of the growing tendrils on the network margins. Under this hypothesis, the main channel downstream from the marginal links is modified by link adjustments and by the development of exterior links directly as offshoots from the main channel, some of which then bifurcate within the limits of nonchannel areas still available for invasion. These adjustments, though involving one or more stochastic mechanisms, apparently place some constraints on complete randomness; the initially simple exponential distribution is modified to produce a mixture of two distributions, with some elements of first-order Markovian dependence.

In our opinion, these findings do not imply that the exponential model may not apply in the nascent stages of stream development. The influence of channel adjustments and development of new tributaries in established channels does, however, influence the structure of predictive equations for total stream length in mature basins, and possibly the relation between total stream length and basin area for large basins.

We have not attempted to suggest a process model for these adjustments, other than to imply that it is stochastic. We have, however, presented a statistical description of various properties of developed channels of moderate to high magnitude that have not been seriously considered before. Obviously, in any adequate theoretical treatment these properties must be explained. We are aware that additional modifications are required in our model for link lengths represented by equation (9). As a possible guide to underlying process elements and other higher-order structures in stream network patterns, we have built our model into a simulation program for generating channel networks that have length distribution properties and frequencies of cis and trans links compatible with those we observe.

We are also a long way from including streams of magnitude lower than ten in our analysis, and there remains the whole question of the length distribution of exterior links at the still growing edges of moderately well developed stream networks. Preliminary data suggest that streams of magnitude 4 with their three interior and four exterior links may be close enough to the initial link-generating process that subsequent channel adjustments may be substantially discounted, except under badland conditions as studied by Schumm (1956). In low magnitude basins, however, we encounter difficulties long recognized in current operational definitions for identification and delineation of exterior links on topographic maps. When only a few exterior links are involved, inclusion or exclusion of one or two doubtful links may introduce significant sampling errors.

One of the main conclusions we reached is that additional field work is imperative for reexamining current and establishing new operational definitions that will furnish the kinds of critical data needed for further analysis. We are of the opinion that the need is not as much for more data of the sorts now becoming increasingly available, as for additional kinds of measurement data that permit closer scrutiny of natural networks, as well as observational data on what actually happens in nature when two cis or trans junctions are very close together. Increasingly, observational and measurement data need to be related to *stream process* rather than to *channel response*, if our main goal is to develop stochastic *process* models.

ACKNOWLEDGMENTS.—We are indebted to John Tukey and John Hartigan of Princeton University for encouragement and guidance in this research. J. S. Smart of the IBM Watson Research Center kindly made available some of his material in manuscript form. We are particularly indebted to R. L. Shreve of the University of California at Los Angeles for detailed discussion and numerous suggestions during the final revision of this manuscript. Financial support from the Geography Branch of the Office of Naval Research under Contract Nonr-1228(36), ONR Task No. 389-150, greatly facilitated this study, as did computer time and other facilities generously extended by the Department of Statistics at Princeton University.

REFERENCES CITED

AITCHISON, J., and BROWN, J. A. C., 1957, The lognormal distribution: London, Cambridge Univ. Press, 176 p.

ANDERSON, T. W., and GOODMAN, L. A., 1957, Statistical inference about Markov chains: Annals Math. Statistics, v. 28, p. 89–110.

FELLER, W., 1966, An introduction to probability theory and its applications: New York, John Wiley & Sons, v. 2, 626 p.

KRUMBEIN, W. C., and GRAYBILL, F. A., 1965, An introduction to statistical models in geology: New York, McGraw-Hill Book Co., 475 p.

LEOPOLD, L. B., and LANGBEIN, W. B., 1962, The concept of entropy in landscape evolution: U.S. Geol. Survey Prof. Paper 500-A, 37 p.

MOOD, A. M., and GRAYBILL, F. A., 1963, Introduction to the theory of statistics (2d ed.): New York, McGraw-Hill Book Co. 443 p.

SCHUMM, S. A., 1956, Evolution of drainage systems and slopes in badlands at Perth Amboy, New Jersey: Geol. Soc. America Bull., v. 67, p. 596–646.

SHREVE, R. L., 1966, Statistical law of stream numbers: Jour. Geology, v. 74, p. 17–37.

——— 1967, Infinite topologically random channel networks: Jour. Geology, v. 75, p. 178–186.

——— 1969, Stream lengths and basin areas in topologically random channel networks: Jour. Geology, v. 77, p. 397–414.

SMART, J. S., 1968, Statistical properties of stream lengths: Water Resources Research, v. 4, p. 1001–1021.

———, SURKAN, A. J., and CONSIDINE, J. P., 1967, Symposium on river morphology, *in* Internat. Assoc. Sci. Hydrology Pub. no. 75, p. 89–98.

STRAHLER, A. N., 1952, Hypsometric (area-altitude) analysis of erosional topography: Geol. Soc. America Bull., v. 63, p. 1117–1142.

——— 1954, Statistical analysis in geomorphic research: Jour. Geology, v. 62, p. 1–25.

13

Reprinted from *Water Resources Research* 7:1558–1566 (1971)

A Classification of Channel Links in Stream Networks

STEVEN J. MOCK

U.S. Army Cold Regions Research and Engineering Laboratory, Hanover, New Hampshire 03755

Recent work by *Shreve* [1966, 1967, 1969] has provided a fundamental probabilistic basis for statistically evaluating the topologic properties of stream networks. The power of this approach has been shown by the fact that the Horton-Strahler law of stream numbers is derivable as a maximum likelihood event. By introducing the concept that links are basic elements of stream networks and by assigning a magnitude to each link, one makes available the necessary elements for systematic analysis of real networks in terms of a viable theoretical model.

A major difficulty with the topologically random model is that the sample size necessary for direct statistical analysis is prohibitive for all except the smallest networks. Comparison of observed stream number sets with those predicted by the topologically random model has been the primary method used for the statistical analysis of data from large networks. *Smart* [1969] has proposed a classification scheme (termed ambilateral) that preserves much of the topologic information lost in stream number sets. Although it is applicable to slightly larger networks than the direct study of distinct topologies, it, too, is limited to small networks because of problems of sample size.

The present paper introduces a classification of channel links by type, presents the necessary equations for calculating their probabilities of occurrence, and illustrates some of the potential uses of this system.

OPERATIONAL DEFINITIONS

The following definitions provide a basis for the objective classification of all the links in a stream network. Where applicable, they follow the rapidly evolving terminology of this field. According to *Shreve* [1966, p. 20], 'The points farthest upstream in a channel network are termed *sources*. The point of confluence of two channels is a *fork*. The term *link* will refer to a section of channel without intervening forks from either a fork or a source at its upstream end to either a fork or the outlet at its downstream end.' *Shreve* [1967, p. 178] also provides the first order of classification: 'The terms *exterior link* and *interior link* will signify links terminating at their upstream ends in sources and forks, respectively.' The magnitude of a link 'is equal to the total number of sources ultimately tributary to it' [*Shreve*, 1967, p. 179], when all sources are assigned a magnitude of 1. Magnitude is additive; i.e., the magnitude of any link is the sum of the magnitudes of the two links that join at its upstream terminating fork.

By means of the concept of magnitude it is possible to define several types of interior links and two types of exterior links. Figure 1 shows an idealized stream network illustrating the various link types.

Exterior links. There are two types of exterior links. (1) The S (source) link is a magnitude 1 link that joins another magnitude 1 link at its downstream fork. (2) The TS (tributary source) link is a magnitude 1 link that joins a link of a magnitude greater than 1 at its downstream fork.

214

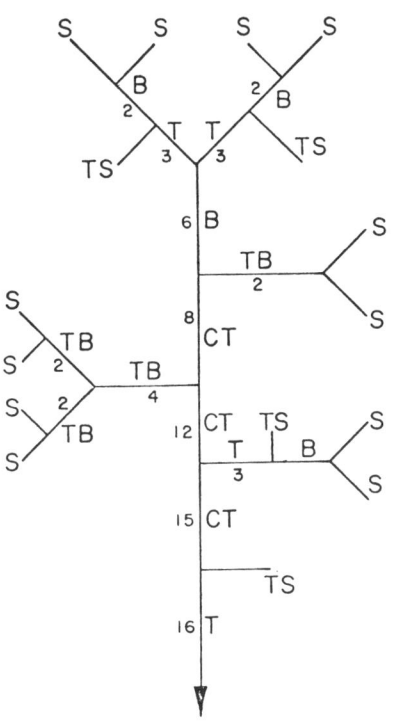

Fig. 1. Idealized network showing link magnitudes and types.

Interior links. Figure 2 shows the upstream and downstream criteria for defining interior links. (1) The B (bifurcating) link is a link of magnitude μ that is formed at its upstream fork by the confluence of two links, each of a magnitude of $\frac{1}{2}\mu$ and that flows at its downstream fork into a link of a magnitude of less than 2μ. (2) The TB (tributary bifurcating) link is a link of magnitude μ that is formed at its upstream fork by the confluence of two links, each of a magnitude of $\frac{1}{2}\mu$ and that flows at its downstream fork into a link of a magnitude greater than or equal to 2μ. (3) The T (tributary) link is a link of magnitude μ that is formed at its upstream fork by the confluence of two links of unequal magnitude and that flows at its downstream fork into a link of a magnitude greater than or equal to 2μ. (4) The CT (cis-trans) link is a link of magnitude μ that is formed at its upstream fork by the confluence of two links of unequal magnitude and that flows at its downstream fork into a link of a magnitude of less than 2μ.

The last downstream link in any system under study, i.e., the highest magnitude link, is arbitrarily defined as either a T or TB link depending on the magnitude relationships at its upstream fork.

James and Krumbein [1969, p. 547] defined two types of interior links (cis and trans) and provided the rules necessary to determine these types. These rules included certain restrictions on the magnitude of a link before it could be considered either a cis or a trans link. The CT links in the present paper are the sum of the cis and trans links and are defined without regard to magnitude restrictions. We do not consider either cis or trans links individually since they are dependent on topologic relationships at successive forks rather than the arithmetic relationships used here.

LINK TYPE PROBABILITIES

The number of topologically distinct arrangements for a network of magnitude M is given by [*Shreve*, 1966, p. 29]:

$$N(M) = \frac{1}{2M-1}\binom{2M-1}{M} \quad (1)$$

The probability of drawing a link of magnitude μ at random from a population of topologically random networks of magnitude M is [*Shreve*, 1967, p. 181]

$$W(\mu; M) = \frac{(M-\mu+1)N(M-\mu+1)N(\mu)}{(2M-1)N(M)} \quad (2)$$

Magnitude of Downstream link \ Magnitude of Upstream link	$= 1/2\,\mu$	$\neq 1/2\,\mu$
$< 2\mu$ S $(\mu; M)$	B-link $P(\mu_B; M)$	CT-link $P(\mu_{CT}; M)$
$\geq 2\mu$ T $(\mu; M)$	TB-link $P(\mu_{TB}; M)$	T-link $P(\mu_T; M)$

(Upper-left cells: Q $(\mu; M)$, K $(\mu; M)$)

Fig. 2. Definition of link types by the magnitude relationships of link of magnitude μ and its adjacent and downstream links.

Since link types have been defined in terms of magnitude relationships, equations 1 and 2 provide the basis for all further probability calculations. Conceptually, we proceed as follows:

1. We draw a link at random from a topologically random population of networks of any specified magnitude M. The possible magnitude of the drawn link (specified μ) is an integer from the set of all integers $1 \cdots M$. (This step is sufficient to define whether the drawn link is an interior or exterior link.)

2. We again draw a link at random but from a topologically random population of magnitude $M - \mu$. At this step we are interested in magnitude relationships at the downstream junction; thus we eliminate from consideration a topologically random population of magnitude μ and are left with the $M - \mu$ magnitude population of networks. (If step 1 results in an exterior link, step 2 defines its type. If step 1 results in an interior link, step 2 defines its downstream relationships.)

3. We again draw a link at random from a topologically random population of magnitude $M = \mu - 1$. We are interested in the magnitude relationships of the links at the upstream fork of the link drawn in step 1. (Steps 2 and 3 define the type of link, if interior, drawn in step 1.)

Exterior links. Exterior links are by definition links of magnitude 1. The probability of drawing an exterior link at random from a topologically random population of networks of magnitude M is given directly by equation 2 as

$$W(1; M) = M/(2M - 1) \quad (3)$$

The probability of drawing an exterior link at random from an infinite topologically random population can be calculated from

$$\lim_{M \to \infty} W(\mu; M) = v(\mu) \quad (4)$$

where

$$v(\mu) = \frac{2^{-(2\mu-1)}}{2\mu - 1}\binom{2\mu - 1}{\mu} \quad (5)$$

[*Shreve*, 1967, p. 181], and

$$v(1) = 0.5 \quad (6)$$

The probability of drawing an S link at random from a topologically random population of magnitude M is equal to the probability of drawing an exterior link at random from a topologically random population of magnitude M and then drawing another exterior link at random from a topologically random population of magnitude $M - 1$. We designate this probability $P(\mu_S; M)$, and thus (from equation 3) $P(\mu_S; M) = W(1; M) W(1; M - 1)$ and

$$P(\mu_S; M) = \frac{M(M - 1)}{(2M - 1)(2M - 3)} \quad (7)$$

for networks of finite M. For an infinite topologically random population, the probability $P(\mu_S)$ of drawing an S link at random is (from equation 7)

$$P(\mu_S) = v(1)^2 = 0.25 \quad (8)$$

The probability of drawing a TS link is defined as the probability of drawing a magnitude 1 link at random from a topologically random population of networks of magnitude M and consecutively drawing a link of a magnitude greater than 1 (an interior link) at random from a topologically random population of networks of magnitude $M - 1$. The probability of drawing an interior link at random is (from equation 3)

$$P(\mu_{INT}; M) = W(\mu; M)$$

$$= 1 - [M/(2M - 1)] \quad \mu > 1$$

and

$$P(\mu_{INT}; M) = (M - 1)/(2M - 1) \quad (9)$$

The probability of drawing a TS link is given by (3) and (9):

$$P(\mu_{TS}; M) = W(1; M)P(\mu_{INT}; M - 1)$$

$$P(\mu_{TS}; M) = \left(\frac{M}{2M - 1}\right)\left(\frac{M - 2}{2M - 3}\right) \quad (10)$$

The probability of drawing a TS link at random from an infinite topologically random network is given by:

$$\lim_{M \to \infty} P(\mu_{TS}; M) = \lim_{M \to \infty} \left(\frac{M}{2M - 1}\right)\left(\frac{M - 2}{2M - 3}\right)$$

and

$$P(\mu_{TS}) = \lim_{M \to \infty} P(\mu_{TS}; M) = 0.25 \quad (11)$$

Interior links. The relationships of the magnitude of a link with those of its nearest upstream and downstream neighbors (which define its type) are shown in Figure 2. We are interested in calculating the joint and marginal probabilities shown in Figure 2.

First consider the probability that a link of magnitude μ drawn at random from a topologically random population of networks of any magnitude bifurcates at its upstream fork: $q(\mu) = W(\mu/2; \mu - 1)$. The probability of such an occurrence in a topologically random population of magnitude M is

$$Q(\mu; M) = \sum_{\mu=1}^{M} W(\mu; M) W(\mu/2; \mu - 1) \quad (12)$$

The probability of the occurrence of links that do not bifurcate is

$$K(\mu; M) = 1 - \sum_{\mu=1}^{M} W(\mu; M) W(\mu/2; \mu - 1) \quad (13)$$

The probability that the next downstream link of a link of magnitude μ drawn at random from a topologically random population of magnitude M would be a link of a magnitude of less than 2μ is equivalent to the probability that that link of magnitude μ would join with one of magnitude γ, where $\gamma < \mu$. This relationship can be calculated from

$$s(\mu; M) = \sum_{\gamma=1}^{\mu-1} W(\gamma; M - \mu)$$

and the probability of occurrence is

$$S(\mu; M) = \sum_{\mu=1}^{M} \sum_{\gamma=1}^{\mu-1} W(\mu; M) W(\gamma; M - \mu) \quad (14)$$

In an analogous manner, the probability that the adjacent downstream link of a link of magnitude μ would be one of a magnitude greater than or equal to 2μ is

$$t(\mu; M) = \sum_{\gamma=\mu}^{M-\mu} W(\gamma; M - \mu)$$

and the probability of occurrence is

$$T(\mu; M) = \sum_{\mu=1}^{M} \sum_{\gamma=\mu}^{M-\mu} W(\mu; M) W(\gamma; M - \mu) \quad (15)$$

We now define the probability of occurrence of each link type in topologically random networks of any specified magnitude M by considering the probability of randomly drawing a link of magnitude μ and the probability of its meeting any combination of two defining criteria. Then by summing over all possibilities, we obtain

$$P(\mu_B; M) = W(\mu; M) q(\mu) s(\mu; M)$$

the probability of drawing a link of magnitude μ that is a B link. The probability of occurrence of a B link is

$$P(\mu_B; M) = \sum_{\mu=1}^{M} \sum_{\gamma=1}^{\mu-1} W(\mu; M) W(\mu/2; \mu - 1) \cdot W(\gamma; M - \mu) \quad (16)$$

The equations defining the probability of occurrence of the other interior link types are:

$$P(\mu_{TB}; M) = \sum_{\mu=1}^{M} \sum_{\gamma=\mu}^{M-\mu} W(\mu; M) \cdot W(\mu/2; \mu - 1) W(\gamma; M - \mu) \quad (17)$$

$$P(\mu_{CT}; M) = \sum_{\mu=1}^{M} \sum_{\gamma=1}^{\mu-1} W(\mu; M) \cdot [1 - W(\mu/2; \mu - 1)] W(\gamma; M - \mu) \quad (18)$$

$$P(\mu_T; M) = \sum_{\mu=1}^{M} \sum_{\gamma=\mu}^{M-\mu} [W(\mu; M) \cdot [1 - W(\mu/2; \mu - 1)] W(\gamma; M - \mu)] - W(1; M) \quad (19)$$

The expression $W(1; M)$ removes the population of exterior links included in the summation of (19).

We are interested in determining the limiting values, if any, of (16)–(19) as M becomes infinite, i.e., for an infinite topologically random network. Our approach is to calculate analytically the marginal probabilities shown in Figure 2 for the infinite case and then evaluate numerically the joint probabilities $P(\mu_B; M)$ and $P(\mu_{TB}; M)$, which are sufficient to define the remaining joint probabilities. It can easily be shown that

$$\sum_{\mu=1}^{M} W(\mu; M) W(\mu/2; \mu - 1)$$
$$= \frac{1}{2} \sum_{\mu=1}^{M} W(\mu/2; M) W[\mu/2; M - (\mu/2)]$$
$$= \frac{1}{2} \sum_{\mu=1}^{M} W(\mu; M) W(\mu; M - \mu)$$

We can rewrite the marginal probability $Q(\mu; M)$ of Figure 2 as

$$Q(\mu; M) = \frac{1}{2} \sum_{\mu=1}^{M} W(\mu; M) W(\mu; M - \mu) \quad (20)$$

and from (4),

$$\lim_{M \to \infty} Q(\mu; M) = \frac{1}{2} \sum_{\mu=1}^{\infty} v(\mu) v(\mu) \quad (21)$$

This summation can be calculated exactly by using the functional relationships satisfied by the gamma function (M. Dacey, personal communication, 1970), which give

$$\lim_{M \to \infty} Q(\mu; M) = \tfrac{1}{2}[(4/\pi) - 1] = 0.13622 \cdots \quad (22)$$

Thus

$$\lim_{M \to \infty} K(\mu; M) = 1 - 0.13662 - 0.5$$
$$= 0.36338 \cdots \quad (23)$$

The remaining marginal probabilities for the infinite topologically random case become

$$\lim_{M \to \infty} S(\mu; M) = \sum_{\mu=1}^{\infty} \sum_{\gamma=1}^{\mu-1} v(\mu) v(\gamma) \quad (24)$$

$$\lim_{M \to \infty} T(\mu; M) = \sum_{\mu=1}^{\infty} \sum_{\gamma=\mu}^{\infty} v(\mu) v(\gamma) \quad (25)$$

Consider now an infinite topologically random network from which we make two consecutive random drawings and designate the magnitude of the first link μ and the second link γ. We

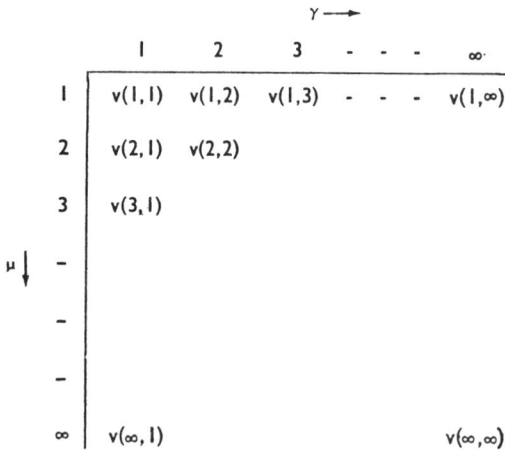

Fig. 3. Probability matrix for an infinite topologically random network.

designate the joint probabilities of $v(\mu)v(\gamma) = v(\mu, \gamma)$, and thus a matrix of probabilities as shown in Figure 3 is symmetric.

Because of symmetry,

$$\sum_{\mu=2}^{\infty} \sum_{\gamma=1}^{\mu-1} v(\mu, \gamma) = \sum_{\mu=1}^{\infty} \sum_{\gamma=\mu+1}^{\infty} v(\mu, \gamma) \quad (26)$$

$$\sum_{\mu=2}^{\infty} \sum_{\gamma=1}^{\mu-1} v(\mu, \gamma) + \sum_{\mu=1}^{\infty} \sum_{\gamma=\mu+1}^{\infty} v(\mu, \gamma)$$
$$+ \sum_{\mu=1}^{\infty} v(\mu, \mu) = 1 \quad (27)$$

but

$$\sum_{\mu=2}^{\infty} \sum_{\gamma=1}^{\mu-1} v(\mu, \gamma)$$
$$= \sum_{\mu=1}^{\infty} \sum_{\gamma=1}^{\mu-1} v(\mu, \gamma) = \lim_{M \to \infty} S(\mu; M)$$

since for $\mu = 1$,

$$\sum_{\gamma=1}^{\mu-1} v(\mu, \gamma) = 0$$

From (26) and (27),

$$2 \lim_{M \to \infty} S(\mu; M) = 1 - \sum_{\mu=1}^{\infty} v(\mu; \mu)$$

$$\lim_{M \to \infty} S(\mu; M) = 0.36338 \quad (28)$$

$$\lim_{M \to \infty} T(\mu; M) = 0.63662 \quad (29)$$

We are now in a position to evaluate the limits of $P(\mu_B; M)$ and $P(\mu_{TB}; M)$ as $M \to \infty$:

$$\lim P(\mu_B; M) + \lim P(\mu_{TB}; M)$$
$$= \lim Q(\mu; M) = 0.13662$$

which is

$$\sum_{\mu=1}^{\infty} \sum_{\gamma=1}^{\mu-1} v(\mu) W(\mu/2; \mu - 1) v(\gamma)$$
$$+ \sum_{\mu=1}^{\infty} \sum_{\gamma=\mu}^{\infty} v(\mu) W(\mu/2; \mu - 1) v(\gamma) = 0.13662 \quad (30)$$

Equation 30 can be rapidly evaluated to five significant figures by means of a computer so that

$$\lim_{M \to \infty} P(\mu_B; M) = 0.07086 \quad (31)$$

TABLE 1. Probability of Occurrence of Link Types for Networks of Various Magnitudes

M	$P(\mu_S; M)$	$P(\mu_{TS}; M)$	$P(\mu_{CT}; M)$	$P(\mu_T; M)$	$P(\mu_B; M)$	$P(\mu_{TB}; M)$
2	0.667			0.333		
3	0.400	0.200		0.200	0.200	
4	0.343	0.229	0.114	0.114	0.114	0.086
5	0.317	0.238	0.159	0.111	0.111	0.063
6	0.303	0.242	0.182	0.100	0.100	0.074
7	0.294	0.245	0.200	0.098	0.098	0.065
8	0.287	0.246	0.213	0.091	0.091	0.071
9	0.282	0.247	0.224	0.090	0.090	0.067
10	0.279	0.248	0.231	0.087	0.087	0.069
20	0.263	0.249	0.264	0.078	0.078	0.067
50	0.255	0.250	0.281	0.074	0.074	0.066
100	0.253	0.250	0.287	0.072	0.072	0.066
200	0.251	0.250	0.290	0.072	0.072	0.066
400	0.251	0.250	0.291	0.071	0.071	0.066
∞	0.250	0.250	0.293	0.071	0.071	0.066

TABLE 2. Relationships between TDCN Ambilateral Classes, Link Type Sets, and Stream Number Sets for Networks with Six Sources

TDCN	Ambilateral Class	Link Type Set						Stream Numbers		
		N_{CT}	N_T	N_B	N_{TB}	N_S	N_{TS}	N_1	N_2	N_3
16		3	1	1	0	2	4	6	1	0
8		2	1	1	1	4	2	6	2	1
8										
4		1	1	1	2	4	2			
4		0	2	2	1	4	2			
2		0	1	1	3	6	0	6	3	1

TABLE 3. Contingency Table with Observed and Expected Frequencies

Link Type	Link Lengths, feet					Total
	0–10	11–20	21–30	31–40	41–∞	
CT	596	459	264	126	159	1604
	(547.01)	(449.39)	(282.76)	(132.95)	(189.63)	
T	76	117	96	51	81	42'
	(143.57)	(117.95)	(74.22)	(34.90)	(49.77)	
B	175	66	66	25	35	421
	(143.57)	(117.95)	(74.22)	(34.90)	(49.77)	
TB	128	105	78	35	63	409
	(139.48)	(114.59)	(72.10)	(33.90)	(48.35)	
Total	975	801	504	237	338	2859

All values are times 40; numbers in parentheses are expected frequencies; $v = 98.02$; $\chi^2 = 28.30$.

$$\lim_{M \to \infty} P(\mu_{TB}; M) = 0.06576 \quad (32)$$

and by means of the remaining marginal probabilities of Figure 3

$$\lim_{M \to \infty} P(\mu_{CT}; M) = 0.29252 \quad (33)$$

$$\lim_{M \to \infty} P(\mu_{T}; M) = 0.07086 \quad (34)$$

Table 1 shows the probability of occurrence of each link type for topologically random populations of various magnitudes.

DISCUSSION

In Table 1 note that the probabilities of occurrence of T links and B links are equal for networks of all magnitudes. By starting at a T link and moving upstream following the main channel (moving up the link of greatest magnitude at each fork), one can continue the process until a B link is encountered. This rule holds true for every distinct channel sequence within a network and illustrates the one-for-one correspondence of T and B links. A channel sequence (as opposed to a channel network) can be defined as a continuous sequence of links terminated downstream by a T link and upstream by a B link. The intermediate links consist exclusively of CT links and can range in number from zero to infinity.

The fact that link types vary in number as a function of topology suggests that the possible combinations can be used to form sets usable for statistical studies.

We define a link type set as a set of integers representing the number of links of each type occurring in a particular stream network and designated in the following order: N_{CT}, N_T, N_B, N_{TB}, N_S, and N_{TS}, where N represents the number of links of the type indicated by the subscript. The analogy with sets of Strahler or Horton stream numbers is obvious, but the motivation for proposing such a schema derives largely from the ambilateral classification of Smart [1969], which sought to provide a classification scheme intermediate between individual topologically distinct channel networks (TDCN) and stream number sets with which to compare networks statistically against predictions of the topologically random model. The essence of Smart's system is that any group of TDCN that can be transformed into a single TDCN by simple left–right transpositions at junctions forms an ambilateral class. Such a classification groups together TDCN with similar hydrologic and geomorphic parameters while it reduces the sample size problem. Link type sets have less commonality in hydrologic and geomorphic properties than ambilateral sets, but they reduce the sampling problems in that one or more ambilateral classes are included in each link type set. Table 2 illustrates the available classification schemes.

The classification system discussed here has evolved as part of a study of stream networks whose geometry is geologically controlled. In the present case a group of stream basins with well-developed trellis or rectangular patterns has been studied.

Twelve networks ranging in magnitude from 51 to 385 formed the study group. Nine of the networks were located in the folded Appalachians

TABLE 4. Goodness-of-Fit Test of Link Number Sets for Magnitude 6 Networks

Link No. Sets	P	Observed	Expected
3 1 1 0 2 4	0.38095	36	37.71
2 1 1 1 4 2	0.38095	34	37.71
1 1 1 2 2 4	0.09524	13	9.43
0 2 2 1 2 4	0.09524	12	9.43
0 1 1 3 0 6	0.04762	4	4.71
Total		99	

$(O - E)^2/E = 2.60$; $\chi^2_{4, 0.05} = 9.488$.

TABLE 5. Goodness-of-Fit Test of Link Number Sets for Magnitude 7 Networks

Link No. Sets	P	Observed	Expected
4 1 1 0 2 5	0.24242	12	16.00
3 1 1 1 4 3	0.36364	22	24.00
2 1 1 2 4 3	0.06061	7	4.00
2 1 1 2 6 1	0.06061	4	4.00
2 2 2 0 4 3	0.12121	11	8.00
1 1 1 3 6 1	0.06061	1	4.00
0 2 2 2 6 1	0.03030	4	2.00
0 3 3 0 4 3	0.06061	5	4.00
Total		66	

$(O - E)^2/E = 9.04$; $\chi^2_{7, 0.05} = 14.07$.

of central Pennsylvania and had well-developed trellis drainage patterns. The other three networks were located in eastern Pennsylvania and New Jersey on moderately northwest-dipping Triassic rocks of the Newark basin. Each of these networks has a geometry that can be classed as rectangular in geomorphic terminology.

Each network was traced out in its entirety on an overlay from modern 1 : 24,000 topographic maps. In the absence of blue lines, V-shaped contours were used as criteria for delineating streams of lesser magnitude. The magnitude of each link was calculated and tabulated along with its type and length. Lengths are straight line measurements between junctions in units of 1/50 inch (equal to 40 feet on the ground).

It is appropriate to inquire whether our classification has any relationship to the physical properties of stream links. The simplest physical property to determine is length, which was measured for all links in the 12 networks. *Smart* [1968] proposed a negative exponential density function for the distribution of interior link lengths. In arriving at this result, he assumed that the lengths of the interior links in a given network were independent random variables drawn from the same population. *Shreve* [1969] used a gamma distribution with a shape parameter of 2 for interior links but noted that although it was a satisfactory model for the purposes of his study it did not provide a very good fit to the observed data. *James and Krumbein* [1969] developed separate gammalike densities for the length distribution of cis and trans links. By means of a contingency table, we will test the hypothesis that interior link lengths and link types are independent. The data are the population of interior links of the 12 networks under study. The contingency table is shown in Table 3,

and the results allow the rejection of the independence hypothesis at the 0.001 level of significance. Examination of the density functions of length properties for each of the link types will be the subject of another paper.

We have examined the magnitude 6, 7, and 8 networks contained in the stream basins under study and have used observed and expected occurrences by link type sets in a goodness-of-fit test of the hypothesis that these sets were drawn from a topologically random model. The distributions are shown in Tables 4, 5, and 6. In each case the topologically random model is acceptable.

We have applied a goodness-of-fit test to

TABLE 6. Goodness-of-Fit Test of Link Number Sets for Magnitude 8 Networks

Link No. Sets	P	Observed	Expected
5 1 1 0 2 6	0.149	8	8.95
4 1 1 1 4 4	0.298	20	17.90
3 2 2 0 4 4	0.149	3	8.95
3 1 1 2 6 2	0.112	5	6.71
3 1 1 2 4 4	0.037	3	2.24
2 1 1 3 6 2	0.056	4	3.36
2 2 2 1 6 2	0.037	1	2.24
2 2 2 1 4 4	0.037	4	2.24
1 2 2 2 6 2	0.037	3	2.24
1 1 1 4 6 2	0.019	1	1.12
1 1 1 4 8 0	0.009	2	0.56
1 3 3 0 4 4	0.037	5	2.24
0 3 3 1 6 2	0.019	0	1.12
0 0 0 7 8 0	0.002	1	0.14
Total		60	

$U = 20.93$; $\chi^2_{13, 0.05} = 22.36$.

TABLE 7. Summary of Goodness-of-Fit Tests for Observed versus Expected Numbers for Each Link Type in 12 Networks

Network	Magnitude	$(O - E^2)/E$
Rhines*	51	2.990
Barton*	102	4.272
Lick*	117	4.283
George*	246	1.028
Willow†	380	13.887
Tusc, east*	385	10.169
Tusc, west*	281	7.341
Horse valley*	175	0.414
Bixler†	274	26.240
Neshanic*	259	3.432
Stony*	274	4.235
Tohichon*	311	6.365
Total		84.656

* Hypothesis accepted.
† Hypothesis rejected.
Degrees of freedom were 5; $\chi_{3,0.05}^2 = 7.82$.

each of 12 large networks and have compared the observed number of links of each type with the expected number for a topologically random population of the same magnitude. The validity of such a test is perhaps suspect, but the topologically random hypothesis can be rejected in only two cases (Table 7).

CONCLUSIONS

The concept of magnitude provides a basis for classifying channel links by types according to their numerical relationships with their upstream and downstream neighbors. The topologically random model of channel networks allows the exact calculation of the probability of occurrence of each link type for topologically random populations of networks of any magnitude. Link type sets have been defined that alleviate to some extent the sampling problems inherent in evaluating real networks statistically from the prediction of the topologically random model. A study of networks with geologically controlled geometry has been used to illustrate the uses of these techniques. The study indicates that each link type may have different length properties and that the topologically random model is a satisfactory model for these networks.

Acknowledgments. I have benefited by the encouragement and interest of Professor W. C. Krumbein, who stimulated these studies. Dr. J. S. Smart has provided helpful criticisms, in particular regarding the defining criteria for interior link types. Dr. M. Dacey lent his mathematical talent directly for evaluating the limits of certain equations. Professor R. L. Shreve provided cogent and detailed criticism. Dr. C. C. Langway and Dr. K. F. Sterrett provided continuing encouragement in this work. DA task 4A062112A89401.

REFERENCES

James, W. R., and W. C. Krumbein, Frequency distribution of stream link lengths, *J. Geol.*, 77(5), 544–565, 1969.

Shreve, R. L., Statistical law of stream numbers, *J. Geol.*, 74(1), 17–37, 1966.

Shreve, R. L., Infinite topologically random channel networks, *J. Geol.*, 75(2), 178–186, 1967.

Shreve, R. L., Stream lengths and basin areas in topologically random channel networks, *J. Geol.*, 77(4), 399–414, 1969.

Smart, J. S., Statistical properties of stream lengths, *Water Resour. Res.*, 4(5), 1001–1014, 1968.

Smart, J. S., Topological properties of channel networks, *Geol. Soc. Amer. Bull.*, 80(9), 1757–1774, 1969.

(Manuscript received June 8, 1971;
revised July 6, 1971.)

Part III

NETWORK GROWTH AND SPACE FILLING

Editors' Comments
on Papers 14 Through 18

14 GLOCK
The Development of Drainage Systems: A Synoptic View

15 HORTON
Excerpt from *Erosional Development of Streams and Their Drainage Basins; Hydrophysical Approach to Quantitative Morphology*

16 SCHUMM
Excerpt from *Evolution of Drainage Systems and Slopes in Badlands at Perth Amboy, New Jersey*

17 MORISAWA
Development of Drainage Systems on an Upraised Lake Floor

18 DACEY and KRUMBEIN
Three Growth Models for Stream Channel Networks

From the time of Davis in the late nineteenth century, fluvial geomorphologists have been greatly concerned with questions of drainage basin evolution and change through time. How do river channels grow and fill space within a drainage basin? How does the network contract as the relief is reduced over time? Studies of network evolution have been hampered by the shortage of historical observations and the need to infer past stages from a contemporary static base. But these questions are central to notions of equilibrium adjustment in drainage basin geomorphology and to the attainment of a steady state in drainage composition.

Glock (Paper 14) suggested a two-stage sequence of network development, first by extension and then by integration. This paper established the principle that drainage networks evolve to fill drainage basin space. After the network has expanded to a state of maximum extension, competition between river valleys modifies the surface that the network drains. Tributaries previously added may be lost by abstraction or absorption. The streams fill space as tributary basins compete for drainage area.

The first quantitative study to provide a theory of stream network development was by Horton (Paper 14). On the basis of his infiltration theory of surface runoff and the geometry of slope erosion by overland flow, Horton proposed an evolutionary model of rill channels becoming coordinated by cross-grading and micropiracy. He developed a space-filling sequence based on subdivision of space in hierarchically nested squares. This sequence generates the laws of drainage composition, although Horton explicitly recognized that the partition of space into squares is artificial. He explained the geometry of stream junction angles in terms of channel gradients. The trigonometry of his solution reduces to the statement that water will run downslope, perpendicular to the contours. As a practical hydrologist, he also discussed the growth implications of changes in surface resistance, such as might be associated with deforestation, overgrazing, or human impact on the destruction of vegetative cover.

Models of two-dimensional spatial structure for channel networks have been investigated for both Horton's laws and the random model of drainage composition. Woldenberg (1969) noted the similarity of Horton's laws to relationships describing the hierarchy of towns and their market areas, as set forth in Christaller's (1933) work on central places. While Horton suggested subdivision of space into nested squares, Christaller generated his geometric-progression laws on the basis of subdivision of space into hexagons. Woldenberg (1968, 1971, 1979) has shown that partitioning of space into hexagons could lead to a least-cost configuration and would generate the laws of number and area. Other laws follow as functions of the basic number law.

In work closely related to the literature of central-place theory and plant ecology, Dacey and Krumbein showed how Shreve's topological randomness does not predicate spatial randomness in the patterns of stream sources and junctions observed in natural river networks (Dacey and Krumbein, 1971; Krumbein and Dacey, 1973). The spatial pattern of stream junctions was also studied by Oeppen and Ongley (1975). Since links are defined by the location of sources and junctions, it follows that the spatial structure in link sequences along mainstreams may perhaps also be understood in terms of optimality, space filling, and spatial competition (see Paper 12; Jarvis and Sham, 1981).

Considering the fact that stream entrance angles contribute so much to the visual impression of a stream pattern, it is surprising that there is not an extensive bibliography on this subject. Besides the theories of Horton and observations by Schumm (Paper 16), the first paper to focus on junction angles was that of Lubowe (1964). She examined Strahler-ordered tributaries and found that the angles between two tributaries of the same order increased with order.

Howard (1971) proposed a minimum power model for optimizing the junction angle. Roy (1982) investigated optimizing models and was able to account for a high percentage of the variation in junction angles and an even higher percentage of the variation in associated tributary and mainstream link lengths.

While streams and their junction angles are immediately perceivable on topographic maps, basin divides and drainage areas are rarely highlighted. The angles between streams and their divides at a junction are clearly important, for they govern the availability of space and ultimately must affect the formation of new tributaries. Flint (1980) has shown that, where a tributary stream joins a main channel, tributaries to the tributary stream upstream from the fork are more likely to be found on the outer side of the tributary stream, rather than in the space between the tributary and main channel. Also, where a large tributary joins a mainstream, the next tributary to the mainstream, upstream of this fork, is more likely to occur on the side of the mainstream opposite to the first tributary. This kind of preemption of space is evident in the mainstream sequences reported by Jarvis and Sham (1981). Abrahams (1980) has shown that these tributary arrangements are related to asymmetries in the semi-divide angles between streams and divides. The distribution of link orientations within entire networks and the relations of link length to orientation within a drainage basin have been investigated by Jarvis (1976). Link length tends to decrease as link orientation diverges from the overall basin axis.

Since stream junction angles seem to be partly explained by mechanical principles, and divides and junction angles regulate the space available for tributary branches, it would seem reasonable that some topologic properties should be related to spatial constraints. Milton (1966, p. 92) suggested that the bifurcation ratio "is set by the angular relationships of the streams and the drainage density." Milton went on to say that wide angles mean a low bifurcation ratio, and vice versa. The argument, though unstated by Milton, could be that with a wide angle and space, tributaries of order u-1 can join to form a stream of order u at a short distance upstream of the mouth of the order u basin. Only a few lower-order tributaries would enter the order u mainstream, thus creating a low bifurcation ratio. These ideas await empirical testing.

Network analysts in biology have pursued ideas along these lines. Honda (1971) proposed that some botanical trees could be modeled by varying branching angle and branch length. Later, Honda and his colleagues examined space filling directly as a modeling principle (Fisher and Honda, 1979a, b; Honda et al., 1982). In a modification of their approach, Honda et al. (1981) simulated branching by accumulation of a critical amount of a hypothetical growth factor, supposedly stimulated by extra sunlight. Botanists have the opportunity to test their models against the growth pattern of trees in real time. This testing is very difficult to do for rivers. Nonetheless, there have been some important attempts to develop, verify, and modify river network growth models by observing natural changes over time.

Schumm (Paper 16) and Morisawa (Paper 17) found situations in nature where an initial unvegetated surface was exposed, and so they could directly document channel network evolution. Schumm extended Horton's work on junction angles and also observed tributary abstraction, lateral shift of main channels, and migration of junction points as slopes evolved. Morisawa mapped network development on a newly exposed lake floor. She related network changes to the initial slope and type of material. She observed rapid attainment of steady state, with expansion and integration occurring simultaneously. Observations of the maximum extension of channel networks and inferences of stream abstraction have also been made by Abrahams (1972, 1976).

Carter and Chorley (1961) used stream order as an index of evolution in valley-side slope form. The growth assumption is fairly reasonable in an actively expanding stream system, where increasing stages of development may be associated with increasing stream order. Network extension and tributary ramification regulate discharge and hence stream capacity to excavate sediment delivered from valley-side slopes. Network evolution must proceed hand in hand with slope evolution. Spatial variation of slope form in a drainage basin was related to stream order by Arnett (1971), and stream order was used to classify valley topographic and soil associations (Arnett and Conacher, 1973).

Most of the networks of interest to geomorphologists were formed long ago, and we are forced to attempt to infer how they might have developed from their present configuration. A probabilistic approach to network growth was developed by Dacey and Krumbein (Paper 18). They used the topology of very small subnetworks to assess the relative importance of various alternative models of network development. Their studies revealed that simple bifurcation at the head of exterior links is not adequate to account for the structure of natural river networks. Similar studies on the development of brain cell networks in the rat also demonstrated how growth processes may be deduced from the frequency of topologies in very small networks (Hollingworth and Berry, 1975; Berry and Bradley, 1976a, 1976b; Berry and Pymm, 1980). However, as noted by Dacey and Krumbein, it is essential to exercise great caution in interpreting some tests of topologic growth models because identical probability distributions for TDCN's or ambilateral classes can be generated by very different growth mechanisms. This work also points out the danger of applying a simple ergodic hypothesis and of substituting space for time in order to interpret network morphology in an evolutionary context.

REFERENCES

Abrahams, A. D., 1972, Factor Analysis of Drainage Basin Properties: Evidence for Stream Abstraction Accompanying the Degradation of Relief, *Water Resources Research* **8:**624-633.

Abrahams, A. D., 1976, Evolutionary Changes in Link Lengths: Further Evidence for Stream Abstraction, *Inst. British Geographers Trans.*, new series **1:**225-230.

Abrahams, A. D., 1980, Divide Angles and Their Relation to Interior Link Lengths in Natural Channel Networks, *Geog. Analysis* **12:**157-171.

Arnett, R. R., 1971, Slope Form and Geomorphological Process: An Australian Example, in *Slopes, Form and Process,* D. Brunsden, ed., Institute of British Geographers Special Publication Number 3, pp. 81-92.

Arnett, R. R., and A. J. Conacher, 1973, Drainage Basin Expansion and the Nine-Unit Landsurface Model, *Australian Geogr.* **12:**237-249.

Berry, M., and P. M. Bradley, 1976a, The Application of Network Analysis to the Study of Branching Patterns of Large Dendritic Fields, *Brain Research* **109:**111-132.

Berry, M., and P. M. Bradley, 1976b, The Growth of the Dendritic Trees of Purkinje Cells in Irradiated Agranular Cerebellar Cortex, *Brain Research* **111:**361-387.

Berry, M., and D. Pymm, 1980, Analysis of Neural Networks, *Adv. Physiol. Sci.* **30:**155-169.

Carter, C. S., and R. J. Chorley, 1961, Early Slope Development in an Expanding Stream System, *Geol. Mag.* **98:**117-130.

Christaller, W., 1933, *Die Zentralen Orte in Süddeutschland,* translated by C. W. Baskin (1966) as *Central Places in Southern Germany,* Prentice-Hall, Englewood Cliffs, New Jersey, 230p.

Dacey, M. F., and W. C. Krumbein, 1971, Comments on Spatial Randomness in Dendritic Stream Channel Networks, *Office of Naval Research Contract N00014-67A0356-0018, Department of Geological Sciences, Northwestern University,* Evanston, Illinois, Technical Report 17.

Fisher, J. B., and H. Honda, 1979a, Branch Geometry and Effective Leaf Area: A Study of Terminalia Branching Patterns. 1. Theoretical Trees, *Am. Jour. Bot.* **66:**633-644.

Fisher, J. B., and H. Honda, 1979b, Branch Geometry and Effective Leaf Area: A Study of Terminalia Branching Pattern. 2. Survey of Real Trees, *Am. Jour. Bot.* **66:**645-655.

Flint, J. J., 1980, Tributary Arrangements in Fluvial Systems, *Am. Jour. Sci.* **280:**26-45.

Hollingworth, T., and M. Berry, 1975, Network Analysis of Dendritic Fields of Pyramidal Cells in the Neocortex and Purkinje Cells in the Cerebellum of the Rat, *Royal Soc. London Philos. Trans.,* ser. B, **270:**227-264.

Honda, H., 1971, Description of the Form of Trees by the Parameters of the Tree-like Body: Effects of the Branching Angle and the Branch Length on the Shape of the Tree-like Body, *Jour. Theor. Biol.* **31:**331-338.

Honda, H., P. B. Tomlinson, and J. B. Fisher, 1981, Computer Simulation of Branch Interaction and Regulation by Unequal Flow Rates in Botanical Trees, *Am. Jour. Bot.* **68:**569-585.

Honda, H., P. B. Tomlinson, and J. B. Fisher, 1982, Two Geometrical Models of Branching of Botanical Trees, *Annals Bot.* **49:**1-11.

Howard, A. D., 1971, Optimal Angles of Stream Junction: Geometric, Stability to Capture, and Minimum Power Criteria, *Water Resources Research* **7:**863-873.

Jarvis, R. S., 1976, Stream Orientation Structures in Drainage Networks, *Jour. Geology* **84:**563-582.

Jarvis, R. S., and C. H. Sham, 1981, Drainage Network Structure and the Diameter-Magnitude Relation, *Water Resources Research* **17:**1019-1027.

Krumbein, W. C., and M. F. Dacey, 1973, Comments on Randomness in Spatial Components of Dendritic Stream Channel Networks, in *Recent Researches in Geology*, Hindustan Publishing Corporation, Delhi, pp. 53-65.

Lubowe, J. K., 1964, Stream Junction Angles in the Dendritic Drainage Pattern, *Am. Jour. Sci.* **262:**325-339.

Milton, L. E., 1966, The Geomorphic Irrelevance of Some Drainage Net Laws, *Australian Geogr. Stud.* **4:**89-95.

Oeppen, B. J., and E. D. Ongley, 1975, Spatial Point Processes Applied to the Distribution of River Junctions, *Geog. Analysis* **7:**153-171.

Roy, A. G., 1982, *Optimality and Its Relationship to the Hydraulic and Angular Geometry of Rivers and Lungs,* Ph.D. dissertation, State University of New York at Buffalo, New York.

Woldenberg, M. J., 1968, *Hierarchical Systems: Cities, Rivers, Alpine Glaciers, Bovine Livers and Trees,* Ph.D. dissertation, Columbia University, New York.

Woldenberg, M. J., 1969, Spatial Order in Fluvial Systems: Horton's Laws Derived from Mixed Hexagonal Hierarchies of Drainage Basin Areas, *Geol. Soc. America Bull.* **80:**97-112.

Woldenberg, M. J., 1971, A Structural Taxonomy of Spatial Hierarchies, in *Regional Forecasting,* M. Chisholm, A. Frey, and P. Haggett eds., Butterworth, London, pp. 147-175.

Woldenberg, M. J., 1979, A Periodic Table of Spatial Hierarchies, in *Philosophy in Geography,* S. Gale and G. Olson, eds., D. Reidel, Dordrecht, Holland, pp. 429-456.

THE DEVELOPMENT OF DRAINAGE SYSTEMS: A SYNOPTIC VIEW*

Waldo S. Glock

Carnegie Institution of Washington

PHYSICAL geography has a dual nature.[1] It includes a static or passive phase involving the detailed form of the land surfaces and a dynamic or active phase involving the agents and processes modifying those surfaces. The first of these phases is known commonly as geomorphology; the second might well be called surficial geodynamics.

The present work desires to confine its attention to streams. It is the purpose of the paper to trace in a summary manner the sequence of pattern during the development of a drainage system after a fashion as nearly ideal as possible for a region of simple rock structure and of humid climate. The following treatment has no intention or wish to ignore the influence of rock and structure nor has it the desire to minimize the fascination in the study of land forms. It does, however, intend to adopt the dynamic viewpoint for the time being.

The sequential stages recognized in the evolution of a drainage system are "extension" and "integration": the first, a stage of increasing complexity; the second, of simplification. The assumption that extension begins on a "new" land surface will be entertained for the present.

The Stage of Extension

Extension may be held to include the genesis (initiation) of streams and thereby the birth of a drainage system, the headward growth (elongation) of the new streams into virgin territory theirs by right of inheritance, and the constant addition (elaboration) of tributaries of decreasing rank up to the time when the system is fully developed from the standpoint of drainage. The form of the drainage system assumed at initiation, which constitutes the first step in the establishment of the system, largely determines the general pattern of the drainage during the early phases of growth. The initial phase of

---

*A summary of parts of a paper presented before the Geological Society of America, Washington, D. C., December 28, 1929. The writer wishes to acknowledge his obligation to the Department of Geological Sciences at Yale University where the investigation into drainage systems was initiated, to the Research Committee of the Graduate School of Ohio State University for a grant of funds which made possible the continuation of the work, to the University's Department of Geology for many valuable favors, and to all three organizations for constant encouragement and material assistance.

[1] Waldo S. Glock: Dual Nature of Physiography, *Science*, No. 1853, Vol. 72, 1930, July 4, pp. 3-5.

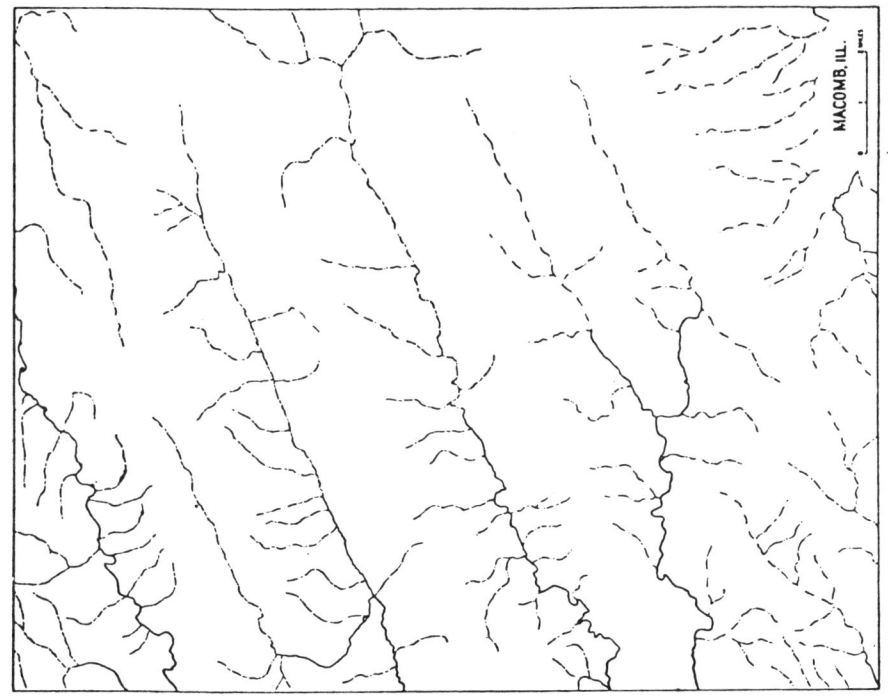

FIG. 2—Elongation is very nearly, or quite, complete, and the framework of the system has been established. In contrast, elaboration has just begun.

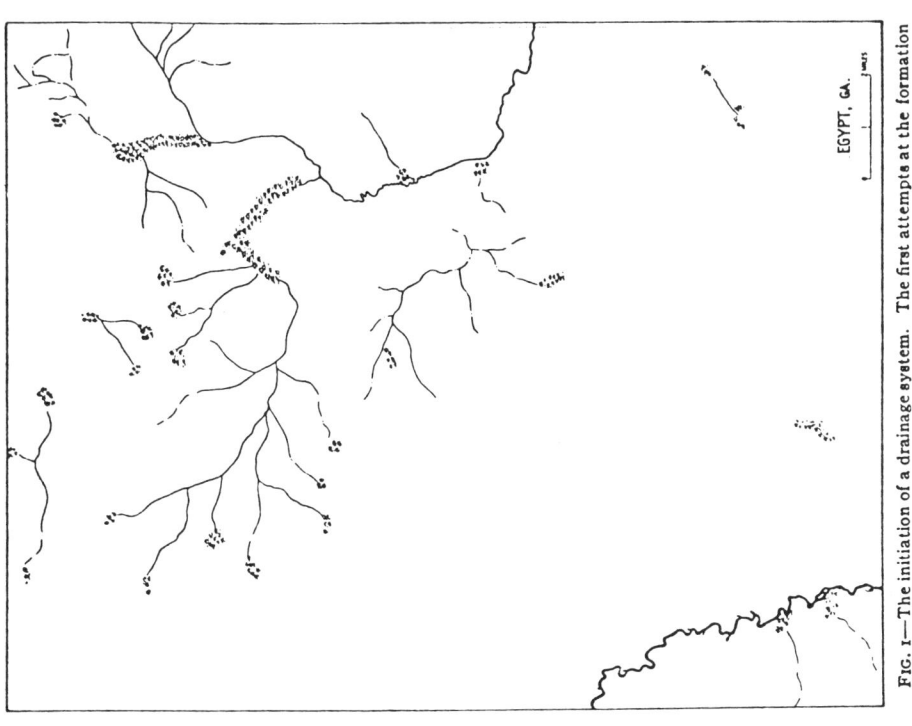

FIG. 1.—The initiation of a drainage system. The first attempts at the formation of definite drainage courses, hence the very beginning of extension.

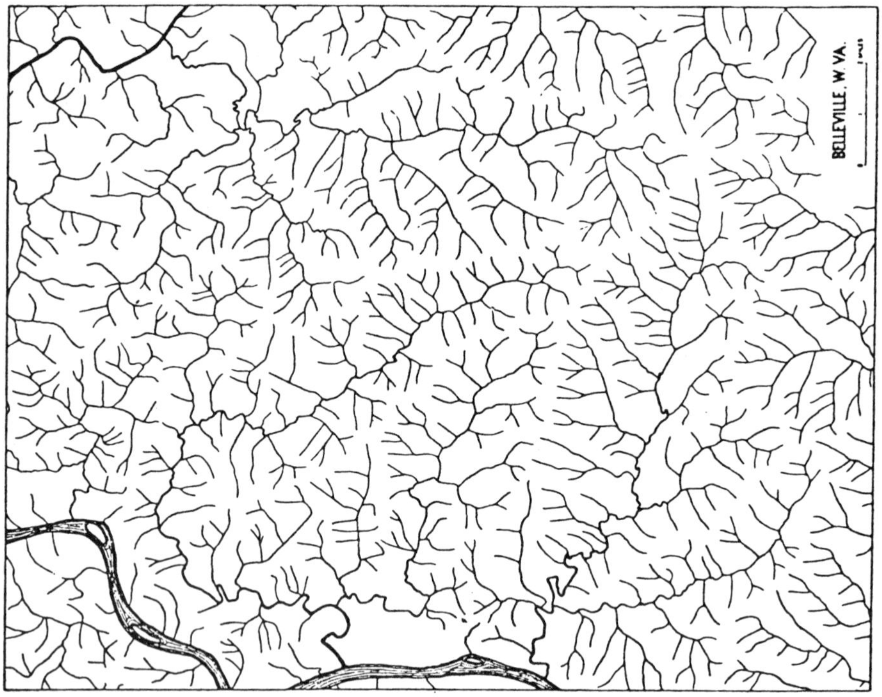

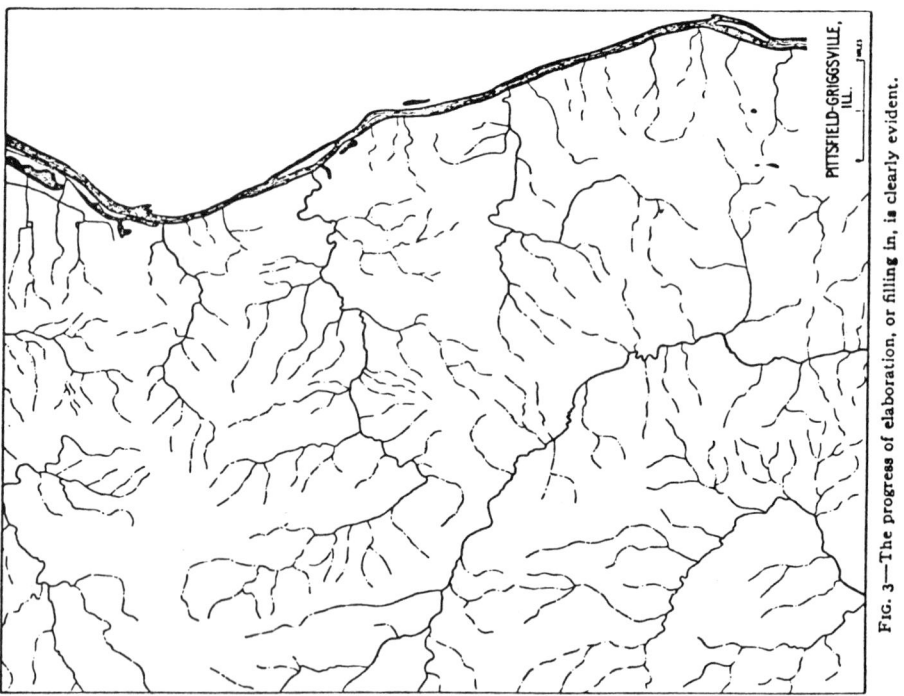

FIG. 4.—Elaboration completed and extension at a maximum. The territory has been wholly occupied by streams.

FIG. 3.—The progress of elaboration, or filling in, is clearly evident.

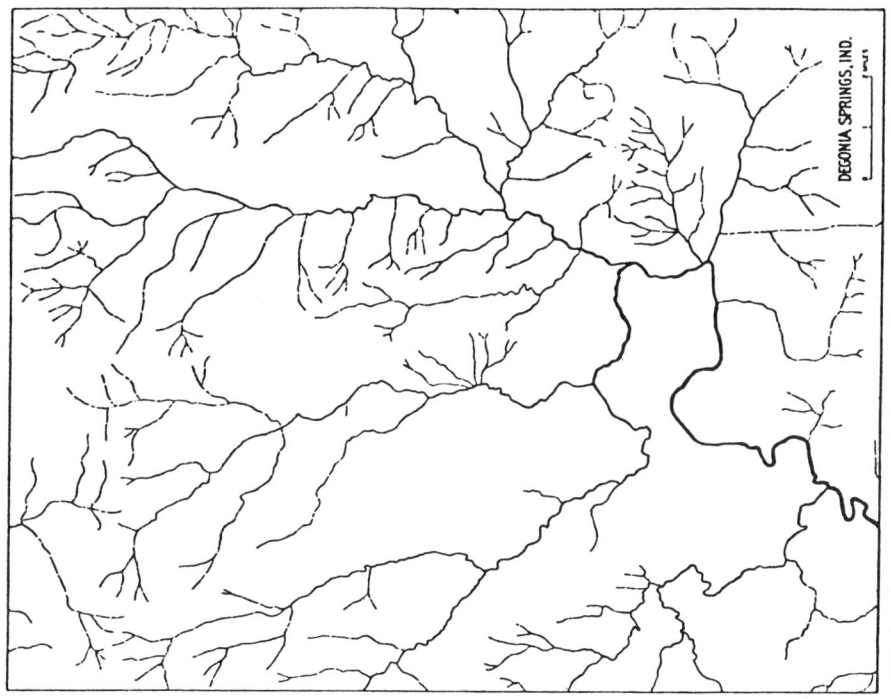

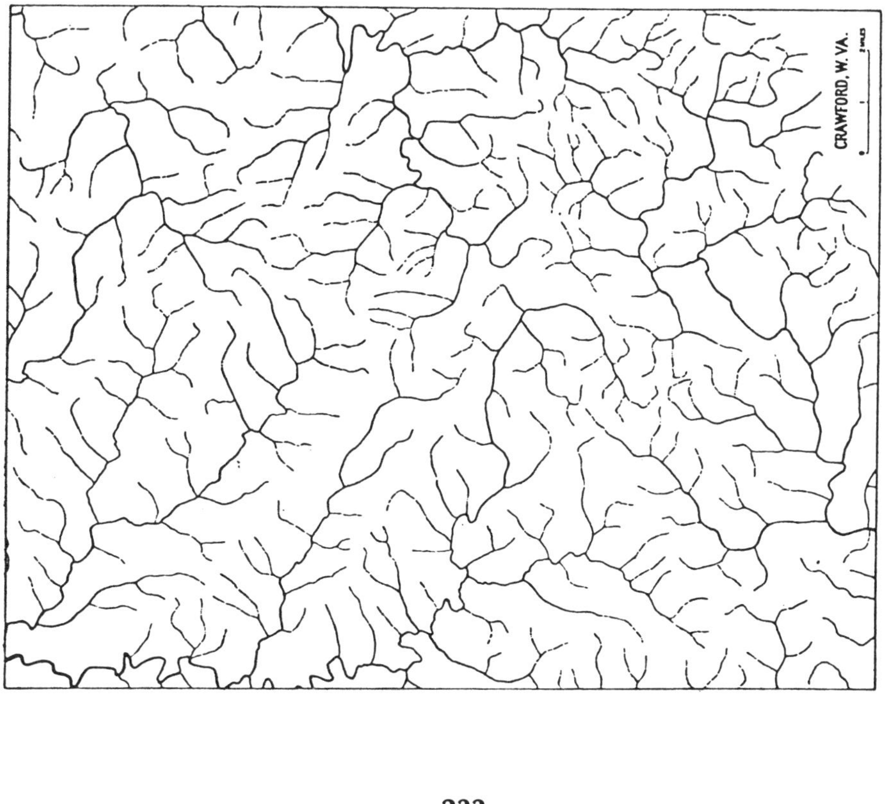

Fig. 5—The nature of the stream pattern and the character of the piracy indicate that maximum extension had existed at some time in the past.

Fig. 6—The reappearance of the skeletonized form, and integration rather well begun.

extension as illustrated by Figure 1 is characterized by a notable lack of streams over a large percentage of surface, by the indefinite termination of many streams without combining into a main stream, and by the failure on the part of the existing streams to have started that active conquest of territory so typical of their future histories. These features are highly typical of the phase initiation but are not necessarily habitual. There is in truth a temptation to say that the drainage system is quite amorphous as yet. However that may be, a time of increasing activity follows the genetic period of hesitation and indecision. The streams begin the conquest of territory, some in a highly aggressive fashion, others in a more or less passive way.

Abbreviated streams and skeletonized systems characterize the stage of extension in a broad way, and these two characteristics must be eliminated before the stage is ended. The growing streams reach out into the territory bequeathed them and take possession of their inheritance by means of headward elongation which begins shortly after the efformation of the system. They sketch in, as it were, the lineaments of the future drainage pattern (Fig. 2). After the area has been thus blocked out the process of elaboration gradually eliminates the skeletal form by means of the addition and growth of minor streams (Fig. 3). A plexus of these accessory tributaries spreads outward from the mains until a veritable network of drainage covers the area first possessed by the elongated streams. With the progress of extension the abbreviated form commonly disappears first while the elimination of the skeletonized pattern, although beginning more slowly, endures throughout the entire stage.

The attainment of complete elaboration may be simply called maximum extension. It is the time of completed territorial conquest and minute invasion—the time of the fully developed drainage system (Fig. 4). The land surface, in other words, has been entirely occupied. Theoretically, the exact position and nature of maximum extension may appear to present unexpected difficulties in view of the almost infinite variation to be found among individual streams. The question may arise whether the elimination of the abbreviated streams on the one hand and the skeletonized system on the other may not lead to different extensional maxima, especially if opposing systems enter into active competition with each other, an activity tending to elongate certain streams at the expense of others. Should lengthening accomplished by piracy after elaboration has been completed fall within the scope of extension? It seems not. Figure 5 shows that a system may grow at the expense of a neighbor after maximum extension has been attained, since the pattern of the captured streams themselves indicates that the territory had been completely occupied when the piracy occurred.

From a practical standpoint, also, the essential termination of the processes of elongation and elaboration may be more readily recognized and circumscribed if held to the simple concept inherent in the attempted description of extension. The scheme of classification

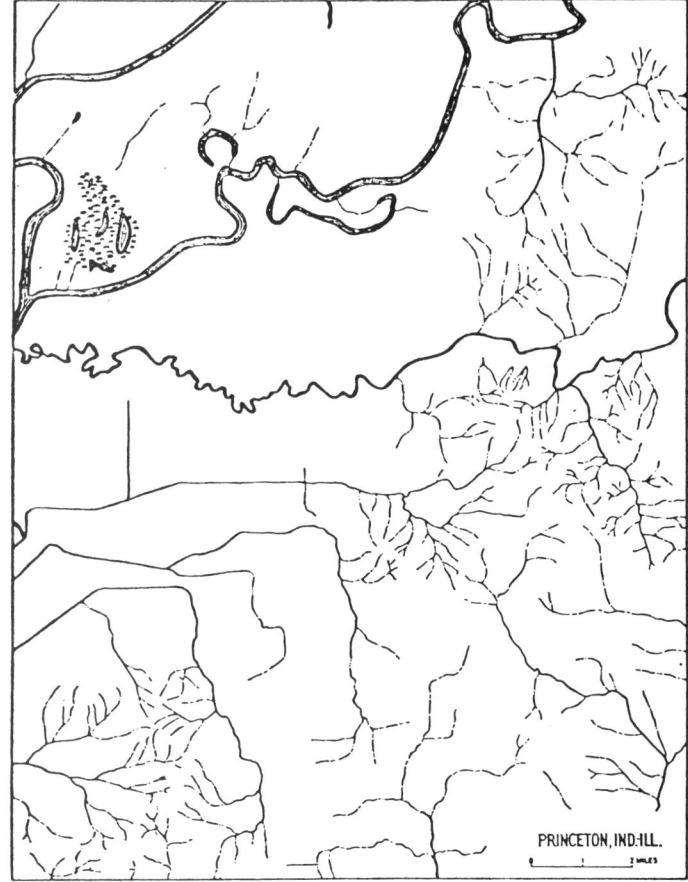

FIG. 7—Master streams and master tributaries late in the stage of integration.

to be desired is the one that is as simple and, at the same time, as adequate as possible. True maximum extension may be considered to refer to the completed invasion of the unoccupied surface within the jurisdiction of a particular drainage system after active elongation into rightfully inherited territory has added all possible area to the system. Hence, the intensity of intersystem strife may wax to a maximum either with, or after, the full development of the drainage systems, and extension may be at a maximum or may have definitely passed away when systems "come to an understanding about their drainage areas." Piracy between systems does not serve as a limiting criterion for extension. Treated, therefore, in the preferred fashion, the scheme is simple enough to conform to the standards which, it is believed, an ideal scheme should follow. Little doubt can exist that such an ideal scheme acts as an axis of variation about which natural phenomena appear to group themselves.

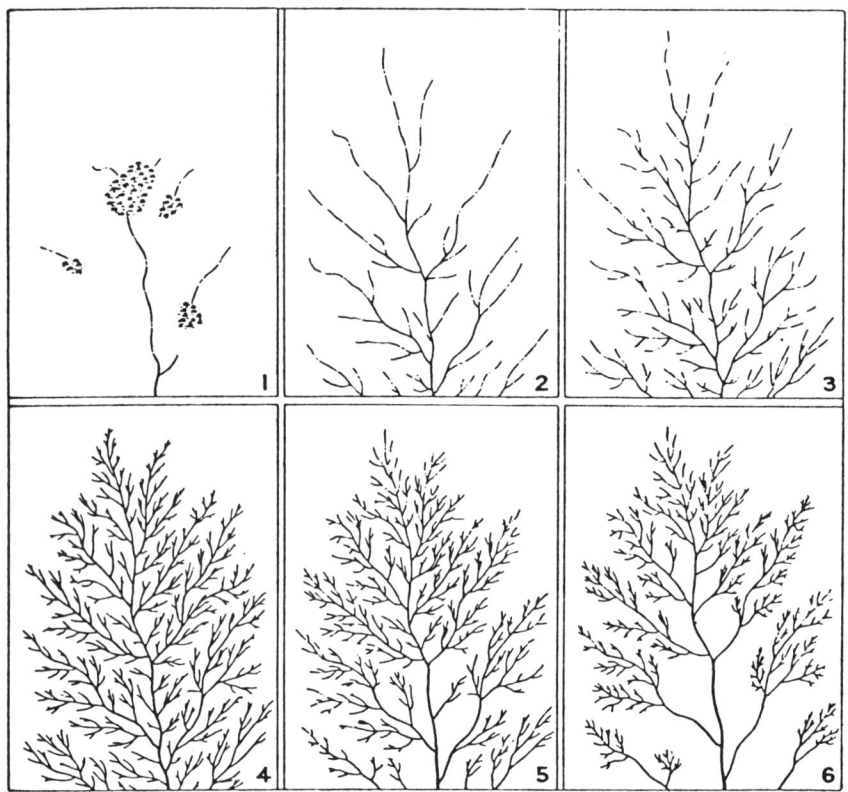

Fig. 8—An ideal diagrammatic summary of the development of a drainage system given for purposes of comparison only. The first four parts show extension, thus: 1, initiation; 2, elongation; 3, elaboration; and 4, maximum extension. Parts 5 and 6 represent steps during integration.

The Stage of Integration

The processes responsible for integration may be designated as follows: (1) abstraction, the loss of identity suffered by a secondary stream at the hands of its primary; (2) absorption, the disappearance of a stream save immediately after rainfall; and (3) a sort of adjustment or aggression, the attempt made by the main stream to reach the sea by the shortest route consistent with regional slope. The reappearance of the skeletonized form out of the intricate plexus of streams some time after maximum extension definitely marks the existence of integration (Fig. 6). It constitutes the second and final stage in the developmental history of a drainage system.

Abstraction refers to the elimination of a secondary stream by its primary. As the stream swings from side to side it constantly increases its own drainage area and thus abstracts territory from its tributaries. The lower portions of a tributary system may be dismembered in this way, all of the shorter branches may be completely destroyed, and the lower part of the chief tributary may lose its identity and independence on the meander belt of the master.

With integration well begun many of the minor tributaries seem to be absorbed and thereafter come into existence only for the purpose of discharging the immediate rainfall. Their disappearance quite likely is involved in the flattening of the local ground-water surface during the progress of integration and the consequent sinking of that surface below stream level.

The third process is less easy, if not impossible, to observe to any great extent at the present day. As integration advances into the final phase, the master stream becomes more and more independent of its environment except for the general slope of its drainage area and its relation to the sea or point of discharge. Aggression is said to take place when the stream attempts to gain the shortest (valley) route to the sea governed solely by the general slope of its drainage area, and then only if that direct route did not exist at initiation or was abandoned for any reason later. A stream having worked out such a course for itself may conveniently be called an integrational consequent and undoubtedly finds abundant illustration in geologic history.

The three processes accomplish the elimination of a host of streams and result in the appearance of the simplified form of integration very similar to the skeletal outline of early extension. Master streams joined by master tributaries (Fig. 7) at last emerge from the plethora of previously existing streams and, if necessary, seek the shortest practicable route to the sea.

In some respects integration appears to reverse the procedure of extension, as for instance the disappearance of minor tributaries, the continuation of which appears constantly to accentuate the original framework of the system. The stages in reality do resemble each other in that the sequence of changes (with one exception) sweeps headward along the trunk streams and thence to the chief branches, arriving finally at the outermost confines of the system—a migration quite naturally anticipated. Here, however, resemblance ceases.

There is no intention to infer that the scheme of development including extension and integration, because of its simplicity, possesses definiteness and perfection to such a degree that each is a distinct stage by itself. In fact, the two may always exist at the same time from a regional standpoint; or, further, extension may be occurring locally among the headwaters while integration is taking place farther down stream. Minor cases of actual overlap should be expected in any detailed study of a drainage system.

EROSIONAL DEVELOPMENT OF STREAMS AND THEIR DRAINAGE BASINS; HYDROPHYSICAL APPROACH TO QUANTITATIVE MORPHOLOGY

R. E. Horton

[Editors' Note: In the original, material precedes this excerpt.]

ORIGIN AND DEVELOPMENT OF STREAM SYSTEMS AND THEIR VALLEYS BY AQUEOUS EROSION

RILL CHANNELS AND RILLED SURFACE

The first step toward the gradation of newly exposed sloping terrain is the development of shallow parallel gullies wherever the length of overland flow is greater than the limiting critical distance x_c. These are "rill channels," and a surface covered with such channels is a "rilled surface." Rill channels are usually relatively uniform, closely spaced, and nearly parallel channels of small dimensions which are initially developed by sheet erosion on a uniform, sloping, homogeneous surface. They are sometimes described as "shoestring gullies," but the term "gully" as ordinarily understood connotes larger and less regular channels developed by sheet erosion at a later stage. A rilled surface presents a striated appearance in plan and a finely serrated appearance in cross section.

Excellent examples of rilled surfaces may be found in newly made road cuts, on the slopes of highway and reservoir embankments, spoil banks, and mine dumps. In road cuts, water often drains onto the newly made slope from above the edge of the cut, in which case the rill channels extend the full length of the slope. If such drainage does not occur then the rill channels invariably begin at a little distance below the top edge of the cut. Actually the value of the critical length x_c may be very small, a few inches to a few feet, on newly exposed steep slopes, and the fact that the rills do not extend to the top of the slope would not ordinarily be noticed. Where a rilled surface develops on a newly exposed slope the usual result is the development of a deep central master rill or gully, with more or less parallel, shallower, shoestring rills, decreasing in depth and frequency, on both sides of the master gully. These shoestring rills do not generally survive. The deeper ones close to the master gully are absorbed by the master rill by bank caving or are destroyed by the breaking down of the narrow ridges between them. Those more remote are later obliterated when lateral slope has developed sufficiently to permit cross flow.

On some newly exposed lands, with high infiltration-capacity and high resistivity to erosion, the length of slope from the major divide to the downslope edge of the area may never exceed x_c. Under these conditions a rilled surface may not develop. This condition often occurs on sand-dune areas and in some glaciated areas with deep permeable soils, especially where grass or other vegetal cover develops soon after the disappearance of glacial ice. In the latter case x_c on the newly formed surface may exceed the values of l_o pertaining to the drainage of melt-water from the ice sheet, a rilled surface may not develop, and the topography will remain much the same as when the ice disappeared, except that gradation by solution may take place. In desert regions, with suitable relations between the rain intensity, infiltration-capacity, surface resistivity, and the slope, a rilled surface may develop with little or no cross-grading, so that surface gradation may never extend beyond the rill stage.

ORIGIN OF RILL CHANNELS

"Sheet erosion" implies the formation of either a rilled or gullied surface. From the discussion thus far it would appear that overland flow downstream from the critical point x_c on a smooth uniform surface should remove a uniform layer of soil instead of producing a rilled surface.

The question may fairly be asked: Why does a drainage basin contain a stream system? Surface runoff starts at the watershed line as true sheet flow, without channels. Even below the critical distance x_c it should apparently continue as such sheet flow combined with sheet erosion. Why, then, do rill channels develop? The answer is that channels start to develop where there is an accidental concentration of sheet flow. Accidental variations of configuration may provide the requisite initial conditions where a local area has a lateral slope joining a longitudinal slope or where two lateral slopes join and form a trough.

Most cases of active erosion observed at present represent conditions where there is or has been a protective vegetal cover and the initial resistivity of the soil surface is greater than that of the immediately underlying subsoil.

Consider a point upslope from x_c. If, as a result of change in cover conditions, either the resistance R_i or the infiltration-capacity is reduced, the point x_c may move upslope from the given point, which will then be susceptible to erosion. When the remaining protective cover is broken through at a given point, a channel or gully will form which will proceed rapidly upslope, chiefly by headward erosion, because of the lower resistivity of the underlying soil.

This, however, is not the mode of origin of rill channels, which, it must be presumed, often form on new terrain without vegetal cover and with a value of R_i sensibly the same at and to some depth below the soil surface. Slight accidental variations of topography may produce a sag in which the depth of sheet flow is a maximum at the point a (Fig. 20), the line bb' representing the water surface at maximum runoff intensity. As a result of the greater depth at a, erosion will be most rapid at that point, and increased channel capacity will be provided at a, and part of the water which originally flowed in shallower depths on the adjacent area will be diverted into this enlarged channel. This may accelerate the process until the entire flow is concentrated in the rill channel (Fig. 20). This does not involve headward erosion in the ordinary sense. However, when a rill channel has once formed, sheet flow coming down the slope upstream from the head of the rill will be deflected toward and diverted into the rill channel, thus providing a means of rapid headward extension of the rill.

This process of rill formation can often be observed on a cultivated slope during heavy runoff. The size and spacing of the rill channels vary with the slope, runoff intensity, and length of overland flow, ranging from a few inches apart on a cultivated slope to many feet or yards apart on long slopes with low runoff intensity and higher erosive resistance. In some areas in abandoned lake beds or exposed coastal

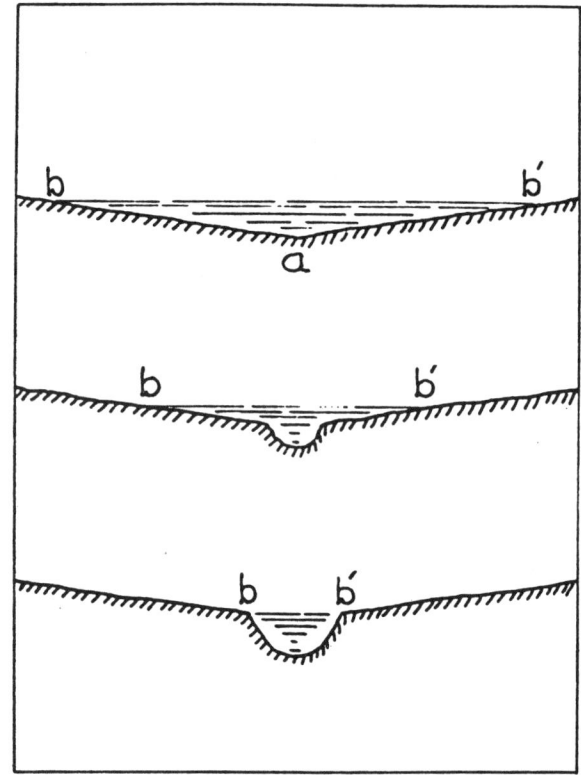

FIGURE 20.—*Successive stages of rill-channel development*

belts in arid regions stream development has never progressed beyond the rill stage. Such an example is given on the Moon Mountain, Arizona-California, quadrangle, U. S. G. S. topographic map (Fig. 21). Later stages of stream-channel development belong to the domain of channel dynamics and involve velocity distribution, silt equilibrium, and other factors which cannot be considered fully here.

The ultimate dimensions of a stream channel are, as indicated by Playfair's law, such that it is adapted to the area which it drains. Stream channels tend to acquire ultimate dimensions such as to carry all or most of the flood waters of the stream. This is largely because most surface erosion and channel erosion occur during floods.

CROSS-GRADING AND MICROPIRACY

A system of parallel shoestring gullies is transformed to a dendritic drainage net as the result of the tendency of the water to flow along the resultant slope lines and

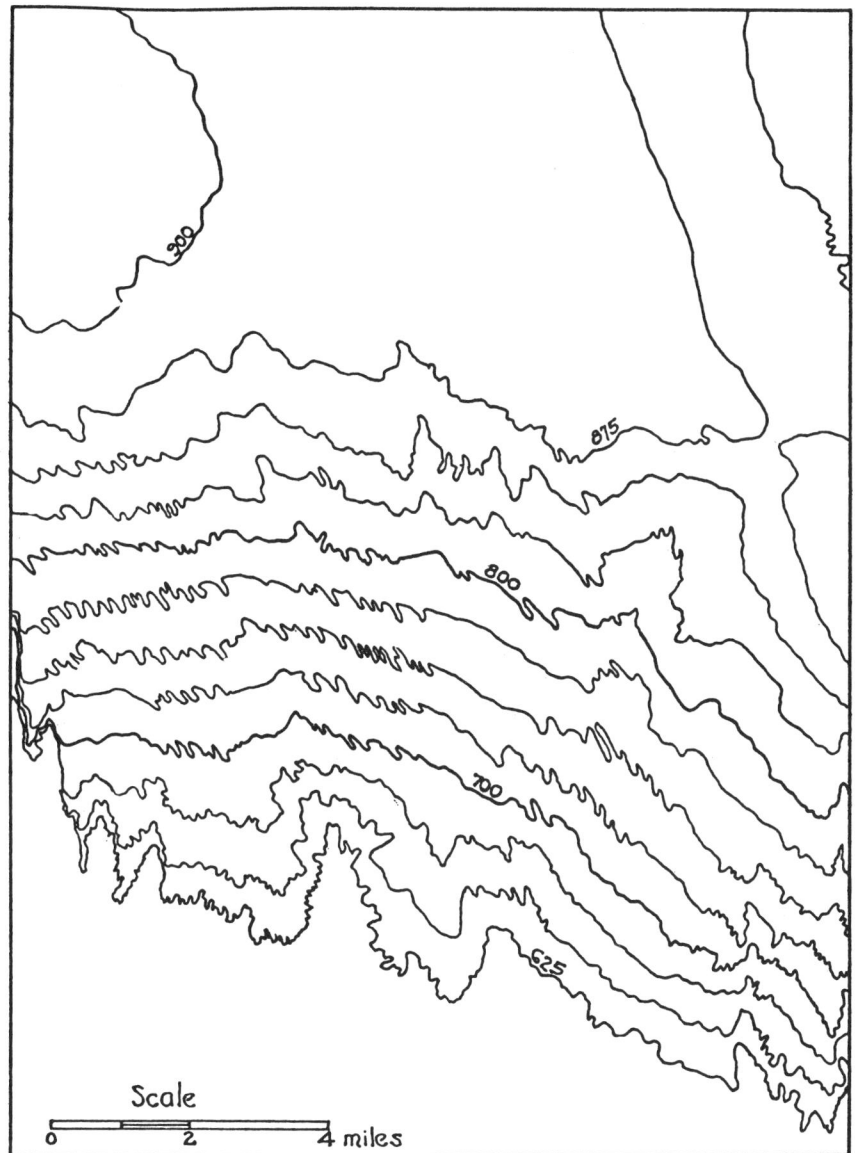

FIGURE 21.—*Portion of Moon Mountain, Ariz.-Calif., quadrangle, U. S. G. S.*

is a direct consequence of the overtopping and breaking down of intermediate ridges between gullies by overland flow during heavier storms.

The deepest and widest rill develops where the net length $l_o - x_c$ in which erosion can occur is greatest. If x_c varies, this may not occur where the total length l_o of overland flow is greatest. The longest, deepest, and strongest rill channel will be called the "master" rill. Owing to smaller values of $l_o - x_c$, proceeding away from the master rill on each side, the rills will be shallower, or, considering two adjacent rills, the bottom of the one farther from the master rill will be higher.

When a storm occurs exceeding in intensity preceding storms on the newly exposed areas, the divide between two rills may be broken down at its weakest point by (1) caving in of the divide between two rills, diverting the higher into the lower rill; (2) erosion of the divide by the deeper or lower rill, thus diverting the higher rill; (3) overtopping of the divide at the low point by the higher rill, again diverting it into the lower rill. This breaking down of divides between adjacent rill channels and diverting the higher into the lower rills is described as micropiracy. Micropiracy much resembles stream capture by lateral corrasion, but micropiracy results chiefly from water overtopping a low spot in the narrow ridge between two rills. Micropiracy obliterates the original system of rills and their intermediate ridges on a uniform newly exposed surface. The process of erosion, in the course of development of a stream system and its accompanying valleys destroys most of the record of their origin. Ultimately the original slope parallel with the stream is replaced on each side of the stream by a new slope deflected toward the stream. This process is described as "cross-grading."

The initiation of cross-grading is illustrated on Figure 22, which shows a plan of a small area of newly exposed land, $aa'bb'$. The line cc' marks the downslope limit of the belt of no erosion, $aa'cc'$. The critical distance x_c is assumed to vary with slope, infiltration-capacity, and initial resistance to erosion. Rills develop downslope from cc', and their development is followed by cross-grading, as shown on the cross sections taken on the line dd' and numbered 1 to 4, inclusive. The line of resultant slope in each case is in the direction shown by the arrows, and the rills increase in depth and degree of gradation at a given time proceeding away from the lateral boundaries toward the initial or master rill. In section 2 (Fig. 22) the rilled surface has developed, but flat "lands" still persist between rills, and the resultant slope is still parallel with the original slope. In section 3 some rills have combined by cross-grading, creating slight cross slopes, but the overland flow is still carried chiefly by rills parallel with the original slope. In section 4, with increased cross slopes and perhaps a heavier storm, active cross-grading has taken place, especially mid-length of and in the lower portion of the original slope; the direction of overland flow is no longer parallel with the original slope, but overland flow takes place partly in the rills and partly across the intervening ridges, somewhat as shown on a larger scale on Figure 23, and in detail for a single pair of rills on Figure 24. This process can sometimes be observed in heavy storms on lands cultivated nearly but not quite parallel with the contours, the tillage marks corresponding to the original rills above described.

In Figure 22, section 5, the original serrated rilled surface has been obliterated by cross-grading and is replaced by an irregularly roughened surface on which a new rilled surface tends to develop, with flow lines parallel with the resultant slope. This represents the end point of the first stage of valley gradation and stream development. At this stage there exists only one stream in the area, and this follows the course of the initial or master rill. This idealized picture of the cross-grading of a rilled surface is based in part on field observations of eroding slopes and in part on the observed manner of erosion of experimental plots, using artificial rainfall. Under natural conditions the results are rarely so uniform as those shown on Figure 22.

A break across a rill divide may result from numerous causes, such as a rock or

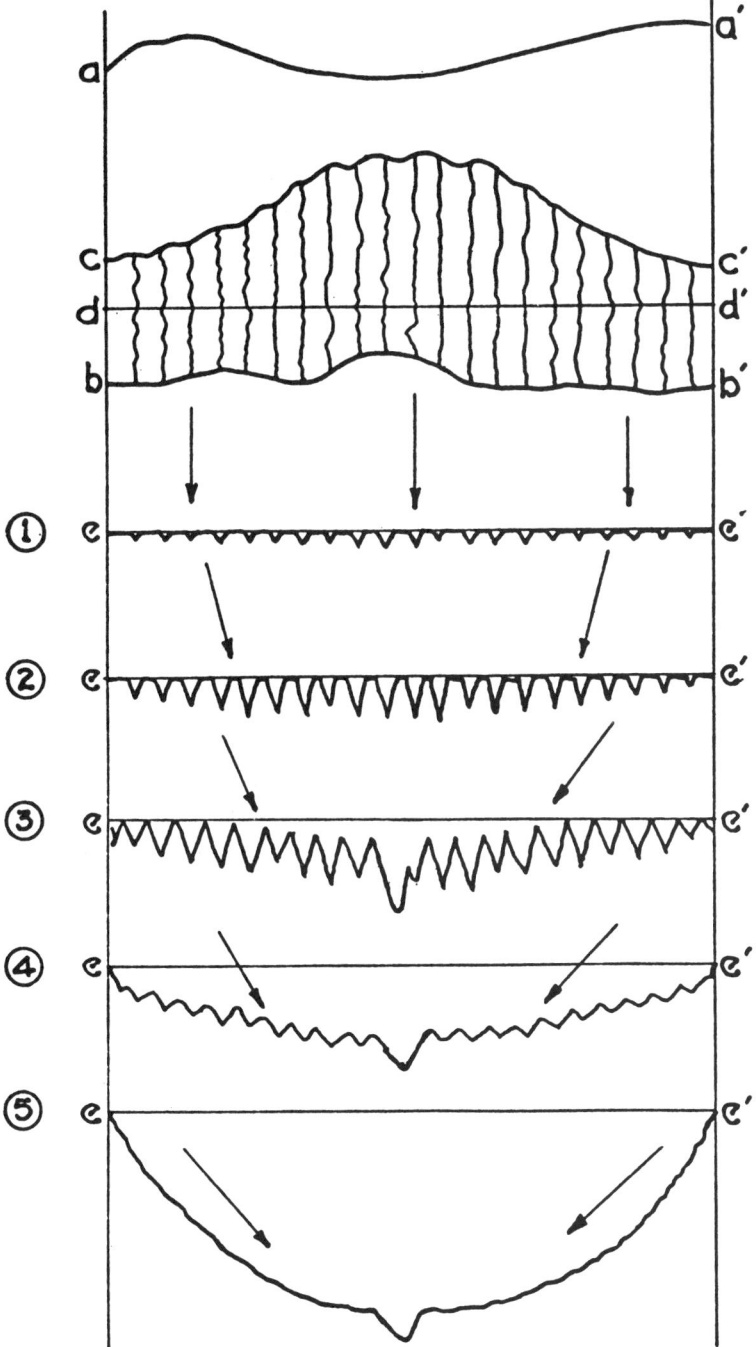

FIGURE 22.—*Development of a valley by cross-grading*

ORIGIN AND DEVELOPMENT OF STREAM SYSTEMS

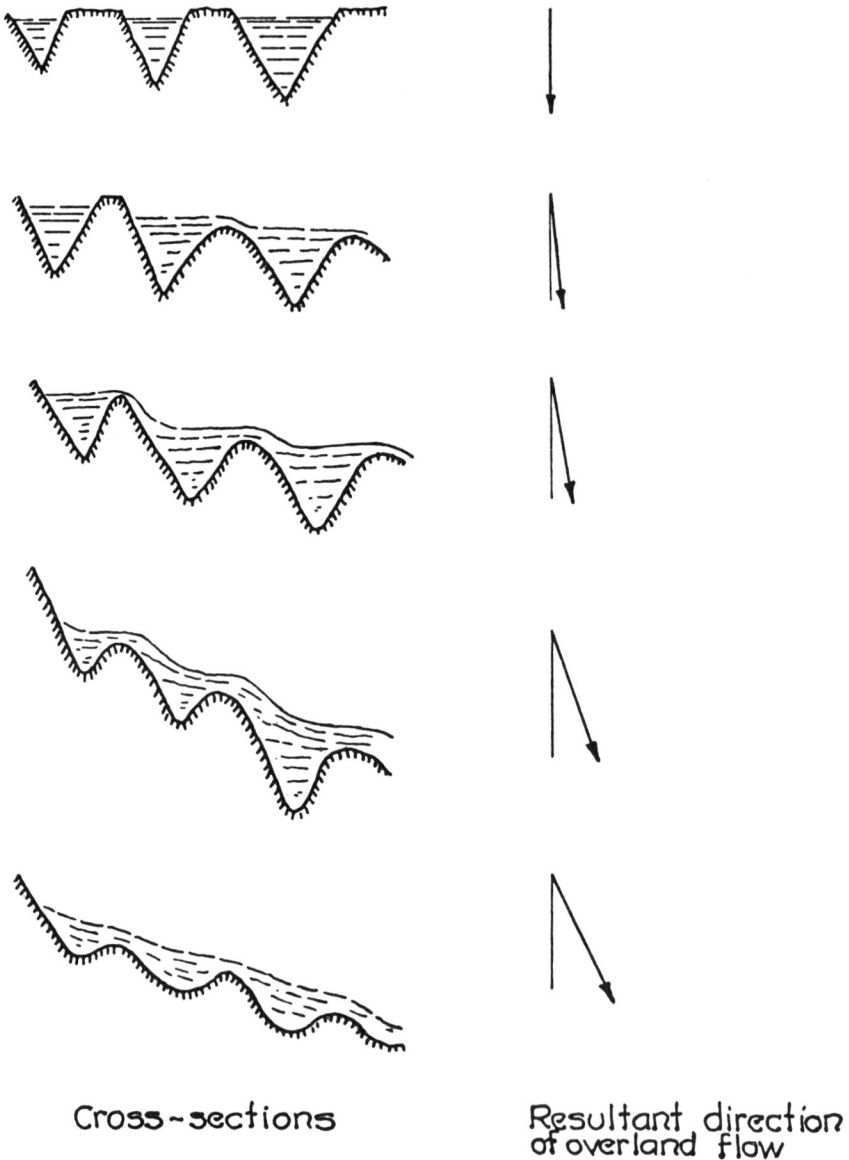

FIGURE 23.—*Successive stages of rill obliteration*

obstruction in the path of the rill, causing back-water upstream therefrom, or the caving in of the bank of the rill, thus obstructing its flow and producing a side outlet. A very common cause is an accidentally low divide between two adjacent rills. In most cases the channel of the diverted rill will be obstructed just downstream from the point of diversion. If the break supplies a free outlet from the diverted rill, then immediately downstream from the break, as at x (Fig. 24, B), there will be little or no flow, and erosion will cease, while erosion just above the break will continue. The channel above x will quickly become deeper than the abandoned rill channel below x. There will be thrust, as indicated by the downslope arrows on Figure 24, at the point of diversion, resulting in a tendency toward the formation of a rounded

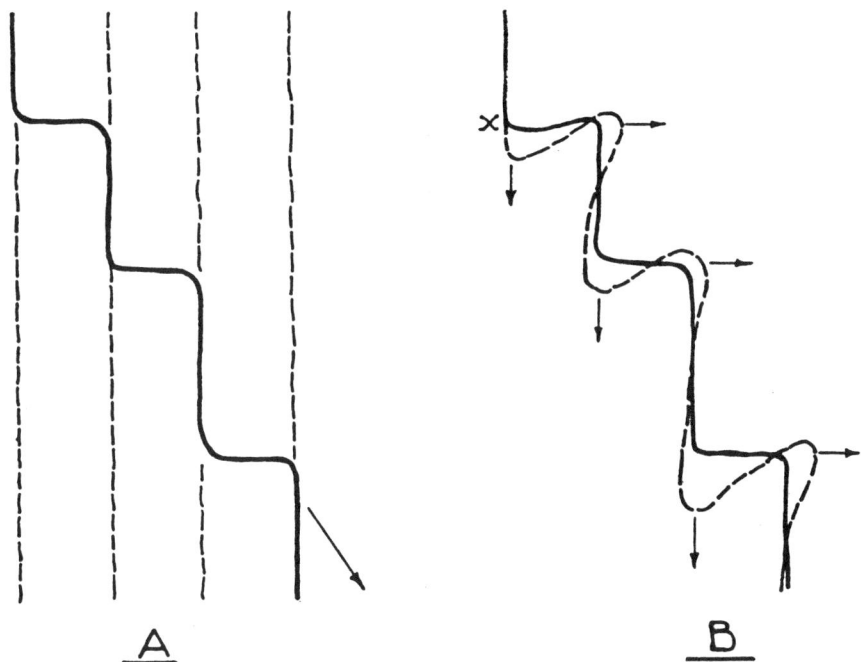

FIGURE 24.—*Development of a stream from a rill system by cross-grading*
(A) Showing angular plan of initial stream; (B) Development of bends by thrust at angles of an initial stream.

bend by impact erosion. Similar thrust across the slope will occur at the second angle of each cross rill diversion, with similar results.

Micropiracy tends to give the resulting stream at first a more or less angular course (Fig. 24) which, as the angular bends are rounded by erosion, will finally develop a more or less tortuous stream course following generally the line of resultant slope. On steeper slopes the resulting stream tends strongly to maintain a straight course and has eroding power sufficient to do so. On flatter slopes, with greatly reduced eroding power, centrifugal force around the initial angular stream bends tends to enlarge their radii. Weak bends merge with stronger ones until ultimately a system of stream meanders is developed. Since the master rill either initially or by cross-grading, on a given slope, ultimately becomes a permanent stream, it appears that conditions favoring the formation of stream bends on flatter slopes are inherent with the origin of the streams.

The elimination of rill systems on gentle slopes is very different from the development of mature meander belts such as those observed in natural streams. Even where stream bends originate in this way the evidence of the intermediate steps is eliminated in the course of the process.

This is not the sole explanation of the origin of stream bends, for individual bends arise from other and accidental causes. The fact that bends occur generally in rather definite systems on flatter stream slopes and in material that is almost perfectly homogeneous seems to require something more than purely fortuitous causes to explain their origin. It is at least significant to find that a stream in its initial stage, as it merges from a rill system, provides the necessary conditions for the development of stream bends on flat slopes.

HYDROPHYSICAL BASIS OF GEOMETRIC-SERIES LAWS OF STREAM NUMBERS AND STREAM LENGTHS

General statement.—A conventionalized illustration is given of the main steps involved in the development of a drainage net, showing the hydrophysical basis of the geometric-series laws of stream numbers and stream lengths. A square area with its diagonal parallel with the direction of slope will be assumed. This roughly approximates in form a typical ovoid drainage basin.

First stage.—On Figure 25, *oabc* is a uniform surface sloping toward *o*. The maximum length of overland flow is the diagonal length $l_o = ob$. A storm produces surface runoff of intensity sufficient to reduce the critical distance x_c to some value $bg < l_o$. Sheet erosion can then occur over the area *ofgh*. The runoff intensity q_1, in cubic feet per second per unit width, will increase proceeding from *a* and *c* toward the center line nearly in proportion to the length of overland flow. There will be no erosion at *f* or *h*. The erosion intensity will increase from these points along the line *fh* toward the center line. The maximum intensity of surface runoff cannot occur until surface detention is built up to a point where the inflow to and outflow from surface storage are equal. Since the unit runoff intensity q_1, other things equal, increases nearly as the length of overland flow, the critical intensity necessary to induce erosion will be exceeded first along the center line of the area and then progressively later proceeding toward *f* and *h* (Fig. 25, a). Sheet erosion will begin first along the diagonal line *og*, spreading more or less rapidly toward the points *f* and *h*. In a typical storm the duration of surface-runoff intensity adequate to produce erosion will also be greatest near the center line of the area, decreasing toward the sides. Consequently, erosion will begin first, be most intense, and last longer near the center line of the area. A series of more or less parallel gullies will develop (Fig. 25, a), decreasing in depth and frequency, proceeding away from *og*, forming a rilled surface.

In Figure 25a the lines of overland flow are parallel with the central or master rill. Actually as the valley develops, the lines of overland flow will follow the resultant slope lines converging toward the central rill first at acute angles and, as the slope increases, at increasingly larger angles, approaching right angles as a limiting case.

This is the first stage of stream and valley development. It may later produce further upslope erosion in more intense storms. At the end of the first stage (Fig. 25a), there is a single central stream, with a V-shaped valley.

Second stage.—The development of the first stream (Fig. 25a) has divided the area and reduced the maximum length of overland flow on the remaining areas on each side to $\frac{1}{2} l_o$ or to half the initial maximum length of overland flow. Lateral tributaries have not yet developed because (1) Lateral flow cannot occur unless there is a lateral component of slope, and (2) until the lateral slope extends far enough from the main stream so that in a given storm the value of the critical length x_c is reduced

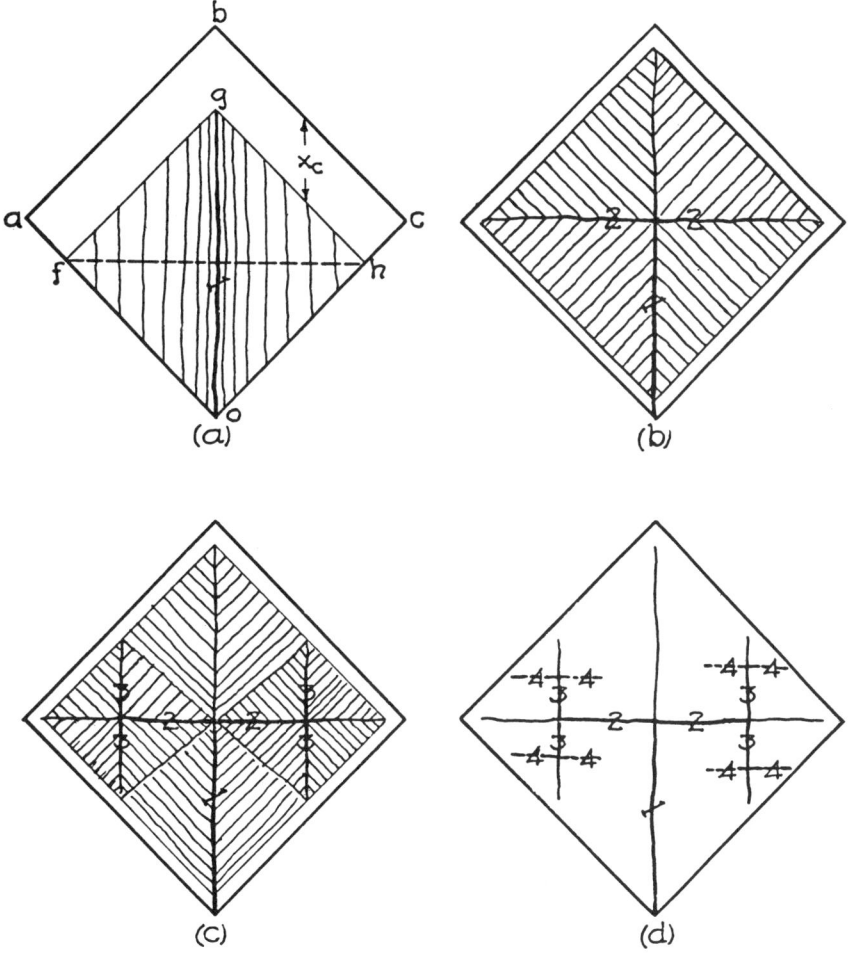

FIGURE 25.—*Development of a drainage net in a stream basin*
(Schematic).

to less than the width of the lateral slope, or in case of complete development of the initial valley, the value x_c must be reduced to less than $\frac{1}{2} l_g$.

The second stage involves the development of lateral tributaries and their valleys. During a storm of sufficient intensity to meet the prerequisites described, a pair of master rills or lateral tributaries with accompanying shoestring gullies will develop, one from each of the equal areas on opposite sides of stream 1 (Fig. 25b). These lateral streams are designated "2," and their development and that of their lateral slopes will follow the same course as in the case of stream 1. At the end of the second stage the area will appear as shown by Figure 25b. In the meantime, further headward development or downward gradation, or both, of the valley of stream 1 may have occurred.

Subsequent stages.—At the end of the second stage the maximum remaining length of overland flow in the area has been again halved or reduced to $\frac{1}{4} l_g$, and a still more intense flood is required to reduce the critical length x_c to a value less than this and permit the development of a third group of lateral tributaries. When such a flood occurs, each of the No. 2 tributaries will develop a pair of lateral tributaries, designated "3" on Figure 25c.

The development of lateral slopes adjacent to a given stream brings in overland flow from additional areas, increasing downstream, and accelerates grading of the main stream and its immediate valley. The stream system at the end of the fourth stage is shown by Figure 25d. The number of the stage of stream development corresponds to the order of the main stream. The main stream is of the 1st order at the end of the 1st stage, and of the 4th order at the end of the 4th stage.

Development of lateral tributaries and the manner in which they develop is the direct consequence of (1) the existence of a critical length x_c of overland flow required to institute erosion; (2) the operation of cross-grading. Drainage patterns, while invariably following the two fundamental geometric-series laws as to stream length and stream numbers, can still develop in an infinite variety of ways.

Two questions naturally arise: (1) What would happen if the newly exposed area was a continuous belt along the coast line, with no lateral boundaries? (2) Why and how are the boundaries of drainage basins developed? This case will be considered later.

ADVENTITIOUS STREAMS

Differences occur between the development of streams under natural conditions and those assumed in the example because:

(1) The drainage area is usually not rectangular but ovoid.

(2) Newly formed tributaries follow in general the resultant slope of the cross-graded areas on which they develop and hence enter the parent stream at more or less acute angles; the steeper the slope, the more acute is the angle of stream entrance. Tributaries thus tend to be longer than if they entered at right angles, and the stream-length ratio is consequently usually greater than 2.0.

(3) There are nearly always variations—sometimes large variations—of infiltration-capacity in different parts of the area.

(4) There are also variations—sometimes extreme—in the initial resistance of the terrain to erosion, as, for example, where part of the area is in consolidated and part in unconsolidated material, or part covered with vegetation and part bare. As a result of these departures from hypothetical conditions, the following results often occur:

In certain parts of the area the length of overland flow to the parent stream or its larger tributaries may be less relative to x_c than on the remaining areas tributary to the last group of streams developed. Then some 1st, and perhaps 2nd, order tributaries develop, entering the main stream or larger streams directly and not through higher-order tributaries. These streams, which result from accidental variations of conditions within the area, may appropriately be designated "adventitious" streams. The development of adventitious streams increases the number of streams of lower orders and tends to make the bifurcation ratio greater than 2.0, as it usually is for natural streams. Lateral slope also increases the length of tributaries and makes the stream-length ratio also greater than 2.0. An increase of r_l is also

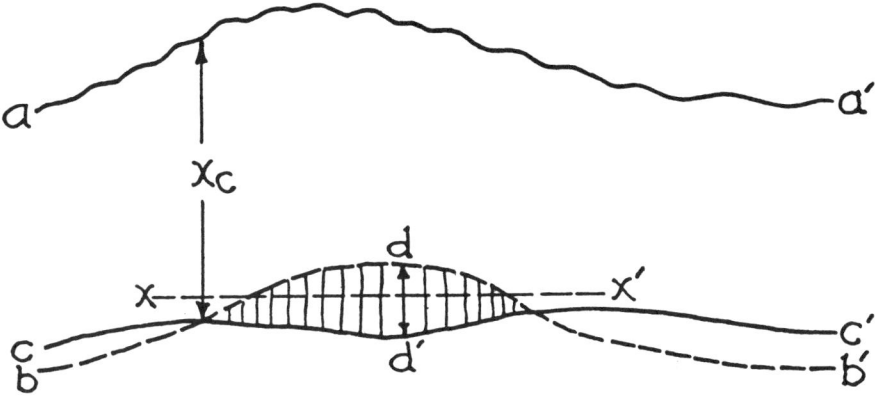

FIGURE 26.—*Beginning of erosion on newly exposed land*

produced because streams do not extend to the watershed line although they may extend by headward erosion to a distance less than the critical minimum value of x_c from the watershed line. Adventitious streams usually increase the bifurcation ratio more than the stream-length ratio is increased by the conditions described, with the result that the ratio $\frac{r_l}{r_b}$ is in general a fraction, and the total length of streams of a given order is not constant but decreases proceeding from the lowest to the highest stream orders. Adventitious streams do not in general develop simultaneously with larger streams in the basin but are developed later as the development of the stream system approaches maturity.

STREAM DEVELOPMENT WITH PROGRESSIVELY INCREASING LAND-EXPOSURE COMPETITION

For illustration the exposure of coast marginal lands will be assumed to be nearly a uniform homogeneous sloping plane, extending from a divide line aa' (Fig. 26) to the new coast line cc'. It is assumed that the soil surface in the newly exposed belt $aa'cc'$ is initially bare and has a certain infiltration-capacity f and a surface resistance to erosion R, such that the critical length x_c required to permit surface erosion to occur in the most intense rain is as shown on the diagram. The dashed line bb' is at a distance x_c from the watershed line aa'. As long as the coast line is within the belt $aa'bb'$, no streams will develop, runoff will be in the form of direct sheet flow to the new coast line, and no erosion takes place. There will be irregularities in the watershed line aa' and in the coast line cc', and, when the length of overland flow exceeds x_c at some point d, erosion will begin at that point. When the coast line has reached the position cc' there will be a small area, as outlined by a dashed line, within which $l_o > x_c$, and within this area sheet flow will produce erosion and a series of rill channels parallel with the direction of the initial slope surface. The first rill channel will be at dd', where the length of overland flow first exceeds the critical length x_c. As the coast line recedes the belt in which erosion can occur will increase laterally and longitudinally, and the system of rill channels will be extended correspondingly

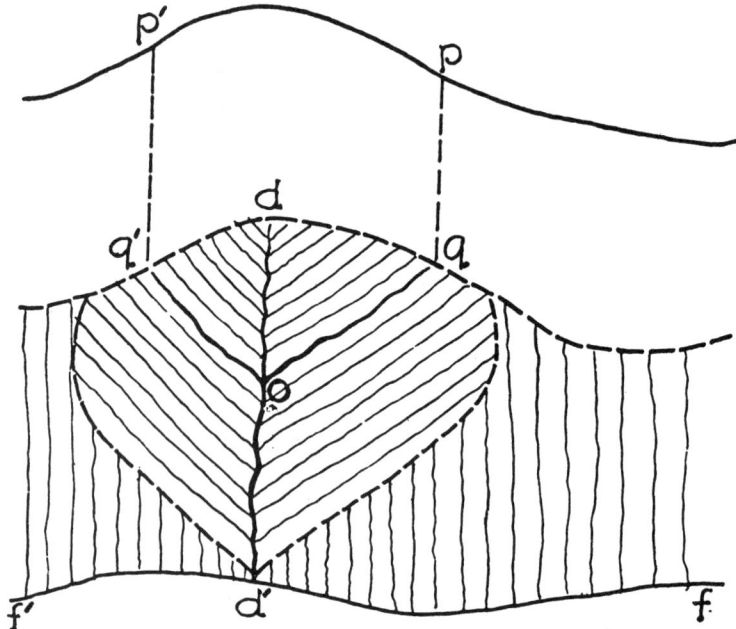

FIGURE 27.—*Development of first pair of tributaries on new stream system*

in both directions. The rill at dd' was first formed and has been longest subject to erosion and will become the master rill. Cross-grading will take place, producing new components of slope toward the rill dd' and obliterating the original rill channels. New rill channels will develop following the new direction of slope, on each side of the original stream dd' (Fig. 27). In general the lengths of these new rill channels will increase proceeding down the slope from the line cc'. At some point o (Fig. 27) a new rill channel will have a greater length oq and greater runoff than rills between o and d. It will have developed earlier than rill channels entering the parent stream dd' between o and d'. It therefore has greater runoff and a longer duration of runoff in which to cut its channel than rills formed farther down the slope. Such rill channels will survive as a tributary stream. Such a rill channel occurs on each side of the parent stream in the vicinity of o, and cross-grading toward these tributary streams will also occur. Cross-grading of the areas adjacent to these two tributaries will produce cross-graded slopes on either side of each tributary (Fig. 28), until there is again a location on each of these areas favorable for the development of tributaries, and new tributaries will develop, usually one on each of the two preceding tributaries, as at m, n, and p (Fig. 28). This process will continue until finally there is no land surface above the mouths of the original tributaries where the length of overland flow exceeds the critical length x_c.

If the coast line recedes farther (Fig. 29), the area upslope from *oo'* on the right hand side of the stream *dd'* is tributary to the stream *oq*. The original rill channels parallel with *dd'* upslope from *oo'* have been obliterated, and the runoff from the area

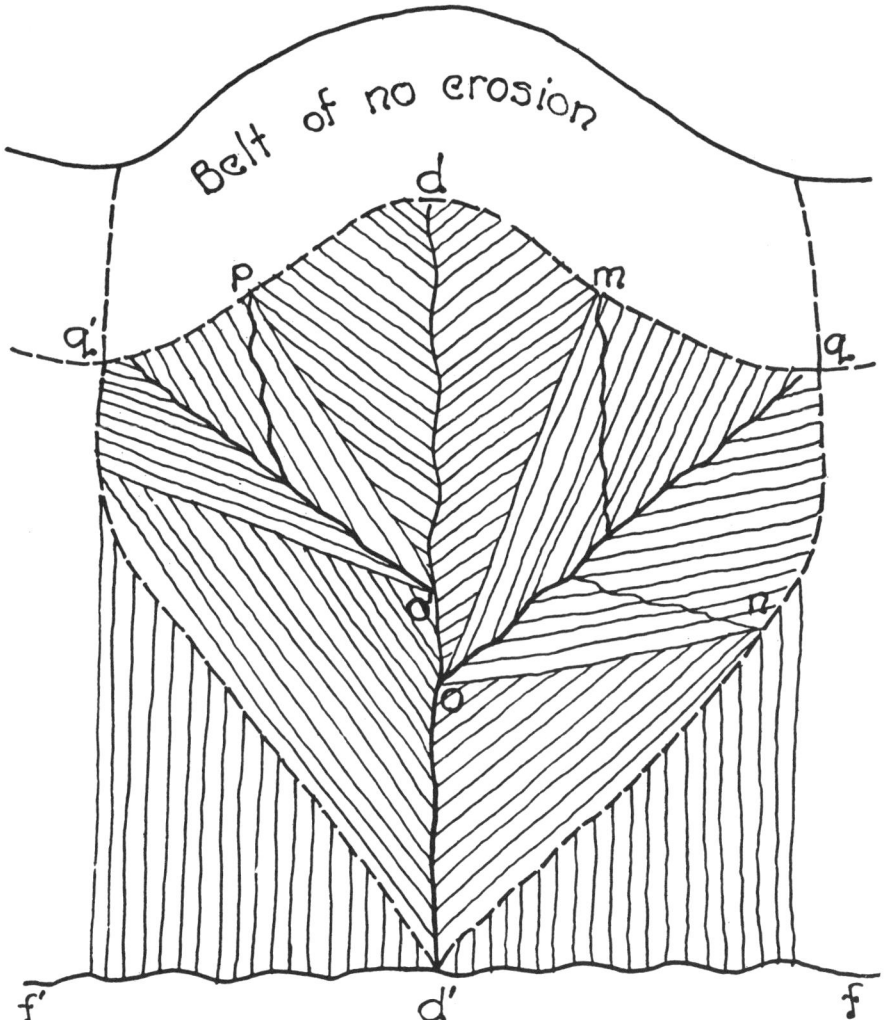

FIGURE 28.—*Lines of flow after cross-grading of first pair of tributary areas*

oo'o'' now enters stream *oq*. As the coast line recedes a new system of rill channels parallel with *dd'* develops downslope from *oo'*, and the area *oo'd'd''* will become cross-graded toward *dd'*. When the length of overland flow within the area *oo'd'd''* becomes sufficiently great at some point *q'*, a new tributary *q'r* will develop along the line of the resultant slope, and its basin will in turn be developed by cross-grading. There must be a certain minimum space or intercept between tributaries of the main stream to provide adequate length of overland flow to permit a lower tributary to the main stream to develop. Furthermore, the tributary $q'r$, having developed much later than the tributary oq, will extend its drainage area laterally more slowly than the latter, with the result that the drainage basin will tend to have an ovoid outline (Fig. 29).

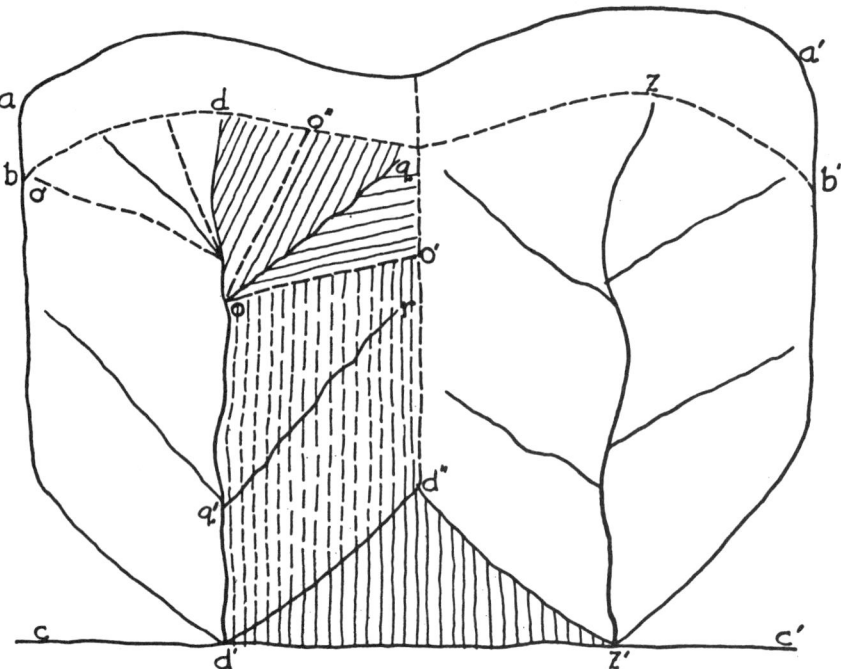

FIGURE 29.—*Development of lower pairs of main tributaries*

Another stream may also develop at zz' in the same manner as the stream at dd'. The development of this stream may have begun either a little earlier or a little later than the stream dd', and the final location of the lateral divide between the two drainage basins will be determined by the conditions of competition. The older stream will absorb the greater part of the area between the two streams. A marginal area of direct drainage $d'd''z'$ is left between the two major drainage basins. If the length of overland flow here becomes sufficient, an intermediate subordinate stream will develop.

The appearance of the final stream systems in the two drainage basins will be somewhat as shown by Figure 30.

Two major factors control the development not only of the drainage basin of a given stream but the systems of drainage basins tributary to a new coast line:

(1) Streams develop successively at points where the length of overland flow becomes greater than the critical length x_c.

(2) Competition results in the survival of those streams which have the earliest start or had the greatest length of overland flow, or both, and which are therefore able to absorb their competitors by cross-grading.

END POINT OF STREAM DEVELOPMENT

Stream development on a newly exposed slope continues until the greatest remaining length of overland flow is less than the critical distance x_c required to institute erosion.

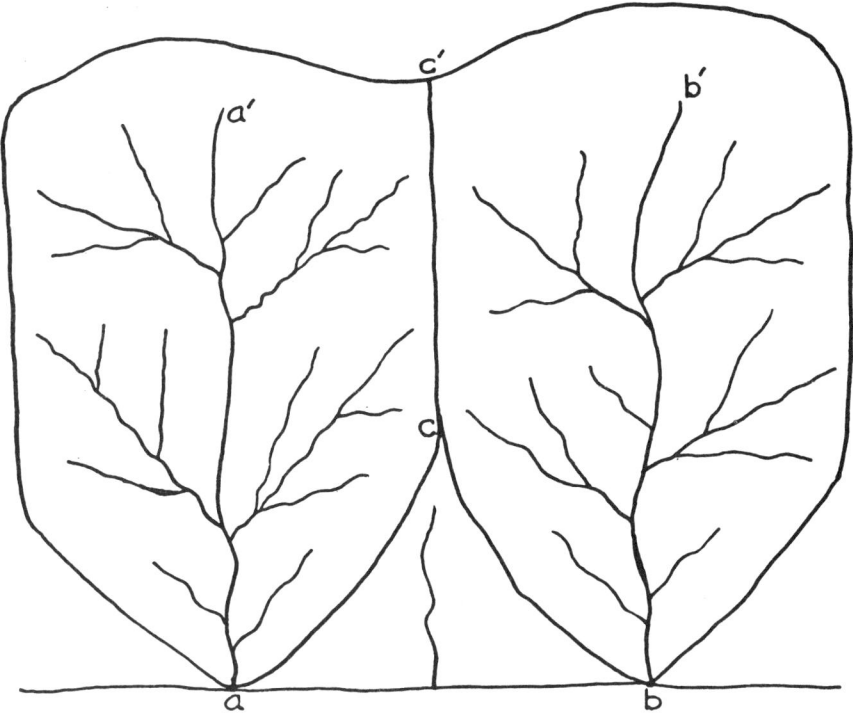

FIGURE 30.—*Final development of two adjacent drainage basins on newly exposed land*

At a certain stage of gradation (Fig. 31) the stream *oa* has developed with a drainage basin *ocd*. Before cross-grading of this area the critical length x_c is, for example, equal to that shown by the line *mm'* on the insert, and this is less than *oa*. After cross-grading of the area *ocd* this critical length is somewhat reduced by increased resultant slope and is now *mn*. The greatest lengths of overland flow on the areas *oca* and *oad* are now along the slope lines *de* and *ce*, but these are both less than *mn*. Hence no additional streams will develop in the area *ocd*.

The upper ends of the streams in a drainage basin will extend at least to the distance x_c from their watershed line, measured in the direction of slope. They may be extended closer to the watershed line by headward erosion, under suitable conditions.

For streams to be perennial at their sources there must be ground-water flow at the head of the stream channel. In regions where there is a permanent ground-water horizon under the drainage basin the most common condition is that the stream is intermittent for a distance downstream from the point where its channel begins. Figure 32 shows the profile at the head of a stream. The watershed line is at *a*, and a definite channel begins at *b*. There is a water table underneath the headwater

ORIGIN AND DEVELOPMENT OF STREAM SYSTEMS

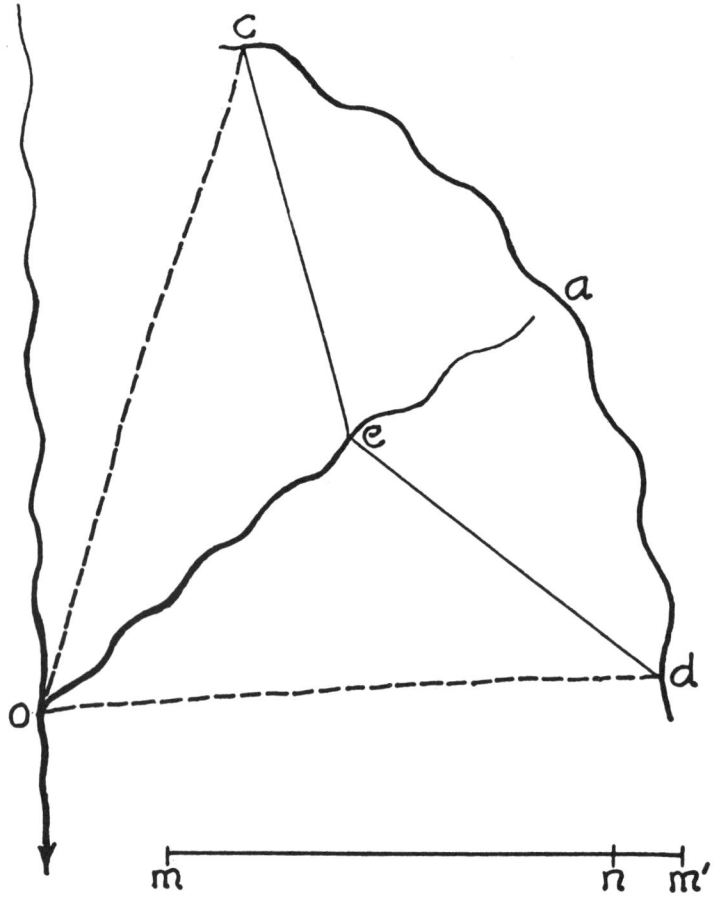

FIGURE 31.—*End point of stream development*

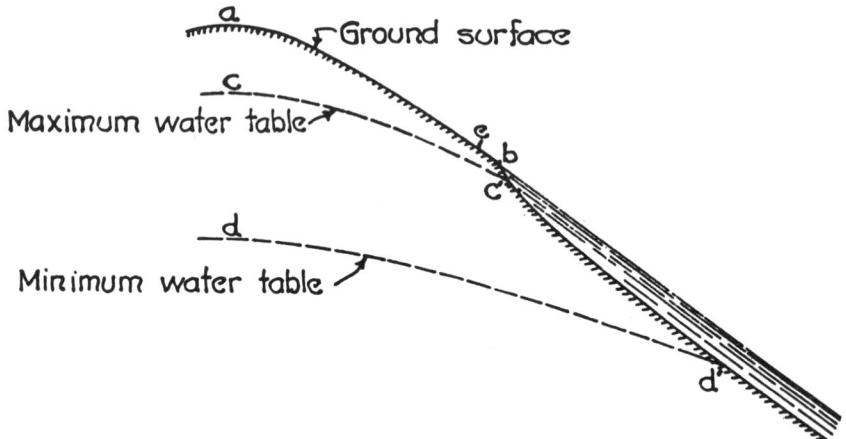

FIGURE 32.—*End point of a definite stream channel*

belt of no erosion ab, the maximum ground-water table is at cc', and the minimum at dd'. Between cc' and dd' the stream is intermittent. At c' part of the infiltration on the upper drainage area enters the stream. At times of maximum surface runoff the ground-water flow may represent a considerable fraction of the total flow. If,

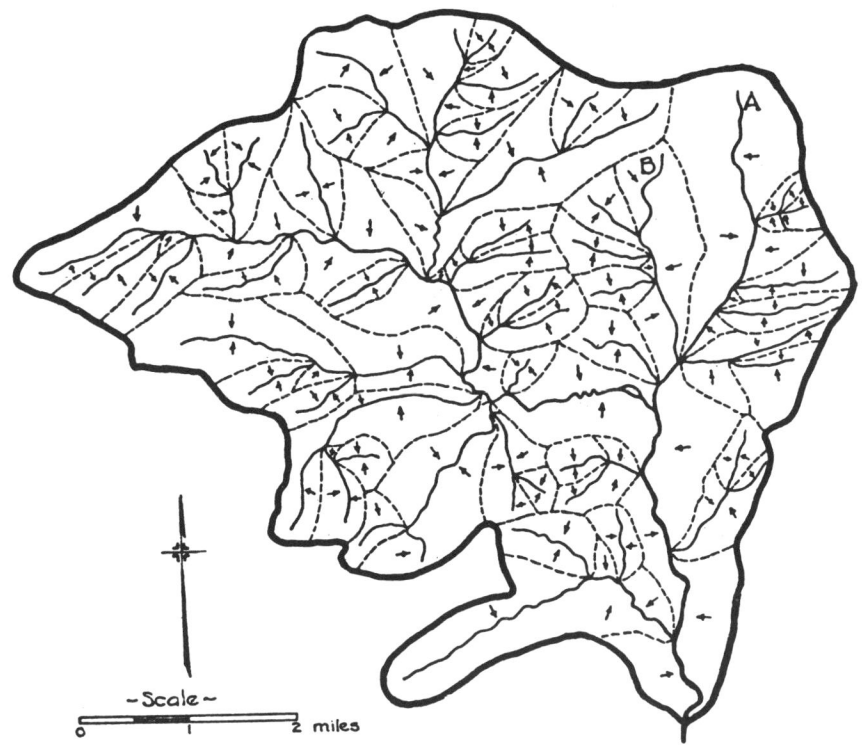

FIGURE 33.—*Drainage basin of Pennypack Creek*
Above Valley Falls, Pa., showing subareas from which surface runoff is derived.

for example, the ground-water flow is one fourth of the total flow at c', then, if the channel extended a little farther upslope to e, the maximum runoff would be reduced one fourth by elimination of ground water. There is therefore an abrupt and sometimes considerable change in the total runoff at about the point where the maximum level of the water table intersects the stream channel. Surface runoff plus ground-water flow can generally extend the channel upstream farther by headward erosion than could surface runoff alone. Hence the channel usually ends near the point where ground-water flow is no longer effective. Ground-water flow at c' is intermittent, but it usually continues much longer than surface runoff and by maintaining the soil at the head of the stream channel moist and soft it promotes extension of the channel by headward erosion and bank caving.

The final results of stream development under natural conditions are illustrated by Figure 33. Some of the streams in the lower part of the basin are clearly adventitious. There are several drainage basins, such as A and B, where tributaries have developed only on one side of the parent stream, leaving, in this case, an isolated plateau in the interfluve area, although the drainage development of the basin is evidently mature.

STREAM-ENTRANCE ANGLES

From geometrical considerations the following equation has been obtained for the entrance angle between a tributary and the higher-order stream which it enters (Horton, 1932)[4]:

$$\cos z_c = \frac{\tan s_c}{\tan s_g}$$

where z_c is the entrance angle between the two streams; s_c is the channel slope of the parent or receiving stream; s_g is the ground slope or resultant slope, which is here assumed to be the same as the slope of the tributary stream.

Values of the entrance angle computed by this equation for different values of the ratio s_c/s_g are as follows:

s_c/s_g =	0.9	0.8	0.7	0.6	0.5	0.4	0.3	0.2	0.1
z_c =	25.5°	36.8°	45.5°	37.0°	60.0°	66.2°	72.3°	78.3°	84.2°

As shown by Table 4, stream slopes are always less than the adjacent ground slope, and tributaries should enter the confluent stream at acute angles when the slopes of the channels of the tributary and confluent streams are nearly the same. The equation takes on the indeterminate form 0/0 if the two slopes s_c and s_g are equal. This means that the two streams will be parallel and will not join. Three cases will be considered for purposes of illustration.

CASE 1—FLAT STREAMS DEVELOPED ON A FLAT AREA: When the parent stream has developed and cross-grading has proceeded to a point where a pair of tributaries develop, the parent stream will in general have cut into the initial surface to some depth, and its stream slope in the vicinity of the debouchure of the tributaries will be materially less steep than the original slope, while the slopes of the tributaries as they approach the parent stream will be materially steeper than the original slope. As a consequence, instead of the ratio s_c/s_g being close to unity, this ratio will seldom have a value greater than 1/2 or 1/3, and the tributaries will not enter the main stream at acute angles, as would be the case if s_c and s_g were nearly equal, but will more generally enter the parent stream at angles of 60° to 80°. On extremely flat surfaces in humid regions a swampy condition often prevails, and stream-entrance angles are but little subject to control by erosion conditions. On semiarid plains where little erosion occurs, acute entrance angles of tributaries to the parent stream may sometimes be observed.

CASE 2—FLAT VALLEY SLOPE WITH MODERATE TO STEEP ADJACENT GROUND SLOPE: Under these conditions the ratio s_c/s_g is nearly always low, and the stream-entrance angles to the main or parent stream are commonly 60° or greater. As the

---

[4] Derivation of this equation is given correctly in the reference cited. Interpretation of the equation as there given is incomplete and not wholly correct.

stream system develops, the slope of the main stream steepens proceeding upstream, and the lateral ground slopes also steepen proceeding upstream. The ratio s_c/s_g may remain sensibly constant, or it may either increase or decrease. Most commonly it decreases to some extent. Quite generally the entrance angles of tributaries to the main or initial stream are quite uniform and range from 60° upward, decreasing somewhat upstream.

CASE 3—TRIBUTARIES ON A STEEP SLOPE: Tributaries developed on the same slope generally run nearly parallel, and if the main valley is relatively flat they will enter the parent stream at an angle of 90°, representing a limiting condition which is approached but not often attained. Tributaries developed on the same lateral slope may of course join and are especially likely to join where drainage development is incipient, as on steep, rocky slopes and in semiarid regions where tributary development has been arrested at the end of the rill stage. Parallel tributaries which join on a steep slope under these conditions commonly have an acute angle of juncture. In this case the ratio s_c/s_g is close to unity.

DRAINAGE PATTERNS

Much has been written regarding the forms of drainage patterns. They are usually classified as dendritic (treelike), rectangular or trellised, radial, and centripetal. The terms radial and centripetal commonly refer to the arrangement of a group of drainage patterns originating at or converging to a common point and do not refer in general to the pattern in an individual drainage basin. All drainage patterns of individual drainage basins are treelike, but different patterns resemble the branchings of different kinds of trees and range from those with branches entering the parent stream nearly at right angles, to those with tributaries nearly parallel and entering their parent streams at small angles. The form of the drainage pattern depends to a large extent on the relation of the slope of the parent stream to the resultant ground slope after cross-grading. If this ratio increases with successive cross-gradings, stream-entrance angles of successive tributaries are somewhat more acute for successively lower-order streams, affording the most usual type of dendritic drainage pattern.

On a relatively flat surface the directions of resultant overland flow after the first cross-grading are nearly at right angles to the initial stream, and the second series of streams developed enter the parent stream nearly at right angles. Cross-grading of the areas tributary to these streams produces but a slight change in the slope ratio s_c/s_g, so that the next order of streams also enters the parent streams more or less nearly at right angles. In this way a rectangular drainage pattern is developed.

If, on a steep, sloping, original surface, the headwater divide forms roughly an arc of a circle, then the first two tributaries developed will enter the parent stream from opposite sides at nearly the same point (Fig. 34). These streams will develop long tributaries nearly parallel with the initial stream, giving rise to a centripetal drainage pattern (Fig. 34).

On flat slopes each successive cross-grading of a given subarea changes the direction of the next stream to develop on the area through an angle approaching 90° as a

ORIGIN AND DEVELOPMENT OF STREAM SYSTEMS 351

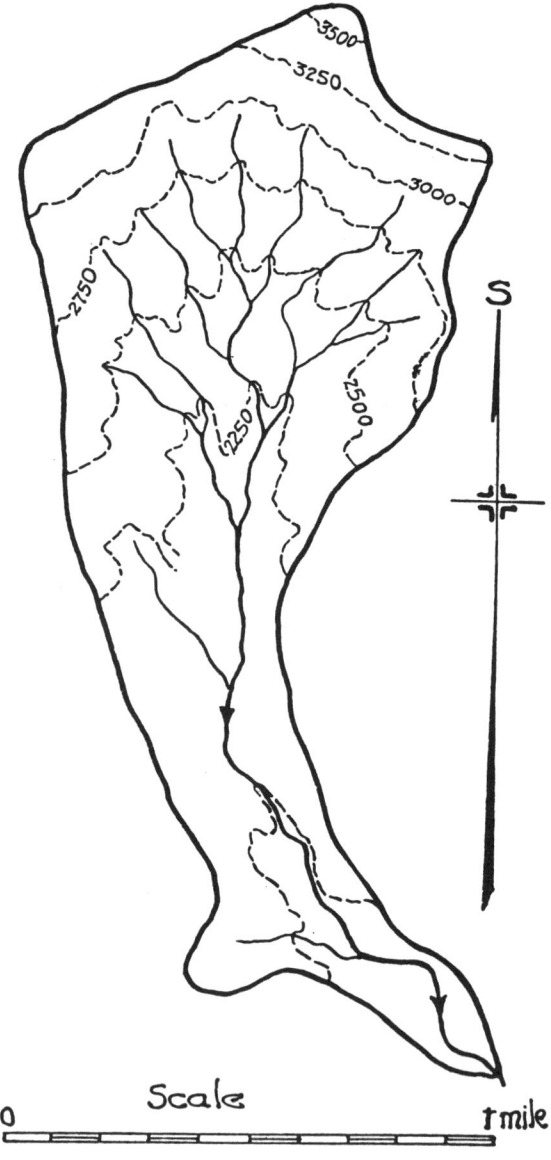

FIGURE 34.—*Centripetal drainage pattern*
Payne Creek, Ga., Mulky Gap quad., U. S. G. S.—T. V. A.

limit and changes the direction of overland flow through a corresponding angle. The direction of resultant cross-graded slope at the end of a given stage becomes the direction of the stream of the next succeeding stage. The directions of streams and of resultant slopes will change through nearly a right angle with each successive stage of stream development and cross-grading, and the directions of streams and of resultant slopes tend generally to be the same in any two stages of stream development which are either both even numbered or both odd numbered.

ASYMMETRICAL DRAINAGE PATTERNS

Because newly developed tributaries enter their parent streams at acute angles, they divide their tributary areas into two parts such that the remaining upslope tributary areas are larger than those on the downslope side, using the terms "upslope" and "downslope" with reference to the two sides of the tributary. Because of inequality of area, width, and slope on the two sides of a tributary, the next lower order of tributaries may develop with two or three tributaries on the upslope side and fewer or none on the downslope side, a common phenomenon, particularly in mountain areas. Since the average elevation of the upslope area is greater than that of the downslope area, this phenomenon is sometimes attributed to increase of rainfall with elevation. It may occur, however, as the result of differences of tributary area and length of overland flow on the upslope and downslope sides of the parent streams, independently of variation of rainfall or runoff on the drainage basin. Burch Creek and Reels Creek drainage basins (Utica, New York, quad., U. S. Geological Survey) afford examples of asymmetrical drainage-basins.

PERCHED OR SIDEHILL STREAMS

In general, streams follow the bottoms of the valleys in which they are located. Small—usually 1st order—streams are occasionally perched precariously on the side slopes of graded valleys of higher-order streams. The course of such a stream is often more nearly parallel with the antecedent slope than with the cross-graded slope. At the foot of the slope the stream often turns abruptly and debouches into the parent stream at nearly a right angle (Fig. 35). Evidently gradation of the valley of the parent stream cd reached the stage shown in the figure before the slope became steep enough to reduce the critical length x_c below the maximum length l_o of overland flow on the right-hand side, and l_o became greater than x_c only when gradation of the valley slope had reached the end point. A weak stream, ab, then developed by micropiracy and cross-grading, but owing to some local cause, such as increased resistivity of the soil to erosion at increased depth below the original surface, this stream was unable to develop a valley of its own by further cross-grading and so remained high above the parent stream on the antecedent rilled surface, until, with increasing volume and slope, it turned nearly a right angle as it entered the parent stream.

REJUVENATED STREAMS; EPICYCLES OF EROSION

In the preceding sections it has been assumed that: (1) Uplift or exposure of new terrain took place continuously though not necessarily at a uniform rate, the region finally becoming stable; (2) the initial resistance R_i of the soil surface to erosion remained constant. The effect of subsequent further elevation or subsequent subsidence of an area on which a stream system has already developed has been extensively discussed in connection with the Davis erosion cycle (Wooldridge and Morgan, 1937) and will not be considered further here. Before leaving the general subject of stream development and valley gradation consideration will be given to the effect of (1) differences between surface and subsurface resistivity to erosion, (2) changes in the surface resistivity to erosion.

ORIGIN AND DEVELOPMENT OF STREAM SYSTEMS 353

The term "rejuvenated stream" is applied to a stream system in which a renewed cycle of erosion begins and which may extend the drainage net after it has reached maturity. Rejuvenation may result from several causes, although in the Davis

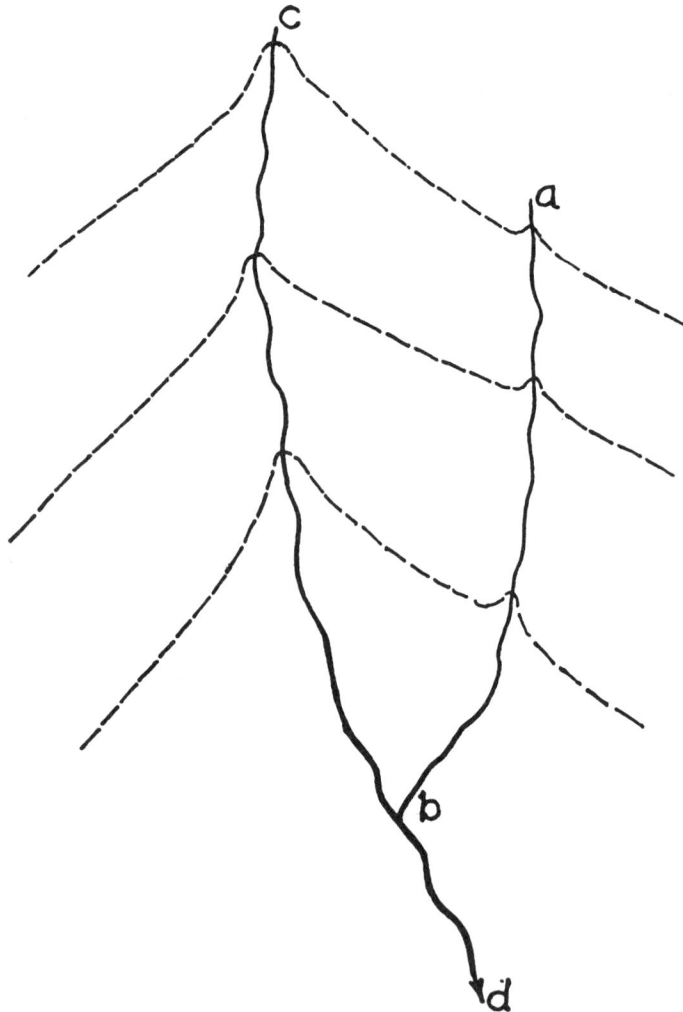

FIGURE 35.—*Perched or hillside stream*

sense the term is applied chiefly where it results from widespread geologic changes such as renewed uplift, folding, and tilting.

Accelerated or decreased erosion may result without any such geologic changes if the original terrain varies in erosional resistivity or infiltration-capacity proceeding downward from the surface. Then, as erosional gradation takes place, changes in the critical length of overland flow x_c will occur, and if these changes are abrupt they may result in important effects, either (1) marked increase in drainage density and extension and number of minor tributaries, if R_i and x_c decrease downward from the surface, or (2) abandonment and fossilization of pre-existing streams and tributaries, if R_i and x_c increase with increased gradation.

A third condition may also bring about changes in erosion rate and stream development which is more common than rejuvenation due to strictly geologic causes. This occurs where, as the result chiefly of climatic or cultural changes, there is a change in the surface-erosional resistivity or infiltration-capacity of the terrain which brings about changes in the critical length x_c and in the consequent development of drainage.

Accelerated erosion due to the removal or replacement of an initially resistant surface by a less resistant surface has been appropriately described by Bailey (1935) as an epicycle of erosion. This term is appropriate since it implies a marked changed in erosional and gradational activity, superposed on the normal erosional conditions. Changes in erosional conditions brought about by dust storms and the formation of loess veneer on soil surfaces, and changes in erosional activity resulting from improper cultivation of the soil, deforestation, fires, or overgrazing of range lands, afford excellent examples of epicycles of erosion.

Where a less permeable and more resistant surface layer of soil or sod overlies weaker or more permeable subsoil, there will be in effect two different values of x_c, one pertaining to the surface layer, the other to the underlying material. This occurs where well-established grass or other vegetal cover overlies a noncohesive sandy soil or where there is a layer of loess or similar fine-textured material, with moderate or high cohesiveness, overlying more permeable and less cohesive material, such as sand.

If the overlying resistive material is broken through, the value of x_c pertaining to the underlying material governs subsequent stream development. In such cases the development of a drainage net is likely to be erratic and sporadic. On much of the area there may be but few streams. This will be true where the larger or surficial value of erosive resistance R_i and critical distance x_c are effective. At other locations where the smaller subsurface values of R_i and x_c have become effective, active and extensive stream development may take place. Extensive plains, for the most part undisturbed by erosion, may be dissected by rapidly growing and irregularly branching systems of gullylike channels. This condition exists in the Pontotoc Ridge region of the Little Tallahatchie, Mississippi, drainage basin, where deep incoherent sand is overlain with a thin veneer of fine uniform loessal silt. In this region x_c for the underlying sand is practically zero, and stream development may extend far above the x_c limit for the surface material as a result of headward erosion. The author has observed gullies in the Pontotoc Ridge region which in some cases have extended not only to but somewhat beyond the topographic boundaries of their drainage basins (Happ et al., 1940). This has resulted from the slumping of masses of earth from the nearly vertical and sometimes undermined scarp formed by the erosion of the deep, incoherent sand.

The destruction of vegetation by smelter fumes early in the present century in the vicinity of Ducktown and Copper Hill, Tennessee, brought about a new erosion cycle. Glenn's early report (1911) and the author's later observations show that forest and hills sometimes protected the sod locally even where the trees were killed, and where the sod was protected no erosion occurred. As described by Glenn (1911, p. 78):

"The erosion starts near the bottom of a slope, and where the soil is porous rapidly cuts a steep-sided gully to a depth of 5 to 12 feet below the surface, where the underlying schist is as a rule still measurably firm. After a gully has reached its limit in depth it widens until its walls coalesce with the walls of adjacent gullies, by which time most of the soil has been removed."

Over much of the denuded area erosion has not been as complete as that above described. Narrow flat lands still persist between the parallel gullies, and uneroded, nearly flat summits of the hills are conspicuous. In some cases the gullies afford excellent examples of cross-grading in progress, with remnants of the antecedent rill surface still visible.

The erosional topography of this region was essentially mature before denudation took place wherever there was a well-established sod cover. The resistivity of the underlying soil to erosion is, however, so small that, lacking protection, the critical distance x_c is reduced nearly but not quite to zero. Consequently the walls between initial parallel ridges on steep slopes have sometimes coalesced, as described by Glenn. Within a few years after destruction of the vegetation the drainage density was increased locally from ten to one hundred fold, and where this occurred the end point of the new erosion cycle was quickly attained.

In the gully formation in the Pontotoc Ridge region in Mississippi and in the vicinity of Ducktown, Tennessee, surface and subsurface resistance R_i differed, the surface resistance being initially greater and the terrain initially stable against erosion. Reduction of surface resistance resulted from improper cultivation in the Pontotoc Ridge region and from partial destruction of vegetal cover by smelter fumes in the Ducktown region, and an active epicycle followed in each case. The formation of arroyos on overgrazed land affords another example of an epicycle of erosion where the value of x_c is less for underlying soil than for undisturbed surface cover.

[Editors' Note: Material has been omitted at this point.]

REFERENCES

[Editors' Note: Only the references cited in the preceding excerpt are reproduced here.]

Bailey, R. W., 1935, Epicycles of Erosion in the Valleys of the Colorado Plateau Province, *Jour. Geol.*, vol. 43, p. 337-355.

Glenn, L. C., 1911, Denudation and Erosion in the Southern Appalachian Region and the Monongahela Basins, *U.S. Geol. Survey, Prof. Paper 72*.

Happ, S. C., Rittenhouse, G., and Dobson, G. C., 1940, Some Principles of Accelerated Stream and Valley Sedimentation, *U. S. Dept. Agric. Tech. Bull.* 695, Washington, D.C.

Horton, R. E., 1932, Drainage Basin Characteristics, *Am. Geophys. Union Tr.*, p. 350-361.

Wooldridge, S. W., and Morgan, R. S., 1937, *The Physical Basis of Geography*, Longmans, Green & Co., London, 435 pages.

16

Reprinted from pages 617–622 of *Geol. Soc. America Bull.* 67:597–646 (1956)

EVOLUTION OF DRAINAGE SYSTEMS AND SLOPES IN BADLANDS AT PERTH AMBOY, NEW JERSEY

S. A. Schumm

[*Editors' Note:* In the original, material precedes this excerpt.]

EVOLUTION OF THE DRAINAGE NETWORK

Effect of Stage on Angles of Junction

In the early stage of basin development stream channels grow headward until they establish major drainage divides; the relief ratio then reaches a fixed value, but changes in channel network continue until a large portion of the basin mass is removed. Thus, the relief ratio becomes fixed before other network characteristics become constant. This is especially true of drainage density in the Perth Amboy area.

Angles of junction of tributaries, resurveyed in 1952, showed some marked differences from corresponding angles in the 1948 map. The writer reasoned that systematic changes were occurring in the drainage pattern as a normal part of the erosional development of the basins.

Horton (1945, p. 349) recognized that the course followed by a new tributary is governed by both the slope of the ground over which it flows and the gradient of the channel to which it is tributary. Where the ground slope is great in relation to the gradient of the master stream a tributary joins at almost right angles; where master-stream gradient and valley-side slope are almost the same the tributary almost parallels the main channel, joining it at a small angle. Horton expresses this as follows:

$$\cos Z_c = \tan S_c / \tan S_g$$

where the cosine of the entrance angle or angle of junction, measured between the tributary and main channel above the point of junction, equals the ratio of the tangent of the main channel gradient to the tangent of the gradient of the tributary stream or of the ground slope over which the tributary flows. It follows that

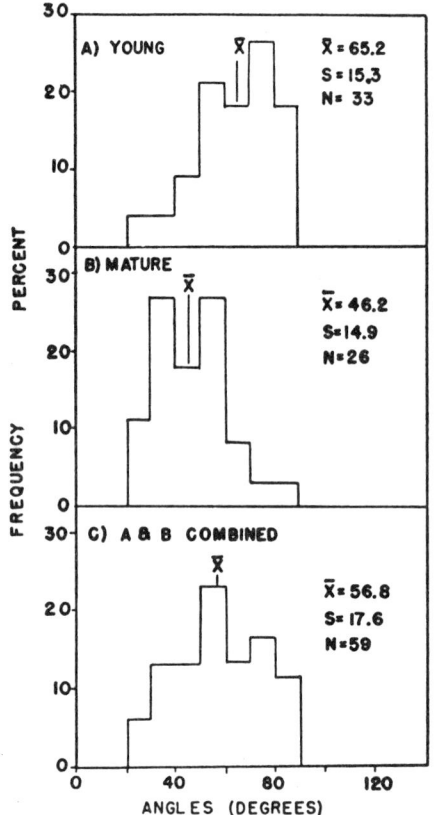

FIGURE 21.—FREQUENCY-DISTRIBUTION HISTOGRAMS OF YOUNG, MATURE, AND COMBINED ANGLES OF JUNCTION

during the early part of basin development, stream-entrance angles change with stream gradients.

Thus, a tributary will develop with an initially large angle of junction; then as the ratio between the two gradients increases the angle of junction decreases. Horton notes that as the ratio increases from 0.3 to 0.9 angles decrease from 72.3° to 25.5°. The decrease is accomplished by lateral migration of the tributary toward the main channel and down-valley shift of the junction.

The writer measured 61 entrance angles on the 1948 Perth Amboy map. The frequency-distribution histogram is broad and flat-topped with angles ranging from 24° to 90° (Fig. 21C; Table 9).

If the assumed changes occur, then by classifying all entrance angles according to stage of development of their tributary drainage basins a significant difference should occur between

TABLE 9.—FREQUENCY DISTRIBUTIONS OF ANGLES OF JUNCTION

Sample	Class mid-values in degrees							$\bar{x}$	s	N
	25	35	45	55	65	75	85			
Combined angles	4	8	8	14	8	10	7	56.8	17.6	59
Mature angles	3	7	5	7	2	1	1	65.2	15.3	26
Young angles	1	1	3	7	6	9	6	46.2	14.9	33

the means of youthful and more mature basins. The basins were separated into two groups on the basis of the existence of flat, undissected areas within the drainage areas, classifying as young basins capable of headward extension or having undissected areas within their drainage areas. The frequency-distribution histograms of each group (Fig. 21) show an expected overlap, but the means of the two groups are significantly different as judged by a t-test. The mean of the youthful class is 65°, that of the older group 46°. The probability that such a difference or greater would occur by chance alone is about 1 in 10,000. A reasonable explanation of the observed difference in angles is the shifting of tributary channels in response to changes in the gradient ratio.

A similar test was applied to angles of bifurcation, defined as the angles between two approximately equal first-order branches. In this case, the stream has bifurcated at its upper end, whereas in the tributary junction referred to above a branch has grown from the trunk of an existing major drainage line. Twenty angles of bifurcation were measured from youthful drainage basins having undissected areas. The mean is 62.1°, compared with the mean of the youthful angles of tributary junction, 65.2°. The frequency distributions of both samples have such great dispersions that this observed difference in means is not significant.

Remapping of the drainage pattern revealed changes in the values of tributary entrance angles and angles of bifurcation. Table 10 shows data for mean entrance angles and angles of bifurcation measured from the 1948 and 1952 drainage maps. There is a decrease of 5.3° in the

TABLE 10.—ANGLES OF BIFURCATION AND ANGLES OF JUNCTION

	Mean angles (degrees)		Standard deviation (s)		Number in sample (N)	
	1948	1952	1948	1952	1948	1952
Angles of bifurcation	62.1	53.3	13.4	17.5	20	12
Angles of junction:						
Total	56.8	53.6	17.6	18.5	59	46
Young	65.2	59.9	15.3	17.1	33	29
Mature	46.2	43.0	14.9	14.9	26	17

mean of the youthful tributary-junction angles, but the standard deviation of each distribution is so large that a statistical test of the significance of difference between the means shows that such a difference would be expected through chance alone 20 per cent of the time and is not significant. This is true also of the difference between the mature angles, 3.2°.

The means of the young angles in both 1948 and 1952 are significantly different from those of the mature angles. It is interesting to note that the means for the total, youthful and mature angles decreased by several degrees during the 4-year period. The difference in each case is not statistically significant but suggests that with more time a significant change might occur.

Only the angles of bifurcation showed a significant reduction, 8.8°, between 1948 and 1952. Only 12 of the 20 original angles could be recognized and measured in 1952. The extreme youthfulness of the newly formed drainage basins, with rapid lowering of channel gradients in progress, is the cause of the great change in bifurcation angle.

A comparison of the drainage patterns showed marked drainage changes. Twelve new tributaries were added to the drainage system between mappings. Coincidentally, 12 others were eliminated, 6 by abstraction or lateral expansion of a more competent neighbor, 2 by angle reduction to the minimum with collapse of the divide and union of the streams, while the remaining 4 were in small, shrinking basins surrounded by headward-growing channels. Two of these channels were originally near the lower limiting area of channel formation, 11.8 and 15.3 square feet. It is interesting to note that both stages of Glock's (1931) drainage-development series are represented here: extension and integration, with abstraction as the major process of integration. Capture occurred in two other instances. Examples of the straightening of the stream channels were numerous.

One other change of pattern noted is the lateral shift of the major tributaries toward the center of the basin. This migration toward a common axis within the system is gradual, but the asymmetry of all high-order transverse-valley profiles testifies to its presence.

A series of drainage patterns traced from the 1948 and 1952 maps (Fig. 22) illustrates some of the changes during that period. The basins illustrated have steep channel gradients, and erosion would be rapid. In addition, the fill is easily eroded and presents few structural obstacles to drainage-channel modifications.

The following generalizations summarize changes in the drainage network at Perth Amboy: A tributary to a channel of higher order develops with an entrance angle dependent on the ratio between channel and ground slope. Because of relatively slower degradation of the main channel, a downstream migration of the point of junction occurs with lessening of the entrance angle. If the ratio between main-channel gradient and tributary gradient remains constant (steady state), no changes in junction will occur except those caused by chance structural irregularities in the fill. As channel gradation spreads throughout the entire system the main-channel gradient will first reach an essentially constant value, but the tributary gradient will continue to lower, with a lessening of the junction angle. When the junction angle becomes very small, lateral planation removes the intervening divide, and the junction migrates upstream. Comparable evolution of stream-entrance angles and drainage patterns in other regions may occur only in youthful areas with a high relief ratio, but similarities between Perth Amboy and other areas in other aspects of drainage-basin morphology suggest that similar

In the initial stage the steep front of the terrace was probably strongly rilled. Because the upper surface of the terrace drained toward the front the rills quickly advanced across the lip of the terrace onto the essentially flat upper

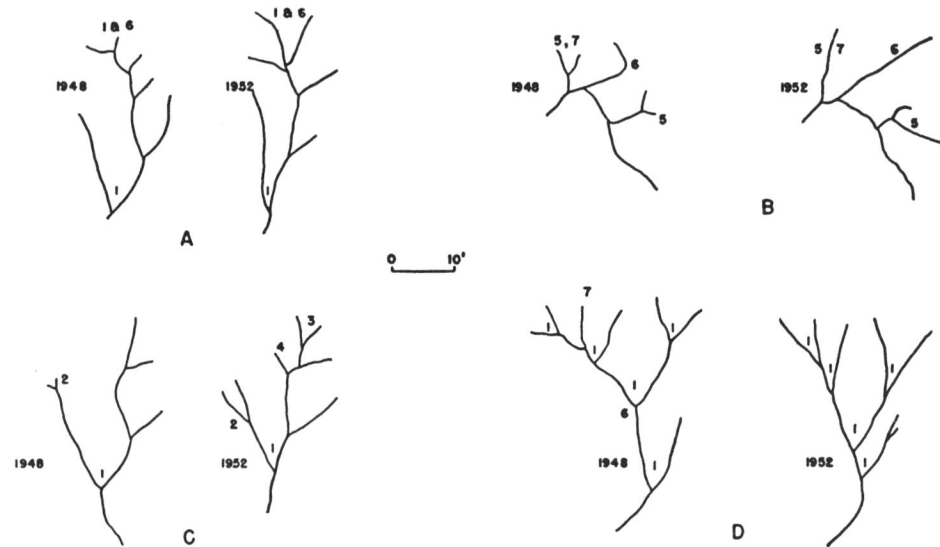

FIGURE 22.—DRAINAGE-PATTERN CHANGES IN SELECTED BASINS BETWEEN 1948 AND 1952 AT PERTH AMBOY

Basins A, C, and D are steep gradient streams. Basin B is a youthful basin on the upper surface of the terrace. Drainage changes are indicated by numbers on the figures:

1 Angle of junction change
2 Migration of junction
3 Bifurcation
4 Addition of tributary

5 Angle of bifurcation change
6 Channel straightening
7 Elimination of tributary

changes although perhaps less obvious, are nevertheless slowly occurring in all expanding drainage systems.

Because the observed drainage-pattern changes were occurring mainly as the stream channels were rapidly downcutting, any uplift of a land surface might initiate the same changes. Studies of drainage patterns on the Pleistocene terraces of the Atlantic Coast, for example, might indicate that height above base level and stage are correlatable with angles of junction.

Evolution of the Perth Amboy Drainage Pattern

From the observed systematic drainage changes at Perth Amboy and the known development of a network within the limiting values of basin area, it may be possible to deduce from the existing pattern the initial and future patterns.

surface. The channels most favored by chance encounter with weak patches of fill deepened and grew rapidly toward the divides of the individual small watersheds. These deeply cut permanent channels followed the path of initial drainage concentration manifested as faint channel traces on the upper surface. Channel traces of this type were observed at Perth Amboy in areas of headward channel development. The permanent channels follow these faint swales on the original surface because there the discharge of runoff is concentrated from the entire watershed. A headward developing incised channel is hydrophilic, advancing always toward maximum water supply.

The most vigorously developing initial rill channel thus dominated its less effective neighbors and established itself as the axis of a broadening ovate drainage basin. Its permanence was decided initially by a favored position in line with the axis of a shallow watershed on the terrace surface from which it was supplied with more runoff than its competitors. It may also have struck zones of weaker material in its bed. The added runoff allowed

stages of the Perth Amboy development, thus forming the first major tributary (Fig. 24, 1, 2). The tributary end grew normal to the main channel until it came under the influence of the forward slope of the terrace when its growth

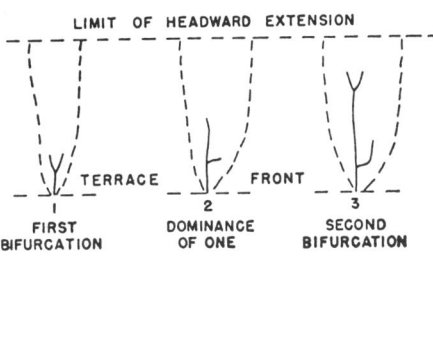

FIGURE 24.—SUGGESTED EVOLUTION OF THE PERTH AMBOY DRAINAGE PATTERN

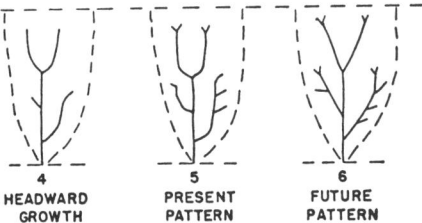

FIGURE 23.—POSSIBLE DEVELOPMENT OF ANGLES OF BIFURCATION

(1) Angle remains unchanged; (2) One channel becomes dominant; (3) On steepest slopes angles decrease and channels unite.

deepening of the drainage channel with corresponding oversteepening and collapse of its valley-side slopes. As soon as lateral expansion of the drainage basin produced sufficiently long slopes, tributary development set in on these slopes.

As the channel outstripped its neighbors the expanding drainage area permitted its bifurcation. The comparison of angles of bifurcation on the 1948 and 1952 maps suggests three predictions of possible future development of a bifurcated channel: (1) both segments of the bifurcated channel continue to grow headward unchanged in angle (Fig. 23, 1); (2) one segment becomes dominant and straightens its channel, while the other segment becomes tributary (Fig. 23, 2); (3) on steep slopes the angle of bifurcation reduces in accordance with the Sc/Sg ratio, and the two segments become one (Fig. 23, 3).

It is postulated that (2) occurred in the early

direction altered and its upper segment developed parallel to the main channel (Fig. 24, 3). Perhaps the next permanent bifurcation was as indicated in Figure 24, 3, followed by headward growth (Fig. 24, 4) and other branches and bifurcations to yield the major elements of the present pattern (Fig. 24, 5; Pl. 1).

As these streams incised their channels secondary tributaries formed on the slopes of the valley walls. These tributaries were under the influence of the rapidly degrading main channels; many still are in the youthful headwater areas. Figure 25 is a frequency-distribution histogram of the angles measured between tributaries and the segments of the main channel (Table 11). The modal class lies between limits of 90° and 100°, indicating a right-angle pattern in accordance with a low Sc/Sg ratio. The earliest-formed of these tributaries became the most important and hindered the development of younger neighbors on adjoining slopes. This is borne out by the fact that the mean distance separating first-order streams along the

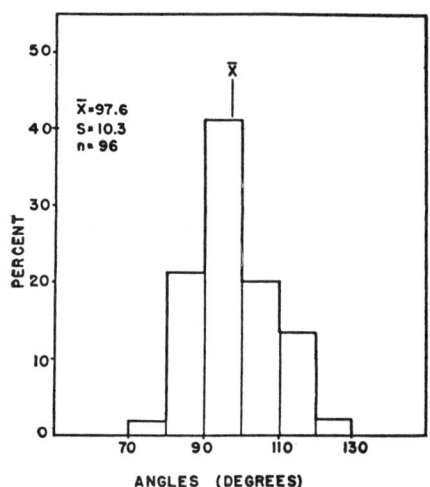

FIGURE 25.—FREQUENCY-DISTRIBUTION HISTOGRAMS OF ANGLES BETWEEN TRIBUTARIES AND SEGMENTS OF THE MAIN CHANNEL

TABLE 11.—FREQUENCY DISTRIBUTION OF ANGLES BETWEEN TRIBUTARIES AND MAIN CHANNEL

Sample	Mid-values in degrees						$\bar{x}$	s	N
	75	85	95	105	115	125			
Angles of junction	2	20	40	19	13	2	97.6	10.3	96

main channel (4.3 feet) is smaller than the mean distance separating first- and second-order stream channels (7.6 feet). Order number thus provides a rough means of classifying channels according to age; the oldest tributary channels have the higher order number.

The present faintly trellised pattern of the principal large-order channels (Fig. 24, 5; Pl. 1) is not considered permanent. It is supposed that the angles of junction become smaller with the increased Sc/Sg ratio, and the lateral shifting of the larger tributaries toward the main channel would result in the acute-angled dendritic drainage pattern that is typical of mature areas of simple structure. This change would involve considerable lateral planation and channel straightening, with a modified final pattern perhaps like that in Figure 24, 6.

If, as previously noted, a positive relationship exists between stream gradients, maximum slopes, and relative relief (expressed as the relief ratio), it follows that the Sc/Sg ratio should vary as the relief ratio. Because entrance angles, and therefore the total drainage pattern, are dependent on this Sc/Sg ratio, similar areas differing only in relative relief probably have recognizable differences in drainage pattern, at least in the early stages of development.

[Editors' Note: Material has been omitted at this point.]

REFERENCES

[Editors' Note: Only the references cited in the preceding excerpt are reproduced here.]

Glock, W. S., 1931, The development of drainage systems: a synoptic view: Geog. Rev., v. 21, p. 475–482

Horton, R. E., 1945, Erosional development of streams and their drainage basins; hydrophysical approach to quantitative morphology: Geol. Soc. America Bull., v. 56, p. 275–370

DEVELOPMENT OF DRAINAGE SYSTEMS ON AN UPRAISED LAKE FLOOR*

MARIE MORISAWA
Antioch College, Yellow Springs, Ohio

ABSTRACT. The newly upraised lake floor at Hebgen Lake, Montana, supplied a natural laboratory on which to observe the origin and development of drainage systems. Analyses of data obtained over a two year period suggest that manner and rate of drainage development, as well as stream morphology, depend upon the slope of the initial land surface and type of material. Silty areas are more susceptible to rapid, ephemeral changes than are sandy regions. Silty flat areas become covered with an intricate network of many short, steep tributaries which flow into wide, shallow, low-gradient valleys. Networks developed on sandy areas are more permanent and simpler with straight streams and narrow valleys. Statistical differences in measurements support the proposition that stream morphology depends upon conditions of geology and topography rather than on stage of the erosion cycle. The development of upper levels in these watersheds are the natural order of events and not the result of several erosion cycles.

Drainage changes are conservative and development of stream pattern follows the original outline. Although there are changes of stream length, gradient, and angle of junction, they are not statistically significant as the watershed quickly reaches a steady state. Integration of the system takes place simultaneously with expansion to maintain the overall dynamic equilibrium of the basin. Just as an individual stream may be graded, so a whole drainage basin moves toward and maintains a steady state.

INTRODUCTION

Many recent advances have been made in the quantitative geomorphology of drainage basins. However, most of this work has been concerned with the morphometry of watersheds formed long ago, with drainage already developed. Glock (1931) and more recently Schumm (1956) discussed the development of drainage systems. Glock's study was of drainage networks, all of which had been established for an undetermined length of time. By astute observation he categorized developing watersheds into the stages of extension and integration, emphasizing that the processes and characteristics of the stages overlapped.

Schumm (1956) studied actual changes in drainage systems developing on badland topography. Although his paper added valuable knowledge to our understanding of the growth of drainage basins, again the network was already well established. His study started in 1948, whereas the area had been exposed to erosion since 1929.

In August, 1959 an earthquake occurred at Hebgen Lake, Montana, which supplied an ideal natural laboratory for the direct observation of the development of drainage systems. As a result of the quake, the lake was tilted so that the north shore was drowned and the south shore was upraised, exposing some 8 to 20 feet of former lake bottom and beach (fig. 1). Here was an opportunity to study the enlargement of drainage systems from the beginning on differing materials and under varying physical conditions. A project was immediately set up for mapping and studying the development of drainage on this newly exposed area.

---

* The research reported in this document has been made possible through support and sponsorship by the United States Department of the Navy, Office of Naval Research, Geography Branch, under Contract Nonr-3254 (00), Project NR 389-130. Reproduction in whole or in part is permitted for any purpose of the United States Government.

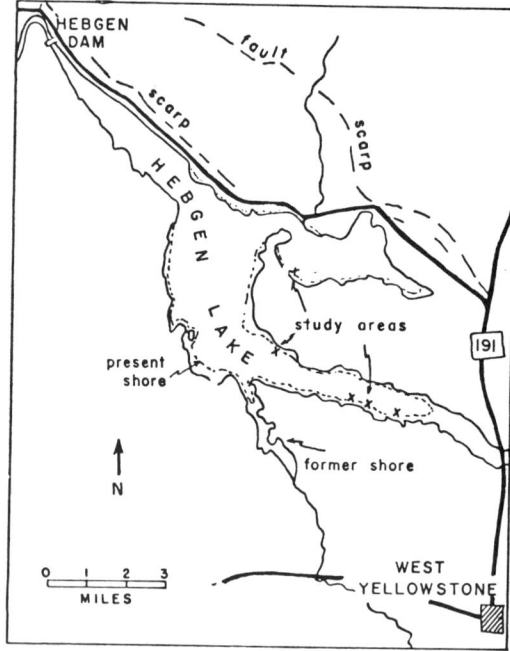

Fig. 1. Index map, Hebgen Lake, Montana.

The research was made possible through support and sponsorship of the Geography Branch, Office of Naval Research under contract Nonr-3254 (00), Project NR 389-130 with Montana State University. Mr. and Mrs. Ian Adams assisted in the field during the summer of 1960, and Ronald K. Fowler assisted in 1961. The writer is indebted to John Hack and Stanley Schumm of the U. S. Geological Survey who read the manuscript and offered valuable criticism and suggestions.

DESCRIPTION OF DRAINAGE AREAS

The exposed lake floor varied in surface conditions and in type of material. Where the lake bottom had sloped gently, wide expanses of level or slightly undulating land were uplifted. Such areas were composed of fine silts and clays and tended to develop mudcracks upon drying out. If the lake had approached the former shore along a cliff, a much steeper and narrower strip was now exposed. Such steeply sloping ground surfaces were composed of coarser materials, sands and gravels.

Gullies and, indeed, whole stream systems have now developed on these surfaces as a result of several factors: (a) initial swash by the rapidly receding water of the lake as it topped the dam during the quake; (b) dessication of the clay and mud, which not only provided initial channelways but also now aids further erosion; (c) numerous new springs which cut valleys during their period of flow (three of these were still flowing in 1961 at the end of the period of study); and (d) the normal erosion caused by rainfall.

Weather records at the Hebgen Dam weather station show that rainfall in the first year of the study was 22.25 inches and for the second year was 30.70 inches. This is reckoned from August through the following July since the quake occurred during August. The increase the second year was mainly as a result of a heavy winter snowfall and a very rainy August. Summer rains are frequent, short, and intense. Winter snowcover is deep, and extreme temperatures indicate that frost heaving is important in the land-shaping processes. Spring melting accelerates both erosion as a result of augmented stream flow and mass movement as a result of soil thaw.

Although the wind was not perceived to erode effectively the landscape in these basins, wind was a factor in removing small loose material from the beach surface. Movement of fine, dry grains was frequent, often creating such "dust devils" that working was uncomfortable.

When newly uplifted, the shore was unvegetated except for former marshy areas which still retained the dead and drying reeds. However, by the second summer, many low flowering plants had begun to spread and take root. These will help stabilize and protect the beach and upraised lake floor.

MORPHOLOGY OF THE DRAINAGE SYSTEMS

These drainage systems are miniature in scale, almost models. However, because they are real and natural, they can tell us much about the principles of drainage development. The basins were carefully mapped, one year and again two years, after exposure so that changes could be noted. Seven basins

TABLE 1

Drainage network characteristics, steep ground slope

Basin	Order	1960 No of streams	1960 Total length*	1960 Mean gradient	1961 No of streams	1961 Total length*	1961 Mean gradient
2B	1	2	10.5	0.207	2	11.3	0.229
	2	1	16.0	0.131	1	15.2	0.105
2C	1	6	15.6	0.162	5	13.8	0.167
	2	2	9.1	0.174	2	8.7	0.174
	3	1	10.4	0.120	1	10.0	0.125
2D	1	4	11.0	0.172	2	27.9	0.124
	2	2	17.2	0.128	1	4.4	0.284
	3	1	4.0	0.250			
2E	1	5	22.7	0.238	4	20.5	0.308
	2	1	13.4	0.186	1	10.0	0.160
2F	1	2	2.0	0.300	1	13.1	0.069
	2	1	10.2	0.127			
2G	1	4	11.5	0.312	3	27.9	0.194
	2	2	11.9	0.268	1	4.4	0.010
	3	1	4.6	0.163			
2H	1	2	19.4	0.210	2	20.1	0.154
	2	1	5.0	0.150	1	5.0	0.140

* feet

on steep ground surfaces and five on flat ground are the basis for discussion in this paper, tables 1 and 2.

The distribution of stream lengths, divided on the basis of initial surface slope, is presented in table 3 and figure 2. Distributions are bimodal, showing a tendency for small streams to develop and a secondary tendency for much longer tributaries to grow. This is particularly pronounced in the case of flat ground and is probably the result of headward growth along mudcracks. As previously noted by Schumm (1956) stream length distributions are strongly skewed toward the shorter lengths.

The watersheds tend to follow Horton's (1945) law of stream numbers, the number of streams of each order forming an inverse geometric series with order (fig. 3). However, all of the basins do not conform to the laws of stream lengths or stream gradients. Aberrations from the straight line proposed by Horton (1945) are caused by abnormally steep and short second order tributaries in some cases, and in others by very long,, low gradient main streams, both characteristics of these networks. The first factor is a result of the quick headward growth of first order tributaries along mudcracks existing on the upper surfaces. Two tributaries forming a mudcrack join to make a second order stream, which then plunges 2 or 3 inches into the main valley (fig. 4). The second factor is a result of rapid erosion and limited available relief. The

TABLE 2

Drainage network characteristics, low ground slope

Basin	Order	1960			1961		
		No of streams	Total length*	Mean gradient	No of streams	Total length*	Mean gradient
1a	1	20	45.2	0.180	30	51.4	0.192
	2	7	18.3	0.324	9	31.6	0.187
	3	2	31.5	0.105	1	75.2	0.037
	4	1	47.4	0.019			
1b	1	25	59.9	0.247	27	64.8	0.206
	2	7	22.8	0.104	10	39.3	0.214
	3	2	21.6	0.069	2	20.8	0.071
	4	1	40.0	0.037	1	47.6	0.034
3	1	49	184.3	0.174	62	209.1	0.183
	2	15	108.3	0.084	23	139.0	0.176
	3	4	162.6	0.024	5	186.3	0.037
	4	1	66.3	0.011	1	71.8	0.018
4	1	11	29.0	0.129	6	36.3	0.159
	2	4	42.4	0.158	3	20.6	0.145
	3	1	20.9	0.112	1	21.3	0.131
	1				2	10.5	0.054
	2				1	29.2	0.140
5	1	19	68.7	0.113	20	60.2	0.126
	2	6	69.7	0.095	6	67.4	0.071
	3	1	74.5	0.067	1	62.2	0.036

* feet

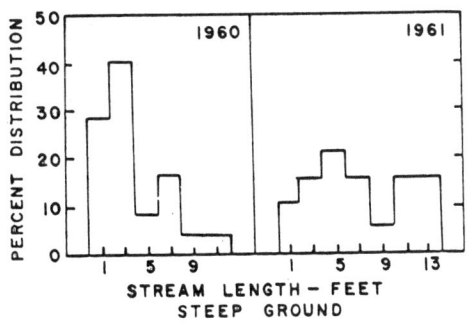
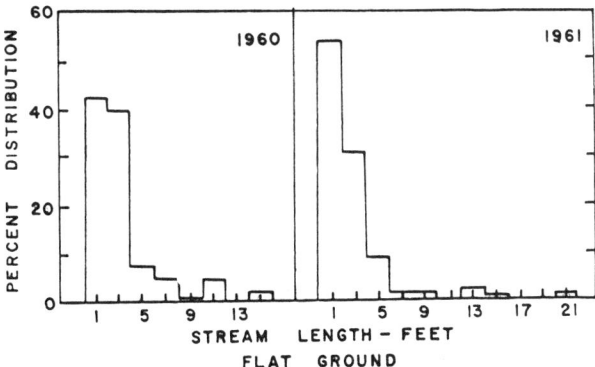

Fig. 2. Histograms of first-order stream length distribution.

TABLE 3

Distribution of first order stream lengths

Length feet	Percent frequency 1960	1961
Steep ground surface		
12-14	—	15.79
10-12	4.00	15.79
8-10	4.00	5.26
6-8	16.00	15.79
4-6	8.00	21.05
2-4	40.00	15.79
0-2	28.00	10.53
Level ground surface		
20-22	—	1.36
14-16	1.61	0.68
12-14	—	2.04
10-12	4.03	—
8-10	0.81	1.36
6-8	4.03	1.36
4-6	7.26	8.84
2-4	39.52	30.61
0-2	42.74	53.74

Development of Drainage Systems on an Upraised Lake Floor 345

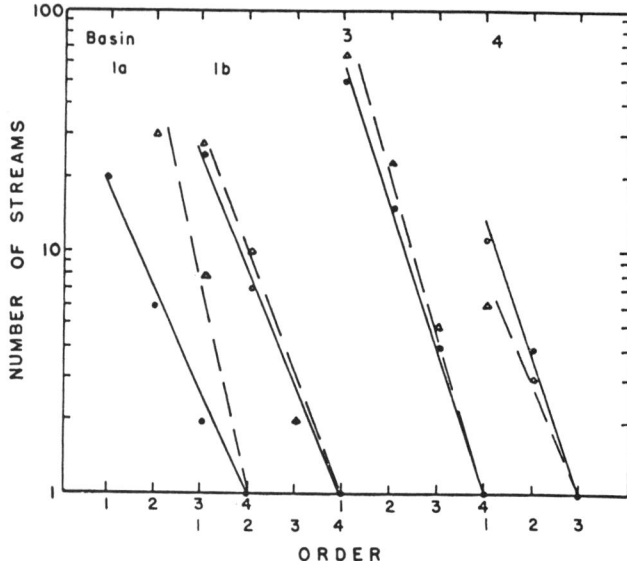

Fig. 3. Relation of number of streams to order.

major streams quickly reach a minimum gradient while the lower orders still maintain a steep grade, flowing down the main valley walls which are vertical.

Sideward and headward expansion of the main valley is aided by both summer dessication and winter freeze and thaw, which loosen blocks of material from the walls. These blocks then disintegrate and the sediment is washed downstream by meltwater or rain, or carried off by the wind. This combined action results in a very wide, shallow, vertical walled main valley, with a very low gradient. Despite the inordinate width of the valleys, there is a definite relationship between channel characteristics in each basin, proceeding downstream. At any point on the main channel, the log of channel length to that

Fig. 4. Drainage basin on flat ground surface.

point and the log of cross section area (width times depth) falls on a straight line (fig. 5).

Although each stream segment may have an "equilibrium" of its own and is "graded", these watersheds as a whole are apparently not yet in a steady state. In using the term steady state, we are treating the whole watershed as an open system. This has been done by other writers, Strahler (1952), Hack (1960) ,and Leopold and Langbein (1962). In an open system material and energy enter and leave the system, and there is a continuous interaction with the environment. In such a system the rate of import and export soon be· becomes balanced so that a point of dynamic equilibrium is reached called the steady state. In this stage the system is self-regulatory, if a change occurs it adjusts itself to compensate for it. When such a basin-wide dynamic equilibrium is reached, it is expected that the watershed will conform to the laws of drainage composition. This steady state has been attained by basin 5, which seems to be stabilized and conforms to the laws of stream numbers, stream length, and gradient. There seems, then, to be a very short time at the beginning stage of drainage development when the watershed is not in a steady state throughout the system. In general, unless it is a result of rock type or geologic structure, this state is transitory and not often observed.

Where it is the result of geologic structure or rock type, such as on the Appalachian Plateau (Morisawa, 1962), it is long-lasting. Here, on the Plateau, the differing lithology of the horizontal strata exerts a control on stream characteristics so that there are aberrations from Horton's laws. So evident is the development of an upper basin level as distinct from the main valley development, that it has called forth explanations by multiple erosion cycles and peneplains. By analogy with these Hebgen Lake watersheds, it is argued that such hypotheses are not necessary. Instead, multiple levels within these basins

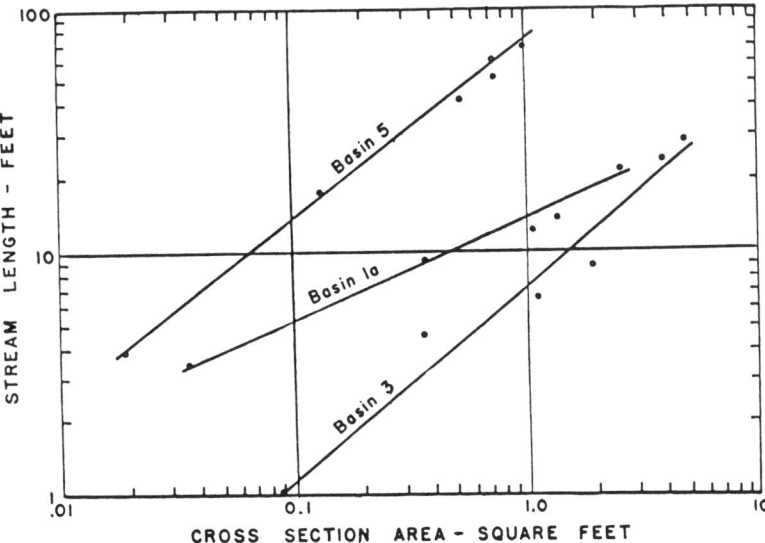

Fig. 5. Relation of stream length to cross section area.

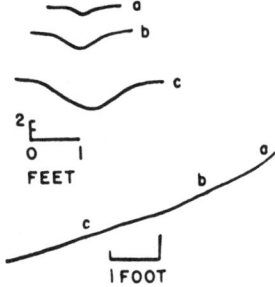

Fig. 6. Stream profiles, steep sandy area.

are assumed to be the regular order of events. The presence of an upper level is simply the result of the orderly development of drainage in a region of horizontal sediments of differing lithology. A more resistant layer merely acts as a local level controlling drainage morphology.

CONTROL OF DRAINAGE BY PHYSICAL CONDITIONS

There is a definite control of morphology by the physical conditions of surface slope and type of material. Examination of the data obtained over this two year period of study indicates that stream networks developed on steep, sandy ground surfaces are straighter and simpler than those that develop on flat, silty surfaces. Streams on sandy beaches, with high infiltration rates, show a slow increase in growth of tributaries or size of drainage net. Their cross-sections are the typical V-shape of "youth" (fig. 6), and first order streams enter the trunk stream at grade. The drainage nets are simple, and streams are straight (figs. 7 and 8).

Streams on silty material on flat ground surfaces, under the same climatic conditions, resemble the arroyo-type transverse profile, with wide, shallow,

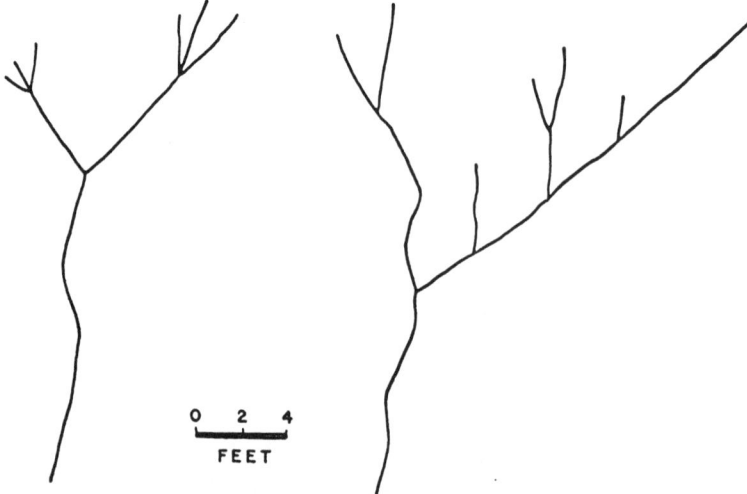

Fig. 7. Drainage net, steep sandy area.

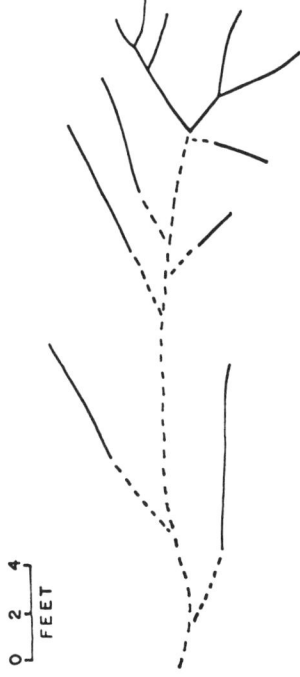

Fig. 8. Drainage net, flat sandy area.

vertically walled valleys (fig. 9). Their drainage nets are intricate and angular (fig. 10), and low order tributaries tend to enter the trunk at ungraded junctions. In these systems, headwater erosion is along cracks formed on the dessicated mud flats. Valley walls are widened and straightened by infall.

First order stream gradients on flat sandy ground averaged 0.114 and on flat silty ground, 0.147. The difference between them was not significant. On steep ground the first order gradient of streams in sand was 0.216, in silt it was

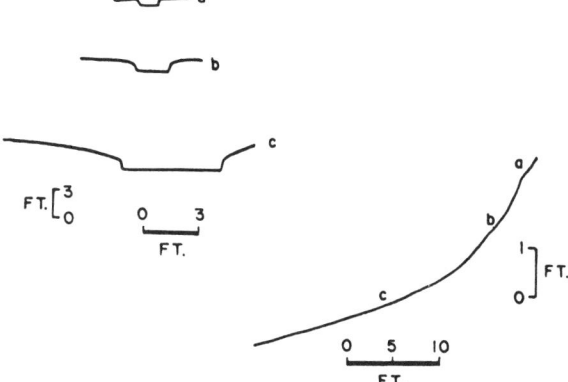

Fig. 9. Stream profiles, flat silty area.

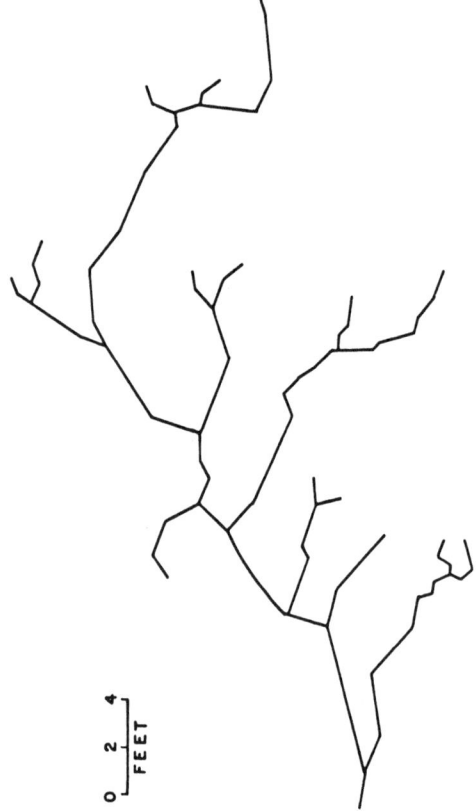

Fig. 10. Drainage net, flat silty area.

0.251. The difference between these two was not significant either. Note, however, that for both slopes, the mean gradient on silt is steeper than on sand This was also found to be true for stream gradients studied by Morisawa (1962) on the Appalachian Plateau.

Analysis of variance of first order stream lengths between flat and steep surfaces and between silty and sandy materials was carried out. The mean first order length on flat ground was 4.8 feet on sand and 3.2 feet on silt. The difference between them was not statistically significant. However, considering the scale of the watersheds, it seems the difference of 1.6 feet ought to be *geologically* significant. For steep surfaces, the mean first order length on sand was 3.7 feet and on silt, 1.4 feet. This was found to be statistically significant. In silty areas there is a significant difference, whether steep or flat. The difference between stream lengths on sandy areas, steep or flat surfaced, was not significant.

On both steep and flat slopes, the first order streams were longer on sandy material than on silty. And, although short, there are many more ephemeral channels on silt, whereas on sand there are fewer, longer streams that, once established, are permanent. Because of the ease of infiltration, each foot of channel needs a larger contributing area on sand than on silt. Hence the con-

TABLE 4

Changes in drainage characteristics

	Low surface slope	Steep surface
Total length all basins	+131.2 feet	+2.2 feet
Stream length per basin	+ 26.24 feet	+0.3 feet
First order length—paired	+ 0.282 feet	– 0.18 feet
Total number of streams	+ 35	–11
Number of streams per basin	+ 7	– 1.4
First order stream gradient—paired	– 0.025	– 0.180

stant of channel maintenance (Schumm, 1956) is greater, and short tributaries never form on sand.

DEVELOPMENT OF DRAINAGE SYSTEMS

Perhaps the most surprising thing about these drainage systems is their stability, even in this early period of growth. This means a very quick adjustment to their environment and attainment of a steady state. Although changes do occur, they are, on the whole, minor and the overall pattern remains essentially as initiated. The main adjustments tend toward establishing a steady state in the system. In general, more changes took place in the basins eroded on the flat silty shore than those on steep sandy beaches, table 4.

On steep surfaces, when the available relief has been reached, simplification and integration of the basin occur to reduce the order of the net and decrease the number of streams. The gradient of stream segments is lowered, generally accompanied by a downstream migration of junctions. As a result of this, main trunks are often shortened but tributaries may or may not be extended. When relief is still available, first order stream lengths increase with a corresponding increase in gradient. Because of the steep ground slope, a slight addition to the length causes a substantial steepening of grade. Although the total first order length increased from 1960 to 1961, the length of those streams that could be recognized from one year to the next actually decreased. The overall increase in first order length was caused by the loss of tributaries so that a second order tributary became a first.

Enlargement of drainage networks along mudcracks in silty areas has already been discussed. A summary of changes from 1960 to 1961 is given in table 4. These basins gained in number of streams as well as in total length. Without pairing the streams (that is, the same stream in 1960 and 1961) there is an overall decrease in mean first order length. This is a result of the addition of numerous tiny tributaries to the network, thus bringing down the average. However, the more permanent first order streams, recognizable from the first to the second year, showed an average gain of length. This difference of +0.282 feet was not significant by a paired t-test (Croxton, 1953). For first order streams, recognizable from one year to the next, the decrease in gradient of –0.025 was not statistically significant either. Changes, then, though they occur are not significant.

Development of Drainage Systems on an Upraised Lake Floor

TABLE 5

Frequency distribution of angles of junction and bifurcation of first order streams

	Class mid-values in degrees							
	25	35	45	55	65	75	85	95
Angle of junction								
1960	7	10	7	13	8	5	15	10
1961	7	9	15	10	13	10	16	11
Angle of bifurcation								
1960	5	13	12	13	12	7	11	8
1961	8	8	9	13	12	10	19	10

Because some of the angles of junction had noticeably changed, and since Schumm (1956) suggested there should be a difference, an analysis of the angles of junction and of bifurcation were carried out. There was found to be

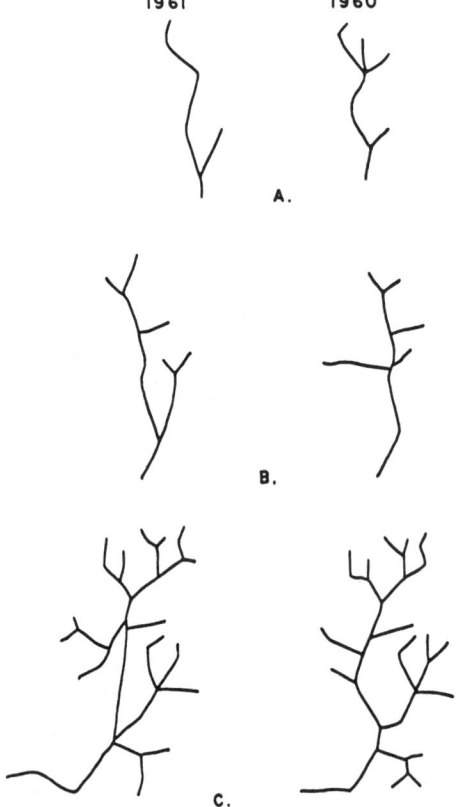

Fig. 11. Changes in drainage networks.

no significant shift in either the angles of junction or in angles of bifurcation (table 5).

In all these basins the process of extension and integration proceed together. Within the same network, the pattern is elaborated by initiation of new tributaries and the elongation of old, and at the same time the system tends toward elimination of tributaries (fig. 11). For example, figure 11C shows changes in one branch of a larger stream system. In some places tributaries have been added, in other places they have been subtracted. Some stream segments have been lengthened, whereas other segments have been shortened. The overall effect in a single basin is very little change in total stream length. This seems to be true in all basins. A loss of length is compensated by added stream length elsewhere. Once a basin has reached a steady state, this seems to be true of other characteristics such as number of streams. Addition of first order streams at the headwaters is balanced by integration downstream.

Hence as the upper part of a basin in the steady state expands, reaching out to enlarge its drainage territory, the lower part of the network becomes integrated, losing numbers and length. When integration or loss of tributaries occurs in the upper part of a watershed, the lower part will increase length by meandering or changing its course. Thus bifurcation ratio, length ratio, gradient ratio, etc. tend to remain constant for a basin that has established a dynamic equilibrium. The whole system seems to be in a steady state, though in a continous compensational flux.

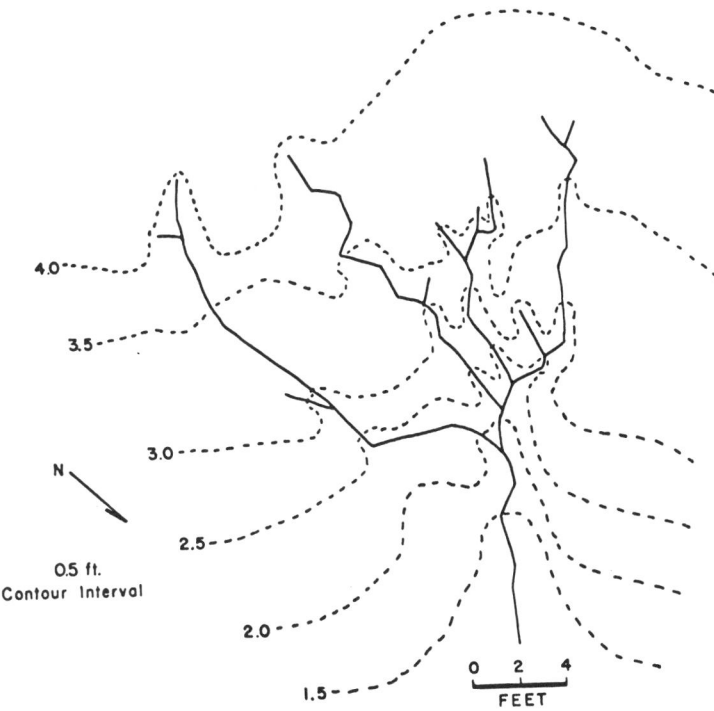

Fig. 12. Basin no. 4, 1960.

Development of Drainage Systems on an Upraised Lake Floor

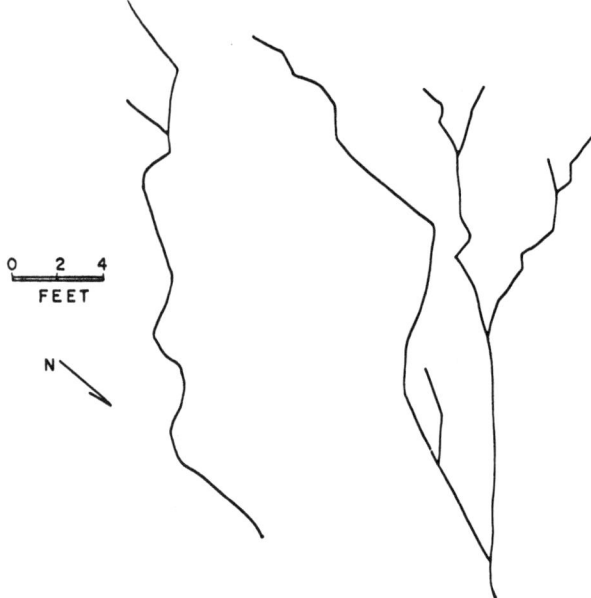

Fig. 13. Basin no. 4, 1961, after capture of part of the watershed.

Figure 11 shows some of the drainage changes that took place and illustrates the balancing that occurs in such a dynamic equilibrium. The top diagram shows integration of tributaries and at the same time an elongation of a lower stream segment. There is also a downstream shift in junction with a narrowing of the entrance angle. The middle nets provide examples of abstraction and elongation, with a major shift in the main channel. A shift of the main channel of these streams is common as the valleys are very wide and flat. At the bottom change is shown by abstraction and the addition of new tributaries. This also illustrates that there is not always a shift of junction downstream.

On the whole drainage changes are conservative, and development tends to follow the outline as initially originated. Growth of the network can be foreseen by studying the area closely, noting faint swales, cracks, flatness of topography, irregularities, heaps of debris, etc. Shifts in the main channel which flows in a wide, flat valley account for many changes in the drainage form (fig. 11).

One case of piracy is shown in figures 12 and 13, diagrams of basin 4. Here an outside tributary has captured part of the basin. It is interesting that, with hindsight, one could see, by examination of the topography, not only the capture but also the other drainage changes that occurred. This is indicated somewhat on the maps (figs. 12 and 13) but is even more evident in the field, where faint drainage traces can be seen.

CONCLUSIONS

On this upraised lake floor, where there is essential homogeneity of material and no structural control, the manner and rate of development depends in great part on the slope of the initial land surface and type of material. Silty areas are more susceptible to rapid, ephemeral changes than sandy areas. Silty, flat regions become covered with an intricate network of many short, steep tributaries which flow into a wide, shallow, long, low-gradient valley. On the other hand, networks developed on sand or steep surfaces are slower to form, more permanent, and simpler, having straight channels with narrow valleys. The difference in aspect of streams on these beaches supports the proposition that stream morphology depends upon physical conditions of topography and geology, rather than on stage of the erosion cycle.

Furthermore, study of these basins indicates that streams, and indeed, whole watersheds quickly reach a steady state in their development. The time during disequilibrium is extremely short. However, in some of these basins, as well as on the Appalachian Plateau, geologic structure or rock type may delay the establishment of a basin-wide steady state. In such regions the presence of an upper level in a watershed is the result of the orderly development of drainage and not of multiple erosion cycles.

On the whole, drainage changes are conservative once the steady state is established, and development follows the outline as initially originated with further growth along drainage traces. Integration of a stream network occurs simultaneously with its expansion. The main adjustments in the system are those that tend toward and maintain the dynamic equilibrium of the watershed as a whole. Just as individual streams become "graded", so a whole drainage area moves toward a steady state.

REFERENCES

Croxton, F. E., 1953, Elementary statistics with application in medicine: New York, Prentice-Hall, Inc., 376 p.

Glock, W. S., 1931, The development of drainage systems: a synoptic view: Geog. Rev., v. 21, p. 475-482.

Hack, J. T., 1960, Interpretation of erosional topography in humid temperate regions: Am. Jour. Sci., Bradley v. 258A, p. 80-97.

Horton, R. E., 1945, Erosional development of streams and their drainage basins, hydrophysical approach to quantitative morphology: Geol. Soc. America Bull., v. 56, p. 275-370.

Leopold, L. B., and Langbein, W. B., 1962, The concept of entropy in landscape evolution: U. S. Geol. Survey Prof. Paper 500A, 20 p.

Morisawa, M. E., 1962, Quantitative geomorphology of some watersheds in the Appalachian Plateau: Geol. Soc. America Bull., v. 73, p. 1025-1046.

Schumm, S. A., 1956, Evolution of drainage systems and slopes in badlands at Perth Amboy, New Jersey: Geol. Soc. America Bull., v. 67, p. 597-646.

Strahler, A. N., 1952, Dynamic basis of geomorphology: Geol. Soc. America Bull., v. 63, p. 923-938.

THREE GROWTH MODELS FOR STREAM CHANNEL NETWORKS

MICHAEL F. DACEY AND W. C. KRUMBEIN

Department of Geography and Department of Geological Sciences,
Northwestern University, Evanston, Illinois 60201

ABSTRACT

Three models that specify allowable branching events during the growth of stream channel networks through time are introduced. These models identify the possible topologic "growth paths" that may be followed as a network grows from a single link to one of magnitude n. The probability of occurrence of channel networks is calculated for magnitudes 2 to 6. One model has probabilities identical with those for Shreve's model of topologically random channel networks. The three models are compared with published data on 12 topologic studies of stream networks of magnitudes 4 to 6. The model with Shreve's probabilities fits 7 of the 12 data sets, a second model also fits 7 of them, and the third model does not fit any. Only one data set is not fit by at least one model. The results suggest that network growth by branching of exterior links alone is not adequate for development of the topologic diversity observed in natural stream channel networks. This conclusion conflicts with the prevalent view of contemporary geomorphology that headward growth is more rapid than sideward growth in dendritic drainage basins of small magnitude.

INTRODUCTION

A recent statement by Shreve (1975) is, in our view, ample justification of the probabilistic-topologic approach to drainage-basin geomorphology. His (1966, 1967) model of topologically random channel networks has successfully predicted a half dozen or more quantitative geomorphological aspects of drainage basins. Shreve's model is morphologic rather than genetic in that it does not specify any particular order of channel branching in basin development, but it does provide a probabilistic foundation for development of genetic models.

The present study extends the probabilistic-topologic approach to drainage-basin geomorphology by identifying a temporal sequence of branching events that generate the varied topologic forms of channel networks. Moreover, by changing the specification of allowable branching events, it identifies three probability distributions for the frequency of occurrence of topologically distinct channel networks of magnitude n, one of which agrees exactly with the probabilities in Shreve's model.

The aspect of network genesis emphasized here is the number of ways (growth paths) by which a channel network of magnitude $n + 1$ can develop from channel networks of magnitude n. Our models are genetic in a topological sense only, with no explicit considerations of link lengths or other basin metrics. Though our treatment is purely probabilistic, it is implicit in our models that normal processes of dendritic growth are involved. Most geomorphologists would probably agree that these include upslope, headward growth of the channels, with bifurcation at the growing tips, and the development of tributary channels farther downstream as the basin and its neighbors approach some optimum drainage density.

Bifurcation seems to appeal to many geomorphologists as the main process of growth, with tributary development secondary. In a strict sense, bifurcation implies an abrupt splitting of a single channel into two channels, each of which then develops its own growth path upslope from the point of bifurcation. Presumably, bifurcation requires some obstacle in the path of growing first-order channel tips. Conceivably a tree or the partial excavation of a boulder could split the channel rather than simply divert it to right or left. Suitable points for the development of tributaries along channel walls may be provided by surface irregularities or by accidental events such as the washing out of animal crossings or the toppling of trees that expose fresh soil. Another possibility that has not been given much attention is tributary development along one side or the other of a growing, first-order channel. One of us (WCK) has seen such a tributary form about 80 feet downstream of a ravine tip, where a glacial boulder excavated by undercutting from relatively soft till had provided the initial notch. A topographic map made after such an event would almost certainly suggest bifurcation rather than tributary development.

In order to include these several possibilities in network growth models, we have selected three sets of conditions involving bifurcation and tributary development. The three resulting models provide varying numbers of growth paths, thus furnishing a range of probabilities for the occurrence of each topologic form and providing values that can be checked against observations on actual stream networks. Comparisons are confined to magnitudes 4, 5, and 6, for which some data are available.

The sets of conditions selected for our models represent only part of a broad spectrum of probabilities associated with allowable events during network growth. As will be seen, our choice is based on sets of events that involve a decreasing probability of exterior link branching as opposed to branching of interior links. In addition, our choice was influenced by the relatively simple tests of the models that can be made with empirical data.

THREE GROWTH MODELS

Each of the three models is specified by two assumptions. The first is common to the models, and it specifies the growth path of channel networks. The second distinguishes the models in terms of the type of branching events that are allowed. To state these assumptions, some terminology is required.

The following terms are specified by

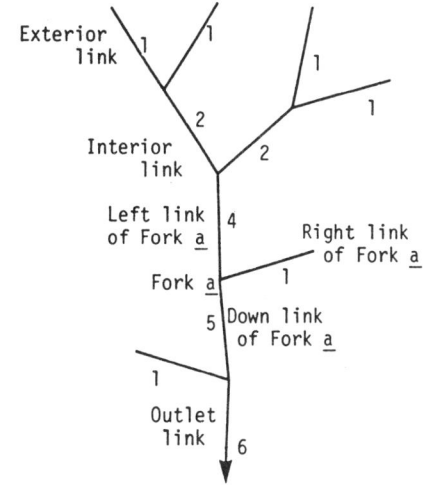

Fig. 1.—Diagram of components in a channel network of magnitude 6. Link magnitude is indicated by number opposite each link.

Shreve (1966, 1967): *channel network of magnitude* n, *link, exterior link, interior link, outlet link, fork, topologically distinct channel networks,* and *topologically identical channel networks.* A term given by Smart (1969) is *ambilateral class.* In addition, the three links that form a fork are called *right-link, left-link,* and *down-link.* Also, the single link of a magnitude 1 channel network is treated as an exterior link. Figure 1 illustrates some of these terms.

The three kinds of branching events that need to be made precise are bifurcation at the growing tips of channel networks and tributary development along the right and left sides of all links.

DEFINITION 1. *Only exterior links can bifurcate. The bifurcation of an exterior link of a channel network replaces that link by three links that form a fork having a left-link and a right-link that are exterior links.*

DEFINITION 2. *Every link can develop a tributary to the right or left. A right-side tributary in a link of a channel network replaces that link by three links that form a fork having a right-link that is an exterior link. A left-side tributary in a link of a channel network replaces that link by three*

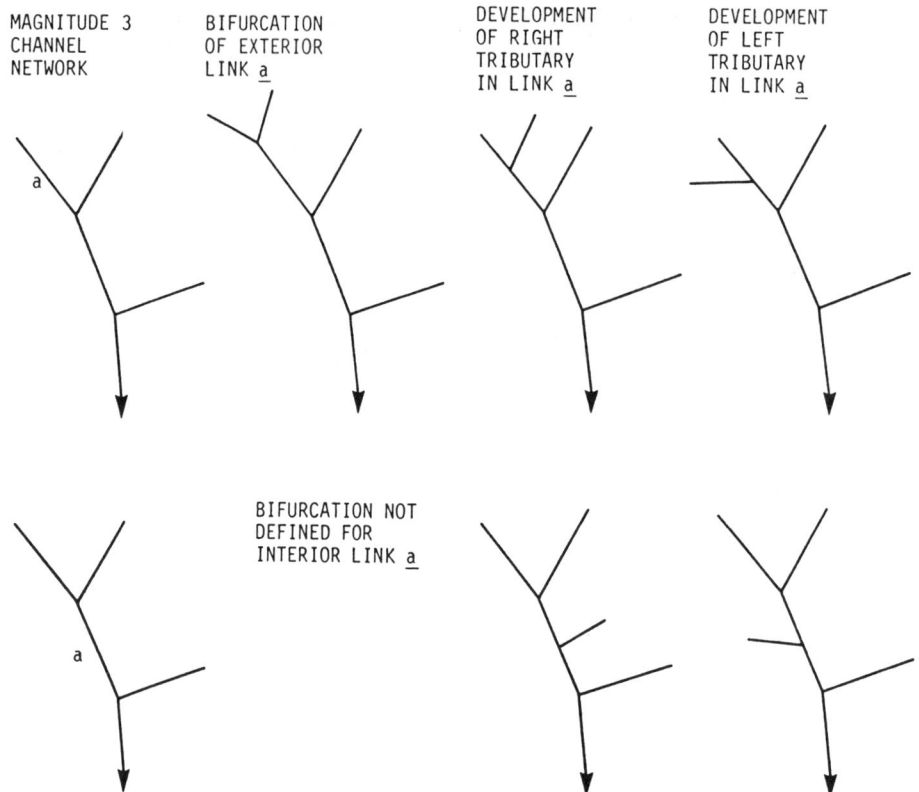

FIG. 2.—Diagrammatic illustration of bifurcation and right and left tributary development in network growth from magnitude 3 to 4.

links that form a fork having a left-link that is an exterior link.

DEFINITION 3. *Bifurcation or tributary development to right or left is a branching of a link in a channel network.*

Figure 2 illustrates these three types of branches. Two properties of branches are noted, and then some well-known properties of magnitude n channel networks are identified. The value of n is restricted to the positive integers.

PROPERTY 1. *The result of bifurcation or tributary development of a link in a magnitude n channel network is a magnitude $n + 1$ channel network.*

PROPERTY 2. *The results of bifurcation or tributary development (right or left) of a specified exterior link of a magnitude n channel network are topologically identical, whereas the results of a right or left tributary development along a specified interior link of a magnitude n channel network are topologically distinct.*

PROPERTY 3. *Every magnitude n channel network has $2n - 1$ links, of which n are exterior links and $n - 1$ are interior links.* Let $N(n)$ be the number of topologically distinct channel networks of magnitude n, and

$$N(n) = \frac{(2n - 2)!}{(n - 1)!\, n!}.$$

The first few values of $N(n)$ are 1, 1, 2, 5, 14, 42. Let $Q(n)$ be the number of ambilateral classes for magnitude n channel networks, and a closed form expression for $Q(n)$ is not known. The first few values of $Q(n)$ are 1, 1, 1, 2, 3, 6.

The model of network growth is specified by two assumptions. The first indicates that at time n there is a channel network of magnitude n that is obtained by branching of a link of the channel network for time $n - 1$. The second assumption specifies the allowable branching events and the probabilities for their occurrence. These allowable branching events are (1) for interior links, right and left tributary developments, and (2) for exterior links, bifurcation and right and left tributary developments. Since Property 2 indicates that the three kinds of branching events on an exterior link produce identical channel networks, these three events are grouped and assigned a single probability.

ASSUMPTION 1. *There is a sequence of channel networks such that at each time* n *there is a channel network of magnitude* n, *and the channel network for time* n + 1 *is the result of branching of a link of the channel network for time* n.

ASSUMPTION 2. *There are nonnegative numbers* u_n *and* v_n *such that the links of the channel network for time* n *have the following probabilities of branching:* P(*each interior link develops a tributary on the right*) $= u_n$, P(*each interior link develops a tributary on the left*) $= u_n$, P(*each exterior link branches*) $= v_n$; *additionally,* $2(n-1)u_n + nv_n = 1$.

Three special cases, out of many permitted by these assumptions, are defined for values of these probabilities. Model A has all $u_n = 0$ and $v_n = 1/n$, model B has $u_n = 1/2(2n - 1)$ and $v_n = 1/(2n - 1)$, and model C has $u_n = v_n = 1/(3n - 2)$.

Notice that the probabilities u_n and v_n for model A are obtained when the only allowable branching events are bifurcations of exterior links, and the n possible branching events for a magnitude n channel network occur with equal probability; those for model B are obtained when the only allowable branching events are right and left tributary developments on all links, and the $2(2n - 1)$ possible branching events for a magnitude n channel network occur with equal probability; those for model C are obtained when the only allowable branching events are right and left tributary developments on interior links and bifurcations on exterior links, and the $3n - 2$ possible branching events for a magnitude n channel network occur with equal probability. In these senses, the three models are defined by branching events that occur with equal probability, but the models differ in the specifications of the allowable kinds of branching events.

Next, a ratio is identified that measures the relative importance to channel network growth of branching of exterior and interior links. It indicates that the three models A, B, and C are ordered by decreasing importance of branching of exterior links.

PROPERTY 4. *Put* $F_n = P$(*interior link of magnitude n channel network branches*)/P(*exterior link of magnitude n channel network branches*). *For the models of Assumptions 1 and 2,* $F_n = 2(n-1)u_n/nv_n$; *for model A,* $F_n = 0$, *for model B* $F_n = 1 - \frac{1}{n}$, *for model C* $F_n = 2\left(1 - \frac{1}{n}\right)$.

Model A does not admit branching of interior links, and $F_n = 0$. For model B, $F_n < 1$ but F_n approaches 1 as n increases; this indicates that during the early growth of stream channel networks branching of exterior links occurs more frequently than tributary development on interior links, but that for larger magnitude channel networks branching of interior and exterior links are equally frequent. For model C and $n \geq 3$, $F_n > 1$; this indicates that tributary development on interior links occurs more frequently than branching of exterior links. Empirical testing of the models thus may yield insights into the relative importance to growth of channel networks by branching of interior and exterior links.

PROBABILITY DISTRIBUTIONS FOR THE MODELS

Although some properties of these three models can be derived theoretically, the probability distributions required for empirical analysis of channel networks of small magnitude are readily obtained by enumerating all possible growth paths. However, one theoretical property of immediate interest is the following demonstration that model B, where tributary development is the only allowable branching event, has the same probabilities as Shreve's (1966, 1967) model of topologically random channel networks.

THEOREM 1. *For model B and each time n, each of the $N(n)$ topologically distinct channel networks of magnitude n occurs with equal probability.*

Proof. Consider a channel network of magnitude n with $n \geq 2$. Corresponding to each of its n exterior links there is a channel network of magnitude $n - 1$ such that the magnitude n channel network is obtained by tributary development on a link of the magnitude $n - 1$ channel network. Thus this magnitude n channel network is obtained from at least n different tributary developments on magnitude $n - 1$ channel networks; moreover, the $N(n)$ topologically distinct, magnitude n channel networks are obtained from at least $nN(n)$ different tributary developments on links of magnitude $n - 1$ channel networks. Next, it is established that each magnitude n channel network is obtained by exactly n different tributary developments on magnitude $n - 1$ channel networks. There are $N(n - 1)$ topologically distinct channel networks of magnitude $n - 1$, each of which has $2n - 3$ links. Hence there are $2(2n - 3)N(n - 1)$ different ways that magnitude n channel networks are obtained by right and left tributary developments on each of the $2n - 3$ links of each of the $N(n - 1)$ topologically distinct, magnitude $n - 1$ channel networks. From Property 3,

$$nN(n) = 2(2n - 3)N(n - 1), \quad n = 2, 3, \ldots.$$

Hence, each of the $N(n)$ topologically distinct, magnitude n channel networks is obtained by n different tributary developments on magnitude $n - 1$ channel networks. Assumption 2 implies that for model B each of the $2(2n - 3)$ possible tributary developments on a magnitude $n - 1$ channel network occurs with equal probability. Since all magnitude $n - 1$ channel networks have $2n - 3$ links, if the $N(n - 1)$ topologically distinct, magnitude $n - 1$ channel networks occur with equal probability, then the $N(n)$ topologically distinct, magnitude n channel networks occur with equal probability $n/2(2n - 3)$. The induction argument is completed by noting there is only one channel network of magnitude 1.

Model B is undoubtedly only one of many growth mechanisms that yield probability distributions for occurrences of channel networks that are identical to those for the model of topologically random channel networks. S. Smart has informed us, by personal communication, that these probabilities are obtained by a growth model in which (1) each exterior link bifurcates or terminates with probabilities 0.5 and (2) if a link bifurcates, each of the two new exterior links bifurcates or terminates with probabilities 0.5. By starting with a magnitude 1 channel network, which terminates with probability 0.5 and bifurcates with the same probability, each of the $N(n)$ topologically distinct channel networks of magnitude n occurs with probability $2^{-(2n-1)}$; this probability reflects that a magnitude n channel network requires that its $n - 1$ interior links bifurcate, each with probability 0.5, and that its n exterior links terminate, each with probability 0.5. So, given that a magnitude n channel network occurs, the probability distribution for occurrences of the $N(n)$ topologically distinct channel networks of magnitude n is identical with that of model B and the model of topologically random channel networks. A different approach to generating the same probability distribution is Werner's (1972) model S that formulates channel network development by merging of streams that are growing downslope.

Smart's model and model A are branch-

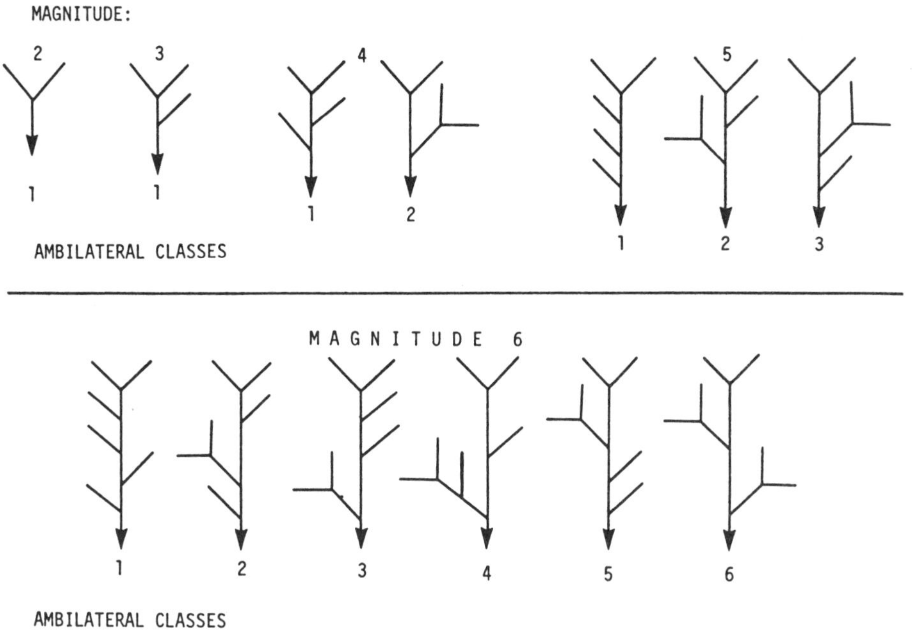

FIG. 3.—One example of each channel network in ambilateral classes for network magnitudes 2, 3, 4, 5 and 6.

ing processes of the type frequently studied in the applied probability literature; one reference is Harris (1964), though most of the models considered in this literature are more involved than simply random bifurcations. Model A is described in sections 3 and 4 of Harding (1971), and he provides many of its properties, but they are not needed for the following analysis.

A limitation on empirical testing of models of topological forms of channel networks is the large number of topologically distinct channel networks for even small magnitudes. A useful strategy for combining channel networks into a smaller number of forms is Smart's (1969) specification of ambilateral class. The following easily verified property also simplifies the calculation of the theoretical probability distributions.

PROPERTY 5. *For each of the three growth models, the topologically distinct channel networks that belong to the same ambilateral class occur with equal probability.*

For magnitudes 2 through 6, figure 3 illustrates a channel network in each ambilateral class. Table 1 gives the number of topologically distinct channel networks in each class, and the probability of occurrence at time n of a single network in each class. The last three columns list the total probability of occurrence at time n of each ambilateral class in the three models. These latter values are simply the product of the number of topologic forms per class times the probability of each form, and they are used in comparing the three models with observational data.

Smart's growth model, mentioned earlier, and model A have different probabilities for ambilateral classes; yet for both models the allowable branching events are restricted to exterior links. For model A, branching events occur one-at-a-time; each of the exterior links of a channel network branches with equal probability, but this probability decreases with magnitude of the channel network. In contrast, for Smart's model it is not

TABLE 1
Probability Distributions for the Three Network Growth Models

Ambilateral Class	Number of Networks	Probability of Occurrence of a Single Network in Ambilateral Class			Probability of Occurrence of All Channel Networks in Ambilateral Class		
		Model A	Model B	Model C	Model A	Model B	Model C
Magnitude 2:							
2–1	1	1.00000	1.00000	1.00000	1.00000	1.00000	1.00000
Magnitude 3:							
3–1	2	.50000	.50000	.50000	1.00000	1.00000	1.00000
Magnitude 4:							
4–1	4	.16667	.20000	.21429	.66667	.80000	.85714
4–2	1	.33333	.20000	.14286	.33333	.20000	.14286
Magnitude 5:							
5–1	8	.04167	.07143	.08571	.33333	.57143	.68571
5–2	4	.12500	.07143	.05000	.50000	.28571	.20000
5–3	2	.08333	.07143	.05714	.16667	.14286	.11429
Magnitude 6:							
6–1	16	.00833	.02381	.03297	.13333	.38095	.52747
6–2	8	.02500	.02381	.01923	.20000	.19048	.15385
6–3	8	.03333	.02381	.01813	.26667	.19048	.14505
6–4	4	.05000	.02381	.01538	.20000	.09524	.06154
6–5	4	.01667	.02381	.02198	.06667	.09524	.08791
6–6	2	.06667	.02381	.01209	.13333	.04762	.02418

necessary to identify a temporal sequence, but each link terminates or branches with probability 0.5, regardless of the magnitude of the network to which this link belongs. Thus the substantial differences between their probability distributions result from subtle differences between their underlying conditions. Analytic comparisons between these two models are difficult because they formulate channel network growth within seemingly incompatible conceptual frameworks. Their availability does emphasize an important methodological principle: an empirical analysis comparing theoretical probabilities with observed frequencies of occurrence of topologic forms in natural drainage basins does not provide sufficient evidence to establish the types and frequencies of branching events that produced the observed topologic forms.

COMPARISON OF GROWTH MODELS WITH OBSERVED DATA

We have located 12 sets of data on natural networks ranging in magnitude from 4 to 6. These data are summarized by ambilateral classes in table 2. The first column lists the ambilateral classes in the order shown in figure 3, and the second column shows the number of observed networks (basins) in each class. The remaining three columns list the expected numbers obtained from the probabilities in table 1. The procedure is illustrated for Howard's (1971) data. Here the observed number of networks is 573. Model A predicts that the number of networks for class 4-1 is 0.66667 × 573 = 355.3, and for class 4-2 is 0.33333 × 573 = 177.7, as against 455 and 78 observed in these two classes.

Goodness of fit was evaluated with conventional chi-square tests, with degrees of freedom one less than the number of classes. The calculated values for models B and C are listed below their expected values. Those values followed by an asterisk or dagger indicate that the fit cannot be rejected at the 0.90 or 0.95 levels, respectively. The following summary applies to table 2.

1. Model A does not fit any data; hence the large chi-square values were not listed.
2. Of the 12 data sets, 11 are satis-

TABLE 2

Comparison of Observed and Calculated Numbers of Channel Networks for 12 Data Sets and Three Growth Models

Ambilateral Class	Observed	Number of Networks		
		Model A	Model B	Model C
Howard (1971):				
4–1............	455	355.3	426.4	456.9
4–2............	78	177.7	106.6	76.1
	533			
			$\chi^2 = 9.59$	$\chi^2 = 0.06$*
Krumbein (1970):				
4–1............	95	76.0	91.2	97.7
4–2............	19	38.0	22.8	16.3
	114			
			$\chi^2 = 0.79$*	$\chi^2 = 0.52$*
Smart (1969), eastern basins:				
4–1............	541	442.0	530.4	568.3
4–2............	122	221.0	132.6	94.7
	663			
			$\chi^2 = 1.06$*	$\chi^2 = 9.18$
Smart (1969), western basins:				
4–1............	409	329.3	395.2	423.4
4–2............	85	164.7	98.8	70.6
	494			
			$\chi^2 = 2.41$*	$\chi^2 = 3.43$†
Howard (1971):				
5–1............	241	123.3	211.4	253.7
5–2............	82	185.0	105.7	74.0
5–3............	47	61.7	52.9	42.3
	370			
			$\chi^2 = 10.12$	$\chi^2 = 2.02$*
Krumbein-Shreve (1970):				
5–1............	102	51.0	87.4	104.9
5–2............	33	76.5	43.7	30.6
5–3............	18	25.5	21.9	17.5
	153			
			$\chi^2 = 5.75$†	$\chi^2 = 0.28$*
Mock (1975), contiguous-seven:				
5–1............	41	24.0	41.1	49.4
5–2............	20	36.0	20.6	14.4
5–3............	11	12.0	10.3	8.2
	72			
			$\chi^2 = 0.07$*	$\chi^2 = 4.56$*
Mock (1975), Triassic-five:				
5–1............	22	14.7	25.1	30.2
5–2............	15	22.0	12.6	8.8
5–3............	7	7.3	6.3	5.0
	44			
			$\chi^2 = 0.92$*	$\chi^2 = 7.39$
Werner (1969):				
5–1............	43	23.7	40.6	48.7
5–2............	18	35.5	20.3	14.2
5–3............	10	11.8	10.1	8.1
	71			
			$\chi^2 = 0.40$*	$\chi^2 = 2.13$*

291

TABLE 2—Continued

Ambilateral Class	Observed	Number of Networks		
		Model A	Model B	Model C
Howard (1971):				
6-1	148	37.6	107.4	148.7
6-2	38	56.4	53.7	43.4
6-3	35	75.2	53.7	40.9
6-4	31	56.4	26.9	17.4
6-5	21	18.8	26.9	24.8
6-6	9	37.6	13.4	6.8
	282			
			$\chi^2 = 29.81$	$\chi^2 = 13.45$
Smart (1969), eastern basins:				
6-1	149	47.9	136.7	189.3
6-2	63	71.8	68.4	55.2
6-3	72	95.7	68.4	52.1
6-4	32	71.8	34.2	22.1
6-5	24	23.9	34.2	31.6
6-6	19	47.9	17.1	8.7
	359			
			$\chi^2 = 5.12$*	$\chi^2 = 35.74$
Smart (1969), western basins:				
6-1	138	36.0	102.9	142.2
6-2	41	54.0	51.4	41.6
6-3	35	72.0	51.4	39.2
6-4	24	54.0	25.7	16.6
6-5	24	18.0	25.7	23.7
6-6	8	38.0	12.9	6.5
	270			
			$\chi^2 = 21.40$	$\chi^2 = 4.24$*

NOTE.—χ^2 is the calculated chi-square goodness-of-fit statistic.
* Denotes fit is acceptable at .90 significance level.
† Denotes fit is acceptable at .95 significance level.

factorily fitted by either model B or model C at the 0.90 significance level.

3. Only 3 data sets are satisfactorily fitted by both models B and C at the 0.90 significance level.

4. Model B fits 7 data sets, of which 4 are not fitted by model C; and model C fits 7 sets of data, of which 4 are not fitted by model B.

It is noted that the test of model B is not equivalent to a test of Shreve's model of topological randomness, even though both models have the same probability distributions for ambilateral classes. This is because Shreve's model is explicitly restricted to stream channel networks that developed "in the absence of strong geologic controls," and this condition may not be satisfied by all of the natural networks summarized in table 2. This restriction does not pertain to the growth models A, B, and C.

IMPLICATIONS TO GEOMORPHOLOGY

Interpretation of table 2 is facilitated by recalling that in model A the only allowable branching events are bifurcations of exterior links. This means that the growth process is confined to the outer edges of the network, with no interior changes of any sort. Models B and C, on the other hand, specify branching events that include both the exterior and interior links.

Inasmuch as model A does not satisfactorily fit any data set, it is rejected as an appropriate model for growth of stream channel networks. As already indicated, this rejection of model A supports, but does not establish, the falsity of the hypothesis that stream channel network growth occurs exclusively by branching of exterior links. Rejection of model A requires rejection of this hypothesis if Assumptions 1 and 2 are valid, but these assumptions are not testable.

Models B and C individually fit slightly more than half the data sets, and together they fit almost all the data. This suggests that network growth involves branching events both at the edges and interiors of networks, and the relative importance of these two types of branching events is indicated by the ratio F_n. For small values of n to which empirical analysis was restricted, the ratios F_n for model B are between 0.67 and 0.8, which suggests that during the growth of stream channel networks the branching of exterior links occurs more frequently than tributary development in interior links. The ratio F_n for model C is greater than 1 for $n \geq 3$, which suggests that tributary development in interior links occurs more frequently than exterior link branching.

If it is accepted that models B and C adequately describe the growth of some stream channel networks, then the following conclusions may be made about the underlying geomorphologic processes. The first conclusion derives from Property 4 and the fact that models B and C fit 11 of 12 data sets.

CONCLUSION 1. *For small values of* n *to which empirical analysis was restricted, branching of both exterior and interior links occurs frequently during the growth of stream channel networks.*

The next conclusion derives from the specifications of models B and C and their good fit to data.

CONCLUSION 2. *Branching events for network growth may have different probabilities of occurrence for interior and exterior links, but the probabilities for links of the same type are equal and are independent of their position within the channel network.*

These conclusions are not definitive because they depend upon the untested Assumptions 1 and 2. Also, there is critical evidence, not taken into account by our empirical analysis, that argues against accepting these conclusions. The consensus of contemporary geomorphologic thought is that headward growth is more rapid than sideward growth in dendritic drainage basins of limited size, perhaps up to magnitude 10 at least. This is supported by the observation that these basins are longer than wide, with a majority having width/length ratios less than 1. For channel networks of small magnitude, this implies a predominance of branching events in the exterior links at the upslope growing tips of the network. Similarly, the probability of interior link tributary development appears from geomorphologic reasoning to be relatively small until the network reaches at least a moderate magnitude, but tributary development in interior links apparently becomes important at higher magnitudes as the network as a whole tends toward some optimum drainage density for the terrain involved.

The conclusions suggested by the models of Assumptions 1 and 2 and supported by the empirical analysis in table 2 are at variance with this concept of network channel growth. Another kind of evidence given in table 2 and figure 3 also favors the models: the topologic forms for ambilateral class 1 of network magnitudes 4, 5, and 6 occur noticeably more frequently than forms in the other classes, and this class typically has more interior link tributaries than forked pairs of exterior links.

Does the empirical evidence imply that geomorphologic consensus is faulty, and that models B and C, supported as they are by empirical data, are valid formulations of network growth? Alternatively, are models B and C faulty because of incorrect postulates or incorrect probabilities, so that no physical significance can be attached to their agreement with empirical data? As a pertinent example, the models of Smart and Werner yield the probability distributions of model B; yet Smart's model does not permit tributary development on interior links and Werner's model postulates that channel networks develop by downstream merging, rather than by branching, of links.

These challenging questions, rising from the present study, suggest the need (1) to develop field and other criteria for quantitative evaluation of the relative importance of true bifurcation as opposed to tributary development in exterior links, (2) to assess the relative incidence of tributary development in interior links as network magnitude increases step by step, and either (3a) to develop alternate models consistent with both the empirical data and geomorphological consensus, or (3b) to revise geomorphologic theory to encompass the findings of this and other models of the probabilistic-topologic approach to geomorphology.

ACKNOWLEDGMENTS.—Useful suggestions by R. L. Shreve and S. Smart are appreciated. Also, the support of the National Science Foundation, Grant SOC 75-16103, is gratefully acknowledged.

REFERENCES CITED

HARDING, E. F., 1971, The probabilities of rooted tree-shapes generated by random bifurcation: Adv. Appl. Probability, v. 3, p. 44–77.

HARRIS, T. C., 1964, The theory of branching processes: Englewood Cliffs, N.J., Prentice-Hall.

HOWARD, A. D., 1971, Simulation model of stream capture: Geol. Soc. America Bull., v. 82, p. 1355–1376.

KRUMBEIN, W. C., 1970, Geological models in transition: in MERRIAM, D. F., ed. Geostatistics: New York, Plenum.

——, and SHREVE, R. L., 1970, Some statistical properties of dendritic channel networks: Evanston, Ill., Northwestern Univ., Dept. Geol. Sci. Off. Naval Research Task 389-150 Tech. Rept. 13; and Los Angeles, Univ. California, Dept. Geology NSF Grant GA-1137 Spec. Proj. Rept.

MOCK, S. J., 1975, Topological properties of some trellis pattern channel networks: Unpub. Ph.D. thesis Northwestern Univ., Evanston, Ill.

SHREVE, R. L., 1966, Statistical law of stream numbers: Jour. Geology, v. 74, p. 17–37.

—— 1967, Infinite topologically random channel networks: Jour. Geology, v. 75, p. 179–186.

—— 1975, The probabilistic-topologic approach to drainage basin geomorphology: Geology, v. 3, p. 527–529.

SMART, J. S., 1969, Topological properties of channel networks: Geol. Soc. America Bull., v. 80, p. 1757–1774.

WERNER, C., 1969, Topological randomness in line patterns: Am. Assoc. Geographers Proc., v. 1, p. 157–162.

—— 1972, Two models for Horton's law of stream numbers: Canadian Geographer, v. 16, p. 50–68.

Part IV

RIVER NETWORKS AND DRAINAGE BASIN GEOMORPHOLOGY

Editors' Comments
on Papers 19 Through 24

19   LEOPOLD and MILLER
Excerpt from *Ephemeral Streams—Hydraulic Factors and Their Relation to the Drainage Net*

20   WARNTZ
Stream Ordering and Contour Mapping

21   CHORLEY and DALE
Cartographic Problems in Stream Channel Delineation

22   GREGORY and WALLING
The Variation of Drainage Density Within a Catchment

23   KIRKBY
Tests of the Random Network Model, and Its Application to Basin Hydrology

24   SMART
Quantitative Characterization of Channel Network Structure

Studies of drainage composition and network growth have indicated how river channel networks coordinate the evolution of drainage basin landforms with the hydrologic processes of routing discharge and sediment through the basin. Each function regulates and adjusts the other. In this final section we examine how some properties of river channel networks have been used to tackle questions in geomorphology and hydrology that go beyond network analysis *per se*. We also address some of the technical and practical questions of acquiring and manipulating river network data. As the subject has grown so rapidly in recent years, and the development of a firm theoretical base has generated so much attention, many of the fundamental issues of data collection and analysis are not covered in standard texts on fluvial geomorphology.

The relationship between Hortonian analysis and hydraulic geometry has long been recognized. Leopold and Miller (Paper 19) show that since the number of streams (basins), basin size, basin length, and stream slope are all related to stream order by geometric progressions, they must be related to each other by power functions. From these they establish the relations between stream order and the components of discharge—namely, width, depth, and velocity. More recently Richards (1980) and Woldenberg (1972) have investigated the changes in hydraulic geometry at stream junctions and related them to the magnitude properties of the confluent tributaries.

Network topology and metric geometry have been viewed by some as best described by relationships based on the laws of probability, and not as being under the predominant control of one or a few physical factors. Others have seen network properties as reflecting some dominant spatial and physical constraints, including some optimizing principle. The same divergence of viewpoints is also true of the hydraulic geometry relationships. Suggestions that hydraulic geometry relationships reflect a most probable state have been reviewed by Williams (1978). Others have proposed that these relationships are based on principles of Newtonian physics and optimization (Smith, 1974; Brebner and Wilson, 1967; Yang et al., 1981).

River channel networks occupy a particular portion of the set of course lines in the general geometry and topology of a fluvial land surface. Warntz (Paper 20) provides a modern restatement and development of early work by Reech (1858), Cayley (1859, 1861), and Maxwell (1870). He relates course lines, ridge lines, and singular points on the topographic surface to stream order and basin hierarchies. He discusses the significance of general surface geomorphology for the cartographic representation of topography. Along with the channel system, ridges form treelike networks in drainage basins, and studies of ridge network topology have contributed important insights on randomness and constraints in fluvial landscapes (Werner, 1972a, 1972b; Mark, 1979). The prominence of ridge and course lines on a topographic surface raises the issue of channel network definition and data acquisition.

Major problems of channel network definition arise from two sources: representation problems in dealing with secondary data bases, and the natural hydrologic variability of network extension. Most work in river network analysis is based on topographic maps. Field survey of all but the smallest tributary systems is practically impossible, and high-quality air-photograph coverage is not always available. Cartographic biases, both methodological and institutional, then become part of the network data. Problems of field identification and channel mapping techniques are examined by Chorley and Dale (Paper 21). Drummond (1974) describes some criteria used by various mapping agencies.

The hydrologic problem in defining a representative drainage network graph is one of natural variation in basin response to different inputs. Every precipitation event activates part of the existing channel network, but which part? The entire network of river valleys includes elements that are presumably activated only by very rare, high-magnitude events. These elements may be utilized by, but could not be formed by, subsequent smaller storms. The extent of seasonal variation in the active drainage net of a small clay catchment is revealed by Blyth and Rodda (1973). Because of such variations, many definitions of channel networks have been used for analysis of drainage composition. Blue lines on topographic maps are commonly taken to infer the extent of perennial channel flow, but this assumption is widely thought to be conservative. Some criteria of contour crenulation are then used to evaluate the likelihood of a dry valley sustaining active channel flow under "normal" hydrologic conditions. Gregory (1966) has investigated the effect of including dry valleys in the analysis of Horton's laws of drainage composition. The problem also haunts, perhaps more seriously, link-based studies. Werritty (1972) examines the accuracy of stream length measurements taken from various editions and scales of topographic maps. Gregory and Walling (Paper 22) make an all too rare attempt to determine the hydrologic regime corresponding to the networks depicted on their topographic map base. Day (1978) provides some evidence of the ways in which networks are related to streamflow hydrographs, and Ovenden and Gregory (1980) demonstrate network change and extension due to human activity since the nineteenth century. Recently there have been attempts to specify objective slope criteria for extending blue-line networks into dry valleys (Shreve, 1974; Kaitanen, 1975; Smart, 1978).

There are related data problems in the analysis of arterial and venous trees and airway networks in lungs. Resin casts fill these systems to the smallest branch, which in the case of the arterial tree is 7 microns. Since the number of exterior links could reach the hundreds of millions, it becomes necessary to sample this distal zone and prune the tree to some standard diameter. There is a serious lack of knowledge about the different effects of pruning to various branch diameters, but many aspects of the network morphometry must be affected. In some cases a link-length criterion is used. The questions become, What is the best criterion for the exterior link or first-order branch? Which differences in morphology reflect real differences in network topology, and which are caused by experimental error or choice of different criteria? There is an additional problem in correcting for broken or missing branches: How can one represent the missing part of the tree? An example of such adjustments can be found in Horsfield and Gordon (1981).

Once the network is defined, the processes of data manipulation and analysis can be greatly facilitated by appropriate data-storage and

-retrieval methods (Jarvis, 1977). Link-associated data can be stored in the sequence of the topologic binary string advocated by Smart (1970), and topologic and geometric properties can be retrieved by means of algorithms presented by Ferguson (1977). An alternative storage sequence is given by Kirkby (Paper 23), and various stream-labeling methods are discussed by Ranalli and Scheidegger (1968).

Finally, some important applications of river network analysis have appeared in recent years. Despite Horton's and Strahler's aims of developing drainage network analysis as a practical hydrological tool, the precise linkages between channel network characteristics and the hydrologic responses of drainage basins have remained rather elusive. Although claims of the hydrologic relevance of network properties—such as Strahler's assertion of a relation between network topologic structure and hydrograph shape (see Paper 5)—are widespread, there are few working relationships with strong empirical justification. A major attempt to remedy this situation is made by Kirkby (Paper 23), who develops the concept of network topologic width and relates it to peak discharge and lag time to peak flow. Other attempts to incorporate network structure in the analysis of flood hydrographs include those of Rogers (1972) and Patton and Baker (1976). Gregory (1977, 1979) defines an index of drainage network power, given by the volume of the channel network divided by the basin relief. This index expresses the potential energy of the network of channels in the basin and correlates well with mean annual flood obtained from a partial duration series.

Analyses of link-associated properties of channel length and drainage area have at last begun to provide measures that can discriminate networks drawn from different geomorphic environments. The use of channel patterns to characterize landscape preceded Horton, but the Hortonian quantification of visually distinctive drainage patterns tended to reveal more similarities than differences. The insensitivity of Hortonian branching ratios to all but the grossest differences in landscape, along with widespread adherence of natural networks to the random topology model, have made it very difficult to recognize basins drawn from different environments on the basis of their channel networks. However, Smart (Paper 24) shows that link lengths and associated drainage areas could be combined in four dimensionless parameters that effectively detect differences in networks attributable to varying lithology and degree of maturity.

REFERENCES

Blyth, K., and J. C. Rodda, 1973, A Stream Length Study, *Water Resources Research* **9**:1454-1461.

Brebner, A., and K. C. Wilson, 1967, Derivation of the Regime Equation from

Relationships for Pressurized Flow by Use of the Principle of Minimum Energy-Degradation Rate, *Inst. Civil Engineers Proc.* **36:**47-62.

Cayley, A., 1859, On Contour and Slope Lines, *London, Edinburgh Dublin Philos. Mag. Jour. Sci.* **18:**264-268.

Cayley, A., 1861, On the Partitions of a Close, *London, Edinburgh Dublin Philos. Mag. Jour. Sci.* **21:**424-428.

Day, D., 1978, Drainage Density Changes During Rainfall, *Earth Surf. Processes* **3:**319-326.

Drummond, R. R., 1974, When is a Stream a Stream? *Prof. Geographer* **26:**34-37.

Ferguson, R. I., 1977, On Determining Distances Through Stream Networks, *Water Resources Research* **13:**672-674.

Gregory, K. J., 1966, Dry Valleys and the Composition of the Drainage Net, *Jour. Hydrology* **4:**327-340.

Gregory, K. J., 1977, Stream Network Volume: An Index of Channel Morphometry, *Geol. Soc. America Bull.* **88:**1075-1080.

Gregory, K. J., 1979, Drainage Network Power, *Water Resources Research* **15:**775-777.

Horsfield, K., and W. I. Gordon, 1981, Morphometry of Pulmonary Veins in Man, *Lung* **159:**211-218.

Kaitanen, V., 1975, Composition and Morphotectonic Interpretation of the Kiellajohka Drainage Basin, Finnish Lapland, *Fennia* **140:**1-54.

Jarvis, R. S., 1977, Drainage Network Analysis, *Prog. Phys. Geogr.* **1:**271-295.

Mark, D. M., 1979, Topology of Ridge Patterns: Randomness and Constraints, *Geol. Soc. America Bull.* **90:**164-172.

Maxwell, J. C., 1870, On Hills and Dales, *London, Edinburgh, Dublin Philos. Mag. Jour. Sci.* **40:**421-427.

Ovenden, J. C., and K. J. Gregory, 1980, The Permanence of Stream Networks in Britain, *Earth Surf. Processes* **5:**47-60.

Patton, P. C. and V. R. Baker, 1976, Morphometry and Floods in Small Drainage Basins Subject to Diverse Hydrogeomorphic Controls, *Water Resources Research* **12:**941-952.

Ranalli, G. and A. E. Scheidegger, 1968, Topological Significance of Stream Labelling Methods, *Internat. Assoc. Sci. Hydrology Bull.* **13**(4):77-85.

Reech, M., 1858, Propriété générale des surfaces fermées, *Journal de l'École Polytechnique* **27:**169-178.

Richards, K. S., 1980, A Note on Changes in Channel Geometry at Tributary Junctions, *Water Resources Research* **16:**241-244.

Rogers, W. F., 1972, New Concept in Hydrograph Analysis, *Water Resources Research* **8:**973-981.

Shreve, R. L., 1974, Variation of Mainstream Length with Basin Area in River Networks, *Water Resources Research* **10:**1167-1177.

Smart, J. S., 1970, Use of Topologic Information in Processing Data for Channel Networks, *Water Resources Research* **6:**932-936.

Smart, J. S., 1978, The Analysis of Drainage Network Composition, *Earth Surf. Processes* **3:**129-170.

Smith, T. R., 1974, A Derivation of the Hydraulic Geometry of Steady-State Channels from Conservation Principles and Sediment Transport Laws, *Jour. Geology* **82:**98-104.

Werner, C., 1972a, Patterns of Drainage Areas with Random Topology, *Geog. Analysis* **4:**119-133.

Werner, C., 1972b, Channel and Ridge Networks in Drainage Basins, *Assoc. Am. Geographers Proc.* **4:**109–114.

Werritty, A., 1972, Accuracy of Stream Link Lengths Derived from Maps, *Water Resources Research* **8:**1255–1264.

Williams, G. P., 1978, Hydraulic Geometry of River Cross Sections Theory of Minimum Variance, *U. S. Geol. Survey Prof. Paper 1029,* 47p.

Woldenberg, M. J., 1972, Relations Between Horton's Laws and Hydraulic Geometry as Applied to Tidal Networks, *Harvard Papers in Theoretical Geography Number 45,* 39p.

Yang, C. T., C. S. Song, and M. J. Woldenberg, 1981, Hydraulic Geometry and Minimum Rate of Energy Dissipation, *Water Resources Research* **17:**1014–1018.

19

Reprinted from pp. 16-24 of *U.S. Geol. Survey Prof. Paper 282-A*, 1956, 36p.

EPHEMERAL STREAMS—HYDRAULIC FACTORS AND THEIR RELATION TO THE DRAINAGE NET

Luna B. Leopold and John P. Miller

[*Editors' Note:* In the original, material precedes this excerpt.]

INTERRELATION OF DRAINAGE NET AND HYDRAULIC FACTORS

RELATION OF STREAM ORDER TO STREAM NUMBER, STREAM LENGTH, AND DRAINAGE AREA

The quantitative description of drainage nets developed by Horton (1945) related stream order to the number, average length, and average slope of streams in a drainage basin. Our purpose in this section is to show how this useful tool may be extended to include the hydraulic as well as drainage-net characteristics.

All the data required for the Horton type of drainage-net description can be obtained from maps. As maps of several different scales were required for our own analysis, some explanation of the procedure is in order.

Figure 12 presents planimetric maps of a sample area near the city of Santa Fe. The map on the right, which shows the drainage net in a typical watershed about 9 miles long by 2 miles wide, was compiled from planimetric maps made by the Soil Conservation Service from aerial photographs at an original scale of 2 inches to the mile. The left map shows in more detail the drainage net in one small tributary which for purposes of this report we will refer to as Arroyo Caliente. This map was made by pace and compass after a planetable traverse had been run for control. Each tributary rill was paced out to its farthest upstream extension in order that the map would include all recognizable channels.

The orders of various channels in the basin of Arroyo Caliente are indicated by numbers appearing in the upper part of the left map of figure 12. A small unbranched tributary is labeled "order 1," and the stream receiving that tributary is labeled "order 2." All streams of orders 3, 4, and 5 are labeled with appropriate numbers near their respective mouths.

On the right map of figure 12, the little basin called Arroyo Caliente is one of the minor tributaries which even on this small-scale map appears to be unbranched like the tributary just west of it. If only this map were available, one would conclude that Arroyo Caliente is a first-order stream. This points up an important qualification to the Horton scheme of stream-order classification; namely, that the definition of a first-order stream depends on the scale of the map used. The first-order stream, by definition, should be the smallest unbranched channel on the ground. The designation of which stream is master and which is tributary is somewhat arbitrary, but we have followed the guide suggested by Horton (1945, p. 281).

The largest drainage basin which is included in the present analysis is that of the Rio Galisteo (fig. 1). At its mouth this basin drains about 670 square miles. Such an area contains a very large number of small tributaries. It was desired to estimate the number of tributaries of various sizes, their lengths, and other characteristics. The task of counting and measuring each individually would be inordinately great but approximate answers could be obtained by a sampling process. Arroyo Caliente is one of the samples used.

The detailed map of Arroyo Caliente was used to determine the number, the average length, and average drainage area of each order of stream in its basin. At its mouth, Arroyo Caliente is of fifth order.

The Arroyo de los Frijoles basin shown in small scale at the right in figure 12 was used as another sample and similar measurements were made. The small, unbranched tributaries on this 1 mile to 2 inch map, of which Arroyo Caliente is one, would be designated order 1, in accordance with the definition of stream order. The detailed study of Arroyo Caliente showed, however, that on the ground this tributary which had appeared unbranched was, in reality, composed of a drainage network of still smaller tributaries. Arroyo Caliente and other channels which appeared as order 1 on the right-hand map are, on the average, actually of 5th order. Thus the true order of any stream determined from the right-hand map of figure 12 is increased by adding 4, so that an order 1 stream on that map becomes order 1+4, or 5.

This provides a way of combining maps of different scales to carry the numbering of stream order from one map to the other. It can be seen in the plot of stream length against stream order (left graph of figure 13) that this relation in stream orders 1 to 5 (average values of Arroyo Caliente) fits well with data from the small-scale maps after the values of stream order were adjusted as described above.

Similarly, this principle was used to obtain the estimate of the number of streams of each order in an 11th order basin in the area studied, as shown in the right diagram in figure 13. An actual count of the number of streams of highest order was made. From the small-scale maps the order of the Rio Galisteo at its mouth (fig. 1) was determined to be 7, which when adjusted by 4, indicates the true order of 11. Because this is the only stream of order 11 in the area studied, the graph must go through the value of 1 on the ordinate scale at an abscissa value of 11. The mean relation was drawn for the numbers of streams of highest orders and extrapolated to determine the number of streams of order 5, the smallest tributaries shown on the small-scale map. The graph of number of streams of orders 1 to 5 in the Arroyo Caliente basin which included only one stream of order 5 was superimposed on the graph determined from the 2 inches to 1 mile map and placed so that the points representing order 5 coincided. By extending the graph to order 1, the number of 1st order tributaries in the 11th order basin could be estimated.

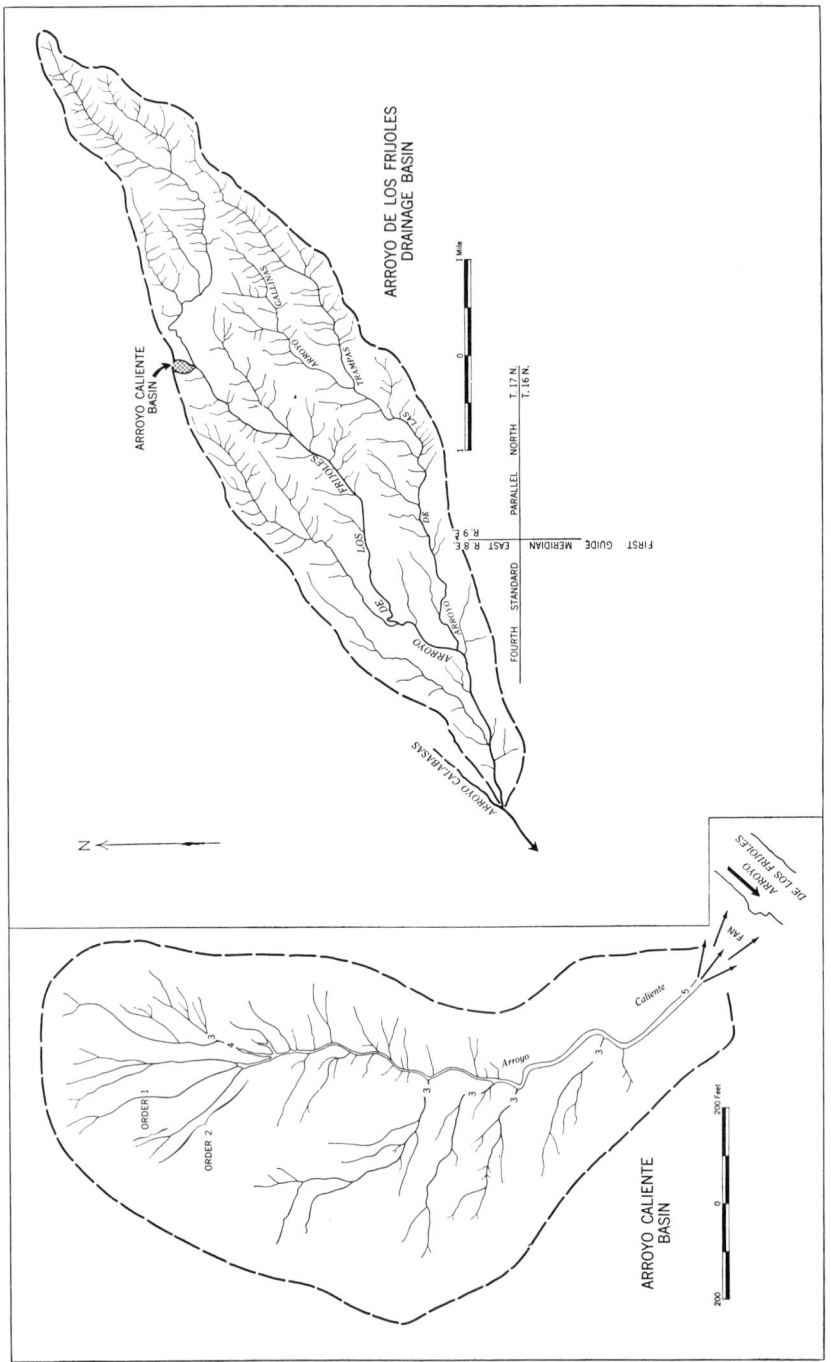

FIGURE 12.—Drainage basin of typical ephemeral arroyo near Santa Fe, N. Mex. Left, basin of Arroyo Caliente, a tributary to Arroyo de los Frijoles; right, basin of Arroyo de los Frijoles showing location of the tributary Arroyo Caliente.

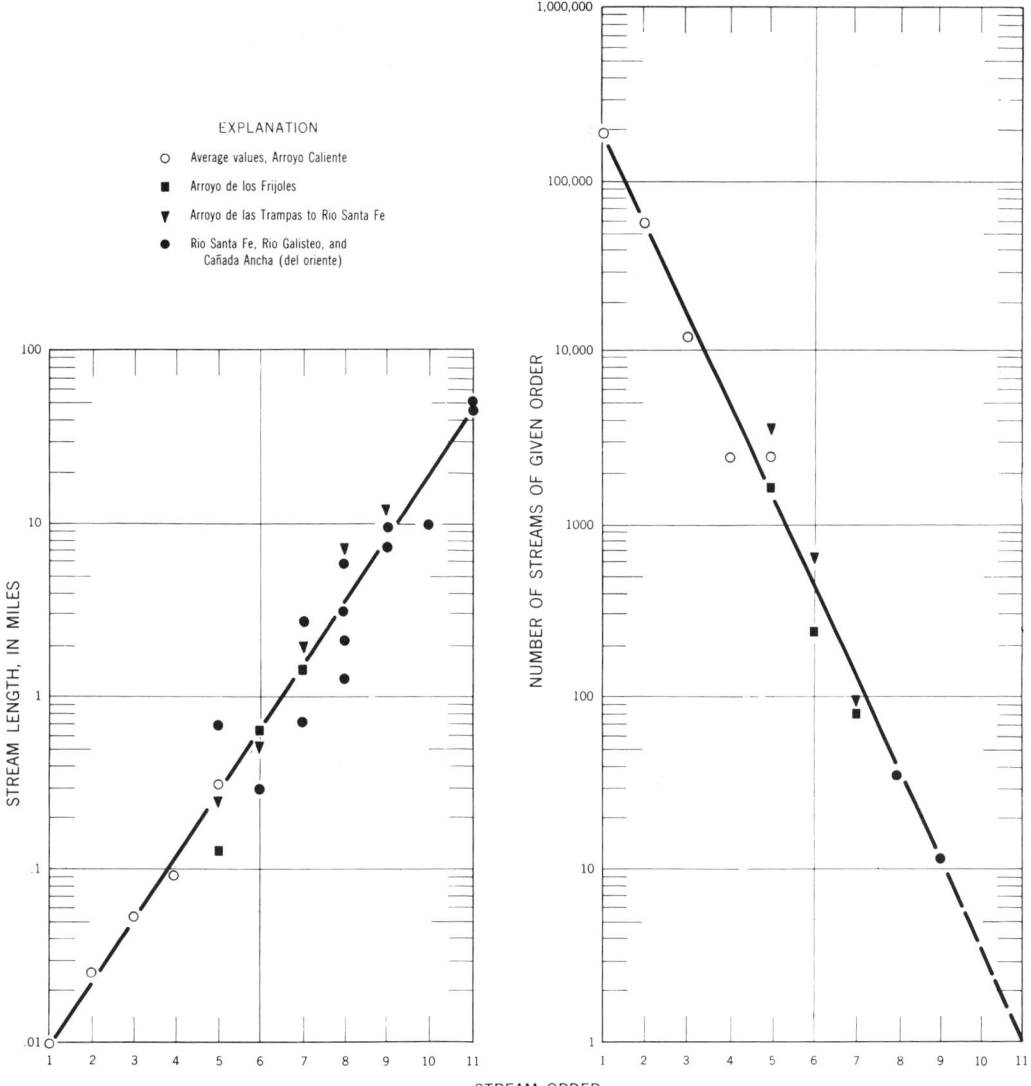

FIGURE 13.—Relation of stream length and number of streams to stream order in basins of 11th order in central New Mexico. Left, stream length plotted against stream order; right, number of individual streams of a given order plotted against order.

This same general procedure was followed for several other sample drainage basins. Order 11 was the highest found, this being for the main stem of Rio Galisteo. The number and average length of streams in each order were determined and the results are included in figure 13.

It will be noted that the plots of stream order against stream length and stream order against number of streams are straight lines on semilogarithmic paper, as Horton discovered. Lengths range from about 50 feet for the 1st order tributaries to 54 miles for the Rio Galisteo.

In order to visualize better the types of channels studied and their relation to stream order, the reader is referred to the photographs in figure 14, which show first-order tributaries in the basin of Arroyo Caliente,

FIGURE 14.—First-order tributaries in basin of Arroyo Caliente. These show the most headward extensions of the smallest tributary rills in the area.

and figure 15 which pictures Arroyo de los Frijoles at a place where its size is typical of an 8th order stream. Channels of order 5 and order 10 can be seen in figures 2 and 3, respectively.

Because maximum stream length is a function of drainage-basin area, it is not unexpected that the relation of drainage area to stream order is also a straight line on semilogarithmic paper, as can be seen in figure 16. The smallest unbranched tributaries, which are rills about 8 inches wide and 1 to 4 inches deep, drain on the average about .00006 square miles or .04 acre. In the 670-square-mile basin of Rio Galisteo there are roughly 190,000 such first-order tributaries, as estimated from figure 13.

EQUATIONS RELATING TO HYDRAULIC AND PHYSIOGRAPHIC FACTORS

From the previous work of Horton or from our data plotted in figures 13 and 16, it is apparent that stream order, O, bears a relation to number of streams, N, in the form

$$O = k \log N \text{ or } O \propto \log N \qquad (1)$$

and a similar relation to stream length, l, slope, s, and drainage area, A_d,

$$O \propto \log l \qquad (2)$$

$$O \propto \log s \qquad (3)$$

$$O \propto \log A_d \qquad (4)$$

FIGURE 15.—Arroyo de los Frijoles at place where it typifies a stream of eighth order.

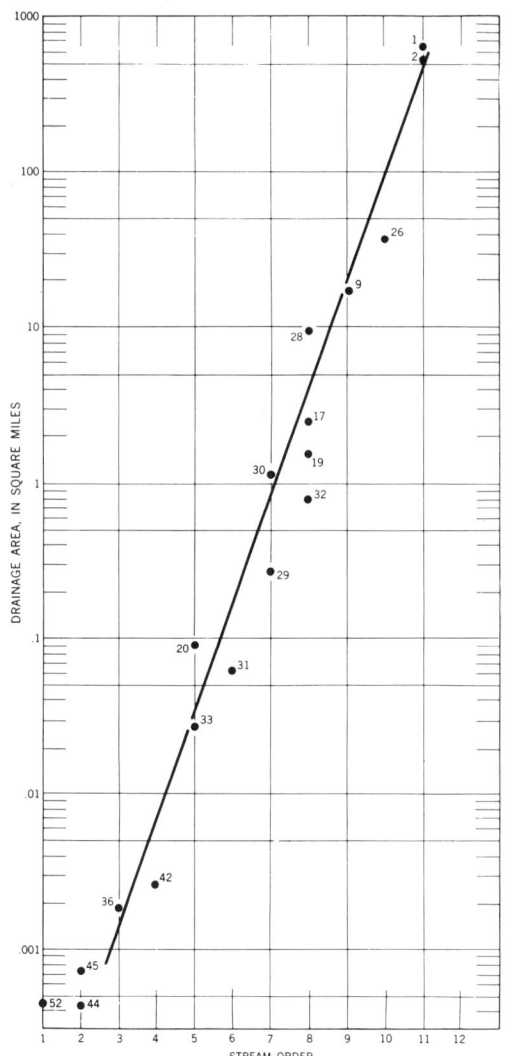

FIGURE 16.—Relation of drainage area to stream order for ephemeral channels in central New Mexico. Number beside point is serial identification keyed to data in appendix.

It follows, then, that there must exist a power-function relation between each two of these variables other than order, in the form

$$l \propto A_d^k, \quad s \propto A_d^k, \quad s \propto l^k$$

where k is some exponent having a particular value in each equation. Moreover, because it is known that discharge, Q, bears a relation to drainage area of the form

$$Q \propto A_d^k \qquad (5)$$

then discharge must be related to stream order according to

$$O \propto \log Q \qquad (6)$$

Reiterating some of the hydraulic relations discussed earlier:

$$w \propto Q^b \qquad (7)$$

$$d \propto Q^f \qquad (8)$$

$$v \propto Q^m \qquad (9)$$

$$L \propto Q^j \qquad (10)$$

$$s \propto Q^z \qquad (11)$$

$$n' \propto Q^y \qquad (12)$$

Where Q = discharge
w = width
d = depth
v = velocity
L = suspended load
s = slope
n' = a roughness parameter
$b, f, m, j, z,$ and y are numerical exponents

It follows from equation (6) and equations (7) to (12) that there definitely is a relation between stream order and width, depth, velocity, suspended load, slope, and roughness of the form

$$O \propto \log \text{(width, depth, etc.)}$$

Also, there are several interrelations among variables in equations (1) to (4), and among those in equations (7) to (12). An example of such a relation is that which would exist between sediment load, L, and drainage area, A_d.

Because $L \propto Q^j$
and $Q \propto A_d^k$
then $L \propto A_d^{jk}$

Thus, it can be seen that a whole series of hydraulic and drainage-network factors are interrelated in the form of power or exponential functions. These equations can be added to the several others derived by

Horton (1945, p. 291) which, in his words, "supplement Playfair's law and make it more definite and more quantitative. They also show that the nice adjustment goes far beyond the matter of declivities."

The equations listed above merely state the condition of proportionality; for them to be definitive the constants involved must be determined. In addition to the values of certain exponents already discussed, data collected during this investigation established the relations among order, slope, and width, as will now be described.

Although channel depth, velocity, and discharge at a particular cross section can be measured only when the stream is flowing, the important hydraulic variables, channel width and channel slope, can be estimated even in a dry stream bed. During the many days when no thunderstorms were occurring in the area studied, our field work included measurement of width and slope in the dry channels. The procedure used will be described briefly.

The width was defined as width near bankfull stage. In Eastern United States where the development of the river flood plain is the rule rather than the exception, the bankfull width is relatively easy to define and measure. It is the width which the water surface would reach when at a stage equal to the level of the flood plain. In dry arroyos where flood plains are the exception and alluvial terraces exceedingly common, it is difficult to point specifically at an elevation which might be called bankfull. Nevertheless, field inspection allows fairly consistent estimates of width corresponding to an effective or dominant discharge, even by different observers. The positions on the stream banks representing the two ends of the cross section were chosen independently by each of us, and the recorded widths represent a compromise between our individual judgments.

Channel slope is somewhat easier to determine. Although there are local dry pools or deeps resulting from both definite patterns of flow and random channel irregularities, a smooth profile of channel bed drawn through several points in a reach provides an estimate of channel slope which is reproducible by successive measurements. Our procedure was to place the planetable in the center of the dry stream bed and take a series of sights both upstream and down as far as the stadia rod could be read with a leveled instrument. In most instances this gave a measurement of slope through a reach of about 600 feet.

Width and slope were measured at more than 100 channel cross sections. Because of the widespread geographic distribution of measured cross sections and because of the lack of adequate maps, we have not determined the order of the streams on which many of these are located. The graphs of figures 17 and 19

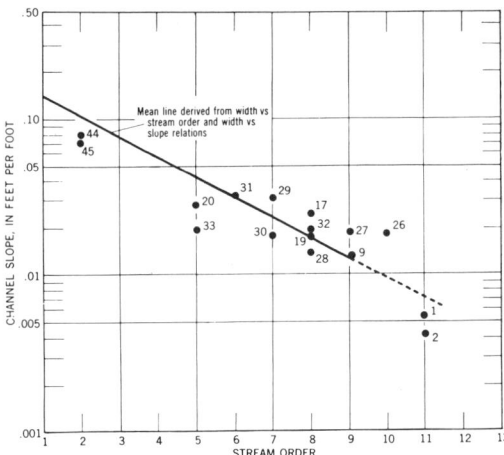

FIGURE 17.—Relation of channel slope to stream order, showing the individual measurements and the mean relation (solid line) derived from other parameters. Number beside point is serial identification keyed to data in appendix.

were plotted from data on cross sections of streams of known order. As expected, order is related to width and slope by equations of the type.

$$O = k \log w \text{ and } O = k \log s$$

The relation between width and slope can be determined by equating the relations above or by direct plotting of the data as in figure 18. To represent the relation in larger streams, a straight line on logarithmic paper has been drawn through the numbered points (fig. 18). The equation of this line is

$$s = 0.12 w^{-0.5}$$

This means that for the area studied, channel slope decreases downstream approximately as the reciprocal of the square root of channel width. This expresses an interrelation and does not imply a direct dependence between these two parameters.

Establishing the relations among width, slope, and order merely requires collecting and plotting the appropriate data. It should be possible to combine those factors which are most easily and definitively measured, and thereby arrive at approximations of other factors which are more difficult to measure. Such a scheme would expand the usefulness of the techniques now available. An example to illustrate this possibility will now be cited.

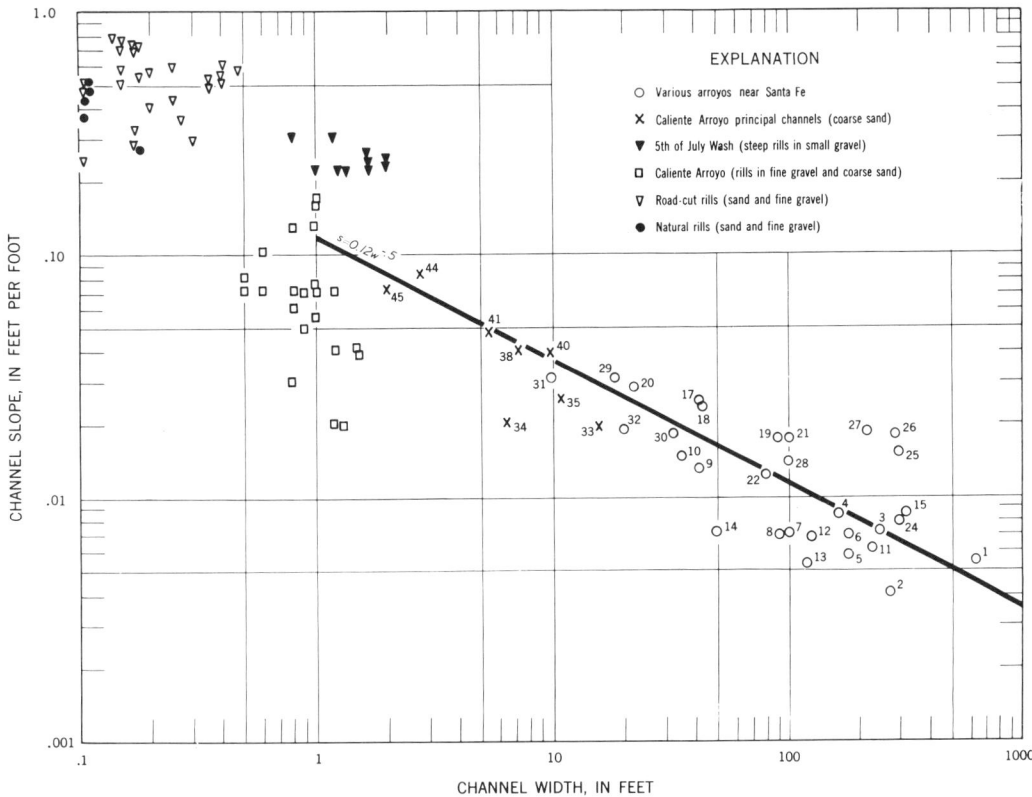

FIGURE 18.—Relation of channel slope to channel width. Data from moderate and large arroyos and differentiated from rills by the different symbols. Number beside point is serial identification keyed to data in appendix.

The manner in which discharge increases with stream order is of particular concern, as it provides the link between the Horton analysis and the hydraulic geometry. For perennial streams, gaging-station data are available in quantity for the larger stream orders. The determination of stream order at a gaging station is laborious but can be made, and order can be plotted directly against discharge of a given frequency derived from gaging-station data. In arid regions there are relatively few gaging stations, and for the most part they are located on the larger streams. To obtain a relation between order and discharge for ephemeral streams requires discharge measurements of the smaller streams. But even these measurements do not provide at a given cross section a specific value of discharge which can be plotted against stream order, for it must be remembered that discharge at any given location may fluctuate through a wide range and that sufficient record is required to allow some kind of frequency analysis.

If the discharge chosen has some specific relation to the position of the cross section along the length of the stream an approximation to constant frequency might result. It is proposed to use that discharge which corresponds to the average width representative of the stream order at the point in question. To obtain this value, the relations already demonstrated can be utilized. Specifically, the relation between width and order indicated on figure 19 will be combined with the relation of downstream increase of width with increasing discharge. The latter is, fortunately, one of the most consistent of the graphs representing the hydraulic variables. From figure 19 the stream width for each order can be obtained and, by use of those values of width, the corresponding discharges can be read from the width-discharge graph of figure 11. In such a manner the relation between stream order and discharge may be derived, and it is plotted as the unbroken line on figure 20.

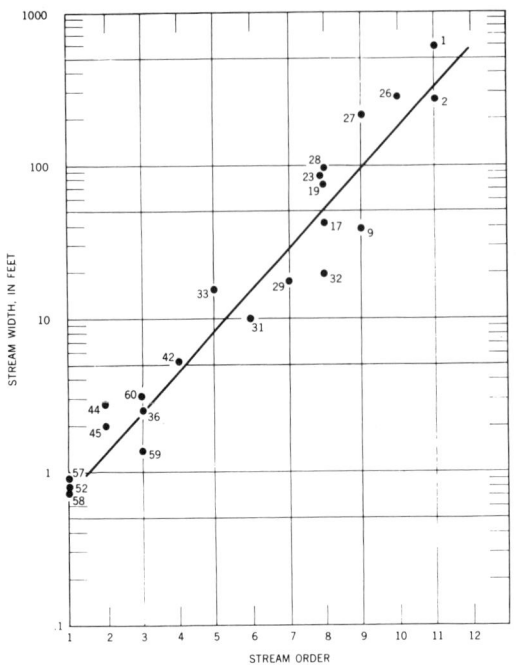

FIGURE 19.—Relation of stream width to stream order in arroyos. Number beside point is serial number in appendix.

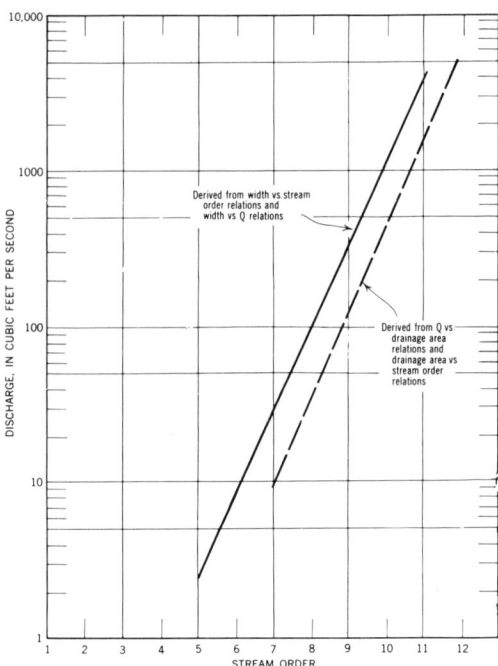

FIGURE 20.—Relation of discharge to stream order derived by two separate types of analyses.

A second approach to the discharge-order relation makes use of flood-frequency analysis. On streams of small and moderate size in central New Mexico there are only a few gaging stations that have a relatively long period of record. Despite the paucity of data, flood-frequency curves for all gaging stations considered applicable to the area being studied were obtained from an unpublished study by H. H. Hudson. Also, the records of some additional stations were analyzed by the authors. In eastern streams the bankfull stage is attained about once a year. A conservative quantity little affected by the length of record is the average of the highest flood each year of record. This is called the mean annual flood. It has a recurrence interval of 2.3 years, and thus we assume roughly approximates the discharge at bankfull stage. The relation between 2.3-year flood discharge and drainage area for gaging stations in central New Mexico is presented on figure 21.

It is known by hydrologists that the discharge of a flood of a given frequency increases somewhat less rapidly than drainage basin size. It is typical for the relation of flood discharge to drainage area to plot as a straight line on logarithmic paper, expressed by the equation

$$Q \propto A_d^k$$

where k is a constant which for the mean annual flood has a value of between 0.7 and 0.8. The slope of line on figure 21 is consistent with values known from other areas. In drainage basins of the same size, those studied in the West produce floods of about one-fifth the magnitude of the typical one in the East.

By combining the discharge-area graph with the order-area graph, discharge can be related to order. The drainage area corresponding to each stream order is read from figure 16, and the value of discharge for an equal drainage area is determined from figure 21. The resulting plot is shown as the dashed line in figure 20.

Thus, the relation between stream order and discharge, which is the link between the Horton analysis and hydraulic geometry, has been derived for a central New Mexico area in two ways which are at least somewhat independent. Comparison between the results is indicated by the two lines in figure 20. Only the slopes

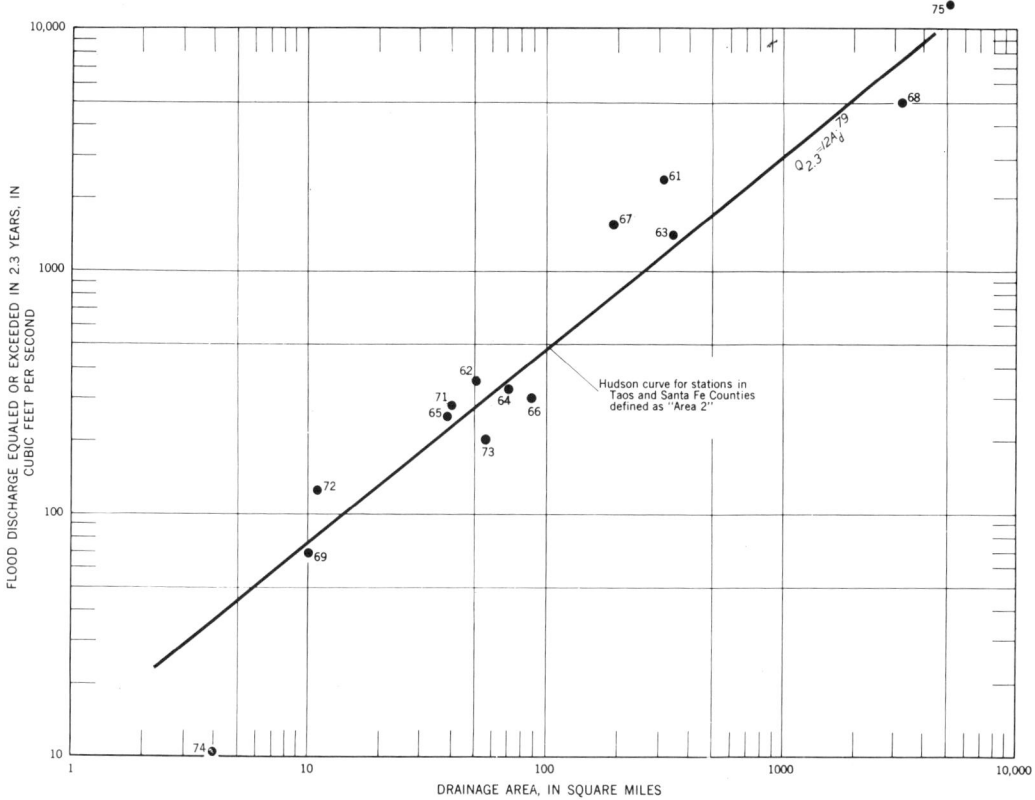

FIGURE 21.—Relation of mean annual flood discharge (equaled or exceeded in 2.3 years) to drainage area. Number beside point is serial number in appendix.

of the two lines should be alike, and indeed, they are similar. The intercepts should not be expected to be exactly the same because the discharge determined from flood-frequency data was chosen to represent a frequency of 2.3 years. The frequency of that discharge which corresponds to full channel width is unknown and need not be identical to the discharge having a 2.3-year recurrence.

It should be recognized that each of the graphical relations presented has considerable scatter owing to the nature of the measurements and the inherent variability of these factors in the field. It should not be inferred that a relation such as that presented between discharge and stream order is considered precise. Rather we are concerned with explaining a methodology by which generalized relations can be obtained, and with demonstrating the nature of the interrelations between a variety of hydraulic and physiographic factors.

In summary, it has been shown that the ephemeral streams in New Mexico are characterized by a uniform downstream increase of width, depth, and velocity with stream order, and also with drainage-basin size. Increasing size of drainage basins is accompanied by a downstream increase in discharge. Furthermore, the interrelations among all of these factors, both hydraulic and physiographic, may be expressed in simple terms, either as exponential or power functions. The method of combining the hydraulic variables with factors measured on a map or obtained in the field from a dry stream bed allows a simple means of obtaining interrelations which cannot be measured directly.

[Editors' Note: Material has been omitted at this point.]

REFERENCE

[Editors' Note: Only the reference cited in the preceding excerpt is reproduced here.]

Horton, R. E., 1945, Erosional development of streams and their drainage basins—hydrophysical approach to quantitative morphology, Geol. Soc. America Bull. v. 56, p. 275-370.

Copyright ©1975 by Elsevier Scientific Publishing Company
Reprinted from *Jour. Hydrology* **25**:209-227 (1975)

STREAM ORDERING AND CONTOUR MAPPING

WILLIAM WARNTZ

Department of Geography, University of Western Ontario, London, Ont. (Canada)

(Accepted for publication September 17, 1974)

ABSTRACT

Warntz, W., 1975. Stream ordering and contour mapping. J. Hydrol., 25: 209—227.

This paper describes the necessary, sufficient, possible, and likely geometrical and topological characteristics of stream drainage basins of various orders. A suggestion is made for experimental topographic mapping to bring it closer to the current theory of spatial hierarchical systems. Stream ordering is examined and a recommendation is offered that streams now considered as of first order be regarded as of zero order. This simplifies mathematical notation for the Horton-Strahler-Woldenberg type of analysis in quantitative geomorphology and has added intellectual interest by facilitating the understanding of the virtually infinite cyclical regress in the patterns of surface features down to individual particle size.

INTRODUCTION

This paper has been prepared in response to what might be regarded, in other arenas of endeavor, as "popular demand". We shall also use it to make a plea for certain changes in topographic mappings. In our first paper in the "Harvard Papers in Theoretical Geography", 16 May 1967, we examined surfaces in general terms but also recognized certain points, lines, and areas on surfaces as singular in their characteristics and worthy of specific delineation in that they represented that minimal part of the spatial structuring that need be known if the flows, if any, on surfaces were to be understood. A simple table was included that grouped the singular geometrical elements by dimensions and by vergency. It is included here subsequently. A hypothetical surface was presented to portray the ideas involved. Following Cayley (1859) and Maxwell 1870) we have discussed the topology and geometry of any surface and the relationship of the points, lines, and areas to flow phenomena. We have found that flows of energy and matter unite various parts of the surface into a system. Fluvial systems, for instance, are highly organized, and show systematic regularity, as Horton (1945) first demonstrated, and as Strahler (1964) and his students have corroborated.

While useful for general "movement theory" purposes, and having been developed with social and economic applications in mind, our hypothetical surface did not contain sufficient "tree-like" or "bifurcation" properties to reveal, for example, the typical, indeed, the necessary, spatial features and their dimensional representation present in even moderately high-order river basins. This present paper, then, is an attempt to clarify these matters and to accede to wishes that we examine river basin geometry explicitly.

None of the illustrations from the paper noted above will be reproduced here. The few following succinct definitions will, it is hoped, suffice.

SELF-CROSSING CONTOUR LINES AND CRITICAL POINTS

A contour line may be regarded as the intersection of two surfaces, the conventional circumstance being that of the intersection of the variable surface under consideration and some specified constant-valued "level" surface. Any two intersecting surfaces do so along a line. This line thus connects points of equal value on the variable surface. Using conventional mathematical notions of surfaces, it is to be seen that the z value is constant along a contour line on a variable surface when x and y values are taken as coordinates on a referent level surface.

The summary of such values with relation to land forms phenomena is conveniently and convincingly displayed by means of a map on which selected contour lines are shown representing the intersections of level surfaces with the variable surface of the phenomenon and with each contour line distinguished by a numeral which shows the level surface to which it belongs.

Let us now relate the nature and significance of contour lines to certain absolute extremum points (local maximum, or minimum) and mixed extrema points on a surface.

The contour "line" at a peak becomes a point. A peak is a local maximum of elevation. Everywhere in the immediate neighborhood on the surface elevation values are lower.

The contour "line" at a pit becomes a point. A pit is a local minimum of elevation. Everywhere in the immediate neighborhood on the surface elevation values are higher.

In general, of course, peaks are at higher elevations than pits. This is not inevitably required to be so for individual peaks or pits. The local condition of the surface determines which, if either, exists.

Peaks and *pits* are to be regarded as singular points and constitute the category we shall call absolute extremum points.

The other kind of singular points, i.e. mixed extrema points, are *passes* and *pales*. A pass or saddle point exists, for example, at the self-crossing point of some contour line that forms two loops, one around each of two adjacent peaks. To find the pass or passes relating to a given peak requires the establishment of the outermost closed contour line.

A pale exists between adjacent pits. The self-crossing contour line for adjacent pits may be either of the inloop or outloop type. The inloop type also consists of two closed curves, one of which, however, lies inside the other

313

Stream Ordering and Contour Mapping 211

except for their shared point. Inloop types occur linking pits within streams and for lakes with outlets.

Within any given loop identified with a given singular point, other singular points and their attendant loops may be found. Through every point on the surface one may consider that there is not only a contour line, but also a slope line. Slope lines indicate the direction of steepest gradient at a given point and, therefore, intersect the contour lines at right angles. We therefore have two families of orthogonal curves on the surface, namely contour lines and slope lines. The property of orthogonality is preserved in a conformal projection to the plane of these two systems.

In general, slope lines have peaks and pits as their termini. In general any one slope line leads to some peak in its "uphill" direction and to some pit in its "downhill" direction. If, however, a particular slope line is found to run from a pit to either a pass or pale, then when continued through that pass or pale, that line will, of necessity, run only to another pit (or in rare cases, the same pit), provided, of course, that the surface be a continuous one as we have stipulated. Similarly any slope line found linking a peak to a pass or pale, must then, when extended through the pass or pale continue only to another peak (or in rare cases, the same peak).

Slope lines linking peaks via passes or pales are designated as *ridge lines*. Slope lines linking pits via passes or pales are designated as *course lines*. All slope lines other than course lines and ridge lines do not encounter passes or pales as they are traced between peaks and pits.

On continuous surfaces the points of the pale and of the pass have at once the attributes of both a local maximum and a local minimum, each resulting in a self-crossing contour. On a map showing the areal variation of the surface for any true field quantity, no flat areas are to be found. There are, of course, singular points on the surface where the instantaneous gradient goes to zero, and direction of slope becomes indeterminate when these points are regarded in isolation. These points are precisely of the kinds mentioned above, peaks, pits, passes, and pales. Peaks and pits have been defined as local maxima and local minima respectively; simple closed contours therefore exist within their immediate neighborhoods. At the point of a pale or of a pass, gradient is zero, but no locally closed contours occur in the immediate neighborhood; for the point of the pale or of the pass has the attributes both of a local maximum and of a local minimum, and a self-crossing of the contour line results. One profile, properly taken, shows the pass at the lowest value between two peaks; a profile through the same point taken at right angles to the first shows the value at the pass to be higher than any other along that cross section. The pale occurs at the high point between pits, but it is a low point along the line at right angles to the line joining the pits.

THE INDICATRIX

To make the above considerations clearer, let us employ the concept of the *indicatrix*, defined as the curve in which a given surface is cut by a plane indefinitely near and parallel to the tangent plane at any point, so called because it indicates the nature of the surface at that point. In addition to contour lines, let lines of steepest slope also be considered and hereafter referred to simply as slope lines. Slope lines, of course, always cross contour lines at right angles. (This property is preserved on these conformal maps.) Through every point on the surface, there is a slope line that, in general, begins at a certain peak and ends at a certain pit. Exceptions are the lines connecting peaks and passes and those connecting pales and pits.

Consider the most distant closed contour line defining a given sample peak or pit. This exterior line is intersected at every one of its points by a slope line. All of these slope lines must intersect all of the interior closed contour lines as well, uniting at an interior point — the peak or the pit. In the general case, the indicatrix at the peak or pit will be an ellipse, as will the contour lines in the immediate neighborhood, with the major and minor axes corresponding to the directions of least and greatest curvature respectively.

Letting a and b for the indicatrix be the semidiameters, major and minor respectively, the equation for the orthogonal trajectory of the ellipse on a plane with x and y coordinates is $y^{b^2} = Cx^{a^2}$. So long as C does not equal infinity, the curve this equation defines touches the axis of x, the direction of least curvature. If C does equal infinity, x becomes zero and the curve touches the axis of the direction of greatest curvature, i.e., y. In general, at the peak or the pit all of the slope curves, save the one limiting case, touch the line indicating the direction of least curvature. The only exception occurs when the indicatrix is truly a circle and the slope lines pass in all directions through the common point at the peak or pit.

At a pale or a pass the indicatrix is, in general, a hyperbola and the trajectory is $C = x^{a^2} y^{b^2}$. When this goes through the pass, C equals zero, and then either x or y equals zero. As a result, only two slope lines occur through the pass, each bisecting the angles made by the branches of the self-crossing contour line. These slope lines therefore intersect at right angles. Let the slope line on which the pass is a point of minimum elevation be termed a ridge line and the other, a course line.

In general, ridge lines pass from peak to peak and course lines from pit to pit. Even with an arbitrary boundary condition it is possible that any one ridge or course line begins and ends on a map at the same peak or pit, thus forming a closed curve, and, in exceptional cases, any one of these lines may be alternately a ridge line or a course line, as is the case with minor peaks on a major one, so that any particular segment must be named with reference to the pass or pale with which it is considered. This consideration must be regarded especially in connection with the self-crossing contour line which is not of the usual figure-eight or outloop type but rather of the inloop type.

Stream Ordering and Contour Mapping 213

SOME TOPOLOGICAL PROPERTIES

To consider additional matters we need to establish symbols. Let: S = number of peaks (summits); I = number of pits (immits); P = number of passes; B = number of pales (bars); C = number of course lines; and R = number of ridge lines.

Within any completely closed contour line on a continuous surface the number of peaks, S, is always one more than the number of passes, P, so that $S = P + 1$. The same rule applies to the number of pits, I, and the number of pales, B, so that $I = B + 1$.

If, in the singular cases of passes and pales, we count each of these as single, double, or n-ple, depending on whether two, three or $n+1$ areas of elevation or depression meet at a pass or pale, respectively, then the above counts can be taken as before, giving each singular point its proper number.

Let P_1 be the number of single passes, P_2 the number of double passes, etc., and B_1, B_2, etc., be the numbers of single, double, etc., pales. Then the number of peaks will be $S = 1 + P_1 + 2P_2 +$ etc., and the number of pits will be $I = 1 + B_1 + 2B_2 +$ etc.

Now, regard any one ridge line or course line as beginning at a pass or a pale and ending at its respective peak or pit. Then the number of ridge lines, R, will be $R = 2(B_1 + P_1) + 3(B_2 + P_2) +$ etc., and the number of course lines, C, will be the same.

With reference to the area enclosed by any one contour line, the following obtains: $(S + I) - (P + B) = 1$.

However, on a closed surface like the spherical earth: $(S + I) - (P + B) = 2$. For, on a sphere, a closed curve bounds two areas.

For a general topological consideration let V be the number of all singular points on the closed surface ($V = S + I + P + B$); let E be the number of lines ($E = R + C$); and let F be the number of separate faces or territories as we shall call them. Then, $F = E - V + 2$.

That is to say the number of faces plus the number of points minus the number of lines equal 2. Again, within any one closed contour line, $F = E - V + 1$.

This general topological relationship among points, lines, and areas was first established by Euler in network analysis (the bridge problem) and was explained in terms of any polyhedron where the number of faces plus the number of vertices minus the number of edges equals two.

Further consideration of the above shows that, for the world's surface, if we put E' equal to the number of ridge lines only, and V' equal to the number of peaks, passes, and pales, then F' is the number of districts of depression (dales) equal to the number of pits. If E'' specifies the number of course lines only and V'' the number of passes, pales, and pits, then F'' is the number of districts of elevation (hills) equal to the number of peaks when the two types of districts are taken independently. Districts whose lines of slope run to the same peaks are the hills, and those whose lines of slope run to the same pits are the dales. The whole closed surface may be divided independently into hills and into dales, each point belonging to a certain hill *and* to a certain dale. Of course, ridge lines are the only slope lines not reaching *pits*, and course lines are the only slope lines not reaching peaks.

SURFACE AND FLOWS

The table concerning flows referred to above is given below. We begin by assuming that "natural" movements on surfaces tend to be along steepest slope lines or gradient paths, i.e. at right angles to the contour lines, and from higher values on the surface toward lower values. These paths are minimum over-the-surface "distances" in each case. This elementary assumption is in keeping with the analysis of potentials and forces in general-field quantity theory. Other assumptions about form and movement are possible especially with regard to additional forces besides the gradient force and also, long-run processes that change surfaces. Here, however, we restrict ourselves to simple gradient movements in the short-run. Our conclusions can be presented in a simple table summarizing converging and diverging flows in terms of dimensions (Table I).

TABLE I

Singular elements: dimensions and vergency

Dimension	Name of surface feature	Vergency
point	peak	divergence
	pit	convergence
	pass	mixed
	pale	mixed
line	course	convergence
	ridge	divergence
area	hill	divergence
	dale	convergence
	territory	mixed

RIVER BASINS: GEOMETRY, TOPOLOGY, AND ORDERS

Let us now relate these ideas specifically to fluvial systems on land forms, particularly to river basins. Fig.1 is an enlarged portion of the Belmont, N.Y., U.S. Geologic Survey Topographic map (contours only). The original linear scale was, of course, 1:62500, the contour interval is 20 ft.

It is often noted when instruction is offered concerning the making or interpreting of contour maps of physical land forms that contours crossing streams (we would say, contours crossing all course lines) are bent so that the "notches" point up stream, i.e., in the direction of higher elevations. We add that the contours crossing ridge lines are bent so that their notches point out precisely the down-hill direction. Even map readers of limited experience should have

Fig.1. Enlarged portion of the Belmont, N.Y., U.S.G.S. Topographic Survey Map (contours only).

no trouble in picking out the most likely positions for streams and their accompanying basin divides on the above noted map in Fig.1.

If we accept these patterns of contour bending as necessary — and indeed they are necessary — we can then follow through, to its final conclusion, the statement about the necessary elements and their dimensional relationships in fluvial systems.

On the following illustration, Fig. 2, a simple first-order stream (i.e. a stream having no tributary) and its basin area bounded by ridge lines are shown. The heaviest lines are ridge lines. The lines of intermediate width represent course lines. The solid part of it represents the portion lying in an actual stream and the dotted portion indicates the position of this line continued back to the pass whence it issued.

The fine thin lines are contour lines. Peaks, pits, passes and pales are labelled, as noted above, as S, I, P, and B, respectively.

The significant features of the contours are the outloops of the figure of eight-type contour with each loop enclosing a peak and with the self-crossing of the contour line occurring at the attendant pass and the inloop type bounding a pit with the self-crossing at the required pale (Fig. 3).

It is well established that any contour is a closed circuit on the earth (although, of course, not necessarily within the area portrayed on any given topographic map). With respect to a first-order drainage basin the only contours that close *within* the basin are those in the immediate vicinity of the *one* pit. Moreover, all of these are within the smaller loop of the inloop type of contour (see Fig. 2 again). The larger loop lies *entirely* outside of the first order basin in question and its path may lead across many basins before closing. Note, however, that any one of the intermediate contour lines shown on Fig. 2 may itself be a segment of the larger loop of some inloop type contour with its smaller loop located entirely within some distant and separate basin. Even

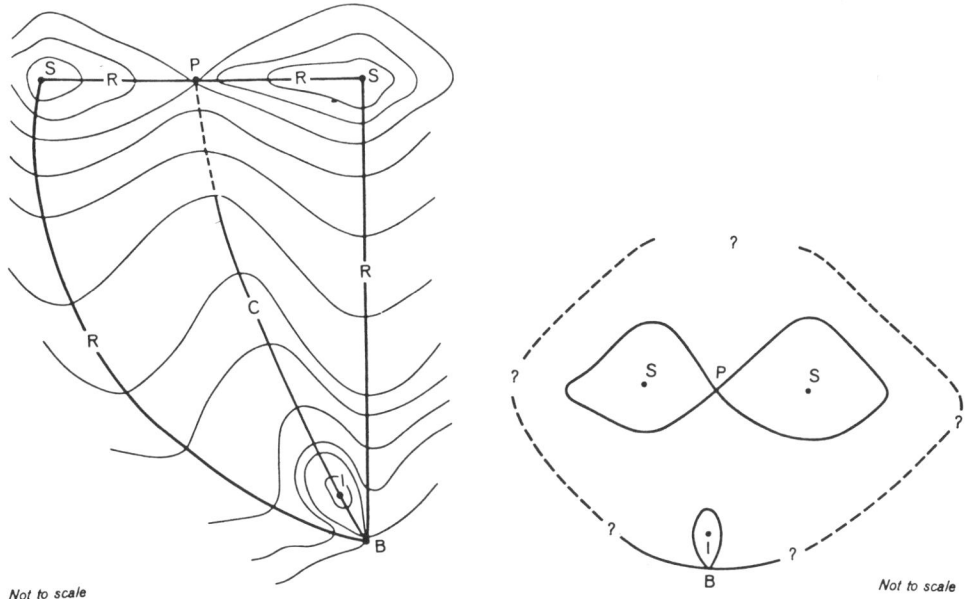

Fig. 2. First-order basin.

Fig. 3. Self-crossing contour lines related to first-order basin.

Stream Ordering and Contour Mapping 217

those contour lines that close in the immediate neighborhood of the peaks in Fig.2 must lie only partly in the basin under consideration and of necessity partly outside it.

If other closed contours (say around some peak or some pit) are found within what has been previously assumed to be a first-order basin, this is evidence that it is really some higher-order basin and that a lower-order one lies entirely within it. In fact on the earth's surface a virtually infinite regress does exist, limited only by particle size at which level the concept of surface is not applicable. We shall speak of that difficulty later in this paper. For the present, we consider the presence of one visually observable unbranched stream — having no tributaries -- as evidence of a first-order stream (and its basin) and carry the accuracy of contour positioning to the level sufficient to delineate only it and not to include those evidences of additional course lines which, however, lack stream channel flows.

Note that course lines or ridge lines connect our designated points. Thus there are two individual and distinct course lines (segments) present within the basin. One runs downhill from the pass to the pit. The other continues from this pit uphill to the pale. For the stream to have a continuous flow there must be sufficient water in its channel to permit it a high enough level to cross the pale. Hence some water must flow uphill for all or any of it to move "downstream". Any stream flowing through several basins has a series of connected pits each with a "downstream" side but actually locally uphill pale. When streams dry up they do not do so in sheet-like fashion. Rather, they reduce to nothing through a series of disconnections of pits with resulting isolated pools of water. A disconnection occurs where and when there is not sufficient water for the flow to cross some pale.

Ridge lines also run between singular points, as for example from a peak to a pass. Another ridge line then goes on to another peak. Also, ridge lines go from peaks to pales.

Ridge lines do not go to pits nor do course lines go to peaks. Both however do go to passes and to pales. If we consider peaks and pits as absolute extremum points and passes and pales as mixed extrema points, then any combination of course lines and/or ridge lines producing a connected continuous path through however many basins desired and of whatever order, do and must exhibit an alternation of absolute extremum and mixed extrema points. (This condition assumes additional importance when we examine below the infinite regress referred to previously.)

When two first-order streams meet, a second-order stream is formed. In Fig.4, a typical example of the essential spatial structure attending the paired first-order basins and the resulting second-order stream is given.

Again we see that the outloop figure of eight-type contour line is present, but this time there are two of them, one of them with both of its loops contained wholly within one of the loops of the other. The situation given in Fig.5 below is, of course, possible, but not likely, the situation portrayed in Fig.4 being the more general case. Fig.6, I shows a section of the inloop type of contour line we considered with the single first-order basin. Fig.6, II shows us that a "rabbit-ears" or "butterfly" double smaller inloop type occurs with the incidence of a second-order stream.

Note on Fig.4 that one ridge line (the "central" one) is shared as a common divide for the two first-order basins.

Fig.7 reveals additional features concerning second-order basins. This illustration is adapted from one by Strahler (1964, p.376). He shows all streams within and the outer ridge line boundary of a fourth-order basin. We have added plausible interior ridge lines and have marked singular points. Again, the heavy lines are ridge lines and the lighter ones are course lines. The second-order stream is shown, as the legend indicates, by a dashed line. This illustration shows that the second-order basin contains at least two first-order basins whose exterior ridge lines it shares and additional area and ridge lines as well. Here the additional area is served by one additional first-order basin and stream flowing into it, but not thereby promoting it to a higher order and by an area of direct drainage through no intermediating stream. Such an area of direct drainage (overland flow) into any stream of higher order than first is

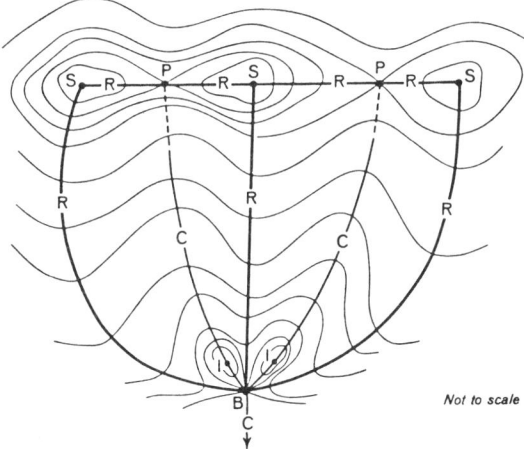

Fig.4. Paired first-order basins producing second-order stream.

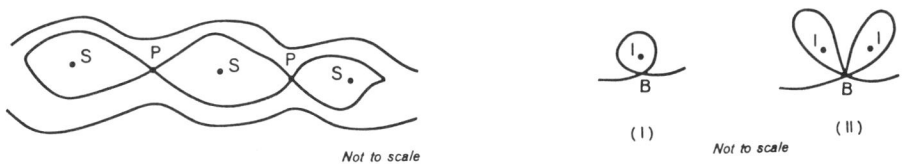

Fig.5. Possible but not typical arrangement of peaks and passes.

Fig.6. Inloop contours for simple first-order streams (I) and paired first-order streams (II).

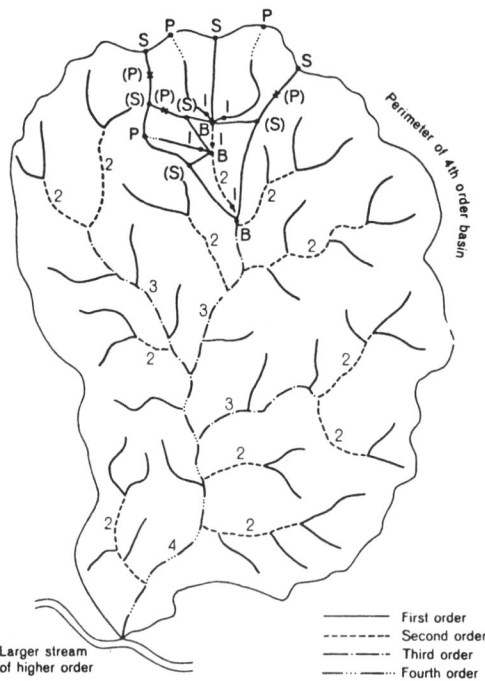

Fig.7. Second-order basin within fourth-order basin. (Modified from Strahler (1960), p.376, Fig.25.7.).

regarded as an interbasin area. We see then that two first-order basins are a necessary but *not* sufficient condition for a second-order basin. At least interbasin area must also exist. Of course additional first-order streams not promoting the basin may develop within it, and indeed higher orders that do promote the basin may sometimes come into existence. Always, however, *some* interbasin area *must* exist within *every* basin of order higher than one and very likely, based on observation, additional non-promoting lower order streams.

Now the other extremely important feature of Fig.7 is that which shows that for basin orders higher than one additional course lines other than those for the first-order streams *must* exist, albeit without channel flow. The x's located on ridge line segments indicate that additional heretofore unregarded passes (P) must exist on these segments. The precise locations of the x's must not be regarded as an attempt specifically to localize these passes but rather to indicate that somewhere on a ridge line segment between any two indicated peaks, S, and/or newly recognized peaks, (S), a pass must occur. (Recall the rule stated earlier concerning alternating absolute extremum and mixed extrema points along any connected path.) Now if these passes exist (and they must, as well as virtually innumerable others) so, too do their course lines, the resulting pits, and pales, and also the ridge lines that pales occasion   along with their additional peaks. These new peaks require additional passes, and so on in new and continually regenerating cycles to the level of separated particles at which level the concept of surface, itself, is no longer applicable. Obviously, the details of the entire structure of any set of nested "basins" (including those without channel flow) cannot be learned so that some threshold must be recognized and defined. It is apparent that all so-called recognizable first-order streams do not contain precisely the same-order course lines. Actual rock type, climate, slope, etc., do determine the length of overland flow preceding channel flow. Moreover, "lower" orders do exist. However there is a demonstrated success that systematic relations among the observed empirical regularities in nested river-basins can be understood by regarding as of first order the streams that have no visibly channeled flow tributaries. Despite variation in the actual course-line order on a surface of so-called first-order streams, the necessity to recognize a threshold exists and the regarding of all unbranched streams as of the same order, namely what has come to be called the first, has proved remarkably convenient and instructive operationally. The slightly different real order that each of the course lines of the so-called first-order streams occupies in the hierarchy of course lines has not served to hide the nature of the system. Rather, the bold operational definition and ordering introduced from empirical observation has helped clarify the relationship in the system. We must remember however that our threshold thus defined has not so much a physical as a statistical meaning.

Fig.7 represents a plausible picture of a second-order basin and indicates a likely basin arrangement based on flow efficiencies. It is, admittedly, possible to construct an entire hypothetical system for a high-order basin in which a bifurcation ratio of two applies throughout and in which peaks are conserved. Thus, the regenerating cycle is avoided. However, either interbasin areas are too large and have inefficient shapes or successively higher-order stream segments then are shorter than preceding ones. For example, we can imagine a third-order basin having only two second-order streams and four first-order streams. If peaks are to be conserved, then only five need exist, all on the exterior set of ridge line segments. Such a portrayal requires, contrary to observed regularities and "least-work" efficiency explanations of them, the inconsistencies noted above. Even a cursory glance at topographic survey maps confirms the notion of efficiency of size and shape of relevant areas and supports the necessity for and the existence of the virtually infinite regress among singular points, lines, and areas. Fig.7, then, presents a "reasonable" set of relations in that they are defensible by theory. Although virtually an infinite number of ridge lines exist, a tendency toward conservation of total ridge line length consistent with a given order of nested basins and work minimization principles seems to be the rule. That is to say, work minimization results in tendencies toward short ridge lines and compact basins. But note also sets of circular basins cannot exhaust an area.

Here then are the geometrical elements, according to their dimensions, present within or on the boundary of a first-order basin, and the number of times each *does and must* occur. This is the geometry that is *necessary and sufficient* to a first-order basin (Table II).

Stream Ordering and Contour Mapping

TABLE II

Geometry of first-order basin

Element and designation	Name and designation	Number of occurrences (necessary and sufficient)
Point (V)	peak (S)	2
	pit (I)	1
	pass (P)	1
	pale (B)	1
Line (E)	course (C)	2
	ridge (R)	4
Area (F)	dale	1
	hill	0 (only parts of two separate hills are present)
	territory	2

The geometrical elements represented in two first-order basins paired to produce a second-order stream (but not including the *additional* features of the second-order basin) are given in Table III.

It is obvious that basin and dale are synonymous. The general principle that $F + V - E = 1$ and its variations including F' and F'' as explained earlier not only holds within any one closed contour line, as it may or may not traverse several basins, but also within any one basin or paired basins. It is also equally obvious that one hill cannot be contained within a first-order basin although single first-order basins contain parts of two hills. It requires parts of four first- or higher-order basins or interbasin areas to comprise one hill. For example, in

TABLE III

Geometry of paired first-order basins

Element and designation	Name and designation	Number of occurrences (necessary and sufficient)
point (V)	peak (S)	3
	pit (I)	2
	pass (P)	2
	pale (B)	1
line (E)	course (C)	4
	ridge (R)	7
area (F)	dale	2
	hill	0 (only parts of three separate hills are present)
	territory	4

TABLE IV

Relationships for the single first-order basin

$S = 2$	$R = 4$	dales = 1
$I = 1$	$C = 2$	hills = 0
		(parts of two separate hills)
$P = 1$		territories = 2

$$F + V - E = 1$$
$$2 + 5 - 6 = 1$$
$$F' + V' - E' = 1$$
$$1 + 4 - 4 = 1$$
$$F'' + V'' - E'' = 1$$
$$0 + 3 - 2 = 1$$

Fig.4 the area within the course lines constitutes part of a hill, the other part lies on the other side of the external connected ridge line segments between the two passes, which connected segments, in terms of topology, serve as an axis of symmetry.

The relationships as given in Table IV (see again Fig.2) hold for the single first-order basin.

The above conditions are those and only those which describe the geometry and topology of the single first-order basin. They are at once necessary and sufficient and cannot be exceeded nor need they be in terms of efficiency.

For the paired first-order basins (see Fig.4), we again find necessary and sufficient geometrical-topological conditions that obtain and that cannot nor need be exceeded for maximum efficiency (Table V).

Now, it is important to notice that the paired first-order basins have an entity that permits them to be regarded as a unit. Their shared internal ridge

TABLE V

Relationships for the paired first-order basin

$S = 3$	$R = 7$	dales = 2
$I = 2$	$C = 4$	hills = 0
		(parts of three separate hills)
$P = 2$		territories = 4
$B = 1$		

$$F + V - E = 1$$
$$4 + 8 - 11 = 1$$
$$F' + V' - E' = 1$$
$$2 + 6 - 7 = 1$$
$$F'' + V'' - E'' = 1$$
$$0 + 5 - 4 = 1$$

line is an axis of symmetry. Woldenberg (1968) has demonstrated that mixed spatial hierarchies based on nested hexagons explain observed phenomena with great precision. It is therefore instructive to attempt to identify the basic hexagon in terms of our geometrical elements. What, for example, constitutes the one face of the modular hexagon? What are its vertices? And its edges?

Fig.8 is offered here as one possible identification. It does not, however, agree with the other details of Woldenberg's discovery and formulation. It is, therefore, only to be regarded as suggestive. In fact, nesting seems difficult. Other identifications are possible and, in fact, the recognition of course lines as edges seems to offer better possibilities in accounting for nestings.

Let us now depart from consideration of the identification of the hexagonal structure, if indeed, that identification is possible or, for that matter, desirable. Let us examine both the minimum second-order basin and the typical second-order basin. It is necessary to make this distinction for the minimum order geometrically cannot freely exist in face of work minimization and spatial efficiency. That is to say, a bifurcation ratio of two is not experienced in nature as the general case.

Fig.9 shows the minimum second-order basin. This condition is necessary, but not sufficient (see Table VI).

The structure in Fig.9 conserves peaks, but is not efficient. A more reasonable one is that shown as noted, in Fig.7. As noted earlier, the additional peaks require additional passes, and hence course lines, ridge lines, and thus pales and pits, and so on in regenerating cycles. It is important to note that the matching of the Euler theorem serves to identify various stages that can be regarded as consistent levels of generalization. The particular level to be shown is, of course, that one essential to the problem at hand.

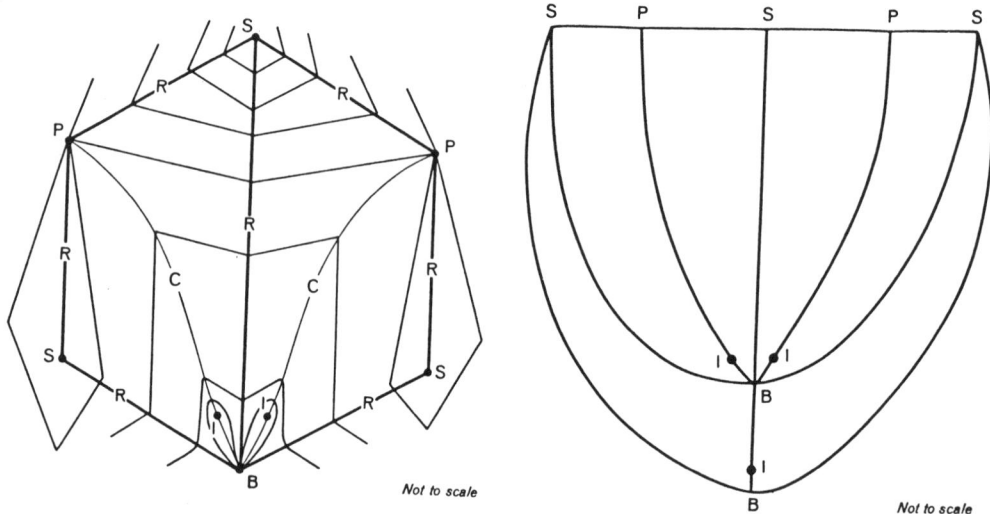

Fig.8. Hypothetical paired first-order basins-hexagonal.

Fig.9. Absolute minimum second-order basin.

TABLE VI

Relationships for the minimum second-order basin

$S = 3$	$R = 9$	dales = 3
$I = 3$	$C = 6$	hills = 0
		(parts of three separate hills)
$P = 2$		territories = 6
$B = 2$		

$$F + V - E = 1$$
$$6 + 10 - 15 = 1$$

$$F' + V' - E' = 1$$
$$3 + 7 - 9 = 1$$

$$F'' + V'' - E'' = 1$$
$$0 + 7 - 6 = 1$$

A RECOMMENDATION FOR TOPOGRAPHIC MAPPING

These are important matters conceptually, in terms of the analysis of surface systems generally, and river-basin systems in particular. They are also important cartographically. Cartographers through the ages have avoided showing the single-valued self-crossing contour lines. These are essential. Surveys should especially determine their precise locations and mapping should, above all else, indicate them, guided by the level of generalization needed.

Conventional topographic mapping practice has not reflected the developments in the understandings of the topology and geometry of surfaces and the study of flows on these surfaces. There is a need now for a new kind of topographic map which will be keyed to more recent knowledge in these fields.

The following paragraphs serve not only to recapitulate the foregoing arguments, but also to recommend new departures in topographic mappings. My colleague, Michael Woldenberg, has assisted in the preparation of these statements.

Specifically, current topographic maps generally use a constant contour interval to indicate gradients on surfaces. This practice is sufficient to describe flows on surfaces in general, if flow were simply overland flow, but of course this is only part of the story. Flows concentrate in channels to gain economies of scale, and hence the end points of course lines, along whose length channel flow begins and ends, must be clearly delineated. Thus a pass is a point and must be defined where some given contour line crosses itself. The pass is also located at the intersection of a course line and ridge line. As the ridge line is followed toward a confluence, it is found to recross the course line at its lower end, and a new point is located, the pale, which again may alternatively be described as the intersection point of a self-crossing contour line.

Thus a whole set of contours is called for, which will serve to delineate these critical passes and pales. Between these contours normal interpolations may be used if desired.

The order reflected in Horton's laws may be reflected in the contour intervals. Suppose that in a river system in a region of youth, developed on a homogeneous surface, detritus is supplied so quickly that materials in the riverbed are not appreciably decreased in size with distance travelled downstream. Then Hack (1957) and Broscoe (1959) suggest the profile of the stream will be logarithmic, and hence the contour interval may well show arithmetic increase, where each contour interval reflects a new stream order.

Suppose the materials in the river bed decline exponentially with distance travelled downstream. Then the profile will be a power function, and the appropriate contour interval will be logarithmic, where each contour interval will correspond to the drop a stream makes for each order basin.

In a word we propose to perform research in developing new topographic maps reflecting the current understanding of spatial order on the earth's surface.

In addition, we propose a small change in the stream ordering system currently employed. In the preceding sections the convenient and operationally significant system employed by Horton (1945) as modified by Strahler (1964) was used. Basically, we suggest merely that what are now regarded as first-order streams and basins must be considered as of zero order and that present second-order be called first and so on. The justification for and the convenience attending such a change are described below.

Horton suggested several laws of fluvial morphology. These may be classified in two ways, direct geometric series, and inverse geometric series. Examples of these follow.

Direct geometric series. In the law of stream lengths, Horton (1945, p.291) stated that: "The average lengths of stream of each of the different orders in a drainage basin tend closely to approximate a direct geometric series in which the first term is the average length of streams of the first order."

The mathematically equivalent statement is:

$$\bar{L}_u = \bar{L}_1 R_L^{u-1}$$

where $\bar{L}_u$ is the average length of the stream of order u; L_1 is the average length of the stream of order 1; and R_L is the length ratio of L_{u+1}/L_u. Schumm (1956, p.606), following the suggestion of Horton (1945, p.294), created an analogous law for stream basin areas:

$$\bar{A}_u = \bar{A}_1 R_a^{u-1}$$

where $\bar{A}_u$ is the mean area of basins of order u; $\bar{A}_1$ is the mean area of the first order basins; and R_a is an area ratio analogous to the length ratio R_L.

Inverse geometric series. Horton's law of stream numbers is as follows (Horton, 1945, p.291): "The numbers of streams of different orders in a given drainage basin tend closely to approximate an inverse geometric series in which the first term is unity and the ratio is the bifurcation ratio."

In symbols:

$$N_u = R_b{}^{k-u}$$

where N_u is the number of streams of order u; R_b is the bifurcation ratio N_u/N_{u+1}; and k is the order of the trunk stream.

As Woldenberg (1966, p.433) has shown, stream order is a logarithm. Logarithms are by definition exponents to some base. Ten is commonly used, and an increase in order of magnitude is equal to 10^{x+1} (where x is any number).

Thus stream order is really stream order of magnitude, to the base of some ratio which may well differ from the commonly used 10. For direct geometric series, the variable y which is the function of stream order may be generalized as:

$$\bar{y}_u = y_1 (R_y)^{u-1}$$

where all terms are analogous to those previously identified.

If the threshold stream were actually of order 0 rather than order 1, this statement could be rewritten as:

$$\bar{y}_u = y_0 (R_y)^u$$

Similarly inverse geometric series would be written as follows:

$$y_u = R_b{}^{k-u}$$

and would be unchanged by the change in the order for threshold streams.

Hence identifying the threshold stream as order 0 simplifies direct geometric series, and has no effect on inverse geometric series. There is another justification as well.

We have pointed out above, the existence of the virtually infinite regress of peaks, pits, passes, pales, course lines, and ridge lines, basins, and hills in regenerating cycles which are implied, but not perceived on a topographic surface. Such course lines do not form channels, and such basins are thus not of threshold size. Therefore, when considering these basins, negative orders may well be used. It is possible to think of orders equal to −5 or −19, etc., which signify basins at very small orders of magnitude.

ACKNOWLEDGEMENT

Professor Warntz gratefully acknowledges the support of the Geography Branch, U.S. Office of Naval Research, Project NR 389-147.

REFERENCES

Broscoe, A., 1959. Quantitative analysis of longitudinal stream profiles of small watersheds. Office of Naval Research Technical Report No.18, Project 389-042, Department of Geology, Columbia University, New York, N.Y., 104 pp.
Cayley, A., 1859. On contour and slope lines. Lond. Edinb. Dublin Philos. Mag. J. Sci., 18: 264—268.
Hack, J.T., 1957. Studies of longitudinal stream profiles in Virginia and Maryland. U.S. Geol. Surv. Prof. Pap. 294-B, 97 pp.
Horton, R.E., 1945. Erosional development of streams and their drainage basins: Hydrophysical approach to quantitative morphology. Geol. Soc. Am. Bull., 56: 275—370.
Maxwell, J.Cl., 1870. On hills and dales. Lond. Edinb. Dublin Philos. Mag. J. Sci., 40 (4th Ser.): 421—427.
Schumm, S., 1956. Evolution of drainage systems and slopes in badlands at Perth Amboy, New Jersey. Geol. Soc. Am. Bull., 67: 597—646.
Strahler, A.N., 1964. Quantitative geomorphology of drainage basins and channel networks. In: Ven Te Chow (Editor), Handbook of Applied Hydrology: Compendium of Water Resources Technology. McGraw-Hill, New York, N.Y., pp.39—76.
U.S. Geological Survey, 1939. Topographic Survey Map of Belmont, N.Y., scale 1:62 500.
Warntz, W. and Woldenberg, M., 1967. Concepts and applications — Spatial order. Harvard Papers in Theoretical Geography No.1, Office of Naval Research Technical Report, Project 389-147, Harvard University, Cambridge, Mass., 196 pp.
Woldenberg, M., 1966. Horton's laws justified in terms of allometric growth and steady state in open systems. Geol. Soc. Am. Bull., 77: 431—434.
Woldenberg, M., 1968. Energy flow and spatial order, with special reference to mixed hexagonal central place hierarchies. Harvard Papers in Theoretical Geography No.8, Office of Naval Research Technical Report, Project 389-147, Harvard University, Cambridge, Mass., 46 pp.

CARTOGRAPHIC PROBLEMS IN STREAM CHANNEL DELINEATION

R. J. Chorley and P. F. Dale
Department of Geography, University of Cambridge

The acquisition of data for stream network analysis is largely dependent on the availability of topographic maps and the accuracy with which data is portrayed thereon. When Yoxall (1969) examined the 1:250,000 series of maps of Ghana, he found inconsistencies in the selection of rivers for mapping. Scheidegger (1966, p. 57) reported that the blue stream lines printed on maps are extremely arbitrary and appeared to depend on the channel flow observed to be present by the surveyor or by means of air photographs. When Morisawa (1957) mapped the channel system of a part of the Appalachian Plateaus in spring she found much more running water in channels than was depicted on the U.S. Geological Survey 1:24,000 topographical maps, even when they were produced from air photographs, it being particularly apparent that many flowing fingertip tributaries had been obscured from the air by overhanging trees. The policy of the U.S. Geological Surveys has been to classify all streams as either perennial (i.e. ones that flow throughout the year) or intermittent (i.e. ones that are dry for a considerable time each year, say for three months or longer). Before criticising such a classification as over-simplistic, it is pertinent to consider the problems in identifying a stream channel network in the field and on maps and air photographs.

Field Identification

The major problem in defining any such network in the field lies in the identification of the most headward fingertip tributaries. Scheidegger (1966, pp. 56-57) has pointed out that, as a channel system is followed upstream, the streamflow becomes intermittent and the channel forks into a network of smaller channels which perhaps lose themselves in a multitude of gullies and rills. The identification of the headward parts of a channel network and the distinction between channels and smaller gullies and rills is of great importance in the generation of parameters which adequately describe the morphometry of fluvially-eroded landforms, especially of drainage density. This identification varies in difficulty depending upon the nature of the erosional environment, being generally simpler in regions of sparse vegetation and little debris cover (e.g. the Perth Amboy and South Dakota badlands: Schumm, 1956) and more difficult where the movement of thick debris may fill and obscure the channels. Even in these semi-arid and arid clay/shale badlands, the problem of channel differentiation is made difficult by the existence of rill networks ramifying from the channel network. In whatever environment one is working, however, the standard channel definition as including "all intermittent and perennial flow lines located in clearly defined valleys" (Strahler, 1964, p. 443) is inadequate.

In the sub-humid Mediterranean climatic environment of the chaparral-covered San Dimas Experimental Forest in Southern California Maxwell (1960, p. 9 and 24) was faced with a situation where the long dry season sometimes causes the smallest ephemeral stream channels to be obscured and indistinct, and where sliding rock debris on slopes often produce discrete debris chute pseudo-channels. He developed four criteria which were particularly valuable in the field definition of true channels:

1. The existence of well-defined, nearly vertical banks; which excluded the chutes.
2. The presence of orientated debris or of debris suspended or draped over branches or roots.
3. The presence of wash marks, ripples and small rill marks within suspected channel margins.
4. The continuity of a suspected channel with a larger one.

In the contrasting well-vegetated and debris-covered Appalachian Plateaus, Morisawa (1959, p. 6) encountered five types of difficulty in defining a channel network:

1. Where is the stream head? This was solved by taking the highest incision of a continuous channel into the surface which showed evidence of water corrosion at any time. The observations by Hack and Goodlett (1960) in the Central Appalachians, however, show this problem to be more complex than the solution assumed.

2. Are recent gullies caused, for example, by a recent heavy downpour to be classed as a channel? Where present and unhealed, these were so classed. The subsequent comments on channel definition from the point of view of their role in terms of runoff has some further bearing on this point.

3. Some channels disappear under debris, emerging further down the valley.

4. Some streams diverge to follow two or more channels and then reunite. Morisawa chose to include the largest channel for the definition of the network.

5. A number of large and deep valleys contained no definite stream channel which could be included in the network. This problem of "dry valleys", often believed to relate to changing runoff conditions of climatic change, must be resolved before any adequate definition of the permanence of channels can be given.

The problem of defining fingertip channels in the broad heads of debris-covered, vegetated basins has been approached in the Central Appalachians by Hack and Goodlett (1960, pp. 5-7) in defining the five characteristic parts of these first-order valleys (Figure 1):

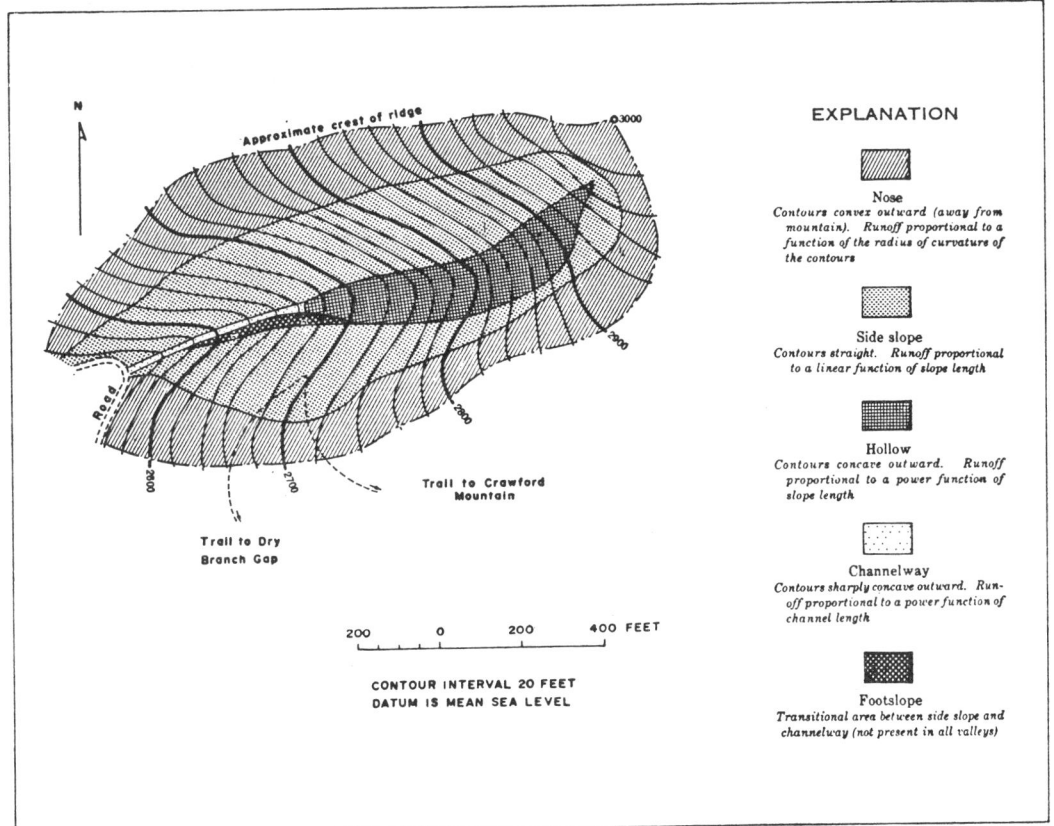

Fig. 1. Contour of the head of a first-order valley on the west side of Crawford Mountain, north-west Virginia, showing a classification of slope and channel areas (from Hack and Goodlett, 1960).

1. Nose. The well-drained ridge crests and adjacent upper slopes where orthogonal flow lines diverge.
2. Side slopes. The straight middle parts of valley-side slopes where flow lines are parallel.
3. Hollow. The poorly-drained, debris-filled upper valley floor (probably excavated by the stream channelway during previous high discharges) where flow lines converge and which is susceptible to channel head invasion during high runoff events
4. Channelway. This is the stream channel proper, bordered by steep banks and covered with coarse rock fragments, within which intermittent concentrated flows prevent the growth of trees and shrubs.
5. Footslope. An occasionally-present low angle slope with converging flow lines bordering the channelway. This is commonly composed of slope or flood debris which is occasionally flushed out by high flows.

Of these, category 4 is the true channel but 3 may be included (Gregory and Walling, 1968).

Some of the above difficulties of giving an adequate operational definition of a stream channel in the field have been highlighted in the following definition by Melton (1957, p. 1) of a channel as "a permanent, clearly defined trench or trough clearly showing evidence of scour by channel flow and bounded by valley sides sloping towards the channel axis. Excluded by this definition are ephemeral or seasonal rills cut in otherwise smooth slopes which do not contribute runoff to the rill and which have no clearly defined watershed and drainage divide". It is clear, then, that five main considerations enter into the problem of defining the existence and extent of a stream channel network: channel size, connectivity with the main network, pattern, permanence, and the role played by the feature in basin runoff.

Natural stream channels are of very differing dimensions and it is not possible to lay down absolute standards of definition according to size which will, for example, include the minute fingertip tributaries of clay badlands but exclude the larger ephemeral rills of some humid valleys. Nevertheless concepts of relative size within a given network system are applicable, but mainly in terms of the relationships between channel length and drainage area. The second consideration of connectivity with a larger channel (Maxwell, 1960, p. 24) is similarly ambiguous in that, for example, stream-bank rills fulfil this requirement. However, all parts of the channel system must by definition, be connected. The third aspect of channel definition, that of pattern, again cannot be applied in isolation. Despite this, when one is dimensionlessly comparing stream systems and rill systems it is usually clear that stream networks are distinctly bifurcating with appreciable entrance angles, whereas rill channels are "relatively uniform, closely-spaced and nearly parallel channels" (Horton, 1945, p. 331).

The feature of permanence (however this may be defined in practice) has been often stressed in field definitions of stream channels, and Horton (1945, pp. 283-284) included in his analysis all permanent network stream channels, both perennial and intermittent. Schumm (1956, p. 601) used this criterion as the basis for his recognition of badlands drainage channels, noting that rills (ascribed by Horton (1945, p. 332) to the accidental local concentrations of sheetflow) are generally ephemeral features, often suffering an annual cycle of formation and destruction (Schumm, 1956, p. 632). However, during periods of active expansion of the "permanent" stream channel network, or during high runoff events of large recurrence interval, rill divides may be broken down by the processes of micro-piracy and master rills develop into truly permanent fingertip channels by cross-grading (Horton, 1945, p. 335). The work of Hack and Goodlett (1960, p. 6) has shown that in debris-mantled terrains channel heads may be choked to become poorly-drained stream head hollows where high discharges may feed temporary sub-debris channel flow or where alternating stream head backcutting and hollow infilling may make the transient stream head position difficult to define (Kirkby and Chorley, 1967, pp. 17-18).

It is natural that implicit in all definitions of stream channels a most important consideration is their functional role in conducting surface runoff. Horton (1945) considered stream channels to result from laterally-concentrated surface runoff and rills from sheetflow, and he included in his determinations of drainage density all intermittent and ephemeral stream channels which carry flood waters (Horton, 1945, p. 284) — a rather difficult definition to enforce in practice. A more satisfactory emphasis is on the relationships between the channel network and its contributing drainage area, and Schumm (1956, p. 632), defining rills as not possessing clearly-defined drainage areas, operated on the assumption that "all channels possessing recognisable drainage areas were considered permanent drainage features and mapped as such" (Schumm, 1956, p. 601). Horton's (1945, pp. 316-317 and 331-332) idea of a "belt of no (sheet) erosion" near drainage divides is of significance here because it implies that, in catchments of less than a limiting length no sheet runoff of sufficient depth to entrain surface debris and initiate rills (some of which might, under the kind of favourable conditions already specified, ultimately develop into fingertip channels) is possible. Schumm (1956, p. 607) developed a similar idea with respect to stream channels in his "constant of channel maintenance" (the minimum limiting area required for the development of a drainage channel). In the Perth Amboy clay badlands he noted that first order channels were reasonably well distinguished from the unchanneled interbasin areas (roughly triangular areas contributing unconcentrated surface runoff directly to a non-fingertip channel) by their magnitude, about 75% of the interbasin areas being less than 50 square feet, and the mean interbasin length of 6.8 feet being significantly less than the 8.3 feet mean length of fingertip (first order) channels. In a single fingertip valley Hack and Goodlett (1960, p. 7) noted that the channelway is distinguished from the stream head hollow by its smaller rate of increase of drainage area as one proceeds downvalley than obtains in the stream head hollow.

Few examples exist of checks having been

carried out on the field mapping of stream channels by a second operator. The most careful of these is reported by Maxwell (1960, pp. 24-25) from the San Dimas Experimental Station in Southern California. Here the main discrepancies were in the mapped lengths of first order streams, the omission of some extremely small first order channels, the precise positions of some of the channel junctions which had a slight effect on the resulting stream ordering, and, finally, differences in the degree of sinuosity recognised. Maxwell (1960, p. 25) concluded that "in the area studied trained observers working independently may be able to enumerate the first-order channels with a reproducibility of approximately five per cent except when the topography is more rugged than usual for the San Gabriel Mountains and when access to the area, both in space and time is limited; then a reproducibility of approximately ten per cent may be expected. The errors of reproducibility in enumeration of higher order channels depends upon the type of junction of incorrectly mapped (omitted) first-order channels".

Channel Mapping

The simplified classification of streams as either perennial or intermittent clearly takes no account of these refined attempts at stream channel network definition and the accuracy of topographic map portrayal of such features must be viewed from the angle of the cartographer. In the topographic instructions to the surveyors of the U.S. Geological Survey (1928, p. 244) it states that:—"The topographer should show all perennial streams and leave for office decision the possible omission of any that may be considered not within the publication scale. Although the map should not be overburdened with insignificant rills and forks, such as abound in well-watered countries, the perennial drainage symbol should be pencilled in all cases of doubt. As the purpose of this symbol is to show where running water may be found, it should be indicated on the field sheets only where the perennial character of the stream is reasonably established; and to this end occasionally inquiry should be made to supplement field observations." In their more recent instructions (1963, book 4, p. 16) it is specified that:—"All perennial drainage is shown regardless of length. Intermittent drainage spurs less than 2,000 feet long usually are omitted unless they emanate from springs or bodies of water. As a general rule, for 1:24,000- and 1:62,500-scale maps those streams selected for publication should be shown as starting not closer than about 1,000 feet from the divide or drainage head. However, problems will arise which require modifications of the general rule." The decision as whether to show an intermittent stream or fingertip tributary will be taken by the cartographer and will depend on such factors as whether it requires a bridge symbol where it may be crossed by a road, on the existing drainage density shown and the requirements of avoiding overcrowding of the map face and the general aesthetic considerations of the map series and the scale of its publication. Topfer and Pillewizer (1966) have shown that the processes of cartographic selection and generalisation tend to follow certain mathematical rules in small scale mapping and by implication these principles can be applied at medium scales (Figure 2).

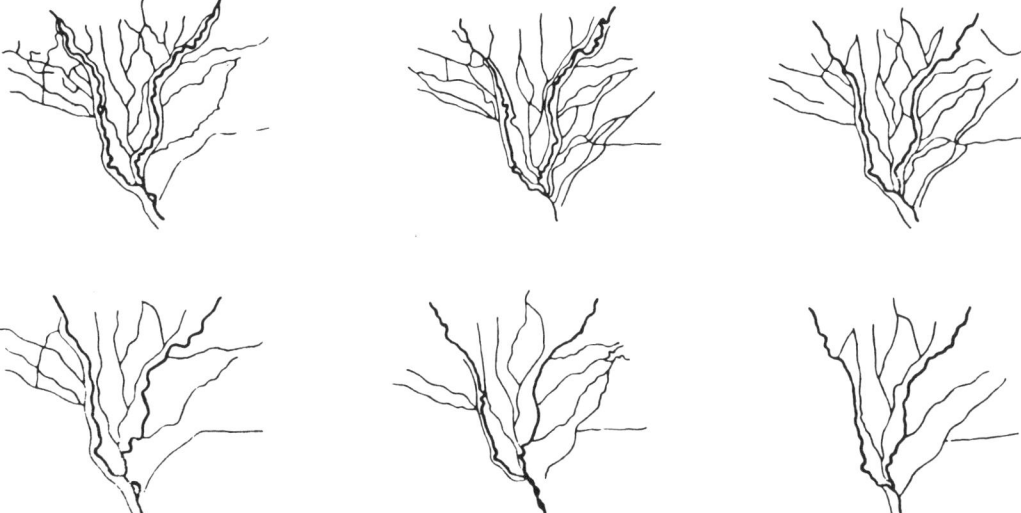

Fig. 2. Examples of generalization of the Nile delta at a scale of 1:500,000 (from Topfer and Pillewizer, 1966.)

Various attempts have been made to infer the existence of stream channels from a study of the contours shown on a map. As Miller (1953, p. 9) put it: "In delimiting the stream channel network it is necesary to pay close attention to contour configuration, and not to depend on the streams shown on the maps. In numerous cases small first order tributaries are clearly indicated by contour crenulations and verified by photographic study, but are not delimited on the maps by the conventional blue stream lines. For this reason, before stream or topographic elements are measured, it is necessary to draw in the missing streams and to extend headward those which are incompletely shown on the map." This approach is to a limited extent legitimate in that it is standard topographic practice to trace in all the drainage lines in the field or on the pencil plot of the air photo compilation and to fit the contours to the drainage pattern. If the cartographer subsequently decides to omit the drainage lines then the contour crenulations will still remain. One is not however justified in assuming that all contour crenulations have been derived in this way, and for the map user, a large element of subjectivity must inevitably enter into any decision regarding the significance of a contour crenulation as an indicator of the existence of a stream channel.

A number of geomorphologists have checked the stream channel networks depicted on topographic maps in the field, and their results are instructive, but somewhat conflicting, depending on the types of map and field/locations. Melton (1957, p. 1) checking basins shown for a number of western States on the U.S. Geological Survey 1:24,000 maps found that a high percentage of first order channels were represented faithfully by the smallest cusps in the contours and that in a few cases contour crenulations did not even represent persistent drainage lines but merely surface irregularities. He concluded that about 95% of the small basins studied in the field required minor channel network corrections on maps compiled from air photographs. Morisawa (1957 and 1959) checked similar 1:24,000 maps produced from aerial photographs by multiplex methods at a contour interval of 20 feet for part of the Appalachian Plateaus. Figure 3 shows an example of one such

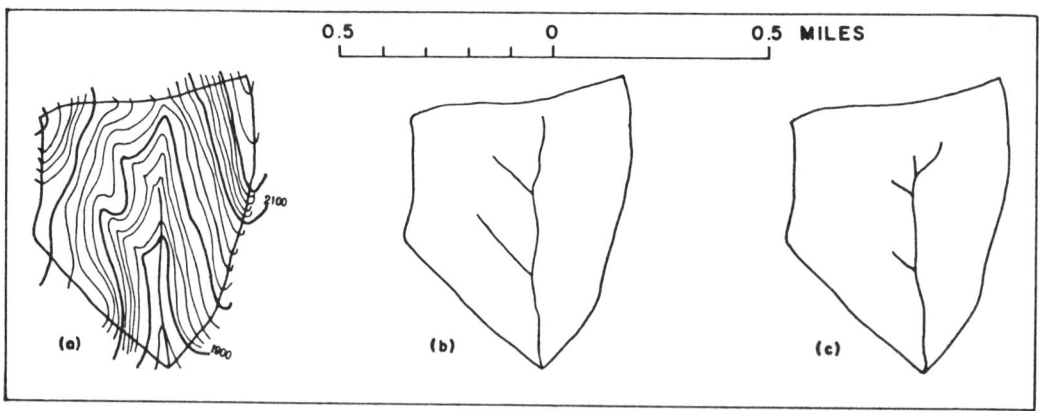

Fig. 3. Contour and drainage map of Heth Run in the Appalachian Plateau: (a) contours and streams shown on the 1:24,000 U.S.G.S. topographic map; (b) drainage net derived from contour crenulations in (a); (c) drainage net as measured in the field (from Morisawa, 1957).

basin, in which the mapped blue lines, the channels defined by contour inflections and the channels mapped in the field have been compared. After correcting measured field distances to horizontal distances, she concluded from an analysis of 18 small basins of less than 2.68 square miles that there was a great discrepancy between the total lengths of blue lines in each basin and the length of channels mapped in the field, but no significant difference between the latter and the channel lengths inferred by means of the contour inference method. Schneider (1961) re-analysed Morisawa's data but considered the correlation between the field measured lengths and the contour inference lengths to be too poor for stream channel lengths to be accurately inferred from these topographic maps. Coates (1958, pp. 24-26) tested the channels inferred from the 1:24,000 map of the Nashville Quadrangle in Southern Illinois (contour interval of 10 feet) with his field maps on a scale of 1:600 and found that fingertip tributaries could seldom be inferred from the U.S.G.S. map, and that most mapped first order channels were in reality third order. In general he found that total stream channel lengths mapped in the field were 3 to 5 times greater than those inferred from the mapped contour crenulations, and that the drainage density obtained from the map was only 20 to 66% of that mapped in the field (Figure 4).

The significance of any crenulations and inflections in the contours is dependent upon the accuracy of the map concerned. Crone (1953) considered the accuracy of topographical maps in terms of qualitative accuracy, planimetric accuracy and the accuracy of the depiction of relief. A variety of other sources are available dealing with the standards of accuracy for topographic maps (Shewell, 1951; Thompson and Davey, 1953; Thompson, 1956 and 1960) but they do not specifically treat the question of contour crenulations. As noted in the *Textbook of Topographic Surveying* (H.M.S.O., 1965, p. 196) the purpose

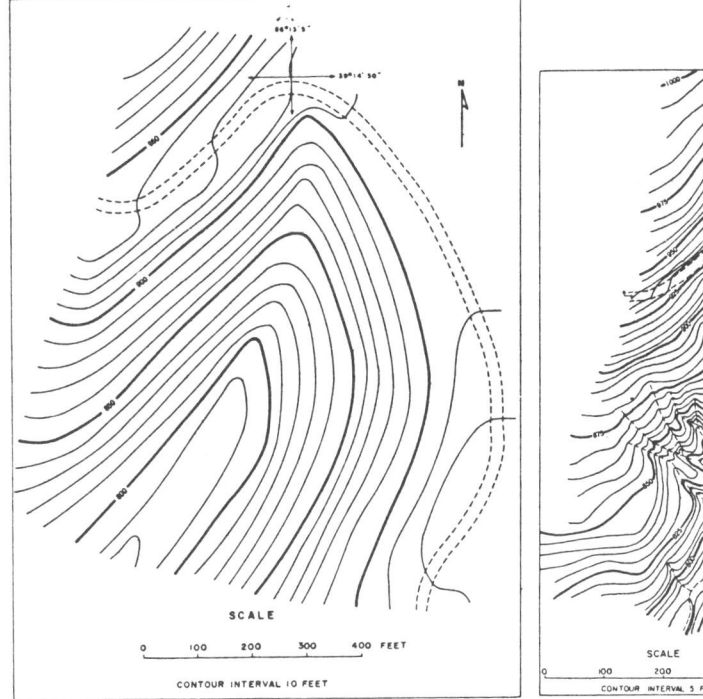
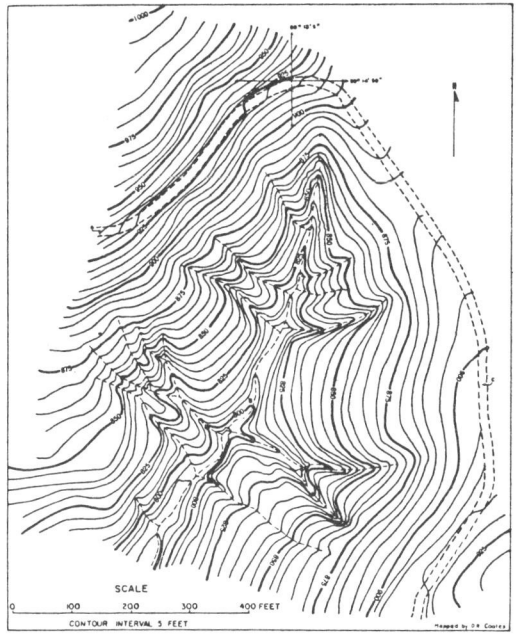

Fig. 4. Part of Lilly Woods, Brown Co., Indiana (from Coates, 1958).
Left: Redrawn and enlarged from the 1:24,000 U.S.G.S. topographic map of the Nashville Quadrangle.
Right: Special large-scale map of the region surveyed in the field by D. R. Coates.

of the contours shown on the British Ordnance Survey maps at scales of 1:10,000 downwards may be defined as follows:—

(a) To show the shape and relative heights of the ground without obscuring cultural detail.
(b) To fulfil the requirements of general engineering reconnaissance and of rough preliminary engineering estimates.
(c) To provide sufficient information for outline planning but not for detail planning.

The United States National Standard for Map Accuracy lays down that where a contour line passes through an identifiable piece of detail then the true height of the point of detail should in 90% of all cases differ from the figure shown by the contour by no more than half the contour interval (Marsden, 1960). This implies that the heights of points as shown by contours may be in error by amounts consistent with a standard deviation of one third of the contour interval. This standard is adopted by most mapping agencies. Thompson (1956) has argued that the vertical accuracy of a map should be expressed in terms of the standard deviation of the contour height error but this is not generally accepted. More stringent accuracy standards have been proposed on the grounds that this would extend the usefulness of the maps but Blakney (1968) has defended the present standards on the basis that higher accuracy can only be achieved at greatly increased costs. When one considers that a line representing any feature such as a contour or stream may be 0.2 mm thick or more and that at 1:25,000 scale this represents 5 metres then the vertical accuracy, assuming a contour interval of 10 metres, is the same as the horizontal.

The traditional methods of fixing contours for medium scale topographic mapping are those involving the interpolation of contours from spot heights and those involving line tracing from air photographs. The first method whereby contours are drawn in the field usually on a plane table, is the least accurate. Maxwell (1960) checked some 1:24,000 maps of the rugged San Dimas Experimental Station in the San Gabriel Mountains of Southern California surveyed between 1925 and 1933 by plane table (contour interval 25 feet) which he photographically enlarged and compared with the channel network observed in the field. This strongly suggested that much of the mapping had been done from the ridge crests giving substantial errors in some cul-de-sac tributary canyons in the central and less accessible parts of the watersheds. Figure 5 gives an example of some of the worst errors, including examples of the incorrect representa-

Fig. 5. Part of Upper East Fork Canyon, San Dimas Experimental Forest, San Gabriel Mountains, California (from Maxwell, 1960).
Above: Enlarged from the 1:24,000 U.S.G.S. topographic map.
Below: Superimposed correct locations of channels (solid) and divides (dashed), as mapped in the field.

tion of first order tributaries. Anyone familiar with the technique of plane tabling will realise that the ability to depict the terrain from a relatively small number of vantage points is one of the great advantages of the technique. That it does not satisfy the geomorphologist's requirements is hardly surprising. The interpolation of contours for 1:24,000 mapping has often been made from points whose height and position have been derived from control points more than a mile away, the contours being interpolated from a similar distance. The topographer deliberately ensures that the contours cut the stream channels at regular intervals so that an even stream profile is shown unless there are rapids or falls in the area. He further ensures that the bends of contours in steep drainage channels and on steep ridges are, in general, in line with one another. In 1928 the U.S. Geological Survey were advising their surveyors:—"Contour lines, unlike most other map features, are largely sketched rather than completely surveyed, and thus contour sketching consists of a free-hand delineation on paper, to the scale of the map, of the surface relief as seen in perspective view, but controlled by locations on the paper corresponding to salient points on the ground. However numerous may be the locations controlling a given contour line, it is always possible, so long as the locations are at an appreciable distance from one another on the paper, to give the line different significant shades of meaning, each equally justified by the control. That contour line therefore is likely to be nearest the truth that is drawn with the fullest comprehension of the character of the feature expressed. The most accurate geometric representation of a land form may appear "wooden" or lifeless on a map unless it is given its true characteristic expression. (U.S. Geol. Sur., 1928, p. 254). And again: "In order to put all possible expressiveness into each contour line and in order to bring out prominent and characteristic relief that otherwise might not be shown, the topographer is occasionally justified in slightly disregarding an elevation determined for no purpose other than contour control. To force a contour into rigid conformity with an instrumental elevation and location where other contours are only sketched may result in a stilted form of detail adjacent to a control point and an appearance of relative absence of detail at a distance from the control point. Where elevations at sharp summits or on broad flats are just under a certain contour elevation, it is permissible license to add or move a contour and thereby bring out a conspicuous form. The need for such license is greatest where the sketching is being done with a large contour interval combined with a small scale, and in such places elevations may be disregarded for as much as 10, 20 or even 30 per cent of the contour interval, the amount depending upon the prominence of the topographic feature and the scale." (U.S. Geol. Sur. 1928, p. 253).

Photogrammetric Methods

The introduction of photogrammetric techniques has greatly improved the quality of terrain representation, including the representation of drainage lines (Shaw, 1953). With modern aerial cameras, plotting machines and the stability of modern film materials the limits of accuracy are primarily financial. Recently contour intervals of 1 inch have been achieved using photography taken from a helicopter. Given satisfactory photography, the contour

interval which can be realised to the standards mentioned previously will depend to a large extent, upon the type of plotting machine used. Each set of photogrammetric equipment has a rating known as its C-factor. The C-factor is a precision factor and is derived empirically. It is used to compute the flying height which will produce photography at a scale that is satisfactory for producing contours to the desired vertical accuracy. It is defined as the ratio:
Flying height/Contour interval.
From this is derived the formula:
Flying height = (contour interval) × (C-factor).

Thus with Multiplex equipment, with a C-factor of about 400, the flying height to achieve a 20 ft vertical interval would have to be 8,000 ft or lower and assuming the use of a camera with a 6 inch focal length lens the scale of the photography would have to be 1:16,000 or larger. Looked at another way, given photography at 1:24,000 (flying height 12,000 ft) Multiplex equipment could only produce contours to the required accuracy with a 30 ft. vertical interval. With the same scale photography and any reasonable modern plotter with a C-factor of 1,500 or so, contours can be produced with a vertical interval of better than 10 ft. whilst with a first order plotter with an automatic contouring system such as that used with the UNAMACE (Bertram, 1969) a C-factor of 5,000 is claimed and contours could theoretically be drawn with a vertical interval of 2½ ft. In practice, however, the greater the precision of the equipment to be used the greater will be the flying height and the smaller the scale of photography, subject to the limitation that the scale must be sufficiently large for the planimetric detail to be resolved. Provided that a clear view of those features that are to be studied is maintained, then doubling the flying height increases the ground coverage per photograph four times and considerably reduces the amount of ground control, the cost of flying and film and the overall time taken to produce the required map. In a final analysis the accuracy with which contours reflect the true height of points on the ground is the same with photogrammetric mapping as with ground interpolation.

The advantage of photogrammetry is the speed and economy with which the contours can be drawn and the greater accuracy with which the form of the land and the intricacy of the contour crenulations can be revealed. Ollier (1967) pointed out that it is possible

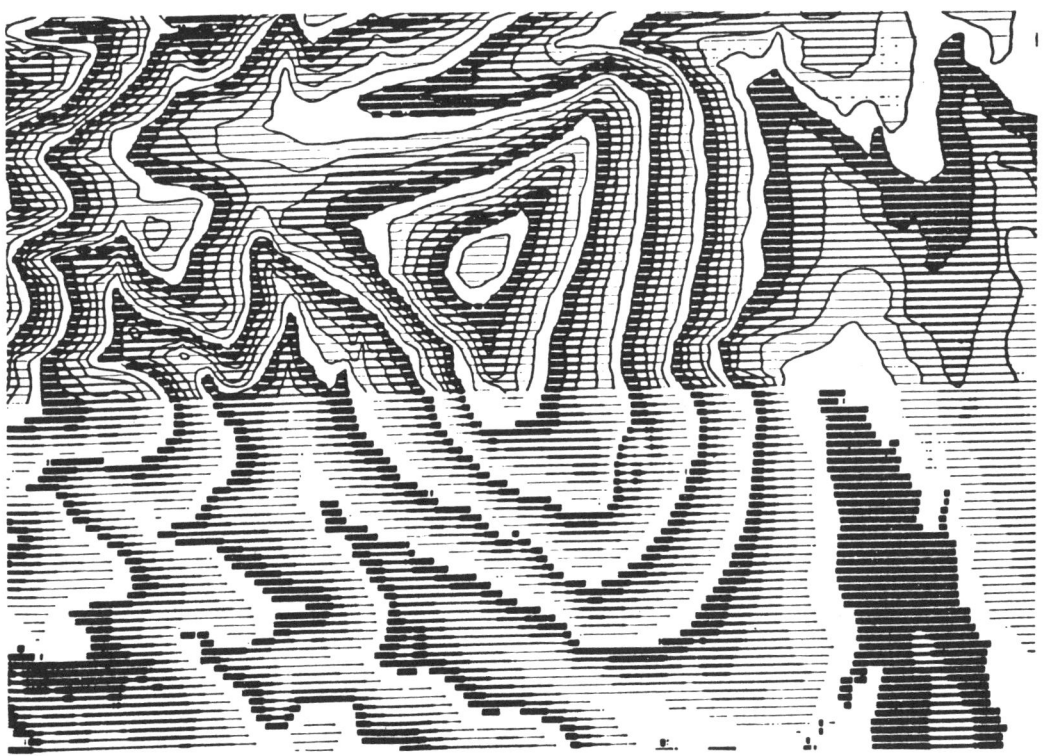

Fig. 6. Example of contouring from automatic drop-line output from a stereoplotter.

to accidentally omit contours around small outlying summits when tracing contours at predetermined elevations. An adequate system of field checking for all map compilations should detect such errors but undoubtedly there are occasions when they do occur. With the introduction of automatic drop-line contouring techniques wherein the whole area of the photograph is scanned in strips and the various contour intervals marked out (Figure 6) the omission of such small features should no longer occur. There still remains the problem of forest cover for, as Jennings (1967) pointed out, where the forest canopy is closed some errors may arise from the inequalities of forest height (Figure 7). Little can be done to avoid this without expensive ground survey.

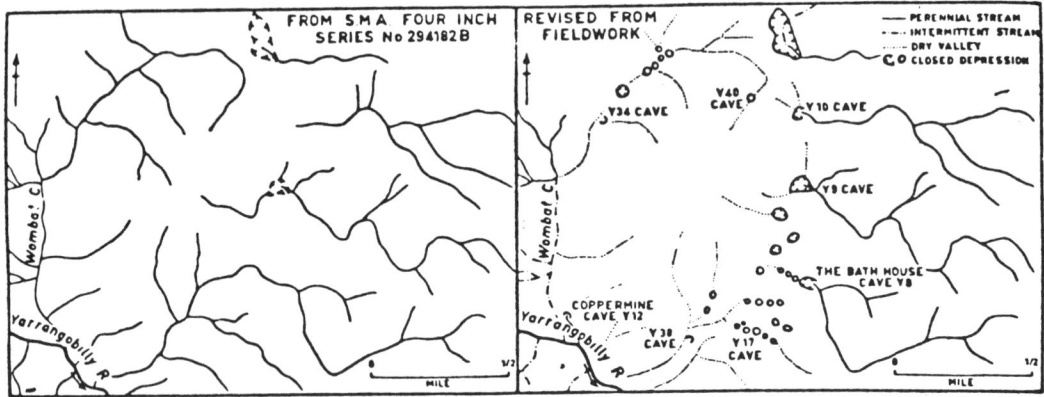

Fig. 7. Comparison of two maps of a limestone area in New South Wales, showing how a forest cover has misled the photogrammetrist who assumed the existance of a normal system of valleys when, in fact, the canopy cover concealed closed depressions (from Jennings, 1967).
Left: From a map produced by photogrammetric methods.
Right: The same map revised by fieldwork.

For many types of terrain the standards of accuracy provided at present on topographic maps are acceptable except in such environments as, for example, small fingertip tributaries in badlands or small channels in densely wooded rolling terrain. Moreover the accuracy with which contours can be depicted on steep slopes of medium scale maps is questionable, particularly when one calculates that the horizontal spacing of 25-foot contours on a 1 in 3 hill slope on a 1:25,000 map is only 0.9 mm. However, Shewell has suggested that a more accurate picture of the form of the ground can be obtained from a large number of comparatively inaccurate contours sketched in the field than from a smaller number of more accurate contours. The visual impression of contour spacing also allows for greater tolerance in interpretation than might be expected and an experiment by Shewell (1951, pp. 201-202) showed that intentional variation in contour spacing on a concave slope (1 in 25 at top and bottom, and 1 in 4 in the middle) produced perceptible distortion only when it reached 33% of the contour spacing. In view of the importance of geomorphic interpretations made from topographic maps, it is not surprising that criticisms have been made at the interpolation of contours, while admitting that this practice, by caricaturing the surface, sometimes emphasizes the form of the ground in a most effective manner (Clayton, 1953, p. 82).

The use of aerial photographs in the preparation of topographic maps which are conventionally employed to delimit drainage networks has already been mentioned, but stereoscopic pairs of photographs can also aid in adding to a network shown on a more conventionally surveyed map. Coates (1958, p. 24) employed these for part of southern Indiana on the U.S.G.S. 1:24,000 scale and found that although true second order channels could be distinguished with some care, the first order channels in this forested region were obscured from the air. A more rigorous attempt to compare the stream channel networks inferred from the contours on published topographic maps with those visible on aerial photographs has been made by Eyles (1966) for Malayan maps on the scale of 1:63,360 with a contour interval of 50 feet. Photographs ranging in scale from 1:8,000 to 1:25,000 (maximum lateral error of 0.04 inches at a scale of 1:15,840) were compared with the topographic maps of 50 third to fifth order basins in open country and it was found that only 7 basins coincided in order between map and photograph, 33 being reduced by one order on the maps and 10 by two orders. The map samples were then divided into three groups:

1. Maps constructed from plane-tabling.
2. Maps made from combined field survey and aerial photography prior to 1960.
3. Maps, similar to group 2, made after 1960.

Figure 8 shows comparisons of the map and aerial photograph drainage densities indicating the greatest accord between stream networks depicted on the group 3 maps and the aerial photographs. The discrepancies between networks delimited from topographic maps (Group 2) and aerial photographs naturally increases where increasing basin slope increases the texture of dissection (Figure 9), and Eyles calculated that the following relationship exists between aerial photograph drainage density (D), drainage density inferred from group 2 map contours (d) and average basin slope (S):

$$D = 1.35d + 0.26S + 2.80$$

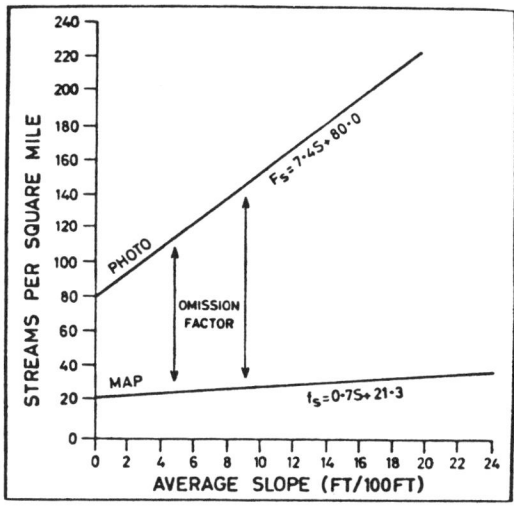

Fig. 9. Regressions showing the general increase of stream number omissions per unit area on Malayan maps with increases in average slope (S) (from Eyles, 1966).

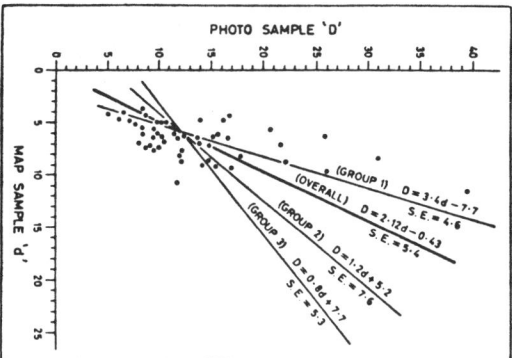

Fig. 8. Relationships of drainage densities (d) determined from three groups of Malayan maps at a scale of 1:63,360 with these (D) determined from aerial photographs (from Eyles, 1966).

From such studies as these it appears that the degree of inaccuracy of channel depiction by medium scale contour maps, even using extrapolation techniques, is very much a function of the scale of the smallest channels (i.e. the drainage density). With the development of the orthophotomap, wherein the base of the map is a compilation of aerial photographs rectified both for tilt displacements and for the variations of ground height, it should be possible to make a better assessment of the existence of stream channels especially when these maps are produced with a "stereo-mate" (i.e. a complimentary map which, when viewed in conjunction with the plane map, gives an effective three dimensional map image) (Collins, 1968).

Great advances have been made recently in the provision of data regarding "earth resources", including stream channel networks, by the use of remote sensors carried by aircraft or space vehicles. Schneider (1968), for example, has investigated the uses of colour photography in evaluating water resources, and Cantrell (1964) showed that infrared photography can detect channels containing water with great facility. Pestrong (1969), in his study of multiband photography for tidal marsh analysis, has shown in addition the superiority of near infrared wavelengths for the differentiation of land and water boundaries and for the detection of drainage channels. The value of radar to channel network studies depends largely upon its resolution (Moore, 1966, p. 22) for, whereas it is presently valuable in the recognition of larger-scale geomorphic lineaments, unclassified radar imagery will only allow the recognition of streams classed as first order on topographic sheets on the scale of 1:62,000 (in some cases of streams so classed on 1:25,000 sheets) (Pierson, Scheps and Simonett, 1965, p. 110). Certainly the resolution necessary to distinguish rock units 5 to 10 metres across, called for by Committee on Geography advisory to the ONR Division of Earth Sciences (National Academy of Sciences, 1966, p. 43), would be inadequate for the general recognition of stream networks. Greysukh (1967) has discussed the possibility of studying landforms by means of digital computers and Jackson (1967) has shown how the technique may be applied to the delineation of surface geologic structures in studies for the petroleum industry. Digital terrain modelling using data extracted from aerial photographs is now an accepted engineering practice for the study of highway designs and has obvious geomorphic applications.

Cartographic Analysis

Returning to the traditional methods of mapping, the problem still remains of interpreting the significance of contour inflections and of trying to establish, for individual terrain types, meaningful and objective definitions of contour crenulations significant in the delimiting of stream channel networks. The terms employed to describe these contour irregularities (*crenulation*—a fine notch or scallop; *cusp*—a point at which two branches of a curve meet; *inflection*—to change curvature from convex to concave; etc) reflect the variety of detailed contour geometry associated with stream channels. Undoubtedly the biggest problem is presented by the broad inflections at the heads of many humid valleys (for example, in the highly permeable chalk) which are only partly associated with distinct channels (see the previous reference to the work of Hack and Goodlett, 1960). Melton (1957, pp. 3-4) is one of the few workers to deal at all rigorously with the contour inflection angles (Ψ) of first order channels (Figure 10), which are rather difficult to measure from maps. Obviously the inflection angle can vary up to the limiting slope of the adjacent valley sides (θ), at which the inflection disappears and the stream channel slope (γ) becomes equal to the valley-side slope. Figure 10 shows a number of inflection angle relationships:

(a) γ approaches θ, giving an obtuse Ψ.

(b) γ is somewhat less than θ, giving an acute Ψ.

(c) γ is much less than θ, giving a very acute Ψ.

(d) Relationships when the floor of the valley is flat.

It is clear that, until general inflection recognition standards are established for differing degrees and types of dissection, there is the very real problem of operator variance in the recognition of the more headward parts of drainage networks from topographic maps. For example, Chorley (1958, p. 210) compared the results of two groups of operators who had defined the stream networks on the same seven drainage basins taken from the Ordance Survey 1:25,000 sheets and exhibiting a drainage density of about 3.5 miles per square mile. It was found that one group recognised 508 fingertip first order tributaries, whereas the other group delimited only 405.

Throughout much of what has been said previously regarding the problems of extracting stream channel network information from topographic maps it has been implicit that, even if one possesses the most accurate topographic maps and presents them for analysis by trained operators in possession of the most rigorous operational definitions of significant contour inflections, the scale of the map must play a large part in determining the faithfulness with which the field network can be inferred from the map. Maps at the scale of about 1:24,000 produced from air photographs appear to represent the stream networks of medium textured terrain with quite a high degree of truth, but this is certainly not the case in areas of high drainage density where, even in the field, the distinction between rills and fingertip channels is difficult to make. Schick (1964), comparing modern topographic maps on scales of 1:20,000 and 1:2,500 found that the former underestimated total stream channel length by 11.1% and drainage density by 9.7% compared with the latter. Leopold, Wolman and Miller (1964, pp. 138-139) give an extreme instance of the role of map scale in the interpretation of stream channel networks. They compared the network inferred for the Arroyo De Los Frijoles, New Mexico, from a U.S. Geological Survey topographic map at 1:31,680, with a field map of the network of one of its first order tributaries. The network mapped within this 0.027 square-mile "first order" basin caused it to be redesignated as fifth order. Such local mapping of sample areas, particularly of first order basins, allows an estimation to be made from the map regarding some of the true features of the stream network in the field in that, in this instance, the orders of all the channels in the Arroyo De Los Frijoles could be increased by 4, and inferences regarding stream numbers, lengths, etc. of orders lower than 5 can be made from Horton-type plots involving stream order. However, as Scheidegger (1966) has pointed out, this simple method of increase of order only holds good for the Strahler system of ordering (1952). For Scheidegger's (1965) own "consistent"

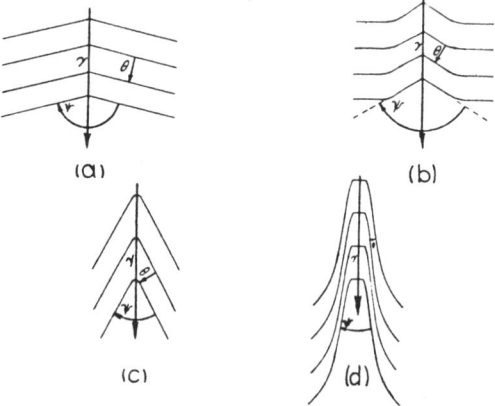

Fig. 10. Inflection angles as measured on various forms of first-order channels (from Melton, 1957).

system of stream ordering, for example, such a simple adjustment is only possible where the original network is extremely regular and the additional mapped channels appear only at the headwaters. In the latter ordering system, random addition of low order channels to the network results in increases of higher order designations by variable amounts.

From the foregoing it is clear that, even for comparative studies, statements involving the length of drainage channels measured from maps, or derivatives of stream length (i.e. drainage density), must be accompanied by background information. Before comparison between such measures is made it is necessary to know, for example:

The method by which the topographic survey was conducted;

The rules governing both the insertion of stream lines and contour crenulations;

The character of the vegetational cover;

The precise operational definition of a stream channel adopted by the investigator.

It should not be assumed from this paper that it is not possible to carry out morphometric analyses involving stream lengths from maps, but that the many vicissitudes besetting map construction and interpretation should be taken into account in an attempt to produce results which are more accurate and comparable.

References

Bertram, S., 1969, The UNAMACE and the Automatic Photomapper; *Photogrammetric Engineering*, Vol. 35, p. 569.

Blakney, W. G. G., 1968, Accuracy Standards for Topographic Mapping; *Photogrammetric Engineering*; Vol. 34, pp. 1040-1042.

Cantrell, J. L., 1964, Infrared geology; *Photogrammetric Engineering*, Vol. 30, pp. 916-922.

Chorley, R. J., 1958, Group operator variance in morphometric work with maps; *American Journal of Science*, Vol. 256, pp. 208-218.

Clayton, K. M., 1953, A note on the 25-foot contours shown on the O.S. 1:25,000 map; *Geography*, Vol. 38, pp. 77-83.

Coates, D. R., 1958, Quantitative geomorphology of small drainage basins of southern Indiana; *Office of Naval Research Project NR 389-042, Technical Report 10, Department of Geology, Columbia University, New York*, 67 pp.

Collins, S. H., 1968, Stereoscopic Orthophoto Maps; *The Canadian Surveyor*, Vol. 22, pp. 167-176.

Crone, D. R., 1953, The Accuracy of Topographical Maps; *Empire Survey Review*, Vol. 12, pp. 64-70.

Eyles, R. J., 1966, Stream representation on Malayan maps; *Journal of Tropical Geography*, Vol. 22, pp. 1-9.

Gregory, K. J., and Walling, D. E., 1968, The variation of drainage density within a catchment; *Bulletin of the International Association of Scientific Hydrology*, Year 13(2), pp. 61-68.

Greysukh, V. L., 1967, The possibilty of studying landforms by means of digital computers; *Soviet Geography*, March, pp. 137-149.

Hack, J. T., and Goodlett, J. C., 1960, Geomorphology and forest ecology of a mountain region in the central Appalachians; *United States Geological Survey, Professional Paper* 347, 66 pp.

Her Majesty's Stationery Office, 1965, *Textbook of Topographic Mapping*; 4th edition.

Horton, R. E., 1945, Erosional development of streams and their drainage basins: Hydrophysical approach to quantitative morphology; *Bulletin of the Geological Society of America*, Vol. 56, pp. 275-370.

Jackson, V. N., 1967, Digital Structural Analysis; *Photogrammetric Engineering*, Vol. 33, pp. 290-296.

Jennings, J. N., 1967, Topographical Maps and the Geomorphologist; *Cartography*, Vol. 6, pp. 73-81.

Kirkby, M. J., and Chorley, R. J., 1967, Throughflow, overland flow and erosion; *Bulletin of the International Association of Scientific Hydrology*, Year 12(3), pp. 5-21.

Leopold, L. B., Wolman, M. G., and Miller, J. P., 1964, *Fluvial Processes in Geomorphology* (Freeman and Co., San Francisco), 522pp.

Marsden, L. E., 1960, How the National Map Accuracy Standards were Developed; *Surveying & Mapping*, Vol. 20, pp. 427-439.

Maxwell, J. C., 1960, Quantitative geomorphology of the San Dimas Experimental forest, California; *Office of Naval Research Project NR 389-042, Technical Report 19, Department of Geology, Columbia University, New York*, 95 pp.

Melton, M. A., 1957, An analysis of the relations among elements of climate, surface properties, and geomorphology; *Office of Naval Research Project NR 389-042, Technical Report 11, Department of Geology, Columbia University, New York*, 102 pp.

Miller, V. C., 1953, A quantitative geomorphic study of drainage basin characteristics in the Clinch Mountain area, Virginia and Tennessee; *Office of Naval Research Project NR 389-042, Technical Report 3, Department of Geology, Columbia University,* New York.

Moore, R. K., 1966, Radar as a sensor; *University of Kansas Center for Research, Engineering Science Division,* Report No. 61-7, 55 pp.

Morisawa, M. E., 1957, Accuracy of determination of stream lengths from topographic maps; *Transactions of the American Geophysical Union,* Vol. 38, pp. 86-88.

Morisawa, M. E., 1959, Relation of quantitative geomorphology to stream flow in representative watersheds of the Appalachian plateau province; *Office of Naval Research Project NR 389-042, Technical Report 20, Department of Geology, Columbia University, New York,* 94 pp.

National Academy of Sciences, 1966, *Spacecraft in Geographic Research;* National Research Council Publication No. 1353, 107 pp.

Ollier, C. D., 1967, Geomorphic Indications of Contour Map Inaccuracy; *Cartography,* Vol. 6, pp. 121-124.

Pestrong, R., 1969, Multiband Photos for a Tidal Marsh; *Photogrammetric Engineering,* Vol. 35, p. 453.

Pierson, W. J., Scheps, B. B., and Simonett, D. S., 1965, Some applications of radar return data to the study of terrestrial and oceanic phenomena; *University of Kansas Center for Research, Engineering Science Division,* Report No. 61-3, 49 pp.

Scheidegger, A. E., 1965, The Algebra of Stream Order Numbers. *U.S. Geological Surveys Prof. Paper* 525-B, pp. 187-189.

Scheidegger, A. E., 1966, Effect of map scale on stream orders; *Bulletin of the International Association of Scientific Hydrology,* Year 11(3), pp. 56-61.

Schick, A. P., 1964, Accuracy of the 1:20,000 topographic maps of Israel for morphometric studies; *Bulletin of the Israel Exploration Society,* Vol. 28, pp. 43-54.

Schneider, W. J., 1961, A note on the accuracy of drainage densities computed from topographic maps; *Journal of Geophysical Research,* Vol. 66, pp. 3617-3618.

Schneider, W. J., 1968, Color Photographs for Water Resources Studies; *Photogrammetric Engineering,* Vol. 34, p. 570.

Schumm, S. A., 1956, The evolution of drainage systems and slopes in badlands at Perth Amboy, New Jersey; *Bulletin of the Geological Society of America,* Vol. 67, pp. 597-646.

Shaw, S. H., 1953, The Value of Air Photographs in the Analysis of Drainage Patterns; *Photogrammetric Record,* Vol. 1, pp. 4-17.

Shewell, H. A. L., 1951, Accuracy of contours; *Journal of the Royal Institution of Chartered Surveyors,* Vol. 31, pp. 195-215.

Strahler, A. N., 1952, Hypsometric (area-altitude) analysis of erosional topography; *Bulletin of the Geological Society of America,* Vol. 63, pp. 1117-1142.

Strahler, A. N., 1964, Quantitative geomorphology of drainage basins and channel networks; Section 4-11 in Chow, Ven Te, (ed.), *Handbook of Applied Hydrology,* (McGraw-Hill, New York), pp. 4-39 to 4-76.

Thompson, M. M., and Davey, C. H., 1953, Vertical accuracy of topographic maps; *Surveying and Mapping,* Vol. 13, pp. 40-48.

Thompson, M. M., 1956, How Accurate is that Map? *Surveying and Mapping,* Vol. 16, pp. 164-173.

Thompson, M. M., 1960, A Current View of National Map Accuracy Standards. *Surveying and Mapping,* Vol. 20, pp. 449-456.

Topfer, F., and Pillewizer, W., 1966, The Principles of Selection; *The Cartographic Journal,* Vol. 3, No. 1, pp. 10-16.

U.S. Geological Survey, 1928, Topographic Instructions of the United States Geological Survey. *Bulletin 788-E.*

U.S. Geological Survey, 1963, *Map Editing and Checking; Provisional Topographic Instructions of the United States Geological Surveys.*

Yoxall, W. H., 1969, Discrepancies in Stream Mapping—The 1:250,000 Series, Ghana Survey. *Journal of Tropical Geography.* Vol. 28, pp. 84-86.

THE VARIATION OF DRAINAGE DENSITY WITHIN A CATCHMENT

K.J. GREGORY and D.E. WALLING
Department of Geography, Exeter University

ABSTRACT

Actual discharges from two experimental catchments are related to the corresponding measurements of the length of channel flow; within a single catchment this is equivalent to drainage density. Drainage densities ranging from less than 1.0 to nearly 10.0 are associated with discharges ranging from 0.15 to nearly 20.0 c.f.s. per square mile. In each catchment all discharge values (Q) and drainage density values (D_d) are related by a function approximately of the form $Q \propto D_d^2$, which is then discussed in relation to studies made of the variation of streamflow and drainage density between catchments. It is suggested that both peak flow and base flow are related to drainage density in the same way. Studies which include drainage density as a basin characteristic and which relate it to water yield should acknowledge that its value varies within any one catchment, and therefore that the drainage density values derived by a particular method can be related only to one type of flow. In Great Britain the watercourses shown on the 1:10,560 maps relate to specific low flow discharges.

INTRODUCTION

Drainage density, since first used by Horton (1945) has been extensively utilised in many hydrological studies. As Gray (1965) noted "The pattern and arrangement of the natural stream channels determine the efficiency of the drainage system. Other factors being constant, the time required for water to flow a given distance is directly proportional to length". Although a better geometrical description of the stream net is desirable (Wooding, 1966), drainage density, defined as the total length of stream channels per unit area, may be used as the best available index to describe a particular stream network. As a parameter in catchment studies drainage density can be used in three main ways. Firstly, it is related to watershed or physiographic characteristics such as relief ratio, rock type and basin shape. Secondly, it is related to input and output of the drainage basin system. Chorley and Morgan (1962) concluded that maximum runoff, which may reflect high intensity rainfall, is a function of drainage density. Melton (1957) has shown that for particular drainage basins, relationships exist between drainage density and both input (precipitation-effectiveness index) and output (runoff-intensity frequency). Thirdly, drainage density may be useful in relation to studies of past (e.g. Schumm, 1965) and future (e.g. Strahler, 1964) conditions. Increased flood discharges in Wales have been partly attributed to recent changes of drainage density, (Howe, Slaymaker, and Harding, 1966). If the relationships between present drainage density and its controlling variables are understood then deductions may be made about past drainage densities and perhaps about the development of this particular basin characteristic in the future.

The usefulness of drainage density as a parameter is necessarily limited by the method used to delimit the drainage net (Gregory, 1966) and by the maps upon which the net is based. A considerable range of values of drainage density has now been recorded from different areas (e.g. Cotton, 1964) but such variations must be viewed to some extent against differences in map scale, map accuracy, methods of construction of the drainage net, and operator variation. Calculation of values of drainage density is rather time-consuming and so various alternative measures have been used and these can provide data which is similar, or related, to the density of streams. A grid method of determining mean-flow distance in a drainage basin was suggested by Busby and Benson (1960) and they showed that results obtained by this method were within ±2.7% of measurements made for the total basin. The length of the longest watercourse has been used as a parameter in many studies of the variation in discharge from drainage basins (e.g. Taylor and Schwarz, 1952). However, this measure is not independent of area and of basin shape, and similarly total stream length in the basin which has been used by Morisawa (1959) and by Brush (1961) does not separate the density of stream channels from their total length.

Many characteristics of water and sediment yield from drainage basins have now been related to drainage density, usually represented as one factor in multivariate analyses. Peak discharge has been related to drainage density in several studies and Benson (1960) related floods of various recurrence intervals to 9 factors, one of which was drainage density. Mean annual runoff, adjusted to mean annual precipitation, was related to drainage density by Hadley and Schumm (1961). In a valuable discussion of drainage density and streamflow, Carlston (1963) demonstrated a relationship between drainage density and average minimum monthly flow. Hydrograph characteristics were analysed by Hickok, Keppel, and Rafferty (1959) who demonstrated that watershed lag time could be expressed as a multiple correlation function of watershed area, average landslope and drainage density. Variations in sediment yield also have been related to values of drainage density, and Hadley and Schumm (1961) demonstrated that sediment yield increased as drainage density increased. Although drainage density has, therefore, been related to peak, mean and low flow rates and also to sediment yield, in some areas it has been shown that it is not easily or significantly related to variations in either water or sediment yield. Bigwood and Thomas (1955) showed that the relationship between mean annual flood and drainage area for Connecticut was not improved by using stream density, and Hidore (1965) demonstrated that spatial variations in runoff in 16 basins were not well-accounted for by variations in drainage density. In the light of these differing views it is perhaps surprising that few studies have been made of the variations in drainage density which occur within a particular catchment. It is the aim of this paper to describe variations in stream length which occurred in two very small instrumented catchments and it is hoped that this will provide an illustration of how drainage density varies while other basin characteristics are maintained constant.

EXPERIMENTAL RESULTS

Several small catchments have been instrumented in south-east Devon, and two of these were selected for a study of the variation of drainage density within a particular catchment, especially in relation to streamflow. Discharge from each catchment was measured by sharp-crested weirs with water levels continuously recorded by vertical water-stage recorders, and stream length was measured, in feet, by reference to pegs set at predetermined positions. On each occasion a record of the discharge at the weir was obtained and then the contributing stream length was measured. Stream length was defined as the total length of concentrated detectable channel flow contributing to the discharge measured at the weir. Each of the two catchments studied includes channels which are perennial, intermittent and ephemeral in nature. Stream length was found to vary considerably with different rates of discharge and so an attempt was made to obtain length measurements associated with a wide range of flows in each catchment.

The initial results of this study show (fig. 1) that there is a definite relationship between stream length and discharge in each of the two catchments. Since area remains constant within the individual catchments, these graphs in fact represent relationships between drainage density and discharge. The range of drainage density values for catchment A is from 1.2 to 5.7 and for catchment B from 1.4 to 10.5. The difference in the range of drainage density shown by the two catchments may be explained by contrasts in land use and slight differences of rock type. Catchment A is almost completely unenclosed moorland and occurs on the outcrop of Upper Greensand (sandstone) covered by clay-with-flints. The same rock type occurs under the highest parts of catchment B but the basin also includes outcrops of the Keuper marl underlying the Greensand, and 75% of the area of the catchment (B) is occupied by enclosed land, which includes arable land and grassland used for grazing. Infiltration is initially greater in catchment B than in A, but peak runoff tends to be greater in B where there is less vegetation to intercept precipitation, and this is further emphasised by the presence of a thin peat layer in A. The same contrasts in catchment characteristics, especially differences in infiltration rates, probably explain why drainage density increases with discharge at a greater rate in B than in A. In A, discharge varies according to $L^{2.9}$ (total length of channel flow) but in B according to L^2. The summer values (fig. 1) do not cover as great a range as the winter ones because evaporation is increased, precipitation intensity is generally less, and vegetation growth, particularly in catchment A where bracken (*Pteridium aquilinum*) is extensive, helps to intercept precipitation.

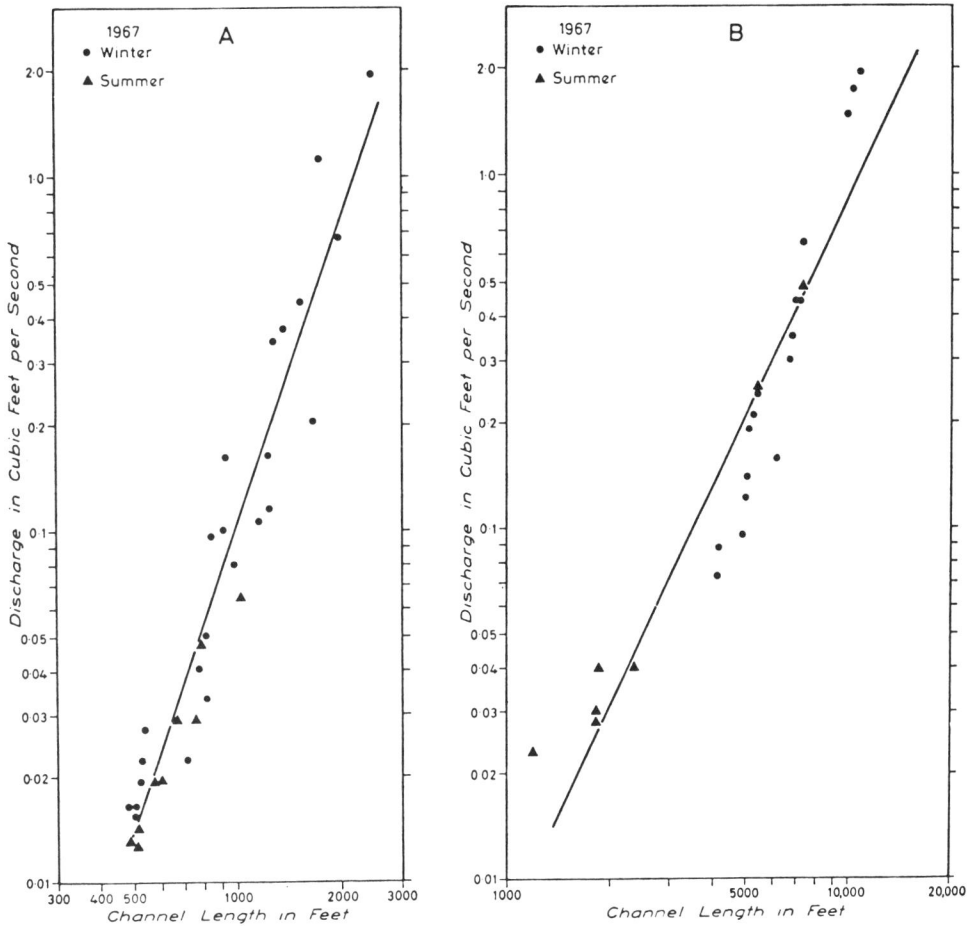

Fig. 1 — The relationship of channel length contributing to actual discharges from two experimental catchments in south-east Devon. The summer values are April-September inclusive. The best fit lines are:

$$A: Q = 9.7 D_d^{2.9}$$
$$B: Q = 8.3 D_d^{2.1}$$

The discharge values plotted (fig. 1) range from very low summer flows to high flows resulting from heavy winter rainfall, and they should therefore include the various elements of flow, namely surface runoff, throughflow, interflow, and base-flow. It it probable, therefore, that all three types of flow, individually or combined, are related to wetted stream length and thus to drainage density by the same type of function. This conclusion is illustrated when the discharge values, which occurred during low flow conditions on August 23rd, 1967, from these two catchments are combined with the flows from three other adjacent instrumented catchments, and the five values are plotted against the corresponding drainage densities operative at that time (fig. 2A). These minimum flows, demonstrated by the hydrographs to be base flow, show that in this case (fig. 2A), base flow discharge varies according to $D_d^{2.2}$. This relationship is based upon values from five catchments which vary in area from 0.08 to 2.5 square miles, have slightly different land use and watershed characteristics, but are on broadly similar rock types. Despite the variations which might be expected, drainage density is seen (fig. 2A) to be related to this particular base flow in a way very similar to the relationship obtained for all types of flow in catchments A and B (fig. 1).

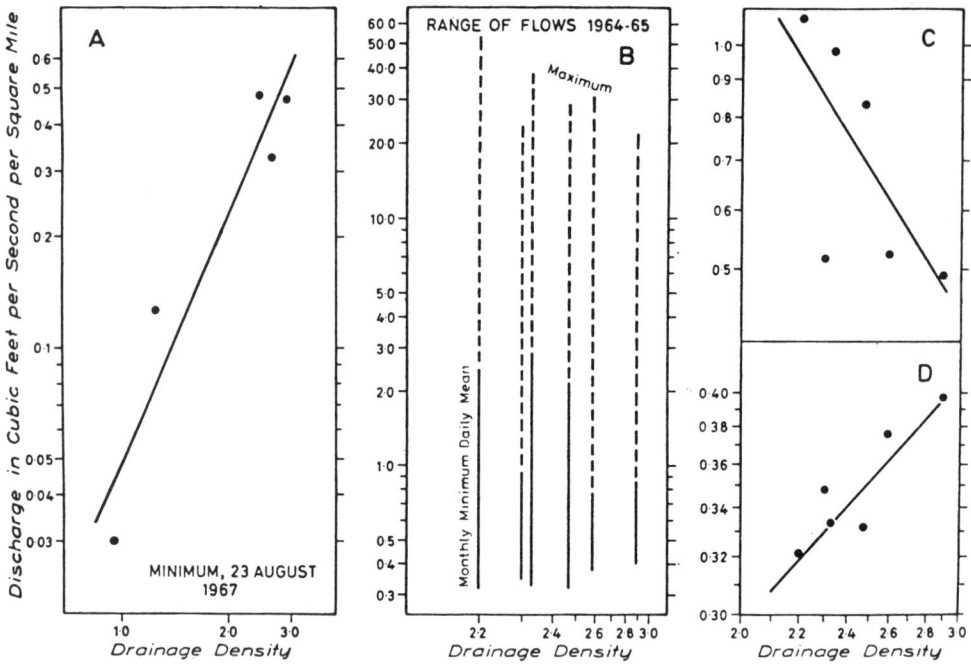

Fig. 2A — The relationship of minimum flow to corresponding drainage densities for 5 experimental catchments in south-east Devon.

Fig. 2B-C-D — The relationship of drainage density, derived from the water-courses shown on 1:10,560 maps, to range of flows 1964-65 water year (B), average monthly minimum flow (C), lowest daily mean for October, 1964 (D). Relationships are:

$$A: Q = 0.05\ D_d^{2.2}$$
$$C: Q = 6.57\ D_d^{-2.5}$$
$$D: Q = 0.17\ D_d^{0.8}$$

IMPLICATIONS

There are several general implications which arise from the results of the preceding study and these will be significant particularly when drainage density is to be used as a parameter to compare different catchments. Firstly, drainage density within a particular catchment is not a static value. When drainage density is to be related to different runoff values (peak, mean or base flow) these flows may often be associated with a range of values of drainage density for each catchment rather than with a single value which has been used in many previous studies. Secondly, the rate of change of drainage density within a catchment may be related to precipitation intensity and to the characteristics of the catchment. Thirdly, it appears that within these catchments streamflow of any origin is related to drainage density by the same power function which is approximately $Q \propto D_d{}^2$. Therefore when attempts are made to relate drainage density and streamflow in several catchments it is necessary to consider carefully the discharge value which is to be related to particular values of drainage density, since this field study has shown that drainage density values from 1 to 10 are associated with discharge variation from 0.15 to nearly 20 c.f.s. per square mile.

C.W. Carlston (1963, 1965) studied the relationship between drainage density and streamflow for 15 basins in the United States and concluded that peak flow, designated by the 2.33 year flood, was related to $D_d{}^2$ whereas baseflow (Q_b) was inversely proportional to $D_d{}^2$ (or $Q_b \propto D_d{}^{-2}$). That two distinct relationships should exist, one for peak runoff and one for base flow, initially seems surprising and would mean that any relationships between mean flow and drainage density might be very difficult to detect. In his analysis, Carlston treated drainage density as a static parameter and related the same density values to both peak flow and base flow. The drainage density values used were derived (for up to 25% of each basin area) by measuring all the marked drainage lines shown on the 1:24,000 maps, supplemented by the extensions into small rills indicated by contour crenulations. These values of drainage density probably represent the upper part of the range of drainage density values in each basin. When water is flowing in all the rills the corresponding discharges will be high. However some workers (e.g. Giusti, 1962; Carlston, 1963) have noted that rivers with the highest peak discharges are frequently those with the lowest baseflows. Therefore by using the same drainage density values an apparently inverse relationship of drainage density and baseflow may be indicated. The highest flood runoff values are associated with the highest drainage densities but these catchments will also have the lowest baseflows.

A further problem concerns the index of base flow which is plotted against drainage density. Although mean annual flood affords a very satisfactory index of peak discharge, Carlston (1965, p. 63) and others have noted that no completely satisfactory method has been devised to accurately designate the base flow or ground-water portion of a stream's discharge. Carlston used the average minimum monthly discharge as one of a number of possibilities for expressing base flow. Although drainage density is difficult to relate to discharge in catchments greater in area than 100 square miles, figure 2C attempts to show the relationship between drainage density (based upon the watercourses shown on 1:10,560 maps) and low flow-discharge for six basins in Devon, England, ranging in size from 7.8 to 232 square miles. The greatest range of flows, in the 1964-65 water year for example, occurs in the catchments with the lowest drainage density (fig. 2B). Thus when mean monthly minimum flow for the year is plotted against drainage density (fig. 2C) the function is of the form $Q \propto D_d{}^{-2.5}$, but when the actual minimum daily mean discharges are plotted for particular months (e.g. October 1964 which was the month in the 1964-65 water year with the lowest daily mean discharges) the relationship is of a different form (fig. 2D), namely $Q \propto D_d{}^{0.8}$. Thus in Great Britain results obtained using average minimum monthly discharge may be of a different form from those obtained by using the actual low flow discharges for particular months. Thus when relating drainage density to discharge it is important to ensure that both the discharge values and the drainage density values from different catchments are directly comparable.

Carlston interpreted his results in the light of the Jacob water table model expressed as:

$$T = \frac{a^2 W}{2 h_0}$$

where
h_0 height of water table above draining stream as measured at the ground water divide;
a horizontal distance from water table divide to stream;
W rate of accretion to water table (recharge);
T Transmissibility.

He then made a proportional to length of overland flow (L_0) and as L_0 is approximately equal to $\frac{1}{2}D_d$ then

$$T = \frac{W}{8 D_d^2 h_0}$$

He then deduced that as ground water discharge into streams would vary directly with transmissibility, ground water discharge (Q_b) should vary according to:

$$Q_b = \frac{W D_d^{-2}}{8 h_0}$$

Then, assuming that W and h_0 remain constant, base flow should be related to drainage density in the form $Q_b \propto D_d^{-2}$ and as flood runoff varies in magnitude inversely with the magnitude of base flow then, on the same assumptions, $Q_{2.33} \propto D_d^2$. Sir Charles Cotton (1964) showed that drainage density does vary substantially with precipitation and therefore in a subsequent paper Carlston (1965) modified the original equation to be $Q_b \propto W D_d^{-2}$, as recharge (W) is roughly proportional to precipitation. But in any one catchment drainage density varies, as shown by the results described above, and therefore the value of L_0 must vary and furthermore L_0 is a function of both a and h_0. Therefore from the original Jacob water table model it is difficult to deduce a model for different types of stream flow, because the drainage density values which apply to peak flows will not apply to base flows (fig. 2B).

These problems are particularly relevant because it is important to know to which discharge values the drainage density values, as shown on topographic maps, really relate. From British maps it is very difficult to obtain the precise equivalent of the drainage densities measured in the United States where rills indicated by contour crenulations can be used with a reasonable degree of accuracy. In Great Britain the landscape has been altered by a long period of human occupance, and the associated pattern of lanes, hedges, and ditches all affect the expanded drainage density obtained during a heavy storm. In general terms Johnson (1966) has suggested that there may be an average of five miles of ditch per square mile of England and Wales, and in some cases the expanded drainage net cannot be detected where it includes field drains. Furthermore dry valleys, well-developed in the areas in which this study was made (figs. 1, 2), and glacial drainage channels are represented unevenly over England and Wales. These elements may be completely independent of the present drainage net and therefore pose a major problem in constructing drainage nets according to the contour crenulations shown on topographic maps (Gregory, 1966). In the light of these problems drainage density for at least some areas in England and Wales is probably best derived from the water courses shown on topographic maps, although man-made diversions which do not affect discharge values can be ignored.

Map scale introduces a further problem as there are variations in the density of watercourses indicated on maps of various scales. Catchment B (fig. 1) has a drainage density of 2.3 on the 1:25,000 map (Prov. Edn. 1963) but a drainage density of 3.6 on the 1:10,560 map (Regular Edition, 1963). Catchment A (fig. 1) has a drainage density of 1.0 on both the 1:25,000 and 1:10,560 maps but the highest discharges are associated with a drainage density of 5.7. The 1:10,560 map provides the best picture of actual surface drainage, and according to field experience in Devon this 1:10,560 net would seem to be that operating during periods of low flow. There is still some variation between basins, however, for whereas the 1:10,560 drainage density for catchment A is that pertaining to very low flows, the 1:10,560 density for catchment B

(fig. 1) corresponds to a discharge ten times as great as those of very low flows. However in five small catchments in Devon (fig. 2A) and in five larger ones (fig. 2D) the values of drainage density, which are broadly those of the 1:10,560 maps, seem to be related most effectively to base flow expressed by specific low flow values. Thus in figure 2D specific low flow values are related to drainage densities derived from the watercourses shown on the 1:10,560 maps. This gives a relationship similar to that indicated by the small catchments (fig. 1). However, if these same drainage density values are plotted against other runoff indices such as average monthly minimum flow (fig. 2C) or maximum recorded discharge (fig 2B) a fundamentally different relationship is obtained. The drainage density values which are associated with high discharges in this part of Devon cannot be satisfactorily indicated by contour crenulations, however, because these give values still appreciably less than those of the completely expanded drainage net.

CONCLUSIONS

Drainage density is a very useful index of basin characteristics and, as Kirkby and Chorley (1967) have recently noted, it affects the magnitude of streamflow from a drainage basin. The relationship of drainage density to actual discharges, representing all types of flow, in two small catchments is shown to be of the form $Q \propto D_d^2$. The fact that discharge varies with D_d in a particular catchment means that when drainage density and streamflow are related for different catchments, consideration must be given to the index of streamflow used and to the method used to derive the drainage density values. These values vary according to the map scale used and also according to whether the net is based upon the valley network, indicated by the contour crenulations, or upon the stream net shown on maps. Although the former method is perhaps the more practical for use in the case of catchments in North America, the analyses in Devon indicate that the stream densities shown on British 1:10,560 topographical maps correspond approximately to those occurring with low flows. Drainage density is the dynamic manifestation of varying inputs into the drainage basin system and its relation to particular inputs reflects the basin characteristics; it is through drainage density that these characteristics influence the output of water and sediment from the system. The relationship between drainage density and streamflow, both within one particular catchment and between catchments, would appear from the above to be of same general nature regardless of the type of flow, and can be expressed in the form $Q \propto D_d^n$.

ACKNOWLEDGEMENT

One of the authors (D.E.W.) is grateful to the Natural Environment Research Council who provided a research studentship.

REFERENCES

BENSON, M. A., 1960, Areal flood frequency analyses in a humid region: *Internat. Assoc. Sci. Hydrology Bull.*, No. 19, pp. 5-15.
BIGWOOD, B. L. and THOMAS, M. P., 1955, A flood-flow formula for Connecticut: *U.S. Geol. Survey Circ.*, No. 365, 16 pp.
BRUSH, L. M., 1961, Drainage basins, channels, and flow characteristics of selected streams in Central Pennsylvania: *U.S. Geol. Survey Prof. Paper*, 282-F.
BUSBY, M. W. and BENSON, M. A., 1960, Grid Method of determining mean flow-distance in a drainage basin: *Internat. Assoc. Sci. Hydrol. Bull.*, No. 20, pp. 32-36.
CARLSTON, C. W., 1963, Drainage density and streamflow: *U.S. Geol. Survey Prof. Paper*, 422-C, 8 pp.
CARLSTON, C. W., 1965, The effect of climate on drainage density and streamflow: *Internat. Assoc. Sci. Hydrol. Bull.*, v. 11, No. 3, pp. 62-69.
CHORLEY, R. J. and MORGAN, M. A., 1962, Comparison of morphometric features, Unaka Mountains, Tennessee and North Carolina, and Dartmoor, England: *Geol. Soc. America Bull.*, v. 73, pp. 17-34.

COTTON, C. A., 1964, The control of drainage density: *New Zealand Journ. of Geol. and Geophys.*, v. 7, pp. 348-352.
GIUSTI, E. V., 1962, A relation between floods and droughts in the Piedmont Province in Virginia: *U. S. Geol. Survey Prof. Paper*, 450-C, pp. C.128-C.129.
GRAY, D. M., 1965, Physiographic characteristics and the runoff pattern: *Proc. of Hydrol. Symp. No. 4, Research Watersheds, National Research Council of Canada*, pp. 147-164.
GREGORY, K. J., 1966, Dry valleys and the composition of the drainage net: *Journ. Hydrology*, v. 4, pp. 327-340.
HADLEY, R. F. and SCHUMM, S. A., 1961, Sediment sources and drainage basin characteristics in Upper Cheyenne River Basin: *U. S. Geol. Survey Water Supply Paper* 1531, part B, pp. 137-196.
HICKOK, R. B., KEPPEL, R. V. and RAFFERTY, B. R., 1959, Hydrograph synthesis for small arid-land watersheds: *Agricultural Engineering*, Oct. 1959, pp. 608-611 and 615.
HIDORE, J. J. 1965, Landform characteristics affecting watershed yields on the Mississippi-Missouri interfluve: *Oklahoma Acad. Sci. Proc.*, v. 45, pp. 201-203.
HORTON, R. E., 1945, Erosional development of streams and their drainage basins: *Geol. Soc. America Bull.*, v. 56, pp. 275-370.
HOWE, G. M., SLAYMAKER, H. O., and HARDING, D. M., 1966. Flood hazard in mid-Wales: *Nature*, v. 212, (5062), 584-585.
JOHNSON, E. A. G., 1966, Land drainage in England and Wales: *River Engineering and Water Conservation works*, Ed. R. B. Thorn, Butterworths, pp. 29-46.
KIRKBY, M. J. and CHORLEY, R. J., 1967, Throughflow, overland flow and erosion: *Internat. Assoc. Sci. Hydrol. Bull.*, v. 12, No. 3, pp. 5-21.
MELTON, M. A., 1957, An analysis of the relations among elements of climate, surface properties, and geomorphology: *Technical Report 11, Department of Geology, Columbia University*.
MORISAWA, M. E., 1959, Relation of morphometric properties to runoff in the Little Mill Creek, Ohio, drainage basin: *Technical Report, No. 17, Department of Geology, Columbia University*.
SCHUMM, S. A. 1965, Quaternary Palaeohydrology: *The Quaternary of the United States*, Eds. H. E. Wright and D. G. Frey. pp. 783-794.
STRAHLER, A. N., 1964, Quantitative geomorphology of drainage basins and channel networks: *Handbook of Applied Hydrology*, Ed. Ven Te Chow, pp. 4:39-4:76.
TAYLOR, A. B. and SCHWARZ, H. E., 1952, Unit hydrograph lag related to basin characteristics: *Am. Geophys. Union Trans.*, v. 33, (1952), pp. 235-246.
WOODING, R. A. 1966, A hydraulic model for the catchment stream problem. III Comparison with runoff observations: *Journ. Hydrol.*, v. 4, pp. 21-37.

TESTS OF THE RANDOM NETWORK MODEL, AND ITS APPLICATION TO BASIN HYDROLOGY

M. J. KIRKBY

School of Geography, University of Leeds, Leeds, England

SUMMARY

If the random model, in which all topologically distinct channel networks are equally likely, is assumed valid, then general explanations of network structure from basin geomorphic processes cannot be expected. Tests for the random model are therefore critical to the direction of future work. Proposed tests are based on frequencies of basins of different magnitudes or diameters, and on network maximum widths. Network topology is also shown to be potentially significant in the prediction of basin hydrographs. Network width commonly varies by a factor of $2\times$ for a given drainage area and drainage density, and is shown to influence peak discharge in proportion. Lag-to-peak can also be predicted better, using network topology. The paper pursues these applications of network topology using random walk theory and simulated random networks.

KEY WORDS   Networks   Hydrology   Topology

INTRODUCTION

Stream networks are components of the landscape which appear to exhibit a high degree of regularity in overall form. One of the principal reasons for studying stream networks is to relate this form to landscape processes. On a long time-span the regularities might, in principle, be understood in terms of sediment transfer processes which mould the landscape. At a qualitative level, Playfair (1802) partially succeeded in doing this. Horton (1945) has made the most serious attempt at a quantitative explanation, but the tendency of almost all dendritic networks to obey Horton's laws of drainage composition (Shreve (1966)) undermines this approach. Shreve's work led him (1966) p. 27 and Smart (1974) to formulate explicitly the 'random' model in which all topologically distinct channel networks (TDCN's) of a given magnitude are equally likely. The first question raised by this model is whether actual networks conform to the model, and one aim of this paper is to discuss possible tests of the random model, although tests to date have shown no significant departures from it. If the random model is accepted empirically, then the problem for theoretical geomorphology is to explain why channel networks are topologically random.

On the short time-span of a few days or months, the network can also be analyzed to assist in predicting its hydrological response to rainfall events. This forms the second component of this paper. It is argued that network topology is significant in influencing both the hydrograph peak and the delay to peak, particularly in basins of more than about $100\,\text{km}^2$ drainage area. It is also argued that the relevant topological factors differ appreciably between 'normal' basins, and do not show the strong convergence to expected values that is shown by Horton or Strahler stream numbers. Since network hydrological response depends on travel times to the basin outlet, the starting point of this paper is to analyze the network as a family tree, describing bifurcation and other properties in terms of numbers of links (generations) from the outflow, or in terms of distance from the outflow. Even if lithology may be assumed homogeneous, there is some reason to suppose that the existence of a large land mass gives a reduced tendency for termination near the sea, and a reduced tendency for branching far inland, near to the continental divide. This is an additional reason for analyzing the network as a family tree.

GENERATION STRUCTURE OF NETWORKS

In the simple random model, topologically distinct channel networks are postulated as being equally likely, for a given network magnitude. One way of generating such a population is by assuming that the network is generated from its outlet, and that probabilities of branching (p) and terminating at a source (q) remain constant throughout the network. For a given magnitude, TDCN's are then necessarily equally likely, since each contains the same number of branches and terminations. The relative frequencies of different network magnitudes are, however, dependent on the choice of the two constant probabilities, p and q ($=1-p$). In this paper the simple random model is explicitly being extended, by specifying p, q, to allow comparisons between networks of differing magnitude. If the nodes of a network are scanned in *any* systematic way, the nodes are signified by a 1 if branching occurs, and a 0 if the node is a stream-tip termination (or *vice-versa*), then each distinct string of 1's and 0's defines a TDCN (Shreve (1967), Scheidegger (1967)). A useful convention is to add an initial 1 to indicate the outflow stream. Then a TDCN of magnitude M, containing M first-order streams and ($2M$-1) links in all, and scanned in any way starting at the outlet, will be uniquely represented by a binary string of M 1's and M 0's with the following characteristics.

(i) The string must commence with two 1's and terminate with two 0's.
(ii) At no point in the sequence must the number of 0's equal or exceed the number of 1's so far.

A further valuable parallel is the isomorphism between the binary string and a random walk presentation in which 1's are indicated by an upward step and 0's by a downward step. The walk, of $2M$ steps, starts and finishes at zero, but lies entirely in the positive (and non-zero) half-plane in between. Each distinct walk of this type if associated with a unique TDCN, and allows random walk theory, particularly that associated with 'first returns' (Feller (1950)), to be applied to TDCN's.

The concept of topologically distinct channel networks (TDCN's) is central to this paper. Two networks have been defined to be topologically identical if one can be made congruent to the other by continuously deforming the links without removing them from the plane (Shreve (1966) p. 27). In the alternative representations, TDCN's correspond to distinct binary strings, or distinct random walks. Figure 1 shows an example of the conversion of a network to a binary string and a random walk, using a scanning method which differs from these previously proposed, in that the network is scanned on a family tree basis, generation by generation. This method has the advantage of grouping nodes according to distance from the outflow, as proposed above. It has the additional advantage that the value of the random walk at any point is related to the 'width' of the network, that is to the number of links at a particular topological distance from the outflow (Shreve (1974) p. 1168). This parameter is thought to be of importance in determining the hydrological response of the catchment in the following way.

If a spatially uniform hydrograph of hillslope flow is delivered uniformly to all channel banks along the network shown in Figure 1(a), and if it is assumed that the time taken to travel each link is constant, then the outflow hydrograph is obtained by convolution of the inflow hydrograph with the link frequency distribution. This distribution consists of the number of links (network width) at successive travel times (corresponding to numbers of links) up from the outflow point. For the network in Figure 1(a), at successive one-link distances, x, the distribution is:

$$x = 0 \quad 1 \quad 2 \quad 3 \quad 4 \quad 5 \quad 6 \quad 7 \quad 8 \quad 9$$
$$w = 1 \quad 1 \quad 2 \quad 2 \quad 4 \quad 4 \quad 4 \quad 4 \quad 2 \quad 0.$$

The timing and magnitude of the outflow hydrograph peak can be shown to depend strongly on this distribution (Surkan (1968), Calver, Kirkby and Weyman (1972)). Although the link frequency distribution may be modelled explicitly, an approximation to it can be obtained from the random walk representation.

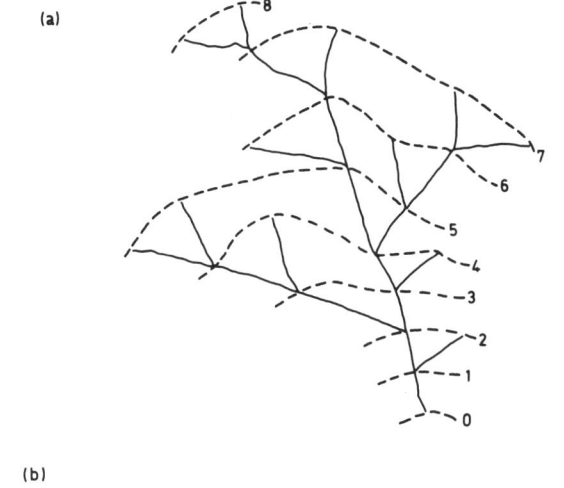

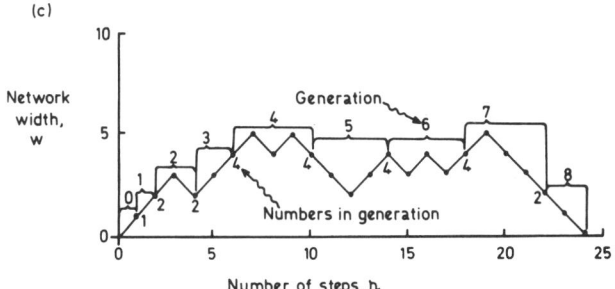

Figure 1. Conversion of a network to a random walk, on the basis of successive generations. (a) The original network. Broken lines indicate successive generations from the outflow point. (b) The binary string, broken into successive generation groupings, each scanned clockwise. 1's indicate a branch, and 0's a source. (c) Random walk representation

At a point where the network topologic width is w_T, then each link adds an average of $1/w_T$ generation. At the end of each completed generation, the random walk width, w_R, is exactly equal to the topologic width, w_T, and elsewhere is approximately equal to it. The number of generation therefore approximates to

$$x = \Sigma(1/w_R). \tag{1}$$

Where link lengths are not equal, but are drawn from some probability distribution, then the simple topological concept breaks down. By adopting the statistical generalization that velocity is more or less spatially uniform (Carlston (1969)), though varying over time; the topologic concept of generation from the outflow need, however, only be replaced by the concept of geometric distance along the network from the outflow. The topologic and geometric measures are compared below.

RANDOM WALKS AND NETWORKS

Random walk theory has been developed as a branch of mathematics and results are quoted here, referring to Feller's (1950) textbook, only as relevant to the context of channel networks. In general, a random walk of the type shown in Figure 1(c), but not restricted to the positive side, is associated with a probability p of increasing at each step, and a probability $q = 1 - p$ of decreasing. After n steps with r increases and $(n - r)$ decreases, the position is given by

$$w = r - (n - r) = 2r - n. \tag{2}$$

The number of all possible paths from the origin to $w = 2r - n$ after n steps is the binomial coefficient

$$\binom{n}{r}$$

and the probability of reaching this position is therefore

$$p_{r,n} = \binom{n}{r} p^r q^{n-r}. \tag{3}$$

The 'reflection principle' (Feller (1950) p. 68) states that route paths (though not their probabilities) are symmetrical with respect to up and down, so that for every possible random walk path, there is another possible route obtained by reflecting part of the path in the $w = 0$ axis or any other horizontal line which it crosses. This intuitive principle is the key to many more complex results. For example, the number of all positive routes to $w = 2r - n$ (>0) after n steps can be obtained (Feller (1950) p. 73, Wilson and Kirkby (1975)) as

$$\frac{2r - n}{n} \binom{n}{r}. \tag{4}$$

Applying this result (the Ballot Theorem) to the number of distinct random walks corresponding to TDCN's by putting $n = 2M - 1$ and $r = M$ (since the walk must finish with a zero), the number of TDCN's for a given network magnitude M is

$$N(M) = \frac{1}{2M - 1} \binom{2M - 1}{M} \sim \frac{2^{2M-2}}{M\sqrt{[\pi(M - 1)]}} \quad \text{for large } M \tag{5}$$

as obtained by Cayley (1859) for trees, and applied to stream networks by Shreve (1966). The probability of this magnitude, given that it begins at all (that is given the initial 1 of the binary string) is (Feller (1950) p. 78)

$$P(M) = \frac{1}{2M - 1} \binom{2M - 1}{M} p^{M-1} q^M. \tag{6}$$

By comparing coefficients of $(pq)^M$ in the binomial expansion for the positive square root $(1 - 4pq)^{1/2}$, the sum of the $P(M)$, which is the probability of some finite magnitude, is given by

$$\sum_0^\infty P(M) = \frac{1}{2p} [1 - (1 - 4pq)^{1/2}]$$

$$= \frac{1}{2p} \{1 - [(p + q)^2 - 4pq]^{1/2}\}$$

$$= \frac{1}{2p} [1 - |(p - q)|]$$

$$= 1 \quad \text{for} \quad 0 < p \leq \tfrac{1}{2}$$

$$= \frac{1 - p}{p} \quad \text{for} \quad \tfrac{1}{2} \leq p \leq 1 \tag{7}$$

Table I. Probabilities of networks of different magnitudes, M

		$M = 1$	2	3	4	5	6	7	8	9	10
p = probability of branching	0·5	1·000	0·500	0·375	0·312	0·273	0·246	0·226	0·209	0·195	0·185
	0·45	1·000	0·450	0·314	0·246	0·205	0·176	0·154	0·138	0·124	0·113
	0·4	1·000	0·400	0·256	0·187	0·145	0·117	0·097	0·082	0·070	0·061
	0·3	1·000	0·300	0·153	0·091	0·069	0·040	0·028	0·020	0·014	0·011
	0·2	1·000	0·200	0·072	0·031	0·015	0·007	0·004	0·001	0·001	0·001

Cumulative probability of a network having magnitude M or greater.

This result may also be obtained using the method outlined in Feller (1950) p. 296–7. It may therefore be seen that for networks with constant p and q throughout, finite network sizes can only be relied upon if $p \leq q$, that is if the probability of branching is not greater than the probability of termination. Equation (6) gives the probabilities of a random network having various magnitudes M, and the cumulative values are listed in Table I.

Goodness of fit to one of these distributions provides one test of the assumption of constant p and q, which corresponds to the concept that all TDCN's are equally likely for a given magnitude. Within a particular network, the same distribution gives some idea of the expected bifurcation structure, by calculating the proportions of different magnitudes for all sub-basins, but it should be remembered that the probability of branching p, is necessarily constrained to an overall value of 0·5, since the particular network necessarily has an equal number of branches (including the outlet as a branch) and terminations, and sub-basins must be drawn from this constrained population.

Because the choice of networks is somewhat arbitrary, except perhaps along a coastline, it may be preferable to weight the networks on an area basis. If constant drainage density is assumed, then area is approximately directly proportional to the total number of links in a basin. For a given total magnitude M, taken at a point where two tributaries come together, the probability of partitioning into two sub-networks with magnitudes M_1 and M_2, where $M_1 + M_2 - M$, is given by

$$p(M_1, M_2) = \frac{N(M_1) \cdot N(M_2)}{N(M)}, \tag{8}$$

since $N(M)$ is the total number of possibilities summed over all possible partitions. This distribution has highest values for M_1 or M_2 small, and much lower values for near-equal partitions. For M_1, M_2 both large, equal to kM and $(1 - k)M$ respectively, then at large M, the probability *density* behaves as

$$\sim \frac{1}{4\pi^{1/2} M^{1/2} \{k(1-k)\}^{3/2}} \quad (0 < k < 1) \tag{9}$$

which becomes progressively smaller at larger M, so that unequal proportional partition (specified by k) becomes more and more likely in larger areas. For large M, and unequal partitions into $r:(M - r)$ where $r \ll M$, the probability behaves as

$$\sim N(r) \, 2^{-2r}. \tag{10}$$

The proportions of partitions into $1:(M - 1)$, $2:(M - 2)$ etc, thus tend towards 1/4, 1/16, 1/32, 5/256 etc, irrespective of the value of M. Conformity to this distribution makes no assumptions about the value of p, the probability of branching, but does test whether it remains constant within the system.

For a network of given magnitude, M, the number of routes through a particular point, $K(r, n)$, (r 1's at the nth step) is given by the number of all-positive routes from the start to this point, multiplied by the number of all-positive routes from this point to the termination point ($r = M$, $n = 2M$). Using the Ballot Theorem; equation (4) above

$$K(r, n) = \frac{2r - n}{n} \binom{n}{r} \frac{2r - n}{2M - n} \binom{2M - n}{M - n + r}. \tag{11}$$

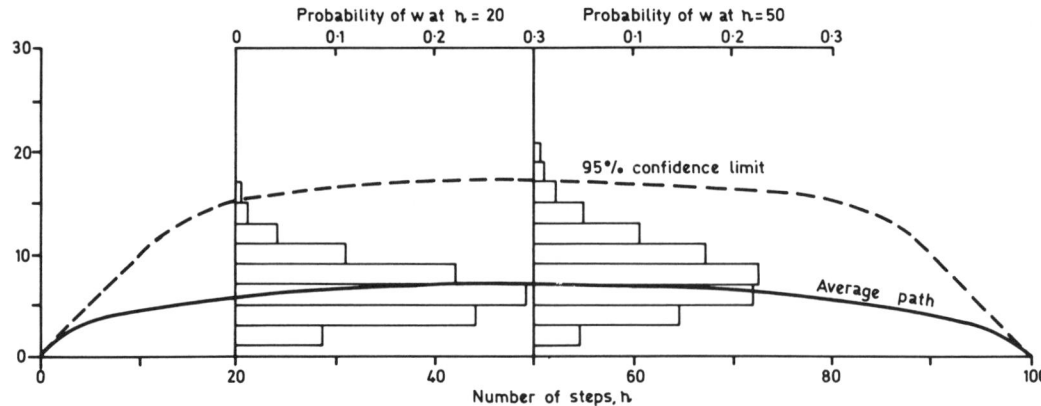

Figure 2. Most probable random walk widths (solid line) and upper 95 per cent confidence limit for path (broken line), corresponding to TDCN's in a network of magnitude 50. Histograms show the probability distribution of walk positions after $n = 20$ and $n = 50$ steps

If we treat $K(r, n)$ as a continuous function of r for a fixed n, then $K(r, n)$ will first increase and then decline. Its peak value will be at approximately that $(r + \frac{1}{2})$ for which

$$\frac{K(r + 1, n)}{K(r, n)} = 1 \cdot 0 \tag{12}$$

substituting from equation (11),

$$\frac{K(r + 1, n)}{K(r, n)} = \frac{(2r + 2 - n)^2}{(2r - n)^2} \cdot \frac{(n - r)(M - r)}{(r + 1)(M - n + r + 1)} = 1 \tag{13}$$

Solving for $2r - n$, and quoting the result for $r + \frac{1}{2}$; the peak value, associated with the most probable value of random walk width is

$$\hat{w}_R = 2r - n = \sqrt{\left[\frac{n(2M - n)}{M} + 1\right]} \tag{14}$$

Figure 2 shows the form of this curve for most probable random walk width which is not the same as the most probable random walk, and a number of frequency distributions for a network of magnitude $M = 50$. Alternatively an expression for the *mean* width may be obtained, subject to the condition that the network is non-zero but without specifying its magnitude. This is given by the sum over valid values of r, roughly $n \geqslant r \geqslant n/2$, of

$$\bar{r} = \sum \left[r \cdot \frac{2r - n}{n} \frac{n}{r} \right] \tag{15}$$

The sum can be expressed in the form

$$\bar{w}_R = 2\bar{r} - n = \frac{2^{n-1}}{\binom{n-1}{\frac{n-1}{2}}} \quad \text{for} \quad n \text{ odd}$$

$$= \frac{2^{n-1}}{\binom{n-1}{n/2}} \quad \text{for} \quad n \text{ even}$$

$$\sim \sqrt{\left(\frac{\pi n}{2}\right)} \quad \text{for} \quad n \text{ large} \tag{16}$$

The flat topped form of curves in Figure 2 demonstrates what has been stated above; namely that the maximum width w_R of the random walk, and so of the topologic network, varies widely both in position (value of n) and in value. We can thus normally expect a considerable variation in hydrologic response between basins of similar magnitude. The flat-peaked form of the curve suggests that the maximum random walk width can be meaningfully estimated, independent of its position along the walk (value of n). By applying the reflection principle repeatedly, it may be shown that the number of all-positive walks (equal to the number of TDCN's) for which the maximum width $w > a$, for a network of magnitude M, is given by (Feller (1950) p 96, Ex 3)

$$L(a, M) = \sum_{K=1}^{K'} \left\{ \left[\frac{2Ka - 1}{2M - 1} \binom{2M - 1}{M + ka - 1} - \frac{2Ka + 1}{2M - 1} \binom{2M - 1}{M + Ka} \right] (-1)^{K-1} \right\} \quad (17)$$

for as many terms are meaningful; that is until $M < (K' + 1)a$. If this expression is divided by $N(M)$, it gives the cumulative probability for the maximum width, as is listed in Table II for $M = 50$. It may be seen that the 95 per cent confidence limits for maximum width are 8 and 18, and the expected maximum width is 12·3.

Table II. Probability that a network of magnitude 50 shall have maximum random walk width $W_R > a$

$a =$	6	7	8	9	10	11	12	13	14	15	16	17	18	19	20	21	22	23
$p(W_R > a)$	1·000	0·998	0·981	0·927	0·826	0·688	0·535	0·391	0·268	0·174	0·106	0·062	0·034	0·018	0·009	0·004	0·002	0·001

The 'average' path of Figure 2 can be used to test deviations of *particular* networks from the modal pattern. The Kolmogorov–Smirnov two-sample test is related to the maximum difference between two cumulative frequency curves, and can be related to the maximum value of a random walk (Feller (1950) p. 71). One possible significance test might be obtained by modifying the theory to test deviations from the mean for all-positive random walks giving the test statistic

$$D = \frac{\text{Max deviation of actual from mean path}}{M = \text{Network magnitude}} \quad (18)$$

and tested for significance against standard tabulated values of D for two samples, both of size M. This test is sensitive to deviations on the high side, but less sensitive on the low side, because of the low value of the 'average' path. An alternative test uses equation (17) to test the absolute maximum value of the width in the random walk. This 'width' test has the advantage that it is sensitive to both high and low values of width, and discriminates almost equally as well as the Kolmogorov–Smirnov test because the mean path is so flat-peaked. Test values are listed in Table III, for magnitudes of 10–200. Against the simplicity of this test, however, must be set the ambiguous meaning of maximum width for the random walk, which is dependent on the sequence of branches and sources within each generation, and so on the method of scanning (eg clockwise or anti-clockwise) within each generation. A less ambiguous measure is the 'topologic width' which is defined as the number in any complete generation. This maximum width is unambiguous in that it is independent of the method of scanning within each generation, and is closely correlated to random walk width. An empirical test for topologic width can be obtained by subtracting 1·5 from the random walk width values shown in Table III. The resulting confidence limits are shown graphically in Figure 3. Plotting of basins and sub-basins on this diagram allows topologically significantly 'broad' or 'narrow' basins to be readily identified.

An alternative to the simple random walk model described above is to model the number in each generation direct as a family tree, using generating functions for the probabilities, but the mathematics is somewhat less tractable. It does, however, lead to a simple alternative to the magnitude test of Table I, by specifying the cumulative probabilities for networks of given topologic diameter (maximum number of links from outflow to a source following the shortest path; that is, the unique path without

Table III. Significance limits for maximum random walk width

Magnitude M	Lower limits for maximum width				Upper limits for maximum width			
	0·999	0·99	0·95	0·90	0·10	0·05	0·01	0·001
10	3	3	3	4	8	8	9	10
20	4	4	5	5	11	11	13	15
30	5	5	6	7	13	14	16	18
40	6	6	7	8	15	16	18	21
50	6	7	8	9	17	18	20	23
60	7	8	9	10	18	20	22	25
70	7	8	10	11	20	21	24	27
80	8	9	10	11	21	23	26	29
90	8	10	11	12	22	24	27	31
100	9	10	12	13	23	25	29	33
150	11	13	14	16	29	31	35	40
200	13	15	17	18	33	35	40	46

Lower limit figures are largest significant value.
Upper limit figures are smallest significant value.

repetition, through the network). The values are listed in Table IV. The family tree model also suggests that the path number classes description of a network (Werner and Smart (1973)) is an appropriate one, consisting as it does of the number of links in successive generations from the outlet (link frequency distribution). This classification contains only marginally less information (Jarvis and Werritty (1975)) than the classification into ambilateral classes (Smart (1969)).

TOPOLOGIC AND GEOMETRIC NETWORK PROPERTIES

In turning from tests of network topology to the hydrological response of networks, it is necessary to relate network width to distance, rather than number of links, from the network outlet. As has been described above, travel times through the network are related to distance, assuming a spatially uniform velocity, and not to numbers of links. It would be simple if the link frequency distributions

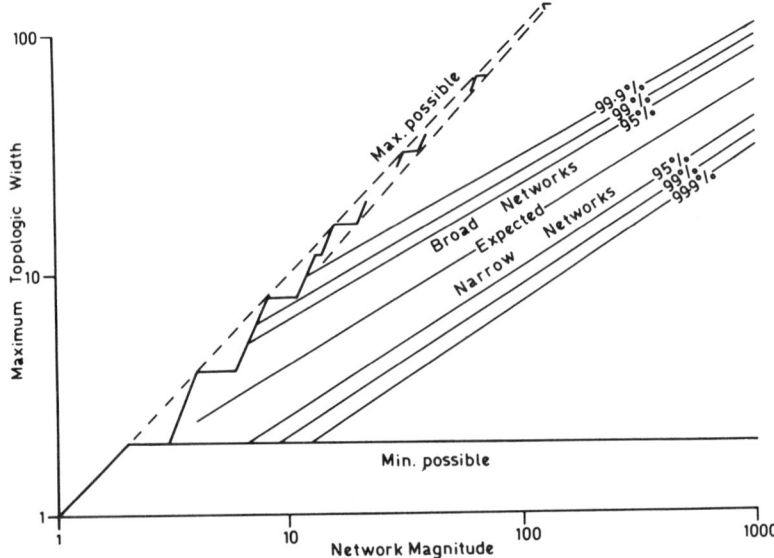

Figure 3. The significance levels for topologic width of a network

Table IV. Probabilities of networks of different topologic diameters. d_T

	$d_T = 1$	2	3	4	5	6	7	8	9	10	15	20
p = probability of branching 0.5	1.000	0.500	0.375	0.305	0.258	0.225	0.200	0.180	0.150	0.139	0.107	0.084
0.4	1.000	0.400	0.256	0.179	0.130	0.097	0.074	0.057	0.044	0.035	0.011	0.003

Cumulative probability of a network having diameter for d_T or greater.

and other basin measures obtained using numbers of links (the 'topologic' measure) were similar to those obtained using distances (the 'geometric' measures), but it will be seen that the two sets differ appreciably.

To examine the relationship between topologic and geometric network measures, a series of networks of magnitude 50 were generated randomly using the method described by Shreve (1974) p. 1172, and each link was assigned a length, drawn from specified distributions for interior and exterior links. In the example described, both were drawn from the exponential distribution with mean 1.0. For each network the following parameters were calculated:

W_R = Maximum random walk width (maximum value of random walk)
W_T = Maximum topologic width (maximum of link frequency distribution with number of links from outlet)
W_G = Maximum geometric width (maximum of link frequency distribution with geometric distance from outlet)
L_G = Total network length in mean link length units
d_T = Topologic diameter
d_G = Geometric diameter in mean link length units
k_T = Mean topologic path length to outlet
k_G = Mean geometric path length to outlet
β_T = Topologic diameter/width
β_G = Geometric diameter/width.

Table V gives the correlation matrix obtained for a set of 30 networks of magnitude 50. The table shows a poor relationship between geometric and topologic measures, especially for the most hydrologically significant measure of those tested, the network width. Both the synthetic measures included, the mean path lengths and diameter-to-width ratios, are dominated by the simplest measure, diameter, and therefore do not appear to be separately justified. It is concluded that the simplicity of the topologic measures recommends them for testing the normality of network structure, as discussed in the previous sections, but that the geometric measures must be preferred for considering the hydrological response of the network. An example of the difference between topologic and geometric link frequency distributions is shown in Figure 4(a) as a further illustration of the real difference between the two that may be expected.

Table V. Correlation matrix for topologic and scalar measures in networks of magnitude 50

	W_R	W_T	W_G	L_G	d_T	d_G	k_T	k_G	T	G
W_R	1.000									
W_T	0.919	1.000								
W_G	0.428	0.410	1.000							
L_G	0.027	0.123	−0.209	1.000						
d_T	−0.776	−0.768	−0.445	0.134	1.000					
d_G	−0.504	−0.496	−0.591	0.608	0.612	1.000				
k_T	−0.730	−0.651	−0.453	0.313	0.856	0.707	1.000			
k_G	−0.476	−0.438	−0.493	0.680	0.584	0.941	0.756	1.000		
T	−0.822	−0.889	−0.416	−0.042	0.920	0.537	0.743	0.472	1.000	
G	−0.480	−0.488	−0.817	0.311	0.543	0.781	0.581	0.652	0.511	1.000

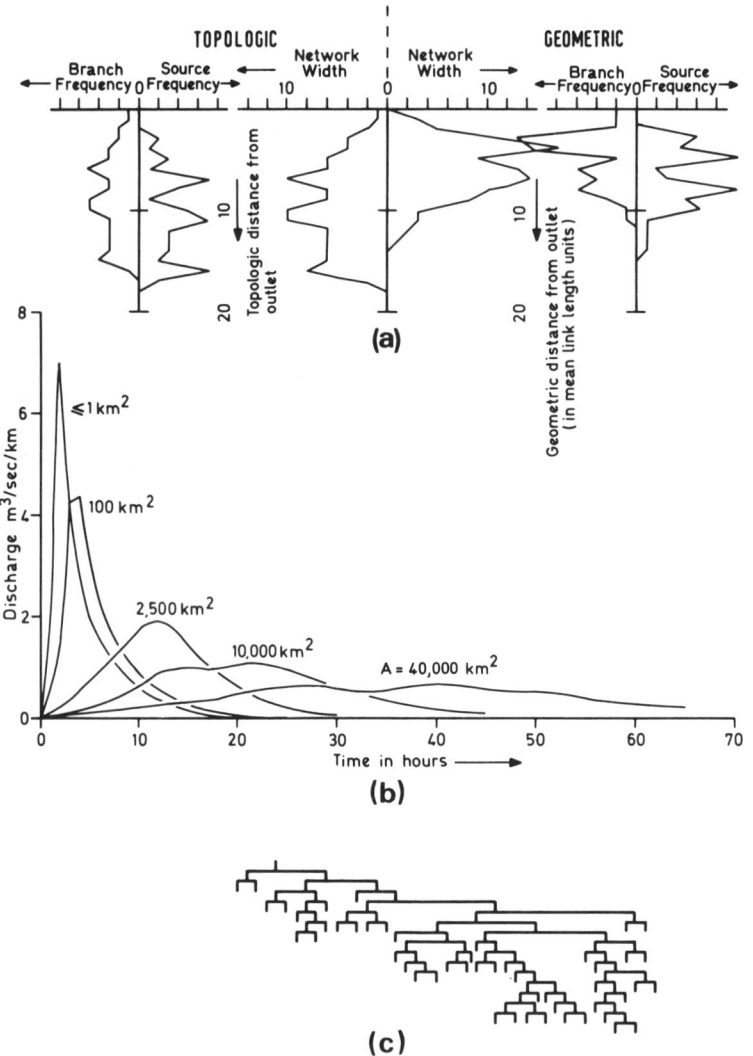

Figure 4. The topology and hydrologic response of a particular network of magnitude 50. (a) Topologic and geometric link frequency analyses. (b) Output hydrographs at different linear scales. (c) Network topology in schematic form

NETWORK HYDROLOGICAL RESPONSE

If hillslopes supply a hydrograph of $q(t)$ per unit length, uniformly along all channel banks, then the stream discharge at time t (Dooge (1959), Wooding (1965), Calver, Kirkby and Weyman (1972) p. 212)

$$Q(t) = 2 \int_{\tau=-\infty}^{t} q(\tau) \cdot W\left[\int_{\tau'=0}^{t-\tau} c(\tau') \, d\tau' \right] c(t-\tau) \, d\tau \qquad (19)$$

where $W(x)$ is the geometric network width at distance x from the outflow, and $c(t)$ is the kinematic wave velocity, assumed spatially uniform, after time t. This assumption is made on the basis of Leopold and Maddock's (1953) and Carlston's (1969) data on downstream variation in velocity for a given recurrence interval. Although not exact for the passage of a flood wave, it is thought to provide a good approximation for network response. An additional term may be added for inflow at stream heads, but is more or less in phase with the side-slope flow, as can be seen from the example in Figure 4(a) from the similarity of the distributions for numbers of streams and numbers of heads. Kinematic wave velocity is obtained by applying Manning's equation at-a-station as the outflow hydrograph $Q(t)$ is sequentially updated. For the example, in this paper, the stream head flow term is ignored, and kinematic wave velocity assumed constant at 1 m/sec at all flow stages. The side-slope hydrograph is also assumed constant, so that the influence of the network can be analyzed in isolation.

The qualitative influence of network scale is illustrated in Figure 4. A network, for which the topology is shown at (c) and the topologic geometric link frequency distributions at (a), has been analyzed at various linear scales. Each scale change alters both drainage area ($\propto$(mean link length)^2) and drainage density ($\propto 1$/mean link length). The same slope hydrograph is supplied to stream banks at all scales. Figure 4(b) shows the output hydrographs, expressed in m^3/sec/km of total network, as the overall basin area is changed. At small drainage areas (<1 km^2) the output hydrograph is indistinguishable from the input slope hydrograph. At larger drainage areas, the peak is relatively reduced and delayed, until at very large drainage areas, the hydrograph begins to look like the geometric link frequency distribution, even to the extent of being bimodal in this example.

The asymptotic behaviour of small and large drainage basins corresponds to the relative travel times for slope and channel flows as described in a more general case by Wooding (1965/6). In very small basins, travel time through the network is negligible and equation (19) tends towards

$$Q(t) = 2L_G \cdot x \cdot q \cdot (t) \tag{20}$$

and where L_G is the total geometric length of the network, measured in mean link length units x is the mean link length. In particular the peak stream discharge

$$Q_{pK} = 2L_G \cdot x \cdot q_{pK} \tag{21}$$

and the delay to peak for the channel

$$t_{CH} = t_G \tag{22}$$

where t_G is the delay to peak for the slope hydrograph, $q(t)$.

For very large basins (provided that $q(t)$ may be assumed as still spatially uniform), the hillslope travel time becomes negligible, and equation (19) gives

$$Q_{pK} = 2c \sum_t q W_G \tag{23}$$

where $\Sigma_t q$ is the total volume of flow from the slopes per unit length of channel bank, and W_G is the network maximum geometric width. The delay to peak is then given by

$$t_{CH} = x n_W / c \tag{24}$$

where n_W is the geometric distance from the outlet to the maximum geometric width, measured in mean link length units. These may take more than one value, corresponding to multiple peaks.

Combining equations (20) and (22) in a dimensionless form

$$\frac{Q_{pK}}{2L_G \cdot q_{pK}} = \phi\left(\frac{u}{x} \cdot \frac{W_G}{L_G}\right) = \phi(2) \tag{25}$$

where

$$u = \frac{c \sum_t q}{q_{pK}}, \quad \text{and} \quad z = \frac{u}{x} \cdot \frac{W_G}{L_G}.$$

u is an equivalent distance which depends mainly on the slope hydrograph. The asymptotic forms show that

$$\phi(z) \to z \text{ as } z \to 0 \quad \text{(large link length, } x\text{), and}$$

$$\phi(z) \to 1 \text{ as } z \to \infty \quad \text{(small link length),}$$

so that there is some hope that $\phi(z)$ may be a single-valued function throughout its range. The bracketed expression for z in equation (25) may be rewritten to separate the influence of basin size from that of its topology. Using the approximate empirical expression, illustrated by Shreve (1974) Fig. 11

$$\bar{a} = \gamma x^2 \tag{26}$$

where the mean link length x, is measured in km,
$\bar{a}$ is the mean area per link in km^2,
and γ is a dimensionless constant approximately equal to 1·5, then the total drainage area

$$A = (2M - 1)\bar{a} = (2M - 1)\gamma x^2 \tag{27}$$

substituting for x, in the expression for z

$$z^2 = \left(\frac{u}{x} \cdot \frac{W_G}{L_G}\right)^2 \left(\frac{\gamma u^2}{A} \cdot \frac{(2M - 1)W_G^2}{L_G^2}\right) \tag{28}$$

or

$$z = \frac{\gamma^{1/2} u}{A^{1/2}} \cdot \left[\frac{(2M - 1)W_G^2}{L_G^2}\right]^{1/2} \tag{29}$$

The left-hand part of the expression is a measure of basin scale relative to the dimension u derived from the slope hydrograph. The right-hand part is a measure of basin topology

$$\frac{(2M - 1)W_G^2}{L_G^2}$$

which for simulated networks of all sizes takes values from about 0·25 to 5·0, with a mean close to 1·0 for basins of magnitude less than 100 and increasing gradually with network magnitude. This expression for z, when substituted into equation (25) thus gives the required separation into scale and network structural components, and indicates the possible importance of the latter.

Figure 5 shows the curve obtained for a series of simulated random networks, of magnitude 20, 50 and 100 and a wide range of internal topologies. The scale of z is also plotted in terms of drainage area for networks of average structure

$$\left[\frac{(2M - 1)W_G^2}{L_G^2} \simeq 1\right],$$

and for the particular value of u (12·5 km) in this simulation. It may be seen that the curve describes the transition between two straight line sections, which intersect at $z = 1$, corresponding to a drainage area of about 230 km^2 in this example.

By comparing equation (25) with empirical prediction equations of high flows, it is first noted that the network parameter

$$\frac{(2M - 1)W_G^2}{L_G^2}$$

has not previously been introduced in the literature. For networks of average structure, equation (25) may be re-written as

$$\frac{Q_{PK}}{2q_{PK} A.D.} = \phi\left[\frac{\gamma^{1/2} u}{A^{1/2}}\right] \tag{30}$$

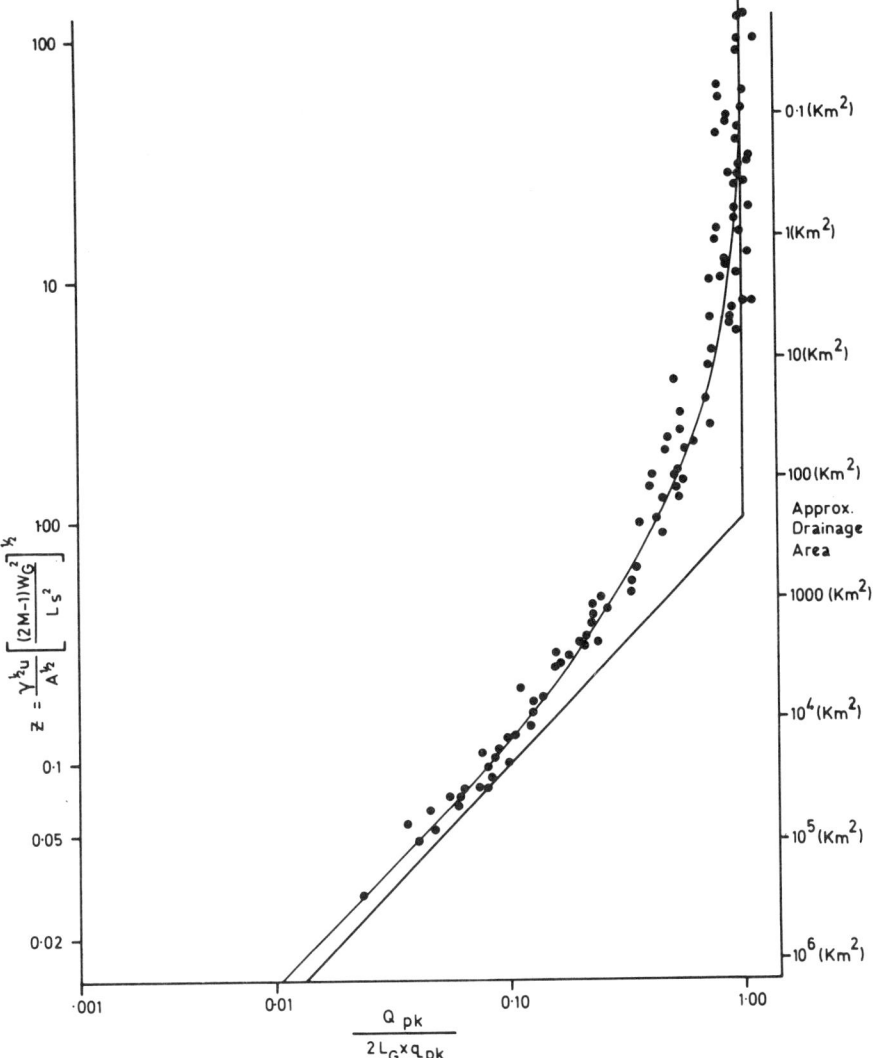

Figure 5. Dimensionless plot of peak discharge against network geometric width for a series of simulated networks. The width scale is also labelled for drainage area, assuming average network structure and the simulated slope hydrograph

where D = drainage density = L_G/A. If the function ϕ is approximated as a power function with exponent $m(0 < m < 1)$, then

$$Q_{PK} \propto 2\gamma^{\frac{1}{2}m} \cdot A^{(1-\frac{1}{2}m)} \cdot D \cdot (q_{PK} \cdot u^m) \qquad (31)$$

in which the bracketed terms refer to the slope hydrology. Comparison may be made with the empirical expressions

$$Q_{2\cdot33} \propto A^{0\cdot77} D^{0\cdot81} \quad \text{(Rodda (1967))} \qquad (32)$$

$$Q_{2\cdot33} \propto A \cdot D^2 \quad \text{(Carlston (1963))} \qquad (33)$$

where $Q_{2\cdot33}$ is the mean annual flood.

The first of these expressions lies close to the prediction of equation (31) for the range of moderate-sized basins used. The second expression, for somewhat smaller basins (and therefore low m), shows a higher exponent of drainage density than predicted. This may be partly explained by the $(q_{PK}u^m)$ term in equation (31). This term is derived from the hillslope hydrograph, which will itself show some dependence on slope gradient and length, and so perhaps on drainage density. Such considerations go beyond the direct influence of the network, and are not considered further here.

Similarly combining equations (22) and (24) a dimensionless expression for lag-to-peak is

$$\frac{t_{CH}}{t_G} = \psi\left(\frac{x}{ct_G} \cdot n_w\right) = \psi\left(\frac{A^{1/2}}{ct_G \gamma^{1/2}} \cdot \frac{n_w}{(2M-1)^{1/2}}\right) \tag{34}$$

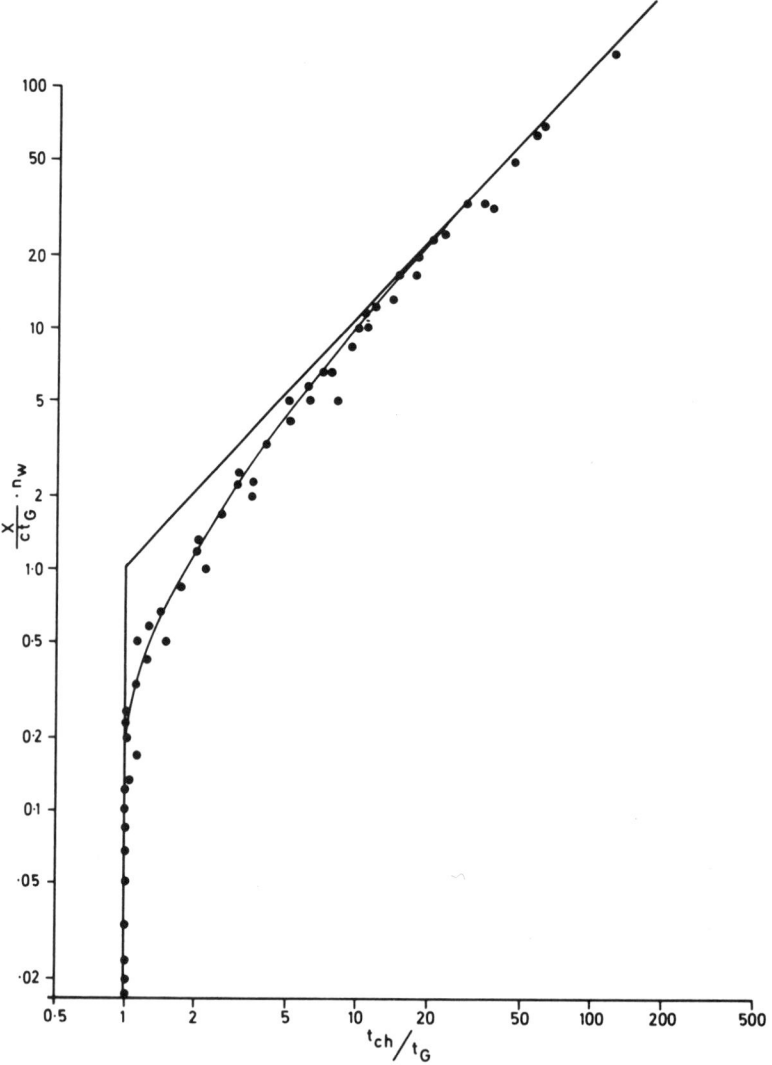

Figure 6. Dimensionless plot of lag-to-peak against distance to maximum network geometric width

Values of this dimensionless expression for the same networks as before are plotted in Figure 6. All peaks were plotted in those cases where network link frequency distributions (LFD's) are multi-peaked because the absolute peak of the hydrograph is not necessarily produced by the absolute maximum of the LFD except in extremely large drainage basins. In moderate-sized basins, later peaks in the LFD (farther from the outlet) tend to dominate, as in the example shown in Figure 4(b) for a drainage area of 10,000 km².

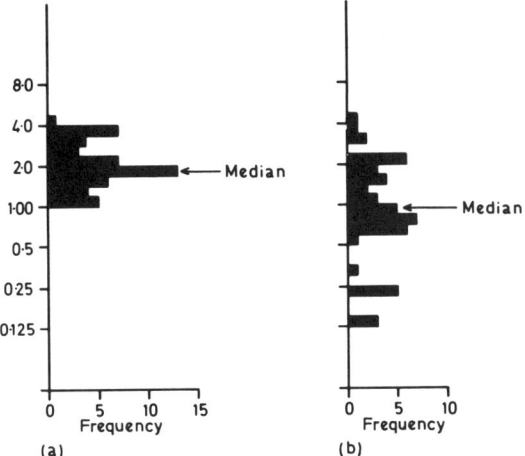

Figure 7. Frequency distributions for 50 simulated networks of magnitude 1,000. (a) Width parameter, $(2M-1)L_G^2/L_G^2$, which is related to peak discharge. (b) Distance to maximum width parameter, $n_w^2/(2M-1)$, which is related to lag-to-peak

It is concluded that the main influence of the network on channel hydrographs is through drainage area, and for peak discharge, drainage density. Even when area and drainage density are held constant, however, the network topology can influence peak discharge over a range of about $2x$ (Figure 7(a)), and influence time to peak over a range of about $4x$ (Figure 7(b)). These influences appear to be highly significant, and suggest that the analysis of drainage networks has a real hydrological value, particularly in drainage basins of more than 50 km² area.

The two directions explored in this paper are seen as important directions for future work on the application of network studies. If networks are shown to be generally random, then work should be concentrated on explanation of anomalous areas, in terms of particular factors influencing the position of each individual stream. If networks are found to differ appreciably from the random model in general, then general explanations for network structure are in order. The second direction for network studies lies in their influence on the landscape, principally through the basin hydrology. Indirectly, of course, the hydrology controls the sediment processes which form the network, so that ultimately the long- and short-term aspects of the network may be related, but at present that goal is very distant.

REFERENCES

Calver, A., Kirkby, M. J., and Weyman, D. R. (1972). 'Modelling hillslope and channel flows', *Spatial Analysis in Geomorphology*, ed. R. J. Chorley, Methuen, London, pp. 197–218.
Carlston, C. W. (1963). 'Drainage density and streamflow', *U.S. Geological Survey*, Professional Paper 422-C, 8 pp.
Carlston, C. W. (1969). 'Downstream variations in the hydraulic geometry of streams: special emphasis in mean velocity', *American Journal of Science*, **64**, No. 2, pp. 241–256.
Dooge, J. C. I. (1959). 'A general theory of the unit hydrograph', *Journal of Geophysical Research*, **64**, No. 2, pp. 241–256.
Feller, W. (1950). *An Introduction to Probability Theory and its Applications*, Vol. 1, Wiley, New York, 509 pp.
Horton, R. E. (1945). 'Erosional development of streams and their drainage basins; hydrophysical approach to quantitative morphology', *Bulletin of the Geological Society of America*, **56**, pp. 275–370.

Jarvis, R. S., and Werrity, A. (1975). 'Some comments on testing random topology stream network models', *Water Resources Research*, **11**, No. 2, pp. 309–318.

Leopold, L. B., and Maddock, T., Jr. (1953). 'The hydraulic geometry of stream channels and some physiographic implications', *U.S. Geological Survey*, Professional Paper 252.

Playfair, J. (1802). *Illustrations of the Huttonian Theory of the Earth*, Edinburgh.

Rodda, J. C. (1967). 'The significance of characteristics of basin rainfall and morphometry in a study of floods in the United Kingdom', *UNESCO Symposium on Floods and their Computation*, Leningrad.

Scheidegger, A. E. (1967). 'On the topology of river nets', *Water Resources Research*, **3**(1), pp. 103–106.

Shreve, R. L. (1966). 'Statistical law of stream numbers', *Journal of Geology*, **74**, pp. 17–37.

Shreve, R. L. (1967). 'Infinite topologically random channel networks', *Journal of Geology*, **75**, pp. 179–186.

Shreve, R. L. (1974). 'Variation of mainstream length with basin area in river networks', *Water Resources Research*, **10**, No. 6, pp. 1167–1177.

Smart, J. S. (1969). 'Topological properties of channel networks', *Bulletin of the Geological Society of America*, **80**, pp. 1757–1774.

Smart, J. S. (1974). 'The random model in fluvial geomorphology', in *Fluvial Geomorphology: Proceedings of the 4th Geomorphology Symposium*, ed. M. Morisawa, Binghampton, State Univ., New York. Pub. Geomorphology, pp. 27–49.

Surkan, A. J. (1968). 'Synthetic hydrographs: effects of network geometry', *Water Resources Research*, **5**, pp. 112–128.

Werner, C., and Smart, J. S. (1973). 'Some new methods of topologic classification of channel networks', *Geographical Analysis*, **5**, pp. 271–295.

Wilson, A. G., and Kirkby, M. J. (1975). *Mathematics for Geographers and Planners*, Oxford University Press, London, 325 pp.

Wooding, R. A. (1965/6). 'A hydraulic model for the catchment-stream problem'. I. 'Kinematic wave theory', *Journal of Hydrology*, **3**, pp. 254–267. II. 'Numerical solutions', *Journal of Hydrology*, **3**, pp. 268–282. III. 'Comparisons with runoff observations', *Journal of Hydrology*, **4**, pp. 21–37.

24

Copyright ©1976 by the American Geophysical Union
Reprinted from *Water Resources Research* **8**:1487–1496 (1972)

Quantitative Characterization of Channel Network Structure

J. S. SMART

IBM Thomas J. Watson Research Center, Yorktown Heights, New York 10598

Abstract. The most commonly used quantitative parameters for characterizing channel networks are derived from a Horton analysis (bifurcation ratios, stream length ratios, and so forth). Although these parameters give useful information about individual networks, they are generally ineffective in distinguishing differences in network structure due to lithologic controls and degree of maturity. As Shreve has noted, this failure is due in part to the random nature of network topology and link lengths and in part to the fact that the Horton analysis tends to average out many of the details that characterize such differences. Parameters derived from considerations of statistical geometric similarity, on the other hand, are relatively successful in characterizing network structure. For a simple example, let l_e and l_i be the mean exterior and interior link lengths, respectively, and a_e and a_i be the means of the associated drainage areas. Four dimensionless parameters that can be constructed from this set are $\lambda = l_e/l_i$, $\alpha = a_e/a_i$, $K_e = l_e^2/a_e$, and $K_i = l_i^2/a_i$. Data on λ, α, K_e, and K_i for natural networks drawn from different geologic populations indicate that these quantities are effective in detecting differences due to varying lithology and degree of maturity.

For many years drainage networks have been classified according to patterns [*Thornbury*, 1969, pp. 117–124]. This classification is purely qualitative and is generally based on either the relative orientations of individual streams in the same channel network (e.g., dendritic, trellis) or the relative orientations of individual channel networks (e.g., radial, parallel). The judgments involved are made purely from visual inspection, with no attempt at quantitative assessment, and in fact the eye can make distinctions considerably finer than those required for pattern assignment. For example, Figures 1–3 show three pairs of dendritic channel networks, each pair being taken from a different geographical location. The eye readily identifies members of the same pair as being more like each other than like members of another pair. *Zernitz* [1932] and *Howard* [1967] suggest that this ability to distinguish network patterns could be more fully used by refining the classification scheme to include modified basic patterns such as subdendritic, pinnate, fault trellis, and recurved trellis.

It would seem that there should be some quantitative procedure for characterizing these small but detectable variations in channel network structure. *Horton* [1945] proposed a method of stream ordering (i.e., numerically ranking the individual channels in a channel network) that could be used to determine two dimensionless network parameters, the bifurcation ratio and the stream length ratio. The so-called 'Horton analysis' has now become a standard procedure for reporting the structural properties of channel networks, although Horton's original ordering scheme has now been generally superseded by *Strahler*'s [1952] modification. *Horton* [1945, pp. 300–306] apparently felt that the bifurcation and stream length ratios would be functions of topography, geology, climate, and other environmental factors and would thus be effective in distinguishing network structures in cases like those in Figures 1–3. These expectations, however, have not been confirmed, although the Horton parameters have proved useful for characterizing individual networks.

Two factors that contribute to this failure have been noted by *Shreve* [1969, p. 414]. First, to a good approximation, channel networks developed in the absence of geologic controls are topologically random, and the exterior and interior link lengths may be regarded as independent random variables with a single common distribution for each type. Thus the distribution of the Horton parameters is mainly determined by this underlying randomness. Second, the

369

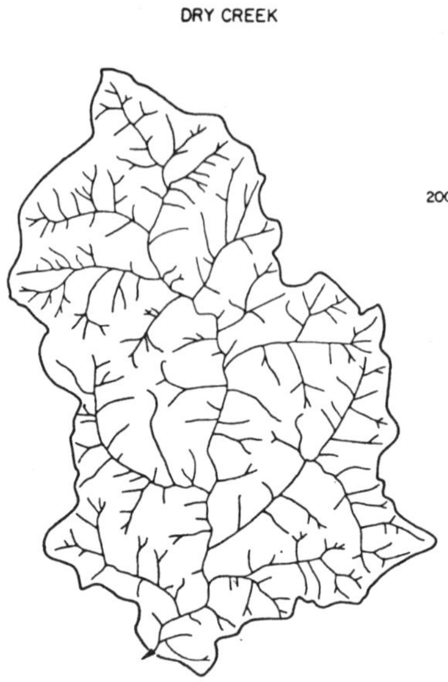

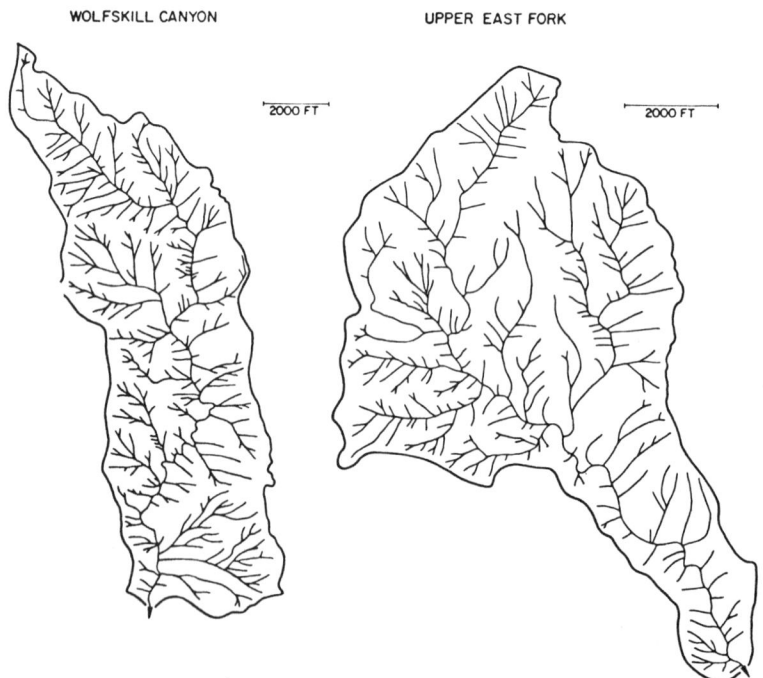

Fig. 1. Channel networks for region A (Miltown, Indiana).

Fig. 2. Channel networks for region B (Glendora–Mt. Baldy, Calif.). These networks were traced from poor reproductions of *Maxwell's* [1960] original plates, and some details may be in error. Note the difference in scale for the two networks.

calculation of the Horton parameters involves summations of a large number of link lengths or their associated areas, so that many of the details responsible for differences in network structure are averaged out.

This paper approaches the problem of distinguishing and characterizing network structure from the standpoint of geometric similarity. *Strahler* [1958, pp. 291-292] first introduced this concept into drainage basin geomorphology. According to his definition, two channel networks have exact geometric similarity if all pairs of corresponding dimensionless variables are numerically equal. This idealized situation is of course not expected to occur in nature, but Strahler suggested that networks developed under the same environmental conditions should have approximate geometric similarity. *Smart and Moruzzi* [1971] made the concept somewhat more precise by proposing that networks developed under the same conditions should have statistical geometric similarity; i.e., all corresponding dimensionless variables should have the same distribution functions.

The bifurcation and stream length ratios are of course the kind of dimensionless variable that one might expect to use in statistical similarity considerations. As was stated above, however, these quantities do not provide any effective discrimination in the classification of network structures. In this study I consider dimensionless variables related to link lengths and their associated drainage areas, since these quantities are the elementary units from which drainage basins are constructed. For example, Figure 6 shows the individual links and drainage areas for a small drainage basin in Pennsylvania. It is likely that many of the features of network structure that can be distinguished visually but not by Horton analysis derive from the statistical properties of these elementary lengths and areas.

DEFINITIONS

Consider a set of N links (which do not necessarily form a complete channel network); let l_j and a_j be the length and associated drainage area, respectively, of the jth link. The random topology and random link length models [*Shreve*, 1966, 1967, 1969; *Smart*, 1968], as well as general geomorphic considerations, suggest that the N pairs of observations (l_j, a_j) may be regarded as correlated random variables drawn from a bivariate population. This section defines some useful statistics that can be derived from the $2N$ observations. The microscopic drainage density δ_j is given by

$$\delta_j = l_j/a_j \qquad j = 1, 2, 3, \cdots, N \qquad (1)$$

The mean microscopic drainage density is then

$$\bar{\delta} = \frac{1}{N} \sum_{j=1}^{N} \frac{l_j}{a_j} \qquad (2)$$

The macroscopic drainage density, which is a more commonly used parameter in geomorphic

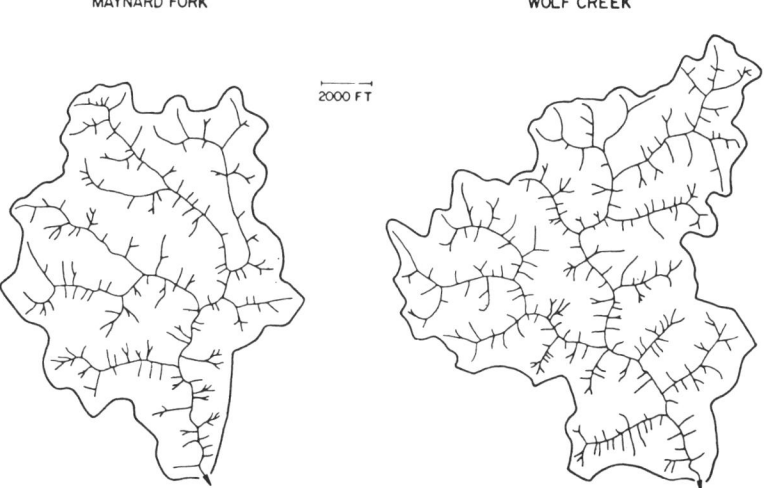

Fig. 3. Channel networks for region C (Thomas, Ky.).

TABLE 1. Values of ϕ for Regular Shapes

Shape	ϕ_{max}	ϕ_{min}
Circle	$4/\pi$	$4/\pi$
Ellipse of eccentricity ϵ	$4/\pi(1-\epsilon^2)^{1/2}$	$4(1-\epsilon^2)^{1/2}/\pi$
Hexagon	$8/3(3^{1/2})$	$2/3^{1/2}$

analysis, is given by

$$D = L/A = \sum_j l_j / \sum_j a_j = \bar{l}_i/\bar{a}_i \quad (3)$$

where L is the total length and A the total area for the set of N links.

Values of $\bar{\delta}$ are also occasionally reported in the literature. Since they are almost invariably given the symbol $\bar{D}$, they are frequently confused with mean values of the D of (3), although in general the two quantities are clearly not the same.

Theoretical studies of drainage basins sometimes invoke the assumption of uniform drainage density; i.e., $\delta_j = \delta_0$ for all j. In this idealized case, $\bar{\delta} = D = \delta_0$.

A quantity that will be useful in statistical similarity considerations is

$$\phi_i = l_i^2/a_i = \delta_i l_i = \delta_i^2 a_i \quad (4)$$

$$j = 1, 2, 3, \cdots, N$$

$$\bar{\phi} = (1/N) \sum_j (l_j^2/a_j) \quad (5)$$

We see that ϕ (which is the reciprocal of the dimensionless coefficient κ previously introduced by *Shreve* [1967, p. 184]) gives somewhat the same information as δ but in a dimensionless form. Its order of magnitude for natural channel networks can be estimated from simple geometric arguments by assuming that the elementary area has a regular shape and is bisected by a straight-line link. Some examples are given in Table 1. The minimum values are of course absolute minimums, whereas the 'maximum' values can be exceeded if the channel segment is not straight. Observations on natural networks, however (e.g., Figure 6), suggest that the ϕ_{max} values are close to practical upper limits. We see that ϕ can be expected to be of the order of unity for elementary drainage areas whose shapes are not excessively elongate.

We also define a macroscopic analog to ϕ:

$$K = \frac{1}{N} \frac{L^2}{A} = \frac{1}{N} \frac{(\sum_j l_j)^2}{\sum_j a_j}$$

$$= D\bar{l}_i = D^2 \bar{a}_i = \frac{\bar{l}_i^2}{\bar{a}_i} \quad (6)$$

For uniform drainage density, $\phi = K = \delta_0 \bar{l} = \delta_0^2 \bar{a}$.

The quantities K and ϕ are evidently related, the exact relation depending on the distributions of l_j and a_j and their degree of correlation. It would appear, however, that, if ϕ is of the order of unity, then K will also be of the order of unity. *Melton* [1960] found that, for mature channel networks of magnitude μ, the factor L^2/A is numerically approximately equal to $2\mu - 1$; this statement is equivalent to saying that $1/K$ is approximately unity.

SELECTION OF DIMENSIONLESS PARAMETERS

The general definition of statistical geometric similarity suggests that we should look for dimensionless functions of link properties, e.g., ϕ, and study their distributions. Thus two channel networks could be classified as alike or different according to whether their ϕ distributions were the same or different. In practice the labor involved in collecting the necessary data is great, and we shall first try the less enterprising alternative of working with the macroscopic analogs, e.g., K.

Although, as was stated above, the definitions of δ, D, ϕ, and K apply formally to any set of links, the observed values are clearly more meaningful if they represent geomorphically significant populations. One well-established property of channel networks is that the exterior and interior link lengths have different distributions, and there is no reason to doubt that this differentiation also occurs for drainage areas. Consequently the data for a channel network of magnitude n will be separated into two groups, one for the n exterior links and one for the $n - 1$ interior links.

The preceding considerations suggest the following four observable dimensionless statistics as a set for characterizing and distinguishing channel network structures:

$$\lambda = \bar{l}_e/\bar{l}_i \quad (7a)$$

$$\alpha = \bar{a}_e/\bar{a}_i \quad (7b)$$

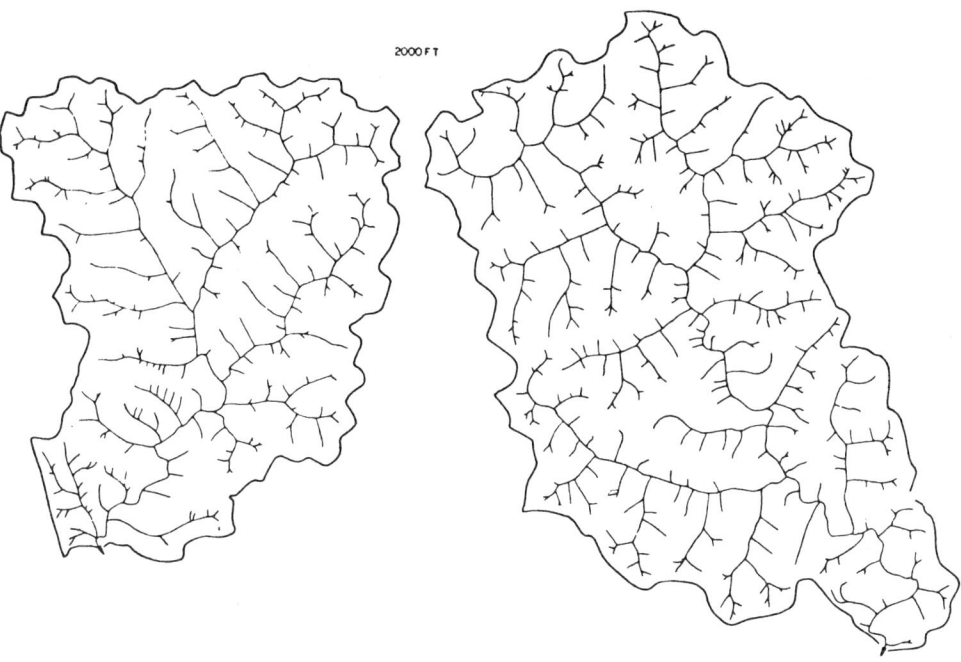

Fig. 4. Channel networks for region D (left, Moundsville, W. Va.; right, Majorsville, W. Va., quadrangle).

$$K_e = \bar{l}_e^2/\bar{a}_e \tag{7c}$$

$$K_i = \bar{l}_i^2/\bar{a}_i \tag{7d}$$

where the subscripts e and i refer to exterior and interior links, respectively. Actually only three of these quantities are independent, since

$$\lambda^2/\alpha = K_e/K_i \tag{8}$$

Note that both K_e and K_i specify a dimensionless property of one particular type of link, whereas λ and α are used to compare mean lengths and drainage areas for two different kinds of links.

DATA COLLECTION

Pairs of networks were selected for study and comparison from each of six different geographical regions. Although all the networks can be classified as dendritic or modified dendritic, the pairs are visually distinctly different (Figures 1–5). The main objective of the selection process was to find dendritic networks representative of regions with differing lithology and degree of maturity.

Brief descriptions of the most obvious topographic and geologic properties of each region are given below. Areas A, B, C, and E–F were previously studied by *Coates* [1958], *Maxwell* [1960], *Krumbein and Shreve* [1970], and *Zakrzewska* [1963], respectively; further details can be found in these references.

Region A. This region in southern Indiana was selected by *Coates* [1958] for its simple uniform lithology and structure. The bedrock is generally flat-lying sandstone interbedded with limestone; the valley side slopes are homogeneous with no signs of benching. Almost 40% of the area is unconsumed upland, and the erosional stage is classified as middle youth.

Region B. This area on the southern slopes of the San Gabriel Mountains in California has a complex geologic and erosional history [*Maxwell*, 1960, pp. 7–8]. The bedrock is a mixture of gneiss, schist, diorite, and granite, intensively fractured by small faults. The topography is fully mature, but a late Pleistocene uplift has produced entrenched meanders and rejuvenated valley sections. There are numerous waterfalls caused by resistant dikes.

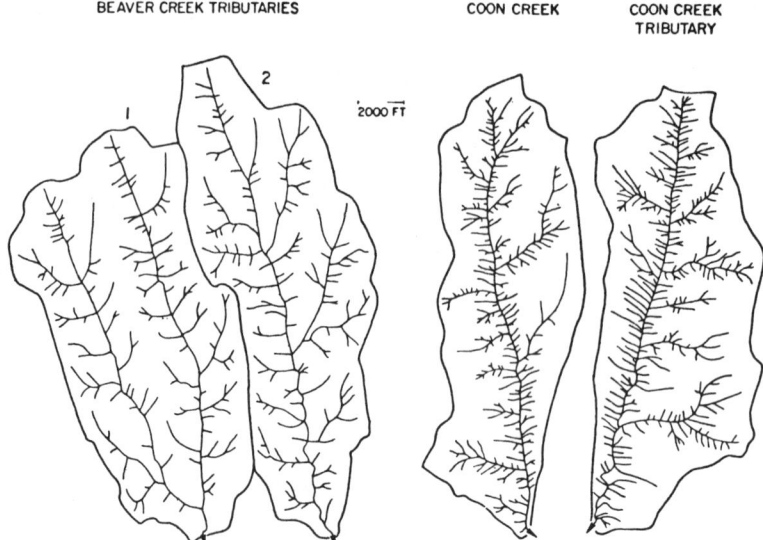

Fig. 5. Channel networks for regions E (Shippee, Nebr.) and F (Quick NE, Nebr.).

Region C. Krumbein and Shreve [1970] describe this eastern Kentucky region as follows:

> The topography of the area is mature, with steep slopes, and narrow, winding valleys and ridges .... The drainage pattern is dendritic and shows no sign of lines of weakness, such as joints or other geologic controls .... The bedrock consists of flat-lying (dips less than 50 feet per mile), relatively homogeneous Pennsylvania sandstone and interbedded siltstone, shale, underclay, and coal. Poorly defined benches and somewhat broad-crested ridges probably attributable to structural control are present, but are widely scattered and nonpersistent. Thus, the area, though not perfect, appears to be a good example of a mature landscape developed in the absence of geologic controls.

One might expect that the drainage networks for regions A and C would be similar at corresponding stages of their erosional history.

Region D. Region D is a highly dissected plateau in the West Virginia panhandle. The bedrock is gently folded and consists of a succession of sandstones, interbedded with shale, limestone, and coal [*Hennen*, 1909, p. 125]. The topography is generally similar to that of region C, though more broad crested ridges are in evidence. The low drainage density is probably attributable to a massive sandstone stratum that caps the plateau in most places. The channel networks are dendritic, but certain regularities in tributary spacing and junction angles suggest the existence of geologic controls, possibly parallel fractures.

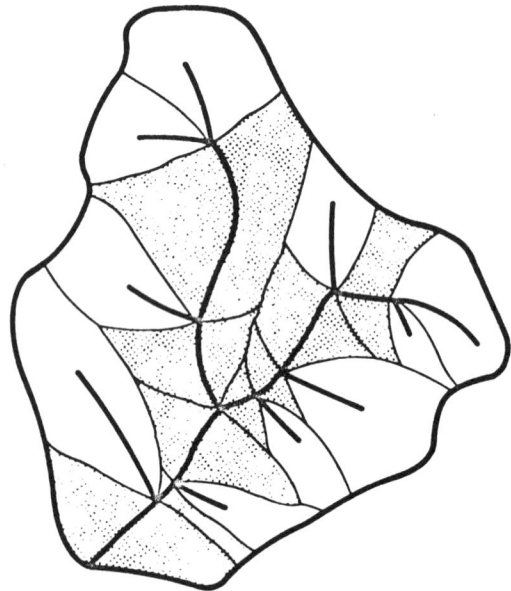

Fig. 6. Exterior and interior links and associated drainage areas for Pritchard Hollow, Oleona, Pennsylvania, quadrangle. Channels and basin boundary are represented by heavy lines; interior drainage divides are represented by light lines. The white area drains into exterior links, and the shaded area drains into interior links.

Regions E and F. In a detailed regional analysis of the topography of the Upper Republican River basin in Nebraska and Kansas *Zakrzewska* [1963] compared the properties of the tributary drainage networks north and south of the Republican River. In both areas the drainage has developed in loess, and for networks of the size shown in Figure 5 only the mainstreams have cut down to bedrock. All four drainage systems are immature, and the drainage patterns in their present form can be classified as pinnate [*Zernitz*, 1932, pp. 512–513]. Despite these similarities the networks in the two regions are easily distinguished; in particular it appears that the northern area will have a much higher drainage density when the drainage development is mature. A possible reason for this difference is that the runoff north of the Republican River is appreciably greater than that south of the river [*Zakrzewska*, 1963, p. 559].

Results of the measurements on the 12 drainage basins are reported in Tables 2 and 3. For regions A and C–F the channel networks were outlined on 1:24,000 U.S. Geological Survey topographic maps by the procedures developed by Strahler and his students. Link lengths were measured to the nearest 1/40 inch with an architect's scale, curved sections being approximated by a series of straight-line segments. Areas were measured with a polar planimeter. In general the results of the measurements agreed well with those of the previous investigators for the corresponding localities.

Maxwell's measurements for region B provided all the data necessary for this study, and I have simply reported his results. Since Maxwell used large-scale maps corrected by field studies, his data are undoubtedly more reliable than those for other areas. It may be noted parenthetically that the absolute accuracy is not too important for testing the effectiveness of the proposed characterization procedures. All that is required is that the maps for each region be interpreted consistently. If the procedures prove satisfactory and are to be used as an aid in geomorphic classification, then of course the question of data reliability becomes extremely important.

DISCUSSION

Table 4 lists the values of the four dimensionless parameters of $(7a)-(7d)$ as well as the related quantities $D_c/D_i = \lambda/\alpha$ and $K_c/K_i =$

TABLE 2. Channel Network Data

Network	U.S. Geol. Surv. 7½-Minute Topographic Sheets	No. of Sources	L, miles	A, mi²	D, mi⁻¹	Outlet Elevation, feet	Relief, feet
Region A	Miltown, Indiana						
Dry Creek		252	57.01	6.51	8.76	540	335
Slick Creek		261	61.21	7.44	8.22	520	380
Region B*	Glendora–Mt. Baldy, Calif.						
Wolfskill Canyon		409	48.00	2.49	19.27	1765	2695
Upper East Fork		347	38.81	2.18	17.81	2565	2560
Region C	Thomas, Ky.						
Maynard Fork		180	31.66	4.21	7.53	700	910
Wolf Creek		252	44.21	5.32	8.31	715	825
Region D	Moundsville–Majorsville–Cameron, W. Va.						
Little Grave Creek		213	53.22	10.55	5.04	700	695
Wolf Run		321	81.31	15.55	5.23	800	710
Region E	Shippee, Nebr.						
Beaver Creek tributary 1		130	26.80	4.04	6.64	2340	200
Beaver Creek tributary 2		136	27.77	3.69	7.52	2330	210
Region F	Quick NE, Nebr.						
Coon Creek		250	32.29	3.15	10.26	2660	260
Coon Creek tributary		266	38.67	3.65	10.58	2620	230

* Data for this region from *Maxwell* [1960].

TABLE 3. Channel Network Data: Exterior and Interior Links

Network	$\bar{l}_e$, feet	$\bar{l}_i$, feet	$\bar{a}_e \times 10^{-5}$, ft²	$\bar{a}_i \times 10^{-5}$, ft²	D_e, mi⁻¹	D_i, mi⁻¹
A1	672	525	3.31	3.91	10.72	7.09
A2	687	553	3.33	4.64	10.91	6.29
B1	376	244	0.97	0.73	20.46	17.67
B2	359	232	1.01	0.75	19.45	17.23
C1	528	403	3.69	2.84	7.55	7.50
C2	571	358	3.64	2.27	8.29	8.34
D1	627	696	7.60	6.24	4.36	5.90
D2	625	714	6.97	6.55	4.74	5.77
E1	593	499	4.95	3.74	6.34	7.07
E2	616	466	4.58	3.01	7.07	8.18
F1	457	226	2.89	0.62	8.34	19.22
F2	555	213	3.23	0.61	9.08	18.59

Network A1 is the first network under Region A in Table 2, i.e., the Dry Creek network. The remaining networks can be identified similarly.

λ^2/α. Since only three of the six entries in each row are independent, the table is somewhat redundant, but it is helpful in interpreting the properties of the networks to have the data displayed in different ways. Before the characterization question is considered, one or two other points of interest may be noted.

All the values of K_i are appreciably less than unity, ranging from 0.57 to 0.82. This fact indicates that the elementary interior drainage areas tend to be elongated in a direction normal to the channel. The behavior of K_e is less easy to interpret, since not only is there a greater range of values (0.52–1.46) but also the exterior links generally do not span the drainage area. *Krumbein and Shreve* [1970, p. 36] suggest that most observers judge the actual channel length to be somewhere between two-thirds and three-quarters of the mesh length; thus values of K_e based on the mesh length would be larger than those reported by about a factor of 2. These things being considered, it appears that a substantial majority of the elementary exterior drainage areas have shapes ranging from roughly circular to elongated in the direction of the channel.

Shreve [1969, p. 413] and *Krumbein and Shreve* [1970, pp. 91–94] have discussed a model of network structure that divides each exterior drainage area a_e into a part a_e', which drains directly into the sides of the channel, and a part a_s, which drains into the tip. Their analysis also assumes that D_e' (i.e., $\bar{l}_e/\bar{a}_e'$) and D_i are equal. In this case we always have $D_e < D_i$. Note that this condition is not satisfied for regions A and B.

Although the data of Table 4 certainly suggest that the dimensionless parameters are reasonably effective in classifying network structures, the degree of success can be seen better in the profile plot of Figure 7. Each profile shows from left to right the values of λ, $\alpha^{1/2}$, $K_e^{1/2}$, and $K_i^{1/2}$, the square roots of the last three

TABLE 4. Channel Network Data: Dimensionless Variables

Network	λ	α	K_e	K_i	λ/α	λ^2/α
A1	1.28	0.85	1.36	0.70	1.51	1.94
A2	1.24	0.72	1.42	0.66	1.73	2.16
B1	1.54	1.33	1.46	0.82	1.16	1.79
B2	1.55	1.35	1.28	0.72	1.15	1.78
C1	1.31	1.30	0.76	0.57	1.01	1.32
C2	1.59	1.60	0.90	0.57	0.99	1.59
D1	0.90	1.22	0.52	0.77	0.74	0.67
D2	0.88	1.07	0.56	0.78	0.82	0.72
E1	1.19	1.32	0.71	0.67	0.90	1.07
E2	1.32	1.52	0.83	0.72	0.87	1.15
F1	2.02	4.64	0.72	0.82	0.44	0.88
F2	2.60	5.32	0.96	0.75	0.49	1.27

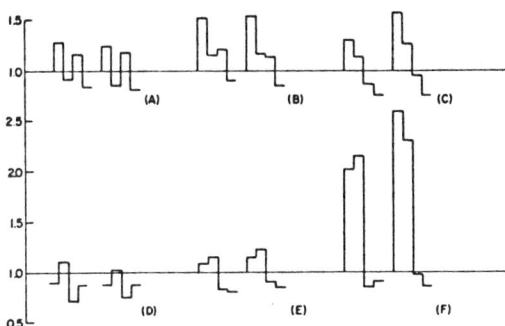

Fig. 7. Profiles of dimensionless variables for the 12 channel networks. In each profile, values of λ, $\alpha^{1/2}$, $K_e^{1/2}$, and $K_t^{1/2}$ are plotted from left to right. Letters A-F identify the regions.

TABLE 5. Values of d_{mn}

	A1	B1	C1	D1	E1	F1
A2	0.15	0.68	0.88	1.08	0.93	4.06
B2	0.57	0.18	0.58	1.01	0.68	3.37
C2	0.93	0.62	0.43	0.88	0.52	3.08
D2	0.92	1.15	0.53	0.16	0.42	3.75
E2	0.86	0.69	0.23	0.60	0.27	3.26
F2	4.68	4.16	4.23	4.46	4.25	0.93

variables being taken simply to reduce the vertical range of the plots. It is clear that members of the same pair of profiles tend to be more like each other than like members of the other pairs, just as was true for the corresponding channel networks of Figures 1–5.

Another, perhaps more quantitative, way of analyzing the data is to let λ, α, and K_e be orthogonal coordinates in a three-dimensional space; then each network is represented by a point in this space, and the Euclidean distance d_{mn} between pairs of points can be used as a measure of similarity or dissimilarity:

$$d_{mn} = [(\lambda_m - \lambda_n)^2 + (\alpha_m - \alpha_n)^2 + (K_{em} - K_{en})^2]^{1/2} \quad (9)$$

The 12 networks in Table 4 yield 66 distinct values of d_{mn}; the main features of the data, however, can be displayed in the 6 × 6 array in Table 5, which has been arranged so that the six distances between networks in the same region appear on the principal diagonal and 30 of the 60 distances between networks in different regions appear as off-diagonal elements.

For each of the regions A, B, D, and F the diagonal element is appreciably less than the other 10 elements in the corresponding row and column; thus the networks in these four regions have been properly sorted. Networks C1, E1, and E2, however, appear to belong to the same group, whereas C2 is not very close to any of the other networks. A second look at Figures 3 and 5 shows that networks C and E have points of similarity that become more apparent if the differences in basin shape are ignored. It is not clear whether the relatively large d value for C1 and C2 reflects differing environmental conditions for these two drainage basins (which are contiguous) or is a consequence of the natural sampling variance for uniform environmental conditions.

Note that the profile analysis leads to somewhat different conclusions concerning networks C and E and in particular does not associate C1 with E1 and E2. This discrepancy is not surprising because the profile and distance analyses emphasize different features of the parameter data of Table 4.

One possible use of statistical similarity procedures is the quantitative comparison of channel networks of different sizes. *Schumm* [1956] studied the geomorphic properties of a small (31,000 ft^2) drainage basin developed on clay–sand fill in Perth Amboy, New Jersey. The values of λ, α, K_e, and K_t deduced from Schumm's data are 1.57, 1.41, 1.20, and 0.69, respectively. Both the profile analysis and the distance analysis indicate that the Perth Amboy network is structurally most like those in region B (San Gabriel Mountains).

The limited data of Table 4 are of course insufficient to make any general inferences about the range of applicability and sensitivity of the proposed method. Detailed statistical studies on much larger samples are needed to establish how the distribution functions of λ, α, and K_e (or any other set of three) depend on environmental factors (e.g., lithology and climate) and degree of maturity. Experience acquired in studying the networks discussed above plus about a dozen others suggests that the sensitivity of the method is such that it can easily detect differences due to operator variation. Consequently the question of map accuracy will be of paramount importance in extending and quantifying the method.

Acknowledgment. This research was supported in part by the Geography Programs, Office of Naval Research, under ONR contract N00014-70-C-0188, task NR 389-155.

REFERENCES

Coates, D. R., Quantitative geomorphology of small drainage basins in southern Indiana, *Proj. NR 389-042, Tech. Rep. 10,* Dep. of Geol., Columbia Univ., New York, 1958.

Hennen, R. V., West Virginia Geological Survey county reports: Marshall, Wetzel, and Tyler counties, p. 125, 1909.

Horton, R. E., Erosional development of streams and their drainage basins: Hydrophysical approach to quantitative morphology, *Geol. Soc. Amer. Bull., 56,* 275–330, 1945.

Howard, A. D., Drainage analysis in geologic interpretation: A summation, *Amer. Ass. Petrol. Geol. Bull., 51,* 2246–2259, 1967.

Krumbein, W. C., and R. L. Shreve, Some statistical properties of dendritic channel networks, *Tech. Rep. 13, ONR Task 389-150,* pp. 36, 91–94, Dep. of Geol. Sci., Northwest. Univ., Evanston, Ill., 1970. (Also *Spec. Proj. Rep. NSF Grant 6A-1137,* Dep. of Geol., Univ. of Calif., Los Angeles, 1970.)

Maxwell, J. C., Quantitative geomorphology of the San Dimas National Forest, California, *Proj. NR 389-042, Tech. Rep. 19,* pp. 7–8, Dep. of Geol., Columbia Univ., New York, 1960.

Melton, M. A., Concept of state of a drainage system, *Geol. Soc. Amer. Bull., 71,* 1928, 1960.

Schumm, S. A., Evolution of drainage systems and slopes in badlands at Perth Amboy, New Jersey, *Geol. Soc. Amer. Bull., 67,* 597–646, 1956.

Shreve, R. L., Statistical law of stream numbers, *J. Geol., 74,* 17–37, 1966.

Shreve, R. L., Infinite topologically random channel networks, *J. Geol., 75,* 179–186, 1967.

Shreve, R. L., Stream lengths and basin areas in topologically random channel networks, *J. Geol., 77,* 397–414, 1969.

Smart, J. S., Statistical properties of stream lengths, *Water Resour. Res., 4,* 1001–1014, 1968.

Smart, J. S., and V. L. Moruzzi, Computer simulation of Clinch Mountain drainage networks, *J. Geol., 79,* 572–584, 1971.

Strahler, A. N., Hypsometric analysis of erosional topography, *Geol. Soc. Amer. Bull., 63,* 1117–1142, 1952.

Strahler, A. N., Dimensional analysis applied to fluvially eroded landforms, *Geol. Soc. Amer. Bull., 69,* 279–299, 1958.

Thornbury, W. D., *Principles of Geomorphology,* 2nd ed., John Wiley, New York, 1969.

Zakrzewska, B., An analysis of landforms in a part of the central Great Plains, *Ann. Ass. Amer. Geogr., 53,* 536–568, 1963.

Zernitz, E. R., Drainage patterns and their significance, *J. Geol., 40,* 498–521, 1932.

(Manuscript received June 12, 1972.)

AUTHOR CITATION INDEX

Abrahams, A. D., 5, 103, 228
Aitchison, J., 155, 212
Anderson, E. M., 103
Anderson, H. W., 188
Anderson, T. W., 212
Arnett, R. R., 228

Bailey, R. W., 262
Baker, V. R., 300
Becker, H. W., 188
Benson, M. A., 93, 351
Berge, C., 164
Berry, M., 103, 104, 105, 106, 228
Bertram, S., 343
Bigwood, B. L., 351
Blakney, W. G. G., 343
Blyth, K., 299
Borchert, R., 103
Bowden, K. L., 13, 103, 128, 155
Bradley, P. M., 103, 228
Brater, E. F., 92
Brebner, A., 299
Broscoe, A. J., 13, 55, 92, 155, 330
Brown, J. A. C., 155, 212
Brown, W. G., 104
Brush, L. M., 128, 351
Busby, M. W., 351

Calef, W., 93
Calver, A., 367
Campbell, R. N., 103
Cantrell, J. L., 343
Carlston, C. W., 92, 351, 367
Carter, C. S., 228
Catalan, E., 104
Cayley, E., 104, 128, 188, 300, 330
Chapman, C. A., 93
Chapman, D. G., 155
Chorley, R. J., 5, 6, 13, 92, 93, 228, 343, 351, 352
Christaller, W., 228
Clayton, K. M., 343
Coates, D. R., 92, 128, 343, 378

Coffman, D. M., 13, 198
Collins, S. H., 343
Conacher, A. J., 228
Considine, J. P., 155, 213
Cotton, C. A., 36, 352
Crone, D. R., 343
Croxton, F. E., 283
Cumming, G., 104, 107
Curtis, L. F., 6

Dacey, M. F., 228, 229
Davey, C. H., 344
Davis, W. M., 6, 36, 91
Day, D., 300
de Segner, J. A., 104
Dobson, G. C., 262
Dooge, J. C. I., 367
Doornkamp, J. C., 6
Drummond, R. R., 300
Duncan, W. J., 91
Dwight, H. B., 155

Etherington, I. M. H., 104, 188
Euler, L., 128
Eyles, R. J., 13, 343

Feller, W., 104, 137, 155, 212, 367
Ferguson, R. I., 104, 300
Fisher, J. B., 228, 229
Flinn, R. M., 103
Flint, J. J., 6, 104, 228
Fok, Y-S, 13
Franck, D. H., 106
Frijters, D., 104

Gilbert, G. K., 6, 93
Giusti, E. V., 352
Glenn, L. C., 262
Glock, W. S., 268, 283
Golding, B. L., 92
Goodlett, J. C., 343
Goodman, L. A., 212
Gordon, W. I., 300

Author Citation Index

Gravelius, H., 6, 13, 36
Gray, D. M., 188, 352
Graybill, F. A., 137, 155, 212, 213
Gregory, K. J., 6, 300, 343, 352
Greysukh, V. L., 343

Hack, J. T., 92, 104, 188, 283, 330, 343
Hadley, R. F., 352
Happ, S. C., 262
Harding, D. M., 352
Harding, E. F., 104, 188, 294
Harris, T. C., 294
Harvard University, Staff of the Computation Laboratory, 128
Hennen, R. V., 378
Henry, J., 93
Her Majesty's Stationery Office, 343
Hickok, R. B., 352
Hidore, J. J., 352
Holland, P. G., 104
Hollingworth, T., 103, 104, 228
Honda, H., 228, 229
Horsfield, K., 104, 105, 107, 300
Horton, R. E., 6, 13, 36, 38, 50, 55, 91, 92, 93, 128, 137, 155, 164, 188, 262, 268, 283, 311, 330, 343, 352, 367, 378
Howard, A. D., 105, 229, 294, 378
Howe, G. M., 352

Jackson, V. N., 343
James, W. R., 6, 188, 222
Jarvis, R. S., 6, 105, 188, 198, 229, 300, 368
Jennings, J. N., 343
Johnson, E. A. G., 352
Joos, G., 164

Kaitanen, V., 300
Kascht, L. J., 106
Keill, J., 14, 105
Keller, E. A., 13, 198
Kennedy, B. A., 5
Keppel, R. V., 352
Kirkby, M. J., 6, 343, 352, 367, 368
Knuth, D. E., 188
Kohler, M. A., 92
Krumbein, W. C., 6, 93, 188, 212, 222, 228, 229, 294, 378
Kuhn, T. S., 6

Lamé, M., 105
Lane, E. W., 93
Langbein, W. B., 91, 92, 128, 155, 188, 213, 283
Leopold, L. B., 14, 92, 93, 105, 128, 155, 213, 283, 343, 368
Liao, K. H., 105, 198

Lindenmayer, A., 104, 105
Linsley, R. K., 92
Listing, J. B., 128
Low, D. E., 92
Lubowe, J. K., 229
Lück, H. B., 105
Lück, J., 105
Lyman, T., 14

McConnell, P., 105
Mackin, J. H., 93
Maddock, T., Jr., 14, 93, 368
Malm, D. E. G., 92
Maner, S. B., 93
Mark, D. M., 300
Marsden, L. E., 343
Maxwell, J. C., 92, 128, 155, 300, 330, 343, 378
Melhorn, W. N., 13, 198
Melton, M. A., 91, 92, 93, 105, 128, 137, 155, 198, 343, 352, 378
Milton, L. E., 14, 229
Miller, J. P., 92, 128, 343
Miller, V. C., 92, 344
Mock, S. J., 6, 188, 294
Mood, A. M., 128, 137, 155, 213
Moore, R. K., 344
Morgan, M. A., 13, 351
Morgan, R. S., 36, 262
Morisawa, M. E., 92, 93, 128, 188, 283, 344, 352
Moruzzi, V. L., 378
Murray, C. D., 105

National Academy of Sciences, 344
Newcomb, R., 93

Oeppen, B. J., 229
Ollier, C. D., 344
Ongley, E. D., 229
Oohata, S., 105
Ordance Survey, 198
Ovenden, J. C., 300

Patton, P. C., 300
Paulhus, J. L. H., 92
Pestrong, R., 344
Pierson, W. J., 344
Pillewizer, W., 344
Playfair, J., 6, 128, 368
Pogorzelski, H. A., 92
Polya, G., 106
Potter, W. D., 93
Prowse, K., 107
Pymm, D., 228

Author Citation Index

Quastler, H., 198

Rafferty, B. R., 352
Raisz, I., 93
Ranalli, G., 300
Reech, M., 300
Richards, K. S., 300
Riordan, J., 14, 38, 128
Rittenhouse, G., 262
Rodda, J. C., 299, 368
Rogers, W. F., 300
Rouane, P., 105
Roy, A. G., 106, 229
Rubey, W. W., 93
Ruhe, R. V., 93

Sadler, M., 106
Scheidegger, A. E., 105, 106, 137, 164, 188, 198, 300, 344, 368
Schenck, H., Jr., 128
Scheps, B. B., 344
Schick, A. P., 344
Schneider, W. J., 344
Schumm, S. A., 14, 55, 92, 93, 128, 137, 155, 213, 283, 330, 344, 352, 378
Schwarz, H. E., 92, 352
Sham, C. H., 6, 105, 229
Shaw, S. H., 344
Shewell, H. A. L., 344
Shidei, T., 105
Shreve, R. L., 6, 106, 137, 155, 188, 198, 213, 222, 294, 300, 368, 378
Shulits, S., 92
Siegel, S., 137
Silberger, D., 106
Simonett, D. S., 344
Singhal, S., 107
Slade, N. A., 103
Slaymaker, H. O., 352
Smart, J. S., 6, 14, 106, 155, 188, 189, 198, 199, 213, 222, 294, 300, 368, 378
Smit, G. J., 106
Smith, G.-H., 93
Smith, K. G., 92, 128
Smith, T. R., 300
Snyder, F. F., 92
Song, C. S., 301
Steingraeber, D. A., 106
Strahler, A. N., 6, 14, 38, 50, 55, 91, 128, 137, 155, 164, 189, 198, 213, 283, 330, 344, 352, 378
Surkan, A. J., 155, 213, 368

Taylor, A. B., 92, 352
Thomas, M. P., 351
Thompson, M. M., 344
Thornbury, W. D., 378
Tomari, D., 106
Tomlinson, P. B., 106, 229
Topfer, F., 344

U.S. Corps of Engineers, 92
U.S. Geological Survey, 330, 344
Uylings, H. B. M., 106

Van Pelt, J., 107
Veldmaat-Wansink, L., 106
Verwer, R. W. H., 107
Von Bertalanffy, L., 91

Walling, D. E., 343
Wallis, J. R., 13, 103, 128, 155
Warntz, W., 330
Wedderburn, J. H. M., 107
Weibel, E., 14
Wentworth, C. K., 93
Werner, C., 106, 189, 198, 199, 294, 300, 301, 368
Werritty, A., 107, 199, 301, 368
Weyman, D. R., 367
Widdett, D., 106
Williams, G. P., 301
Wilson, A. G., 368
Wilson, K. C., 299
Winthrop, J., 14
Wisler, C. O., 92
Woldenberg, M. J., 6, 14, 106, 107, 229, 301, 330
Wolman, M. G., 93, 128, 343
Woodford, A. O., 93
Wooding, R. A., 352, 368
Wooldridge, S. W., 36, 262

Yang, C. T., 14, 301
Yatsu, E., 93
Young, T., 6, 14, 107
Yoxall, W. H., 344

Zakrzewska, B., 378
Zernitz, E. R., 6, 378

SUBJECT INDEX

Absorption, 237
Abstraction, 224, 227, 236-237, 265, 279-283
Adventitious streams, 248-249. See also Network growth
Aggression, 237. See also Competition
Allometry, 63, 67. See also Scale dependency
Altitude. See Diameter
Ambilateral class, 98, 101-103, 170-172, 190-192, 285-294
Angle
　stream/divide, 226
　stream entrance, 225, 251, 256, 344
　stream junction, 225-227, 256-257, 263-268, 279-283
Arborescence, bifurcating, 157
Area-discharge relation, 67
Arterial trees, 9-10, 13, 101, 298
Astrophyton, 9
Asymmetric branching, 9, 103, 257-259

Basin area, 11, 20, 46-49, 65, 67, 185-186
　related to order, 306. See also Laws of drainage composition
　and stream discharge, 67, 307
Basin geometry, relation to climatic factors
　basin perimeter, 84
　basin relief, 52-53
　basin shape, 68
Basin shape, 12, 51-53, 68-69
　relation to hydrograph, 68
Belt of no erosion, 242-243, 251
Bifurcating links. See Link types
Bifurcating, 284. See also Network growth
Bifurcation ratio, 11-13, 21-31, 41, 61-62, 100-101, 109-117, 162-164, 169, 226, 281
Binary string of network topology, 134, 157-159, 161-163, 167, 299, 354-355
Blue lines, 19, 43-44, 297-298. See also Network identification
Botanical trees, 13, 100-101, 226-227
Brain cells, 13, 100-101
Broken branch correction, 298

Cascading subsystem, 3
Central place theory, 225
Chains, 99-100, 204-213
Channel network, 166
Cis links. See Link types
Cis-trans links. See Link types
Combinatorial analysis, 11, 37-38, 101-103, 119-127, 130-136, 138-155, 214-222, 284-294, 357-359
Competition, 249, 252
Complete network, 139
Composition of drainage net, 21
Connectivity matrix, 101
Constant of channel maintenance, 45, 49, 71
Contour crenulation, 298, 342
Contour line, 313
Course lines, 297, 314
Critical length, 238-239, 252-253. See also Rill channels
Cross-grading, 240-251
Cross-sectional geometry of channel, 78

Data manipulation, 298-299
Davisian cycle, 1-3, 13, 58
Diameter, 98, 157-160, 174, 179-181, 191-198, 360-367
Dimensional analysis, 58-59, 86-87
Discharge, 67, 302-311, 347-350, 362-367
　relation to basin geometry, 89-90
　relation to order, 307, 309. See also Hydrograph and network topology
Divides, 226
Drainage basin space, 4
Drainage density, 2-4, 18-19, 27-35, 52-53, 69-71, 86-88, 135-136, 341, 345-352, 362-367
Drainage patterns, 1-2, 230-237, 257-262
Dry valleys, 19, 298, 332-352
Dynamic equilibrium, 3, 57-58, 88-89, 224, 275-283

Ephemeral streams, 19, 303-311
Epicycles of erosion, 260-262

Subject Index

Ergodic hypothesis, 157, 227-228
Erosion proportionality factor, 52-53
Evolution of basin, 57, 266-268. See also Network growth
Extension, maximum, 224, 227, 265, 281-282
Exterior links. See Link types
Exterior path length, 98. See also Diameter

Field mapping, 53, 332-344. See also Network identification
First order basin, 62, 319
Fork, 111, 118
Free vertex, 157
Frequency-density relationship, 73, 136

Generation, 354-355. See also Diameter; Stream order
Geometric series laws, 9-11. See also Laws of drainage composition
Geometry number, 85
Gradient, channel, 20, 73, 78, 277
Graph, 156-164
Graph height, 157-158, 160. See also Diameter; Topologic path length

Headward erosion, 247-248. See also Network growth
Headward growth, 247-248, 284, 354. See also Network growth
Height. See Diameter
Hierarchies, 13
Horton number, 87-88
Hortonian analysis, 3-5, 108-128, 138-155, 169. See also Laws of drainage composition
Horton's laws and power functions, 306-311
Horton-type laws of hydraulic parameters, 307
Hydraulic geometry, 10, 12, 296-297, 303, 307
Hydrograph
　and basin shape, 68, 362-367
　and network topology, 61, 64, 169-170, 298-299
Hydrologic variability of networks, 16, 297-298
Hypsometric analysis, 85-86

Indicatrix of a surface, 314
Infinite regress of drainage net, 323
Infinite topologically random networks, 97, 129-137
Information content, 98, 190-199
Integration, 236, 279-283
Interbasin areas, 46-49, 65-66, 322
Interbasin lengths, 64
Interior links. See Link types

Junction, 166
　angle. See Angle, stream junction
　down-valley shift, 264-265, 279

Labeling of lung networks, 298. See also Network identification
Laws of drainage composition, 9, 10, 13, 21-26, 30, 40-45, 51-53, 60-78, 135-136, 169, 224-225, 328, 369
　basin areas, 11, 28-30, 43-45, 52, 65-66, 136, 151-155
　basin relief, 12, 52-53
　channel frequency, 53, 55
　constant of channel maintenance, 11, 45, 71-72, 136, 153-155
　discharge, 12, 67
　drainage density, 52, 54
　link numbers, 135
　stream lengths, 9-11, 23-28, 41-42, 53, 62-64, 135, 143-151, 271-273, 278, 306
　stream numbers, 9, 23-26, 41, 52-53, 60-62, 108-127, 135, 162-163, 191, 274
　　derivation from geometric series, 115-117
　stream slopes, 30, 43, 77-78
Length, total, in a basin, 26-27, 135
　related to discharge, 347
　related to order, 306
Length of overland flow, 19. See also Critical length
Length ratio, 31, 169
Length-area relationship, 11-12, 63, 66-67, 98
Link, 111, 118
　area ratio, 373
　density, 371
　distance. See Topologic path length
　length ratio, 373
　lengths, 97-100, 141-148, 200-213, 221-222, 271-273
　slope, 100
　types, 4, 129-130, 139, 166, 187, 200-213, 214-222
　　probabilities, 200-213, 214-222
Livers, 101
Longitudinal profile. See Stream profile
Lung networks, 100-102, 298

Magnitude, 5, 97, 130-136, 139, 166
Mapping of networks, 19, 43-44, 297, 312-327, 335-343. See also Network identification
Maximum source height. See Diameter
Mean source height, 192. See also Topologic path length
Micropiracy. See Cross-grading
Morphological subsystem, 3
Multiple erosion cycles. See Rejuvenation

Subject Index

Network growth, 10-11, 46-49, 211-213, 224-294, 354
Network identification
 lungs, 226
 rivers, 19, 43-44, 53, 254, 298, 312-330, 332-344
Network power, 299
Network state, 254
Network structure, 369-378. *See also* Topologic structure
Nodes, 4, 37-38

Open systems, 57, 275
Optimality, 101, 225, 297
Order. *See* Stream order
Order-area relation, 28
Orientation, 99, 226
Outlet, 166
Overland flow, 4, 19-20, 64, 71, 225, 238-256

Pales, 313
Passes, 313
Path length. *See* Topologic path length
Path numbers, 172-175, 191-192. *See also* Topologic path length
Peaks, 313
Pendant vertex, 157
Peneplain, 275
Photographic identification of river nets, 338-343. *See also* Network identification
Pits, 313
Planation, lateral, 265
Planted tree, 166
Playfair's law, 2, 16, 28, 71
Point patterns, 225
Pore velocity, 160
Porous media, dispersion in, 98, 156-164
Power, 13, 99, 101
Power functions derived from Horton's laws, 306-311
Precipitation-effectiveness index, 70
Probability distributions
 for network analysis, 130-133, 139-151
 for network growth, 287-290
Purkinje cells. *See* Brain cells

Random topology model, 5, 12-13, 96-99, 118-127, 129-137, 156-199, 211-222, 353-369
Random walks, 103, 133-135, 356-359
Rejuvenation, 13, 88-89, 259-262, 275
Relief
 available, 279
 basin, 12, 82
 and drainage pattern, 268

Relief ratio, 52, 83-84, 100, 268
Ridge lines, 297, 314
Rill channels, 238-246, 266-268
River capture, 230-237, 240-251, 265, 282
Ruggedness number, 84-85

Sampling, 59, 80-83
Scale dependency, 63-64, 98. *See also* Allometry
Second order basin, 321
Sediment yield, 78-84
Segmental growth, 284-287. *See also* Network growth
Sheet erosion. *See* Rill channels
Similarity, geometrical, 12, 58-59, 371
Simplification, 279
Simulation, 101, 117, 158, 162, 181-184, 227, 354
Singular points, 297
Slope
 evolution, 227
 ground, 20
 line, 314
 related to order, 306
Source, 111, 139, 166, 253
Source links. *See* Link types
Space filling, 2, 5, 10-11, 45-49, 86-90, 97-101, 224-228, 230-294
Statistical analysis, 57, 59-60
Steady state. *See* Dynamic equilibrium
Stream frequency, 12, 20, 52-53, 72-73, 136
Stream lengths, 11, 21-27, 62-64, 66-67
Stream order
 determination by extrapolation, 34
 generations (centrifugal), 3, 8-10, 16, 227, 354-355
 Horton (centripetal), 3, 8-10, 16-18, 52, 108-118
 Scheidegger, 130
 Strahler, 10-11, 37-38, 52, 60-62, 108-118, 169
Stream profile, 12, 73-78, 276-283
Substitution of space for time. *See* Ergodic hypothesis

Topographic maps, 19, 297-298, 312-352
Topologic path length, 98-99, 157-161, 170-188, 191-198, 360-367
Topological randomness, 122-128, 168
Topologically distinct channel networks (TDCN), 5, 97-99, 117-127, 129-135, 165-170, 191-199
Topologically identical channel networks, 118-119
Topologic structure, 196-199

Subject Index

Topology, 4-5, 10-11, 37-38, 108-135, 165-189, 312-330
  and geomorphic environment, 299
  spatial constraints on, 226, 297
Total number of streams, 62
Total stream length, 28, 64
Transient state, 57, 88, 275
Trans links. *See* Link types
Tributaries, lateral migration, 263

Tributary links. *See* Link types
Tributary bifurcating links. *See* Link types
Tributary source links. *See* Link types

Valleyside slope, 20, 78-81, 227

Width
  channel, related to order, 307
  topologic, 103, 354

About the Editors

RICHARD S. JARVIS received the B.A. degree in 1970 and the Ph.D. in 1975, both in geography from Cambridge University, England. After teaching for one year at Durham University in England, he took a position at the State University of New York at Buffalo in 1974, where he is currently associate professor of geography. He has published several papers on fluvial networks, along with other research in biogeography, icthyology, and climatology.

MICHAEL J. WOLDENBERG received the B.S. degree in 1956 and the M.S. degree in 1957, both in geology from the University of Wisconsin in Madison. He received the Ph.D. in 1968 in geography from Columbia University. From 1968 to 1975 he worked in the City Planning Department, Graduate School of Design, Harvard University. Since 1975 he has been with the Department of Geography at the State University of New York at Buffalo. He has published on fluvial and biological networks, and on central place theory. His current research is interdisciplinary and involves rivers, airways, blood vessels, and other biological trees.

DISCARDED